Accessing the WAN
CCNA Exploration Companion Guide

Bob Vachon
Rick Graziani

Cisco Press

800 East 96th Street

Indianapolis, Indiana 46240 USA

Accessing the WAN, CCNA Exploration Companion Guide

Bob Vachon, Rick Graziani

Copyright© 2008 Cisco Systems, Inc.

Published by:
Cisco Press
800 East 96th Street
Indianapolis, IN 46240 USA

Printed in the United States of America

First Printing December 2011

Library of Congress Cataloging-in-Publication Data:

Vachon, Bob.

  Accessing the WAN : CCNA exploration companion guide / Bob Vachon,

Rick Graziani.

    p. cm.

  ISBN 978-1-58713-205-6 (hardcover w/cd)

  1. Electronic data processing personnel--Certification. 2. Wide area

networks (Computer networks) 3. Computer networks--Examinations--Study

guides. I. Graziani, Rick. II. Cisco Systems, Inc. III. Title.

  QA76.3.V334 2008

  004.6--dc22

                      2008011637

ISBN-13: 978-1-58713-349-7
ISBN-10: 1-58713-349-0

Publisher
Paul Boger

Associate Publisher
Dave Dusthimer

Cisco Representative
Anthony Wolfenden

Cisco Press Program Manager
Jeff Brady

Executive Editor
Mary Beth Ray

Production Manager
Patrick Kanouse

Senior Development Editor
Christopher Cleveland

Senior Project Editor
San Dee Phillips

Copy Editor
Gayle Johnson

Technical Editors
Nolan Fretz
Charles Hannon
Snezhy Neshkova
Matt Swinford

Editorial Assistant
Vanessa Evans

Book and Cover Designer
Louisa Adair

Composition
Mark Shirar

Indexer
Tim Wright

Proofreader
Kathy Ruiz

cisco

Trademark Acknowledgments

All terms mentioned in this book that are known to be trademarks or service marks have been appropriately capitalized. Cisco Press or Cisco Systems, Inc. cannot attest to the accuracy of this information. Use of a term in this book should not be regarded as affecting the validity of any trademark or service mark.

Warning and Disclaimer

This book is designed to provide information about the *Accessing the WAN* course of the Cisco Networking Academy CCNA Exploration curriculum. Every effort has been made to make this book as complete and accurate as possible, but no warranty or fitness is implied.

The information is provided on an "as is" basis. The authors, Cisco Press, and Cisco Systems, Inc. shall have neither liability nor responsibility to any person or entity with respect to any loss or damages arising from the information contained in this book or from the use of the discs or programs that may accompany it.

The opinions expressed in this book belong to the authors and are not necessarily those of Cisco Systems, Inc.

Corporate and Government Sales

The publisher offers excellent discounts on this book when ordered in quantity for bulk purchases or special sales, which may include electronic versions and/or custom covers and content particular to your business, training goals, marketing focus, and branding interests. For more information, please contact:

U.S. Corporate and Government Sales
1-800-382-3419
corpsales@pearsontechgroup.com

For sales outside the United States please contact:

International Sales
international@pearsoned.com

Feedback Information

At Cisco Press, our goal is to create in-depth technical books of the highest quality and value. Each book is crafted with care and precision, undergoing rigorous development that involves the unique expertise of members of the professional technical community.

Reader feedback is a natural continuation of this process. If you have any comments about how we could improve the quality of this book, or otherwise alter it to better suit your needs, you can contact us through e-mail at feedback@ciscopress.com. Please be sure to include the book title and ISBN in your message.

We greatly appreciate your assistance.

Americas Headquarters	Asia Pacific Headquarters	Europe Headquarters
Cisco Systems, Inc.	Cisco Systems, Inc.	Cisco Systems International BV
170 West Tasman Drive	168 Robinson Road	Haarlerbergpark
San Jose, CA 95134-1706	#28-01 Capital Tower	Haarlerbergweg 13-19
USA	Singapore 068912	1101 CH Amsterdam
www.cisco.com	www.cisco.com	The Netherlands
Tel: 408 526-4000	Tel: +65 6317 7777	www-europe.cisco.com
800 553-NETS (6387)	Fax: +65 6317 7799	Tel: +31 0 800 020 0791
Fax: 408 527-0883		Fax: +31 0 20 357 1100

Cisco has more than 200 offices worldwide. Addresses, phone numbers, and fax numbers are listed on the Cisco Website at **www.cisco.com/go/offices.**

About the Authors

Bob Vachon is the coordinator of the Computer Systems Technology program at Cambrian College in Sudbury, Ontario, Canada, where he teaches networking infrastructure courses. He has worked and taught in the computer networking and information technology field since 1984. He is a scholar graduate of Cambrian College, and he received the prestigious Teaching Excellence Award in 1997. Vachon has been a Cisco Networking Academy instructor since 1999 and has been CCNP certified since 2002. He has worked with Cisco as team lead, author, CCNP certification assessment developer, and subject matter expert on a variety of projects, including CCNA, CCNP, and global partner training courses. He enjoys playing the guitar and being outdoors, either working in his gardens or white-water canoe tripping.

Rick Graziani teaches computer science and computer networking courses at Cabrillo College in Aptos, California. He has worked and taught in the computer networking and information technology fields for almost 30 years. Before that, he worked in IT for various companies, including Santa Cruz Operation, Tandem Computers, and Lockheed Missiles and Space Corporation. He holds an M.A. in computer science and systems theory from California State University Monterey Bay. Graziani also does consulting work for Cisco and other companies. When he is not working, he is most likely surfing. He is an avid surfer who enjoys longboarding at his favorite Santa Cruz surf breaks.

About the Technical Reviewers

Nolan Fretz is a college professor in network and telecommunications engineering technology at Okanagan College in Kelowna, British Columbia. He has almost 20 years of experience in implementing and maintaining IP networks and has been sharing his experiences by educating students in computer networking for the past nine years. He holds a master's degree in information technology.

Charles Hannon is an assistant professor of network design and administration at Southwestern Illinois College. He has been a Cisco Certified Academy instructor since 1998. He has a master of arts degree in education from Maryville University in St. Louis. He holds a valid CCNA certification and has eight years of experience in managing information systems. His priority is to empower students to become successful and compassionate lifelong learners.

Snezhy Neshkova, CCIE No. 11931, is a technical manager with the Cisco Networking Academy. She has more than 20 years of networking experience including field services and support, management, and networking education. She has developed and taught a number of different courses in the networking field including Cisco Networking Academy curricula. Snezhy holds a master of science degree in computer science from the Technical University of Sofia, Bulgaria.

Matt Swinford, associate professor of network design and administration at Southwestern Illinois College, has been an active Cisco Certified Academy instructor since 1999. He is dedicated to fostering a learning environment that produces certified students and quality IT professionals. He has a master of business administration degree from Southern Illinois University at Edwardsville and holds valid CCNP, A+, and Microsoft certifications.

Dedications

For my wife, Teri. Without your patience and understanding, I would not have been able to participate in this project. Thank you for your love and support throughout the countless hours it took me to complete this book and for your understanding that I still needed time to surf.
—Rick Graziani

To my wife, Judy, who, through good times and hard times, helped me keep body and soul together. Without her support and encouragement, I would not have been involved with this project.
—Bob Vachon

Acknowledgments

From Rick Graziani:

First of all, I want to thank my good friend Bob Vachon for the pleasure of writing this book with him. Bob's expertise with and commitment to the Cisco Networking Academy have always been extraordinary. His work in the creation of this book has been another example of his exceptional talents.

This book was not the work of any one or two individuals but literally was a team effort. Jeremy Creech headed a team that included Gail Behrend, Koksal Cengiz, Don Chipman, Sonya Coker, Allan Johnson, David Kotfila, Jeff Luman, Bob Vachon, Alan Weiler, and me. My sincere gratitude and thanks to Jeremy and the team for letting me be part of such an outstanding team. I am honored and humbled to work with such a fine group of dedicated people.

Special thanks to Mary Beth Ray for her patience and understanding throughout this long process. Mary Beth always provided that voice of calm reassurance and guidance whenever needed.

Thank you, Chris Cleveland, for your help in the editing and production stages. I am amazed at the level of cooperation and teamwork required to produce a technical book, and I am grateful for all your help.

Thanks to all the technical editors for providing feedback and suggestions. Nolan Fretz, Charles Hannon, Snezhy Neshkova, and Matt Swinford did more than just technical editing; they helped take these topics and made sure that they were understandable and accurate.

Finally, I want to thank all my students over the years. For some reason, I always get the best students. You make my job fun and are the reason why I love teaching.

From Bob Vachon:

I would first like to thank Rick Graziani for providing guidance and assistance when I needed it most. They say you can measure a man by the amount of respect he gets. Rick, you are a giant. Thank you. It has been a pleasure writing this book with you.

I would also like to thank my friends Jeremy Creech and John Behrens of Cisco for their continued support and for asking me to be part of a great development team. My sincere gratitude to the entire development team for their outstanding contribution. I am honored to work with such a fine group of dedicated people.

Special thanks to the folks at Cisco Press. A big thank-you goes to Mary Beth Ray for providing me the opportunity to be part of this project and to Chris Cleveland for your editing insight and patience. Thanks to the technical editors for providing a fresh set of eyes when reviewing the book.

A great big thanks to the folks at Cambrian College—specifically, Liz Moratz, Geoff Dalton, Sonia Del Missier, and Sylvia Barnard for your encouragement and support. I would also like to thank Betty Freelandt for providing me with the opportunity to discover the Cisco Networking Academy.

Finally, thanks to all my students. You're the reason why we're here. I learn so much from you, and you make me thankful for having the best job in the world!

Contents at a Glance

Contents

Icons Used in This Book

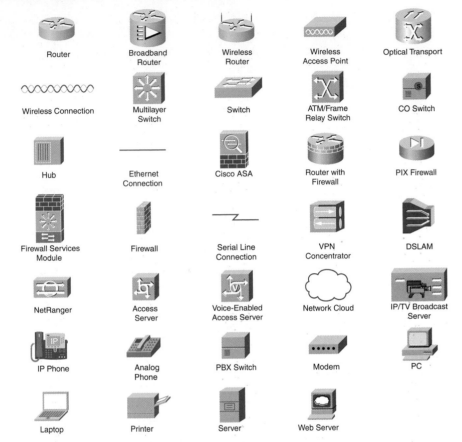

Router

Broadband Router

Wireless Router

Wireless Access Point

Optical Transport

Wireless Connection

Multilayer Switch

Switch

ATM/Frame Relay Switch

CO Switch

Hub

Ethernet Connection

Cisco ASA

Router with Firewall

PIX Firewall

Firewall Services Module

Firewall

Serial Line Connection

VPN Concentrator

DSLAM

NetRanger

Access Server

Voice-Enabled Access Server

Network Cloud

IP/TV Broadcast Server

IP Phone

Analog Phone

PBX Switch

Modem

PC

Laptop

Printer

Server

Web Server

Command Syntax Conventions

The conventions used to present command syntax in this book are the same conventions used in the IOS Command Reference. The Command Reference describes these conventions as follows:

- **Bold** indicates commands and keywords that are entered literally as shown. In actual configuration examples and output (not general command syntax), bold indicates commands that the user enters (such as a **show** command).

- *Italic* indicates arguments for which you supply actual values.

- Vertical bars (|) separate alternative, mutually exclusive elements.

- Square brackets ([ ]) indicate an optional element.

- Braces ({ }) indicate a required choice.

- Braces within brackets ([{ }]) indicate a required choice within an optional element.

Introduction

The Cisco Networking Academy is a comprehensive e-learning program that provides students with Internet technology skills. A Networking Academy delivers web-based content, online assessment, student performance tracking, and hands-on labs to prepare students for industry-standard certifications. The CCNA curriculum includes four courses oriented around the topics on the Cisco Certified Network Associate (CCNA) certification.

Accessing the WAN, CCNA Exploration Companion Guide is the official supplement textbook to be used with version 4 of the CCNA Exploration Accessing the WAN online curriculum of the Networking Academy.

This book goes beyond earlier editions of the Cisco Press *Companion Guides* by providing many alternative explanations and examples as compared with the course. You can use the online curriculum as normal and use this *Companion Guide* to help solidify your understanding of all the topics through the alternative examples.

The basis for this book as well as the online curriculum is to help you understand several WAN technologies, including PPP and Frame Relay, and related topics, such as access control lists and Network Address Translation. This book also introduces other WAN technologies, such as DSL, cable modems, and Virtual Private Networks (VPNs).

Goals of This Book

First and foremost, by providing a fresh, complementary perspective on the topics, this book is intended to help you learn all the required materials of the Exploration Accessing the WAN course in the Networking Academy CCNA curriculum. As a secondary goal, the text is intended as a mobile replacement for the online curriculum for individuals who do not always have Internet access. In those cases, you can instead read the appropriate sections of the book, as directed by your instructor, and learn the same material that is covered in the online curriculum. Another secondary goal is to serve as your offline study material and help you prepare for the CCNA exam.

Audience for This Book

This book's main audience is anyone taking the CCNA Exploration Accessing the WAN course of the Cisco Networking Academy curriculum. Many Academies use this textbook as a required tool in the course, and other Academies recommend the Companion Guides as an additional source of study and practice materials.

The secondary audience for this book includes people taking CCNA-related classes from professional training organizations. This book can also be used for college- and university-level networking courses, as well as by anyone who wants to gain a detailed understanding of wide-area networks.

Book Features

The educational features of this book focus on supporting topic coverage, readability, and practice of the course material to facilitate your full understanding of the course material.

Topic Coverage

The following features give you a thorough overview of the topics covered in each chapter so that you can make constructive use of your study time:

- **Objectives**: Listed at the beginning of each chapter, the objectives reference the core concepts covered in the chapter. The objectives match the objectives stated in the corresponding chapters of the online curriculum. However, the question format in the *Companion Guide* encourages you to think about finding the answers as you read the chapter.

- **"How-to" feature**: When this book covers a set of steps that you need to perform for certain tasks, this book lists the steps as a how-to list. When you are studying, the How To icon helps you easily find this feature as you skim through the book.

- **Notes, tips, cautions, and warnings**: These are sidebars that point out interesting facts, time-saving methods, and important safety issues.

- **Chapter summaries**: At the end of each chapter is a summary of the chapter's key concepts. It provides a synopsis of the chapter and serves as a study aid.

Readability

The authors have compiled, edited, and in some cases rewritten the material so that it has a more conversational tone that follows a consistent and accessible reading level. In addition, the following features have been updated to aid your understanding of the networking vocabulary:

- **Key terms**: Each chapter begins with a list of key terms, along with a page number reference. The terms are listed in the order in which they are explained in the chapter. This handy reference allows you to see a term, flip to the page where it appears, and see it used in context. The glossary defines all the key terms.

- **Glossary**: This book contains an all-new glossary with more than 240 terms.

Practice

Practice makes perfect. This new *Companion Guide* offers you ample opportunities to put what you learn into practice. You will find the following features valuable and effective in reinforcing the instruction that you receive:

- **Check Your Understanding questions and answer key**: Updated review questions are presented at the end of each chapter as a self-assessment tool. These questions match the style of questions that you see in the online course. The appendix, "Check Your Understanding and Challenge Questions Answer Key," provides the answers to all the questions and includes an explanation of each answer.

- **(New) Challenge questions and activities**: Additional—and more challenging—review questions and activities are presented at the end of each chapter. These questions are designed to be similar to the more complex styles of questions you might see on the CCNA exam. This section might also include activities to help prepare you for the exams. Appendix A provides the answers.

- **Packet Tracer activities**: Interspersed throughout the chapters, you'll find many opportunities to work with the Cisco Packet Tracer tool. Packet Tracer allows you to create networks, visualize how packets flow in the network, and use basic testing tools to determine whether the network would work. When you see this icon, you can use Packet Tracer with the listed file to perform a task suggested in this book. The activity files are available on this book's CD-ROM; Packet Tracer software is available through the Academy Connection website. Ask your instructor for access to Packet Tracer.

Labs and Study Guide

The supplementary book *Accessing the WAN, CCNA Exploration Labs and Study Guide* by Cisco Press (ISBN: 1-58713-201-x) contains all the labs from the curriculum plus additional challenge labs and study guide material. The end of each chapter of this *Companion Guide* indicates with icons what labs, activities, and Packet Tracer activities are available in the *Labs and Study Guide*.

- **Lab references**: This icon notes the hands-on labs created for this chapter in the online curriculum. In *Accessing the WAN, CCNA Exploration Labs and Study Guide* you will also find additional labs and study guide material created by the author of that book.

- **(New) Packet Tracer Companion activities**: Many of the hands-on labs include Packet Tracer Companion activities, where you can use Packet Tracer to complete a simulation of the lab. Look for this icon in *Accessing the WAN, CCNA Exploration Labs and Study Guide* for hands-on labs that have a Packet Tracer Companion.

- **(New) Packet Tracer Skills Integration Challenge activities**: These activities require you to pull together several skills you learned from the chapter to successfully complete one comprehensive exercise. Look for this icon in *Accessing the WAN, CCNA Exploration Labs and Study Guide* for instructions on how to perform the Packet Tracer Skills Integration Challenge for this chapter.

A Word About Packet Tracer Software and Activities

Packet Tracer is a self-paced, visual, interactive teaching and learning tool developed by Cisco. Lab activities are an important part of networking education. However, lab equipment can be a scarce resource. Packet Tracer provides a visual simulation of equipment and network processes to offset the challenge of limited equipment. Students can spend as much time as they like completing standard lab exercises through Packet Tracer, and they have the option to work from home. Although Packet Tracer is not a substitute for real equipment, it allows students to practice using a command-line interface. This "e-doing" capability is a fundamental component of learning how to configure routers and switches from the command line.

Packet Tracer version 4.*x* is available only to Cisco Networking Academies through the Academy Connection website. Ask your instructor for access to Packet Tracer.

The course essentially includes three different types of Packet Tracer activities. This book uses icons to indicate which type of Packet Tracer activity is available. The icons are intended to give you a sense of the activity's purpose and the amount of time you'll need to complete it. The three types of Packet Tracer activities are as follows:

- **Packet Tracer Activity**: This icon identifies straightforward exercises interspersed throughout the chapters, where you can practice or visualize a specific topic. The activity files for these exercises are available on the book's CD-ROM. These activities take less time to complete than the Packet Tracer Companion and Challenge activities.

- **Packet Tracer Companion**: This icon identifies exercises that correspond to the course's hands-on labs. You can use Packet Tracer to complete a simulation of the hands-on lab or complete a similar "lab." The *Companion Guide* points these out at the end of each chapter, but look for this icon and the associated exercise file in *Accessing the WAN, CCNA Exploration Labs and Study Guide* for hands-on labs that have a Packet Tracer Companion.

- **Packet Tracer Skills Integration Challenge**: This icon identifies activities that require you to pull together several skills you learned from the chapter to successfully complete one comprehensive exercise. The *Companion Guide* points these out at the end of each chapter, but look for this icon in *Accessing the WAN, CCNA Exploration Labs and Study Guide* for instructions on how to perform the Packet Tracer Skills Integration Challenge for this chapter.

How This Book Is Organized

The book covers the major topic headings in the same sequence as the online curriculum for the CCNA Exploration Accessing the WAN course. This book has eight chapters, with the same numbers and similar names as the online course chapters.

If you're reading this book without being in the CCNA Accessing the WAN class, or if you're just using this book for self-study, the sequence of topics in each chapter provides a logical sequence for learning the material presented.

- **Chapter 1, "Introduction to WANs,"** provides an overview of the options available for designing enterprise WANs, the technologies available to implement them, and the terminology used to discuss them. You will learn about selecting the appropriate WAN technologies, services, and devices to meet the changing business requirements of an evolving enterprise.

- **Chapter 2, "PPP,"** examines PPP, including its roots in HDLC, PPP concepts, PPP layered architecture, and configuring PPP. Configuring PPP with authentication using PAP and CHAP are also discussed.

- **Chapter 3, "Frame Relay,"** examines the Frame Relay protocol. Basic Frame Relay concepts are discussed, including encapsulation, topologies, and address mapping. Various Frame Relay configuration techniques are examined, including the use of static Frame Relay maps, the use of inverse ARP, and configuring Frame Relay on subinterfaces.

- **Chapter 4, "Network Security,"** covers the threats and attacks that face many of today's networks. Security policies and mitigation techniques are discussed. Securing networks and devices is examined, including an introduction to Cisco SDM. Managing Cisco IOS images is also discussed in this chapter, including password recovery and restoring IOS images.

- **Chapter 5, "ACLs,"** discusses ACL operation and guidelines using standard, extended, and named ACLs. Configuring ACLs is examined, including using wildcard masks, monitoring ACLs, and applying ACLs to interfaces. Dynamic ACLs, reflexive ACLs, and time-based ACLs are introduced.

- **Chapter 6, "Teleworker Services,"** discusses how organizations can provide secure, fast, and reliable remote network connections for teleworkers. This chapter introduces DSL, cable modem, and broadband wireless. VPNs and IPsec also are discussed.

- **Chapter 7, "IP Addressing Services,"** discusses DHCP, NAT, and IPv6. This chapter includes both the concepts and configurations needed to implement these technologies.

- **Chapter 8, "Network Troubleshooting,"** discusses documenting your network, creating a baseline, and the troubleshooting tools and methodologies used in diagnosing network issues.

- The **appendix, "Check Your Understanding and Challenge Questions Answer Key,"** provides the answers to the Check Your Understanding questions at the end of each chapter. It also includes answers for the Challenge Questions and Activities that conclude most chapters.

- The **glossary** defines all the key terms that appear throughout this book.

About the CD-ROM

The CD-ROM included with this book provides many useful tools and information to support your education:

- **Packet Tracer Activity files:** These are files to work through the Packet Tracer Activities referenced throughout the book, as indicated by the Packet Tracer Activity icon.

- **Taking Notes:** This section includes a .txt file of the chapter objectives to serve as a general outline of the key topics of which you need to take note. The practice of taking clear, consistent notes is an important skill not only for learning and studying the material but for on-the-job success as well. Also included in this section is "A Guide to Using a Networker's Journal" PDF booklet providing important insight into the value of the practice of using a journal, how to organize a professional journal, and some best practices on what, and what not, to take note of in your journal.

- **IT Career Information:** This section includes a student guide to applying the toolkit approach to your career development. Learn more about entering the world of information technology as a career by reading two informational chapters excerpted from The IT Career Builder's Toolkit: "The Job Search" and "The Interview."

- **Lifelong Learning in Networking:** As you embark on a technology career, you will notice that it is ever-changing and evolving. This career path provides new and exciting opportunities to learn new technologies and their applications. Cisco Press is one of the key resources to plug into on your quest for knowledge. This section of the CD-ROM provides an orientation to the information available to you and tips on how to tap into these resources for lifelong learning.

About the Cisco Press Website for This Book

Cisco Press may provide additional content that you can access by registering your book at the ciscopress.com website. Becoming a member and registering is free, and you then gain access to exclusive deals on other resources from Cisco Press.

To register this book, go to *http://www.ciscopress.com/bookstore/register.asp* and enter the book's ISBN, located on the back cover. You'll then be prompted to log in or to join ciscopress.com to continue the registration.

After you register this book, a link to the supplemental content will be listed on your My Registered Books page.

CHAPTER 1

Introduction to WANs

Objectives

After completing this chapter, you should be able to answer the following questions:

■ How does the Cisco enterprise architecture provide integrated services over an enterprise network?

■ What are the key WAN technology concepts?

■ What appropriate WAN technologies are used to meet different enterprise business requirements?

Key Terms

This chapter uses the following key terms. You can find the definitions in the glossary at the end of the book.

When an enterprise grows to include branch offices, e-commerce services, or global operations, a single local-area network (LAN) is no longer sufficient to meet its business requirements. *Wide-area network (WAN)* access has become essential for larger businesses today.

A variety of WAN technologies meet the different needs of businesses, and there are many ways to scale the network. Adding WAN access introduces other considerations, such as network security and address management. Consequently, designing a WAN and choosing the correct carrier network services is not a simple matter.

In this chapter, you will begin exploring some of the options available for designing enterprise WANs, the technologies available to implement them, and the terminology used to discuss them. You will learn about selecting the appropriate WAN technologies, services, and devices to meet the changing business requirements of an evolving enterprise. The activities and labs confirm and reinforce your learning.

After completing this chapter, you will be able to identify and describe the appropriate WAN technologies to enable integrated WAN services over a multilocation *enterprise network*.

Introducing Wide-Area Networks (WANs)

One way to categorize networks is to divide them into local-area networks (LAN) and wide-area networks (WAN). LANs typically are connected workstations, printers, and other devices within a limited geographic area such as a building. All the devices in the LAN are under the common administration of the owner of that LAN, such as a company or an educational institution. Most LANs today are Ethernet LANs.

WANs are networks that span a larger geographic area and usually require the services of a common carrier. Examples of WAN technologies and protocols include Frame Relay, ATM, and DSL.

What Is a WAN?

A WAN is a *data communications* network that operates beyond the geographic scope of a LAN. Figure 1-1 shows the relative location of a LAN and WAN.

Figure 1-1   WAN Location

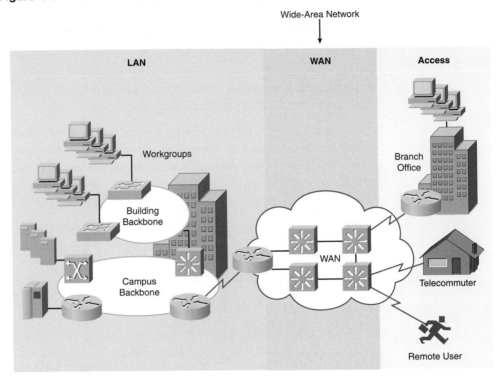

WANs differ from LANs in several ways. Whereas a LAN connects computers, peripherals, and other devices in a single building or other small geographic area, a WAN allows the transmission of data across greater geographic distances. In addition, an enterprise must subscribe to a WAN service provider to use WAN carrier network services. LANs typically are owned by the company or organization that uses them.

WANs use facilities provided by a service provider, or carrier, such as a telephone or cable company, to connect the locations of an organization to each other, to locations of other organizations, to external services, and to remote users. WANs provide network capabilities to support a variety of mission-critical traffic such as voice, video, and data.

Here are the three major characteristics of WANs:

- WANs generally connect devices that are separated by a broader geographic area than can be served by a LAN.

- WANs use the services of carriers, such as telephone companies, cable companies, satellite systems, and network providers.

- WANs use serial connections of various types to provide access to bandwidth over large geographic areas.

Why Are WANs Necessary?

LAN technologies provide both speed and cost efficiency for the transmission of data in organizations over relatively small geographic areas. However, other business needs require communication among remote sites, including the following:

- People in the regional or branch offices of an organization need to be able to communicate and share resources with the central site.

- Organizations often want to share information with other organizations across large distances. For example, software manufacturers routinely communicate product and promotion information to distributors that sell their products to end users.

- Employees who frequently travel on company business need to access information that resides on their corporate networks.

In addition, home computer users need to send and receive data across increasingly larger distances. Here are some examples:

- It is now common in many households for consumers to communicate with banks, stores, and a variety of providers of goods and services via computers.

- Students do research for classes by accessing library catalogs and publications located in other parts of their country and in other parts of the world.

Because it is obviously not feasible to connect computers across a country or around the world in the same way that they are connected in a LAN with cables, different technologies have evolved to support this need. The Internet has become and continues to be an inexpensive alternative for WAN connectivity. New technologies are available to businesses to provide security and privacy for their Internet communications and *transactions*. WANs used by themselves, or in concert with the Internet, allow organizations and individuals to meet their wide-area communication needs.

The Evolving Enterprise

As companies grow, they hire more employees, open branch offices, and expand into global markets. These changes also influence companies' requirements for integrated services and drive their network requirements. This section explores how company networks evolve to accommodate companies' changing business requirements.

Businesses and Their Networks

Every business is unique. How an organization grows depends on many factors, such as the type of products or services the business sells, the owners' management philosophy, and the economic climate of the country in which the business operates.

In slow economic times, many businesses focus on increasing their profitability by improving the efficiency of the existing operations, increasing employee productivity, and lowering operating costs. Establishing and managing networks can represent significant installation and operating expenses. To justify such a large expense, companies expect their networks to perform optimally and to be able to deliver an ever-increasing array of services and applications to support productivity and profitability.

To illustrate, we'll use a fictitious company called Span Engineering as an example. You'll watch how its network requirements change as the company grows from a small local business into a global enterprise.

Small Office (Single LAN)

Span Engineering, an environmental consulting firm, has developed a special process for converting household waste into electricity. It is developing a small pilot project for a municipal government in its local area. The company, which has been in business for four years, has grown to include 15 employees: six engineers, four computer-aided drawing (CAD) designers, two senior partners, a receptionist, and two office assistants.

Span Engineering's management is hoping that the company will have full-scale projects after the pilot project successfully demonstrates the feasibility of its process. Until then, the company must manage its costs carefully.

For its small office, shown in Figure 1-2, Span Engineering uses a single LAN to share information between computers and to share peripherals, such as a printer, a large-scale plotter (to print engineering drawings), and fax equipment. The company recently upgraded its LAN to provide inexpensive *voice over IP (VoIP)* service to save on the costs of separate phone lines for its employees.

The company connects to the Internet through a common *broadband* service called Digital Subscriber Line (DSL), which is supplied by the local telephone service provider. With so few employees, bandwidth is not a significant problem.

The company cannot afford in-house information technology (IT) support staff, so it uses support services purchased from the same service provider. The company also uses a hosting service rather than purchasing and operating its own FTP and e-mail servers.

Campus (Multiple LANs)

Five years later, Span Engineering has grown rapidly. As the owners had hoped, the company was contracted to design and implement a full-sized waste conversion facility soon after the successful implementation of their first pilot plant. Since then, other projects have also been won in neighboring municipalities and in other parts of the country.

Figure 1-2   Small-Office LAN

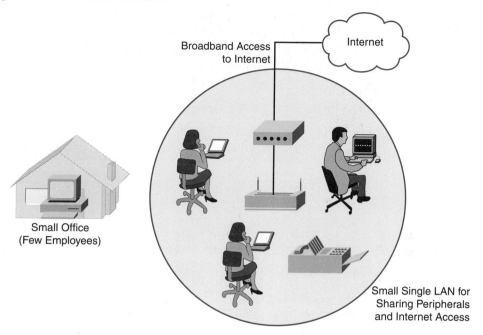

To handle the additional workload, the business has hired more staff and leased more office space. It is now a small to medium-sized business with several hundred employees. Many projects are being developed at the same time, and each requires a project manager and support staff. The company has organized itself into functional departments, with each department having its own organizational team. To meet its growing needs, the company has moved into several floors of a larger office building.

As the business has expanded, the network has also grown. Instead of a single small LAN, the network now consists of several subnetworks, each devoted to a different department. For example, all the engineering staff are on one LAN, and the marketing staff is on another LAN. These multiple LANs are joined to create a company-wide network, or campus, which spans several floors of the building. Figure 1-3 shows Span Engineering's expanded campus LAN.

The business now has in-house IT staff to support and maintain the network. The network includes servers for e-mail, data transfer and file storage, web-based productivity tools, and applications. The network includes a company intranet to provide in-house documents and information to employees. In addition, the company has an extranet that provides project information only to designated customers.

Figure 1-3 Campus (Multiple LANs)

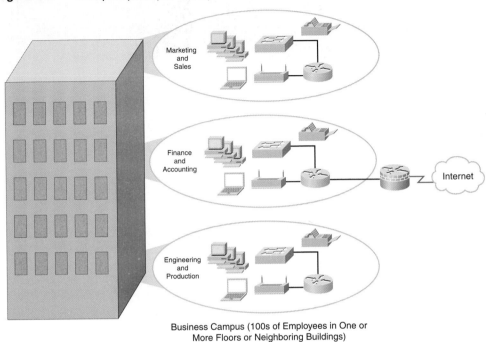

Business Campus (100s of Employees in One or
More Floors or Neighboring Buildings)

Branch (WAN)

Another five years later, Span Engineering has been so successful with its patented process that demand for its services has skyrocketed. New projects are now being built in other cities. To manage those projects, the company has opened small branch offices closer to the project sites.

This situation presents new challenges to the IT team. To manage the delivery of information and services throughout the company, Span Engineering now has a data center, which houses the company's various databases and servers. To ensure that all parts of the business can access the same services and applications regardless of where the offices are located, the company now needs to implement a WAN.

For its branch and regional offices that are in nearby cities, the company decides to use private dedicated lines through its local service provider, as shown in Figure 1-4. However, for the offices that are located in other countries, the Internet is now an attractive WAN connection option. Although connecting offices through the Internet is economical, it introduces security and privacy issues that the IT team must address.

Figure 1-4   Branch (WAN)

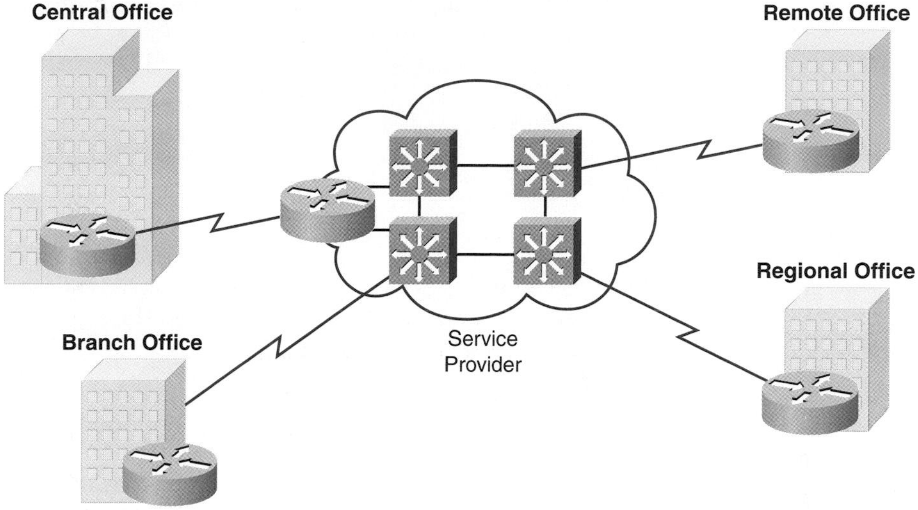

Distributed (Global)

Span Engineering has now been in business for 20 years and has grown to thousands of employees distributed in offices worldwide. The cost of the network and its related services is a significant expense. The company is looking to provide its employees with the best network services at the lowest cost. Optimized network services would allow each employee to work at high efficiency.

To increase profitability, Span Engineering needs to reduce its operating expenses. It has relocated some of its office facilities to less expensive areas. The company is also encouraging teleworking and virtual teams. Web-based applications—including web conferencing, e-learning, and online collaboration tools—are being used to increase productivity and reduce costs. Site-to-site and remote-access Virtual Private Networks (VPN) enable the company to use the Internet to connect easily and securely with employees and facilities around the world. To meet these requirements, the network must provide the necessary converged services and secure Internet WAN connectivity to remote offices and individuals. Figure 1-5 shows SPAN Engineering's new distributed or global network.

Figure 1-5   Distributed (Global)

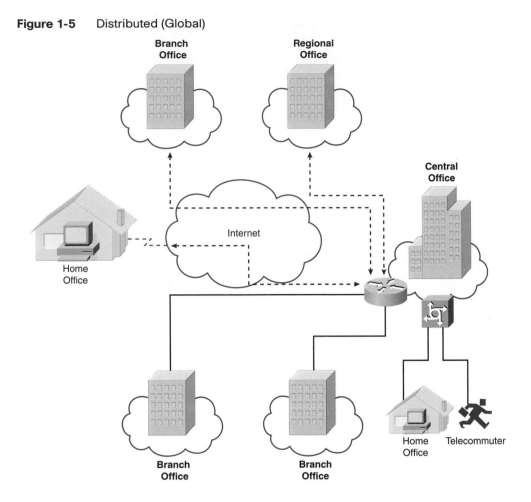

As you can see from this example, a company's network requirements can change dramatically as the company grows over time. Distributing employees saves costs in many ways, but it puts increased demands on the network. Not only must a network meet the business's day-to-day operational needs, but it also needs to be able to adapt and grow as the company changes. Network designers and administrators meet these challenges by carefully choosing network technologies, protocols, and service providers, and by optimizing their networks using many of the techniques we teach in this series of courses. The next sections describe a model for designing networks that can accommodate the changing needs of today's evolving businesses.

The Evolving Network Model

The hierarchical network model is a framework that helps you visualize and design networks. Several variations of this model exist, and it can be adapted for specific implementations.

The Hierarchical Design Model

Figure 1-6 shows the hierarchical network model, which is a useful high-level tool for designing a reliable network infrastructure. It provides a modular view of a network, making it easier to design and build a scalable network. The figure conceptually displays the model and identifies its major responsibilities.

Figure 1-6   Hierarchical Network Model

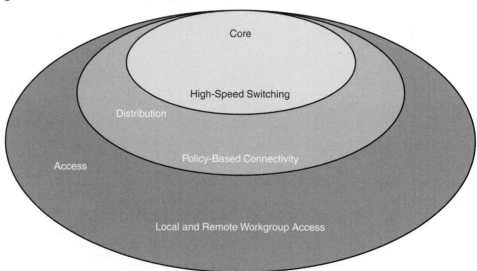

The Hierarchical Network Model

As you may recall from *CCNA Exploration: LAN Switching and Wireless*, the hierarchical network model divides a network into three layers:

- The access layer grants user access to network devices. In a network campus, the access layer generally incorporates switched LAN devices with ports that provide connectivity to workstations and servers. In the WAN environment, it may give *teleworkers* or remote sites access to the corporate network across WAN technology.

- The distribution layer aggregates the *wiring closets*, using switches to segment workgroups and isolate network problems in a campus environment. Similarly, the distribution layer aggregates WAN connections at the edge of the campus and provides policy-based connectivity.

■ The core layer (also called the backbone) is a high-speed *backbone* that is designed to switch packets as fast as possible. Because the core is critical for connectivity, it must provide a high level of availability and adapt to changes very quickly. It also provides scalability and fast convergence.

Figure 1-7 represents the Hierarchical Network Model in campus environments. The Hierarchical Network Model provides a modular framework that allows flexibility in network design and facilitates ease of implementation and troubleshooting in the infrastructure. However, it is important to understand that the network infrastructure is only the foundation of a comprehensive architecture.

Figure 1-7   Hierarchical Network Model in Campus Environments

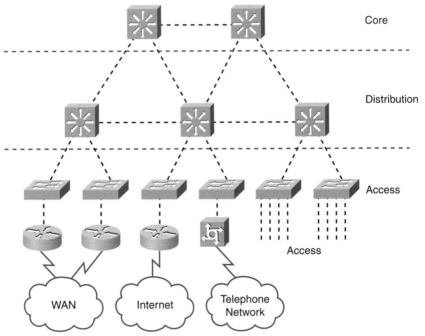

Networking technologies have advanced considerably in recent years, resulting in networks that are increasingly intelligent. The current network elements are more aware of traffic characteristics and can be configured to deliver specialized services based on such things as the types of data they carry, the data's priority, and even the security needs. Although most of these various infrastructure services are outside the scope of this course, it is important to understand that they influence network design. The next sections explore the Cisco Enterprise Architecture, which expands on the hierarchical model by making use of network intelligence to address the network infrastructure.

The Enterprise Architecture

As described earlier, different businesses need different types of networks, depending on how the business is organized and its business goals. Unfortunately, all too often networks grow in a haphazard way as new components are added in response to immediate needs. Over time, those networks become complex and expensive to manage. Because the network is a mixture of newer and older technologies, it can be difficult to support and maintain. Outages and poor performance are a constant source of trouble for network administrators.

To help prevent this situation, Cisco has developed a recommended architecture called the Cisco Enterprise Architecture. It has relevance to the different stages of a business's growth, as shown in Figure 1-8. This architecture is designed to give network planners a road map for network growth as the business moves through different stages. By following the suggested road map, IT managers can plan for future network upgrades that will integrate seamlessly into the existing network and support the ever-growing need for services.

Figure 1-8   Cisco Enterprise Architecture

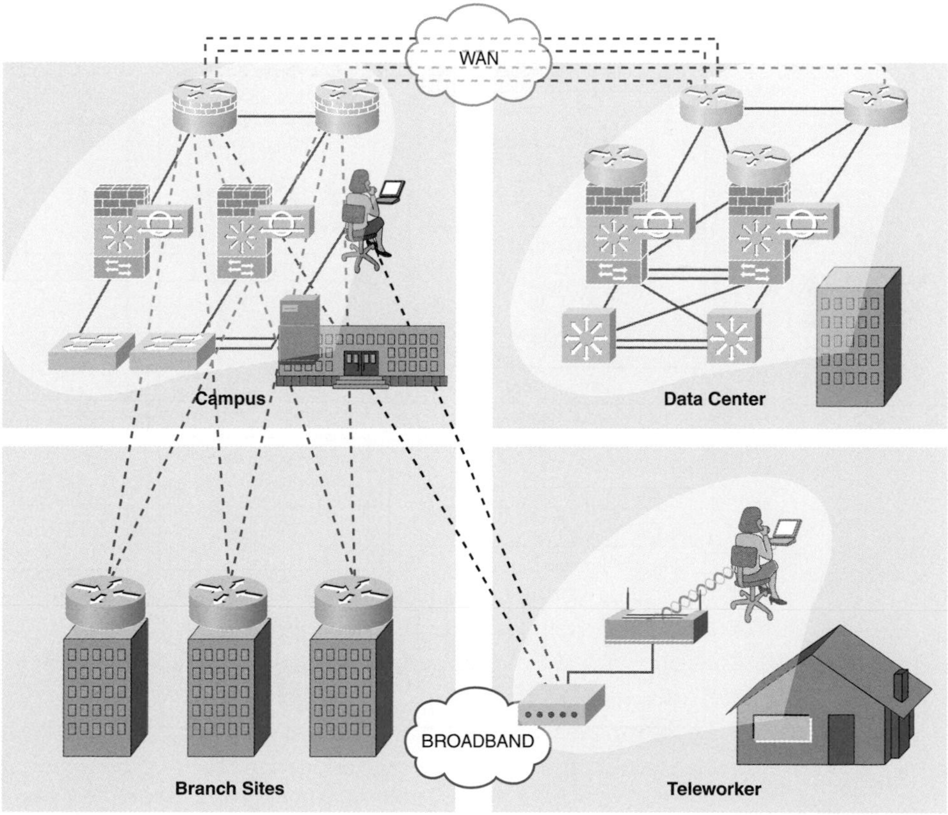

The Cisco Enterprise Architecture consists of modules representing focused views that target each place in the network. Each module has a distinct network infrastructure with services and network applications that extend across the modules. The following are some of the modules within the architecture that are relevant to the Span Engineering scenario described earlier:

- Enterprise Campus Architecture

- Enterprise Branch Architecture

- Enterprise Data Center Architecture

- Enterprise Teleworker Architecture

Figure 1-9 shows the Cisco Enterprise Architecture, which consists of modules representing focused views that target each place in the network. Each module has a distinct network infrastructure with services and network applications that extend across the modules.

Figure 1-9   Modules of the Enterprise Architecture

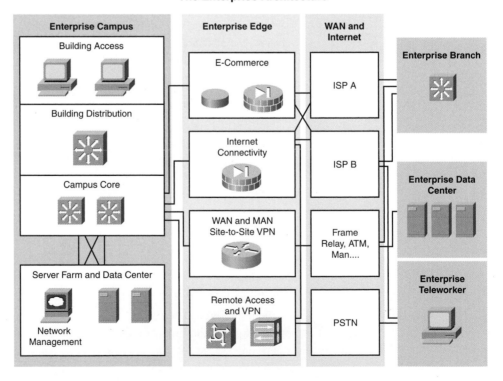

The Cisco Enterprise Architecture includes the following modules, each of which is described in greater detail in the following sections:

- Enterprise Campus Architecture

- Enterprise Edge Architecture

- Enterprise Branch Architecture

- Enterprise Data Center Architecture

- Enterprise Teleworker Architecture

Enterprise Campus Architecture

A campus network is a building or group of buildings connected into one enterprise network that consists of many LANs. A campus generally is limited to a fixed geographic area, but it can span several neighboring buildings, such as an industrial complex or business park environment. In the Span Engineering example, the campus spans multiple floors of the same building.

The Enterprise Campus Architecture describes the recommended methods to create a scalable network while addressing the needs of campus-style business operations. The architecture is modular and can easily expand to include additional campus buildings or floors as the enterprise grows. The Enterprise Campus Architecture, as illustrated in Figure 1-9, is composed of four submodules:

- The building access contains end-user workstations, IP phones, and Layer 2 access switches that connect devices to the building distribution submodule.

- The building distribution provides aggregation of building access devices, often using Layer 3 switching. This submodule performs routing, quality control, and access control.

- The campus core provides redundant and fast-converging connectivity between buildings and the server farm and enterprise edge.

- The server farm contains e-mail and corporate servers providing application, file, print, e-mail, and Domain Name System (DNS) services to internal users.

The enterprise campus module describes the connections between users, the campus network, the server farm, and the Enterprise Edge modules.

Enterprise Edge Architecture

This module, as illustrated in Figure 1-9, often functions as a liaison between the campus module and the other modules in the Enterprise Architecture. It offers connectivity to voice, video, and data services outside the enterprise. It enables the enterprise to use Internet and partner resources and provide resources for its customers. The Enterprise WAN and *metropolitan-area network (MAN)* Architecture, which the technologies covered later in this course are relevant to, are considered part of this module.

The enterprise edge aggregates the connectivity from the various functional areas at the enterprise edge (e-commerce, Internet connectivity, and VPNs) and routes the traffic into the campus core submodule.

Enterprise Branch Architecture

This module, as illustrated in Figure 1-9, allows businesses to extend the applications and services found at the campus to thousands of remote locations and users or to a small group of branches. Much of this course focuses on the technologies that are often implemented in this module.

Enterprise Data Center Architecture

Data centers provide management for many data systems that are vital to modern business operations. Employees, partners, and customers rely on data and resources in the data center to effectively create, collaborate, and interact. Over the last decade, the rise of Internet and web-based technologies has made the data center more important than ever, improving productivity, enhancing business processes, and accelerating change.

The enterprise data center, as illustrated in Figure 1-9, manages and maintains centralized data systems for the entire enterprise.

Enterprise Teleworker Architecture

Many businesses today offer a flexible work environment to their employees, allowing them to telecommute from home offices. To telecommute is to leverage the network resources of the enterprise from home. The teleworker module, as illustrated in Figure 1-9, recommends that connections from home using broadband services such as cable modem or DSL connect to the Internet and from there to the corporate network. Because the Internet introduces significant security risks to businesses, special measures need to be taken to ensure that teleworker communications are secure and private.

The enterprise teleworker module connects individual employees to network resources remotely, typically from their homes.

Figure 1-10 shows how all the Enterprise Architecture modules can be used to build a business network topology.

Figure 1-10   Sample Enterprise Architecture Topology

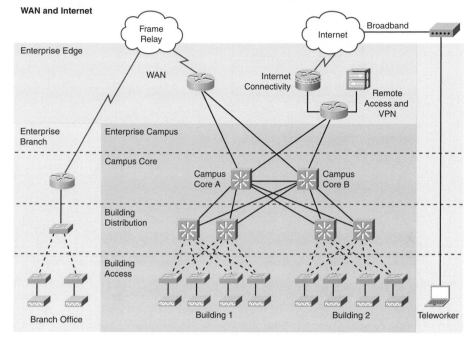

WAN Technology Concepts

This section discusses the physical and data link layer concepts of wide-area networks, including an introduction to some of the standards and protocols.

WAN Technology Overview

A variety of protocols and technologies are used in wide-area networks. Some of these services, such as HDLC and Frame Relay, are explained in more detail later in this book.

As described in relation to the OSI reference model, WAN operations focus primarily on Layer 1 and Layer 2, as shown in Figure 1-11. WAN access standards typically describe both physical layer delivery methods and data link layer requirements, including physical addressing, flow control, and encapsulation. WAN access standards are defined and managed by a number of recognized authorities, including the International Organization for Standardization (ISO), the Telecommunication Industry Association (TIA), and the Electronic Industries Alliance (EIA).

Figure 1-11   OSI and WAN Services

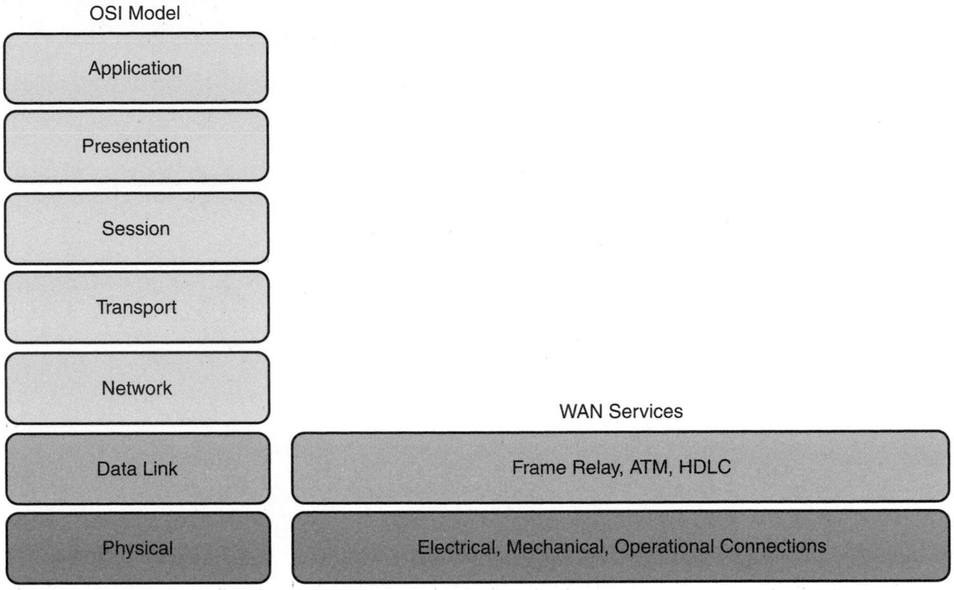

OSI Model

| Application |
| Presentation |
| Session |
| Transport |
| Network |

WAN Services

| Data Link | | Frame Relay, ATM, HDLC |
| Physical | | Electrical, Mechanical, Operational Connections |

As highlighted in Figure 1-11, the physical layer (OSI Layer 1) protocols describe how to provide electrical, mechanical, operational, and functional connections to the services of a communications service provider.

The data link layer (OSI Layer 2) protocols define how data is encapsulated for transmission toward a remote location and the mechanisms for transferring the resulting frames. A variety of technologies are used, such as *Frame Relay* and *Asynchronous Transfer Mode (ATM)*. Some of these protocols use the same basic framing mechanism, *High-Level Data Link Control (HDLC)*, an ISO standard, or one of its subsets or variants.

WAN Physical Layer Concepts

The WAN physical layer includes several devices and terms specific to wide-area networks, as described in the following sections.

WAN Physical Layer Terminology

One primary difference between a WAN and a LAN is that for a company or organization to use WAN carrier network services, it must subscribe to an outside WAN service provider. A WAN uses data links provided by carrier services to access or connect the locations of an organization to each other, to locations of other organizations, to external services, and to remote users. The WAN access physical layer describes the physical connection between the company network and the service provider network.

Figure 1-12 illustrates the terminology commonly used to describe physical WAN connections, as described in further detail in the following list:

- *Customer Premises Equipment (CPE)*: The devices and inside wiring located at the premises of the subscriber, connected with a telecommunication *channel* of a carrier. The subscriber either owns or leases the CPE. A subscriber, in this context, is a company that arranges for WAN services from a service provider or carrier.

- *Data Communications Equipment (DCE)*: Also called data circuit-terminating equipment, the DCE consists of devices that put data on the local loop. The DCE primarily provides an interface to connect subscribers to a communication link on the WAN cloud.

- *Data Terminal Equipment (DTE)*: The customer devices that pass the data from a customer network or host computer for transmission over the WAN. The DTE connects to the local loop through the DCE.

- *Local loop*: The copper or fiber *cable* that connects the CPE at the subscriber site to the central office (CO) of the service provider. The local loop is sometimes called the "last mile."

- *Demarcation point*: A point established in a building or complex to separate customer equipment from service provider equipment. Physically, the demarcation point is the cabling junction box, located on the customer premises, that connects the CPE wiring to the local loop. It is usually placed for easy access by a technician. The demarcation point is the place where the responsibility for the connection changes from the user to the service provider. This is very important, because when problems arise, it is necessary to determine whether the user or the service provider is responsible for troubleshooting or repair.

- *Central office (CO)*: A local service provider facility or building where local cables link to long-haul, all-digital, fiber-optic *communications lines* through a system of switches and other equipment.

Figure 1-12   WAN Physical Layer Terminology

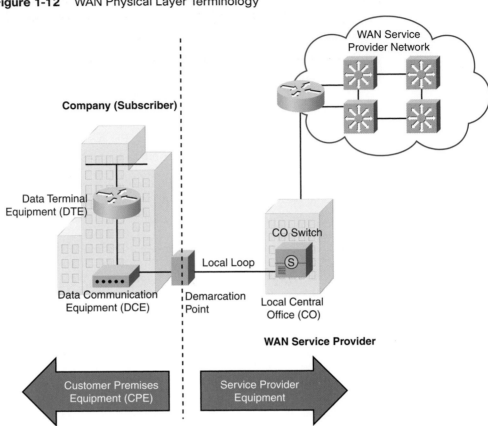

WAN Devices

WANs use numerous types of devices that are specific to WAN environments:

- *Modem*: Modulates an analog carrier signal to encode digital information, and also demodulates the carrier signal to decode the transmitted information. A voiceband modem converts the digital signals produced by a computer into voice frequencies that can be transmitted over the analog lines of the public telephone network. On the other side of the connection, another modem converts the sounds back into a digital signal for input to a computer or network connection. Faster modems, such as cable modems and DSL modems, transmit using higher broadband frequencies.

- **CSU/DSU**: Digital lines, such as *T1* and *T3* carrier lines, require a *channel service unit (CSU)* and a *data service unit (DSU)*. The two are often combined into a single piece of equipment, called the CSU/DSU. The CSU provides termination for the digital signal and ensures connection integrity through error correction and line monitoring. The DSU converts the *T-carrier* line frames into frames that the LAN can interpret and vice versa.

- *Access server*: Concentrates dial-in and dial-out user communications. An access server may have a mixture of analog and digital interfaces and support hundreds of simultaneous users.

- **WAN switch**: A multiport internetworking device used in carrier networks. These devices typically switch traffic such as Frame Relay, ATM, or *X.25* and operate at the data link layer of the OSI reference model. *Public switched telephone network (PSTN)* switches may also be used within the cloud for circuit-switched connections such as *Integrated Services Digital Network (ISDN)* or analog dialup.

- **Router**: Provides internetworking and WAN access interface ports that are used to connect to the service provider network. These interfaces may be serial connections or other WAN interfaces. With some types of WAN interfaces, an external device such as a DSU/CSU or modem (analog, cable, or DSL) is required to connect the router to the service provider's local *point of presence (POP)*.

- *Core router*: A router that resides within the middle or backbone of the WAN rather than at its periphery. To fulfill this role, a router must be able to support multiple telecommunications interfaces of the highest speed in use in the WAN core, and it must be able to forward IP packets at full speed on all those interfaces. The router must also support the routing protocols being used in the core.

Figure 1-13 shows the location of each device.

Figure 1-13   WAN Devices

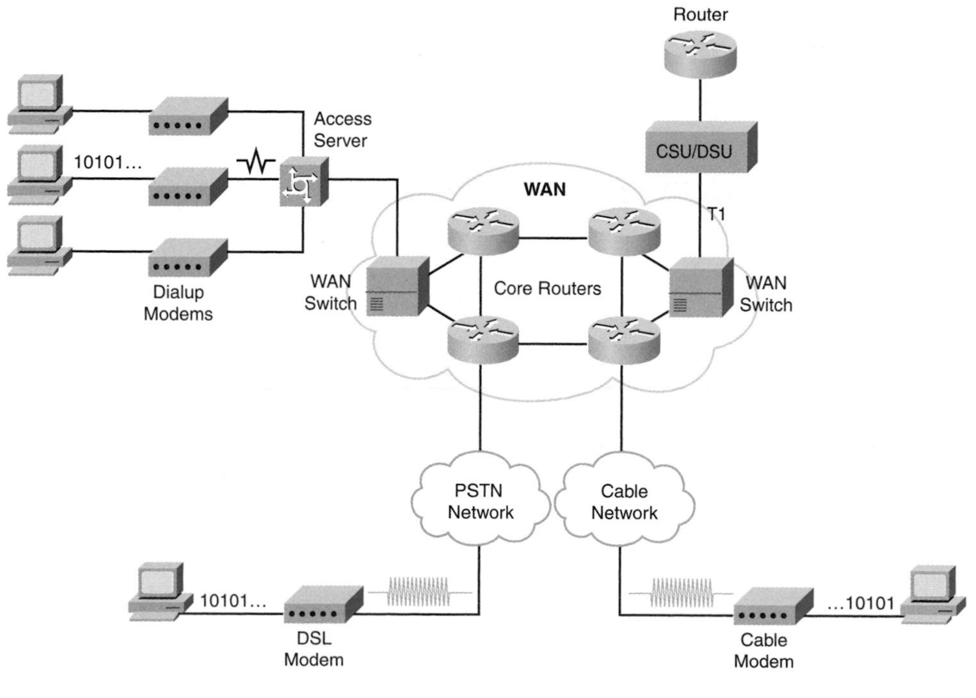

WAN Physical Layer Standards

WAN physical-layer protocols describe how to provide electrical, mechanical, operational, and functional connections for WAN services. The WAN physical layer also describes the interface between the DTE and DCE.

The DTE/DCE interface uses various physical layer protocols:

- **EIA/TIA-232**: This protocol allows signal speeds of up to 64 kbps on a 25-pin D-connector over short distances. It was formerly known as RS-232. The ITU-T V.24 specification is effectively the same.

- **EIA/TIA-449/530**: This protocol is a faster (up to 2 Mbps) version of EIA/TIA-232. It uses a 36-pin D-connector and is capable of longer cable runs. Several versions exist. This standard is also known as RS-422 and RS-423.

- **EIA/TIA-612/613**: This standard describes the *High-Speed Serial Interface (HSSI)* protocol, which provides access to services up to 52 Mbps on a 60-pin D-connector.

- **V.35**: This is the ITU-T standard for synchronous communications between a network access device and a packet network. Originally specified to support data rates of 48 kbps, it now supports speeds of up to 2.048 Mbps using a 34-pin rectangular connector.

- **X.21**: This protocol is an ITU-T standard for synchronous digital communications. It uses a 15-pin D-connector.

These protocols establish the codes and electrical parameters the devices use to communicate with each other. Choosing a protocol is largely determined by the service provider's method of facilitation.

Figure 1-14 illustrates the types of cable connectors associated with each physical layer protocol.

Figure 1-14   WAN Cable Connectors

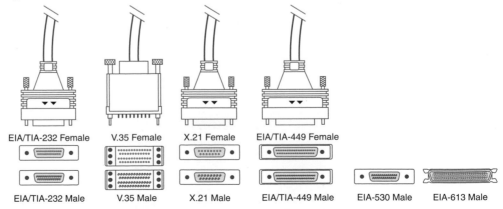

WAN Data Link Layer Concepts

In addition to physical layer devices, WANs require data link layer protocols to establish the link across the communication line from the sending to the receiving device. This section describes the common data link protocols that are used in today's enterprise networks to implement WAN connections.

Data Link Protocols

Data link layer protocols define how data is encapsulated for transmission to remote sites and the mechanisms for transferring the resulting frames. A variety of technologies are used, such as ISDN, Frame Relay, or ATM, as shown in Figure 1-15. Many of these protocols use the same basic framing mechanism, HDLC, an ISO standard, or one of its subsets or variants. ATM is different from the others, because it uses small fixed-size cells of 53 bytes (48 bytes for data), unlike the other packet-switched technologies, which use variable-sized packets.

Figure 1-15   Data Link Layer Protocols

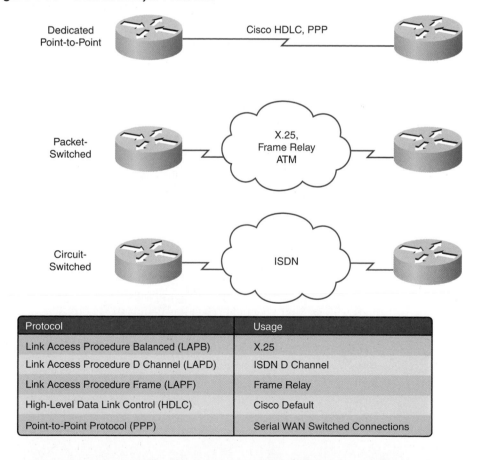

Protocol	Usage
Link Access Procedure Balanced (LAPB)	X.25
Link Access Procedure D Channel (LAPD)	ISDN D Channel
Link Access Procedure Frame (LAPF)	Frame Relay
High-Level Data Link Control (HDLC)	Cisco Default
Point-to-Point Protocol (PPP)	Serial WAN Switched Connections

The most common WAN data-link protocols are as follows:

- HDLC

- *Point-to-Point Protocol (PPP)*

- Frame Relay

- ATM

ISDN and X.25 are older data-link protocols that are less frequently used today. However, ISDN is still covered in this course because of its use when provisioning a VoIP network using PRI links. X.25 is mentioned to help explain the relevance of Frame Relay. As well, X.25 is still in use in developing countries where packet data networks (PDN) are used to transmit credit card and debit card transactions from retailers.

> **Note**
>
> Another data link layer protocol is Multiprotocol Label Switching (MPLS). MPLS is increasingly being deployed by service providers as an economical solution to carry circuit-switched as well as packet-switched network traffic. It can operate over any existing infrastructure, such as IP, Frame Relay, ATM, or Ethernet. It sits between Layer 2 and Layer 3 and is sometimes referred to as a Layer 2.5 protocol. MPLS is beyond the scope of this course, but it is covered on the CCNP: Implementing Secure Converged Wide Area Networks course.

WAN Encapsulation

Data from the network layer is passed to the data link layer for delivery on a physical link, which normally is point-to-point on a WAN connection. The data link layer builds a frame around the network layer data so that the necessary checks and controls can be applied. Each WAN connection type uses a Layer 2 protocol to encapsulate a packet while it is crossing the WAN link. To ensure that the correct encapsulation protocol is used, the Layer 2 encapsulation type used for each router serial interface must be configured. The choice of encapsulation protocols depends on the WAN technology and the equipment. HDLC was first proposed in 1979; for this reason, most framing protocols that were developed afterwards are based on it.

Figure 1-16 shows how WAN data link protocols encapsulate traffic.

Examining the header portion of an HDLC frame, shown in Figure 1-17, helps you identify common fields used by many WAN encapsulation protocols. The frame always starts and ends with an 8-bit Flag field. The bit pattern is 01111110. The Address field is not needed for WAN links, which are almost always point-to-point. The Address field is still present and may be 1 or 2 bytes long. The Control field is protocol-dependent, but it usually indicates whether the data is control information or network layer data. The Control field normally is 1 byte.

Figure 1-16   WAN Encapsulation

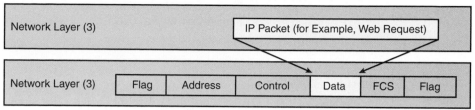

Network data is encapsulated in an HDLC frame.

Figure 1-17   WAN Frame Encapsulation Formats

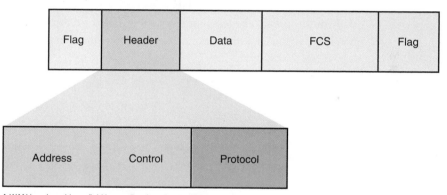

A WAN header address field is usually a broadcast address on a point-to point link. The control field identifies the data portion as either information or control. The protocol field identifies the intended layer 3 protocol (e.g., IP, IPX).

The Address and Control fields, as illustrated in Figure 1-17, are called the frame header. The encapsulated data follows the Control field. Then a frame check sequence (FCS) uses the cyclic redundancy check (CRC) mechanism to establish a 2- or 4-byte field.

Several types of WAN encapsulation formats exist, including subsets and proprietary versions of HDLC. Both PPP and the Cisco version of HDLC have an extra field in the header to identify the network layer protocol of the encapsulated data.

WAN Switching Concepts

WAN switched networks are categorized as either circuit-switched or packet-switched, as described in greater detail in the following sections.

Circuit Switching

A circuit-switched network is one that establishes a dedicated *circuit* (or channel) between nodes and terminals before the users may communicate.

As an example, Figure 1-18 shows that when a subscriber makes a telephone call, the dialed number is used to set switches in the exchanges along the call's route so that a continuous circuit exists from the caller to the called party. Because of the switching operation used to establish the circuit, the telephone system is called a circuit-switched network. If the telephones are replaced with modems, the switched circuit can carry computer data.

Figure 1-18   Circuit Switching

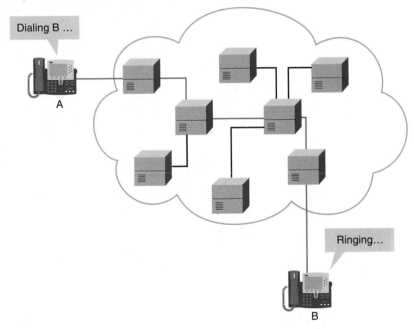

The internal path taken by the circuit between exchanges is shared by a number of conversations. *Time-division multiplexing (TDM)* gives each conversation a share of the connection in turn. TDM ensures that a fixed-capacity connection is made available to the subscriber.

If the circuit carries computer data, the usage of this fixed capacity may be inefficient. For example, if the circuit is used to access the Internet, a burst of activity occurs on the circuit while a web page is transferred. This could be followed by no activity while the user reads the page, and then another burst of activity while the next page is transferred. This variation in usage between none and maximum is typical of computer network traffic. Because the subscriber has sole use of the fixed-capacity allocation, switched circuits generally are an expensive way of moving data.

PSTN and ISDN are two types of *circuit-switching* technology that may be used to implement a WAN in an enterprise setting.

Packet Switching

In contrast to circuit switching, *packet switching* splits traffic data into packets that are routed over a shared network. Packet-switching networks do not require a circuit to be established, and they allow many pairs of nodes to communicate over the same channel.

The switches in a *packet-switched network* determine which link the packet must be sent on next from the addressing information in each packet. There are two approaches to this link determination:

- *Connectionless* systems, such as the Internet, carry full addressing information in each packet. Each switch must evaluate the address to determine where to send the packet.

- *Connection-oriented* systems predetermine a packet's route, and each packet only has to carry an identifier. In the case of Frame Relay, these are called *Data Link Connection Identifiers (DLCI)*. The switch determines the onward route by looking up the identifier in tables held in memory. The set of entries in the tables identifies a particular route or circuit through the system. If this circuit exists only while a packet travels through it, it is called a *virtual circuit (VC)*. A virtual circuit is a logical circuit between two network devices to help ensure reliable communications.

Because the internal links between the switches are shared between many users, the costs of packet switching are lower than those of circuit switching. Delays (latency) and variability of delay (jitter) are greater in packet-switched networks than in circuit-switched networks. This is because the links are shared, and packets must be entirely received at one switch before moving to the next. Despite the latency and jitter inherent in shared networks, modern technology allows satisfactory transport of voice and even video communications on these networks.

In Figure 1-19, Server A is sending data to Server B. Packets may not necessarily always take the same path to reach the destination. Each packet may take different routes to reach Server B.

Figure 1-19   Packet Switching

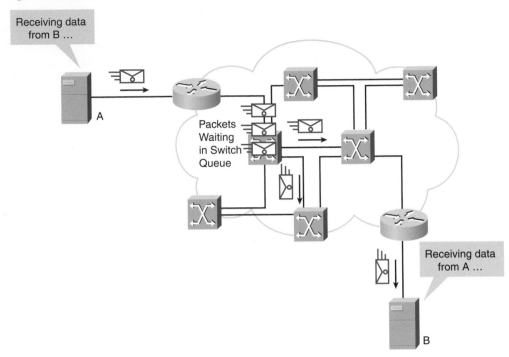

Virtual Circuits

Packet-switched networks may establish routes through the switches for particular end-to-end connections. These routes are called virtual circuits (VC). A VC is a logical circuit created within a shared network between two network devices. Two types of VCs exist:

- *Permanent virtual circuit (PVC)*: A permanently established virtual circuit that consists of one mode: data transfer. PVCs are used in situations in which data transfer between devices is constant. PVCs decrease the bandwidth use associated with establishing and terminating VCs, but they increase costs because of constant virtual circuit availability. PVCs generally are configured by the service provider when an order is placed for service.

- *Switched virtual circuit (SVC)*: A VC that is dynamically established on demand and terminated when transmission is complete. Communication over an SVC consists of three phases: circuit establishment, data transfer, and circuit termination. The establishment phase involves creating the VC between the source and destination devices, with SVC entries stored in lookup tables held in memory. Data transfer involves transmitting data between the devices over the VC, and the circuit termination phase involves tearing down the VC between the source and destination devices. SVCs are used in situations in which data transmission between devices is intermittent, largely to save costs. SVCs release the circuit when transmission is complete, which results in less expensive connection charges than those incurred by PVCs, which maintain constant virtual circuit availability.

Note

Virtual circuits are discussed in more detail in Chapter 3, "Frame Relay."

Connecting to a Packet-Switched Network

To connect to a packet-switched network, a subscriber needs a local loop to the nearest location where the provider makes the service available. This is called the service's point of presence (POP). Normally this is a dedicated leased line. This line is much shorter than a leased line connected directly between the subscriber locations. In addition, this one line to the POP can carry several VCs, allowing it to provide connections to multiple destinations. Because it is likely that not all the VCs require maximum demand simultaneously, the capacity of the *leased line* can be smaller than the sum of the individual VCs. Examples of packet- or cell-switched connections include

- X.25

- Frame Relay

- ATM

WAN Connection Options

This section covers various WAN connection options, including private dedicated links, private switched links, and public connection options using the Internet.

WAN Link Connection Options

Many options for implementing WAN solutions are currently available. They differ in technology, speed, and cost. Familiarity with these technologies is an important part of network design and evaluation:

Figure 1-20 provides a high-level view of the various WAN link connection options:

- **Private WAN connection options**: Private WAN connections include both dedicated and switched communication link options:

  - **Dedicated communication links**: When permanent dedicated connections are required, point-to-point lines are used with various capacities that are limited only by the underlying physical facilities and the willingness of users to pay for these dedicated lines. A point-to-point link provides a preestablished WAN communications path from the customer premises through the provider network to a remote destination. Point-to-point lines usually are leased from a carrier and are also called leased lines.

- **Switched communication links**: Switched communication links can be either circuit-switched or packet-switched:

  Circuit-switched communication links: Circuit switching dynamically establishes a dedicated connection for voice or data between a sender and a receiver. Before communication can start, it is necessary to establish the connection through the service provider's network. Examples of circuit-switched communication links are analog dialup (PSTN) and ISDN.

  Packet-switched communication links: Many WAN users do not make efficient use of the fixed bandwidth that is available with dedicated, switched, or permanent circuits, because the data flow fluctuates. Communications providers have data networks available to more appropriately service these users. In packet-switched networks, the data is transmitted in labeled frames, cells, or packets. Packet-switched communication links include Frame Relay, ATM, X.25, and Metro Ethernet.

- **Public WAN connection options**: Public connections use the global Internet infrastructure. Until recently, the Internet was not a viable networking option for many businesses because of the significant security risks and lack of adequate performance guarantees in an end-to-end Internet connection. With the development of VPN technology, however, the Internet is now an inexpensive and secure option for connecting to teleworkers and remote offices where performance guarantees are not critical. Internet WAN connection links are through broadband services such as DSL, cable modem, and broadband wireless, and they are combined with VPN technology to provide privacy across the Internet.

Figure 1-20 WAN Link Connection Options

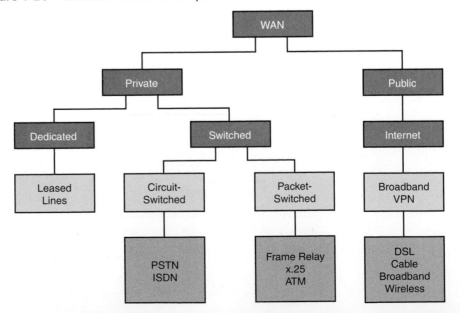

Dedicated Connection Link Options

When permanent dedicated connections are required, a point-to-point link is used to provide a preestablished WAN communications path from the customer premises through the provider network to a remote destination.

Point-to-point lines usually are leased from a carrier and are called leased lines. Figure 1-21 shows a T3 and E3 circuit. This section describes how enterprises use leased lines to provide a dedicated WAN connection.

Figure 1-21   Leased Lines

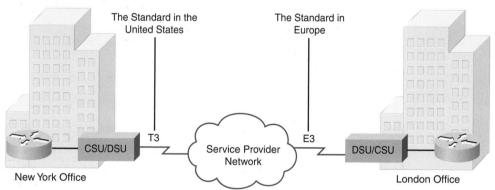

Leased lines are available in different capacities. They generally are priced based on the bandwidth required and the distance between the two connected points.

Table 1-1 lists the available leased-line types and their bit-rate capacities.

Table 1-1   Leased-Line Types and Capacities

Line Type	Bit Rate Capacity	Line Type	Bit Rate Capacity
56	56 kbps	OC-9	466.56 Mbps
64	64 kbps	OC-12	622.08 Mbps
T1	1.544 Mbps	OC-18	933.12 Mbps
E1	2.048 Mbps	OC-24	1244.16 Mbps
J1	2.048 Mbps	OC-36	1866.24 Mbps
E3	34.064 Mbps	OC-48	2488.32 Mbps
T3	44.736 Mbps	OC-96	4976.64 Mbps
OC-1	51.84 Mbps	OC-192	9953.28 Mbps
OC-3	155.54 Mbps	OC-768	39,813.12 Mbps

Point-to-point links usually are more expensive than shared services such as Frame Relay. The cost of leased-line solutions can become significant when they are used to connect many sites over increasing distances. However, sometimes the benefits outweigh the cost of the leased line. The dedicated capacity removes latency and jitter between the endpoints. Constant availability is essential for some applications, such as VoIP and video over IP.

A router serial port is required for each leased-line connection. A CSU/DSU and the actual circuit from the service provider are also required.

Leased lines provide permanent dedicated capacity and are used extensively to build WANs. They have been the traditional connection of choice but have a number of disadvantages. Leased lines have a fixed capacity; however, WAN traffic is often variable, leaving some of the capacity unused. In addition, each endpoint needs a separate physical interface on the router, which increases equipment costs. Any changes to the leased line generally require a site visit by the carrier.

Circuit-Switched Connection Options

Circuit-switched networks establish a dedicated connection for voice or data between a sender and a receiver. Before any communications can begin, it is necessary to establish the connection through the service provider's network.

Analog Dialup

When intermittent, low-volume data transfers are needed, modems and analog dialed telephone lines provide low capacity and dedicated switched connections.

This section describes the pros and cons of using analog dialup connection options and describes the types of business scenarios that benefit most from this type of option. Figure 1-22 shows an analog dialup connection.

Figure 1-22   WAN Built with an Intermittent Connection Using a Modem and the Voice Telephone Network

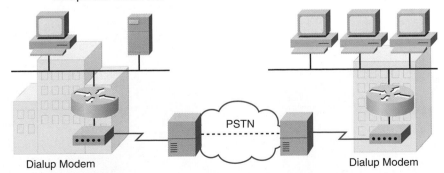

Traditional *telephony* uses a copper cable, called the local loop, to connect the telephone handset in the subscriber premises to the CO. The signal on the local loop during a call is a continuously varying electronic signal that is a translation of the subscriber analog voice signal.

Traditional local loops can transport binary computer data through the voice telephone network using a modem. The modem modulates the binary data into an analog signal at the source and demodulates the analog signal into binary data at the destination. The physical characteristics of the local loop and its connection to the PSTN limit the signal's rate to less than 56 kbps.

For small businesses, these relatively low-speed dialup connections are adequate for the exchange of sales figures, prices, routine reports, and e-mail. Using automatic dialup at night or on weekends for large file transfers and data backup can take advantage of lower off-peak tariffs (line charges). Tariffs are based on the distance between the endpoints, time of day, and the call's duration.

The advantages of modem and analog lines are simplicity, availability, and low implementation cost. The disadvantages are the low data rates and a relatively long connection time. The dedicated circuit has little delay or jitter for point-to-point traffic, but voice or video traffic does not operate adequately at these low bit rates.

Integrated Services Digital Network

Integrated Services Digital Network (ISDN) is a circuit-switching technology that enables the local loop of a PSTN to carry digital signals, resulting in higher-capacity switched connections. ISDN changes the internal connections of the PSTN from carrying analog signals to time-division multiplexed (TDM) digital signals. TDM allows two or more signals or bit streams to be transferred as subchannels in one communication channel. The signals appear to transfer simultaneously, but physically they take turns on the channel. A data block of subchannel 1 is transmitted during time slot 1, subchannel 2 during time slot 2, and so on. One TDM frame consists of one time slot per subchannel. TDM is described in more detail in Chapter 2, "PPP."

ISDN turns the local loop into a TDM digital connection. This change enables the local loop to carry digital signals that result in higher-capacity switched connections. The connection uses 64-kbps *bearer (B) channels* to carry voice or data and a *signaling, delta channel* for call setup and other purposes.

There are two types of ISDN interfaces:

- *Basic Rate Interface (BRI)*: ISDN is intended for the home and small enterprise and provides two 64-kbps B channels and a 16-kbps D channel. The BRI D channel is designed for control and often is underused, because it has only two B channels to control. Therefore, some providers allow the D channel to carry data at low bit rates, such as X.25 connections at 9.6 kbps.

■ *Primary Rate Interface (PRI)*: ISDN is also available for larger installations. PRI delivers 23 B channels with 64 kbps and one D channel with 64 kbps in North America, for a total bit rate of up to 1.544 Mbps. This includes some additional overhead for *synchronization*. In Europe, Australia, and other parts of the world, ISDN PRI provides 30 B channels and one D channel, for a total bit rate of up to 2.048 Mbps, including synchronization overhead. In North America, PRI corresponds to a T1 connection. The PRI rate of lines outside North America corresponds to an *E1* or *J1* connection.

Figure 1-23 illustrates the various differences between ISDN BRI and PRI lines.

Figure 1-23   ISDN Network Infrastructure and PRI/BRI Line Capacity

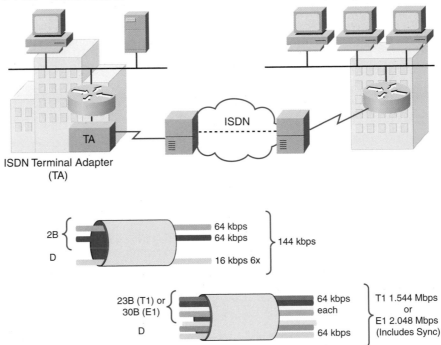

For WAN links, which require low bandwidth, the BRI ISDN can provide an ideal connection mechanism. BRI has a *call setup time* that is less than a second, and the 64-kbps B channel provides greater capacity than an analog modem link. If greater capacity is required, a second B channel can be activated to provide a total of 128 kbps. Although this is inadequate for video, it permits several simultaneous voice conversations in addition to data traffic.

Another common application of ISDN is to provide additional capacity as needed on a leased-line connection. The leased line is sized to carry average traffic loads, and ISDN is added during peak demand periods. ISDN is also used as a backup if the leased line fails. ISDN tariffs are based on a per-B-channel basis and are similar to those of analog voice connections.

With PRI ISDN, multiple B channels can be connected between two endpoints. This allows for videoconferencing and high-bandwidth data connections with no latency or jitter. However, multiple connections can be very expensive over long distances.

Note

Although ISDN is still an important technology for telephone service provider networks, it is declining in popularity as an Internet connection option with the introduction of high-speed DSL and other broadband services. The "Consumer and Industry Perspectives" section at *http://en.wikipedia.org/wiki/ISDN* provides a good discussion of ISDN worldwide trends.

Packet-Switched Connection Options

The most common packet-switching technologies used in today's enterprise WANs include legacy X.25, Frame Relay, and ATM, as described in the following sections.

X.25

Figure 1-24 shows an X.25 network. X.25 is a legacy network-layer protocol that provides subscribers with a network address. Virtual circuits can be established through the network with call request packets to the target address. The resulting SVC is identified by a channel number. Data packets labeled with the channel number are delivered to the corresponding address. Multiple channels can be active on a single connection.

Figure 1-24   X.25 Network

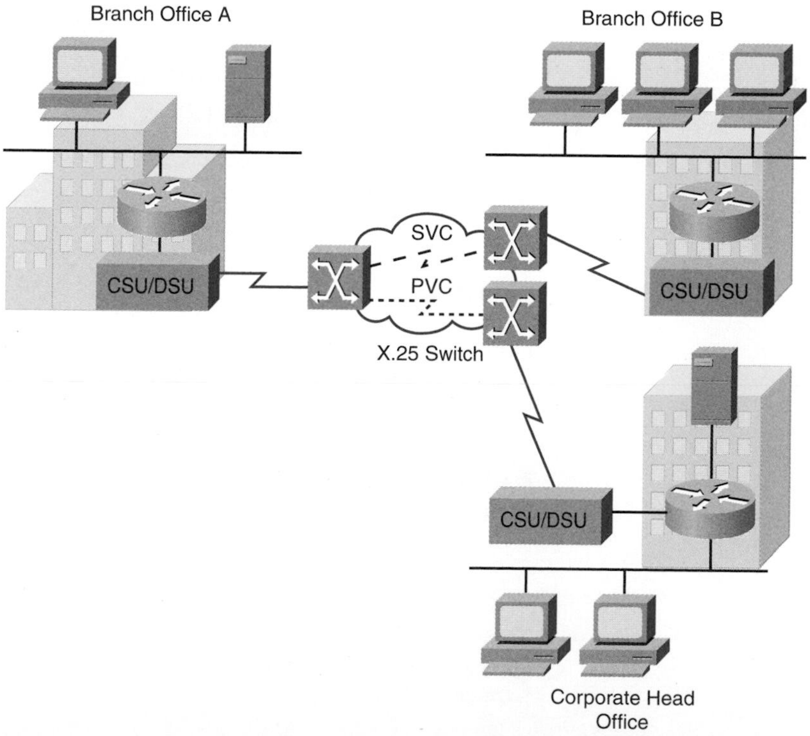

Typical X.25 applications are point-of-sale card readers. These readers use X.25 in dialup mode to validate transactions on a central computer. For these applications, the low bandwidth and high latency are not a concern, and the low cost makes X.25 affordable.

X.25 link speeds vary from 2400 bps up to 2 Mbps. However, public networks usually are low-capacity, with speeds rarely exceeding 64 kbps.

X.25 networks are now in dramatic decline, being replaced by newer Layer 2 technologies such as Frame Relay, ATM, and ADSL. However, they are still in use in many portions of the developing world, which have limited access to newer technologies.

Frame Relay

Figure 1-25 shows a Frame Relay network. Although the network layout appears similar to X.25, Frame Relay differs from X.25 in several ways. Most importantly, it is a much simpler protocol, operating strictly at Layer 2, whereas X.25 additionally provides Layer 3 services. Frame Relay implements no error or flow control. The simplified handling of frames leads to reduced latency, and measures taken to avoid frame buildup at intermediate switches help reduce jitter. Frame Relay offers data rates up to 4 Mbps, with some providers offering even higher rates.

Figure 1-25   Frame Relay Network

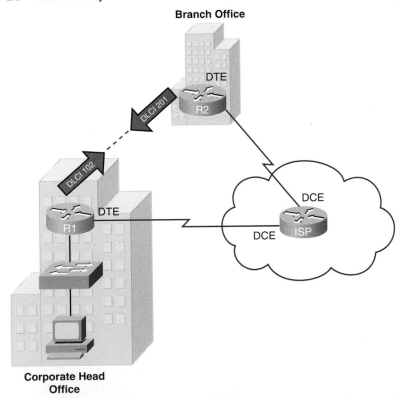

Frame Relay VCs are uniquely identified by a DLCI, which ensures bidirectional communication from one DTE device to another. Most Frame Relay connections are PVCs rather than SVCs.

Frame Relay provides permanent, shared, medium-bandwidth connectivity that carries both voice and data traffic. Frame Relay is ideal for connecting enterprise LANs. The router on the LAN needs only a single interface, even when multiple VCs are used. The short-leased line to the Frame Relay network edge allows cost-effective connections between widely scattered LANs.

Frame Relay is described in more detail in Chapter 3.

ATM

Figure 1-26 shows an ATM network. Asynchronous Transfer Mode (ATM) technology can transfer voice, video, and data through private and public networks. It is built on a cell-based architecture rather than on a frame-based architecture. ATM cells are always a fixed length of 53 bytes. The ATM cell contains a 5-byte ATM header followed by 48 bytes of ATM payload. Small, fixed-length cells are well suited for carrying voice and video traffic, because this traffic is intolerant of delay. Video and voice traffic do not have to wait for a larger data packet to be transmitted.

Figure 1-26   ATM Network

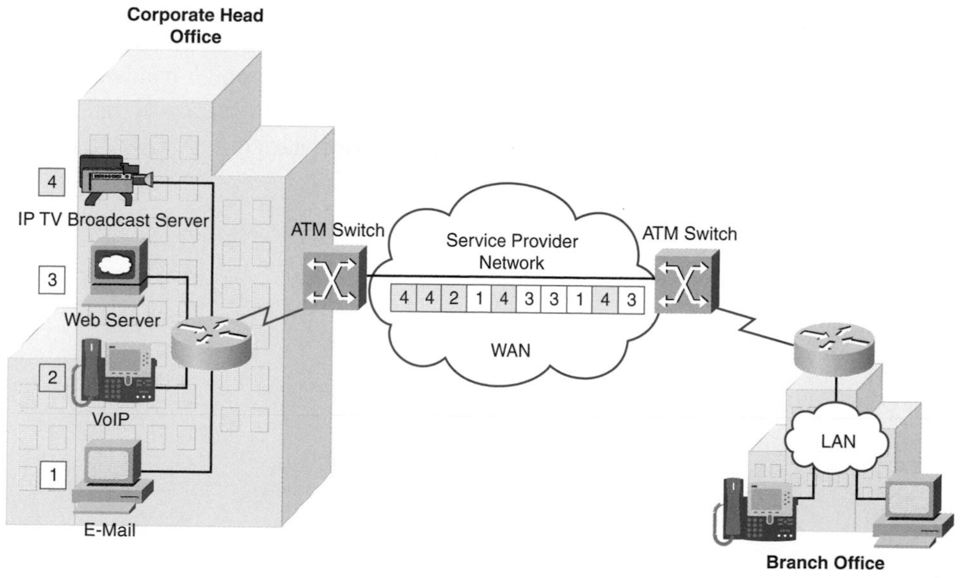

The 53-byte ATM *cell* is less efficient than the bigger frames and packets of Frame Relay and X.25. Furthermore, the ATM cell has at least 5 bytes of overhead for each 48-byte payload. When the cell is carrying segmented network layer packets, the overhead is higher, because the ATM switch must be able to reassemble the packets at the destination. A typical ATM line needs almost 20 percent more bandwidth than Frame Relay to carry the same volume of network layer data.

ATM was designed to be extremely scalable. It can support link speeds of T1/E1 to OC-12 (622 Mbps) and higher.

ATM offers both PVCs and SVCs, although PVCs are more common with WANs. And as with other shared technologies, ATM allows multiple VCs on a single leased-line connection to the network edge.

Internet Connection Options

The Internet is an inexpensive and secure option for connecting to teleworkers and remote offices where performance guarantees are not critical.

Broadband connection options typically are used to connect telecommuting employees to a corporate site over the Internet. These options include DSL, cable, and wireless.

DSL

DSL technology, shown in Figure 1-27, is an always-on connection technology that uses existing twisted-pair telephone lines to transport high-bandwidth data and provides IP services to subscribers. A DSL modem converts an Ethernet signal from the user device into a DSL signal, which is transmitted to the central office.

Figure 1-27   DSL

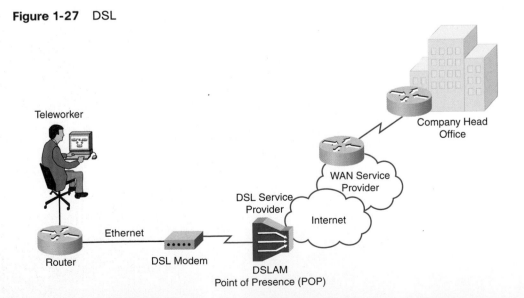

Multiple DSL subscriber lines are multiplexed into a single high-capacity link using a DSL access multiplexer (DSLAM) at the provider location. DSLAMs incorporate TDM technology to aggregate many subscriber lines into a single medium, generally a T3 (DS3) connection. Current DSL technologies use sophisticated coding and modulation techniques to achieve data rates of up to 8.192 Mbps.

A wide variety of DSL types, standards, and emerging technologies exist. DSL is now a popular choice for enterprise IT departments to support home workers. Generally, a subscriber cannot choose to connect to an enterprise network directly. The subscriber must first connect to an ISP, and then an IP connection is made through the Internet to the enterprise. Security risks are incurred in this process, but they can be mediated with security measures.

Cable Modem

Coaxial cable is widely used in urban areas to distribute television signals. Network access is available from some *cable television* networks. This allows for greater bandwidth than the conventional telephone local loop.

Cable modems provide an always-on connection and a simple installation. Figure 1-28 shows how a subscriber connects a computer or LAN router to the cable modem, which translates the digital signals into the broadband frequencies used for transmitting on a cable television network. The local cable TV office, which is called the cable headend, contains the computer system and databases needed to provide Internet access. The most important component located at the *headend* is the cable modem termination system (CMTS). It sends and receives digital cable modem signals on a cable network and is necessary for providing Internet services to cable subscribers.

Figure 1-28   Cable Modem

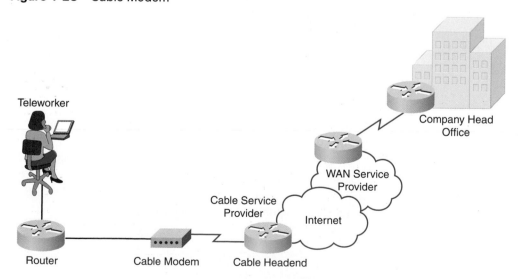

Cable modem subscribers must use the ISP associated with the service provider. All the local subscribers share the same cable bandwidth. As more users join the service, available bandwidth may be below the expected rate.

Broadband Wireless

Wireless technology uses the unlicensed radio spectrum to send and receive data. The unlicensed spectrum is accessible to anyone who has a wireless router and wireless technology in the device he or she is using.

Until recently, one limitation of wireless access has been the need to be within the local transmission range (typically less than 100 feet) of a wireless router or a wireless modem that has a wired connection to the Internet. The following new developments in broadband wireless technology are changing this situation:

- **Municipal Wi-Fi**: Many cities have begun setting up municipal wireless networks. Some of these networks provide high-speed Internet access for free or for substantially less than the price of other broadband services. Others are for city use only, allowing police and fire departments and other city employees to do certain aspects of their jobs remotely. To connect to a municipal Wi-Fi, a subscriber typically needs a wireless modem, which provides a stronger radio and directional antenna than conventional wireless adapters. Most service providers provide the necessary equipment for free or for a fee, much like they do with DSL or cable modems.

- **WiMAX**: Worldwide Interoperability for *Microwave* Access (WiMAX) is a new technology that is just beginning to come into use. It is described in IEEE standard 802.16. WiMAX provides high-speed broadband service with wireless access and provides broad coverage like a cell phone network rather than through small Wi-Fi hotspots. WiMAX operates in a similar way to Wi-Fi, but at higher speeds, over greater distances, and for a greater number of users. It uses a network of WiMAX towers that are similar to cell phone towers, as shown in Figure 1-29. To access a WiMAX network, subscribers must subscribe to an ISP that has a WiMAX tower within 10 miles of their location. They also need a WiMAX-enabled computer and a special encryption code to get access to the base station.

- **Satellite Internet**: This is typically used by rural users where cable and DSL are unavailable. A satellite dish provides two-way (upload and download) data communications. The upload speed is about one-tenth of the 500-kbps download speed. Cable and DSL have higher download speeds, but satellite systems are about ten times faster than an analog modem. To access satellite Internet services, subscribers need a satellite dish, two modems (uplink and downlink), and coaxial cables between the dish and the modem.

Figure 1-29   Broadband Wireless

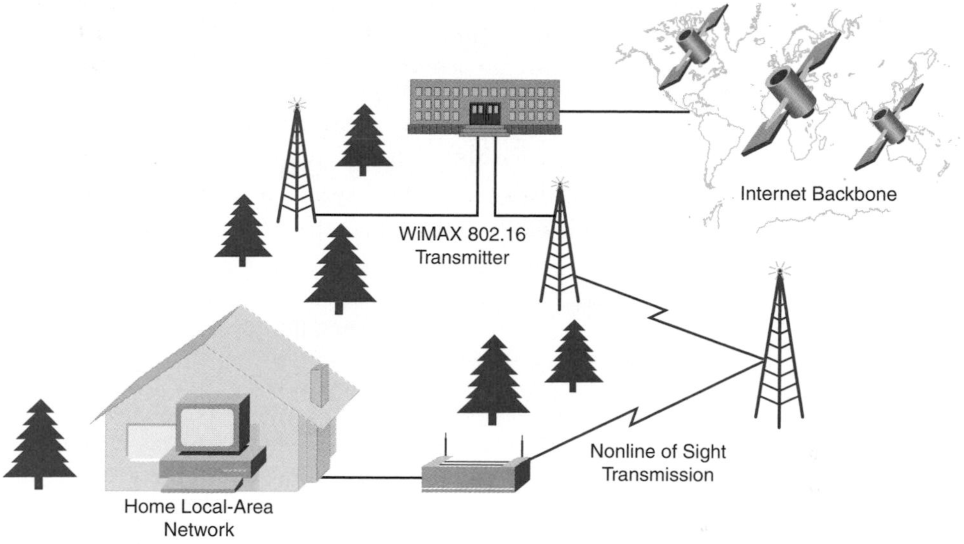

DSL, cable, and wireless broadband services are described in more detail in Chapter 6, "Teleworker Services."

VPN Technology

Security risks are incurred when a teleworker or remote office uses broadband services to access the corporate WAN over the Internet. To address security concerns, broadband services provide capabilities for using Virtual Private Network (VPN) connections to a VPN server, which typically is located at the corporate site.

A VPN is an encrypted connection between private networks over a public network such as the Internet. Instead of using a dedicated Layer 2 connection such as a leased line, a VPN uses virtual connections called VPN tunnels, which are routed through the Internet from the company's private network to the remote site or employee host.

VPN Benefits

Benefits of VPN include the following:

- **Cost savings**: VPNs enable organizations to use the global Internet to connect remote offices and remote users to the main corporate site, thus eliminating expensive dedicated WAN links and modem banks.

- **Security**: VPNs provide the highest level of security by using advanced encryption and authentication protocols that protect data from unauthorized access.

- **Scalability**: Because VPNs use the Internet infrastructure within ISPs and devices, it is easy to add new users. Corporations can add large amounts of capacity without adding significant infrastructure.

- **Compatibility with broadband technology**: VPN technology is supported by broadband service providers such as DSL and cable, so mobile workers and telecommuters can take advantage of their home high-speed Internet service to access their corporate networks. Business-grade, high-speed broadband connections can also provide a cost-effective solution for connecting remote offices.

Types of VPN Access

Two types of VPN access exist:

- **Site-to-site VPNs**: Site-to-site VPNs connect entire networks to each other. For example, they can connect a branch office network to a company headquarters network, as shown in Figure 1-30. Each site is equipped with a VPN gateway, such as a router, *firewall*, VPN concentrator, or security appliance. In the figure, a remote branch office uses a site-to-site VPN to connect with the corporate head office.

- **Remote-access VPNs**: Remote-access VPNs enable individual hosts, such as telecommuters, mobile users, and extranet consumers, to access a company network securely over the Internet, as shown in Figure 1-31. Each host typically has VPN client software loaded or uses a web-based client.

Figure 1-30   Site-to-Site VPNs

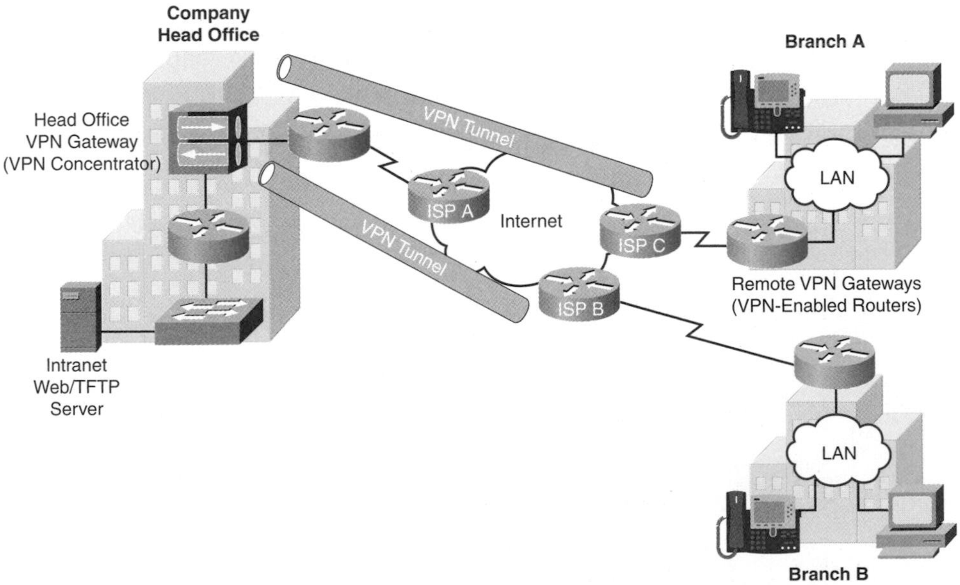

Figure 1-31   Remote-Access VPNs

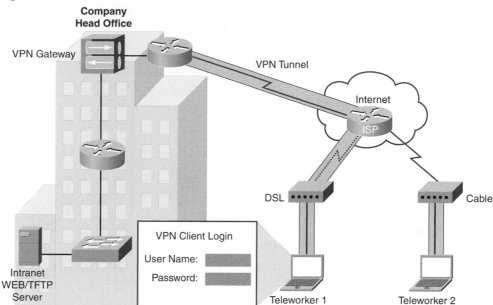

Metro Ethernet

Metro Ethernet is a rapidly maturing networking technology that broadens Ethernet to the public networks run by telecommunications companies. IP-aware Ethernet switches enable service providers to offer enterprises converged voice, data, and video services such as IP telephony, video streaming, imaging, and data storage. Figure 1-32 shows that by extending Ethernet to the metropolitan area, companies can provide their remote offices with reliable access to applications and data on the corporate headquarters LAN.

Here are some benefits of Metro Ethernet:

- **Reduced expenses and administration**: Metro Ethernet provides a switched, high-bandwidth Layer 2 network that can manage data, voice, and video all on the same infrastructure. This characteristic increases bandwidth and eliminates expensive conversions to ATM and Frame Relay. The technology enables businesses to inexpensively connect numerous sites in a metropolitan area to each other and to the Internet.

- **Easy integration with existing networks**: Metro Ethernet connects easily to existing Ethernet LANs, reducing installation costs and time.

- **Enhanced business productivity**: Metro Ethernet enables businesses to take advantage of productivity-enhancing IP applications that are difficult to implement on TDM or Frame Relay networks, such as hosted IP communications, VoIP, and streaming and broadcast video.

Figure 1-32   Service Provider Metro Ethernet

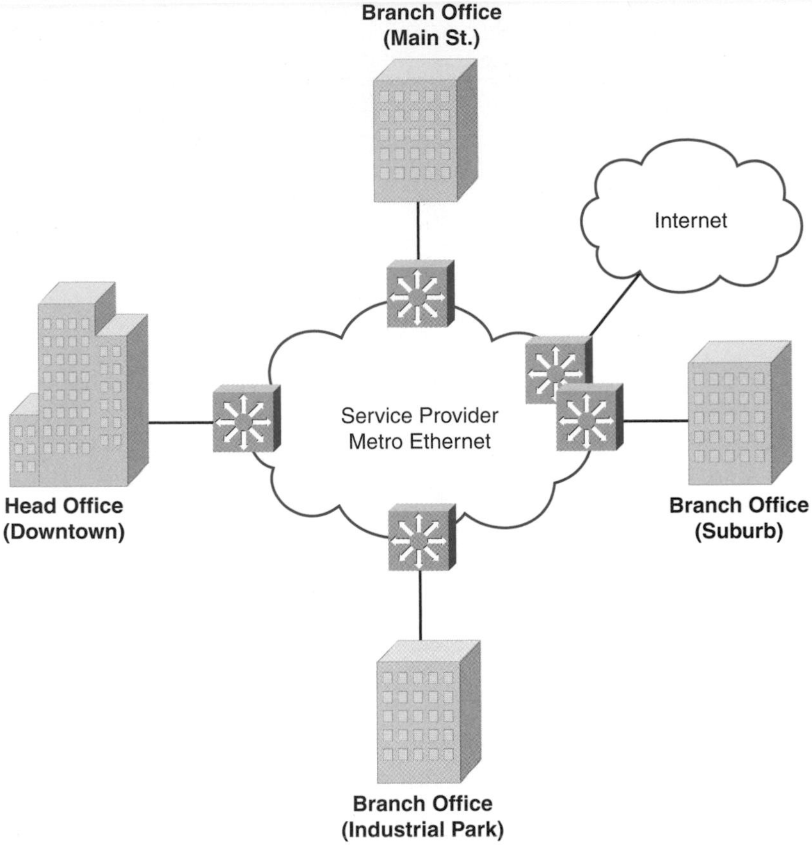

Choosing a WAN Link Connection

Now that you have looked at the variety of WAN connection options, how do you choose the best technology to meet the requirements of a specific business? Table 1-2 compares the advantages and disadvantages of the WAN connection options that we have discussed in this chapter.

Table 1-2   Choosing a WAN Link Connection

Option	Description	Advantages	Disadvantages	Sample Protocols
Leased line	Point-to-point connection between two computers' LANs.	Most secure	Expensive	PPP, HDLC, SDLC
Circuit switching	A dedicated circuit path is created between endpoints. Best example is dialup connections.	Less expensive	Call setup	PPP, ISDN
Packet switching	Devices transport packets via a shared single point-to-point or point-to-multipoint link across a carrier inter network. Variable-length packets are transmitted over PVCs or SVCs.	Highly efficient use of bandwidth	Shared media across link	X.25, Frame Relay
Cell relay	Similar to packet switching, but uses fixed-length cells instead of variable-length packets. Data is divided into fixed-length cells and then transported across virtual circuits.	Best for simultaneous use of voice and data	Overhead can be considerable	ATM
Internet	Connectionless packet switching using the Internet as the WAN infrastructure. Uses network addressing to deliver packets. Because of security issues, VPN technology must be used.	Least expensive, globally available	Least secure	VPN, DSL, cable modem, wireless

This information is a good start. In addition, to help you in the decision-making process, the following sections list some questions to ask yourself when choosing a WAN connection option.

What Is the Purpose of the WAN?

Do you want to connect local branches in the same city area, connect remote branches, connect to a single branch, connect to customers, connect to business partners, or some combination of these? If the WAN is for providing authorized customers or business partners limited access to the company intranet, what is the best option?

What Is the Geographic Scope?

Is it local, regional, global, one-to-one (single branch), one-to-many branches, many-to-many (distributed)? Depending on the range, some WAN connection options may be better than others.

What Are the Traffic Requirements?

Traffic requirements to consider include the following:

- Traffic type (data only, VoIP, video, large files, streaming files) determines the quality and performance requirements. For example, if you are sending a lot of voice or streaming video traffic, ATM may be the best choice.

- Traffic volumes depending on type (voice, video, or data) for each destination determine the bandwidth capacity required for the WAN connection to the ISP.

- Quality requirements may limit your choices. If your traffic is highly sensitive to latency and jitter, you can eliminate any WAN connection options that cannot provide the required quality.

- Security requirements (data integrity, confidentiality, and security) are an important factor if the traffic is of a highly confidential nature or if provides essential services, such as emergency response.

Should the WAN Use a Private or Public Infrastructure?

A private infrastructure offers the best security and confidentiality, whereas the public Internet infrastructure offers the most flexibility and lowest ongoing expense. Your choice depends on the purpose of the WAN, the types of traffic it carries, and the available operating budget. For example, if the purpose is to provide a nearby branch with high-speed secure services, a private dedicated or switched connection may be best. If the purpose is to connect many remote offices, a public WAN using the Internet may be the best choice. For distributed operations, a combination of options may be the best solution.

For a Private WAN, Should It Be Dedicated or Switched?

Real-time, high-volume transactions have special requirements that could favor a dedicated line, such as traffic flowing between the data center and the corporate head office. If you are connecting to a local single branch, you could use a dedicated leased line. However, that option would become very expensive for a WAN connecting multiple offices. In that case, a switched connection might be better.

For a Public WAN, What Type of VPN Access Do You Need?

If the purpose of the WAN is to connect a remote office, a site-to-site VPN may be the best choice. To connect teleworkers or customers, remote-access VPNs are a better option. If the WAN is serving a mixture of remote offices, teleworkers, and authorized customers, such as a global company with distributed operations, a combination of VPN options may be required.

Which Connection Options Are Available Locally?

In some areas, not all WAN connection options are available. In this case, your selection process is simplified, although the resulting WAN may provide less-than-optimal perform-ance. For example, in a rural or remote area, the only option may be broadband satellite Internet access.

What Is the Cost of the Available Connection Options?

Depending on the option you choose, the WAN can be a significant ongoing expense. The cost of a particular option must be weighed against how well it meets your other require-ments. For example, a dedicated leased line is the most expensive option, but the expense may be justified if it is critical to ensure secure transmission of high volumes of real-time data. For less-demanding applications, a cheaper switched or Internet connection option may be more suitable. Also, wireless point-to-point bridges are becoming a potential alter-native to leased lines.

As you can see, you must consider many important factors when choosing an appropriate WAN connection. Following the guidelines just described, as well as those described by the Cisco Enterprise Architecture, you should now be able to choose an appropriate WAN con-nection to meet the requirements of different business scenarios.

Summary

A WAN is a data communications network that operates beyond the geographic scope of a LAN.

As companies grow, adding more employees, opening branch offices, and expanding into global markets, their requirements for integrated services change. These business requirements drive companies' network requirements.

The Cisco Enterprise Architecture expands on the Hierarchical Network Model by further dividing the enterprise network into physical, logical, and functional areas.

Implementing a Cisco Enterprise Architecture provides a secure, robust network with high availability that facilitates the deployment of converged networks.

WANs operate in relation to the OSI reference model, primarily on Layers 1 and 2.

Devices that put data on the local loop are called data circuit-terminating equipment or data communications equipment (DCE). The customer devices that pass the data to the DCE are called data terminal equipment (DTE). The DCE primarily provides an interface for the DTE into the communication link on the WAN cloud.

The physical demarcation point is the place where the responsibility for the connection changes from the enterprise to the service provider.

Data link layer protocols define how data is encapsulated for transmission to remote sites and the mechanisms for transferring the resulting frames.

A circuit-switching network establishes a dedicated circuit (or channel) between nodes and terminals before the users may communicate.

A packet-switching network splits traffic data into packets that are routed over a shared network. Packet-switching networks do not require a circuit to be established and allow many pairs of nodes to communicate over the same channel.

A point-to-point link provides a preestablished WAN communications path from the customer premises through the provider network to a remote destination. Point-to-point links use leased lines to provide a dedicated connection.

Circuit-switching WAN options include analog dialup and ISDN. Packet-switching WAN options include X.25, Frame Relay, and ATM. ATM transmits data in 53-byte cells rather than frames. ATM is best suited to video traffic.

Internet WAN connection options include broadband services, such as DSL, cable modem or broadband wireless, and Metro Ethernet. VPN technology enables businesses to provide secure teleworker access through the Internet over broadband services.

Labs

The activities and labs available in the companion *Accessing the WAN, CCNA Exploration Labs and Study Guide* (ISBN 1-58713-212-5) provide hands-on practice with the following topic introduced in this chapter:

Lab 1-1: Challenge Review (1.4.1)

In this lab, you review basic routing and switching concepts. Try to do as much on your own as possible. Refer to previous material when you cannot proceed on your own.

Note

Configuring three separate routing protocols—RIP, OSPF, and EIGRP—to route the same network definitely is not a best practice. It should be considered a *worst* practice and is not something that would be done in a production network. It is done here so that you can review the major routing protocols before proceeding and see a dramatic illustration of the concept of administrative distance.

Packet Tracer
☐ Companion

Many of the Hands-on Labs include Packet Tracer Companion Activities, where you can use Packet Tracer to complete a simulation of the lab. Look for this icon in *Accessing the WAN, CCNA Exploration Labs and Study Guide* for Hands-on Labs that have a Packet Tracer Companion.

Check Your Understanding

Complete all the review questions listed here to test your understanding of the topics and concepts in this chapter. Answers are listed in Appendix, "Check Your Understanding and Challenge Questions Answer Key."

1. Which of the following items are considered WAN devices? (Choose three.)

   A. Bridge

   B. Modem

   C. Router

   D. Ethernet switch

   E. Access server

   F. Repeater

2. Which layer of the hierarchical network design model is often called the backbone?

   A. Access

   B. Distribution

   C. Network

   D. Core

   E. Workgroup

   F. WAN

3. Match each term with its definition:

   Circuit switching

   Packet switching

   Connection-oriented packet switching

   Connectionless packet switching

   A. A switching technology in which each switch must evaluate the packet's address to determine where to send it.

   B. A switching technology in which a virtual circuit exists only while a packet travels through it.

   C. A switching technology that establishes routes through the switches for particular end-to-end connections.

   D. A switching technology that has a preestablished dedicated circuit (or channel) between nodes and terminals.

4. Match each term with its packet-switched technology definition:

Metro Ethernet

X.25

ATM

Frame Relay

A. Provides a high-bandwidth Layer 2 network that can manage data, voice, and video all on the same infrastructure.

B. Built on a cell-based architecture in which the cell has a fixed length of 53 bytes.

C. Operates at the data link layer, and the PVC is identified by a Data Link Control Identifier.

D. Operates at the network layer, and the SVC is identified by a channel number.

5. Which device is commonly used as Data Terminal Equipment?

A. ISDN

B. Modem

C. Router

D. CSU/DSU

6. Which type of WAN connection should you choose when a dedicated point-to-point WAN communications path from the customer premises through the provider network to a remote destination is required?

A. ISDN

B. Analog dialup

C. ATM

D. Frame Relay

E. Leased line

7. How are Frame Relay virtual circuits identified?

A. CIR

B. DLCI

C. VPI

D. MAC

E. SPID

8. What WAN technology is designed to deliver data, voice, and video simultaneously built on a cell-based architecture?

A. ATM

B. Cable

C. Frame Relay

D. ISDN

9. Which architecture enables enterprises to offer important network services—such as security, new communication services, and improved application performance—to every office, regardless of its size or proximity to headquarters?

A. Cisco Enterprise Campus Architecture

B. Cisco Enterprise Data Center Architecture

C. Cisco Enterprise Branch Architecture

D. Cisco Enterprise Teleworker Architecture

10. At which layer of the hierarchical network model do users connect to the network?

A. Application

B. Access

C. Distribution

D. Network

E. Core

11. ISDN PRI is composed of how many B channels in North America?

A. 2

B. 16

C. 23

D. 30

E. 64

12. The ability to connect securely to a private network over a public network is provided by which WAN technology?

A. DSL

B. Frame Relay

C. ISDN

D. PSTN

E. VPN

13. Which hierarchical network model layer is responsible for containing network problems to the workgroups in which they occur?

A. Application

B. Access

C. Distribution

D. Network

E. Core

14. What term describes the cabling that connects the customer site to the nearest exchange of the WAN service provider?

A. CPE

B. CO

C. Local loop

D. DCE

E. DTE

15. Which goal can be accomplished by implementing the Cisco Enterprise Teleworker Architecture?

A. It allows the enterprise to add large branch sites that span geographic areas.

B. It allows the enterprise to deliver secure voice and data services to workers no matter where or when they work.

C. To reduce remote security threats, it forces users who are located at main sites to log on to resources.

D. It satisfies telephony requirements for users who are located at medium to large enterprise sites.

16. Describe the three layers of the hierarchical network model.

17. Describe the five modules of the Cisco Enterprise Architecture.

18. Compare and contrast the following WAN terms: CPE, CO, local loop, DCE, DTE, and demarcation point.

19. Compare and contrast the following WAN devices: modem, CSU/DSU, access server, WAN switch, and router.

20. Compare and contrast X.25, Frame Relay, and ATM.

Challenge Questions and Activities

1. Explain the advantages and disadvantages of circuit-switched networks.

2. What are the differences between a site-to-site VPN and a remote-access VPN?

CHAPTER 2

PPP

Objectives

After completing this chapter, you should be able to answer the following questions:

- What are the fundamental concepts of point-to-point serial communication?

- What are the key concepts of PPP?

- What commands are used to configure PPP encapsulation?

- What commands are used to configure PAP and CHAP authentication?

Key Terms

This chapter uses the following key terms. You can find the definitions in the glossary at the end of the book.

This chapter starts your exploration of WAN technologies by introducing point-to-point communications and Point-to-Point Protocol (PPP).

One of the most common types of WAN connections is the point-to-point connection using PPP as the Layer 2 protocol. *Point-to-point connections* are used to connect LANs to service provider WANs and to connect LAN segments within an Enterprise network. A LAN-to-WAN point-to-point connection is also called a serial connection or leased-line connection, because the lines are leased from a carrier (usually a telephone company) and are dedicated for use by the company leasing the lines. Companies pay for a continuous connection between two remote sites, and the line is continuously active and available. Understanding how point-to-point communication links function to provide access to a WAN is important to an overall understanding of how WANs function.

Point-to-Point Protocol (PPP) provides multiprotocol LAN-to-WAN connections handling TCP/IP, IPX, and AppleTalk simultaneously. It can be used over twisted pair, fiber-optic lines, and satellite transmission. PPP provides transport over WAN technologies such as ATM, Frame Relay, ISDN, and optical links. These technologies are discussed later.

In modern networks, security is a key concern. PPP allows you to authenticate connections using either *Password Authentication Protocol (PAP)* or the more effective *Challenge Handshake Authentication Protocol (CHAP)*.

In this chapter you will also learn about the key concepts of serial communications and how to configure and troubleshoot a PPP serial connection on a Cisco router.

Introducing Serial Communications

Serial communication is the process of transmitting a single bit at a time over a communications circuit or channel.

How Does Serial Communication Work?

You know that most PCs have both serial and parallel ports. You also know that electricity can move at only one speed. To transfer data quicker, it can be compressed and therefore require fewer bits to be transmitted. An alternative method is to transmit the bits simultaneously, as done in computers with parallel connections. Computers use relatively short parallel connections between interior components, but they use a serial bus to convert signals for most external communications. Let's compare serial and parallel communications.

With a serial connection, information is sent across one wire, one data bit at a time. The nine-pin serial connector on most PCs uses two loops of wire, one in each direction, for data communication, plus additional wires to control the flow of information. In any given direction, data is still flowing over a single wire.

A parallel connection sends the bits over more wires simultaneously. In the case of the 25-pin parallel port on your PC, eight data-carrying wires carry 8 bits simultaneously. Because eight wires carry the data, the parallel link theoretically transfers data eight times faster than a serial connection. So, based on this theory, a parallel connection sends a byte in the same amount of time a serial connection takes to send a bit.

In Figure 2-1, the serial connection sends 1 bit at a time, while the parallel connection sends 8 bits at a time. Notice that the serial connection has sent 4 bits and is currently sending the fifth bit, while the parallel connection has already sent 4 bytes.

Figure 2-1   Serial and Parallel Communication

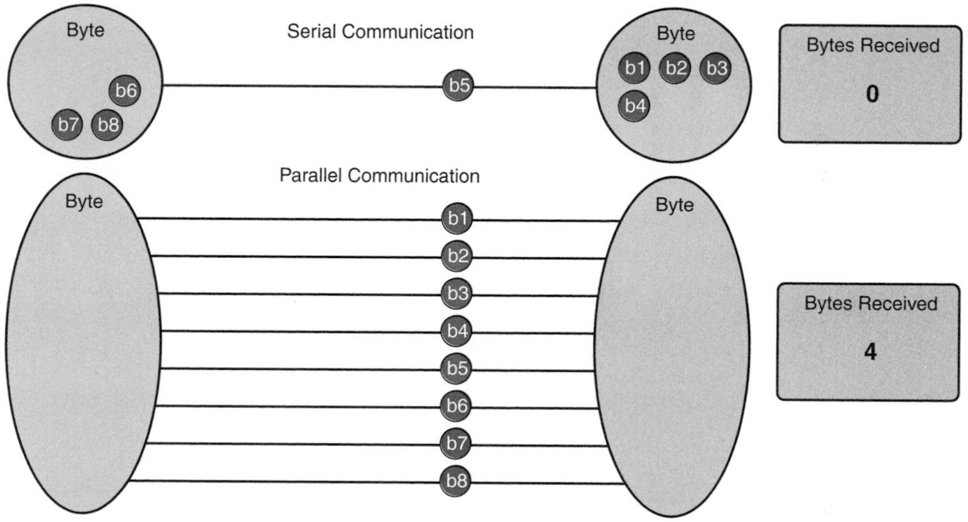

This explanation brings up some questions. What is meant by "theoretically faster"? If parallel is theoretically faster than serial, is parallel better suited for connecting to a WAN? It would initially seem that a serial link must be inferior to a parallel one, because it can transmit less data at each clock tick. However, serial links can be clocked considerably faster than parallel links and therefore can achieve faster data rates. As well, parallel links are limited to shorter distances because of the effects of clock skew and crosstalk interference.

For instance, in a parallel connection, it is wrong to assume that the 8 bits leaving the sender at the same time arrive at the receiver at the same time. Rather, some of the bits get there later than others. This is known as *clock skew*. Overcoming clock skew is not trivial. The receiving end must synchronize itself with the transmitter and then wait until all the bits have arrived. The process of reading, waiting, latching, waiting for clock signal, and transmitting the 8 bits adds time to the transmission. In parallel communications, a latch is a data storage system used to store information in sequential logic systems. The more wires you use and the farther the connection reaches, this compounds the problem and adds delay. The need for clocking slows parallel transmission well below theoretical expectations. Clock skew is not a factor with serial links, because it has only one channel to transmit on.

In Figure 2-2, notice that the bits of the parallel connection do not arrive at the same time due to clock skew.

Figure 2-2   Clock Skew

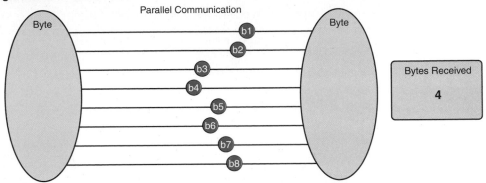

Parallel wires are physically bundled in a parallel cable, and signals can imprint themselves on each other, making the cable more susceptible to crosstalk. The possibility of crosstalk across the wires requires more processing, especially at higher frequencies.

The serial buses on computers and routers compensate for crosstalk before transmitting the bits. Because serial cables have fewer wires, less crosstalk occurs, and network devices transmit serial communications at higher, more efficient frequencies.

In Figure 2-3, bits 1, 2, 7, and 8 are experiencing some crosstalk, but bits 5 and 6 are not. Bits 3 and 4 have encountered too much crosstalk and therefore are dropped.

Figure 2-3   Crosstalk

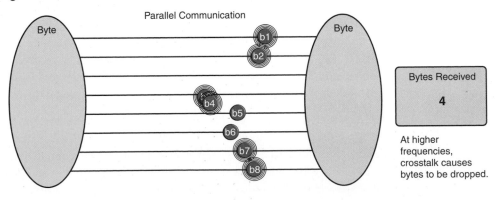

In most cases, serial communications are considerably cheaper to implement. Serial communications use fewer wires, cheaper cables, and fewer connector pins.

Serial Communication Standards

All long-haul communications and most computer networks use serial connections, because the cost of cable and synchronization difficulties makes parallel connections impractical. The most significant advantage is simpler wiring. Also, serial cables can be longer than parallel cables, because much less interaction (crosstalk) occurs among the conductors in the cable. In this chapter, we will confine our consideration of serial communications to those connecting LANs to WANs.

Figure 2-4 is a simple representation of serial communication. The sending router encapsulates the data using PPP. The encapsulated PPP frame is sent on a physical medium to the WAN. There are various ways to traverse the WAN, but the receiving router uses the same communications protocol to unencapsulate the frame when it arrives.

Figure 2-4   Serial Communication

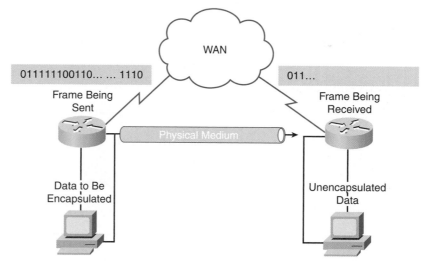

There are many different serial communication standards, each one using a different signaling method. Three key serial communication standards affect LAN-to-WAN connections:

- **RS-232**: Most serial ports on PCs conform to the RS-232C standard or the newer RS-422 and RS-423 standards. Although the standard defines a nine-pin connector and a 25-pin connector, the nine-pin connector is more commonly implemented. A serial port is a general-purpose interface that can be used for almost any type of device, including modems, mice, and printers. Many network devices use RJ-45 connectors that also conform to the RS-232 standard. Figure 2-5 shows an RS-232 connector.

- **V.35**: Typically used for modem-to-multiplexer communication, this ITU standard for high-speed, synchronous data exchange combines the bandwidth of several telephone circuits. In the United States, V.35 is the interface standard used by most routers and DSUs that connect to T1 carriers. V.35 cables are high-speed serial assemblies designed to support higher data rates and connectivity between DTEs and DCEs over digital lines. You'll read more about DTEs and DCEs later in this section.

■ **HSSI**: A High-Speed Serial Interface (HSSI) supports transmission rates of up to 52 Mbps. Engineers use HSSI to connect routers on LANs with WANs over high-speed lines such as T3 lines. Engineers also use HSSI to provide high-speed connectivity between LANs, using Token Ring or Ethernet. HSSI is a DTE/DCE interface developed by Cisco Systems and T3plus Networking to address the need for high-speed communication over WAN links.

Figure 2-5   Nine-Pin RS-232 Connector

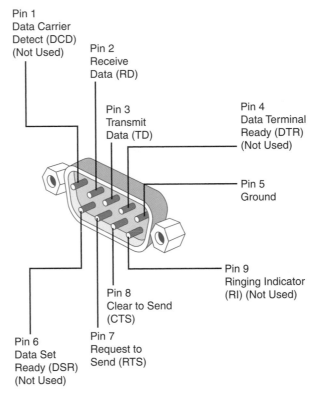

As well as using different signaling methods, each of these standards uses different types of cables and connectors. Each standard plays a different role in a LAN-to-WAN topology. This course does not examine the details of V.35 and HSSI pinning schemes. However, a quick look at a nine-pin RS-232 connector used to connect a PC to a modem helps illustrate the concept, as shown in Figure 2-5. A later section looks at V.35 and HSSI cables.

■ Pin 1: Data Carrier Detect (DCD) indicates that the carrier for the transmit data is ON.

■ Pin 2: The receive pin (RD) carries data from the serial device to the computer.

- Pin 3: The transmit pin (TD) carries data from the computer to the serial device.

- Pin 4: *Data Terminal Ready (DTR)* tells the modem that the computer is ready to transmit.

- Pin 5: Ground.

- Pin 6: *Data Set Ready (DSR)* is similar to DTR. It indicates that the Data set is ON.

- Pin 7: The RTS pin requests clearance to send data to a modem.

- Pin 8: The serial device uses the *Clear to Send (CTS)* pin to acknowledge the computer's RTS signal. In most situations, RTS and CTS are constantly ON throughout the communication session.

- Pin 9: An auto-answer modem uses the Ring Indicator (RI) to signal receipt of a telephone ring signal.

The DCD and RI pins are available only in connections to a modem. These two lines are rarely used. Most modems transmit status information to a PC when a carrier signal is detected (when a connection is made to another modem) or when the modem receives a ring signal from the telephone line.

Note

The pinning scheme for the nine-pin RS-232 connector is included only as an example. If you are interested in a more complete explanation, consult other sources, such as *http://www.camiresearch.com/Data_Com_Basics/RS232_standard.html#anchor1154232*.

TDM

In the early 1960s, Bell Laboratories developed *time-division multiplexing (TDM)* to maximize the amount of voice traffic carried over a medium. Before multiplexing, each telephone call required its own physical link. This was an expensive and unscalable solution.

TDM is a signaling method that divides the bandwidth of a single link into separate channels or time slots. TDM transmits two or more channels over the same link by allocating a different time interval (time slot) for the transmission of each channel. In effect, the channels take turns using the link.

Time Division Multiplexing

TDM is a physical layer concept. It has no regard for the nature of the information that is being multiplexed onto the output channel. TDM is independent of the Layer 2 protocol that is used by the input channels.

TDM can be explained by an analogy to highway traffic. To transport traffic from four roads to another city, you can send all the traffic on one highway lane if the feeding roads are equally serviced and the traffic is synchronized. So, if each of the four roads puts a car on the highway every four seconds, the highway receives one car each second. As long as the speed of all the cars is synchronized, no collisions occur. At the destination, the reverse happens: the cars are taken off the highway and are fed to the local roads by the same synchronous mechanism.

This is the principle used in synchronous TDM when sending data over a link. TDM increases the capacity of the *transmission link* by slicing time into smaller intervals so that the link carries the bits from multiple input sources. This effectively increases the number of bits transmitted per second. With TDM, the transmitter and receiver both know exactly which signal is being sent.

In Figure 2-6, a multiplexer (MUX) at the transmitter accepts three separate signals, depicted as D, E, and F. The MUX divides each signal into segments and puts each segment into a single channel by inserting each segment into a time slot. The figure shows multiple time slots, starting with time slot 0 (TS0).

Figure 2-6 TDM

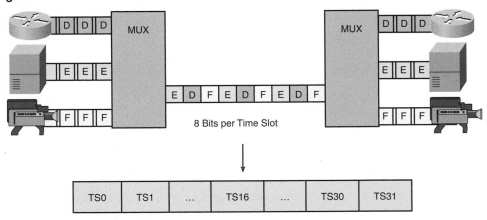

A MUX at the receiving end reassembles the TDM stream into the three separate *data streams* based on only the timing of the arrival of each bit. A technique called bit interleaving keeps track of the number and sequence of the bits from each specific transmission so that they can be quickly and efficiently reassembled into their original form upon receipt. Byte interleaving performs the same functions, but because there are 8 bits in each byte, the process needs a bigger or longer time slot.

For more information on TDM, refer to *http://www.networkdictionary.com/telecom/tdm.php*.

Statistical Time Division Multiplexing

In another analogy, compare TDM to a train with 32 railroad cars. Each car is owned by a different freight company, and every day the train leaves with the 32 cars attached. If one of the companies has cargo to send, that car is loaded. If the company has nothing to send, the car remains empty but stays on the train. Shipping empty containers is not very efficient. TDM shares this inefficiency when traffic is intermittent, because the time slot is still allocated even when the channel has no data to transmit.

Statistical time-division multiplexing (STDM) is a variation of TDM that was developed to overcome this inefficiency. STDM uses a variable time slot length, allowing channels to compete for any free slot space, as shown in Figure 2-7.

Figure 2-7   Statistical TDM

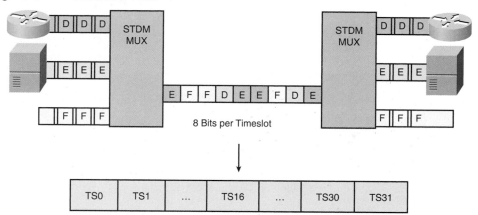

In the TDM example, signals D, E, and F were always sent in sequential order. Notice that in Figure 2-7, the signal transmissions are no longer sent sequentially. Instead, STDM embeds the signals as required into any available time slot. To do so, it employs *buffer* memory that temporarily stores the data during periods of peak traffic. STDM does not waste high-speed line time with inactive channels using this scheme. However, STDM requires each transmission to carry identification information (a channel identifier).

TDM Examples: ISDN and SONET

An example of a technology that uses synchronous TDM is ISDN. ISDN basic rate interface (BRI) has three channels: two 64-kbps B channels (B1 and B2) and a 16-kbps D channel. The TDM has ten time slots, which are repeated in the sequence shown in Figure 2-8.

Figure 2-8   TDM Example: ISDN

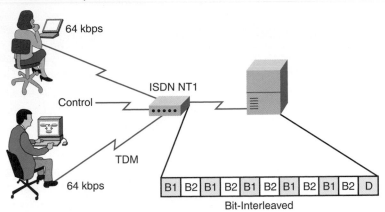

On a larger scale, the telecommunications industry uses the *SONET* or SDH standard for optical transport of TDM data. SONET, used in North America, and SDH, used elsewhere, are two closely related standards that specify interface parameters, rates, framing formats, multiplexing methods, and management for synchronous TDM over fiber.

Figure 2-9 shows an example of statistical TDM. SONET/SDH takes n bit streams, multiplexes them, and optically modulates the signal, sending it out using a light-emitting device over fiber with a bit rate equal to (incoming bit rate) $*$ n. Thus, traffic arriving at the SONET multiplexer from four places at 2.5 Gbps goes out as a single stream at 4 $*$ 2.5 Gbps, or 10 Gbps. This principle is illustrated in the figure, which shows an increase in the bit rate by a factor of 4 in time slot T.

Figure 2-9   STDM Example: SONET

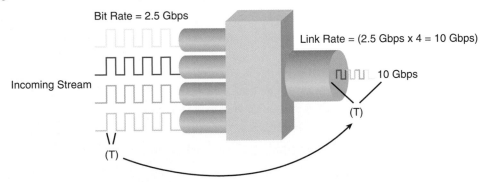

The original unit used in multiplexing telephone calls is 64 kbps, which represents one phone call. This is referred to as a *DS0 (digital signal level zero)*. In North America, 24 DS0 units are multiplexed using TDM into a higher bit-rate signal with an aggregate speed of

1.544 Mbps for transmission over T1 lines. Outside North America, 32 DS0 units are multiplexed for E1 transmission at 2.048 Mbps.

Table 2-1 shows the signal level hierarchy for multiplexing telephone calls. As an aside, although it is common to refer to a 1.544-Mbps transmission as a T1, it is more correct to call it DS1.

Table 2-1   DS0 Units

Signal Bit	Rate	Voice Slots
DS0	64 kbps	1 DS0
DS1	1.544 Mbps	24 DS0s
DS2	6.312 Mbps	96 DS0s
DS3	44.736 Mbps	672 DS0s or 28 DS1s

T-carrier refers to the bundling of DS0s. For example, a T1 equals 24 DS0s, a T1C equals 48 DS0s (or two T1s), and so on. Figure 2-10 shows a sample T-carrier infrastructure hierarchy. The E-carrier hierarchy is similar.

Note

For more information, refer to *http://www.atis.org/tg2k/_t-carrier.html*.

Figure 2-10   T-Carrier Hierarchy

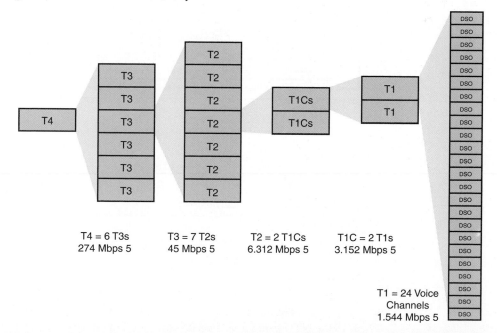

T4 = 6 T3s
274 Mbps 5

T3 = 7 T2s
45 Mbps 5

T2 = 2 T1Cs
6.312 Mbps 5

T1C = 2 T1s
3.152 Mbps 5

T1 = 24 Voice
Channels
1.544 Mbps 5

Demarcation Point

Before deregulation in North America and other countries, telephone companies owned the local loop, including the wiring and equipment on the premises of the customers. Deregulation forced telephone companies to unbundle their local loop infrastructure to allow other suppliers to provide equipment and services. This led to a need to delineate which part of the network the telephone company owned and which part the customer owned. This point of delineation is the demarcation point, or demarc.

Demarc

The demarcation point marks the point where your network interfaces with the network owned by another organization. In telephone terminology, this is the interface between customer premises equipment (CPE) and network service provider equipment. The demarcation point is the point in the network where the responsibility of the service provider ends.

Figure 2-11 shows an ISDN scenario. In the United States, a service provider provides the local loop to the customer premises, and the customer provides the active equipment such as the channel service unit/data service unit (CSU/DSU) on which the local loop is terminated. This termination often occurs in a telecommunications closet, and the customer is responsible for maintaining, replacing, or repairing the equipment.

Figure 2-11   Demarcation Point

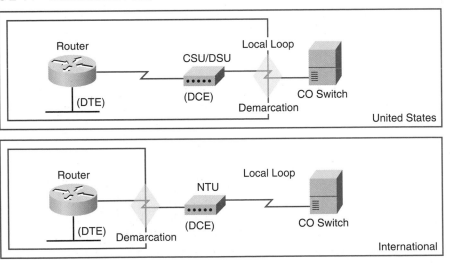

In other countries, the network terminating unit (NTU) is provided and managed by the service provider. Therefore, the demarcation point is now located between the provider's NTU and the customer's router. The provider can now actively manage and troubleshoot the local loop. The customer connects a CPE device, such as a router or *Frame Relay access device*, to the NTU using a V.35 or RS-232 serial interface.

Data Terminal Equipment and Data Communications Equipment

The term Data Terminal Equipment (DTE) refers to the device at the user end of the user-network interface. It serves as a data source, destination, or both. The DTE connects to a data network through Data Communications Equipment (DCE).

The DCE provides the physical connection to the network. It provides the clocking signal, which is used to synchronize the data transmission between the DCE and DTE, and forwards traffic.

DTE-DCE

From the point of view of connecting to the WAN, a serial connection has a DTE device at one end of the connection and a DCE device at the other end. The connection between the two DCE devices is the WAN service provider transmission network, as shown in Figure 2-12. In this case:

- The CPE, which generally is a router, is the DTE. The DTE could also be a terminal, computer, printer, or fax machine if they connect directly to the service provider network.

- The DCE, commonly a modem or CSU/DSU, is the device used to convert the user data from the DTE into a form acceptable to the WAN service provider transmission link. This signal is received at the remote DCE, which decodes the signal into a sequence of bits. The remote DCE then signals this sequence to the remote DTE.

Figure 2-12   Serial DCE and DTE Connections

The Electronics Industry Association (EIA) and the International Telecommunication Union Telecommunications Standardization Sector (ITU-T) have been most active in developing standards that allow DTEs to communicate with DCEs. The EIA calls the DCE data communications equipment, and the ITU-T calls the DCE data circuit-terminating equipment.

Cable Standards

Originally, the concept of DCEs and DTEs was based on two types of equipment: terminal equipment that generated or received data, and communication equipment that only relayed data. In the development of the RS-232 standard, there were reasons why 25-pin RS-232 connectors on these two types of equipment needed to be wired differently. These reasons are no longer significant, but we are left with two different types of cables: one for connecting a DTE to a DCE, and another for connecting two DTEs directly to each other.

The DTE/DCE interface for a particular standard defines the following specifications:

- **Mechanical/physical**: The number of pins and connector type.

- **Electrical**: Defines voltage levels for 0 and 1.

- **Functional**: Specifies the functions that are performed by assigning meanings to each of the signaling lines in the interface.

- **Procedural**: Specifies the sequence of events for transmitting data.

The original RS-232 standard defined only the connection of DTEs with DCEs, which were modems. However, if you want to directly connect two DTEs, such as two computers or two routers, as we do in our labs, a special serial cable called a *null modem* eliminates the need for a DCE. It provides the same functionality as a crossover cable connected to the Ethernet interfaces of a PC. However, a null modem cable is used to connect the serial interfaces of the DTEs. Notice that with a null modem connection, the transmit (Tx) and receive (Rx) wires are crosslinked, as shown in Figure 2-13.

Figure 2-13   Null Modem to Connect Two DTEs

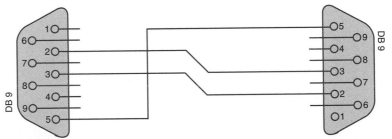

Connector 1	Connector 2	Function
2	3	Rx ← Tx
3	2	Rx → Tx
5	5	Signal ground

Note the crosslinks: Pin 2 to Pin 3 and Pin 3 Pin 2

Note

A null modem cable also requires additional wires to be crossed. However, in this example we are simply focusing on the transmit and receive wires.

The cable for the DTE-to-DCE connection is a shielded serial transition cable. The router end of the shielded serial transition cable may be a DB-60 connector, which connects to the

DB-60 port on a serial WAN interface card. The other end of the serial transition cable is available with the connector appropriate for the standard that is to be used. The WAN provider or the CSU/DSU usually dictates this cable type. Cisco devices support the EIA/TIA-232, EIA/TIA-449, V.35, X.21, and EIA/TIA-530 serial standards, as shown in Figure 2-14.

Figure 2-14   WAN Serial Connection Options

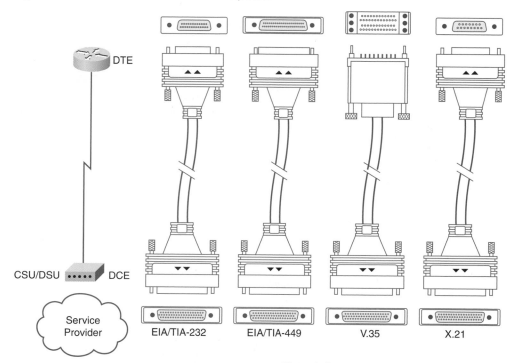

Network Connections at the CSU DSU

Figure 2-15 shows the DB-60 connector on a Cisco router.

Figure 2-15   DB-60 Router Connector

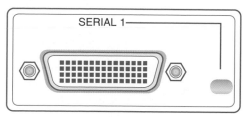

To support higher port densities in a smaller form factor, Cisco has introduced a Smart Serial cable. The router interface end of the Smart Serial cable is a 26-pin connector that is significantly more compact than the DB-60 connector.

Figure 2-16 shows the Smart Serial cable and connection on a Cisco router. Notice that this connector contains two serial interfaces occupying the space that one DB-60 connector would take.

Figure 2-16   Smart Serial Router Connection

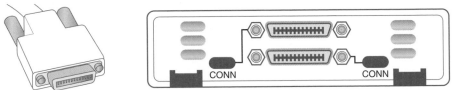

When using a null modem, keep in mind that synchronous connections require a clock signal. An external device can generate the signal, or one of the DTEs can generate the clock signal. When a DTE and DCE are connected, the serial port on a router is the DTE end of the connection by default, and the clock signal typically is provided by a CSU/DSU or similar DCE device, as shown in Figure 2-17. However, when you use a null modem cable in a router-to-router connection, one of the serial interfaces must be configured as the DCE end to provide the clock signal for the connection.

Figure 2-17   Serial WAN Connection in the Lab

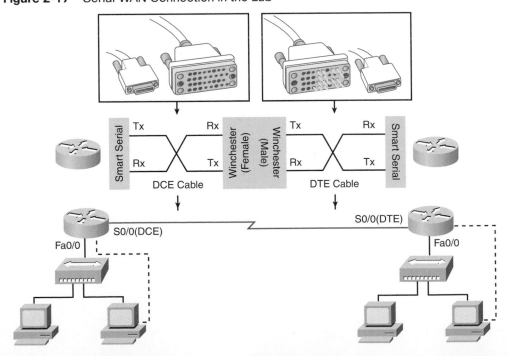

Parallel-to-Serial Conversion

The terms DTE and DCE are relative with respect to what part of a network you are observing. RS-232C is the recommended standard (RS) describing the physical interface and protocol for relatively low-speed serial data communication between computers and related devices. The EIA originally defined RS-232C for teletypewriter devices in the early 1960s. The DTE is the RS-232C interface that a computer uses to exchange data with a modem or other serial device. The DCE is the RS-232C interface that a modem or other serial device uses in exchanging data with the computer.

Note

In the early 1990s, the EIA renamed the RS-232 standard EIA232. However, both terms are still acceptable when referring to the standard.

For instance, as shown in Figure 2-18, your PC typically uses an RS-232C interface to communicate and exchange data with connected serial devices such as a modem. Your PC also has a *Universal Asynchronous Receiver/Transmitter (UART)* chip on the motherboard. Because the data in your PC flows along parallel circuits, the UART chip converts the groups of bits in parallel to a serial stream of bits. To work faster, a UART chip has buffers so that it can cache data coming from the system bus while it processes data going out the serial port. The UART is the DTE agent of your PC. It communicates with the modem or other serial device, which, in accordance with the RS-232C standard, has a complementary interface called the DCE interface.

Figure 2-18 Parallel-to-Serial Conversion Example

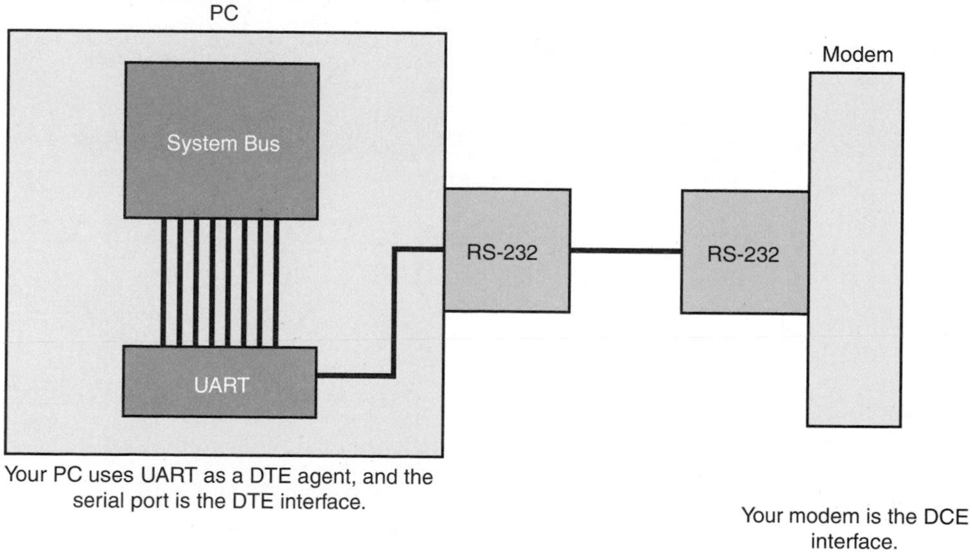

Your PC uses UART as a DTE agent, and the serial port is the DTE interface.

Your modem is the DCE interface.

HDLC Encapsulation

WANs use several different types of Layer 2 protocols, including PPP, Frame Relay, ATM, X.25, and HDLC. The HDLC protocol is introduced a little later.

Layer 2 WAN Encapsulation Protocols

On each WAN connection, data is encapsulated into frames before crossing the WAN link. To ensure that the correct protocol is used, you need to configure the appropriate Layer 2 encapsulation type. The choice of protocol depends on the WAN technology and the communicating equipment.

Figure 2-19 shows the more common WAN protocols and where they are used.

Figure 2-19   WAN Encapsulation Protocols

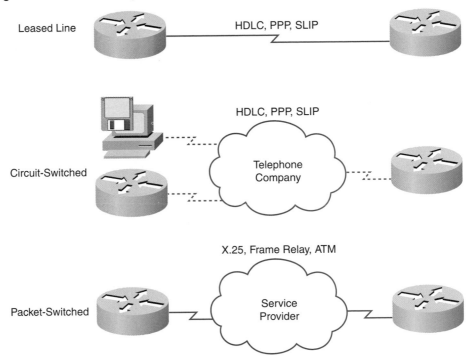

The following are short descriptions of the WAN protocols:

- **HDLC**: The default encapsulation type on point-to-point connections, dedicated links, and circuit-switched connections when the link uses two Cisco devices. HDLC is now the basis for synchronous PPP used by many servers to connect to a WAN, most commonly the Internet.

- **PPP**: Provides router-to-router and host-to-network connections over synchronous and asynchronous circuits. PPP works with several network layer protocols, such as IP and *Internetwork Packet Exchange (IPX)*. PPP also has built-in security mechanisms such as PAP and CHAP. Most of this chapter deals with PPP.

- *Serial Line Internet Protocol (SLIP)*: A standard protocol for point-to-point serial connections using TCP/IP. SLIP has been largely displaced by PPP.

- **X.25**/*Link Access Procedure, Balanced (LAPB)*: An ITU-T standard that defines how connections between a DTE and DCE are maintained for remote terminal access and computer communications in public data networks. X.25 specifies LAPB, a data link layer protocol. X.25 is a predecessor to Frame Relay.

- **Frame Relay**: An industry-standard, switched, data link layer protocol that handles multiple virtual circuits. Frame Relay is a next-generation protocol after X.25. Frame Relay eliminates some of the overhead (such as error correction and flow control) employed in X.25. The next chapter is devoted to Frame Relay.

- **ATM**: The international standard for *cell relay* in which devices send multiple service types (such as voice, video, or data) in fixed-length (53-byte) cells. Fixed-length cells allow processing to occur in hardware, thereby reducing transit delays. ATM takes advantage of high-speed transmission media such as *E3*, SONET, and T3.

HDLC Encapsulation

High-level Data Link Control (HDLC) is a *bit-oriented* synchronous data link layer protocol developed by the International Organization for Standardization (ISO). The current standard for HDLC is ISO 13239. HDLC was developed from the *Synchronous Data Link Control (SDLC)* standard proposed in the 1970s. HDLC provides both connection-oriented and connectionless service.

HDLC uses synchronous serial transmission to provide error-free communication between two points. HDLC defines a Layer 2 framing structure that allows for flow control and error control through the use of acknowledgments. Each frame has the same format, whether it is a data frame or a control frame.

When you want to transmit frames over synchronous or asynchronous links, you must remember that those links have no mechanism to mark the beginnings or ends of frames. HDLC uses a frame delimiter, or flag, to mark the beginning and end of each frame.

Cisco has developed an extension to the HDLC protocol to solve the inability to provide multiprotocol support. In fact, HDLC is the default encapsulation protocol on all Cisco serial interfaces. Although Cisco HDLC (also called cHDLC) is proprietary, Cisco has allowed many other network equipment vendors to implement it. Cisco HDLC frames contain a field for identifying the network protocol being encapsulated. Figure 2-20 compares HDLC to Cisco HDLC.

Figure 2-20   Standard and Cisco HDLC Frame Format

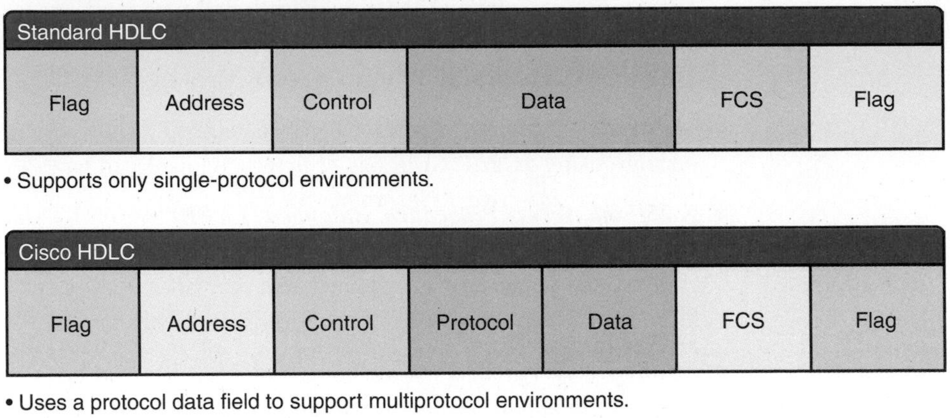

Standard HDLC					
Flag	Address	Control	Data	FCS	Flag

• Supports only single-protocol environments.

Cisco HDLC						
Flag	Address	Control	Protocol	Data	FCS	Flag

• Uses a protocol data field to support multiprotocol environments.

HDLC defines three types of frames, each with a different Control field format. The following descriptions summarize the fields illustrated in the figure:

- **Flag**: The Flag field initiates and terminates error checking. The frame always starts and ends with an 8-bit Flag field. The bit pattern is 01111110. Because there is a likelihood that this pattern occurs in the actual data, the sending HDLC system always inserts a 0 bit after every five 1s in the Data field, so in practice the flag sequence can occur only at the frame ends. The receiving system strips out the inserted bits. When frames are transmitted consecutively, the end flag of the first frame is used as the start flag of the next frame.

- **Address**: The HDLC standard can be configured in point-to-point and multipoint connections. In point-to-point HDLC connections, this field is empty.

- **Control**: The Control field uses three different formats, depending on the type of HDLC frame used: Information, Supervisory, and Unnumbered frames.

- **Protocol** (used only in Cisco HDLC): This field specifies the protocol type encapsulated within the frame (such as 0x0800 for IP).

- **Data**: A variable-length field that contains Layer 3 packets.

- **Frame check sequence (FCS)**: The FCS precedes the ending flag delimiter and usually is a cyclic redundancy check (CRC) calculation remainder. The CRC calculation is redone in the receiver. If the result differs from the value in the original frame, an error is assumed.

Figure 2-21 and the following list summarize the control frames:

- **Information (I) frame**: I-frames carry upper-layer information and some control information. This frame sends and receives sequence numbers, and the poll final (P/F) bit performs flow and error control. The send sequence number refers to the number of the frame to be sent next. The receive sequence number provides the number of the frame to be received next. Both sender and receiver maintain send and receive sequence numbers. A ***primary station*** uses the P/F bit to tell the secondary whether it requires an immediate response. A secondary station uses the P/F bit to tell the primary whether the current frame is the last in its current response.

- **Supervisory (S) frame**: S-frames provide control information. An S-frame can request and suspend transmission, report on status, and acknowledge receipt of I-frames. S-frames do not have an Information field.

- **Unnumbered (U) frame**: U-frames support control purposes and are not sequenced. A U-frame can be used to initialize secondaries. Depending on the function of the U-frame, its Control field is 1 or 2 bytes. Some U-frames have an Information field.

Figure 2-21   HDLC Frame Types

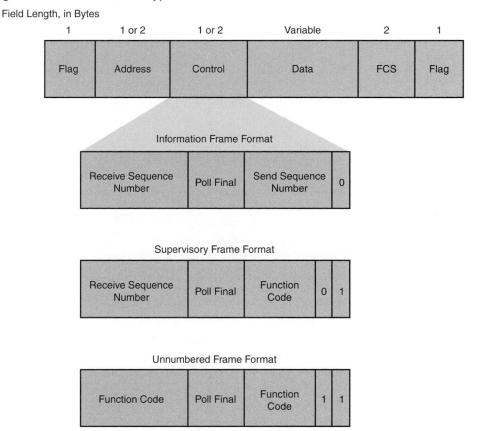

Configuring HDLC Encapsulation

Cisco HDLC is the default encapsulation method used by Cisco devices on synchronous serial lines.

You use Cisco HDLC as a point-to-point protocol on leased lines between two Cisco devices. If you are connecting to a non-Cisco device, use synchronous PPP.

If the default encapsulation method has been changed, use the **encapsulation hdlc** command in privileged mode to reenable HDLC.

There are two steps to enable HDLC encapsulation:

Step 1.   Enter the interface configuration mode of the serial interface.

Step 2.   Enter the **encapsulation hdlc** command to specify the encapsulation protocol on the interface.

To configure HDLC on a serial interface, you would enter the following configuration:

```
R1(config)# interface serial 0/0/0
R1(config-if)# encapsulation hdlc
```

Troubleshooting Serial Interfaces

The output of the **show interfaces serial** command displays information specific to serial interfaces. When HDLC is configured, "Encapsulation HDLC" should be reflected in the output, as highlighted in Example 2-1.

Example 2-1 Verifying a Serial PPP Encapsulation Configuration

```
R1# show interfaces serial 0/0/0

Serial0/0/0 is up, line protocol is up
  Hardware is GT96K Serial
  Internet address is 172.16.0.1/30
  MTU 1500 bytes, BW 128 Kbit, DLY 20000 usec,
     reliability 255/255, txload 1/255, rxload 1/255
  Encapsulation HDLC, loopback not set
  Keepalive set (10 sec)
  Last input 00:00:03, output 00:00:04, output hang never
  Last clearing of "show interface" counters 1w0d
  Input queue: 0/75/0/0 (size/max/drops/flushes); Total output drops: 0
  Queueing strategy: fifo
  Output queue: 0/40 (size/max)
  5 minute input rate 0 bits/sec, 0 packets/sec
  5 minute output rate 0 bits/sec, 0 packets/sec
     219 packets input, 15632 bytes, 0 no buffer
     Received 218 broadcasts, 0 runts, 0 giants, 0 throttles
     0 input errors, 0 CRC, 0 frame, 0 overrun, 0 ignored, 0 abort
     217 packets output, 14919 bytes, 0 underruns
     0 output errors, 0 collisions, 107 interface resets
     0 output buffer failures, 0 output buffers swapped out
     12 carrier transitions
     DCD=up  DSR=up  DTR=up  RTS=up  CTS=up
```

The **show interfaces serial** command returns one of six possible states. You can see any of the following possible states in the interface status line:

- Serial *x* is up, line protocol is up

- Serial *x* is down, line protocol is down

- Serial *x* is up, line protocol is down

- Serial *x* is up, line protocol is up (looped)

- Serial *x* is up, line protocol is down (disabled)

- Serial *x* is administratively down, line protocol is down

Table 2-2 explains some of the possible conditions and solutions.

Table 2-2   Troubleshooting a Serial Interface

Status Line	Possible Condition	Problem/Solution
Serial *x* is up, line protocol is up	This is the proper status line condition.	No action is required.
Serial *x* is down, line protocol is down (DTE mode)	The router is not sensing a CD signal, which means the CD is not active.	1. Check the LEDs on the CSU/DSU to see whether the CD is active, or insert a break-out box on the line to check for the CD signal.
	A WAN carrier service provider problem has occurred, which means the line is down or is not connected to the CSU/DSU.	2. Verify that the proper cable and interface are being used by looking at the hardware installation documentation.
	Cabling is faulty or incorrect.	3. Insert a breakout box, and check all control leads.
	Hardware failure has occurred (CSU/DSU).	4. Contact the leased-line or other carrier service to see whether there is a problem.
		5. Swap faulty parts.
		6. If faulty router hardware is suspected, change the serial line to another port. If the connection comes up, the previously connected interface has a problem.

continues

Table 2-2   Troubleshooting a Serial Interface

Status Line	Possible Condition	Problem/Solution
Serial x is up, line protocol is down (DTE mode)	A local or remote router is misconfigured. The remote router is not sending keepalives. A leased-line or other carrier service problem has occurred, which means a noisy line or misconfigured or failed switch. A timing problem has occurred on the cable, which means serial clock transmit external (SCTE) is not set on the CSU/DSU. SCTE is designed to compensate for clock phase shift on long cables. When the DCE device uses SCTE instead of its internal clock to sample data from the DTE, it is better able to sample the data without error, even if there is a phase shift in the cable. A local or remote CSU/DSU has failed. Router hardware, which could be either local or remote, has failed.	1. Put the modem, CSU, or DSU in local loopback mode, and use the **show interfaces serial** command to see whether the line protocol comes up. If it does, a WAN carrier service provider problem or a failed remote router is the likely problem. 2. If the problem appears to be on the remote end, repeat Step 1 on the remote modem, CSU, or DSU. 3. Verify all cabling. Make certain that the cable is attached to the correct interface, the correct CSU/DSU, and the correct WAN carrier service provider network termination point. Use the **show controllers** EXEC command to determine which cable is attached to which interface. 4. Enable the **debug serial interface** EXEC command. 5. If the line protocol does not come up in local loopback mode, and if the output of the **debug serial interface** EXEC command shows that the keepalive counter is not incrementing, a router hardware problem is likely. Swap the router interface hardware.

Table 2-2	Troubleshooting a Serial Interface	
Status Line	**Possible Condition**	**Problem/Solution**
		6. If the line protocol comes up and the keepalive counter increments, the problem is not in the local router.
		7. If faulty router hardware is suspected, change the serial line to an unused port. If the connection comes up, the previously connected interface has a problem.
Serial x is up, line protocol is down (DCE mode)	The **clockrate** interface configuration command is missing.	1. Add the **clockrate** interface configuration command on the serial interface.
	The DTE device does not support or is not set up for SCTE mode (terminal timing).	Syntax: **clockrate** *bps*
		Syntax description: *bps* is the desired clock rate in bits per second: 1200, 2400, 4800, 9600, 19200, 38400, 56000, 64000, 72000, 125000, 148000, 250000, 500000, 800000, 1000000, 1300000, 2000000, 4000000, or 8000000.
	The remote CSU or DSU has failed.	
		2. If the problem appears to be on the remote end, repeat Step 1 on the remote modem, CSU, or DSU.
		3. Verify that the correct cable is being used.
		4. If the line protocol is still down, there is a possible hardware failure or cabling problem. Insert a breakout box, and observe the leads.
		5. Replace faulty parts as necessary.

continues

Table 2-2   Troubleshooting a Serial Interface

Status Line	Possible Condition	Problem/Solution
Serial *x* is up, line protocol is up (looped)	A loop exists in the circuit. The sequence number in the keepalive packet changes to a random number when a loop is initially detected. If the same random number is returned over the link, a loop exists.	1. Use the **show running-config** privileged EXEC command to look for any loopback interface configuration command entries. 2. If there is a **loopback** interface configuration command entry, use the **no loopback** interface configuration command to remove the loop. 3. If there is no **loopback** interface configuration command, examine the CSU/DSU to determine whether they are configured in manual loopback mode. If they are, disable manual loopback. 4. After disabling loopback mode on the CSU/DSU, reset the CSU/DSU, and inspect the line status. If the line protocol comes up, no other action is needed. 5. If, upon inspection, the CSU or DSU cannot be manually set, contact the leased-line or other carrier service for line troubleshooting assistance.

Table 2-2   Troubleshooting a Serial Interface

Status Line	Possible Condition	Problem/Solution
Serial *x* is up, line protocol is down (disabled)	A high error rate has occurred due to a WAN service provider problem. A CSU or DSU hardware problem has occurred. Router hardware (interface) is bad.	1. Troubleshoot the line with a serial analyzer and breakout box. Look for toggling CTS and DSR signals. 2. Loop the CSU/DSU (DTE loop). If the problem continues, it is likely that there is a hardware problem. If the problem does not continue, it is likely that there is a WAN service provider problem. 3. Swap out bad hardware as required (CSU, DSU, switch, local or remote router).
Serial *x* is administratively down, line protocol is down	The router configuration includes the **shutdown** interface configuration command. A duplicate IP address exists.	1. Check the router configuration for the **shutdown** command. 2. Use the **no shutdown** interface configuration command to remove the **shutdown** command. 3. Verify that no identical IP addresses are using the **show running-config** privileged EXEC command or the **show interfaces** EXEC command. 4. If there are duplicate addresses, resolve the conflict by changing one of the IP addresses.

The **show controllers** command is another important diagnostic tool when you're troubleshooting serial lines. The output indicates the state of the interface channels and whether a cable is attached to the interface.

In Example 2-2, serial interface 0/0/0 has a V.35 DCE cable attached. The command syntax varies, depending on the platform. *Cisco 7000* series routers use a cBus controller card to connect serial links. With these routers, use the **show controllers cbus** command.

Example 2-2 Verifying a Serial PPP Encapsulation Configuration

```
R1# show controllers serial 0/0/0

Interface Serial0/0/0
Hardware is GT96K
DCE V.35, clock rate 64000
idb at 0x62938244, driver data structure at 0x6293A608
wic_info 0x6293AC04
Physical Port 0, SCC Num 0
MPSC Registers:
MMCR_L=0x000304C0, MMCR_H=0x00000000, MPCR=0x00000000
CHR1=0x00FE007E, CHR2=0x00000000, CHR3=0x000005F4, CHR4=0x00000000
CHR5=0x00000000, CHR6=0x00000000, CHR7=0x00000000, CHR8=0x00000000
CHR9=0x00000000, CHR10=0x00003008
SDMA Registers:
SDC=0x00002201, SDCM=0x00000080, SGC=0x0000C000
CRDP=0x073BD020, CTDP=0x073BD450, FTDB=0x073BD450
Main Routing Register=0x00038E00 BRG Conf Register=0x0005023F
Rx Clk Routing Register=0x76583888 Tx Clk Routing Register=0x76593910
GPP Registers:
Conf=0x43430002, Io=0x4646CA50, Data=0x7F6B3FAD, Level=0x80004
Conf0=0x43430002, Io0=0x4646CA50, Data0=0x7F6B3FAD, Level0=0x80004
0 input aborts on receiving flag sequence
0 throttles, 0 enables
0 overruns
0 transmitter underruns
 --More--
```

If the electrical interface output is shown as UNKNOWN instead of V.35, EIA/TIA-449, or some other electrical interface type, the likely problem is an improperly connected cable. A problem with the card's internal wiring is also possible. If the electrical interface is unknown, the corresponding display for the **show interfaces serial** *x* command shows that the interface and line protocol are down.

Packet Tracer
☐ **Activity**

Troubleshooting a Serial Interface 2.1.7

In this activity, you practice troubleshooting serial interfaces. Detailed instructions are provided within the activity. Use File e4-217.pka on the CD-ROM that accompanies this book to perform this activity using Packet Tracer.

PPP Concepts

This section examines Point-to-Point Protocol (PPP) in more detail.

Introducing PPP

Recall that HDLC is the default serial encapsulation method when you connect two Cisco routers. With an added Protocol Type field, the Cisco version of HDLC is proprietary. Thus, Cisco HDLC can work only with other Cisco devices. However, when you need to connect to a non-Cisco router, you should use PPP encapsulation.

What Is PPP?

PPP encapsulation has been carefully designed to retain compatibility with most commonly used supporting hardware. PPP encapsulates data frames for transmission over physical links. PPP establishes a direct connection using serial cables, phone lines, *trunk* lines, cellular telephones, specialized radio links, or fiber-optic links. Using PPP has many advantages, including the fact that it is not proprietary. Moreover, it includes many features not available in HDLC:

- The link quality management feature monitors the quality of the link. If too many errors are detected, PPP takes the link down.

- PPP supports PAP and CHAP authentication. This feature is explained and practiced in a later section.

PPP contains three main components:

- It uses the HDLC protocol as a basis for encapsulating datagrams over point-to-point links.

- It uses an extended version of *Link Control Protocol (LCP)* to establish, configure, and test the data link connection.

- It has a family of *Network Control Protocols (NCP)* to establish and configure different network layer protocols. PPP allows the simultaneous use of multiple network layer protocols. Some of the more common NCPs are Internet Protocol Control Protocol, AppleTalk Control Protocol, *Novell IPX* Control Protocol, Cisco Systems Control Protocol, *SNA Control Protocol*, and Compression Control Protocol.

Figure 2-22 shows the default HDLC encapsulation on Cisco routers, as well as the more common PPP encapsulation and its three main components.

Figure 2-22   What Is PPP?

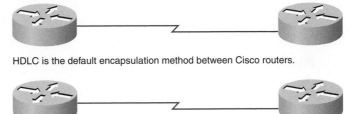

HDLC is the default encapsulation method between Cisco routers.

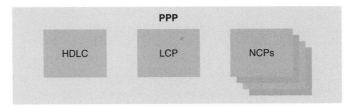

Use PPP encapsulation to connect to a non-Cisco router.

PPP Layered Architecture

A layered architecture is a logical model, design, or blueprint that aids communication between interconnecting layers.

PPP Architecture

Figure 2-23 maps the layered architecture of PPP against the Open Systems Interconnection (OSI) model. PPP and OSI share the same physical layer, but PPP distributes the functions of LCP and NCP differently.

Figure 2-23   PPP Layered Architecture: Physical Layer

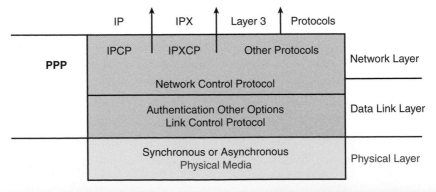

At the physical layer, you can configure PPP on a range of interfaces:

- Asynchronous serial
- Synchronous serial
- HSSI
- ISDN

PPP operates across any DTE/DCE interface (RS-232-C, RS-422, RS-423, or V.35). The only absolute requirement imposed by PPP is a duplex circuit, either dedicated or switched, that can operate in either an asynchronous or synchronous bit-serial mode, transparent to PPP link layer frames. PPP does not impose any transmission rate restrictions other than those imposed by the particular DTE/DCE interface in use.

Most of the work done by PPP is at the data link and network layers by the LCP and NCPs. The LCP sets up the PPP connection and its parameters, the NCPs handle higher-layer protocol configurations, and the LCP terminates the PPP connection.

PPP Architecture: Link Control Protocol Layer

The LCP is the real working part of PPP. The LCP sits on top of the physical layer and has a role in establishing, configuring, and testing the data-link connection between devices.

The LCP, as shown in Figure 2-24, establishes the point-to-point link. The LCP also negotiates and sets up control options on the WAN data link, which are handled by the NCPs.

Figure 2-24   PPP Layered Architecture: LCP Layer

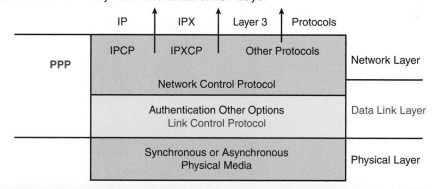

The LCP provides automatic configuration of the interfaces at each end, including the following:

- Handling varying limits on packet size

- Detecting common misconfiguration errors

- Terminating the link

- Determining when a link is functioning properly or when it is failing

PPP also uses the LCP to agree automatically on encapsulation formats (authentication, compression, error detection) as soon as the link is established.

PPP Architecture: Network Control Protocol Layer

Point-to-point links tend to worsen many problems with the current family of network protocols. For instance, assigning and managing IP addresses, which is a problem even in LAN environments, is especially difficult over circuit-switched point-to-point links (such as dialup modem servers). PPP addresses these issues using NCPs.

PPP permits multiple network layer protocols to operate on the same communications link. For every network layer protocol used, PPP uses a separate NCP, as shown in Figure 2-25. For example, IP uses the IP Control Protocol (IPCP), and IPX uses the Novell IPX Control Protocol (IPXCP).

Figure 2-25   PPP Architecture: Network Layer

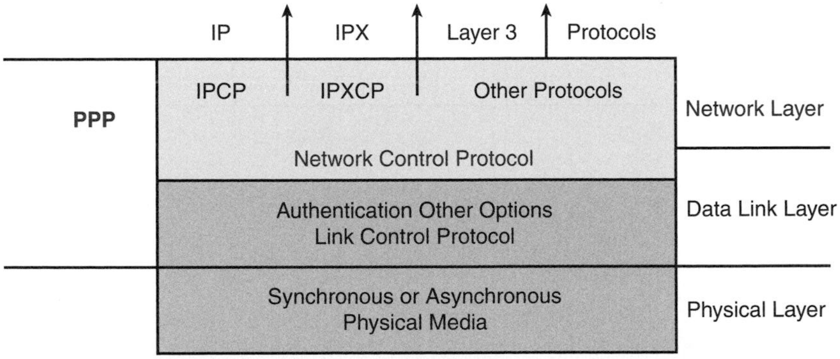

With its higher level functions, PPP carries packets from several network layer protocols in NCPs. These are functional fields containing standardized codes to indicate the network layer protocol type that PPP encapsulates.

NCPs include functional fields containing standardized codes (PPP protocol field numbers, as shown in Table 2-3) to indicate the network layer protocol that PPP encapsulates.

Table 2-3   NCPs

Value (in Hex)	Protocol Name
8021	Internet Protocol Control Protocol
8023	OSI Network Layer Control Protocol
8029	AppleTalk Control Protocol
802b	Novell IPX Control Protocol
C021	Link Control Protocol
C023	Password Authentication Protocol
C223	Challenge Handshake Authentication Protocol

Each NCP manages the specific needs of its respective network layer protocols. The various NCP components encapsulate and negotiate options for multiple network layer protocols. Using NCPs to configure the various network layer protocols is explained and practiced later in this chapter.

PPP Frame Structure

A PPP frame has six fields, as shown in Figure 2-26.

Figure 2-26   PPP Frame Fields

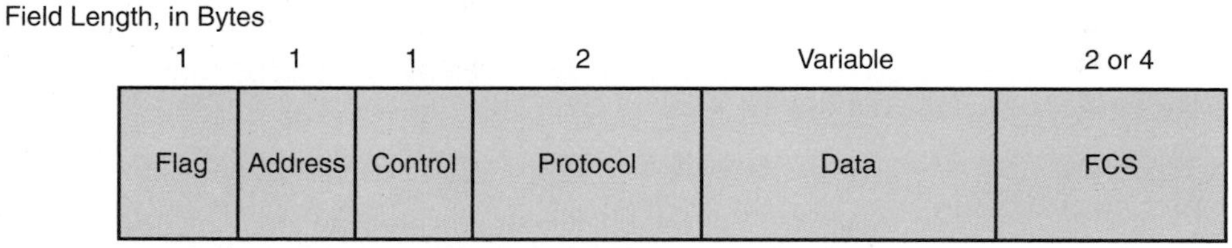

Field Length, in Bytes

The fields in the PPP frame contain the following information:

- **Flag**: Indicates the beginning or end of a frame. Consists of the binary sequence 01111110 to identify a PPP frame. The value is set to 0x7E (bit sequence 011111110) to signify the start and end of a PPP frame. In successive PPP frames, only a single flag character is used.

- **Address**: Consists of the standard broadcast address, which is the binary sequence 11111111. PPP does not assign individual station addresses.

- **Control**: 1 byte that consists of the binary sequence 00000011, which calls for transmission of user data in an unsequenced frame. This provides a connectionless link service that does not require you to establish data links or link stations. In HDLC environments, the Address field is used to address the frame to the destination node. On a point-to-point link, the destination node does not need to be addressed. Therefore, for PPP, the Address field is set to 0xFF, the broadcast address. If both PPP peers agree to perform Address and Control field compression during LCP negotiation, the Address field is not included.

■ **Protocol**: As shown in Figure 2-26, the Protocol field consists of 2 bytes that identify the protocol encapsulated in the frame's Data field. The 2-byte Protocol ID field identifies the protocol of the PPP payload. If both PPP peers agree to perform Protocol field compression during LCP negotiation, the Protocol ID field is 1 byte for Protocol IDs in the range 0x00-00 to 0x00-FF.

■ **Data**: 0 or more bytes that contain the datagram for the protocol specified in the Protocol field. The 2 bytes of the Frame Check Sequence (FCS) field, followed by the closing flag (not displayed), mark the end of the Data field. The default maximum length of the Data field is 1500 bytes.

■ **Frame Check Sequence (FCS)**: A 16-bit checksum that is used to check for bit-level errors in the PPP frame. If the receiver's calculation of the FCS does not match the FCS in the PPP frame, the PPP frame is silently discarded. By prior agreement, consenting PPP implementations can use a 32-bit (4-byte) FCS for improved error detection.

The LCP can negotiate modifications to the standard PPP frame structure.

Establishing a PPP Session

Establishing a PPP session consists of three phases performed by the LCP.

Establishing a PPP Session

Figure 2-27 shows the three phases of establishing a PPP session:

■ **Phase 1: Link establishment and configuration negotiation**: Before PPP exchanges any network layer datagrams (such as IP), the LCP must open the connection and negotiate configuration options. This phase is complete when the receiving router sends a configuration-acknowledgment frame back to the router, initiating the connection.

■ **Phase 2: Link quality determination (optional)**: The LCP tests the link to determine whether the link quality is sufficient to bring up network layer protocols. The LCP can delay transmission of network layer protocol information until this phase is complete.

■ **Phase 3: Network layer protocol configuration negotiation**: After the LCP has finished the link quality determination phase, the appropriate NCP can separately configure the network layer protocols, and bring them up and take them down at any time. If the LCP closes the link, it informs the network layer protocols so that they can take appropriate action.

Figure 2-27   Establishing a PPP Session

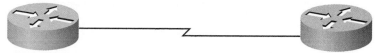

Phase 1 - Link Establishment: "Let's negotiate."

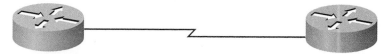

Phase 2 - Determine Link Quality: "Maybe we should discuss some details about quality. Or maybe not...."

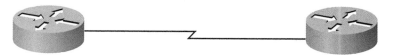

Phase 3 - Network Protocol Negotiation: "Okay, I will leave it to the NCPs to discuss higher-level details."

The LCP does all the talking.

The link remains configured for communications until explicit LCP or NCP frames close the link, or until some external event occurs (for example, an inactivity timer expires or a user intervenes). The LCP can terminate the link at any time. This usually is done when one of the routers requests termination, but it can happen because of a physical event, such as the loss of a carrier or the expiration of an idle-period timer.

Establishing a Link with LCP

LCP operation includes provisions for link establishment, link maintenance, and link termination.

LCP Operation

LCP operation uses three classes of LCP frames to accomplish the work of each LCP phase:

- Link-establishment frames establish and configure a link (Configure-Request, Configure-Ack, Configure-Nak, and Configure-Reject).

- Link-maintenance frames manage and debug a link (Code-Reject, Protocol-Reject, Echo-Request, Echo-Reply, and Discard-Request).

- Link-termination frames terminate a link (Terminate-Request and Terminate-Ack).

Figure 2-28 shows the LCP process. The first phase of LCP operation is link establishment. This phase must complete successfully before any network layer packets can be exchanged. During link establishment, the LCP opens the connection and negotiates the configuration parameters.

Figure 2-28 Establishing the Link

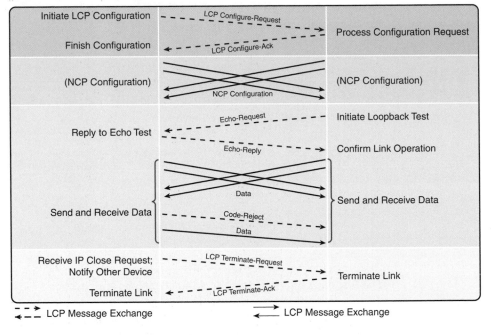

The link establishment process starts with the initiating device sending a Configure-Request frame to the responder. The Configure-Request frame includes a variable number of configuration options needed to set up on the link. In other words, the initiator sends a "wish list" to the responder.

The initiator's wish list includes options for how it wants the link created, including protocol or authentication parameters. The responder processes the wish list. If it is acceptable, the responder responds with a Configure-Ack message. After receiving the Configure-Ack message, the process moves on to the authentication stage.

If the options are unacceptable or unrecognized, the responder sends a Configure-Nak or Configure-Reject. If a Configure-Ack is received, the operation of the link is handed over to the NCP. If either a Configure-Nak or Configure-Reject message is sent to the requester, the link is not established. If the negotiation fails, the initiator needs to restart the process with new options.

During link maintenance, LCP can use messages to provide feedback and test the link:

- **Code-Reject and Protocol-Reject**: These frame types provide feedback when one device receives an invalid frame due to either an unrecognized LCP code (LCP frame type) or a bad protocol identifier. For example, if an uninterpretable packet is received from the peer, a Code-Reject packet is sent in response.

- **Echo-Request, Echo-Reply, and Discard-Request**: These frames can be used to test the link.

When the transfer of data at the network layer is complete, the LCP terminates the link. In the figure, notice that the NCP only terminates the network layer and NCP link. The link remains open until the LCP terminates it. If the LCP terminates the link before the NCP, the NCP session is also terminated.

PPP can terminate the link at any time. This might happen because of the loss of the carrier, authentication failure, link quality failure, the expiration of an idle-period timer, or the administrative closing of the link. The LCP closes the link by exchanging Terminate packets. The device initiating the shutdown sends a Terminate-Request message. The other device replies with a Terminate-Ack. A termination request indicates that the device sending it needs to close the link. When the link is closing, PPP informs the network layer protocols so that they may take appropriate action.

Figure 2-29 shows a logical diagram of the LCP link negotiation process.

Figure 2-29   LCP Link Negotiation Process

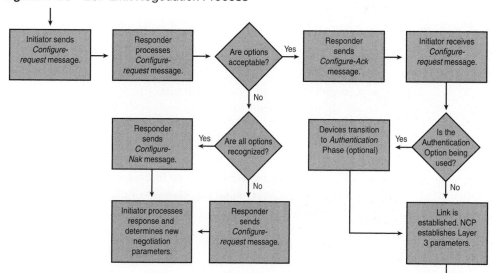

LCP Packet

Each LCP packet is a single LCP message consisting of an LCP Code field identifying the type of LCP packet, an Identifier field so that requests and replies can be matched, and a Length field indicating the size of the LCP packet and LCP packet type-specific data.

Figure 2-30 shows the fields in an LCP packet.

Figure 2-30   LCP Packet Codes

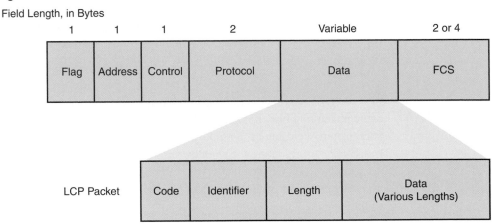

An LCP packet contains the following information:

- **Code**: The Code field is one octet in length and identifies the type of LCP packet.

- **Identifier**: The Identifier field is one octet in length and is used to match packet requests and replies.

- **Length**: The Length field is two octets in length and indicates the total length (including all fields) of the LCP packet.

- **Data**: The Data field is zero or more octets, as indicated by the Length field. The format of this field is determined by the code.

Each LCP packet has a specific function in the exchange of configuration information, depending on its packet type. The Code field of the LCP packet identifies the packet type, as shown in Table 2-4.

Table 2-4   LCP Packet Fields

LCP Code	LCP Packet Type	Description
1	Configure-Request	Sent to open or reset a PPP connection. Configure-Request contains a list of LCP options with changes to default option values.
2	Configure-Ack	Sent when all the values of all the LCP options in the last Configure-Request received are recognized and acceptable. When both PPP peers send and receive Configure-Acks, the LCP negotiation is complete.
3	Configure-Nak	Sent when all the LCP options are recognized, but the values of some options are unacceptable. Configure-Nak includes the offending options and their acceptable values.
4	Configure-Reject	Sent when LCP options are unrecognized or unacceptable for negotiation. Configure-Reject includes the unrecognized or nonnegotiable options.
5	Terminate-Request	Optionally sent to close the PPP connection.
6	Terminate-Ack	Sent in response to the Terminate-Request.
7	Code-Reject	Sent when the LCP code is unknown. The Code-Reject message includes the offending LCP packet.
8	Protocol-Reject	Sent when the PPP frame contains an unknown Protocol ID. The Protocol-Reject message includes the offending LCP packet. Protocol-Reject typically is sent by a PPP peer in response to a PPP NCP for a LAN protocol not enabled on the PPP peer.
9	Echo-Request	Optionally sent to test the PPP connection.
10	Echo-Reply	Sent in response to an Echo-Request. The PPP Echo-Request and Echo-Reply are not related to the ICMP Echo Request and Echo Reply messages.
11	Discard-Request	Optionally sent to exercise the link in the outbound direction.

PPP Configuration Options

As shown in Figure 2-31, PPP can be configured to support various functions, including

- Authentication using either PAP or CHAP

- Compression using either Stacker or Predictor

- Multilink, which combines two or more channels to increase the WAN bandwidth

Figure 2-31   PPP Configuration Options

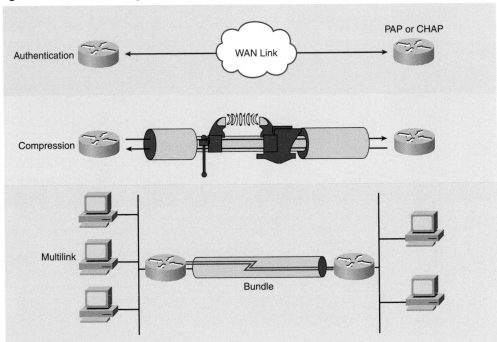

These options are discussed in more detail in the next section.

To negotiate the use of these PPP options, the LCP link-establishment frames contain Option information in the Data field of the LCP frame, as shown in Figure 2-32. If a configuration option is not included in an LCP frame, the default value for that configuration option is assumed.

Figure 2-32 LCP Option Field

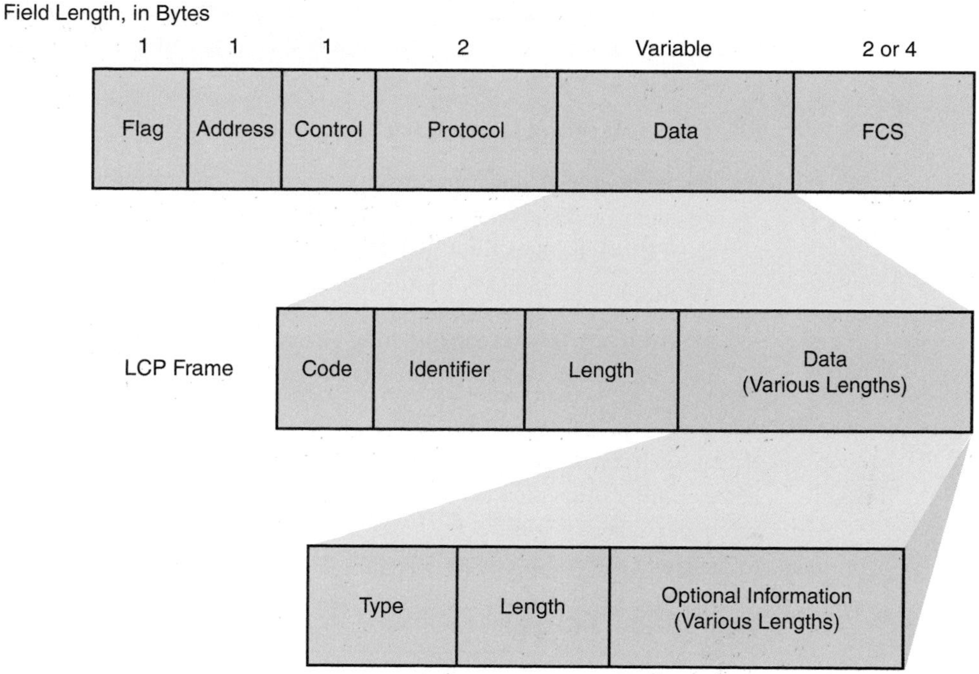

Field Length, in Bytes

1	1	1	2	Variable	2 or 4
Flag	Address	Control	Protocol	Data	FCS

LCP Frame

Code	Identifier	Length	Data (Various Lengths)

Type	Length	Optional Information (Various Lengths)

This phase is complete when a configuration acknowledgment frame has been sent and received.

NCP Explained

After the link has been initiated, the LCP passes control to the appropriate NCP. Although initially designed for IP datagrams, PPP can carry data from many types of network layer protocols by using a modular approach in its implementation. It can also carry two or more Layer 3 protocols simultaneously. Its modular model allows the LCP to set up the link and then hand the details of a network protocol to a specific NCP. Each network protocol has a corresponding NCP. Each NCP has a corresponding RFC. There are NCPs for IP, IPX, AppleTalk, and others. NCPs use the same packet format as the LCPs.

NCP Process

After the LCP has configured and authenticated the basic link, the appropriate NCP is invoked to complete the specific configuration of the network layer protocol being used. When the NCP has successfully configured the network layer protocol, the network protocol is in the open state on the established LCP link. At this point, PPP can carry the corresponding network layer protocol packets.

As an example of how the NCP layer works, IP, which is the most common Layer 3 protocol, is used. After LCP has established the link, the routers exchange IPCP messages, nego-
tiating options specific to the protocol. IPCP is responsible for configuring, enabling, and
disabling the IP modules on both ends of the link.

IPCP negotiates two options:

- **Compression**: Allows devices to negotiate an algorithm to compress TCP and IP headers and save bandwidth. Van Jacobson TCP/IP header compression reduces the size of
  the TCP/IP headers to as few as 3 bytes. This can be a significant improvement on slow
  serial lines, particularly for interactive traffic.

- **IP-Address**: Allows the initiating device to specify an IP address to use for routing IP
  over the PPP link, or to request an IP address for the responder. Dialup network links
  commonly use the IP address option.

When the NCP process is complete, the link goes into the open state, and LCP takes over
again. Link traffic consists of any possible combination of LCP, NCP, and network layer
protocol packets. Figure 2-33 shows how LCP messages can then be used by either device
to manage or debug the link.

Figure 2-33   NCP Process

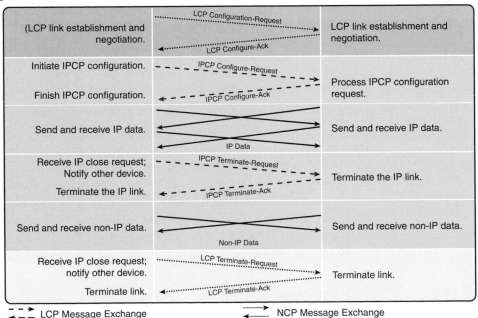

PPP Configuration Options

Basic PPP configuration is similar to configuring other Layer 2 protocols such as HDLC. PPP also includes several configuration options, including authentication and compression.

PPP Configuration Options

In the preceding section, you were introduced to the LCP options you can configure to meet specific WAN connection requirements. PPP may include the following LCP options:

- **Authentication**: Peer routers exchange authentication messages. Two authentication choices are Password Authentication Protocol (PAP) and Challenge Handshake Authentication Protocol (CHAP). Authentication is explained in the next section.

- **Compression**: Increases the effective throughput on PPP connections by reducing the amount of data in the frame that must travel across the link. The protocol decompresses the frame at its destination. Two compression protocols available in Cisco routers are Stacker and Predictor.

- **Error detection**: Identifies fault conditions. The Quality and Magic Number options help ensure a reliable, loop-free data link. The Magic Number field helps detect links that are in a looped-back condition. Until the Magic-Number Configuration Option has been successfully negotiated, the Magic Number must be transmitted as 0. Magic numbers are generated randomly at each end of the connection.

- **Multilink**: Cisco IOS software Release 11.1 and later support Multilink PPP. This alternative provides load balancing over the router interfaces that PPP uses. Multilink PPP (also called MP, MPPP, MLP, or Multilink) provides a method for spreading traffic across multiple physical WAN links while providing packet *fragmentation* and *reassembly*, proper sequencing, multivendor interoperability, and load balancing on inbound and outbound traffic.

- **PPP Callback**: To enhance security, Cisco IOS software Release 11.1 and later offer callback over PPP. With this LCP option, a Cisco router can act as a callback client or callback server. The client makes the initial call, requests that the server call it back, and terminates its initial call. The callback router answers the initial call and makes the return call to the client based on its configuration statements. The command is **ppp callback** [**accept** | **request**].

When options are configured, a corresponding field value is inserted into the LCP option field. Table 2-5 highlights the valid LCP option values.

Table 2-5   Configurable Option Field Codes

Option Name	Option Type	Option Length	Description
Maximum Receive Unit (MRU)	1	4	The maximum size of a PPP frame. Cannot exceed 65,535 bytes. The default is 1500 bytes. If neither peer is changing the default, it is not negotiated.
Asynchronous Control Character Map (ACCM)	2	6	A bit map that enables character escapes for asynchronous links. By default, character escapes are used.
Authentication Protocol	3	5 or 6	This field indicates the authentication protocol, either PAP or CHAP.
Magic Number	5	6	A random number chosen to distinguish a peer and detect looped-back lines.
Protocol Compression	7	2	A flag indicating that the PPP protocol ID be compressed into a single octet when the 2-byte protocol ID is in the range 0x00-00 to 0x00-FF.
Address and Control Field Compression	8	2	A flag indicating that the PPP Address field (always set to 0xFF) and the PPP Control field (always set to 0x03) should be removed from the PPP header.
Callback	13 or 0x0D	3	A one-octet indicator of how callback is to be determined.

PPP Configuration Commands

This series of examples shows you how to configure PPP and some of the options.

Example 1: Enabling PPP on an Interface

To set PPP as the encapsulation method used by a serial or ISDN interface, use the **encapsulation ppp** interface configuration command.

Example 2-3 enables PPP encapsulation on serial interface 0/0/0.

Example 2-3 Configuring PPP Encapsulation

```
R3# configure terminal
R3(config)# interface serial 0/0/0
R3(config-if)# encapsulation ppp
```

The **encapsulation ppp** command has no arguments. However, you must first configure the router with an IP routing protocol to use PPP encapsulation. You should recall that if you do not configure PPP on a Cisco router, the default encapsulation for serial interfaces is HDLC.

Example 2: Compression

You can configure point-to-point software compression on serial interfaces after you have enabled PPP encapsulation. Because this option invokes a software compression process, it can affect system performance. If the traffic already consists of compressed files (.zip, .tar, or .mpeg, for example), using compression on the router would achieve little benefit. The command syntax for the **compress** command is as follows:

```
Router(config-if)# compress [predictor | stac]
```

where

- **predictor** (optional) specifies that a predictor compression algorithm will be used.

- **stac** (optional) specifies that a Stacker (LZS) compression algorithm will be used.

Example 2-4 configures compression over PPP.

Example 2-4 Configuring Compression

```
R3(config)# interface serial 0/0/0
R3(config-if)# encapsulation ppp
R3(config-if)# compress [predictor | stac]
```

Example 3: Link Quality Monitoring

Recall from our discussion of LCP phases that LCP provides an optional link quality determination phase. In this phase, LCP tests the link to determine whether the link quality is sufficient to use Layer 3 protocols. The following command ensures that the link meets the quality requirement you set; otherwise, the link closes down:

```
Router(config-if)#ppp quality percentage
```

The *percentage* parameter specifies the link quality threshold. The range is 1 to 100.

The percentages are calculated for both incoming and outgoing directions. The outgoing quality is calculated by comparing the total number of packets and bytes sent to the total number of packets and bytes received by the destination node. The incoming quality is calculated by comparing the total number of packets and bytes received to the total number of packets and bytes sent by the destination node.

If the link quality percentage is not maintained, the link is deemed to be of poor quality and is taken down. Link Quality Monitoring (LQM) implements a time lag so that the link does not bounce up and down.

Example 2-5 configuration monitors the data dropped on the link and avoids frame looping.

Example 2-5 Configuring Link Quality Monitoring

```
R3(config)# interface serial 0/0/0
R3(config-if)# encapsulation ppp
R3(config-if)# ppp quality 80
```

Use the **no ppp quality** command to disable LQM.

Example 4: Load Balancing Across Links

Multilink PPP (also called MP, MPPP, MLP, or Multilink) provides a method for spreading traffic across multiple physical WAN links while providing packet fragmentation and reassembly, proper sequencing, multivendor interoperability, and load balancing on inbound and outbound traffic.

MPPP allows packets to be fragmented. It sends these fragments simultaneously over multiple point-to-point links to the same remote address. The multiple physical links come up in response to a user-defined load threshold. MPPP can measure the load on just inbound traffic, or on just outbound traffic, but not on the combined load of both inbound and outbound traffic.

The commands shown in Example 2-6 perform load balancing across multiple links.

Example 2-6 Configuring Load Balancing

```
R3(config)# interface serial 0/0/0
R3(config-if)# encapsulation ppp
R3(config-if)# ppp multilink
```

The **multilink** command has no arguments. To disable PPP multilink, use the **no ppp multilink** command.

Verifying a Serial PPP Encapsulation Configuration

Use the **show interfaces serial** command to verify proper configuration of HDLC or PPP encapsulation. The command output in Example 2-7 shows a PPP configuration.

Example 2-7 Verifying a Serial PPP Encapsulation Configuration

```
R2# show interfaces serial 0/0/0

Serial0/0/0 is up, line protocol is up
  Hardware is GT96K Serial
  MTU 1500 bytes, BW 128 Kbit, DLY 20000 usec,
     reliability 255/255, txload 1/255, rxload 1/255
  Encapsulation PPP, LCP Open
  Open: CDPCP, loopback not set
  Keepalive set (10 sec)
  Last input 00:00:07, output 00:00:07, output hang never
  Last clearing of "show interface" counters 00:00:11
  Input queue: 0/75/0/0 (size/max/drops/flushes); Total output drops: 0
  Queueing strategy: weighted fair
  Output queue: 0/1000/64/0 (size/max total/threshold/drops)
     Conversations  0/1/32 (active/max active/max total)
     Reserved Conversations 0/0 (allocated/max allocated)
     Available Bandwidth 96 kilobits/sec
  5 minute input rate 0 bits/sec, 0 packets/sec
  5 minute output rate 0 bits/sec, 0 packets/sec
     6 packets input, 76 bytes, 0 no buffer
     Received 0 broadcasts, 0 runts, 0 giants, 0 throttles
     0 input errors, 0 CRC, 0 frame, 0 overrun, 0 ignored, 0 abort
     7 packets output, 84 bytes, 0 underruns
     0 output errors, 0 collisions, 0 interface resets
     0 output buffer failures, 0 output buffers swapped out
     0 carrier transitions
     DCD=up  DSR=up  DTR=up  RTS=up  CTS=up
```

When you configure HDLC, the output of the **show interfaces serial** command should show **Encapsulation HDLC**. When you configure PPP, you can check its LCP and NCP states.

Table 2-6 summarizes commands used when verifying PPP.

Table 2-6   Verifying and Debugging Commands

Command	Description
show interfaces	Displays statistics for all interfaces configured on the router or access server.
show interfaces serial	Displays information about a serial interface.
debug ppp	Debugs PPP.
undebug all	Turns off all debugging displays.

Troubleshooting PPP Encapsulation

By now you are aware that the **debug** command is used for troubleshooting and is accessed from privileged EXEC mode of the command-line interface. **debug** displays information in real time about various router operations and the related traffic the router generates or receives, as well as any error messages. It is a very useful and informative tool, but you must always remember that Cisco IOS treats **debug** as a high-priority task. It can consume a significant amount of resources, and the router is forced to process-switch the packets being debugged. **debug** must not be used as a monitoring tool; it is meant to be used for a short period of time for troubleshooting. When troubleshooting a serial connection, you use the same approach you have used in other configuration tasks.

Troubleshooting the Serial Encapsulation Configuration

Use the **debug ppp** command to display information about the operation of PPP. The command syntax for this command is as follows:

```
debug ppp {packet | negotiation | error | authentication | compression | cbcp}
```

The **no** form of this command disables debugging output.

Table 2-7 explains the command parameters for the **debug ppp** command.

Table 2-7   **debug ppp** Command Parameters

Parameter	Usage
packet	Displays PPP packets being sent and received. (This command displays low-level packet dumps.)
negotiation	Displays PPP packets transmitted during PPP startup, where PPP options are negotiated.

Table 2-7   **debug ppp** Command Parameters

Parameter	Usage
error	Displays protocol errors and error statistics associated with PPP connection negotiation and operation.
authentication	Displays authentication protocol messages, including Challenge Handshake Authentication Protocol (CHAP) packet exchanges and Password Authentication Protocol (PAP) exchanges.
compression	Displays information specific to the exchange of PPP connections using Microsoft Point-to-Point Compression (MPPC). This command is useful for obtaining incorrect packet sequence number information where MPPC compression is enabled.
cbcp	Displays protocol errors and statistics associated with PPP connection negotiations using Microsoft Callback Control Protocol (MSCB).

Output of the **debug ppp packet** Command

A good command to use when troubleshooting serial interface encapsulation is **debug ppp packet**.

The topology shown in Figure 2-34 will be used for the next series of output examples.

Figure 2-34   Sample Topology

Example 2-8 is output from the **debug ppp packet** command as seen from the Link Quality Monitor (LQM) side of the connection. The output shows the packet exchange between router R1 and router R3 during normal PPP operation.

Example 2-8 Output of the **debug ppp packet** Command

```
R3# debug ppp packet

PPP Serial2(o): lcp_slqr() state = OPEN magic = D21B4, len = 48
PPP Serial2(i): pkt type 0xC025, datagramsize 52
PPP Serial2(i): lcp_rlqr() state = OPEN magic = D3454, len = 48
PPP Serial2(i): pkt type 0xC021, datagramsize 16
PPP Serial2: I LCP ECHOREQ(9) id 3  magic D3454
PPP Serial2: input(C021) state = OPEN code = ECHOREQ(9) id = 3 len = 12
PPP Serial2: O LCP ECHOREP(A) id 3  magic D21B4
PPP Serial2(o): lcp_slqr() state = OPEN magic = D21B4, len = 48
PPP Serial2(i): pkt type 0xC025, datagramsize 52
PPP Serial2(i): lcp_rlqr() state = OPEN magic = D3454, len = 48
PPP Serial2(i): pkt type 0xC021, datagramsize 16
PPP Serial2: I LCP ECHOREQ(9) id 4  magic D3454
PPP Serial2: input(C021) state = OPEN code = ECHOREQ(9) id = 4 len = 12
PPP Serial2: O LCP ECHOREP(A) id 4  magic D21B4
PPP Serial2(o): lcp_slqr() state = OPEN magic = D21B4, len = 48
PPP Serial2(i): pkt type 0xC025, datagramsize 52
PPP Serial2(i): lcp_rlqr() state = OPEN magic = D3454, len = 48
PPP Serial2(i): pkt type 0xC021, datagramsize 16
PPP Serial2: I LCP ECHOREQ(9) id 5  magic D3454
PPP Serial2: input(C021) state = OPEN code = ECHOREQ(9) id = 5 len = 12
PPP Serial2: O LCP ECHOREP(A) id 5  magic D21B4
PPP Serial2(o): lcp_slqr() state = OPEN magic = D21B4, len = 48
PPP Serial2(i): pkt type 0xC025, datagramsize 52
PPP Serial2(i): lcp_rlqr() state = OPEN magic = D3454, len = 48
PPP Serial2(i): pkt type 0xC021, datagramsize 16
PPP Serial2: I LCP ECHOREQ(9) id 6  magic D3454
PPP Serial2: input(C021) state = OPEN code = ECHOREQ(9) id = 6 len = 12
PPP Serial2: O LCP ECHOREP(A) id 6  magic D21B4
PPP Serial2(o): lcp_slqr() state = OPEN magic = D21B4, len = 48
PPP Serial2(i): pkt type 0xC025, datagramsize 52
PPP Serial2(i): lcp_rlqr() state = OPEN magic = D3454, len = 48
PPP Serial2(i): pkt type 0xC021, datagramsize 16
PPP Serial2: I LCP ECHOREQ(9) id 7  magic D3454
PPP Serial2: input(C021) state = OPEN code = ECHOREQ(9) id = 7 len = 12
PPP Serial2: O LCP ECHOREP(A) id 7  magic D21B4
PPP Serial2(o): lcp_slqr() state = OPEN magic = D21B4, len = 48
```

This display example depicts packet exchanges under normal PPP operation. This is only a partial listing, but it's enough to get you ready for the practice lab.

Look at each line in the output, and match it to the meaning of the field. Although it's beyond the scope of this course, use the following to guide your examination of the output.

- **PPP**: PPP debugging output.

- **Serial2**: The interface number associated with this debugging information.

- **(o), O**: The detected packet is an output packet.

- **(i), I**: The detected packet is an input packet.

- **lcp_slqr()**: Procedure name; running LQM, send a Link Quality Report (LQR).

- **lcp_rlqr()**: Procedure name; running LQM, received an LQR.

- **input (C021)**: Router received a packet of the specified packet type (in hexadecimal). A value of C025 indicates a packet of type LQM.

- **state = OPEN**: PPP state; normal state is OPEN.

- **magic = D21B4**: Magic Number for indicated node. When output is indicated, this is the Magic Number of the node on which debugging is enabled. The actual Magic Number depends on whether the packet detected is indicated as I or O.

- **datagramsize = 52**: Packet length, including header.

- **code = ECHOREQ(9)**: Identifies the type of packet received in both string and hexadecimal form.

- **len = 48**: Packet length without header.

- **id = 3**: ID number per Link Control Protocol (LCP) packet format.

- **pkt type 0xC025**: Packet type in hexadecimal. Typical packet types are C025 for LQM and C021 for LCP.

- **LCP ECHOREQ (9)**: Echo Request. Value in parentheses is the hexadecimal representation of the LCP type.

- **LCP ECHOREP (A)**: Echo Reply. Value in parentheses is the hexadecimal representation of the LCP type.

Output of the **debug ppp negotiation** Command

Example 2-9 shows the output of the **debug ppp negotiation** command in a normal negotiation, where both sides agree on network control program (NCP) parameters.

Example 2-9 Output of the **debug ppp negotiation** Command

```
R1# debug ppp negotiation

ppp: sending CONFREQ, type = 4 (CI_QUALITYTYPE), value = C025/3E8
ppp: sending CONFREQ, type = 5 (CI_MAGICNUMBER), value = 3D56CAC
ppp: received config for type = 4 (QUALITYTYPE) acked
ppp: received config for type = 5 (MAGICNUMBER) value = 3D567F8 acked (ok)
PPP Serial2: state = ACKSENT fsm_rconfack(C021): rcvd id 5
ppp: config ACK received, type = 4 (CI_QUALITYTYPE), value = C025
ppp: config ACK received, type = 5 (CI_MAGICNUMBER), value = 3D56CAC
ppp: ipcp_reqci: returning CONFACK. (ok)
PPP Serial2: state = ACKSENT fsm_rconfack(8021): rcvd id 4
```

In this case, protocol type IP is proposed and acknowledged. Let's take the output a line or two at a time.

The first two lines indicate that the router is trying to bring up the LCP and will use the indicated negotiation options (Quality Protocol and Magic Number):

```
ppp: sending CONFREQ, type = 4 (CI_QUALITYTYPE), value = C025/3E8
ppp: sending CONFREQ, type = 5 (CI_MAGICNUMBER), value = 3D56CAC
```

The value fields are the values of the options themselves. C025/3E8 translates to Quality Protocol LQM. 3E8 is the reporting period (in hundredths of a second). 3D56CAC is the value of the Magic Number for the router.

The next two lines indicate that the other side negotiated for options 4 and 5 and that it requested and acknowledged both:

```
ppp: received config for type = 4 (QUALITYTYPE) acked
ppp: received config for type = 5 (MAGICNUMBER) value = 3D567F8 acked (ok)
```

If the responding end does not support the options, the responding node sends a CONFREJ. If the responding end does not accept the value of the option, it sends a CONFNAK with the value field modified.

The next three lines indicate that the router received a CONFACK from the responding side and displays accepted option values:

```
PPP Serial4: state = ACKSENT fsm_rconfack(C021): rcvd id 5
ppp: config ACK received, type = 4 (CI_QUALITYTYPE), value = C025
ppp: config ACK received, type = 5 (CI_MAGICNUMBER), value = 3D56CAC
```

Use the rcvd id field to verify that the CONFREQ and CONFACK have the same ID field.

The next line indicates that the router has IP routing enabled on this interface and that the IPCP NCP negotiated successfully:

```
ppp: ipcp_reqci: returning CONFACK
(ok)
```

Output of the **debug ppp error** Command

You can use the **debug ppp error** command to display protocol errors and error statistics associated with PPP connection negotiation and operation, as shown in Example 2-10. These messages might appear when the Quality Protocol option is enabled on an interface that is already running PPP.

Example 2-10   Output of the **debug ppp error** Command

```
R1# debug ppp error

PPP Serial3(i): rlqr receive failure. successes = 15
PPP: myrcvdiffp = 159 peerxmitdiffp = 41091
PPP: myrcvdiffo = 2183 peerxmitdiffo = 1714439
PPP: threshold = 25
PPP Serial2(i): rlqr transmit failure. successes = 15
PPP: myxmitdiffp = 41091 peerrcvdiffp = 159
PPP: myxmitdiffo = 1714439 peerrcvdiffo = 2183
PPP: l->OutLQRs = 1 LastOutLQRs = 1
PPP: threshold = 25
PPP Serial3(i): lqr_protrej() Stop sending LQRs.
PPP Serial3(i): The link appears to be looped back.
```

Look at each line in the output, and match it to the meaning of the field. Again, this is beyond the scope of this course, but you can use the following to guide your examination of the output.

- **PPP**: PPP debugging output.

- **Serial3(i)**: The interface number associated with this debugging information. Indicates that this is an input packet.

- **rlqr receive failure**: The receiver does not accept the request to negotiate the Quality Protocol option.

- **myrcvdiffp = 159**: The number of packets received over the time period specified.

- **peerxmitdiffp = 41091**: The number of packets sent by the remote node over this period.

- **myrcvdiffo = 2183**: The number of octets received over this period.

- **peerxmitdiffo = 1714439**: The number of octets sent by the remote node over this period.

- **threshold = 25**: The maximum error percentage acceptable on this interface. You calculate this percentage using a value of 100 minus the threshold value entered in the **ppp quality** *percentage* interface configuration command. In this case, the maximum error percentage calculated is set to 25% which means that the interface was configured using the **ppp quality 75** command ($100 - 75 = 25$). This means that the local router must maintain a minimum 75 percent nonerror percentage (or a 25% maximum error percentage), or the PPP link closes down.

- **OutLQRs = 1**: The current send LQR sequence number of the local router.

- **LastOutLQRs = 1**: The last sequence number that the remote node side has seen from the local node.

Configuring Point-to-Point Encapsulations 2.3.4

In this activity, you will practice changing the encapsulation on serial interfaces. Detailed instructions are provided within the activity. Use File e4-234.pka on the CD-ROM that accompanies this book to perform this activity using Packet Tracer.

PPP Authentication Protocols

PPP defines an extensible version of LCP that allows negotiation of an authentication protocol for a router to authenticate its peer before allowing network layer protocols to transmit over the link.

PPP Authentication Protocol

RFC 1334 defines two protocols for authentication, as shown in Figure 2-35.

Figure 2-35   PPP Authentication Protocols

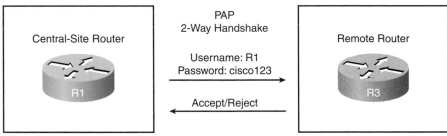

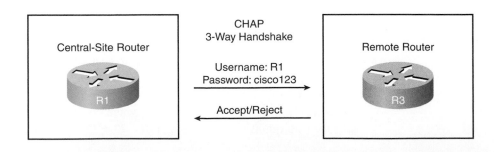

Password Authentication Protocol (PAP) is a basic two-way process. There is no encryption, because the username and password are sent in plain text. If it is accepted, the connection is allowed. Challenge Handshake Authentication Protocol (CHAP) is more secure than PAP. It involves a three-way exchange of a shared secret. The process is described later in this section.

The authentication phase of a PPP session is optional. If it is used, you can authenticate the peer after the LCP establishes the link and choose the authentication protocol. If it is used, authentication takes place before the network layer protocol configuration phase begins.

The authentication options require that the calling side of the link enter authentication information. This helps ensure that the user has permission from the network administrator to make the call. Peer routers exchange authentication messages.

Password Authentication Protocol

One of the many features of PPP is that it performs Layer 2 authentication in addition to other layers of authentication, encryption, access control, and general security procedures.

Initiating PAP

PAP provides a simple method for a remote node to establish its identity using a two-way handshake. PAP is not interactive. When the **ppp authentication pap** command is used, the username and password are sent as one LCP data package, rather than the server's sending a login prompt and waiting for a response.

Figure 2-36 shows that after PPP completes the link establishment phase, the remote node repeatedly sends a username-password pair across the link until the sending node acknowledges it or terminates the connection.

Figure 2-36   Initiating PAP

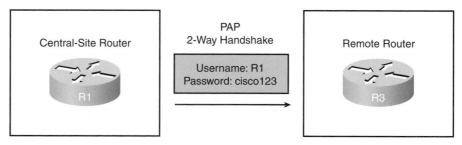

Router R1 sends its PAP username and password to Router R3.

Figure 2-37 shows that at the receiving node, the router (or an authentication server) checks the username-password. It either allows or denies the connection. An accept or reject message is returned to the requester.

Figure 2-37 Completing PAP

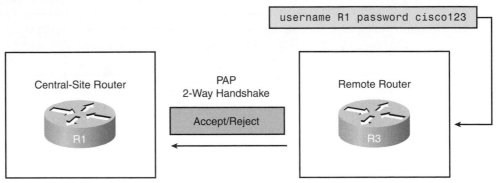

Router R3 evaluates R1's username and password against its local database. If it matches, it accepts the connection. If not, it rejects the connection.

PAP is not a strong authentication protocol. Using PAP, you send passwords across the link in clear text, and there is no protection from playback or repeated trial-and-error attacks. The remote node is in control of the frequency and timing of the login attempts.

Nonetheless, sometimes using PAP can be justified. For example, despite its shortcomings, PAP may be used in the following environments:

- A large installed base of client applications that do not support CHAP

- Incompatibilities between different vendor implementations of CHAP

- Situations in which a plain-text password must be available to simulate a login at the remote host

Challenge Handshake Authentication Protocol (CHAP)

Challenge Handshake Authentication Protocol (CHAP), defined in RFC 1994, verifies the peer's identity by means of a three-way handshake. CHAP is considered a stronger authentication method than PAP.

PAP authenticates only once. After authentication is established, PAP essentially stops working, because it can't reauthenticate during the session. This leaves the network vulnerable to attack. Unlike PAP, which authenticates only once, CHAP conducts periodic challenges to make sure that the remote node still has a valid password value. The password value is variable and changes unpredictably while the link exists.

After the PPP link establishment phase is complete, the local router sends a challenge message to the remote node, as shown in Figure 2-38.

Figure 2-38   Initiating CHAP

Router R3 initiates the 3-way handshake and sends a challenge message to Router R1.

Figure 2-39 shows that the remote node responds with a value calculated using a one-way hash function, which typically is *Message Digest 5 (MD5)*, based on the password and challenge message. These steps are explained in the next section.

Figure 2-39   Responding to CHAP

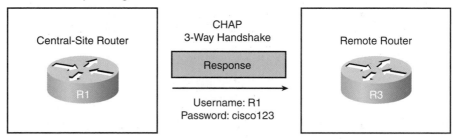

R1 responds R3's CHAP challenge by sending its CHAP username and password.

In Figure 2-40, the local router checks the response against its own calculation of the expected hash value. If the values match, the initiating node acknowledges the authentication. Otherwise, it immediately terminates the connection.

Figure 2-40   Completing CHAP

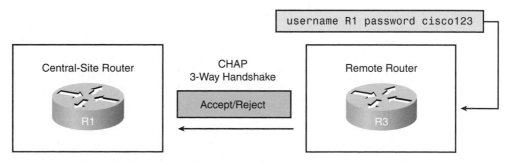

Router R3 evaluates R1's username and password against its local database. If it matches, it accepts the connection. If not, it rejects the connection.

CHAP provides protection against playback attack by using a variable challenge value that is unique and unpredictable. Because the challenge is unique and random, the resulting hash value is also unique and random. The use of repeated challenges limits the time of exposure to any single attack. The local router or a third-party authentication server is in control of the frequency and timing of the challenges.

PPP Encapsulation and Authentication Process

You can use the flowchart shown in Figure 2-41 to help understand the PPP authentication process when configuring PPP. The flowchart provides a visual example of the logic decisions that PPP makes.

Figure 2-41   PPP Encapsulation and Authentication Process

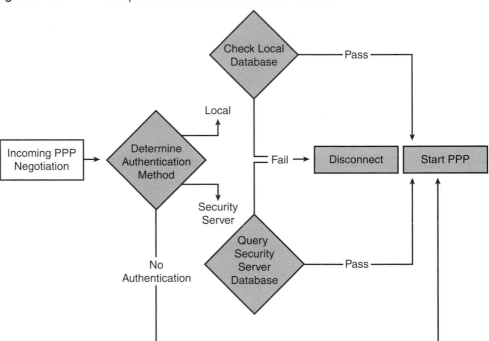

For example, if an incoming PPP request requires no authentication, PPP progresses to the next level. If an incoming PPP request requires authentication, it can be authenticated using either the local database or a security server. As illustrated in the flowchart, successful authentication progresses to the next level, whereas an authentication failure disconnects and drops the incoming PPP request.

Follow these steps to see how router R1 establishes an authenticated PPP CHAP connection with Router R2:

Step 1.   As shown in Figure 2-42, router R1 initially negotiates the link connection using LCP with router R2, and the two systems agree to use CHAP authentication during the PPP LCP negotiation.

Figure 2-42   Establishing a Link

Step 2.   As shown in Figure 2-43, router R2 generates an ID and a random number and sends that plus its username as a CHAP challenge packet to R1.

Figure 2-43   Sending a CHAP Challenge to R1

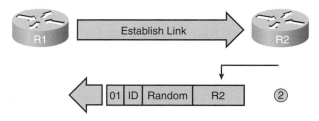

Step 3.   As shown in Figure 2-44, router R1 uses the username of the challenger (R2) and cross-references it with its local database to find its associated password. R1 then generates a unique MD5 hash number using R2's username, ID, random number, and the shared secret password.

Figure 2-44   R1 Validates R2

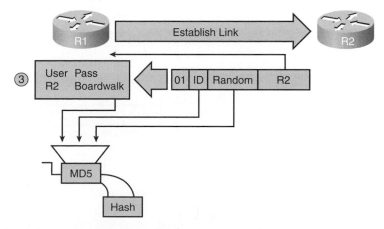

Step 4.   As shown in Figure 2-45, router R1 validates router R2's hash and then sends the challenge ID, the hashed value, and its username (R1) to R2.

Figure 2-45   R1 Sends the Challenge to R2

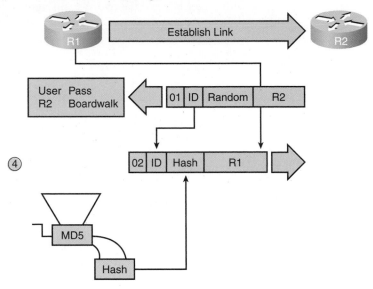

Step 5.   As shown in Figure 2-46, router R2 generates its own hash value using the ID, the shared secret password, and the random number it originally sent to R1.

Figure 2-46   R2 Validates R1

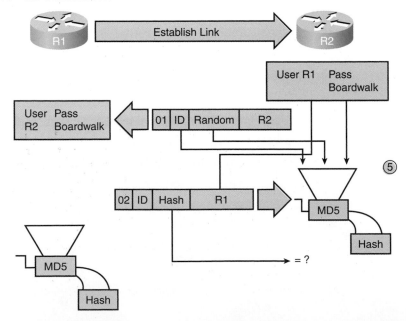

Step 6.   As shown in Figure 2-47, router R2 compares its hash value with the hash value sent by R1. If the values are the same, R2 sends a link established response to R1.

Figure 2-47   R2 Establishes the Link

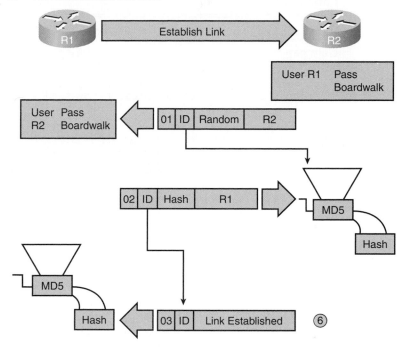

If the authentication fails, a CHAP failure packet is built from the following components:

- 04 = CHAP failure message type

- id = copied from the response packet

- "Authentication failure" or a similar message, which is meant to be a user-readable explanation

Note that the shared secret password must be identical on R1 and R2.

Configuring PPP with Authentication

To specify the order in which the CHAP or PAP protocols are requested on the interface, use the **ppp authentication** interface configuration command, the syntax for which is as follows:

```
ppp authentication {chap | chap pap | pap chap | pap} [if-needed]
   [list-name | default [callin]
```

Use the **no** form of the command to disable this authentication.

Table 2-8 describes the **ppp authentication** command parameters.

Table 2-8   ppp authentication Command Parameters

Parameter	Usage
chap	Enables CHAP on a serial interface.
chap pap	Enables both CHAP and PAP and performs CHAP authentication before PAP.
pap chap	Enables both CHAP and PAP and performs PAP authentication before CHAP.
pap	Enables PAP on a serial interface.
if-needed	(Optional) Used with TACACS and XTACACS. Do not perform CHAP or PAP authentication if the user has already provided authentication. This option is available only on asynchronous interfaces.
list-name	(Optional) Used with AAA/TACACS+. Specifies the name of a list of TACACS+ authentication methods to use. If no list name is specified, the system uses the default. Lists are created with the **aaa authentication ppp** command.
default	(Optional) Used with AAA/TACACS+. Created with the **aaa authentication ppp** command.
callin	Specifies authentication on incoming (received) calls only.

After you have enabled CHAP or PAP authentication, or both, the local router requires the remote device to prove its identity before allowing data traffic to flow. This is done as follows:

- PAP authentication requires that the remote device send a name and password to be checked against a matching entry in the local username database or in the remote TACACS/TACACS+ database.

- CHAP authentication sends a challenge to the remote device. The remote device must encrypt the challenge value with a shared secret and return the encrypted value and its name to the local router in a response message. The local router uses the name of the remote device to look up the appropriate secret in the local username or remote *TACACS/TACACS+* database. It uses the looked-up secret to encrypt the original challenge and verify that the encrypted values match.

Note

AAA/TACACS is a dedicated server used to authenticate users. AAA stands for authentication, authorization, and accounting. TACACS clients send a query to a TACACS authentication server. The server can authenticate the user, authorize what the user can do, and track what the user has done.

You may enable PAP or CHAP or both. If both methods are enabled, the first method specified is requested during link negotiation. If the peer suggests using the second method or simply refuses the first method, the second method is tried. Some remote devices support CHAP only and some PAP only. The order in which you specify the methods is based on your concerns about the ability of the remote device to correctly negotiate the appropriate method as well as your concern about data line security. PAP usernames and passwords are sent as clear-text strings and can be intercepted and reused. CHAP has eliminated most of the known security holes.

Figure 2-48 shows a sample topology.

Figure 2-48   Sample Topology

Examples 2-11 and 2-12 show a two-way PAP authentication configuration.

Example 2-11   Sample PAP Configuration on R1

```
hostname R1
username R3 password someone
!
int serial 0/0
ip address 128.0.1.1 255.255.255.0
encapsulation ppp
ppp authentication PAP
ppp pap sent-username R1 password someone
```

Example 2-12   Sample PAP Configuration on R3

```
hostname R3
username R1 password someone
!
int serial 0/0
ip address 128.0.1.2 255.255.255.0
encapsulation ppp
ppp authentication PAP
ppp pap sent-username R3 password someone
```

Both routers authenticate and are authenticated, so the PAP authentication commands mirror each other. The PAP username and password that each router sends must match those specified with the **username** *name* **password** *password* command of the other router.

PAP provides a simple method for a remote node to establish its identity using a two-way handshake. This is done only on initial link establishment. The hostname on one router must match the username the other router has configured. The passwords must also match and are case-sensitive.

CHAP periodically verifies the identity of the remote node using a three-way handshake. The hostname on one router must match the username the other router has configured. The passwords must also match. This occurs on initial link establishment and can be repeated any time after the link has been established. Examples 2-13 and 2-14 show a CHAP configuration.

Example 2-13   Sample CHAP Configuration on R1

```
hostname R1
username R3 password sameone
!
int serial 0/0
ip address 128.0.1.1 255.255.255.0
encapsulation ppp
ppp authentication CHAP
```

Example 2-14   Sample CHAP Configuration on R3

```
hostname R3
username R1 password sameone
!
int serial 0/0
ip address 128.0.1.2 255.255.255.0
encapsulation ppp
ppp authentication CHAP
```

Troubleshooting a PPP Configuration with Authentication

Authentication is a feature that needs to be implemented correctly, or the security of your serial connection may be compromised. Always verify your configuration with the **show interfaces serial** command, in the same way as you did without authentication.

Never assume that your authentication configuration works without testing it. Debugging allows you to confirm your configuration and correct any deficiencies. The command for debugging PPP authentication is **debug ppp authentication**.

Example 2-15 shows sample output for the **debug ppp authentication** command.

Example 2-15   Troubleshooting a PPP Configuration with Authentication

```
R1# debug ppp authentication

Serial0: Unable to authenticate. No name received from peer
Serial0: Unable to validate CHAP response. USERNAME R3 not found.
Serial0: Unable to validate CHAP response. No password defined for USERNAME R3
Serial0: Failed CHAP authentication with remote.
Remote message is Unknown name
Serial0: remote passed CHAP authentication.
Serial0: Passed CHAP authentication with remote.
Serial0: CHAP input code = 4 id = 3 len = 48
```

The following is an interpretation of the output:

Line 1 says that the router is unable to authenticate on interface Serial0 because the peer did not send a name.

Line 2 says the router was unable to validate the CHAP response because USERNAME R3 was not found.

Line 3 says that no password was found for R3. Other possible responses at this line might have been no name received to authenticate, unknown name, no secret for given name, short MD5 response received, or MD5 compare failed.

In the last line, **code = 4** means a failure has occurred. Other code values are as follows:

- 1 = Challenge

- 2 = Response

- 3 = Success

- 4 = Failure

id = 3 is the ID number per LCP packet format.

len = 48 is the packet length without the header.

Configuring PAP and CHAP Authentication 2.4.6

PPP encapsulation allows two different types of authentication: Password Authentication Protocol (PAP) and Challenge Handshake Authentication Protocol (CHAP). PAP uses a clear-text password, whereas CHAP invokes a one-way hash that provides more security than PAP. In this activity, you configure both PAP and CHAP as well as review OSPF routing configuration. Detailed instructions are provided within the activity. Use File e4-246.pka on the CD-ROM that accompanies this book to perform this activity using Packet Tracer.

Summary

On completing this chapter, you can describe in conceptual and practical terms why serial point-to-point communications are used to connect your LAN to your service provider WAN, rather than using a connection where communications bits are sent in parallel, which might intuitively seem faster. You can explain how multiplexing allows efficient communications and maximizes the amount of data that can be passed over a communications link. You learned the functions of key components and protocols of serial communications, and you can configure a serial interface with HDLC encapsulation on a Cisco router.

This chapter provided a good basis for comprehending PPP, including its features, components, and architectures. You can explain how a PPP session is established using the functions of the LCP and NCPs. You learned the syntax of the configuration commands and learned about the use of the various options required to configure a PPP connection. You also learned how to use PAP or CHAP authentication protocols to ensure a secure connection. The steps required for verifying and troubleshooting PPP were described. You are now ready to confirm your knowledge in the lab, where you will configure your router to use PPP to connect to a WAN.

Labs

The activities and labs available in the companion *Accessing the WAN, CCNA Exploration Labs and Study Guide* (ISBN 1-58713-212-5) provide hands-on practice with the following topics introduced in this chapter:

Lab 2-1: Basic PPP Configuration (2.5.1)

In this lab, you learn how to configure PPP encapsulation on serial links using the network shown in the topology diagram. You also learn how to restore serial links to their default HDLC encapsulation. Pay special attention to the router's output when you intentionally break PPP encapsulation. This will assist you in the Troubleshooting lab associated with this chapter. Finally, you configure PPP PAP authentication and PPP CHAP authentication.

Lab 2-2: Challenge PPP Configuration (2.5.2)

In this lab, you learn how to configure PPP encapsulation on serial links using the network shown in the topology diagram. You also configure PPP CHAP authentication. If you need assistance, refer to the Basic PPP Configuration lab, but try to do as much on your own as possible.

Lab 2-3: Troubleshooting PPP Configuration (2.5.3)

The routers at your company were configured by an inexperienced network engineer. Several errors in the configuration have resulted in connectivity issues. Your boss has asked you to troubleshoot and correct the configuration errors and document your work. Using your knowledge of PPP and standard testing methods, find and correct the errors. Make sure that all the serial links use PPP CHAP authentication and that all the networks can be reached.

Packet Tracer
☐ Companion

Many of the Hands-on Labs include Packet Tracer Companion Activities, where you can use Packet Tracer to complete a simulation of the lab. Look for this icon in *Accessing the WAN, CCNA Exploration Labs and Study Guide* for Hands-on Labs that have a Packet Tracer Companion.

Check Your Understanding

Complete all the review questions listed here to test your understanding of the topics and concepts in this chapter. Answers are listed in Appendix, "Check Your Understanding and Challenge Questions Answer Key."

1. Match each PPP establishment step with its appropriate sequence number:

   Step 1

   Step 2

   Step 3

   Step 4

   Step 5

   A. Test link quality (optional).

   B. Negotiate Layer 3 protocol options.

   C. Send link-establishment frames to negotiate options such as MTU size, compression, and authentication.

   D. Send configuration-acknowledgment frames.

   E. NCP reaches Open state.

2. Which output from the **show interfaces s0/0/0** command indicates that the far end of a point-to-point link has a different encapsulation set than the local router?

   A. serial 0/0/0 is down, line protocol is down

   B. serial 0/0/0 is up, line protocol is down

   C. serial 0/0/0 is up, line protocol is up (looped)

   D. serial 0/0/0 is up, line protocol is down (disabled)

   E. serial 0/0/0 is administratively down, line protocol is down

3. What is the default encapsulation for serial interfaces on a Cisco router?

   A. HDLC

   B. PPP

   C. Frame Relay

   D. X.25

4. What is the function of the Protocol field in a PPP frame?

   A. It identifies the application layer protocol that will process the frame.

   B. It identifies the transport layer protocol that will process the frame.

   C. It identifies the data link layer protocol encapsulation in the frame's Date field.

   D. It identifies the network layer protocol encapsulated in the frame's Data field.

5. Match each description with its corresponding term:

Error control

Authentication protocols

Allows load balancing

Compression protocols

A. Stacker/predictor

B. Magic number

C. Multilink

D. CHAP/PAP

E. Call in

6. Which of the following statements describe the function of statistical time-division multiplexing (STDM)? (Choose three.)

A. Multiple data streams share one common channel.

B. Bit interleaving controls the timing mechanism that places data on the channel.

C. Time slots are used on a first-come, first-served basis.

D. STDM was developed to overcome the inefficiency caused by time slots still being allocated even when the channel has no data to transmit.

E. Sources of data alternate during transmission and are reconstructed at the receiving end.

F. Priority can be dedicated to one data source.

7. Which of the following describes the serial connection between two routers using the High-level Data Link Control (HDLC) protocol?

A. Synchronous or asynchronous bit-oriented transmissions using a universal frame format

B. Synchronous bit-oriented transmissions using a frame format that allows flow control and error detection

C. Asynchronous bit-oriented transmissions using a frame format derived from the Synchronous Data Link Control (SDLC) protocol

D. Asynchronous bit-oriented transmissions using a V.35 DTE/DCE interface

8. If an authentication protocol is configured for PPP operation, when is the client or user workstation authenticated?

    A. Before link establishment

    B. During the link establishment phase

    C. Before the network layer protocol configuration begins

    D. After the network layer protocol configuration has ended

9. Why are Network Control Protocols used in PPP?

    A. To establish and terminate data links

    B. To provide authentication capabilities to PPP

    C. To manage network congestion and to allow quality testing of the link

    D. To allow multiple Layer 3 protocols to operate over the same physical link

10. Which statement describes the PAP authentication protocol?

    A. It sends encrypted passwords by default.

    B. It uses a two-way handshake to establish identity.

    C. It protects against repeated trial-and-error attacks.

    D. It requires the same username to be configured on every router.

11. A technician testing the functionality of a recently installed router is unable to ping the serial interface of a remote router. The technician executes the **show interfaces serial 0/0/0** command on the local router and sees the following line in the router:

    Serial0/0/0 is down, line protocol is down

    What are two possible causes of this command output?

    A. The **clock rate** command is missing.

    B. The carrier detect signal is not sensed.

    C. Keepalives are not being sent.

    D. The interface is disabled due to a high error rate.

    E. The interface is shut down.

    F. The cabling is faulty or incorrect.

12. The network administrator is configuring Router1 to connect to Router2 using three-way handshake authentication. Match each description with the command necessary to configure Router1:

Configure the username and password

Enter interface configuration mode

Specify the encapsulation type

Configure authentication

   A. **username Router2 password cisco**

   B. **username Router1 password cisco**

   C. **interface serial 0/1/0**

   D. **encapsulation ppp**

   E. **encapsulation hdlc**

   F. **ppp authentication pap**

   G. **ppp authentication chap**

13. What is required to successfully establish a connection between two routers using CHAP authentication?

   A. The hostnames of both routers must be the same.

   B. The usernames of both routers must be the same.

   C. The enable secret passwords configured on both routers must be the same.

   D. The password configured with the router's username must be the same on both routers.

   E. The **ppp chap sent-username** command must be configured the same on both routers.

14. For each characteristic, indicate whether it is associated with PAP or CHAP:

Two-way handshake

Three-way handshake

Open to trial-and-error attacks

Password sent in clear text

Periodic verification

Uses a one-way hash function

15. For each description, indicate whether it is associated with LCP or NCP:

   Negotiates link establishment parameters

   Negotiates Layer 3 protocol parameters

   Maintains/debugs a link

   Can negotiate multiple Layer 3 protocols

   Terminates a link

16. Describe four of the six types of WAN encapsulation protocols.

17. Describe the functions of LCP and NCP.

18. Describe the five configurable LCP encapsulation options.

19. Refer to the following configurations for Router R1 and Router R3:

```
hostname R1
username R1 password cisco123
!
int serial 0/0
ip address 128.0.1.1 255.255.255.0
encapsulation ppp
ppp authentication pap
```

```
hostname R3
username R1 password cisco
!
int serial 0/0
ip address 128.0.1.2 255.255.255.0
encapsulation ppp
ppp authentication CHAP
```

Router R1 is unable to connect with Router R3. On the basis of the information presented, which configuration changes on Router R1 would correct the problem?

Challenge Questions and Activities

1. The following outputs are a result of the **debug ppp negotiation** command. Which of these outputs are the result of using PAP authentication, and which are the result of using CHAP authentication?

```
Serial1 PPP: Phase is AUTHENTICATING, by both
Serial1 PPP: Phase is AUTHENTICATING, by the peer
Serial1 PPP: Phase is AUTHENTICATING, by this end
```

CHAPTER 3

Frame Relay

Objectives

After completing this chapter, you should be able to answer the following questions:

- What are the fundamental concepts of Frame Relay technology in terms of enterprise WAN services, including operation, implementation requirements, Frame Relay maps, and Local Management Interface (LMI) operation?

- How do you configure a basic Frame Relay permanent virtual circuit (PVC), including configuring and troubleshooting Frame Relay on a router serial interface and configuring a static Frame Relay map?

- What are the advanced concepts of Frame Relay technology in terms of enterprise WAN services, including subinterfaces, bandwidth, and flow control?

- How do you configure advanced Frame Relay PVC, including solving reachability issues, configuring subinterfaces, and verifying and troubleshooting a Frame Relay configuration?

Key Terms

This chapter uses the following key terms. You can find the definitions in the glossary at the end of the book.

Introduction

Frame Relay is a high-performance WAN protocol that operates at the physical and data link layers of the OSI reference model.

Eric Scace, an engineer at Sprint International, invented Frame Relay as a simpler version of the X.25 protocol to use across Integrated Services Digital Network (ISDN) interfaces. Today, it is used over a variety of other network interfaces as well. When Sprint first implemented Frame Relay in its public network, it used StrataCom switches. Cisco's acquisition of StrataCom in 1996 marked its entry into the carrier market.

Network providers commonly implement Frame Relay for voice and data as an encapsulation technique, used between LANs over a WAN. Each end user gets a private line (or leased line) to a Frame Relay node. The Frame Relay network handles the transmission over multiple paths, transparent to all end users.

Frame Relay has become one of the most extensively used WAN protocols, primarily because it is inexpensive compared to *dedicated lines*. In addition, configuring user equipment in a Frame Relay network is very simple. Frame Relay connections are created by configuring Customer Premises Equipment (CPE) routers or other devices to communicate with a service provider Frame Relay switch. The service provider configures the Frame Relay switch, which helps keep end-user configuration tasks to a minimum.

This chapter describes Frame Relay and explains how to configure Frame Relay on a Cisco router.

Basic Frame Relay Concepts

Frame Relay has become the most widely used WAN technology in the world. Large enterprises, governments, ISPs, and small businesses use Frame Relay, primarily because of its price and flexibility.

Introducing Frame Relay

As organizations grow and depend more and more on reliable data transport, traditional leased-line solutions are prohibitively expensive. The pace of technological change, along with companies expanding geographically into other areas, demand and require more flexibility.

Frame Relay: An Efficient and Flexible WAN Technology

Frame Relay reduces network costs by using less equipment, less complexity, and an easier implementation. Moreover, Frame Relay provides greater bandwidth, reliability, and resiliency than private or leased lines. With increasing globalization and the growth of one-to-many branch office topologies, Frame Relay offers simpler network architecture and lower cost of ownership.

Using an example of a large enterprise network helps illustrate the benefits of using a Frame Relay WAN. In Figure 3-1, Span Engineering has five campuses across North America. As with most organizations, Span's bandwidth requirements do not match a "one size fits all" solution.

Figure 3-1   Corporate Bandwidth Requirements

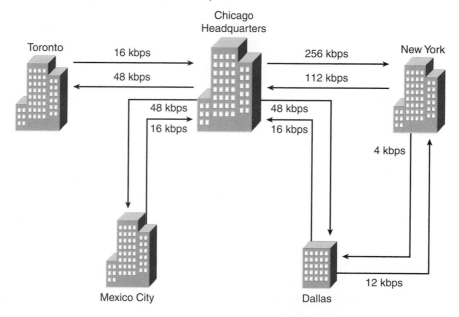

The first thing to consider is the bandwidth requirements of each site. Working out from the headquarters, the Chicago-to-New York connection requires a maximum speed of 256 kbps. Three other sites need a maximum speed of 48 kbps connecting to the headquarters. The connection between the New York and Dallas branch offices requires only 12 kbps.

Before Frame Relay became available, Span leased dedicated lines.

Using leased lines, each Span site is connected through a switch at the local telephone company's central office (CO) through the local loop, and then across the entire network, as shown in Figure 3-2. The Chicago and New York sites each use a dedicated T1 line (equivalent to 24 DS0 channels) to connect to the switch, and other sites use ISDN connections (56 kbps). Because the Dallas site connects with both New York and Chicago, it has two locally leased lines. The service providers have given Span one DS0 between the respective COs, except for the larger pipe connecting Chicago to New York, which has four DS0s. DS0s are priced differently from region to region and usually are offered at a fixed price. These lines are truly dedicated in that the network provider reserves that line for Span's own use. No sharing occurs. Span pays for the end-to-end circuit regardless of how much bandwidth it uses.

Figure 3-2   Dedicated Line WAN Requirements

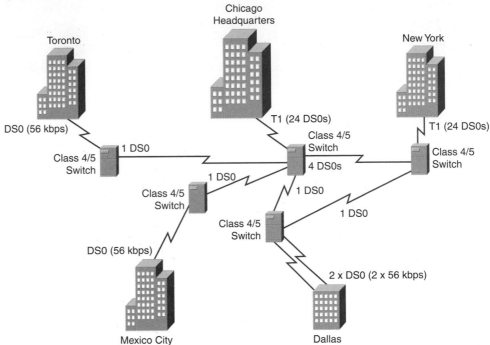

A dedicated line provides little practical opportunity for a one-to-many connection without getting more lines from the network provider. In the Span Engineering example, almost all communication must flow through the corporate headquarters, simply to reduce the cost of additional lines.

If you examine what each site requires in terms of bandwidth, you notice a lack of efficiency:

- Of the 24 DS0 channels available in the T1 connection, the Chicago site uses only seven. Some carriers offer fractional T1 connections in increments of 64 kbps, but this requires a specialized multiplexer at the customer end to channelize the signals. In this case, Span has opted for the full T1 service.

- Similarly, the New York site uses only five of its available 24 DS0s.

- Because Dallas needs to connect to Chicago and New York, two lines connect through the CO to each site.

The leased-line design also limits flexibility. Unless circuits are already installed, connecting new sites typically requires new circuit installations and takes considerable time to implement. From a network reliability point of view, imagine the additional costs in money and complexity of adding spare and redundant circuits.

In Figure 3-3, Span's Frame Relay network uses permanent virtual circuits (PVC). A PVC is the logical path along an originating Frame Relay link, through the network, and along a terminating Frame Relay link to its ultimate destination. Compare this to the physical path used by a dedicated connection. In a network with Frame Relay access, a PVC uniquely defines the path between two endpoints. The concept of virtual circuits is discussed in more detail later in this section.

Figure 3-3   Frame Relay WAN Requirements

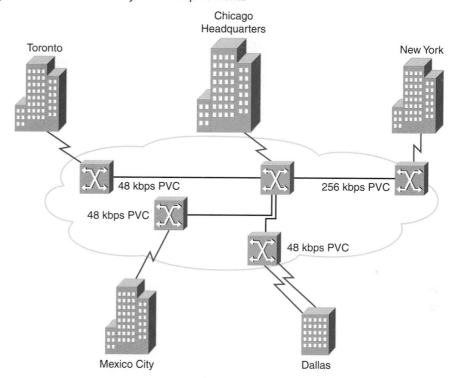

Span's Frame Relay solution provides both cost effectiveness and flexibility.

Cost Effectiveness of Frame Relay

Frame Relay is a more cost-effective option for two reasons. First, with dedicated lines, customers pay for an end-to-end connection. That includes the local loop and the network link within the WAN cloud. With Frame Relay, customers pay for only the local loop and the bandwidth they purchase from the network provider. Distance between nodes is not important. In a dedicated-line model, customers use dedicated lines provided in increments of 64 kbps. However, Frame Relay customers can define their virtual-circuit needs in far greater granularity, often in increments as small as 4 kbps.

The second reason for Frame Relay's cost effectiveness is that it shares bandwidth across a larger base of customers. Typically, a service provider can service 40 or more 56-kbps customers over one T1 circuit. Using dedicated lines would require more DSU/CSUs (one for each line) and more complicated routing and switching. Service providers save because there is less equipment to purchase and maintain.

Table 3-1 shows a representative cost comparison (in U.S. dollars) for comparable ISDN and Frame Relay connections. Although initial costs for Frame Relay are higher than for ISDN, the monthly cost is considerably lower. Frame Relay is easier to manage and configure than ISDN. In addition, customers can increase their bandwidth as their needs grow in the future. Frame Relay customers pay for only the bandwidth they need. Frame Relay incurs no hourly charges. ISDN calls are metered and can result in unexpectedly high monthly charges from the telephone company if a full-time connection is maintained.

Table 3-1   Frame Relay Costs

	64-kbps ISDN	56-kbps Frame Relay
Local loop monthly charge	$185	$85
ISP setup	$380	$750
Equipment	$700 (ISDN router)	$1600 (Cisco router)
ISP monthly charge	$195	$195
One-time charges	$1080	$2660
Monthly charges	$380	$280

Flexibility of Frame Relay

A virtual circuit provides considerable flexibility in network design. Looking at the figure, you can see that Span's offices all connect to the Frame Relay cloud over their respective local loops. What happens in the cloud is really of no concern at this time. All that matters is that when any Span office wants to communicate with any other Span office, all it needs to do is connect to a virtual circuit leading to the other office. In Frame Relay, the end of each connection has a number to identify it called a *Data Link Connection Identifier (DLCI)*. Any station can connect with any other simply by stating the address of that station and DLCI number of the line it needs to use. In a later section, you will learn that when Frame Relay is configured, all the data from all the configured DLCIs flows through the same port of the router. Try to picture the same flexibility using dedicated lines. Not only is it complicated, but it also requires considerably more equipment.

The next few topics will expand your understanding of Frame Relay by defining the key concepts introduced in the example.

Frame Relay WAN

In the late 1970s and into the early 1990s, the WAN technology joining the end sites typically used the X.25 protocol. Now considered a legacy protocol, X.25 was a popular packet-switching technology because it provided a reliable connection over unreliable cabling infrastructures. It did so by including additional error control and flow control. However, these additional features added overhead to the protocol. Its major application was for processing credit card authorizations and automatic teller machines. This course mentions X.25 only for historical purposes.

When you build a WAN, regardless of the transport you choose, the WAN always has a minimum of three basic components, or groups of components, connecting any two sites, as shown in Figure 3-4. Each site needs its own equipment (DTE) to access the telephone company's CO serving the area (DCE). The third component sits in the middle, joining the two sites. In the figure, this is the portion supplied by the Frame Relay backbone, the area within the cloud.

Figure 3-4   Frame Relay WAN

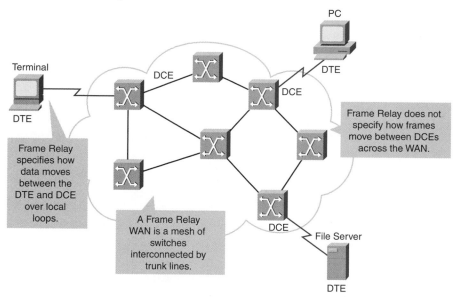

Frame Relay differs significantly from X.25 in its functionality and format. In particular, Frame Relay is a more streamlined protocol, facilitating higher performance and greater efficiency. For example, Frame Relay does not provide error correction. Modern WAN facilities offer more reliable connection services and a higher degree of reliability than older facilities. The Frame Relay node simply drops packets without notification when it detects errors. Any necessary error correction, such as retransmission of data, is left to the endpoints. This makes propagation from customer end to customer end through the network very fast.

Frame Relay operates between an end-user device, such as a LAN bridge or router, and a network. The network itself can use any transmission method that is compatible with the speed and efficiency that Frame Relay applications require. Some networks use Frame Relay itself, but others use digital circuit switching or ATM cell relay systems.

Frame Relay Operation

The connection between a DTE device and a DCE device consists of both a physical layer component and a data link layer component:

- The physical component defines the mechanical, electrical, functional, and procedural specifications for the connection between the devices. One of the most commonly used physical layer interface specifications is the RS-232 specification.

- The data link layer component defines the protocol that establishes the connection between the DTE device, such as a router, and the DCE device, such as a switch.

Figure 3-5 illustrates Frame Relay operation. When carriers use Frame Relay to interconnect LANs, a router on each LAN is the DTE. A serial connection, such as a T1/E1 leased line, connects the router to the carrier's Frame Relay switch at the nearest point of presence (POP) for the carrier. The Frame Relay switch is a DCE device. Network switches move frames from one DTE across the network and deliver frames to other DTEs by way of DCEs. Computing equipment that is not on a LAN may also send data across a Frame Relay network. The computing equipment uses a ***Frame Relay access device (FRAD)*** as the DTE. The FRAD is sometimes called a Frame Relay assembler/dissembler and is a dedicated appliance or a router configured to support Frame Relay. It is located on the customer's premises and connects to a switch port on the service provider's network. In turn, the service provider interconnects the Frame Relay switches.

Virtual Circuits

Virtual circuits provide a bidirectional communication path from one DTE device to another and are uniquely identified by a DLCI. The circuits are virtual because there is no direct electrical connection from end to end. The connection is logical, and data moves from end to end without a direct electrical circuit. With virtual circuits (VC), Frame Relay shares the bandwidth among multiple users, and any single site can communicate with any other single site without using multiple dedicated physical lines.

Frame Relay virtual circuits fall into two categories: switched virtual circuits (SVC) and permanent virtual circuits (PVC):

- SVCs are temporary connections used in situations requiring only sporadic transfer between DTE devices across the Frame Relay network. A communication session across an SVC consists of four operational states: call setup, data transfer, idle, and call termination.

Figure 3-5   Frame Relay Operation

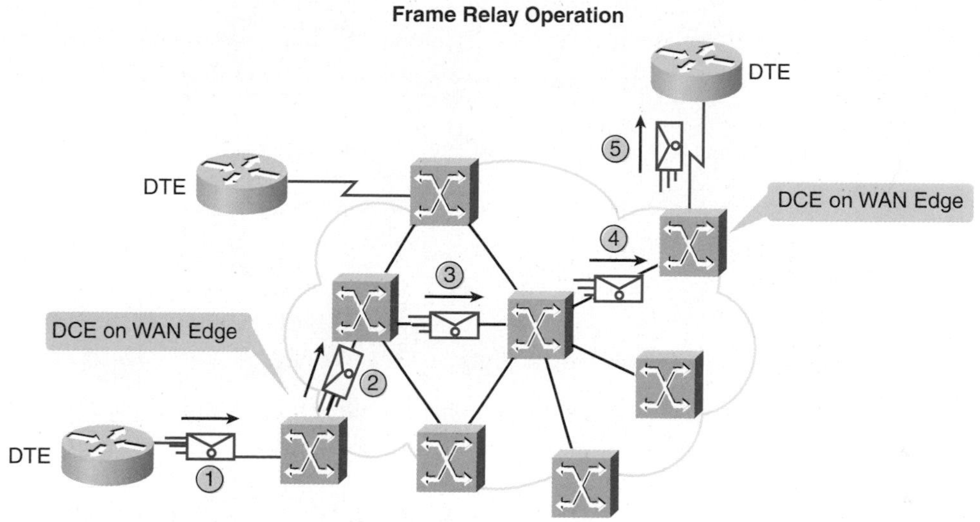

Frame Relay Operation

1   The DTE sends frames to the DCE switch on the WAN edge.

2-4 The frames move from switch to switch across the WAN to the destination DCE switch on the WAN edge.

5   The destination DCE delivers the frames to the destination DTE.

- PVCs are permanently established connections that are used for frequent and consistent data transfers between DTE devices across the Frame Relay network. Communication across a PVC does not require the call setup and termination states that are used with SVCs. PVCs always operate in one of two operational states: data transfer or idle mode. Note that some publications refer to PVCs as private VCs.

Figure 3-6 shows a VC between the sending and receiving nodes. The VC follows the path A, B, C, D. Frame Relay creates a VC by storing input-port-to-output-port mapping in the memory of each switch and thus links one switch to another until a continuous path from one end of the circuit to the other is identified. A VC can pass through any number of intermediate devices (switches) located in the Frame Relay network.

Figure 3-6   Virtual Circuits

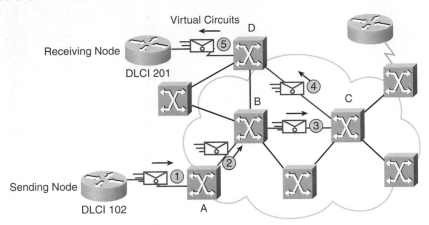

At this point, you might be wondering how the various nodes and switches are identified.

VCs provide a bidirectional communication path from one device to another. VCs are identified by DLCIs, as shown in Figure 3-7. DLCI values typically are assigned by the Frame Relay service provider (for example, the telephone company). Frame Relay DLCIs have local significance, which means that the values themselves are not unique in the Frame Relay WAN. A DLCI identifies a VC to the equipment at an endpoint. A DLCI has no significance beyond the single link. Two devices connected by a VC may use a different DLCI value to refer to the same connection.

Figure 3-7   Local Significance of DLCIs

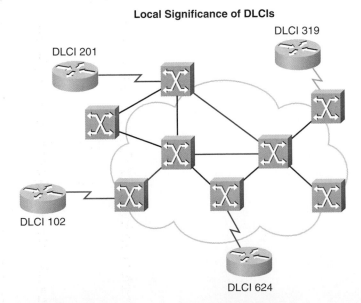

Locally significant DLCIs have become the primary method of addressing, because the same address can be reused in several different locations to refer to completely different connections. Local addressing prevents a customer from running out of DLCIs as the network grows.

Figure 3-8 is the same network as shown in Figure 3-7, but this time, as the frame moves across the network, Frame Relay labels each VC with a DLCI. The DLCI is stored in the address field of every frame transmitted to tell the network how the frame should be switched. The Frame Relay service provider assigns DLCI numbers. Usually, DLCIs 0 to 15 and 1008 to 1023 are reserved for special purposes. Therefore, service providers typically assign DLCIs in the range of 16 to 1007.

Figure 3-8   Identifying VCs

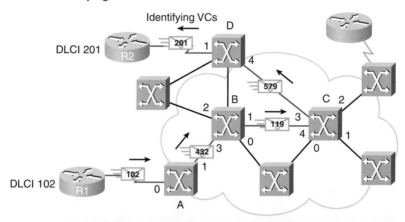

Leg	VC	Port	VC	Port
A	102	0	432	1
B	432	3	119	1
C	119	4	579	3
D	579	4	201	1

In Figure 3-8, the frame uses DLCI 102. It leaves the router (R1) using Port 0 and VC 102. At switch A, the frame exits Port 1 using VC 432. This process of VC-port mapping continues through the WAN until the frame reaches its destination at DLCI 201. The DLCI is stored in the Address field of every Frame Relay data link frame transmitted.

Multiple VCs

Frame Relay is statistically multiplexed, meaning that it transmits only one frame at a time, but many logical connections can coexist on a single physical line. The Frame Relay access device (FRAD) or router connected to the Frame Relay network may have multiple VCs connecting it to various endpoints. Multiple VCs on a single physical line are distinguished because each VC has its own DLCI. Remember that the DLCI has only local significance and may be different at each end of a VC.

Figure 3-9 shows two VCs on a single access line, each with its own DLCI, attaching to a router (R1).

Figure 3-9   Multiple VCs on a Single Access Line

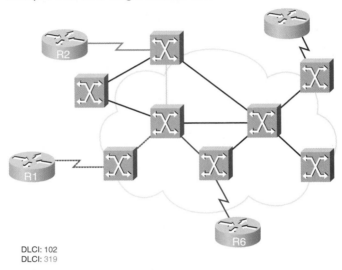

DLCI: 102
DLCI: 319

Multiple VCs on the same access link are distinguishable by the DLCI.

This capability often reduces the equipment and network complexity required to connect multiple devices, making it a very cost-effective replacement for a *mesh* of access lines. With this configuration, each endpoint needs only a single access line and interface. More savings arise because the capacity of the access line is based on the average bandwidth requirements of the VCs, rather than on the maximum bandwidth requirement.

For example, in Figure 3-10, Span Engineering has five locations, along with its headquarters in Chicago. Table 3-2 lists each router's local DLCI used to reach the Chicago network. Chicago is connected to the network using five VCs, and each VC is given a DLCI. The DLCIs on the Chicago router do not need to be the same values as the DLCIs on the remote routers.

Figure 3-10   Span Engineering's DLCIs from Chicago

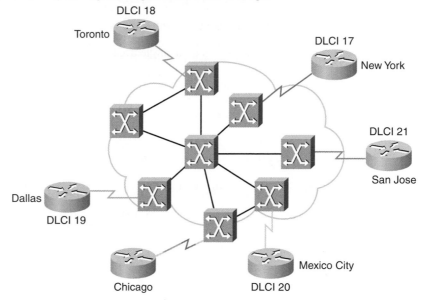

Table 3-2   Span Engineering's DLCIs

Local Router	Local DLCI	Destination Network
New York	17	Chicago
Toronto	18	Chicago
Dallas	19	Chicago
Mexico City	20	Chicago
San Jose	21	Chicago

Cost Benefits of Multiple VCs

Recall the earlier example of how Span Engineering evolved from a dedicated-line network to a Frame Relay network. Specifically, look back at Table 3-1, which compares the cost of a single Frame Relay connection to a similar-sized ISDN connection. Note that with Frame Relay, customers pay for the bandwidth they use. In effect, they pay for a Frame Relay port. When they increase the number of ports, as described earlier, they pay for more bandwidth. But will they pay for more equipment? The short answer is "no," because the ports are virtual. The physical infrastructure doesn't change. Compare this to purchasing more bandwidth using dedicated lines.

Frame Relay Encapsulation

Frame Relay takes data packets from a network layer protocol, such as IP or IPX. It encapsulates them as the data portion of a Frame Relay frame and then passes the frame to the physical layer for delivery on the wire. To understand how this process works, it is helpful to understand how it relates to the lower levels of the OSI model.

The Frame Relay Encapsulation Process

Figure 3-11 shows how Frame Relay encapsulates data for transport and moves it down to the physical layer for delivery.

Figure 3-11   Frame Relay Encapsulation and the OSI Model

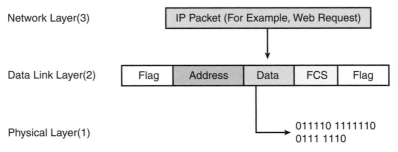

First, Frame Relay accepts a packet from a network layer protocol such as IP. It then wraps it with an Address field that contains the DLCI and a checksum. Flag fields are added to indicate the beginning and end of the frame and are always the same. The flags are represented as either the hexadecimal number 7E or the binary number 01111110. After the packet is encapsulated, Frame Relay passes the frame to the physical layer for transport.

The CPE router encapsulates each Layer 3 packet inside a Frame Relay header and trailer before sending it across the VC. The header and trailer are defined by the *Link Access Procedure for Frame Relay (LAPF)* Bearer Services specification, ITU Q.922-A. Specifically, the Frame Relay header (Address field), shown in Figure 3-12, contains the following:

- **DLCI**: The 10-bit DLCI is the essence of the Frame Relay header. This value represents the virtual connection between the DTE device and the switch. Each virtual connection that is multiplexed onto the physical channel is represented by a unique DLCI. The DLCI values have local significance only, which means that they are unique only to the physical channel on which they reside. Therefore, devices at opposite ends of a connection can use different DLCI values to refer to the same virtual connection.

- **C/R**: The bit that follows the most significant DLCI byte in the Address field. The C/R bit is not currently defined.

- **Extended Address (EA)**: If the value of the EA field is 1, the current byte is determined to be the last DLCI octet. Although current Frame Relay implementations all use a two-octet DLCI, this capability does allow longer DLCIs in the future. The eighth bit of each byte of the Address field indicates the EA.

- *Congestion* **control**: Contains 3 bits that control the Frame Relay congestion-notification mechanisms. The *Forward Explicit Congestion Notification (FECN)*, *Backward Explicit Congestion Notification (BECN)*, and Discard Eligibility (DE) bits are the last 3 bits in the Address field. Congestion control is discussed in a later section.

Figure 3-12   Standard Frame Relay Frame

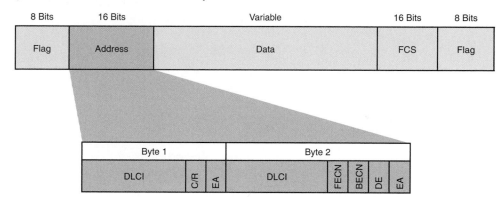

The physical layer typically is EIA/TIA-232, 449, or 530; V.35; or X.21. The Frame Relay frame is a subset of the HDLC frame type. Therefore, it is delimited with Flag fields. The 1-byte flag uses the bit pattern 01111110. The FCS determines whether any errors in the Layer 2 Address field occurred during transmission. The FCS is calculated before transmission by the sending node, and the result is inserted in the FCS field. At the distant end, a second FCS value is calculated and compared to the FCS in the frame. If the results are the same, the frame is processed. If there is a difference, the frame is discarded. Frame Relay does not notify the source when a frame is discarded. Error control is left to the upper layers of the OSI model.

Frame Relay Topologies

When more than two sites are to be connected, you must consider the topology of the connections between them. A topology is the map or visual layout of the Frame Relay network. You need to consider the topology from several perspectives to understand the network and the equipment used to build the network. Complete topologies for design, implementation, operation, and maintenance include overview maps, logical connection maps, functional maps, and address maps showing the detailed equipment and channel links.

Cost-effective Frame Relay networks link dozens and even hundreds of sites. Considering that a corporate network might span any number of service providers and include networks from acquired businesses differing in basic design, documenting topologies can be a very complicated process. However, every network or network segment can be viewed as being one of three topology types: star, full mesh, or partial mesh.

Star Topology (Hub and Spoke)

The simplest WAN topology is a *star topology*, as shown in Figure 3-13. In this topology, Span Engineering has a central site in Chicago that acts as a hub and hosts the primary services. Notice that Span has grown and recently opened an office in San Jose. Using Frame Relay made this expansion relatively easy.

Figure 3-13   Star (Hub-and-Spoke) Topology

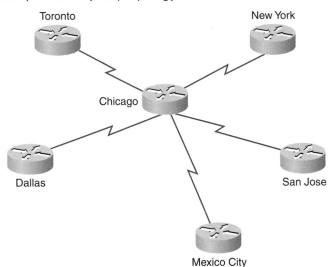

Star Topology-Hub with Five Physical Links (Spokes)

Connections to each of the five remote sites act as spokes. In a star topology, the location of the hub usually is chosen by the lowest leased-line cost. When implementing a star topology with Frame Relay, each remote site has an access link to the Frame Relay cloud with a single VC.

Figure 3-14 shows the star topology in the context of a Frame Relay cloud. The *hub* at Chicago has an access link with multiple VCs, one for each remote site. The lines going out from the cloud represent the connections from the Frame Relay service provider and terminate at the customer premises. These typically are lines ranging in speed from 56,000 bps to E1 (2.048 Mbps) and faster. One or more DLCI numbers are assigned to each line endpoint.

Because Frame Relay costs are not distance-related, the hub does not need to be in the geographic center of the network.

Figure 3-14   Frame Relay Star Topology

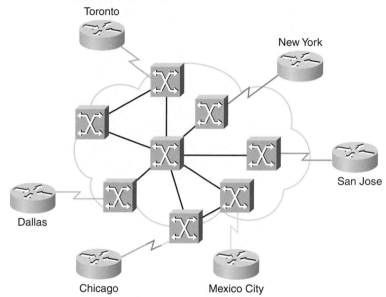

Frame Relay Star-Hub with One Physical Link Carrying Five VCs

Full-Mesh Topology

Figure 3-15 shows a *full-mesh topology* using dedicated lines. A full-mesh topology suits a situation in which the services to be accessed are geographically dispersed and highly reliable access to them is required. A full-mesh topology connects every site to every other site. Using leased-line interconnections, additional serial interfaces and lines add costs. In this example, ten dedicated lines are required to interconnect each site in a full-mesh topology.

Using Frame Relay, a network designer can build multiple connections simply by configuring additional VCs on each existing link. This software upgrade grows the star topology to a full-mesh topology without the expense of additional hardware or dedicated lines. Because VCs use statistical multiplexing, multiple VCs on an access link generally make better use of Frame Relay than single VCs. Figure 3-16 shows how Span Engineering has used four VCs on each link to scale its network without adding new hardware. Service providers will charge for the additional bandwidth, but this solution usually is more cost-effective than using dedicated lines.

Figure 3-15   Full-Mesh Topology

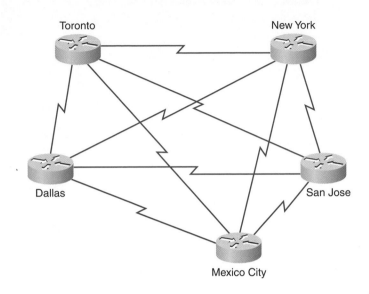

Full-Mesh Topology

Figure 3-16   Frame Relay Mesh Topology

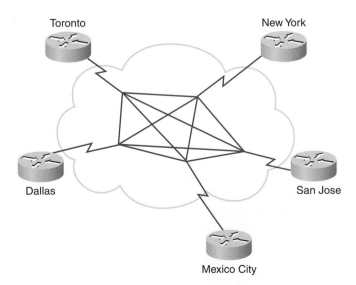

Full Relay Mesh

Partial-Mesh Topology

For large networks, a full-mesh topology is seldom affordable because the number of links required increases dramatically. The issue is not with the cost of the hardware, but because there is a theoretical limit of fewer than 1000 VCs per link. In practice, the limit is less than that.

For this reason, larger networks generally are configured in a *partial-mesh topology*. Partial mesh has more interconnections than are required for a star arrangement, but not as many as for a full mesh. The actual pattern depends on the data flow requirements.

Frame Relay Address Mapping

Before a Cisco router can transmit data over Frame Relay, it needs to know which local DLCI maps to the Layer 3 address of the remote destination. Cisco routers support all network layer protocols over Frame Relay, such as IP, IPX, and AppleTalk. This address-to-DLCI mapping can be accomplished by either static or dynamic mapping.

Inverse ARP

Inverse Address Resolution Protocol (ARP) obtains Layer 3 addresses of other stations from Layer 2 addresses, such as the DLCI in Frame Relay networks. It is used primarily in Frame Relay and ATM networks, where Layer 2 addresses of VCs are sometimes obtained from Layer 2 signaling, and the corresponding Layer 3 addresses must be available before these VCs can be used. Whereas ARP translates Layer 3 addresses to Layer 2 addresses, Inverse ARP does the opposite.

Dynamic Mapping

Dynamic address mapping relies on Inverse ARP to resolve a next-hop network protocol address to a local DLCI value. The Frame Relay router sends out Inverse ARP requests on its PVC to discover the protocol address of the remote device connected to the Frame Relay network. The router uses the responses to populate an address-to-DLCI mapping table on the Frame Relay router or access server. The router builds and maintains this mapping table, which contains dynamic entries from resolved Inverse ARP requests and static entries from manual configuration.

Example 3-1 shows the output of the **show frame-relay map** command. You can see that the interface is up and that the destination IP address is 10.1.1.2. The DLCI identifies the logical connection being used to reach this interface. This value is displayed in three ways: its decimal value (102), its hexadecimal value (0x66), and its value as it would appear in the two-octet Address field as it goes on the wire (0x1860). This is a static entry, not a dynamic entry. The link is using Cisco encapsulation as opposed to IETF encapsulation.

Example 3-1 show frame-relay map Command for Router R1

```
R1# show frame-relay map

Serial0/0/1 (up): ip 10.1.1.2 dlci 102 (0x66,0x1860), static
             broadcast,
             CISCO, status defined, active
R1#
```

On Cisco routers, Inverse ARP is enabled by default for all protocols enabled on the physical interface. Inverse ARP packets are not sent out for protocols that are not enabled on the interface.

The user can choose to override dynamic Inverse ARP mapping by supplying a manual static mapping for the next-hop protocol address to a local DLCI. A static map works similarly to dynamic Inverse ARP by associating a specified next-hop protocol address to a local Frame Relay DLCI. You cannot use Inverse ARP and a map statement for the same DLCI and protocol.

An example of using static address mapping is a situation in which the router at the other side of the Frame Relay network does not support dynamic Inverse ARP for a specific network protocol. To provide accessibility, a static mapping is required to complete the remote network layer address to local DLCI resolution.

Another example is on a hub-and-spoke Frame Relay network. You would use static address mapping on the spoke routers to provide spoke-to-spoke reachability. Because the spoke routers do not have direct connectivity with each other, dynamic Inverse ARP would not work between them. Dynamic Inverse ARP relies on the presence of a direct point-to-point connection between two ends. In this case, dynamic Inverse ARP works only between hub and spoke, and the spokes require static mapping to provide reachability to each other.

Configuring Static Mapping

Establishing static mapping depends on your network needs.

To map between a next-hop protocol address and a local DLCI address, use the following command:

```
Router(config)# frame-relay map protocol protocol-address dlci [broadcast] [ietf]
    [cisco]
```

Use the keyword **ietf** when connecting to a non-Cisco router.

You can greatly simplify the configuration for the Open Shortest Path First (OSPF) protocol by adding the optional **broadcast** keyword when performing this task.

Figure 3-17 shows the topology used for the next example. Example 3-2 provides the configuration commands for statically mapping a DLCI on a Cisco router. In this example, static address mapping is performed on R1's interface serial 0/0/0, and the Frame Relay encapsulation used on DLCI 102 is CISCO. As shown in the configuration steps, static mapping of the address using the **frame-relay map** command allows users to select the type of Frame Relay encapsulation used on a per-VC basis. Static mapping configuration is discussed in more detail in the next major section.

Figure 3-17   Static Frame Relay Mapping

Static FR Address Mappping

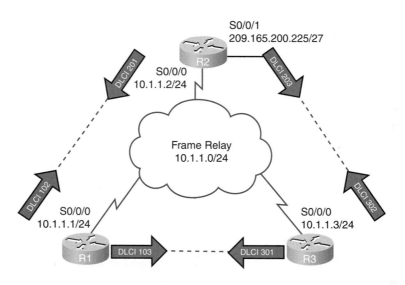

Example 3-2   Static Mapping Configuration for Router R1

```
R1(config)# interface serial0/0/0
R1(config-if)# ip address 10.1.1.1 255.255.255.0
R1(config-if)# encapsulation frame-relay
R1(config-if)# no frame-relay inverse-arp
R1(config-if)# frame-relay map ip 10.1.1.2 102 broadcast cisco
R1(config-if)# no shut
R1(config-if)#
*Oct 16 03:37:03.391: %LINK-3-UPDOWN: Interface Serial0/0/0, Changed state to up
*Oct 16 03:37:14.443: %LINEPROTO-5-UPDOWN: Line protocol on Interface Serial0/0/0,
  changed state to up
```

Local Management Interface (LMI)

A review of networking history will help you understand the role played by the *Local Management Interface (LMI)*. The Frame Relay design provides packet-switched data transfer with minimum end-to-end delays. The original design omits anything that might contribute to delay.

When vendors implemented Frame Relay as a separate technology rather than as one component of ISDN, they decided that there was a need for DTEs to dynamically acquire information about the network's status. However, the original design did not include this feature. A consortium of Cisco, Digital Equipment Corporation (DEC), Northern Telecom, and StrataCom extended the Frame Relay protocol to provide additional capabilities for complex internetworking environments. These extensions are collectively referred to as the LMI.

Basically, the LMI is a keepalive mechanism that provides status information about Frame Relay connections between the router (DTE) and the Frame Relay switch (DCE). Every 10 seconds or so, the end device polls the network, requesting either a dumb sequenced response or channel status information. If the network does not respond with the requested information, the user device may consider the connection down. When the network responds with a FULL STATUS response, it includes status information about DLCIs that are allocated to that line. The end device can use this information to determine whether the logical connections can pass data.

Using the topology shown in Figure 3-17, Example 3-3 shows the output of the **show frame-relay lmi** command. The output shows the LMI type used by the Frame Relay interface and the counters for the LMI status exchange sequence, including errors such as LMI timeouts.

Example 3-3 show frame-relay lmi Command for Router R1

```
R1# show frame-relay lmi

LMI Statistics for interface Serial1 (Frame Relay DTE) LMI TYPE = ANSI
  Invalid Unnumbered info 0        Invalid Prot Disc 0
  Invalid dummy Call Ref 0         Invalid Msg Type 0
  Invalid Status Message 0         Invalid Lock Shift 0
  Invalid Information ID 0         Invalid Report IE Len 0
  Invalid Report Request 0         Invalid Keep IE Len 0
  Num Status Enq. Sent 9          Num Status msgs Rcvd 0
  Num Update Status Rcvd 0        Num Status Timeouts 9
```

It is easy to confuse the LMI and encapsulation. The LMI is a definition of the messages used between the DTE (R1) and the DCE (the Frame Relay switch owned by the service provider). Encapsulation defines the headers used by a DTE to communicate information to the DTE at the other end of a VC. The switch and its connected router care about using the same LMI. The switch does not care about the encapsulation. The endpoint routers (DTEs) do care about the encapsulation.

LMI Extensions

In addition to the Frame Relay protocol functions for transferring data, the Frame Relay specification includes optional LMI extensions that are extremely useful in an internetworking environment. The LMI enhancements offer a number of features for managing complex internetworks, including the following:

- **VC status messages** provide information about PVC integrity by communicating and synchronizing between devices, periodically reporting the existence of new PVCs and the deletion of already existing PVCs. VC status messages prevent data from being sent into black holes (PVCs that no longer exist).

- **Multicasting** allows a sender to transmit a single frame that is delivered to multiple recipients. Multicasting supports the efficient delivery of routing protocol messages and address resolution procedures that typically are sent to many destinations simultaneously.

- **Global addressing** gives connection identifiers global rather than local significance, allowing them to be used to identify a specific interface to the Frame Relay network. Global addressing makes the Frame Relay network resemble a LAN in terms of addressing, and ARPs perform exactly as they do over a LAN.

- **Simple flow control** provides an XON/XOFF flow-control mechanism that applies to the entire Frame Relay interface. It is intended for devices whose higher layers cannot use the congestion notification bits and need some level of flow control.

Table 3-3 lists the LMI identifiers. The 10-bit DLCI field supports 1024 VC identifiers: 0 through 1023. The LMI extensions reserve some of these identifiers, thereby reducing the number of permitted VCs. LMI messages are exchanged between the DTE and DCE using these reserved DLCIs.

Table 3-3   LMI Identifiers

VC Identifiers	VC Types
0	LMI (ANSI, ITU)
1 to 15	Reserved for future use
1008 to 1022	Reserved for future use (ANSI, ITU)
1019 and 1020	Multicasting (Cisco)
1023	LMI (Cisco)

There are several LMI types, each of which is incompatible with the others. The LMI type configured on the router must match the type used by the service provider. Cisco routers support three types of LMIs:

- **Cisco**: Original LMI extension
- **Ansi**: Corresponds to the ANSI standard T1.617 Annex D
- **q933a**: Corresponds to the ITU standard Q933 Annex A

Starting with Cisco IOS software Release 11.2, the default LMI autosense feature detects the LMI type supported by the directly connected Frame Relay switch. Based on the LMI status messages it receives from the Frame Relay switch, the router automatically configures its interface with the supported LMI type acknowledged by the Frame Relay switch.

If it is necessary to set the LMI type, use the following interface configuration command:

```
frame-relay lmi-type [cisco | ansi | q933a]
```

Configuring the LMI type disables the autosense feature.

When manually setting up the LMI type, you must configure the *keepalive interval* on the Frame Relay interface to prevent status exchanges between the router and switch from timing out. The LMI status exchange messages determine the status of the PVC connection. For example, a large mismatch in the keepalive interval on the router and the switch can cause the switch to declare the router dead.

By default, the keepalive time interval is 10 seconds on Cisco serial interfaces. You can change the keepalive interval with the **keepalive** interface configuration command.

You'll set the LMI type and configure the keepalive in a later activity.

LMI Frame Format

Figure 3-18 shows an LMI frame format. LMI messages are carried in a variant of LAPF frames. The Address field carries one of the reserved DLCIs. Following the DLCI field are the Unnumbered Information Indicator, Protocol Discriminator, and Call Reference fields, which do not change. The fourth field indicates the LMI message type.

Status messages help verify the integrity of logical and physical links. This information is critical in a routing environment because routing protocols make decisions based on link integrity.

Using LMI and Inverse ARP to Map Addresses

LMI status messages combined with Inverse ARP messages allow a router to associate network layer and data link layer addresses.

In Figure 3-19, when R1 connects to the Frame Relay network, it sends an LMI status inquiry message to the network. The network replies with an LMI status message containing the details of every VC configured on the access link.

Figure 3-18 LMI Frame Format

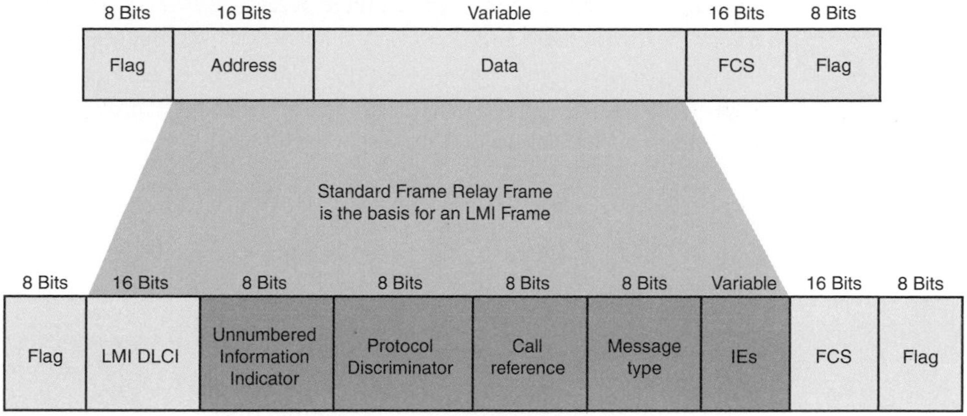

8 Bits
16 Bits
Variable
16 Bits
8 Bits
Flag
Address
Data
FCS
Flag
Standard Frame Relay Frame
is the basis for an LMI Frame
8 Bits
16 Bits
8 Bits
8 Bits
8 Bits
8 Bits
Variable
16 Bits
8 Bits
Flag
LMI DLCI
Unnumbered Information Indicator
Protocol Discriminator
Call reference
Message type
IEs
FCS
Flag

Figure 3-19 Stages of Inverse ARP and LMI Operation

DCLI 101
DCLI 102
DCLI 103
DCLI 104
1
75
R1
7D
2

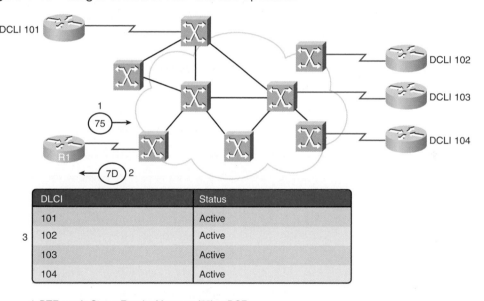

DLCI	Status
101	Active
102	Active
103	Active
104	Active

3

1 DTE sends Status Enquiry Message (75) to DCE.

2 DCE responds with Status Message (7D) – includes configured DLCIs.

3 DTE learns what VCs it has.

Periodically, the router repeats the status inquiry, but subsequent responses include only status changes. After a set number of these abbreviated responses, the network sends a full status message.

If the router needs to map the VCs to network layer addresses, it sends an Inverse ARP message on each VC, as shown in Figure 3-20. The Inverse ARP message includes the router's network layer address, so the remote DTE, or router, can also perform the mapping. The Inverse ARP reply allows the router to make the necessary mapping entries in its address-to-DLCI mapping table. If several network layer protocols are supported on the link, Inverse ARP messages are sent for each one.

Figure 3-20   Using LMI and Inverse ARP to Map Addresses

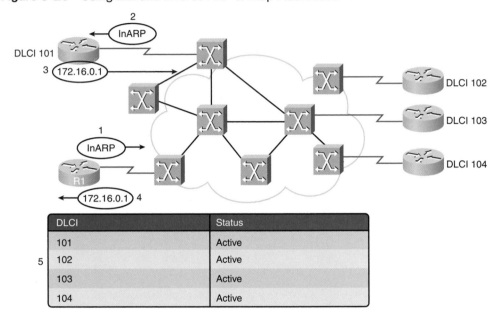

DLCI	Status
101	Active
102	Active
103	Active
104	Active

1,2 DTE sends inverse ARP on a VC, mapping VC to network address.

3,4 Remote DTE replies with Layer 3 address.

5   DTE maps Layer 2–Layer 3.

This process is repeated for each VC and each Layer 3 protocol.

Configuring Frame Relay

Frame Relay is configured on a Cisco router from the Cisco IOS command-line interface (CLI).

This section outlines the required steps to enable Frame Relay on your network, as well as some of the optional steps you can follow to enhance or customize your configuration.

Figure 3-21 shows the basic setup model used for this discussion. Later in this section, additional hardware will be added to the diagram to help explain more-complex configuration tasks.

Figure 3-21   Frame Relay Topology for Configuration

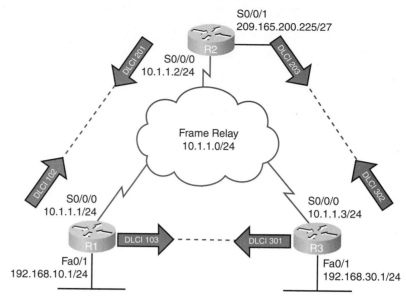

In this section, you will configure the Cisco routers as Frame Relay access devices, or DTE, connected directly to a dedicated Frame Relay switch, or DCE. The following are the required and optional tasks for configuring Frame Relay:

Required tasks:

- Enable Frame Relay encapsulation on an interface.
- Configure dynamic or static address mapping.

Optional tasks:

- Configure the LMI.
- Configure Frame Relay SVCs.
- Configure Frame Relay traffic shaping.
- Customize Frame Relay for your network.
- Monitor and maintain Frame Relay connections.

Enabling Frame Relay Encapsulation

Using the topology shown in Figure 3-21, Examples 3-4 and 3-5 show how Frame Relay has been configured on the serial interfaces for routers R1 and R2. This involves assigning an IP address, setting the encapsulation type, and allocating bandwidth.

Example 3-4 Router R1 Configuration Script

```
interface s0/0/0
ip address 10.1.1.1 255.255.255.0
encapsulation frame-relay
bandwidth 64
```

Example 3-5 Router R2 Configuration Script

```
interface s0/0/0
ip address 10.1.1.2 255.255.255.0
encapsulation frame-relay
bandwidth 64
```

The steps for enabling Frame Relay encapsulation are as follows:

Step 1. **Set the IP address on the interface.** On a Cisco router, Frame Relay is most commonly supported on synchronous serial interfaces. Use the **ip address** command to set the interface's IP address. You can see in Figure 3-21 that R1 has been assigned IP address 10.1.1.1/24, and R2 has been assigned 10.1.1.2/24.

Step 2. **Configure the encapsulation.** The **encapsulation frame-relay** interface configuration command enables Frame Relay encapsulation and allows Frame Relay processing on the supported interface. You can choose from two encapsulation options, as described next.

Step 3. **Set the bandwidth (optional).** If needed, use the **bandwidth** command to set the bandwidth of the serial interface. You specify the bandwidth in kbps. This command notifies the routing protocol that bandwidth is statically configured on the link. The EIGRP and OSPF routing protocols use the bandwidth value to calculate and determine the link's metric.

Step 4. **Set the LMI type (optional).** This step is optional because Cisco routers autosense the LMI type. Recall that Cisco supports three LMI types—Cisco, ANSI Annex D, and Q933-A Annex A—and that the default LMI type for Cisco routers is cisco.

Recall that the default encapsulation type on a serial interface on a Cisco router is the Cisco-proprietary version of HDLC. To change the encapsulation from HDLC to Frame Relay, use the following command:

```
encapsulation frame-relay [cisco | ietf]
```

The **no** form of this command removes the Frame Relay encapsulation on the interface and returns the interface to the default HDLC encapsulation.

The default Frame Relay encapsulation enabled on supported interfaces is the Cisco encapsulation. Use this option if you're connecting to another Cisco router. Many non-Cisco devices also support this encapsulation type. It uses a 4-byte header, with 2 bytes to identify the DLCI and 2 bytes to identify the packet type.

The IETF encapsulation type complies with RFC 1490 and RFC 2427. Use this option if you're connecting to a non-Cisco router.

The output of the **show interfaces serial** command shown in Examples 3-6 and 3-7 verifies the configuration for routers R1 and R2.

Example 3-6 show interface serial Command for Router R1

```
R1# show interface serial0/0/0

Serial0/0/0 is up, line protocol is up
  Hardware is GT96K Serial
  Internet address is 10.1.1.1/24
  MTU 1500 bytes, BW 1544 Kbit, DLY 20000 usec,
     reliability 255/255, txload 1/255, rxload 1/255
  Encapsulation FRAME-RELAY, loopback not set
  Keepalive set (10 sec)
  LMI enq sent 18, LMI stat recvd 19, LMI upd recvd 0, DTE LMI up
  LMI enq recvd 0, LMI stat sent 0, LMI upd sent 0
  LMI DLCI 1023 LMI type is CISCO frame relay DTE
  FR SVC disabled, LAPF state down
  Broadcast queue 0/64, broadcasts sent/dropped 0/0, interface broadcasts 0
  Last input 00:00:08, output 00:00:08, output hang never
  Last clearing of "show interface" counters 00:04:06
  Input queue: 0/75/0/0 (size/max/drops/flushes); Total output drops: 0
  Queueing strategy: weighted fair
  Output queue: 0/1000/64/0 (size/max total/threshold/drops)
     Conversations 0/1/256 (active/max active/max total)
     Reserved Conversations 0/0 (allocated/max allocated)
     Available Bandwidth 1558 kilobits/sec
  5 minute input rate 0 bits/sec, 0 packets/sec
  5 minute output rate 0 bits/sec, 0 packets/sec
     24 packets input, 815 bytes, 0 no buffer
     Received 0 broadcasts, 0 runts, 0 giants, 0 throttles
     0 input errors, 0 CRC, 0 frame, 0 overrun, 0 ignored, 0 abort
     27 packets output, 807 bytes, 0 underruns
     0 output errors, 0 collisions, 1 interface resets
     0 output buffer failures, 0 output buffers swapped out
     2 carrier transitions
     DCD=up DSR=up DTR=up RTS=up CTS=up
```

Example 3-7 show interface serial Command for Router R2

```
R2# show interface serial0/0/0

Serial0/0/0 is up, line protocol is up
 Hardware is GT96K Serial
 Internet address is 10.1.1.2/24
 MTU 1500 bytes, BW 1544 Kbit, DLY 20000 usec,
    reliability 255/255, txload 1/255, rxload 1/255
 Encapsulation FRAME-RELAY, loopback not set
 Keepalive set (10 sec)
 LMI enq sent 17, LMI stat recvd 18, LMI upd recvd 0, DTE LMI up
 LMI enq recvd 0, LMI stat sent 0, LMI upd sent 0
 LMI DLCI 1023 LMI type is CISCO frame relay DTE
 FR SVC disabled, LAPF state down
 Broadcast queue 0/64, broadcasts sent/dropped 0/0, interface broadcasts 0
 Last input 00:00:07, output 00:00:07, output hang never
 Last clearing of "show interface" counters 00:03:40
 Input queue: 0/75/0/0 (size/max/drops/flushes); Total output drops: 0
 Queueing strategy: weighted fair
 Output queue: 0/1000/64/0 (size/max total/threshold/drops)
    Conversations 0/1/256 (active/max active/max total)
    Reserved Conversations 0/0 (allocated/max allocated)
    Available Bandwidth 1558 kilobits/sec
 5 minute input rate 0 bits/sec, 0 packets/sec
 5 minute output rate 0 bits/sec, 0 packets/sec
    23 packets input, 786 bytes, 0 no buffer
    Received 0 broadcasts, 0 runts, 0 giants, 0 throttles
    0 input errors, 0 CRC, 0 frame, 0 overrun, 0 ignored, 0 abort
    29 packets output, 1197 bytes, 0 underruns
    0 output errors, 0 collisions, 1 interface resets
    0 output buffer failures, 0 output buffers swapped out
    0 carrier transitions
    DCD=up DSR=up DTR=up RTS=up CTS=up
```

Configuring Static Frame Relay Maps

Cisco routers support all network layer protocols over Frame Relay, such as IP, IPX, and AppleTalk. The address-to-DLCI mapping can be accomplished by either dynamic or static address mapping.

Dynamic mapping is performed by the Inverse ARP feature. Because Inverse ARP is enabled by default, no additional command is required to configure dynamic mapping on an interface.

Static mapping is manually configured on a router. Establishing static mapping depends on your network needs. To map between a next-hop protocol address and a DLCI destination address, use the following command:

```
frame-relay map protocol protocol-address dlci [broadcast]
```

Table 3-4 shows how to use the **frame-relay map** command parameters when configuring static address maps.

Table 3-4   Command Parameters

Command Parameter	Description
protocol	Defines the supported protocol, bridging, or logical link control. Possible values are **appletalk**, **decnet**, **dlsw**, **ip**, **ipx**, **llc2**, **rsrb**, **vines**, and **xns**.
protocol-address	Defines the network layer address of the destination router interface.
dlci	Defines the local DLCI used to connect to the remote protocol address.
broadcast	(Optional) Allows broadcasts and multicasts over the VC. This permits the use of dynamic routing protocols over the VC.

Frame Relay, ATM, and X.25 are *nonbroadcast multiaccess (NBMA)* networks. NBMA networks only allow data transfer from one computer to another over a VC or across a switching device. NBMA networks do not support multicast or broadcast traffic, so a single packet cannot reach all destinations. To achieve a broadcast, you are required to replicate the packets manually to all destinations.

Some routing protocols may require additional configuration options. For example, RIP, EIGRP, and OSPF require additional configurations to be supported on NBMA networks.

Because NBMA does not support broadcast traffic, using the **broadcast** keyword for the **frame-relay map** command is a simplified way of forwarding routing updates. The **broadcast** keyword allows broadcasts and multicasts over the PVC and, in effect, turns the broadcast into a unicast so that the other node gets the routing updates.

Using the topology shown in Figure 3-22, R1 uses the **frame-relay map** command to map the VC to R2, as shown in Example 3-8.

Figure 3-22   Configuring the Static Frame Relay Map

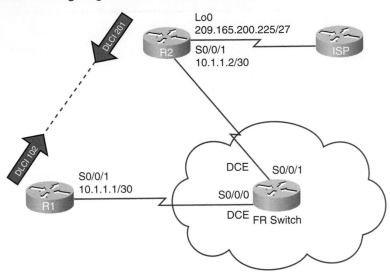

Note: The Frame Relay switch is shown as a router in this graphic. Routers can be configured as a Frame Relay switches.

Example 3-8 Static Map Configuration for Router R1

```
R1#(config)# interface s0/0/1
R1#(config-if)# ip address 10.1.1.1 255.255.255.252
R1#(config-if)# encapsulation frame-relay
R1#(config-if)# bandwidth 64
R1#(config-if)# frame-relay map ip 10.1.1.2 102 broadcast
```

To verify the Frame Relay mapping, use the **show frame-relay map** command, as shown in Example 3-9 for router R1 and in Example 3-10 for router R2.

Example 3-9 Verifying a Static Frame Relay Map on R1

```
R1# show frame-relay map

Serial0/0/1 (up): ip 10.1.1.2 dlci 102(0x66,0x1860), static,
  broadcast,
  CISCO, status defined, active
```

Example 3-10   Verifying a Static Frame Relay Map on R2

```
R2# show frame-relay map

Serial0/0/1 (up): ip 10.1.1.1 dlci 201(0xC9,0x3090), static,
  broadcast,
  CISCO, status defined, active
```

Packet Tracer
☐ **Activity**

Configuring Basic Frame Relay with Static Maps (3.2.2)

In this activity, you configure two static Frame Relay maps on each router to reach two other routers. Although the LMI type is autosensed on the routers, you will statically assign the type by manually configuring the LMI. Detailed instructions are provided within the activity. Use File e4-322.pka on the CD-ROM that accompanies this book to perform this activity using Packet Tracer.

Advanced Frame Relay Concepts

Frame Relay involves several advanced concepts, including understanding the effects of routing protocols that use split horizon, the use of subinterfaces, and the complexities of cost structure used by Frame Relay providers.

Solving Reachability Issues

By default, a Frame Relay network provides NBMA connectivity between remote sites. NBMA clouds usually use a hub-and-spoke topology. Unfortunately, a basic routing operation based on the split-horizon principle can cause reachability issues on a Frame Relay NBMA network.

Split Horizon

Recall that split horizon is a technique used to prevent a routing loop in networks using distance vector routing protocols. Split-horizon updates reduce routing loops by preventing a routing update received on one interface from being forwarded out the same interface.

Figure 3-23 shows R2, a spoke router, sending a broadcast routing update to R1, the hub router.

Figure 3-23   Split-Horizon Rule

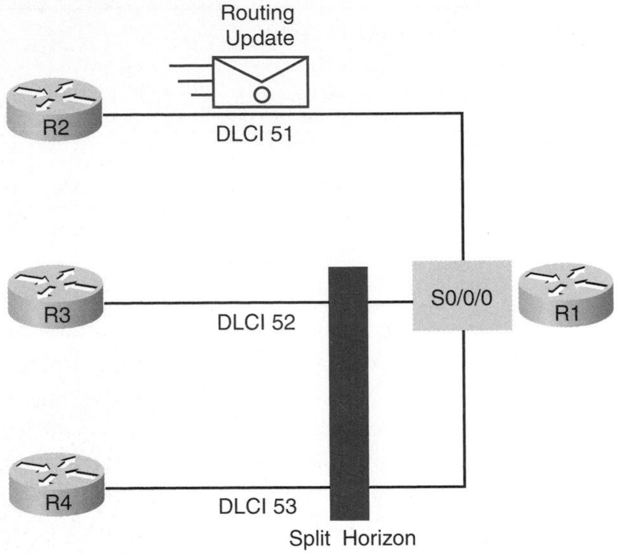

Routers that support multiple connections over a single physical interface have many PVCs terminating on a single interface. R1 must replicate broadcast packets, such as routing update broadcasts, on each PVC to the remote routers. The replicated broadcast packets can consume bandwidth and cause significant latency to user traffic. The amount of broadcast traffic and the number of VCs terminating at each router should be evaluated during the design of a Frame Relay network. Overhead traffic, such as routing updates, can affect the delivery of critical user data, especially when the delivery path contains low-bandwidth (56-kbps) links.

In Figure 3-23, router R1 has multiple PVCs on a single physical interface. The split-horizon rule prevents R1 from forwarding the routing updates, initially coming from router R2, through the same physical interface to other remote spoke routers (R3 and R4).

Disabling split horizon may seem like a simple solution, because it allows routing updates to be forwarded out the same physical interface from which they came. However, only IP allows you to disable split horizon; IPX and AppleTalk do not. Also, disabling split horizon increases the chance of routing loops in any network. Split horizon could be disabled for physical interfaces with a single PVC.

The next obvious solution to solve the split-horizon problem is to use a fully meshed topology. However, this is expensive because more PVCs are required. The preferred solution is to use subinterfaces, as explained in the next section.

Frame Relay Subinterfaces

Frame Relay can partition a physical interface into multiple virtual interfaces called subinterfaces. A subinterface is simply a logical interface that is directly associated with a physical interface. Therefore, a Frame Relay subinterface can be configured for each of the PVCs coming into a physical serial interface.

To enable the forwarding of broadcast routing updates in a Frame Relay network, you can configure the router with logically assigned subinterfaces. A partially meshed network can be divided into a number of smaller, fully meshed, point-to-point networks. Each point-to-point subnetwork can be assigned a unique network address. This allows packets received on a physical interface to be sent out the same physical interface, because the packets are forwarded on VCs in different subinterfaces.

Frame Relay subinterfaces can be configured in either point-to-point or multipoint mode:

- **Point-to-point**: A single point-to-point subinterface establishes one PVC connection to another physical interface or subinterface on a remote router. In this case, each pair of the point-to-point routers is on its own subnet, and each point-to-point subinterface has a single DLCI. In a point-to-point environment, each subinterface acts like a separate, conventional point-to-point interface. Typically, each point-to-point VC has a separate subnet. Therefore, routing update traffic is not subject to the split-horizon rule.

- **Multipoint**: A single multipoint subinterface establishes multiple PVC connections to multiple physical interfaces or subinterfaces on remote routers. All the participating interfaces are in the same subnet. The subinterface acts like an NBMA Frame Relay interface, so routing update traffic is subject to the split-horizon rule. Typically, all multipoint VCs belong to the same subnet.

Figure 3-24 shows two types of subinterfaces that Cisco routers support: point-to-point and multipoint.

Figure 3-24 Frame Relay Subinterfaces

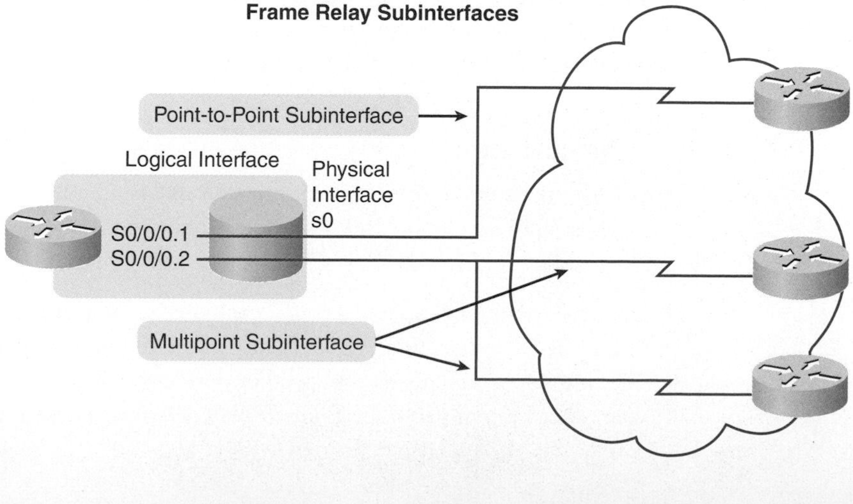

In split-horizon routing environments, routing updates received on one subinterface can be sent out another subinterface. In a subinterface configuration, each VC can be configured as a point-to-point connection. This allows each subinterface to act similarly to a leased line. Using a Frame Relay point-to-point subinterface, each pair of the point-to-point routers is on its own subnet.

The **encapsulation frame-relay** command is assigned to the physical interface. All other configuration items, such as the network layer address and DLCIs, are assigned to the subinterface.

You can use multipoint configurations to conserve addresses. This can be especially helpful if Variable-Length Subnet Masking (VLSM) is not being used. However, multipoint configurations may not work properly given the broadcast traffic and split-horizon considerations. The point-to-point subinterface option was created to avoid these issues.

The following list summarizes point-to-point subinterfaces and multipoint subinterfaces:

Point-to-point subinterfaces (in hub-and-spoke topologies):

- They act as leased lines.

- Each point-to-point subinterface requires its own subnet.

Multipoint subinterfaces (in partial-mesh and full-mesh topologies):

- They act as NBMA, so they do not resolve the split-horizon issue.

- They can save address space, because it uses a single subnet.

You will learn more about how to configure subinterfaces in the later section "Configuring Frame Relay Subinterfaces."

Paying for Frame Relay

Service providers build Frame Relay networks using very large and powerful switches, but as a customer, your devices see only the switch interface of the service provider. Customers usually are not exposed to the network's inner workings, which may be built on very high-speed technologies, such as T1, T3, SONET, or ATM.

Key Terminology

From a customer's point of view, then, Frame Relay is an interface and one or more PVCs. Customers simply buy Frame Relay services from a service provider. However, before considering how to pay for Frame Relay services, you need to know some key terms and concepts:

- **Access rate or port speed:** From a customer's point of view, the service provider provides a serial connection or access link to the Frame Relay network over a leased line. The line's speed is the access speed or port speed. The access rate is the rate at which your access circuits join the Frame Relay network. These typically are 56 kbps, T1

(1.536 Mbps), or Fractional T1 (a multiple of 56 kbps or 64 kbps). Port speeds are clocked on the Frame Relay switch. It is not possible to send data at higher than port speed.

- *Committed Information Rate (CIR)*: Customers negotiate CIRs with service providers for each PVC. The CIR is the amount of data that the network receives from the access circuit. The service provider guarantees that the customer can send data at the CIR. All frames received at or below the CIR are accepted.

A great advantage of Frame Relay is that any unused network capacity is made available or shared with all customers, usually at no extra charge. This allows customers to "burst" over their CIR as a bonus. Bursting is explained in a moment.

In this example, aside from any CPE costs, the customer pays for three Frame Relay cost components:

- **Access or port speed:** The cost of the access line from the DTE to the DCE (customer to service provider). This line is charged based on the port speed that has been negotiated and installed.

- **PVC:** This cost component is based on the PVCs. After a PVC is established, the additional cost to increase CIR typically is small and can be done in small (4-kbps) increments.

- **CIR:** Customers normally choose a CIR lower than the port speed or access rate. This allows them to take advantage of bursts.

In Figure 3-25, the customer is paying for the following:

- An access line with a rate of 64 kbps connecting the customer's DCE to the DCE of the service provider through serial port S0/0/0.

- Two virtual ports, one at 32 kbps and the other at 16 kbps.

- A CIR of 48 kbps across the entire Frame Relay network. This usually is a flat charge and is not connected to the distance.

Oversubscription

Service providers sometimes sell more capacity than they have on the assumption that not everyone will demand their entitled capacity all the time. This oversubscription is analogous to airlines selling more seats than they have in the expectation that some of the booked customers will not show up. Because of oversubscription, there will be instances when the sum of CIRs from multiple PVCs to a given location is higher than the port or access channel rate. This can cause traffic issues, such as congestion and dropped traffic.

Figure 3-25   Frame Relay Charges Example

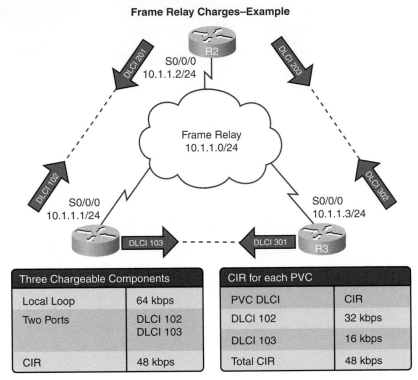

Three Chargeable Components	
Local Loop	64 kbps
Two Ports	DLCI 102 DLCI 103
CIR	48 kbps

CIR for each PVC	
PVC DLCI	CIR
DLCI 102	32 kbps
DLCI 103	16 kbps
Total CIR	48 kbps

Bursting

As stated earlier, Frame Relay takes advantage of any unused network capacity, making it available to other customer and usually at no extra charge.

Using the topology shown in Figure 3-25, Table 3-5 shows an access rate on serial port S0/0/0 of router R1 of 64 kbps. This is higher than the combined CIRs of the two PVCs. Under normal circumstances, the two PVCs should not transmit more than 32 kbps and 16 kbps, respectively. If the amount of data the two PVCs are sending does not exceed the combined CIR, the data should get through the network.

Table 3-5   Access Rates

PVC DLCI	CIR (Normal)	CBIR (Example)	BE
DLCI 102	32 kbps	48 kbps	16 kbps
DLCI 103	16 kbps	0 kbps	48 kbps
	All frames are forwarded	Frames are forwarded but marked DE	Frames most likely will be dropped

Because the physical circuits of the Frame Relay network are shared between subscribers, there are often times when excess bandwidth is available. Frame Relay can allow customers to dynamically access this extra bandwidth and "burst" over their CIR for free.

Bursting allows devices that temporarily need additional bandwidth to borrow it at no extra cost from other devices that aren't using it. For example, if PVC 102 is transferring a large file, it could use any of the 16 kbps not being used by PVC 103. A device can burst up to the access rate and still expect the data to get through. The duration of a burst transmission should be short—less than 3 or 4 seconds.

Various terms are used to describe burst rates, including Committed Burst Information Rate (CBIR) and *Excess Burst Size (BE)*.

The CBIR is a negotiated rate above the CIR that the customer can use to transmit for short bursts. It allows traffic to burst to higher speeds, as available network bandwidth permits. However, it cannot exceed the port speed of the link. A device can burst up to the CBIR and still expect the data to get through. If long bursts persist, a higher CIR should be purchased.

For example, DLCI 102 has a CIR of 32 kbps, with an additional CBIR of 16 kbps, for a total of up to 48 kbps. Frames submitted at the CBIR level are marked as *Discard Eligible (DE)* in the frame header, indicating that they may be dropped if congestion occurs or the network doesn't have enough capacity. Frames within the negotiated CIR are ineligible for discard (DE = 0). Frames above the CIR have the DE bit set to 1, marking it as eligible to be discarded if the network becomes congested.

BE is the term used to describe the bandwidth available above the CBIR up to the access rate of the link. Unlike the CBIR, it is not negotiated. Frames may be transmitted at this level but most likely will be dropped.

Figure 3-26 illustrates the relationship between the various bursting terms.

Figure 3-26   Frame Relay Bursting

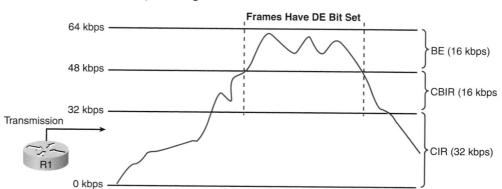

Frame Relay Flow Control

Frame Relay reduces network overhead by implementing simple congestion-notification mechanisms rather than explicit, per-VC flow control. These congestion-notification mechanisms are Forward Explicit Congestion Notification (FECN) and Backward Explicit Congestion Notification (BECN).

To help you understand the mechanisms, Figure 3-27 reviews the structure of the Frame Relay frame. FECN and BECN are each controlled by a single bit contained in the frame header. They let the router know that congestion is occurring and that the router may implement traffic shaping or throttling until the condition is reversed. BECN is a direct notification. FECN is an indirect one.

Figure 3-27   Standard Frame Relay Frame

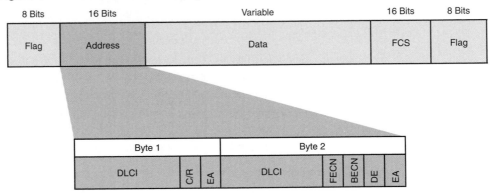

The frame header also contains a Discard Eligibility (DE) bit, which identifies "less important" traffic that can be dropped during periods of congestion. DTE devices can set the value of the DE bit to 1 to indicate that the frame has lower importance than other frames. When the network becomes congested, DCE devices discard the frames that have the DE bit set to 1 before discarding those that do not. This reduces the likelihood of this data's being dropped during periods of congestion.

Note

The concept of "importance" and the Discard Eligibility (DE) bit can be decided by various factors, including quality of service (QoS) mechanisms and or whether this is burst traffic.

In periods of congestion, the provider's Frame Relay switch applies the following logic rules to each incoming frame based on whether the CIR is exceeded:

- If the incoming frame does not exceed the CBIR, the frame is passed.

- If an incoming frame exceeds the CBIR, it is marked DE.

- If an incoming frame exceeds the CBIR plus the BE, it is discarded.

Frames arriving at a switch are queued or buffered before forwarding. As in any queuing system, it is possible that an excessive buildup of frames will occur at a switch. This causes delays. Delays lead to unnecessary retransmissions that occur when higher-level protocols receive no acknowledgment within a set time. In severe cases, this can cause a serious drop in network throughput. To avoid this problem, Frame Relay incorporates a flow-control feature.

Figures 3-28 through 3-30 show a switch with a filling queue. To reduce the flow of frames to the queue, the switch notifies DTEs of the problem using the Explicit Congestion Notification bits in the frame's Address field:

- The FECN bit, indicated by an F in Figure 3-29, is set on every frame that the switch receives on the congested link.

- The BECN bit, indicated by the B in Figure 3-30, is set on every frame forwarded to the downstream sending switches.

To summarize, Figure 3-28 shows that while switch A is putting a large frame on interface 1, other frames for this interface are queued causing congestion. In Figure 3-29, switch A sets the FECN bit on frames forwarded to the upstream destination switch to warn them about the congested queue. In Figure 3-30, switch A sets the BECN bit to inform the downstream sending devices about the congested queue—even though they may not have contributed to the congestion.

DTEs receiving frames with the BECN bit set are expected to try to reduce the flow of frames until the congestion clears.

Figure 3-28   Frame Relay Bandwidth Control: Queuing

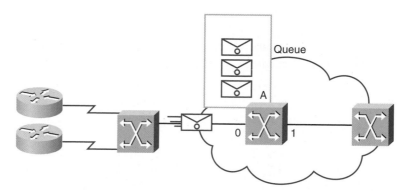

Figure 3-29   Frame Relay Bandwidth Control: FECN

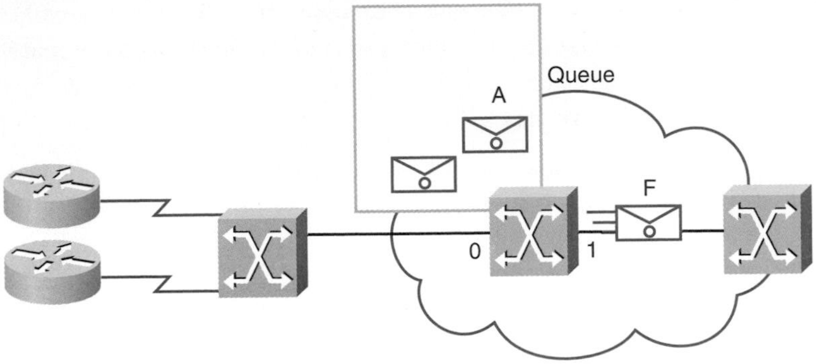

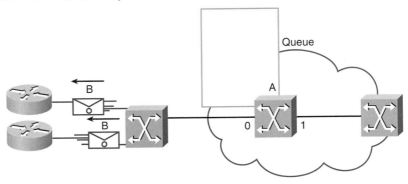

Figure 3-30   Frame Relay Bandwidth Control: BECN

If the congestion occurs on an internal trunk, DTEs may be notified even though they are not the cause of the congestion.

Configuring Advanced Frame Relay

Advanced Frame Relay configuration includes configuring subinterfaces and DLCI information. Configuring Frame Relay on subinterfaces is a little different from configuring it on physical interfaces.

Configuring Frame Relay Subinterfaces

Recall that using Frame Relay subinterfaces ensures that a single physical interface is treated as multiple virtual interfaces to overcome split-horizon rules. Packets received on one virtual interface can be forwarded to another virtual interface, even if they are configured on the same physical interface.

Subinterfaces address the limitations of Frame Relay networks by providing a way to subdivide a partially meshed Frame Relay network into a number of smaller, fully meshed (or point-to-point) subnetworks. Each subnetwork is assigned its own network number and appears to the protocols as if it can be reached through a separate interface. Point-to-point subinterfaces can be unnumbered for use with IP, reducing the addressing burden that might otherwise result.

To create a subinterface, use the **interface serial** command. You can do this in either global configuration mode (config) or interface configuration mode (config-if). Specify the port number, followed by a period (.) and the subinterface number. To make troubleshooting easier, use the DLCI as the subinterface number. You must also specify whether the interface is point-to-point or point-to-multipoint using either the **multipoint** or **point-to-point** keyword, because there is no default. It is important to note that the **encapsulation frame-relay** command must be configured on the physical interface before the subinterfaces can be created. The command syntax for configuring subinterfaces is as follows:

```
router(config-if)# interface serial number.subinterface-number [multipoint |
  point-to-point]
```

Table 3-6 defines the parameters for this command.

Table 3-6   Point-to-Point **interface serial** Command Parameters

interface serial Command Parameters	Description
number.subinterface-number	A subinterface number in the range of 1 to 4294967293. The interface number that precedes the period (.) must match the physical interface number to which this subinterface belongs.
multipoint	Select this if all routers exist in the same subnet.
point-to-point	Select this for each pair of point-to-point routers to have its own subnet. Point-to-point links normally use a subnet mask of 255.255.255.252.

To create a point-to-point subinterface for PVC 103 to R3, you would enter the following:

```
R1(config-if)# interface serial 0/0/0.103 point-to-point
```

If the subinterface is configured as point-to-point, the local DLCI for the subinterface must also be configured to distinguish it from the physical interface. The DLCI is also required for multipoint subinterfaces for which Inverse ARP is enabled. It is not required for multipoint subinterfaces configured with static route maps.

The Frame Relay service provider assigns the DLCI numbers. These numbers range from 16 to 992 and usually have only local significance. The range varies depending on the LMI used.

The **frame-relay interface-dlci** command configures the local DLCI on the subinterface. The command syntax for the **frame-relay interface-dlci** command is as follows:

```
router(config-subif)# frame-relay interface-dlci dlci-number
```

where the *dlci-number* parameter defines the local DLCI number being linked to the subinterface. This is the only way to link an LMI-derived DLCI to a subinterface, because LMI does not know about subinterfaces. Use the **frame-relay interface-dlci** command on subinterfaces only.

Here's an example:

```
R1(config-subif)# frame-relay interface-dlci 103
```

> **Note**
>
> Unfortunately, altering an existing Frame Relay subinterface configuration may fail to provide the expected result. In these situations, it may be necessary to save the configuration and reload the router.

Consider the following example of configuring Frame Relay subinterfaces.

In Figure 3-31, R1 has two point-to-point subinterfaces. The s0/0/0.102 subinterface connects to R2, and the s0/0/0.103 subinterface connects to R3. Each subinterface is on a different subnet.

Figure 3-31   Configuring Point-to-Point Subinterfaces

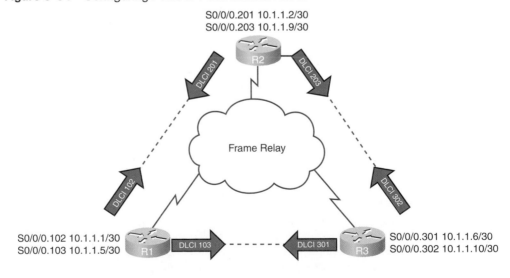

To configure subinterfaces on a physical interface, follow these steps:

Step 1.   Remove any network layer address assigned to the physical interface. If the physical interface has an address, frames are not received by the local subinterfaces.

Step 2. Configure Frame Relay encapsulation on the physical interface using the **encapsulation frame-relay** command.

Step 3. For each of the defined PVCs, create a logical subinterface. Specify the port number, followed by a period (.) and the subinterface number. To make troubleshooting easier, it is suggested that the subinterface number match the DLCI number.

Step 4. Configure an IP address for the subinterface, and set the bandwidth.

At this point, you will configure the DLCI. Recall that the Frame Relay service provider assigns the DLCI numbers.

Step 5. Configure the local DLCI on the subinterface using the **frame-relay interface-dlci** command.

Figure 3-32 illustrates these configuration steps for R1.

Figure 3-32   Point-to-Point Subinterface Configuration Steps

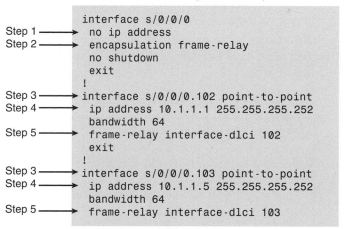

```
                    interface s/0/0/0
Step 1 ───────►      no ip address
Step 2 ───────►      encapsulation frame-relay
                     no shutdown
                     exit
                    !
Step 3 ───────► interface s/0/0/0.102 point-to-point
Step 4 ───────►      ip address 10.1.1.1 255.255.255.252
                     bandwidth 64
Step 5 ───────►      frame-relay interface-dlci 102
                     exit
                    !
Step 3 ───────► interface s/0/0/0.103 point-to-point
Step 4 ───────►      ip address 10.1.1.5 255.255.255.252
                     bandwidth 64
Step 5 ───────►      frame-relay interface-dlci 103
```

Verifying Frame Relay Operation

Frame Relay generally is a very reliable service. Nonetheless, there are times when the network performs at less than expected levels and troubleshooting is necessary. For example, users may report slow and intermittent connections across the circuit. Circuits may go down. Regardless of the reason, network outages are very expensive in terms of lost productivity. A recommended best practice is to verify your configuration before problems appear.

In this section, you will step though a verification procedure to ensure that everything is working correctly before you launch your configuration on a live network.

Verifying Frame Relay Interface Configuration

After configuring a Frame Relay PVC and when troubleshooting an issue, you should verify that Frame Relay is operating correctly on that interface using the **show interfaces** command.

> **Note**
>
> Recall that with Frame Relay, the router normally is considered a DTE device. However, a Cisco router can be configured as a Frame Relay switch. In such cases, the router becomes a DCE device when it is configured as a Frame Relay switch.

The **show interfaces** command displays how the encapsulation is set up, along with useful Layer 1 and Layer 2 status information, including

- LMI type

- LMI DLCI

- Frame Relay DTE/DCE type

The first step is always to confirm that the interfaces are properly configured. Examples 3-11 and 3-12 show sample output for the **show interfaces** command for R1 and R2. Among other things, you can see details about the encapsulation, the DLCI on the Frame Relay-configured serial interface, and the DLCI used for the LMI. You should confirm that these values are the expected values. If not, you may need to make changes.

Example 3-11   show interface serial Commands for Router R1

```
R1# show interface serial 0/0/0

Serial0/0/0 is up, line protocol is up
  Hardware is GT96K Serial
  MTU 1500 bytes, BW 1544 Kbit, DLY 20000 usec,
     reliability 255/255, txload 1/255, rxload 1/255
  Encapsulation FRAME-RELAY, loopback not set
  Keepalive set (10 sec)
  CRC checking enabled
  LMI enq sent  59, LMI stat recvd 59, LMI upd recvd 0, DTE LMI up
  LMI enq recvd 0, LMI stat sent  0, LMI upd sent  0
  LMI DLCI 1023  LMI type is CISCO  frame relay DTE
  FR SVC disabled, LAPF state down
  Broadcast queue 0/64, broadcasts sent/dropped 11/0, interface broadcasts 0
  Last input 00:00:05, output 00:00:05, output hang never
  Last clearing of "show interface" counters 00:09:55
  Input queue: 0/75/0/0 (size/max/drops/flushes); Total output drops: 0
  Queueing strategy: weighted fair
  Output queue: 0/1000/64/0 (size/max total/threshold/drops)
     Conversations  0/1/256 (active/max active/max total)
     Reserved Conversations 0/0 (allocated/max allocated)
```

```
      Available Bandwidth 1158 kilobits/sec
   5 minute input rate 0 bits/sec, 0 packets/sec
   5 minute output rate 0 bits/sec, 0 packets/sec
      67 packets input, 2367 bytes, 0 no buffer
      Received 0 broadcasts, 0 runts, 0 giants, 0 throttles
      0 input errors, 0 CRC, 0 frame, 0 overrun, 0 ignored, 0 abort
      75 packets output, 4906 bytes, 0 underruns
      0 output errors, 0 collisions, 2 interface resets
      0 output buffer failures, 0 output buffers swapped out
      0 carrier transitions
      DCD=up  DSR=up  DTR=up  RTS=up  CTS=up

R1# show interface serial 0/0/0.102

Serial0/0/0.102 is up, line protocol is up
  Hardware is GT96K Serial
  Internet address is 10.1.1.1/30
  MTU 1500 bytes, BW 1544 Kbit, DLY 20000 usec,
     reliability 255/255, txload 1/255, rxload 1/255
  Encapsulation FRAME-RELAY
  CRC checking enabled
  Last clearing of "show interface" counters never
```

Example 3-12   show interface serial Commands for Router R2

```
R2# show interface serial0/0/0

Serial0/0/0 is up, line protocol is up
  Hardware is GT96K Serial
  MTU 1500 bytes, BW 1544 Kbit, DLY 20000 usec,
     reliability 255/255, txload 1/255, rxload 1/255
  Encapsulation FRAME-RELAY, loopback not set
  Keepalive set (10 sec)
  LMI enq sent  37, LMI stat recvd 37, LMI upd recvd 0, DTE LMI up
  LMI enq recvd 0, LMI stat sent  0, LMI upd sent  0
  LMI DLCI 1023  LMI type is CISCO  frame relay DTE
  FR SVC disabled, LAPF state down
  Broadcast queue 0/64, broadcasts sent/dropped 5/0, interface broadcasts 0
  Last input 00:00:06, output 00:00:06, output hang never
  Last clearing of "show interface" counters 00:06:16
  Input queue: 0/75/0/0 (size/max/drops/flushes); Total output drops: 0
  Queueing strategy: weighted fair
  Output queue: 0/1000/64/0 (size/max total/threshold/drops)
```

```
       Conversations  0/1/256 (active/max active/max total)
       Reserved Conversations 0/0 (allocated/max allocated)
       Available Bandwidth 1158 kilobits/sec
  5 minute input rate 0 bits/sec, 0 packets/sec
  5 minute output rate 0 bits/sec, 0 packets/sec
     46 packets input, 3498 bytes, 0 no buffer
     Received 0 broadcasts, 0 runts, 0 giants, 0 throttles
     0 input errors, 0 CRC, 0 frame, 0 overrun, 0 ignored, 0 abort
     42 packets output, 2121 bytes, 0 underruns
     0 output errors, 0 collisions, 2 interface resets
     0 output buffer failures, 0 output buffers swapped out
     0 carrier transitions
     DCD=up  DSR=up  DTR=up  RTS=up  CTS=up


R2# show interface serial0/0/0.201

Serial0/0/0.201 is up, line protocol is up
  Hardware is GT96K Serial
  Internet address is 10.1.1.2/30
  MTU 1500 bytes, BW 1544 Kbit, DLY 20000 usec,
     reliability 255/255, txload 1/255, rxload 1/255
  Encapsulation FRAME-RELAY
  Last clearing of "show interface" counters never
```

Verifying LMI Statistics to Confirm Communication Between Routers and Provider

The next step is to look at some LMI statistics using the **show frame-relay lmi** command, as shown in Examples 3-13 and 3-14. In the output, look for any nonzero "Invalid" items. This helps isolate the problem to a Frame Relay communication issue between the carrier's switch and your router.

Example 3-13   show frame-relay lmi Command for Router R1

```
R1# show frame-relay lmi

LMI Statistics for interface Serial0/0/0 (Frame Relay DTE) LMI TYPE = CISCO
  Invalid Unnumbered info 0          Invalid Prot Disc 0
  Invalid dummy Call Ref 0           Invalid Msg Type 0
  Invalid Status Message 0           Invalid Lock Shift 0
  Invalid Information ID 0           Invalid Report IE Len 0
  Invalid Report Request 0          Invalid Keep IE Len 0
  Num Status Enq. Sent 76            Num Status msgs Rcvd 76
  Num Update Status Rcvd 0           Num Status Timeouts 0
  Last Full Status Req 00:00:48      Last Full Status Rcvd 00:00:48
```

Example 3-14   show frame-relay lmi Command for Router R2

```
R2# show frame-relay lmi

LMI Statistics for interface Serial0/0/0 (Frame Relay DTE) LMI TYPE = CISCO
  Invalid Unnumbered info 0        Invalid Prot Disc 0
  Invalid dummy Call Ref 0         Invalid Msg Type 0
  Invalid Status Message 0         Invalid Lock Shift 0
  Invalid Information ID 0         Invalid Report IE Len 0
  Invalid Report Request 0         Invalid Keep IE Len 0
  Num Status Enq. Sent 78          Num Status msgs Rcvd 78
  Num Update Status Rcvd 0         Num Status Timeouts 0
  Last Full Status Req 00:00:02    Last Full Status Rcvd 00:00:02
```

Examples 3-13 and 3-14 show the number of status messages exchanged between the local router and the local Frame Relay switch.

Now look at the statistics for the interface.

Displaying PVC and Traffic Statistics

Use the **show frame-relay pvc** [**interface** *interface*] [**dlci**] command to view PVC and traffic statistics, as shown in Examples 3-15 and 3-16. This command is also useful for viewing the number of BECN and FECN packets received by the router. The PVC status can be active, inactive, or deleted.

Example 3-15   show frame-relay pvc Command for Router R1

```
R1# show frame-relay pvc 102

PVC Statistics for interface Serial0/0/0 (Frame Relay DTE)
DLCI = 102, DLCI USAGE = LOCAL, PVC STATUS = ACTIVE, INTERFACE = Serial0/0/0.102
  input pkts 12          output pkts 20          in bytes 2816
  out bytes 5455         dropped pkts 0          in pkts dropped 0
  out pkts dropped 0            out bytes dropped 0
  in FECN pkts 0         in BECN pkts 0          out FECN pkts 0
  out BECN pkts 0        in DE pkts 0            out DE pkts 0
  out bcast pkts 15      out bcast bytes 4935
  5 minute input rate 0 bits/sec, 0 packets/sec
  5 minute output rate 0 bits/sec, 0 packets/sec
  pvc create time 00:13:27, last time pvc status changed 00:07:47
```

Example 3-16   show frame-relay pvc Command for Router R2

```
R2# show frame-relay pvc 201

PVC Statistics for interface Serial0/0/0 (Frame Relay DTE)
DLCI = 201, DLCI USAGE = LOCAL, PVC STATUS = ACTIVE, INTERFACE = Serial0/0/0.201
  input pkts 11             output pkts 8            in bytes 3619
  out bytes 2624            dropped pkts 0           in pkts dropped 0
  out pkts dropped 0                out bytes dropped 0
  in FECN pkts 0            in BECN pkts 0           out FECN pkts 0
  out BECN pkts 0           in DE pkts 0             out DE pkts 0
  out bcast pkts 8          out bcast bytes 2624
  5 minute input rate 0 bits/sec, 0 packets/sec
  5 minute output rate 0 bits/sec, 0 packets/sec
  pvc create time 00:08:23, last time pvc status changed 00:08:23
```

The **show frame-relay pvc** command displays the status of all the PVCs configured on the router. You can also specify a particular PVC.

When an Inverse ARP request is made, the router updates its map table with three possible LMI connection states:

- ACTIVE state indicates a successful end-to-end (DTE-to-DTE) circuit.

- INACTIVE state indicates a successful connection to the switch (DTE-to-DCE) without a DTE detected on the other end of the PVC. This can occur because of residual or incorrect configuration on the switch.

- DELETED state indicates that the DTE is configured for a DLCI the switch does not recognize as valid for that interface.

The possible values of the Status field are as follows:

- **0x0**: The switch has this DLCI programmed, but for some reason it is unusable. The reason could possibly be that the other end of the PVC is down.

- **0x2**: The Frame Relay switch has the DLCI, and everything is operational.

- **0x4**: The Frame Relay switch does not have this DLCI programmed for the router, but it was programmed at some point in the past. This could also be caused by the DLCIs being reversed on the router, or by the PVC being deleted by the service provider in the Frame Relay cloud.

As soon as you have gathered all the statistics, use the **clear counters** command to reset the statistics counters. Wait 5 or 10 minutes after clearing the counters before issuing the **show** commands again. Note any additional errors. If you need to contact the carrier, these statistics help resolve the issues.

Verifying Remote IP Address-to-Local DLCI Translation

A final task is to confirm whether the **frame-relay inverse-arp** command resolved a remote IP address to a local DLCI. Use the **show frame-relay map** command to display the current map entries and information about the connections, as shown in Example 3-17.

Example 3-17   show frame-relay map Command for Router R1

```
R1# show frame-relay map

Serial0/0/0.102 (up): ip 10.1.1.2 dlci 100(0x64,0x1840), dynamic broadcast,
        CISCO, status defined, active
```

The output shows the following information:

- 10.1.1.2 is the IP address of the remote router, dynamically learned via the Inverse ARP process.

- 100 is the decimal value of the local DLCI number.

- 0x64 is the hex conversion of the DLCI number; 0x64 = 100 decimal.

- 0x1840 is the value as it would appear on the wire because of the way the DLCI bits are spread out in the Address field of the Frame Relay frame.

- Broadcast/multicast is enabled on the PVC.

- PVC status is active.

To clear dynamically created Frame Relay maps that are created using Inverse ARP, use the **clear frame-relay inarp** command, as shown in Examples 3-18 and 3-19. It may take several moments for the Inverse ARP process. So you may not see any output until this process is complete, before you issue the **show frame-relay map** command.

Example 3-18   clear frame-relay inarp and **show frame-relay map** Commands for Router R1

```
R1# clear frame-relay inarp
R1# show frame-relay map

Serial0/0/0.102 (up): point-to-point dlci, dlci 102(0x66,0x1860), broadcast
        status defined, active
```

Example 3-19   **clear frame-relay inarp** and **show frame-relay map** Commands for
Router R2

```
R2# clear frame-relay inarp
R2# show frame-relay map

Serial0/0/0.201 (up): point-to-point dlci, dlci 201(0xC9,0x3090), broadcast
          status defined, active
```

Troubleshooting Frame Relay Configuration

If the verification procedure indicates that your Frame Relay configuration is not working
properly, you need to troubleshoot the configuration.

Use the **debug frame-relay lmi** command to determine whether the router and the Frame
Relay switch are sending and receiving LMI packets properly.

Look at Examples 3-20 and 3-21. Examine the output of an LMI exchange.

Example 3-20   **debug frame-relay lmi** Command for Router R1

```
R1# debug frame-relay lmi

Frame Relay LMI debugging is on
Displaying all Frame Relay LMI data
R1#
*Sep 12 00:09:35.425: Serial0/0/0(out): StEnq, myseq 110, yourseen 109, DTE up
*Sep 12 00:09:35.425: datagramstart = 0x3F4055D4, datagramsize = 13
*Sep 12 00:09:35.425: FR encap = 0xFCF10309
*Sep 12 00:09:35.425: 00 75 01 01 01 03 02 6E 6D
*Sep 12 00:09:35.425:
*Sep 12 00:09:35.425: Serial0/0/0(in): Status, myseq 110, pak size 13
*Sep 12 00:09:35.425: RT IE 1, length 1, type 1
*Sep 12 00:09:35.425: KA IE 3, length 2, yourseq 110, myseq 110
R1#
*Sep 12 00:09:45.425: Serial0/0/0(out): StEnq, myseq 111, yourseen 110, DTE up
*Sep 12 00:09:45.425: datagramstart = 0x3F4050D4, datagramsize = 13
*Sep 12 00:09:45.425: FR encap = 0xFCF10309
*Sep 12 00:09:45.425: 00 75 01 01 01 03 02 6F 6E
*Sep 12 00:09:45.425:
*Sep 12 00:09:45.425: Serial0/0/0(in): Status, myseq 111, pak size 13
*Sep 12 00:09:45.425: RT IE 1, length 1, type 1
*Sep 12 00:09:45.425: KA IE 3, length 2, yourseq 111, myseq 111
R1# undebug all

All possible debugging has been turned off
R1#
```

Example 3-21   **debug frame-relay lmi** Command for Router R2

```
R2# debug frame-relay lmi

Frame Relay LMI debugging is on
Displaying all Frame Relay LMI data
R2#
*Sep 12 00:07:12.773: Serial0/0/0(out): StEnq, myseq 82, yourseen 81, DTE up
*Sep 12 00:07:12.773: datagramstart = 0x3F401B14, datagramsize = 13
*Sep 12 00:07:12.773: FR encap = 0xFCF10309
*Sep 12 00:07:12.773: 00 75 01 01 01 03 02 52 51
*Sep 12 00:07:12.773:
*Sep 12 00:07:12.773: Serial0/0/0(in): Status, myseq 82, pak size 13
*Sep 12 00:07:12.773: RT IE 1, length 1, type 1
*Sep 12 00:07:12.773: KA IE 3, length 2, yourseq 82, myseq 82
R2#
*Sep 12 00:07:22.773: Serial0/0/0(out): StEnq, myseq 83, yourseen 82, DTE up
*Sep 12 00:07:22.773: datagramstart = 0x3F6AEFD4, datagramsize = 13
*Sep 12 00:07:22.773: FR encap = 0xFCF10309
*Sep 12 00:07:22.773: 00 75 01 01 01 03 02 53 52
*Sep 12 00:07:22.773:
*Sep 12 00:07:22.773: Serial0/0/0(in): Status, myseq 83, pak size 13
*Sep 12 00:07:22.773: RT IE 1, length 1, type 1
*Sep 12 00:07:22.773: KA IE 3, length 2, yourseq 83, myseq 83
*Sep 12 00:07:22.773: PVC IE 0x7 , length 0x3 , dlci 100, status 0x2
R2# undebug all

All possible debugging has been turned off
R2#
```

Some of the information in the **debug frame-relay lmi** command is explained as follows:

- "out" is an LMI status message sent by the router.

- "in" is a message received from the Frame Relay switch.

- A full LMI status message is a "type 0" (not shown in either example).

- An LMI exchange is a "type 1."

- "dlci 100, status 0x2" means that the status of DLCI 100 is active.

Summary

Frame Relay provides greater bandwidth, reliability, and resiliency than private or leased lines. Frame Relay has reduced network costs by using less equipment, by being less complex, and by being easier to implement. For these reasons, Frame Relay has become the most widely used WAN technology in the world.

A Frame Relay connection between a DTE device at the LAN edge and a DCE device at the carrier edge has a link layer component and a physical layer component. Frame Relay takes data packets and encapsulates them in a Frame Relay frame and then passes the frame to the physical layer for delivery on the wire. The connection across the carrier network is a VC identified by a DLCI. Multiple VCs can be multiplexed using a FRAD. Frame Relay networks usually use a partial-mesh topology optimized to the data flow requirements of the carrier's customer base.

Frame Relay uses Inverse ARP to map DLCIs to the IP addresses of remote locations. Dynamic address mapping relies on Inverse ARP to resolve a next-hop network protocol address to a local DLCI value. The Frame Relay router sends out Inverse ARP requests on its PVC to discover the protocol address of the remote device connected to the Frame Relay network. DTE Frame Relay routers use the LMI to provide status information about their connection with the DCE Frame Relay switch. LMI extensions provide additional internetworking information.

The first two tasks in configuring Frame Relay on a Cisco router are to enable Frame Relay encapsulation on the interface and then to configure either static of dynamic mapping. After this, a number of optional tasks can be completed as required, including configuring the LMI and VCs, traffic shaping, and customizing Frame Relay on your network. Monitoring and maintaining Frame Relay connections is the final task.

Frame Relay configuration must consider the split-horizon problem that arises when multiple VCs converge on a single physical interface. Frame Relay can partition a physical interface into multiple virtual interfaces called subinterfaces. Subinterface configuration was also explained and practiced.

The configuration of Frame Relay is affected by the way service providers charge for connections using units of access rates and committed information rates (CIR). An advantage of these charging schemes is that unused network capacity is available to or shared with all customers, usually at no extra charge. This allows users to burst traffic for short periods.

Configuring flow control in a Frame Relay network is also affected by service provider charging schemes. You can configure queuing and shape traffic according to the CIR. DTEs can be prompted to control congestion in the network by adding BECN and FECN bits to frame addresses. DTEs can also be configured to set a discard eligible (DE) bit indicating that the frame may be discarded in preference to other frames if congestion occurs. Frames that are sent in excess of the CIR are marked as DE, which means that they can be dropped if congestion occurs within the Frame Relay network.

Finally, after configuring Frame Relay, you learned how to verify and troubleshoot the connections.

Labs

The activities and labs available in the companion *Accessing the WAN, CCNA Exploration Labs and Study Guide* (ISBN 1-58713-201-x) provide hands-on practice with the following topics introduced in this chapter:

Lab 3-1: Basic Frame Relay (3.5.1)

In this lab, you learn how to configure Frame Relay encapsulation on serial links using the network shown in the topology diagram. You also learn how to configure a router as a Frame Relay switch. Both Cisco standards and Open standards apply to Frame Relay. You will learn about both. Pay special attention in the lab section, in which you intentionally break the Frame Relay configurations. This will help you in the Troubleshooting lab associated with this chapter.

Lab 3-2: Challenge Frame Relay Configuration (3.5.2)

In this lab, you configure Frame Relay using the network shown in the topology diagram. If you need assistance, refer to the Basic Frame Relay lab. However, try to do as much on your own as possible.

Lab 3-3: Troubleshooting Frame Relay (3.5.3)

In this lab, you practice troubleshooting a misconfigured Frame Relay environment. Load or have your instructor load the configurations into your routers. Locate and repair all errors in the configurations, and establish end-to-end connectivity. Your final configuration should match the topology diagram and addressing table.

Many of the Hands-on Labs include Packet Tracer Companion Activities where you can use Packet Tracer to complete a simulation of the lab. Look for this icon in the *Accessing the WAN, CCNA Exploration Labs and Study Guide* for Hands-on Labs that have a Packet Tracer Companion.

Check Your Understanding

Complete all the review questions listed here to test your understanding of the topics and concepts in this chapter. Answers are listed in Appendix, "Check Your Understanding and Challenge Questions Answer Key."

1. What is used to identify the path to the next Frame Relay switch in a Frame Relay network?

   A. CIR

   B. DLCI

   C. FECN

   D. BECN

2. Why are Frame Relay paths referred to as virtual?

   A. There are no dedicated circuits to and from the Frame Relay carrier.

   B. Frame Relay PVCs are created and discarded on demand.

   C. The connections between PVC endpoints act like dialup circuits.

   D. There are no dedicated circuits inside the Frame Relay carrier cloud.

3. Which statement accurately describes the split-horizon problem with regard to a multipoint topology?

   A. Split horizon must be disabled for all non-IP protocols.

   B. Split horizon creates IP routing loops in multipoint domains.

   C. Split horizon does not apply to broadcasts, so it does not protect protocols that use broadcast updates.

   D. Split horizon prevents any interface from accepting a valid update and forwarding to all the other interfaces.

4. Why is Frame Relay more cost-effective than leased lines? (Choose two.)

   A. Time division multiplexing

   B. It uses less equipment.

   C. Optimized packet routing

   D. It shares bandwidth across a large customer base.

   E. Dynamic IP addressing

5. Match each status from the **show frame-relay pvc** command with its meaning:

Active

Inactive

Deleted

A. The DLCI is programmed in the Frame Relay switch, but the other end of the PVC may be down.

B. The DLCI does not exist on the router.

C. The DLCI is programmed in the Frame Relay switch and is usable.

D. The DLCI does not exist on the Frame Relay switch for this router.

E. The DLCI is programmed on the other end of the PVC for this router.

6. What reliability advantage does Frame Relay offer over leased lines?

A. Frame Relay access circuits are higher-grade circuits than leased lines.

B. The pathways for virtual circuits inside the carrier are meshed.

C. From end to end, a single virtual circuit uses a fixed error-checked path.

D. Frame Relay uses more-sophisticated error-detection methods.

7. Refer to Figure 3-33. What is placed in the Address field of a frame that will travel from the Orlando office to the DC office?

Figure 3-33 Network Topology for Question 7

A. MAC address of the Orlando router

B. MAC address of the DC router

C. 192.168.1.25

D. 192.168.1.26

E. DLCI 100

F. DLCI 200

8. Which situation favors a multipoint topology over point-to-point?

   A. When VLSM cannot be used to conserve addresses

   B. When using routing protocols other than IP

   C. When using a frame mesh topology to save access circuits

   D. When using a routing protocol that requires broadcast updates

9. What is an advantage of configuring subinterfaces in a Frame Relay environment?

   A. It makes the DLCIs globally significant.

   B. It eliminates the need for using Inverse ARP.

   C. It solves split-horizon issues.

   D. It improves flow control and bandwidth usage.

10. Which protocol can provide error correction for data that is transmitted over a Frame Relay link?

    A. FECN

    B. FTP

    C. LMI

    D. TCP

    E. UDP

11. Match each command with its description:

    show interface

    show frame-relay lmi

    show frame-relay pvc

    show frame-relay map

    debug frame-relay lmi

    A. Shows the status of the virtual circuit and FECN/BECN statistics

    B. Verifies that the router and Frame Relay switch are sending and receiving LMI packets properly

    C. Verifies encapsulation, LMI type, LMI DLCI, and LMI status

    D. Verifies LMI statistics

    E. Verifies the destination IP address mapping to the DLCI

12. At which rate does a service provider guarantee to transfer data into the Frame Relay network?

    A. Baud rate

    B. Timing rate

    C. Data transfer rate

    D. Committed information rate

13. How are DLCI numbers assigned?

    A. They are assigned by a DLCI server.

    B. They are assigned arbitrarily by the user.

    C. They are assigned by the service provider.

    D. They are assigned based on the host IP address.

14. A router can reach multiple networks through a Frame Relay interface. How does the router know which DLCI to assign to the IP address of the destination network?

    A. It consults the Frame Relay map.

    B. It consults the routing table to find the DLCI.

    C. It uses Frame Relay switching tables to map DLCIs to IP addresses.

    D. It uses RARP to find the IP address of the corresponding DLCI.

15. Match each term with its definition:

    CIR

    DE

    FECN

    BECN

    A. A bit that marks the frame to be dropped when congestion is present

    B. A bit set on every frame that a switch places on a congested link

    C. The rate at which the service provider agrees to accept bits on the VC

    D. A bit set on every frame that a switch receives on a congested link

16. Compare and contrast the following terms: DLCI, LMI, and Inverse ARP.

17. Refer to Figure 3-34.

Figure 3-34   Network Topology for Question 17

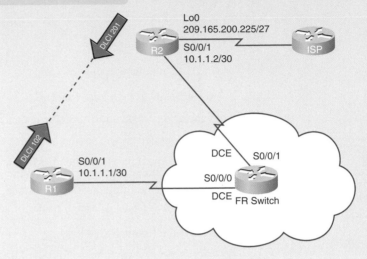

```
interface s0/0/1
ip address 10.1.1.1 255.255.255.252
encapsulation frame-relay
bandwidth 64
```

The following configuration is for router R1:

```
interface s0/0/1
ip address 10.1.1.1 255.255.255.252
encapsulation frame-relay
bandwidth 64
```

What command on R1 is required to statically configure a Frame Relay connection to R2? Traffic between sites must also support OSPF.

18. Compare and contrast the following terms: access rate, CIR, CBIR, and BE.

19. Refer to Figure 3-35 and the following configuration. R1 cannot establish connectivity with the routers over the Frame Relay cloud. What are the problems with this configuration?

Figure 3-35 Network Topology for Question 19

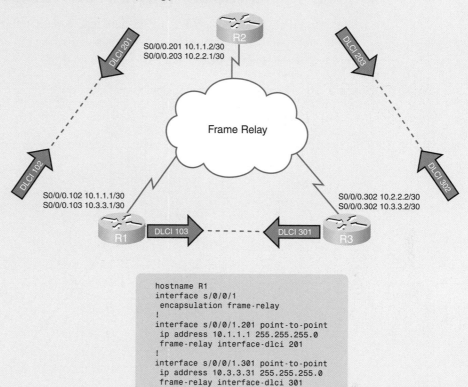

```
hostname R1
interface s/0/0/1
 encapsulation frame-relay
!
interface s/0/0/1.201 point-to-point
 ip address 10.1.1.1 255.255.255.0
 frame-relay interface-dlci 201
!
interface s/0/0/1.301 point-to-point
 ip address 10.3.3.31 255.255.255.0
 frame-relay interface-dlci 301
```

```
hostname R1
interface s0/0/1
  encapsulation frame-relay
!
interface s0/0/1.201 point-to-point
  ip address 10.1.1.1 255.255.255.0
  frame-relay interface-dlci 201
!
interface s0/0/1.301 point-to-point
  ip address 10.3.3.1 255.255.255.0
  frame-relay interface-dlci 301
!
```

Challenge Questions and Activities

1. Refer to Figure 3-36. Routers R2 and R3 both have Frame Relay connections to the R1 router. R1 is acting as the hub router in this hub-and-spoke topology. R2 is using Inverse ARP to map its DLCI with R1's network address.

Figure 3-36 Network Topology for Challenge Question 1

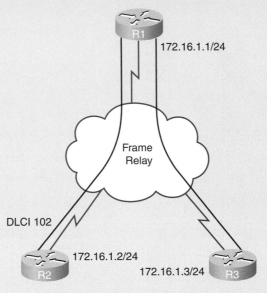

To reach R3, the network administrator configured the following static map on R2:

```
frame-relay map ip 172.16.1.3 102
```

This seems to work, giving R2 reachability to both R1 and R3 (assuming that R3 has also been appropriately configured). However, when the router is reloaded (the running-config was saved to the startup config), R2 can no longer reach R1. The **show frame-relay map** command on R2 shows only the static map to R3; it no longer shows the dynamic Inverse ARP map to R1. What happened? What would be the solution?

To Learn More

Here are some suggested books for further reading on Frame Relay:

- *Cisco Frame Relay Solutions Guide* by Jonathan Chin (Cisco Press, 2004)

- *Frame Relay: Technology and Practice* by Jeff T. Buckwalter (Addison-Wesley Professional, 1999)

CHAPTER 4

Network Security

Objectives

After completing this chapter, you should be able to answer the following questions:

- What are common security threats to enterprise networks?

- What are some methods to mitigate security threats to enterprise networks?

- How do you configure basic router security?

- How do you disable unused router services and interfaces?

- How do you use the Cisco SDM one-step lockdown feature?

- How do you manage files and software images with the Cisco IOS Integrated File System (IFS)?

Key Terms

This chapter uses the following key terms. You can find the definitions in the glossary at the end of the book.

Security has moved to the forefront of network management and implementation. The overall security challenge is to find a balance between two important requirements: the need to open networks to support evolving business opportunities, and the need to protect private, personal, and strategic business information.

Applying an effective *security policy* is the most important step that an organization can take to protect its network. This policy provides guidelines about the activities to be carried out and the resources to be used to secure an organization's network.

Layer 2 security is not discussed in this chapter. For information about Layer 2 LAN security measures, refer to the *Exploration: LAN Switching and Wireless* course.

Introduction to Network Security

Computer networks have grown in both size and importance in a very short time. This growth has pushed the requirement to secure networks.

Why Is Network Security Important?

If the network's security is compromised, serious consequences could occur, such as loss of privacy, theft of information, and even legal liability. To make the situation even more challenging, the types of potential threats to network security are always evolving.

As shown in Figure 4-1, attackers can launch attacks from various locations.

Figure 4-1   Why Is Network Security Important?

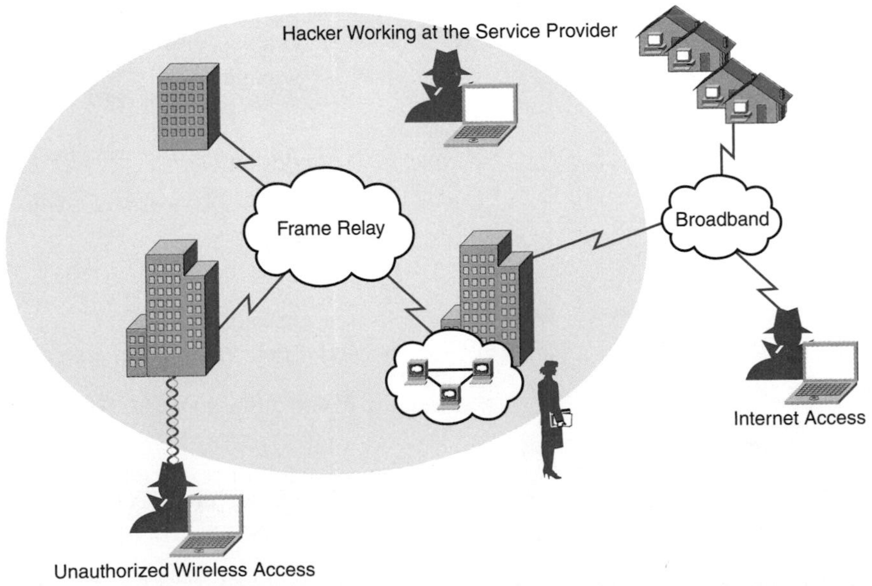

Today's networks must balance accessibility to network resources with the protection of sensitive data from theft.

As e-business and Internet applications continue to grow, finding the balance between being isolated and being open is critical. In addition, the rise of mobile commerce and wireless networks demands that security solutions become seamlessly integrated, more transparent, and more flexible.

Network administrators must carefully balance accessibility to network resources with security.

This chapter takes you on a tour of the world of network security. You will learn about different types of threats, the development of organizational security policies, mitigation techniques, and Cisco IOS software tools to help secure networks. The chapter ends with a look at managing Cisco IOS software images. Although this may not seem like a security issue, Cisco IOS software images and configurations can be deleted. Devices compromised in this way pose security risks.

The Increasing Threat to Security

Over the years, network attack tools and methods have evolved. Here are some examples of attacks:

- 1985: Password guessing and code replication

- 1990: Password cracking and war dialing

- 1995: Viruses, including Love bug, Nimda, and Code Red

- 2000: Trojan horses such as Back Orifice

- 2005 to the present: Worms including Blaster, MyDoom, and Slammer

As shown in Figure 4-2, in 1985 an attacker had to have a sophisticated computer, as well as programming and networking knowledge, to make use of rudimentary tools and carry out basic attacks.

As time went on, and attackers' methods and tools improved, attackers no longer required the same level of sophisticated knowledge. This has effectively lowered the entry-level requirements for attackers. People who previously would not have participated in computer crime now can do so.

As the types of threats, attacks, and exploits have evolved, various terms have been coined to describe the individuals involved. Some of the most common terms are as follows:

- *White hat*: An individual who looks for vulnerabilities in systems or networks and then reports these vulnerabilities to the system's owners so that they can be fixed. This person is ethically opposed to the abuse of computer systems. A white hat generally focuses on securing IT systems, whereas a black hat (the opposite) wants to break into them.

Figure 4-2   Increasing Threat of Attackers

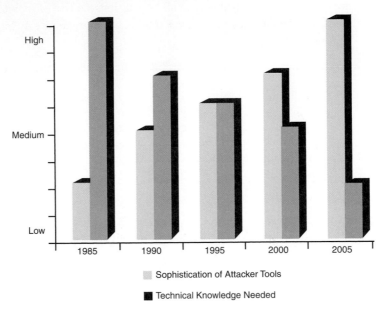

■ Sophistication of Attacker Tools

■ Technical Knowledge Needed

Threats continue to become more sophisticated as the technical knowledge required to implement attacks diminishes.

- *Hacker*: A general term that has historically been used to describe a computer programming expert. More recently, this term is often used in a negative way to describe an individual who attempts to gain unauthorized access to network resources with malicious intent.

- *Black hat*: Another term for individuals who use their knowledge of computer systems to break into systems or networks that they are not authorized to use, usually for personal or financial gain. A cracker is an example of a black hat.

- *Cracker*: A more accurate term to describe someone who tries to gain unauthorized access to network resources with malicious intent.

- **Phreaker**: An individual who manipulates the phone network to cause it to perform a function that is not allowed. A common goal of phreaking is breaking into the phone network, usually through a pay phone, to make free long-distance calls.

- *Spammer*: An individual who sends large quantities of unsolicited e-mail messages. Spammers often use viruses to take control of home computers and use them to send bulk messages.

- *Phisher*: Uses e-mail or other means to trick others into providing sensitive information, such as credit card numbers or passwords. A phisher masquerades as a trusted party that would have a legitimate need for the sensitive information.

Think Like an Attacker

The attacker's goal is to compromise a network target or an application running within a network. To understand your enemy, you must become your enemy. Your best defense is to know how an attacker can compromise your network.

Many attackers use this seven-step process to gain information and start an attack:

Step 1.   **Perform footprint analysis (reconnaissance).** A company web page can lead to information, such as the IP addresses of servers. From there, an attacker can create a picture of the company's security profile or "footprint."

Step 2.   **Enumerate information.** An attacker can expand on the footprint by monitoring network traffic with a packet sniffer such as Wireshark, finding information such as version numbers of FTP servers and mail servers. A cross-reference with vulnerability databases exposes the company's applications to potential exploits.

Step 3.   **Manipulate users to gain access.** Sometimes employees choose passwords that are easily crackable. In other instances, employees can be duped by talented attackers into giving up sensitive access-related information.

Step 4.   **Escalate privileges.** After attackers gain basic access, they use their skills to increase their network privileges.

Step 5.   **Gather additional passwords and secrets.** With improved access privileges, attackers use their talents to gain access to well-guarded, sensitive information.

Step 6.   **Install back doors.** Back doors give the attacker a way to enter the system without being detected. The most common back door is an open listening TCP or UDP port.

Step 7.   **Leverage the compromised system.** After a system is compromised, an attacker uses it to stage attacks on other hosts in the network.

Types of Computer Crime

As security measures have improved over the years, some of the most common types of attacks have diminished in frequency, but new ones have emerged. Implementing network security solutions begins with an appreciation of the complete scope of computer crime. These are the most commonly reported acts of computer crime that have network security implications:

- Insider abuse of network access

- Viruses

- Mobile device theft

- Phishing, in which an organization is fraudulently represented as the sender

- Instant-messaging (IM) misuse

- Denial of service

- Unauthorized access to information

- *Bots* within the organization

- Theft of customer or employee data

- Abuse of a wireless network

- System penetration

- Financial fraud

- Password sniffing

- Key logging

- Website defacement

- Misuse of a public web application

- Theft of proprietary information

- Exploiting an organization's DNS server

- Telecom fraud

- Sabotage

Computer crimes that can be mitigated by effective and vigilant network management include the following:

- Insider abuse of network access

- Denial of service

- System penetration

- Password sniffing

Note

In certain countries, some of these activities may not be a crime, but they are still a problem.

Open Versus Closed Networks

Figure 4-3 illustrates the overall security challenge facing network administrators. Organizations must find a balance between two important needs:

- Keeping networks open to support evolving business requirements

- Protecting private, personal, and strategic business information

Figure 4-3   Balancing Access and Security in a Network

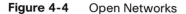

Network administrators seek to find a balance between access and security.

To address these needs, network security models follow a progressive scale. On one end is "open," which means that any service is permitted unless it is expressly denied. On the other end is "restrictive," which means that services are denied by default unless deemed necessary.

For example, in Figure 4-4, the scales are tipped to provide open access to network users.

Figure 4-4   Open Networks

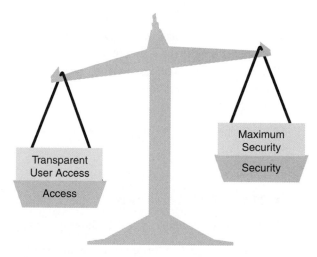

Although the security risks are self-evident, there are some advantages to consider:

- Easy to configure and administer

- Easy for end users to access network resources

- Security costs are much less

In Figure 4-5, the scales are balanced to create more restrictive access for network users.

Figure 4-5   Restrictive Networks

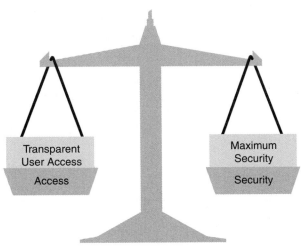

In the case of the restrictive network, the rules for what are permitted are defined in the form of a policy by an individual or group in the organization. A change in access policy may be as simple as asking a network administrator to enable a service. Depending on the company, a change could require an amendment to the enterprise security policy before the administrator is allowed to enable the service. For example, a security policy could disallow the use of IM services; however, demand from employees may cause the company to change the policy.

Although the benefits of implementing security are evident, it does present some draw-backs:

- More difficult to configure and administer

- More difficult for end users to access resources

- Security costs are greater than those for an open network

An extreme alternative for managing security is to close a network to the outside world, as shown in Figure 4-6, with the scales tipped to security.

Figure 4-6   Closed Networks

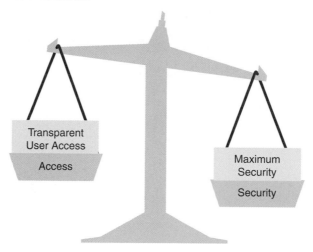

A closed network provides connectivity only to known, trusted parties and sites. It does not allow connectivity to public networks and for this reason is considered safer from outside attacks. However, internal threats still exist. A closed network is still susceptible to attacks from within the enterprise.

A closed network has the same drawbacks as a restrictive network and is also the most expensive to implement.

Developing a Security Policy

The first step any organization should take to protect its data and itself from a liability challenge is to develop a security policy. A security policy is a set of principles that guides decision-making processes and enable leaders in an organization to distribute authority confidently. RFC 2196 states that a "security policy is a formal statement of the rules by which people who are given access to an organization's technology and information assets must abide."

A security policy can be as simple as a brief "Acceptable Use Policy" for network resources, or it can be several hundred pages long and detail every element of connectivity and associated policies. The security policy also varies based on business type, company size, number of users, type of industry, threats, and vulnerabilities. Figure 4-7 shows sample topics that could be included in a security policy document.

Figure 4-7   Security Policy

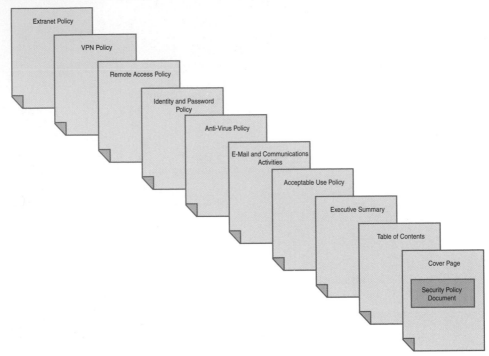

A security policy meets these goals:

■ It informs users, staff, and managers of their obligations for protecting technology and information assets.

■ It specifies the mechanisms through which these requirements can be met.

■ It provides a baseline from which to acquire, configure, and audit computer systems and networks for compliance with the policy.

Assembling a security policy can be daunting if it is undertaken without guidance. For this reason, the International Organization for Standardization (ISO) and the International Electrotechnical Commission (IEC) have published dozens of information security documents. Of specific interest is a security standards document called ISO/IEC 27002. This document refers specifically to information technology and outlines a code of practice for information security management.

ISO/IEC 27002 is intended to be a common basis and practical guidelines for developing organizational security standards and effective security management practices. This document has 12 sections:

■ Risk assessment

■ Security policy

- Organization of information security

- Asset management

- Human resources security

- Physical and environmental security

- Communications and operations management

- Access control

- Information systems acquisition, development, and maintenance

- Information security incident management

- Business continuity management

- Compliance

Tip

This chapter focuses on the security policy section. The actual document is available for purchase on the IEC website. To read more about ISO/IEC 27002, visit the ISO website at *http://www.iso.org/iso/home.htm*.

The development of the network security policy document is discussed later in this chapter.

Cisco provides a tool called the Security Policy Builder that can help you create a custom security policy tailored to an organization's specific requirements. You simply complete a short interview that covers key security issues and concerns, and a custom security policy is e-mailed to you in Microsoft Word format.

To access the Cisco Security Policy Builder, go to *http://www.ciscowebtools.com/spb/*.

Common Security Threats

When discussing network security, three common factors are vulnerabilities, threats, and attacks. The following sections cover these in more detail.

Vulnerabilities

Vulnerability is the degree of weakness that is inherent in every network and device. This includes routers, switches, desktops, servers, and even security devices. Vulnerability also includes the users. Even when the infrastructure and devices are secured, employees can be targets of social-engineering attacks.

Threats are people who are interested in and capable of taking advantage of each security weakness. Such individuals can be expected to continually search for new exploits and weaknesses.

Threats use a variety of tools, scripts, and programs to launch attacks against networks and network devices. Typically, the network devices under attack are the endpoints, such as servers and desktop computers.

The three primary categories of vulnerabilities are

- Technological weaknesses
- Configuration weaknesses
- Security policy weaknesses

Table 4-1 describes technological weaknesses.

Table 4-1   Technological Weaknesses

Technological Weakness	Examples
TCP/IP protocol	Hypertext Transfer Protocol (HTTP), File Transfer Protocol (FTP), and Internet Control Message Protocol (ICMP) are inherently insecure. Simple Network Management Protocol (SNMP), Simple Mail Transfer Protocol (SMTP), and SYN floods are related to the inherently insecure structure upon which TCP was designed.
Operating system	Operating systems have security problems that must be addressed: UNIX, Linux, Mac OS, Mac OS X, and Windows NT, 9x, 2000, XP, and Vista. These problems are documented in the Computer Emergency Response Team (CERT) archives at *http://www.cert.org*.
Network equipment	Various types of network equipment, such as routers, firewalls, and switches, have security weaknesses that must be recognized and protected against. These include password protection, lack of authentication, routing protocols, and firewall holes. Computer and network technologies have intrinsic security weaknesses. These include TCP/IP protocol, operating system, and network equipment weaknesses.

Network administrators or network engineers need to learn about the configuration weaknesses of their networks and correctly configure their network devices to compensate. Table 4-2 describes configuration weaknesses.

Table 4-2   Configuration Weaknesses

Configuration Weakness	How the Weakness Is Exploited
Unsecured user accounts	User account information may be transmitted insecurely across the network, exposing usernames and passwords to snoopers.
System accounts with easily guessed passwords	This common problem is the result of poorly selected user passwords.
Misconfigured Internet services	A common problem is to turn on JavaScript in web browsers, enabling attacks by way of hostile JavaScript when accessing untrusted sites. IIS, FTP, and Terminal Services also pose problems.
Unsecured default settings within products	Many products have default settings that enable security holes.
Misconfigured network equipment	Misconfigurations of the equipment itself can cause significant security problems. For example, misconfigured access lists, routing protocols, or SNMP community strings can open large security holes.

Security risks to the network exist if users do not follow the security policy. Table 4-3 describes some common security policy weaknesses and how they are exploited.

Table 4-3   Policy Weaknesses

Policy Weakness	Examples
Lack of written security policy	An unwritten policy cannot be consistently applied or enforced.
Corporate politics	Political battles and turf wars within the organization can make it difficult to implement a consistent security policy.
Lack of continuity	Poorly chosen, easily cracked, or default passwords can allow unauthorized access to the network.
Logical access controls are not applied	Inadequate monitoring and auditing allow attacks and unauthorized use to continue, wasting company resources. This could result in legal action against or termination of IT technicians, IT management, or even company leadership that allows these unsafe conditions to persist.

continues

Table 4-3   Policy Weaknesses

Policy Weakness	Examples
Software and hardware installation and changes do not follow policy	Unauthorized changes to the network topology or the installation of unapproved applications creates security holes.
Disaster recovery plan is nonexistent	The lack of a disaster recovery plan allows chaos, panic, and confusion to occur when someone attacks the enterprise.

Threats to Physical Infrastructure

When you think of network security, or even computer security, you may imagine attackers exploiting software vulnerabilities. A less glamorous, but no less important, class of threat is the physical security of devices. An attacker can deny the use of network resources if those resources can be physically compromised.

The four classes of physical threats are as follows:

- **Hardware threats**: Theft or vandalism causing physical damage to servers, routers, switches, cabling plant, and workstations

- **Environmental threats**: Temperature extremes (too hot or too cold) or humidity extremes (too wet or too dry)

- **Electrical threats**: Voltage spikes, insufficient supply voltage (brownouts), unconditioned power (noise), and total power loss

- **Maintenance threats**: Poor handling of key electrical components (electrostatic discharge), lack of critical spare parts, poor cabling, and poor labeling

Some of these issues must be dealt with in an organizational policy. Some of them are subject to good leadership and management in the organization. The consequences of natural or other disasters can wreak havoc in a network if the physical security is not sufficiently prepared.

Here are some ways to mitigate physical threats:

- Hardware threat mitigation

- Environmental threat mitigation

- Electrical threat mitigation

- Maintenance threat mitigation

Hardware Threat Mitigation

Figure 4-8 is a floor plan for a small computer center. Be sure to secure physical access to all infrastructure and sensitive equipment. In the figure, the card reader protects physical access to the server room.

Figure 4-8   Computer Center Floor Plan

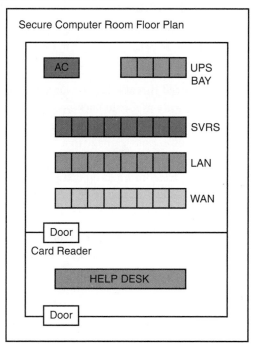

To mitigate hardware threats or vulnerabilities, lock the wiring closet and allow access to only authorized personnel. Block access through any dropped ceiling, raised floor, window, ductwork, or point of entry other than the secured access point. Use electronic access control, and log all entry attempts. Monitor facilities with security cameras.

Environmental Threat Mitigation

To mitigate environmental threats or vulnerabilities, limit damage by creating a proper operating environment through temperature control, humidity control, positive air flow, remote environmental alarming, and recording and monitoring.

Electrical Threat Mitigation

To mitigate electrical supply threats or vulnerabilities, install uninterruptible power supply (UPS) systems and generator sets, follow a preventive maintenance plan, and install redundant power supplies. Services to provide offsite monitoring should also be implemented.

Maintenance Threat Mitigation

To mitigate maintenance threats or vulnerabilities, use properly installed cables and cable runs, label critical cables and components, use electrostatic discharge procedures, stock spares of critical cables, and control access to console ports.

Threats to Networks

Earlier in this chapter, the common computer crimes that have implications for network security were listed. These crimes can be grouped into two primary classes of threats to networks:

- **Unstructured threats**: Unstructured threats consist of mostly inexperienced individuals using easily available hacking tools, such as shell scripts and password crackers. Even unstructured threats that are executed only with the intent of testing an attacker's skills can do serious damage to a network. For example, if a company website is hacked, the company's reputation may be damaged. Even if the website is separated from the private information that sits behind a protective firewall, the public does not know that. What the public perceives is that the site might not be a safe environment in which to conduct business.

- **Structured threats**: Structured threats come from individuals or groups that are more highly motivated and technically competent. These people know system vulnerabilities and use sophisticated hacking techniques to penetrate unsuspecting businesses. They break into business and government computers to commit fraud, destroy or alter records, or simply create havoc. These groups often are involved with major fraud and theft cases reported to law enforcement agencies. Their hacking is so complex and sophisticated that only specially trained investigators understand what is happening.

  In 1995, Kevin Mitnick was convicted of accessing interstate computers in the United States for criminal purposes. He broke into the California Department of Motor Vehicles database, routinely took control of New York and California telephone switching hubs, and stole credit card numbers.

These two primary classes of threats can further be categorized as follows:

- **External threats**: External threats can arise from individuals or organizations working outside of a company who do not have authorized access to the computer systems or network. They work their way into a network mainly from the Internet or dialup access servers. External threats can vary in severity, depending on the expertise of the attacker—either amateurish (unstructured) or expert (structured).

- **Internal threats**: Internal threats occur when someone has authorized access to the network with either an account or physical access. Just as with external threats, the severity of an internal threat depends on the attacker's expertise.

Social Engineering

The easiest attack involves no computer skills at all. If an intruder can trick a member of an organization into giving out valuable information, such as the location of files or passwords, the process of hacking is much easier. This type of attack is called social engineering, and it preys on personal vulnerabilities that talented attackers can discover. It can include appeals to an employee's ego, or it can be a disguised person or faked document that causes someone to provide sensitive information.

Phishing is a type of social engineering attack that involves using e-mail or other types of messages in an attempt to trick others into providing sensitive information, such as credit card numbers or passwords. The phisher masquerades as a trusted party that has a seemingly legitimate need for the sensitive information.

Frequently, phishing scams involve sending spam e-mails that appear to be from known online banking or auction sites. Figure 4-9 shows a replica of such an e-mail. The actual company used as the lure in this example has been changed.

Figure 4-9   Phishing Email Example

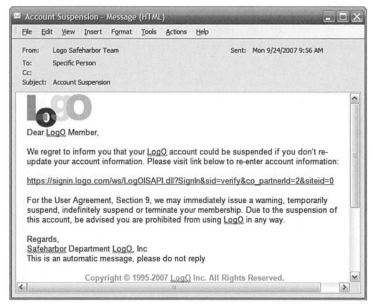

These e-mails contain hyperlinks that appear to be legitimate, but they actually take users to a fake website set up by the phisher to capture their information. The site appears to belong to the party that is faked in the e-mail. When the user enters his or her information, it is recorded for the phisher to use.

Phishing attacks can be prevented by educating users and implementing reporting guidelines for when they receive suspicious e-mail. Administrators can also block access to certain websites and configure filters that block suspicious e-mail.

Types of Network Attacks

Various types of attacks can be launched against an organization. Understanding these attacks is the first step in being able to stop the attackers from disrupting your operations.

There are four primary classes of attacks:

- Reconnaissance
- Access
- Denial of service
- Malicious code (worms, viruses, and Trojan horses)

The following sections cover these classes of attacks in greater detail.

Reconnaissance Attacks

Reconnaissance is the unauthorized discovery and mapping of systems, services, or vulnerabilities. It is also known as information gathering, and, in most cases, it precedes another type of attack. Reconnaissance is similar to a thief casing a neighborhood for vulnerable homes to break into, such as an unoccupied residence, or one with easy-to-open doors or open windows.

Reconnaissance attacks can consist of the following:

- Internet information queries
- Ping sweeps
- Port scans
- Packet sniffers

External attackers can use Internet tools, such as the nslookup and whois utilities, to easily determine the IP address space assigned to a given corporation or entity. After the IP address space is determined, an attacker can ping the publicly available IP addresses to identify the addresses that are active. To help automate this step, an attacker may use a ping sweep tool, such as fping or gping, which systematically pings all network addresses in a given range or subnet. This is similar to going through a section of a telephone book and calling each number to see who answers.

When the active IP addresses are identified, the intruder uses a port scanner to determine which network services or ports are active on the live IP addresses. A port scanner is software, such as Nmap or Superscan, that is designed to search a network host for open ports. The port scanner queries the ports to determine the application type and version, as well as the type and version of operating system (OS) running on the target host. Based on this information, the intruder can determine if a possible vulnerability that can be exploited exists. A network exploration tool such as Nmap can be used to conduct host discovery, port scanning, version detection, and OS detection. Many of these tools are available and easy to use.

Attack tools can also be categorized as noninvasive or invasive. Noninvasive tools are not detectible. Typically these tools only listen to traffic. Invasive tools leave their mark behind. They not only listen to traffic but also can alter or delete traffic.

Internal attackers may attempt to "eavesdrop" on network traffic.

Network snooping and packet sniffing are common terms for eavesdropping. The information gathered by eavesdropping can be used to pose other attacks to the network.

Two common uses of eavesdropping are as follows:

- **Information gathering**: Network intruders can identify usernames, passwords, or information carried in a packet. The goal of this activity is to accumulate as much information as possible about the target.

- **Information theft**: The theft can occur as data is transmitted over the internal or external network. The network intruder can also steal data from networked computers by gaining unauthorized access. Examples include breaking into or eavesdropping on financial institutions and obtaining credit card numbers. The goal of this activity is to use the stolen information for personal gain or malicious reasons.

An example of data susceptible to eavesdropping is SNMP version 1 *community strings*, which are sent in clear text. SNMP is a management protocol that provides a means for network devices to collect information about their status and to send it to an administrator. An intruder could eavesdrop on SNMP queries and gather valuable data on network equipment configuration. Another example is the capture of usernames and passwords as they cross a network.

A common method of eavesdropping on communications is to capture TCP/IP or other protocol packets and decode the contents using a *protocol analyzer* or a similar utility. An example of such a program is Wireshark, which you have been using extensively throughout the Exploration courses. After packets are captured, they can be examined for vulnerable information.

Three of the most effective methods for counteracting eavesdropping are as follows:

- Use switched networks instead of hubs. In this case, the use of a packet sniffer is essentially worthless, because traffic is not broadcast to all endpoints or network hosts.

- Using *encryption* that meets the organization's data security needs without imposing an excessive burden on system resources or users.

- Implementing and enforcing a policy directive that forbids the use of protocols with known susceptibilities to eavesdropping. For example, the company policy may stipulate to use only SNMP version 3 and disallow other versions of SNMP.

Encryption provides protection for data susceptible to eavesdropping attacks, password crackers, or manipulation. Almost every company has transactions that could have negative consequences if viewed by an eavesdropper. Encryption ensures that when sensitive data passes over a medium susceptible to eavesdropping, it cannot be altered or observed. *Decryption* is necessary when the data reaches the destination host.

For example, a common method of encryption is called payload-only encryption. This method encrypts the payload section (data section) after a User Datagram Protocol (UDP) or TCP header. This enables Cisco IOS routers and switches to read the network layer information and forward the traffic as any other IP packet. Payload-only encryption allows flow switching and all access list features to work with the encrypted traffic just as they would with plain-text traffic, thereby preserving desired quality of service (QoS) for all data.

Access Attacks

Unauthorized system access is when an intruder gains access to a device for which he or she does not have an account or a password. Entering or accessing systems usually involves running a hack, script, or tool that exploits a known vulnerability of the system or application being attacked.

Access attacks exploit known vulnerabilities in authentication services, FTP services, and web services to gain entry to web accounts, confidential databases, and other sensitive information.

Password Attacks

Password attacks can be implemented using a packet sniffer to yield user accounts and passwords that are transmitted as clear text. Password attacks usually refer to repeated attempts to log in to a shared resource, such as a server or router, to identify a user account, password, or both. These repeated attempts are called dictionary attacks or brute-force attacks.

To conduct a dictionary attack, attackers can use tools such as L0phtCrack (see Figure 4-10) or Cain.

These programs repeatedly attempt to log in as a user using words from a dictionary. Dictionary attacks often succeed because users have a tendency to choose simple passwords that are short, single words or that are simple variations that are easy to predict, such as adding the number 1 to a word.

Another password attack method uses rainbow tables. A rainbow table contains precomputed series of passwords that are constructed by building chains of possible plaintext passwords. Each chain is developed by starting with a randomly selected "guess" of the plaintext password and then successively applying variations to it. The attack software applies the passwords in the rainbow table until it solves the password. To conduct a rainbow table attack, attackers can use a tool such as L0phtCrack.

Figure 4-10   L0phtCrack

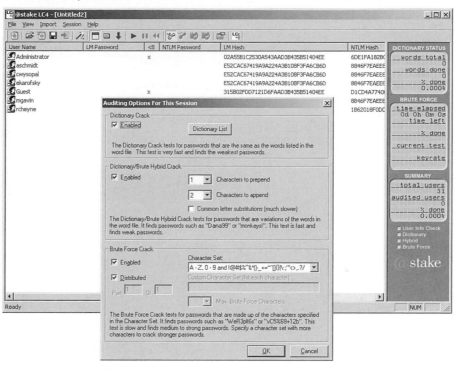

A brute-force attack tool is more sophisticated because it searches exhaustively using combinations of character sets to compute every possible password made up of those characters. The downside is that more time is required to complete this type of attack. Brute-force attack tools have been known to solve simple passwords in less than a minute. Longer, more complex passwords may take days or weeks to resolve.

Password attacks can be mitigated by setting the minimum password length and implementing policies that enforce users to use long, complex passwords consisting of numbers and symbols.

Trust Exploitation

The goal of a trust exploitation attack is to compromise a trusted host, using it to stage attacks on other hosts in a network. If a host in a company's network is protected by a firewall (inside host) but is accessible to a trusted host outside the firewall (outside host), the inside host can be attacked through the trusted outside host.

For example, in Figure 4-11, the attacker at the bottom of the figure gains access to the outside host, System B. As soon as System B is compromised, the attacker can use System B to gain access to the internal host, System A.

Figure 4-11   Trust Exploitation Example

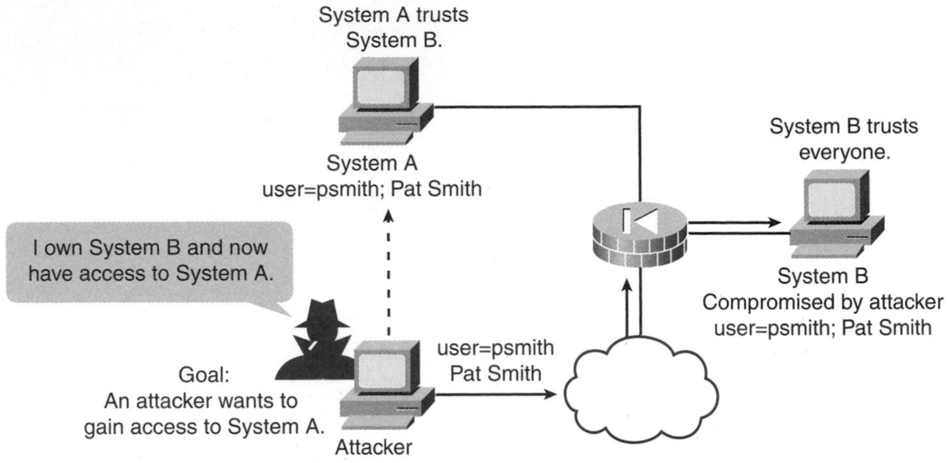

The means used by attackers to gain access to the trusted outside host, as well as the details of trust exploitation, are not discussed in this chapter. For information about trust exploitation, refer to the *Networking Academy Network Security* courses.

Trust exploitation-based attacks can be mitigated through tight constraints on trust levels within a network. For example, private VLANs can be deployed in public-service segments where multiple public servers are available. Systems on the outside of a firewall should never be absolutely trusted by systems on the inside of a firewall. Such trust should be limited to specific protocols and should be authenticated by something other than an IP address where possible.

Port Redirection

A port redirection attack is a type of trust exploitation attack that uses a compromised host to pass traffic through a firewall that would otherwise be blocked.

For example, in Figure 4-12, the attacker gains access to Host A, which is in the publicly accessible *demilitarized zone (DMZ)*.

As soon as Host A is compromised, the attacker can install software to redirect traffic from the outside host directly to the inside host. Although neither communication violates the rules implemented in the firewall, the outside host has now achieved connectivity to the inside host through the port redirection process on the public services host. An example of a utility that can provide this type of access is netcat.

Port redirection can be mitigated primarily through the use of proper trust models, which are network-specific (as mentioned earlier). When a system is under attack, a host-based *intrusion detection system (IDS)* can help detect an attacker and prevent installation of such utilities on a host.

Figure 4-12   Port Redirection Example

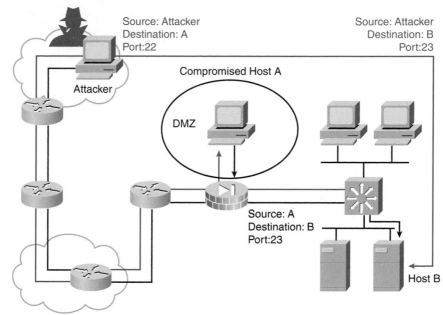

Man-in-the-Middle Attacks

A *man-in-the-middle (MITM)* attack is carried out by attackers who manage to position themselves between two legitimate hosts. The attacker may allow the normal transactions between hosts to occur and only periodically manipulate the conversation between the two.

An attacker can position himself between two hosts in many ways. The details of these methods are beyond the scope of this course, but a brief description of one popular method, the transparent proxy, will help illustrate the nature of MITM attacks.

In a transparent proxy attack, an attacker may catch a victim by using a phishing e-mail or by defacing a website. Then the URL of a legitimate website has the attacker's URL added to the front of it (prepended). For instance, http://www.legitimate.com becomes http://www.attacker.com/http://www.legitimate.com.

Figure 4-13 shows an MITM attack sequence of events:

1. When a victim requests a web page, the victim's host makes the request of the attacker's host.

2. The attacker's host receives the request and fetches the real page from the legitimate website.

3. The attacker can alter the legitimate web page and change the data however he wants.

4. The attacker forwards the requested page to the victim.

Figure 4-13   Man-in-the-Middle Attack Example

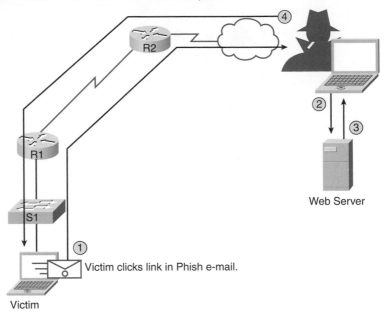

Other sorts of MITM attacks are potentially even more harmful. If attackers manage to get into a strategic position, they can steal information, hijack an ongoing session to gain access to private network resources, conduct *denial-of-service (DoS) attacks*, corrupt transmitted data, or introduce new information into network sessions.

MITM attacks may occur across either a WAN or LAN. WAN MITM attack mitigation is achieved by using virtual private network (VPN) tunnels, which allow the attacker to see only the encrypted, undecipherable text. LAN MITM attacks use such tools as ettercap and ARP poisoning. Most LAN MITM attacks usually can be mitigated by configuring port security on LAN switches.

DoS Attacks

Denial of service (DoS) is when an attacker disables or corrupts networks, systems, or services with the intent to deny services to intended users. DoS attacks involve rendering a system unavailable. This can be accomplished by physically disconnecting a system, crashing the system, or slowing it down to the point that it is unusable. But DoS can also be as simple as deleting or corrupting information. In most cases, performing the attack simply involves running a hack or script. For this reason, DoS attacks are the most feared.

In Figure 4-14, an attacker overwhelms a host and server by sending them multiple packets.

Figure 4-14 DoS Attack

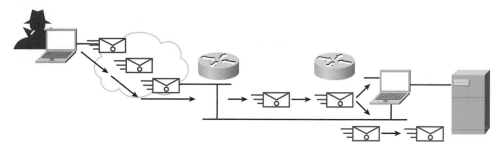

DoS attacks prevent authorized people from using a service by using up system resources.

DoS attacks are the most publicized form of attack and also are among the most difficult to eliminate. Even within the attacker community, DoS attacks are considered trivial and are not highly regarded, because they require so little effort to execute. But because of their ease of implementation and potentially significant damage, DoS attacks deserve special attention from security administrators.

DoS attacks take many forms. Ultimately, they prevent authorized people from using a service by consuming system resources. The following sections describe some examples of common DoS threats.

Ping-of-Death Attacks

The ping-of-death attack gained popularity back in the late 1990s. It took advantage of vulnerabilities in older operating systems. This attack modified the IP portion of a ping packet header to indicate that there was more data in the packet than there actually was. A ping normally is 64 to 84 bytes, whereas a ping of death could be up to 65,535 bytes. Sending a ping of this size may crash an older target computer. Most networks are no longer susceptible to this type of attack.

SYN Flood Attacks

A SYN flood attack exploits the TCP three-way handshake. It involves sending multiple SYN requests (more than 1000) to a targeted server. The server replies with the usual SYN-ACK response, but the malicious host never responds with the final ACK to complete the handshake. This ties up the server until it eventually runs out of resources and cannot respond to a valid host request.

In Figure 4-15, the attacker initiates thousands of TCP sessions with a server.

Figure 4-15   SYN Flood Attack

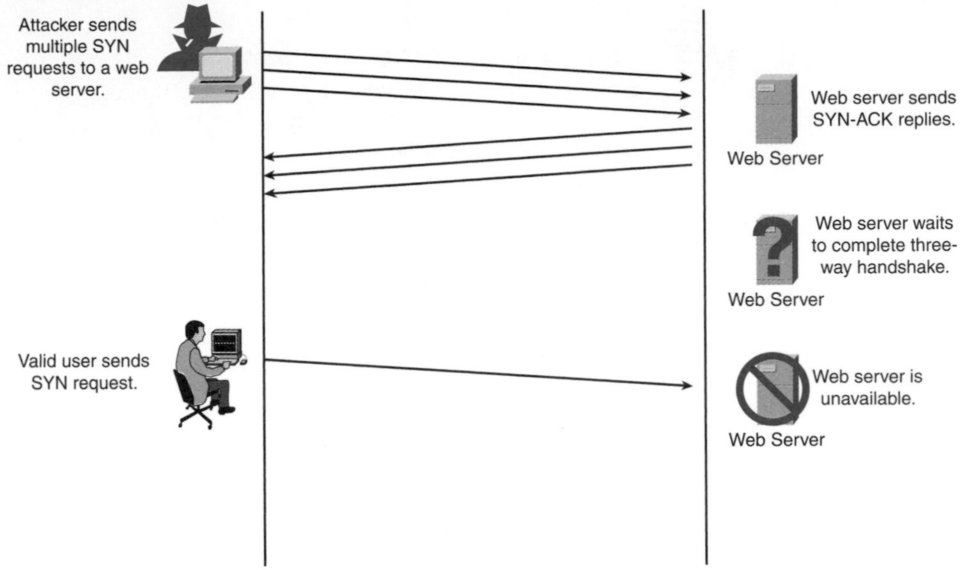

Although the figure shows only three arrows, assume that the attacker is sending thousands of TCP session requests. The server responds with the SYN-ACK response, but the attacker never completes the three-way handshake. In the meantime, the server uses resources to keep track of each individual session. Eventually the server crashes or runs out of resources and is unavailable when a legitimate user attempts to access it.

Other DoS Attacks

Other types of DoS attacks include the following:

- **E-mail bombs**: Programs send bulk e-mails to individuals, lists, or domains, monopolizing e-mail services.

- **Malicious applets**: These attacks are Java, JavaScript, or ActiveX programs that cause destruction or tie up computer resources.

DDoS Attacks

Distributed DoS (DDoS) attacks are designed to saturate network links with illegitimate data. This data can overwhelm an Internet link, causing legitimate traffic to be dropped. DDoS uses attack methods similar to standard DoS attacks but operates on a much larger scale. Typically, hundreds or thousands of attack points attempt to overwhelm a target.

Typically, a DDoS attack has three components, as shown in Figure 4-16:

- The client typically controls the handlers and agents that can be used to launch the attack.

- A handler is a compromised host that is running the attacker program. Each handler can control multiple agents.

- An agent is a compromised host that is running the attacker program. It is responsible for generating a stream of packets that is directed toward the intended victim.

Figure 4-16   DDoS Components

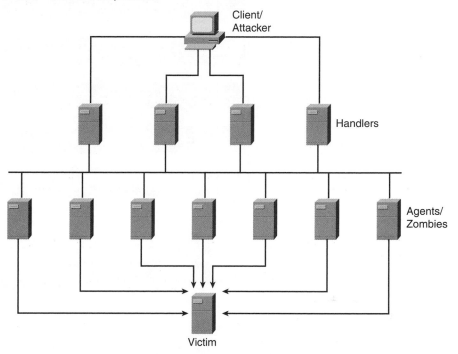

Examples of DDoS attacks include the following:

- Smurf attack

- Tribe Flood Network (TFN)

- Stacheldraht

- MyDoom

Smurf Attacks

The Smurf attack uses spoofed broadcast ping messages to flood a target system. In Figure 4-17, an attacker spoofs the router's IP address, 172.18.1.2, and sends an ICMP echo request to the broadcast network address 209.165.200.255. This makes every host on the 209.165.200.0 network simultaneously reply to the spoofed IP address.

Figure 4-17   Smurf Attack

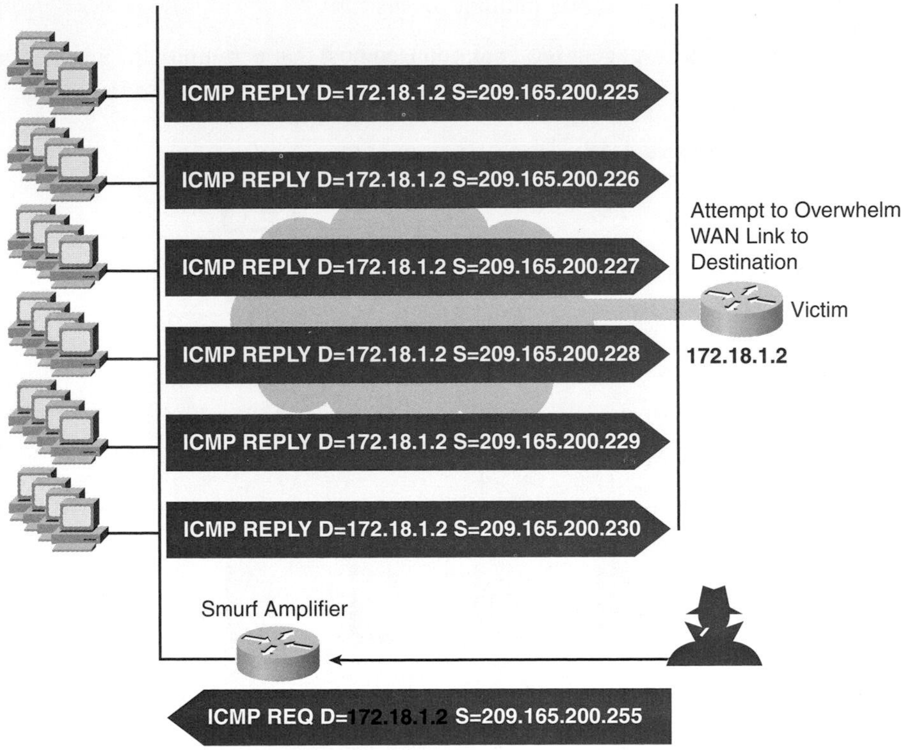

A router, called a Smurf amplifier, could perform the Layer 3 broadcast-to-Layer 2 broadcast function. Each host responds with an ICMP echo reply, multiplying the traffic by the number of hosts responding. On a multiaccess broadcast network, potentially hundreds of machines could reply to each echo packet.

For example, assume that the network has 100 hosts and that the attacker has a high-performance T1 link. The attacker sends a 768-kbps stream of ICMP echo request packets with a spoofed source address of the victim to the broadcast address of a targeted network (called a bounce site). These ping packets hit the bounce site on the broadcast network of 100 hosts, and each takes the packet and responds to it, creating 100 outbound ping replies. A total of 76.8 Mbps of bandwidth is used outbound from the bounce site after the traffic is multiplied. This is then sent to the victim or the spoofed source of the originating packets.

Turning off directed broadcast capability in the network infrastructure prevents the network from being used as a bounce site. Directed broadcast capability is now turned off by default beginning with Cisco IOS Software Release 12.0.

Mitigating DoS and DDoS Attacks

DoS and DDoS attacks can be mitigated by implementing special antispoof and anti-DoS access control lists. ISPs can also implement a traffic rate policy, limiting the amount of nonessential traffic that crosses network segments. A common example is to limit the amount of ICMP traffic that is allowed into a network, because this traffic is used only for diagnostic purposes.

Details of the operation of these attacks is beyond the scope of this course. For more information, refer to the *Networking Academy Network Security* courses.

Malicious Code Attacks

Malicious software can be inserted onto a host to damage or corrupt a system; replicate itself; or deny access to networks, systems, or services. Common names for this type of software are worms, viruses, and Trojan horses.

The following sections describe these attacks in greater detail.

Worms

As illustrated in Figure 4-18, a *worm* executes code and installs copies of itself in the memory of the infected computer, which can, in turn, infect other hosts.

Figure 4-18   Worm

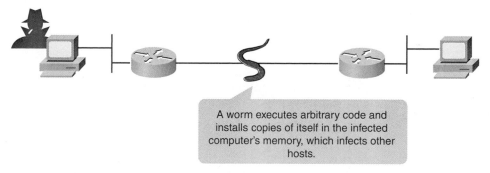

A worm executes arbitrary code and installs copies of itself in the infected computer's memory, which infects other hosts.

The anatomy of a worm attack is as follows:

1. **The enabling vulnerability**: A worm installs itself by exploiting known vulnerabilities in systems, such as naive end users who open unverified executable attachments in e-mails.

2. **Propagation mechanism**: After gaining access to a host, a worm copies itself to that host and then selects new targets.

3. **Payload**: As soon as a host is infected with a worm, the attacker has access to the host, often as a privileged user. Attackers can use a local exploit to escalate their privilege level to administrator.

Typically, worms are self-replicating programs that attack a system and try to exploit a specific vulnerability in the target. Upon successful exploitation of the vulnerability, the worm copies its program from the attacking host to the newly exploited system to restart the cycle. In January 2007, a worm infected the popular MySpace community. Unsuspecting users enabled propagation of the worm, which began to replicate itself on user sites with the defacement "w0rm.EricAndrew."

Worm attack mitigation requires diligence on the part of system and network administrators. Coordination between system administration, network engineering, and security operations personnel is critical in responding effectively to a worm incident. The following are the recommended steps for worm attack mitigation:

How To

Step 1.   **Containment**: Contain the spread of the worm in and within the network. Compartmentalize uninfected parts of the network.

Step 2.   **Inoculation**: Start patching all systems and, if possible, scanning for vulnerable systems.

Step 3.   **Quarantine**: Track down each infected machine inside the network. Disconnect, remove, or block infected machines from the network.

Step 4.   **Treatment**: Clean and patch each infected system. Some worms may require complete core system reinstallations to clean the system.

Viruses

A *virus* is malicious software that is attached to another program to execute a particular unwanted function on a workstation (see Figure 4-19). An example is a program that is attached to command.com (the primary interpreter for Windows systems) and that deletes certain files and infects any other versions of command.com that it can find.

Figure 4-19   Virus

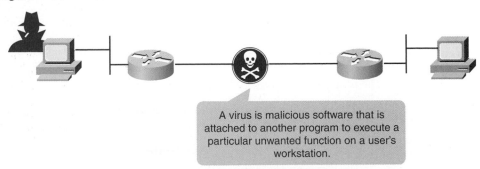

A virus is malicious software that is attached to another program to execute a particular unwanted function on a user's workstation.

A virus normally requires a delivery mechanism (a vector), such as a zip file or some other executable file attached to an e-mail, to carry the virus code from one system to another. The key element that distinguishes a computer worm from a computer virus is that human interaction is required to facilitate the spread of a virus.

These kinds of applications can be contained through the effective use of antivirus software at the user level, and potentially at the network level. Antivirus software can detect most viruses and many Trojan horse applications and prevent them from spreading in the network. Keeping up to date with the latest developments in these sorts of attacks can also lead to a more effective posture toward these attacks. Enterprises need to stay current with the latest versions of antivirus definitions, because new viruses or Trojan applications are continually being released.

Trojan Horse Attacks

As illustrated in Figure 4-20, a *Trojan horse* differs from a worm or virus only in that the entire application is written to look like something else, when in fact it is an attack tool. An example of a Trojan horse is a software application that runs a simple game on a workstation. While the user is occupied with the game, the Trojan horse mails a copy of itself to every address in the user's address book. The other users receive the game and play it, thereby spreading the Trojan horse to the addresses in each address book.

Figure 4-20   Trojan Horse

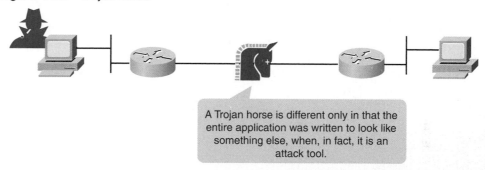

A Trojan horse is different only in that the entire application was written to look like something else, when, in fact, it is an attack tool.

Sub7, or subseven, is a common Trojan horse that installs a backdoor program on user systems. It is popular for both unstructured and structured attacks. As an unstructured threat, inexperienced attackers can use the program to cause the mouse cursor to disappear. As a structured threat, crackers can use the program to install keystroke loggers (programs that record all user keystrokes) to capture sensitive information.

As previously stated, Trojan horses can be contained through the effective use of antivirus software at the user level, and potentially at the network level.

General Mitigation Techniques

Now that you've explored the various types of network-related attacks, this section covers general mitigation techniques.

Host- and Server-Based Security

Host- and server-based security must be applied to all network systems. Mitigation techniques for these devices include

- Device hardening
- Antivirus software
- Personal firewalls
- Operating system patches

The following sections describe these mitigation techniques in greater detail.

Device Hardening

When a new operating system is installed on a device, the security settings are set to the default values. In most cases, this level of security is inadequate. You should take some simple steps that apply to most operating systems:

- Default usernames and passwords should be changed immediately.
- Access to system resources should be restricted to individuals who are authorized to use those resources.
- Any unnecessary services and applications should be turned off and uninstalled when possible.
- Configure system logging and tracking.

Antivirus Software

Install host antivirus software to protect against known viruses. Antivirus software can detect most viruses and many Trojan horse applications and prevent them from spreading in the network.

Antivirus software does this in two ways:

- It scans files, comparing their contents to known virus signatures. Matches are flagged in a manner defined by the end user.
- It monitors suspicious processes running on a host that might indicate infection. This monitoring may include data captures, port monitoring, and other methods.

Most commercial antivirus software uses both of these approaches. Keep in mind that antivirus software is good only if the definitions are up to date. Update antivirus software vigilantly, as shown in Figure 4-21.

Figure 4-21 Update Antivirus Definitions

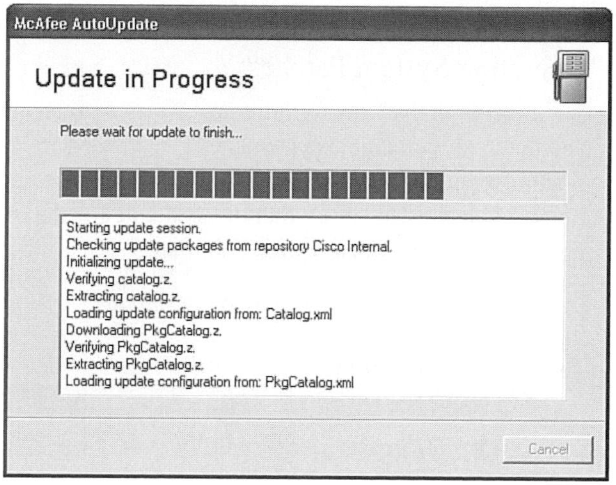

Personal Firewalls

PCs connected to the Internet through a dialup connection, DSL, or cable modem are as vulnerable as corporate networks. Personal firewalls reside on the user's PC and attempt to prevent attacks. Personal firewalls are not designed for LAN implementations when compared to appliance-based or server-based firewalls, and they may prevent network access if installed with other networking clients, services, protocols, or adapters. Figure 4-22 shows the main screen of Norton Personal Firewall by Symantec.

Figure 4-22 Norton Personal Firewall

Other personal firewall software vendors include McAfee and Zone Labs.

Operating System Patches

The most effective way to mitigate a worm and its variants is to download security updates and patch all vulnerable systems. OS patches typically are downloaded from the operating system vendor, such as Microsoft or Apple. However, Linux is available in several distributions or flavors. Updates would be available for the specific Linux distribution or from reputable links in the open-source community.

Figure 4-23 shows Microsoft Windows updates being downloaded.

Figure 4-23   Installing OS Patches

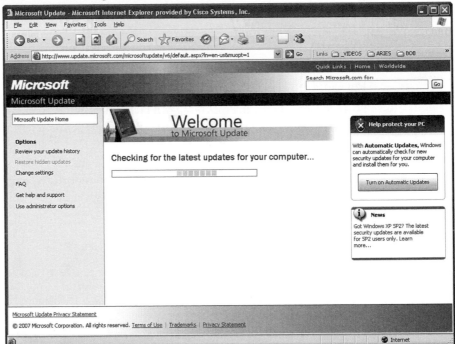

It is critical to protect network hosts, such as workstation PCs and servers. These hosts need to be secured as they are added to the network, and they should be updated with security patches as these updates become available. Additional steps can be taken to secure these hosts. Antivirus, firewall, and intrusion detection are valuable tools that can be used to secure network hosts. Because many business resources may be contained on a single file server, it is especially important for servers to be accessible and available.

Updating numerous systems is difficult with uncontrolled user systems in the local network, and it's even more troublesome if these systems are remotely connected to the network via a VPN or remote-access server (RAS). Administering numerous systems involves creating a standard software image (operating system and accredited applications that are authorized for use on deployed client systems) that is deployed on new or upgraded systems. These images may not contain the latest patches, and the process of continually rebuilding the image to integrate the latest patch may quickly become administratively time-consuming. Pushing patches out to all systems requires that those systems be connected in some way to the network, which may not be possible.

One solution to managing critical security patches is to create a central patch server that all systems must communicate with after a set period of time. Any patches that are not applied to a host are automatically downloaded from the patch server and installed without user intervention. This solution could be enforced using the Cisco NAC appliance.

In addition to performing security updates from the OS vendor, you can simplify the process of determining which devices can be exploited by using security auditing tools that look for vulnerabilities.

Intrusion Detection and Prevention

Intrusion detection systems (IDS) detect attacks against a network and send logs to a management console. ***Intrusion prevention systems (IPS)*** prevent attacks against the network and should provide the following active defense mechanisms in addition to detection:

- **Prevention**: Stops the detected attack from executing.
- **Reaction**: Immunizes the system from future attacks from a malicious source.

Either technology can be implemented at the network level or host level, or both for maximum protection.

Host-Based Intrusion Detection Systems

Depending on the vendor, host-based intrusion typically is implemented as one of the following:

- Passive technology, which was the first-generation technology, is called a host-based intrusion detection system (HIDS). HIDS sends logs to a management console after the attack has occurred and the damage is done.
- Inline technology, called a host-based intrusion prevention system (HIPS), actually stops the attack, prevents damage, and blocks the propagation of worms and viruses.

Active detection can be set to shut down the network connection or to stop impacted services automatically. Corrective action can be taken immediately. Cisco provides HIPS using the Cisco Security Agent software.

HIPS software must be installed on each host, either the server or desktop, to monitor activity performed on and against the host. This software is called agent software. It performs intrusion detection analysis and prevention. Agent software also sends logs and alerts to a centralized management/policy server.

The advantage of HIPS is that it can monitor operating system processes and protect critical system resources, including files that may exist only on that specific host. This means it can notify network managers when some external process tries to modify a system file in a way that may include a hidden back door program.

Figure 4-24 shows a typical HIPS deployment using Cisco Security Agent.

Figure 4-24   Cisco Security Agent

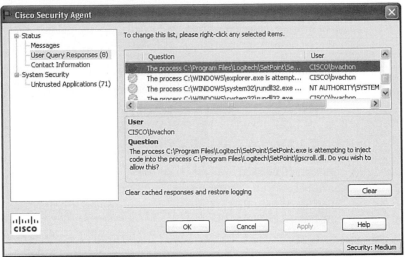

Agents are installed on publicly accessible servers and corporate mail and application servers. The agent reports events to a central console server located inside the corporate firewall. As an alternative, agents on the host can send logs as e-mail to an administrator.

Common Security Appliances and Applications

Security is a top consideration whenever you plan a network. In the past, the one device that would come to mind for network security was the firewall. A firewall by itself is no longer adequate for securing a network. An integrated approach involving a firewall, intrusion prevention, and a VPN may be necessary.

An integrated approach to security, and the necessary devices to make it happen, follows these building blocks:

- **Threat control**: Regulates network access, isolates infected systems, prevents intrusions, and protects assets by counteracting malicious traffic, such as worms and viruses. Devices and applications that provide threat control solutions include the following:
  - Cisco ASA 5500 series Adaptive Security Appliances (ASA)
  - Integrated Services Routers (ISR)

- Network Admission Control (NAC)

- Cisco Security Agent for Desktops

- Cisco Intrusion Prevention Systems (IPS)

Figure 4-25 shows the various security appliances.

Figure 4-25   Common Security Appliances

Cisco ASA 5500

Cisco NAC Appliance

Cisco IPS 4200 Series Sensors

- **Secure communications**: Secures network endpoints with a VPN. The devices that allow an organization to deploy a VPN are Cisco ISR routers with a Cisco IOS VPN solution, and the Cisco 5500 ASA and Cisco Catalyst 6500 switches.

- **Network admission control**: Provides a roles-based method of preventing unauthorized access to a network. Cisco offers a NAC appliance. In-depth coverage of these appliances is beyond the scope of this course; however, the following sections provide a brief overview of each. Refer to the *CCNP: Implementing Secure Converged Wide-Area Networks* course and the *Network Security 1 and 2* course for more information.

Cisco IOS Software on Cisco Integrated Services Routers (ISR)

Cisco provides many of the required security measures for customers within Cisco IOS software. Cisco IOS software provides built-in Cisco IOS Firewall, IPsec, SSL VPN, and IPS services.

Cisco ASA 5500 Series Adaptive Security Appliance

At one time, the PIX firewall was the one device that a secure network would deploy. The PIX has evolved into a platform that integrates many different security features, called the Cisco Adaptive Security Appliance (ASA). The Cisco ASA integrates firewall, voice security, SSL and IPsec VPN, IPS, and content security services in one device.

Cisco IPS 4200 Series Sensors

For larger networks, an inline intrusion prevention system is provided by the Cisco IPS 4200 series sensors. This sensor identifies, classifies, and stops malicious traffic on the network.

Cisco NAC Appliance

The Cisco NAC appliance uses the network infrastructure to enforce security policy compliance on all devices seeking to access network computing resources.

Cisco Security Agent (CSA)

Cisco Security Agent software provides threat protection capabilities for server, desktop, and point-of-service (POS) computing systems. CSA defends these systems against targeted attacks, data leakage, spyware, rootkits, and day-zero attacks.

The Network Security Wheel

Most security incidents occur because system administrators do not implement available countermeasures, and attackers or disgruntled employees exploit the oversight. Therefore, the issue is not just one of confirming that a technical vulnerability exists and finding a countermeasure that works. It is also critical to verify that the countermeasure is in place and working properly.

To assist with the compliance of a security policy, the *Network Security Wheel*, a continuous process, has proven to be an effective approach. Figure 4-26 illustrates the Security Wheel.

Figure 4-26   Network Security Wheel

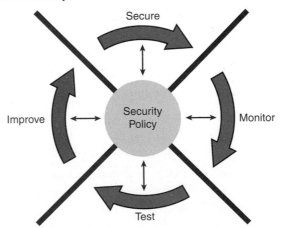

The Network Security Wheel promotes retesting and reapplying updated security measures on a continuous basis. To begin the Network Security Wheel process, first develop a security policy that enables the application of security measures. A security policy establishes the following:

- Identifies the organization's security objectives.

- Documents the resources to be protected.

- Identifies the network infrastructure with current maps and inventories.

- Identifies the critical resources that need to be protected, such as research and development, finance, and human resources. This is called a risk analysis.

The security policy is the hub upon which the four steps of the Security Wheel are based:

Step 1.   Secure

Step 2.   Monitor

Step 3.   Test

Step 4.   Improve

Step 1: Secure

Secure the network by applying the security policy and implementing the following security solutions:

- **Threat defense**: Implement device-hardening techniques, antivirus, spyware tools.

- **Intrusion prevention systems**: Deploy at the network and host level to actively stop malicious traffic.

- **Vulnerability patching**: Apply OS fixes or measures to stop the exploitation of known vulnerabilities.

- **Disable unnecessary services**: The fewer services that are enabled, the harder it is for attackers to gain access.

- **Stateful inspection and packet filtering**: Filter network traffic to allow only valid traffic and services.

Note

Stateful inspection is when a firewall keeps information on the state of a connection in a state table. By doing this, it can recognize changes in the connection that could mean an attacker is attempting to hijack a session or otherwise manipulate a connection.

The following security connectivity solutions must also be considered:

- **VPNs**: Encrypt network traffic to prevent unwanted disclosure to unauthorized or malicious individuals. This is especially important when traversing the public Internet.

- **Trust and identity**: Implement tight constraints on trust levels within a network. For example, systems on the inside of a firewall should never completely trust systems on the outside of a firewall.

- **Authentication**: Give access to authorized users only. One example of this is using one-time passwords.

- **Policy enforcement**: Ensure that users and end devices are in compliance with the corporate policy.

Step 2: Monitor

Monitoring security involves both active and passive methods of detecting security violations. The most commonly used active method is to audit host-level log files. Most operating systems include auditing functionality. System administrators must ensure that all sensitive and vital hosts on the network are being audited. They must also take the time to check and interpret the log file entries.

Passive methods include using IDS devices to automatically detect intrusion. This method requires less attention from network security administrators than active methods. These systems can detect security violations in real time and can be configured to automatically respond before an intruder does any damage.

An added benefit of network monitoring is verifying that the security measures implemented in Step 1 of the Security Wheel have been configured and are working properly.

Step 3: Test

In the testing phase of the Security Wheel, the security measures are proactively tested. Specifically, the functionality of the security solutions implemented in Step 1 and the system auditing and intrusion detection methods implemented in Step 2 are verified. Vulnerability assessment tools such as SATAN, Nessus, and Nmap are useful for periodically testing the network security measures at the network and host level.

Step 4: Improve

The improvement phase of the Security Wheel involves analyzing the data collected during the monitoring and testing phases. This analysis contributes to developing and implementing improvement mechanisms that augment the security policy and results in adding items to Step 1.

With the information collected from the monitoring and testing phases, IDSs can be used to implement improvements to the security. The security policy should be adjusted as new security vulnerabilities and risks are discovered.

To keep a network as secure as possible, the cycle of the Security Wheel must be continually repeated, because new network vulnerabilities and risks are emerging every day.

The Enterprise Security Policy

As defined in RFC 2196, *Site Security Handbook*:

> "A security policy is a formal statement of the rules by which people who are given access to an organization's technology and information assets must abide."

A security policy is a set of guidelines established to safeguard the network from attacks, from both inside and outside a company. Forming a policy starts with asking questions of the organization's management:

- How does the network help the organization achieve its vision, mission, and strategic plan?

- What implications do business requirements have for network security?

- How do those business requirements get translated into the purchase of specialized equipment and the configurations loaded onto devices?

A security policy benefits an organization in the following ways:

- It provides a means to audit existing network security and compare the requirements to what is in place.

- It helps you plan security improvements, including equipment, software, and procedures.

- It defines the roles and responsibilities of the company executives, administrators, and users.

- It defines which network and computer activities are and are not allowed.

- It defines a process for handling network security incidents.

- It enables global network security implementation and enforcement by acting as a standard between sites.

- It creates a basis for legal action if necessary.

A security policy is a living document, meaning that the document is continuously updated as technology and employee requirements change. It acts as a bridge between management objectives and specific security requirements.

Functions of a Security Policy

A comprehensive security policy fulfills these essential functions:

- It protects people and information.

- It sets the rules for expected behavior by users, system administrators, management, and security personnel.

- It authorizes security personnel to monitor, probe, and investigate.

- It defines and authorizes the consequences of violations.

The security policy is for everyone, including employees, contractors, suppliers, and customers who have access to the network. However, the security policy should treat each of these groups differently. Each group should be shown only the portion of the policy appropriate to their work and level of access to the network.

For example, an explanation for why something is being done is not always necessary. You can assume that the technical staff already know why a particular requirement is included. Managers are not likely to be interested in the technical aspects of a particular requirement; they may want just a high-level overview or the principle supporting the requirement. However, when end users know why a particular security control has been included, they are more likely to comply with the policy. Therefore, one document is not likely to meet the needs of the entire audience in a large organization.

Components of a Security Policy

The SANS Institute (*http://www.sans.org*) provides guidelines developed in cooperation with a number of industry leaders, including Cisco, for developing comprehensive security policies for organizations large and small. Not all organizations need all these policies.

The following are general security policies that an organization may invoke:

- **Statement of authority and scope**: Defines who in the organization sponsors the security policy, who is responsible for implementing it, and what areas the policy covers.

- **Acceptable use policy (AUP)**: Defines the acceptable use of equipment and computing services, and the appropriate employee security measures to protect the organization's corporate resources and proprietary information.

- **Identification and authentication policy**: Defines which technologies the company uses to ensure that only authorized personnel have access to its data.

- **Password policy**: Defines the standards for creating, protecting, and changing strong passwords.

- **Internet access policy**: Defines what the company will and will not tolerate with respect to the use of its Internet connectivity by employees and guests.

- **Campus access policy**: Defines acceptable use of campus technology resources by employees and guests.

- **Remote-access policy**: Defines how remote users can use the company's remote-access infrastructure.

- **Incident-handling procedure**: Specifies who will respond to security incidents and how they will be handled.

In addition to these key security policy sections, some others may be necessary in certain organizations:

- **Account access request policy**: Formalizes the account and access request process within the organization. Users and system administrators who bypass the standard processes for account and access requests can lead to legal action against the organization.

- **Acquisition assessment policy**: Defines the responsibilities for corporate acquisitions and defines the minimum requirements of an acquisition assessment that the information security group must complete.

- **Audit policy**: Defines audit policies to ensure the integrity of information and resources. This includes a process to investigate incidents, ensure conformance to security policies, and monitor user and system activity where appropriate.

- **Information sensitivity policy**: Defines the requirements for classifying and securing information in a manner appropriate to its sensitivity level.

- **Risk assessment policy**: Defines the requirements and provides the authority for the information security team to identify, assess, and remediate risks to the information infrastructure associated with conducting business.

- **Global web server policy**: Defines the standards required by all web hosts.

With the extensive use of e-mail, an organization may also want policies specifically related to e-mail, such as the following:

- **Automatically forwarded e-mail policy**: Documents the policy restricting automatic e-mail forwarding to an external destination without prior approval from the appropriate manager or director.

- **E-mail policy**: Defines content standards to keep from tarnishing the organization's public image.

- **Spam policy**: Defines how spam should be reported and treated.

Remote-access policies might include the following:

- **Dial-in access policy**: Defines the appropriate dial-in access and its use by authorized personnel.

- **VPN security policy**: Defines the requirements for VPN connections to the organization's network.

It should be noted that users who defy or violate the rules in a security policy may be subject to disciplinary action, up to and including termination of employment.

Securing Cisco Routers

You know that you can build a LAN by connecting devices with basic Layer 2 LAN switches. You can then use a router to route traffic between different networks based on Layer 3 IP addresses. Routers interconnect different networks.

Router Security Issues

Router security is a critical element in any security deployment. Routers are definite targets for network attackers. If an attacker can compromise and access a router, it can be a potential aid to him or her. Knowing the roles that routers fulfill in the network helps you understand their vulnerabilities.

The Role of Routers in Network Security

Routers fulfill the following roles, as shown in Figure 4-27:

- They advertise networks and filter who can use them.

- They provide access to network segments and subnetworks.

Figure 4-27   Role of Routers in Network Security

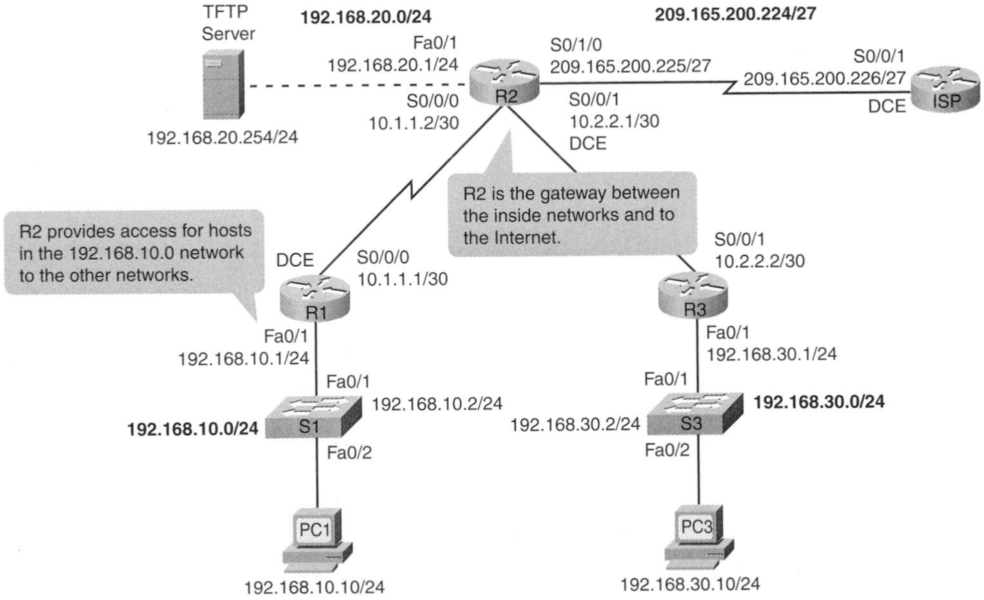

Routers Are Targets

Because routers provide gateways to other networks, they are obvious targets and are subject to a variety of attacks, as shown in Figure 4-28.

Figure 4-28   Routers Are Targets

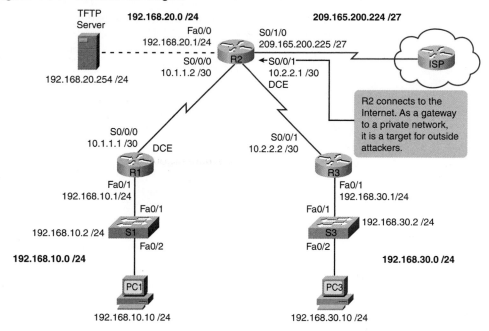

The following are examples of various security problems that can occur with a compromised router:

- Compromising the access control can expose network configuration details, thereby facilitating attacks against other network components.

- Compromising the route tables can reduce performance, deny network communication services, and expose sensitive data by rerouting information to a compromised host.

- Misconfiguring a router traffic filter can expose internal network components to scans and attacks, making it easier for attackers to avoid detection.

Attackers can compromise routers in different ways, so network administrators have no single approach to combat them. The ways in which routers are compromised are similar to the types of attacks you learned about earlier in this chapter, including trust exploitation attacks, IP spoofing, session hijacking, and MITM attacks.

Note

This section focuses on securing routers. Most of the best practices discussed can also be used to secure switches. However, this section does not cover Layer 2 threats, such as MAC address flooding attacks and STP attacks, because these are covered in *CCNA Exploration: LAN Switching and Wireless*.

Securing Your Network

Securing routers at the network perimeter is an important first step in securing the network, as shown in Figure 4-29.

Figure 4-29   Securing Your Network

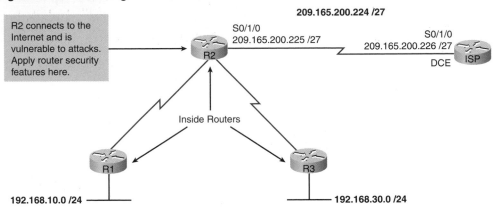

Think about router security in terms of these categories:

- **Physical security**: To provide physical security, locate the router in a locked room or locked cabinet that is accessible to only authorized personnel. It should also be free of any electrostatic or magnetic interference and should have controls for temperature and humidity. To reduce the possibility of DoS due to a power failure, install an uninterruptible power supply (UPS), and keep spare components available.

  Physical devices such as switches and CSUs/DSUs connected to the router should be stored in a locked facility, or they should remain in the possession of a trustworthy individual so that they are not compromised. A device that is left in the open could have Trojans or some other sort of executable file stored on it.

- **Update the router whenever advisable**: Give the router the maximum amount of memory possible. Availability of memory can help protect against some DoS attacks while supporting the widest range of security services.

  The security features in an operating system evolve over time. However, the latest version of an operating system may not be the most stable version available. To get the best security performance from your operating system, use the latest stable release that meets your network's feature requirements.

- **Back up the router configuration and IOS**: Always have a backup copy of a configuration and IOS on hand in case a router fails. Keep a secure copy of the router operating system image and router configuration file on a CD or other storage device. Otherwise, a *TFTP server* is commonly used for backup purposes.

- **Harden the router to eliminate the potential abuse of unused ports and services**: Harden the router to make it as secure as possible. A router has many services enabled by default. Many of these services are unnecessary and may be used by an attacker for information gathering or exploitation. You should harden your router configuration by disabling unnecessary services.

Applying Cisco IOS Security Features to Routers

Before you configure security features on a router, you need a plan for all the Cisco IOS security configuration steps. The following are the steps to safeguard a router:

Step 1. Manage router security.

Step 2. Secure remote administrative access to routers.

Step 3. Log router activity.

Step 4. Secure vulnerable router services and interfaces.

Step 5. Secure routing protocols.

Step 6. Control and filter network traffic.

The first five steps are discussed in this chapter. Step 6 is accomplished by using access control lists (ACL). ACLs are a critical security feature and must be configured to control and filter network traffic. Chapter 5, "ACLs," discusses ACLs in detail.

Steps 1, 2, and 3 are covered in the following sections. Step 4 is covered in the section "Securing Router Network Services." Step 5 is covered in the section "Routing Protocol Authentication Overview." Step 6 is covered in the next chapter.

Step 1 of Safeguarding a Router: Manage Router Security

One of the elements of basic router security is configuring passwords. A strong password is a fundamental element of controlling secure access to a router. For this reason, strong passwords should always be configured.

Good password practices include the following:

- Do not write down passwords and leave them in obvious places such as on your desk or monitor.

- Avoid dictionary words, names, phone numbers, and dates. Using dictionary words makes passwords vulnerable to dictionary attacks.

- Combine letters, numbers, and symbols. Include at least one lowercase letter, uppercase letter, digit, and special character.

- Deliberately misspell a password. For example, **Smith** can be spelled **Smyth** or can also include a number, such as **5mYth**. Another example could be **Security** spelled as **5ecur1ty**.

- Make passwords lengthy. The best practice is to have a minimum of eight characters. You can enforce the minimum length using a feature that is available on Cisco IOS routers, discussed later in this section.

- Change passwords as often as possible. You should have a policy defining when and how often the passwords must be changed. Changing passwords frequently provides two advantages. This practice limits the window of opportunity in which a hacker can crack a password and limits the window of exposure after a password has been compromised.

Note

Spaces before a password are ignored, but all spaces after the first character are not ignored.

Passphrases

A recommended method of creating strong, complex passwords is to use *passphrases* and then use either the entire phrase or its acronym as your password. A passphrase is basically a sentence or phrase that serves as a more secure password. Make sure that the phrase is long enough to be hard to guess but also is easy to remember and type accurately.

Use a sentence, quote from a book, or song lyric that you can easily remember as the basis of your strong password or passphrase. The following are examples of using the acronym of passphrases as passwords:

- "All people seem to need data processing" would translate to **Apstndp**.

- "My favorite spy is James Bond 007" would translate to **MfsiJB007**.

- "It was the best of times, it was the worst of times" would translate to **Iwtbotiwtwot**.

- "Fly me to the moon. And let me play among the stars" would translate to **Fmttm.Almpats**.

Securing Router Passwords

By default, Cisco IOS software leaves most passwords in plain text when they are entered on a router. This is not secure, because anyone walking behind you when you are looking at a router configuration could snoop over your shoulder and see the passwords.

This applies to the **line console**, **line vty**, **enable password**, and **username** *username* **password** *password* commands.

Plaintext passwords are identified as being type 0. For example, in Example 4-1, the 0 displayed in the running configuration indicates that the username password is unencrypted and therefore is not hidden.

Example 4-1   Default Password Encryption

```
R1(config)# username Student password cisco123
R1(config)# do show run | include username
username Student password 0 cisco123
R1(config)#
```

For security reasons, all passwords should be encrypted in a configuration file. To do so, Cisco IOS provides two password protection schemes:

- **Simple encryption, called a Type 7 scheme**: Uses the Cisco-defined encryption algorithm and hides the password using a simple encryption algorithm.

- **Complex encryption, called a Type 5 scheme**: Uses a more secure MD5 hash.

Simple Type 7 Encryption

Type 7 encryption can be used by the **enable password**, **username**, and line **password** commands, including VTY, line console, and AUX port. It does not offer much protection, because it only hides the password using a simple encryption algorithm. Although not as secure as Type 5 encryption, it is still better than no encryption.

The **service password-encryption** command prevents all plaintext passwords that are displayed on the screen from being readable. To encrypt passwords using Type 7 encryption, use the **service password-encryption** global configuration command, as shown in Example 4-2.

Example 4-2   Encrypting All Passwords

```
R1(config)# service password-encryption
R1(config)# do show run | include username

username Student password 7 03075218050061
R1(config)#
```

Notice that the username password has been assigned as Type 7 to indicate that the password is now hidden.

In Figure 4-30, router R1 is being configured to encrypt all passwords. The partial output in Example 4-3 shows that the line console password is now hidden.

Figure 4-30   service password-encryption Command

Administrator encrypts all passwords in the configuration file.

Example 4-3   Verifying Password Encryption

```
R1# show running-config

<Output omitted>
line con 0
password 7 0956F57A109A
<Output omitted>
```

Complex Type 5 Encryption

Cisco recommends that Type 5 encryption be used instead of Type 7 whenever possible. MD5 encryption is a strong encryption method and therefore should be used whenever possible.

It is configured by replacing the keyword **password** with **secret**. For example, the **enable password** and **username password** commands can be rendered more secure by instead using the **enable secret** and **username secret** commands.

Protect the Enable Password

To protect the privileged EXEC level as much as possible, always configure the **enable secret** command instead of using the **enable password** command. Also make sure that the secret password is unique and does not match any other user password.

A router always uses the secret password over the enable password. For this reason, the **enable password** command should never be configured, because it may give away a system password.

For example, router R1 in Figure 4-31 is configured to use the Type 5 enable password.

Figure 4-31   enable secret Command

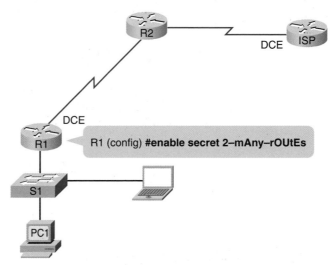

Administrator encrypts a Type 5 (MD5 hash) password.

Example 4-4 also includes the **no enable password** command to remove the existing, unencrypted enable password.

Example 4-4   Removing the Existing Enable Password

```
R1(config)# enable secret 2-mAny-rOUtEs
R1(config)# no enable password
R1(config)#
```

Note

If you forget the privileged EXEC password, you will have to perform the *password recovery* procedure. This procedure is covered later in this chapter.

Protect Username Passwords

The local database usernames should also be protected by configuring the **username** *username* **secret** *password* global configuration command, as shown in Example 4-5.

Example 4-5   Configuring an Encrypted Username

```
R1(config)# username Student secret cisco123
R1(config)# do show run | include username

username Student secret 5 $1$0/dp$A3SCbDWjr1MFHy3FByDLi0
R1(config)#
```

Note

A username cannot have a user password and a user secret password. If the username has already been configured using the **username** *username* **password** command, first it must be removed using the **no username** *username* **password** command.

Note

Some processes may not be able to use Type 5 encrypted passwords. For example, PAP and CHAP require cleartext passwords and cannot use MD5 encrypted passwords.

Configure a Minimum Password Length

Cisco IOS Software Release 12.3(1) and later allow administrators to set the minimum character length for all router passwords using the **security passwords min-length** global configuration command, as shown in Figure 4-32.

Figure 4-32   security passwords min-length Command

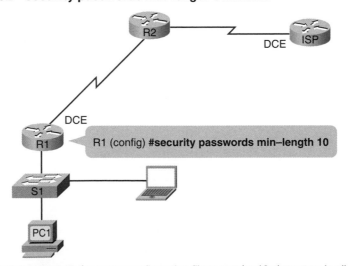

R1 (config) #security passwords min–length 10

Administrator sets the router configuration file to require 10 characters in all passwords.

This command provides enhanced security access to the router by allowing you to specify a minimum password length, eliminating common passwords that are prevalent on most networks, such as "lab" and "cisco."

This command affects any new user passwords, enable passwords and secrets, and line passwords created after the command was executed. This command does not affect existing router passwords. Example 4-6 displays a scenario in which the minimum-length password is set to ten characters. It also shows what happens when you attempt to configure a shorter password.

Example 4-6   Configuring the Minimum Password Length

```
R1(config)# security passwords min-length ?

  <0-16>  Minimum length of all user/enable passwords

R1(config)# security passwords min-length 10
R1(config)# username Student secret cisco123

% Password too short - must be at least 10 characters. Password configuration
  failed
R1(config)# username Student secret cisco12345
R1(config)#
```

Step 2 of Safeguarding a Router: Secure Remote Administrative Access to Routers

Network administrators can connect to a router or switch locally using the console port or remotely using Telnet, as shown in Figure 4-33.

Local access through the console port is the most secure way for an administrator to connect to a device to manage it. However, as companies get bigger and the number of routers and switches in the network increases, the administrator workload to physically connect to all devices may become overwhelming.

Remote administrative access is more convenient than local access for administrators who have many devices to manage. However, if it is not implemented securely, an attacker could collect valuable confidential information.

For example, implementing remote administrative access using Telnet can be very insecure, because Telnet forwards all network traffic in clear text. An attacker could capture network traffic while an administrator is logged in remotely to a router and sniff the administrator passwords or router configuration information. Therefore, remote administrative access must be configured with additional security precautions.

Figure 4-33   Administrative Access to Routers

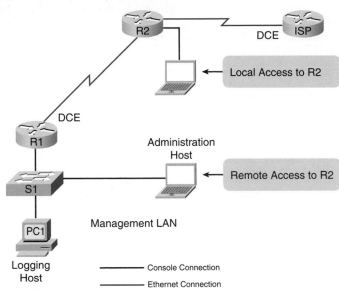

To secure administrative access to routers and switches, first you secure the administrative lines (VTY, AUX), and then you configure the network device to encrypt traffic in an SSH tunnel.

Remote Administrative Access with Telnet and SSH

Having remote access to network devices is critical to effectively managing a network. Remote administrative access typically involves allowing Telnet, *Secure Shell (SSH)*, HTTP, secure HTTP (HTTPS), or SNMP connections to the router from an administrative host on the same internetwork.

Administrative traffic must be protected at all times. If remote administrative access is required, your options are as follows:

- Establish a dedicated management network. The management network should include only identified administrative hosts and connections to infrastructure devices. This typically is accomplished using a management VLAN. However, an additional physical network could be used to connect the devices as well.

- You could also encrypt all traffic between the administrator computer and the router.

An access control list (ACL) should also be configured to allow only the identified administrative hosts and protocol to access the router. For example, if an administrative host had a static IP address assigned, you could only permit the administrative host IP address to establish an SSH connection to the routers and switches in the network.

Also remember that remote access applies not only to the router's VTY line, but also to the auxiliary (AUX) port and the TTY lines, as shown in Figure 4-34.

Figure 4-34   Secure All VTY, AUX, and TTY Lines

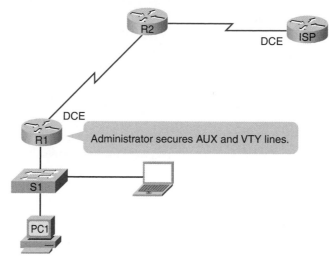

The AUX port and TTY lines provide asynchronous access to a router using a modem. Although they are less common than they once were, they still exist in some installations to provide remote access to a misconfigured router. Securing these ports is as important as securing local terminal ports.

Administrators should make sure that logins on all lines are controlled using an authentication mechanism, even on devices that are supposed to be inaccessible from untrusted networks. You can prevent logins on any line by configuring the router using the **login** command without a password configured. This is the default configuration for VTYs, but not for TTYs and the AUX port. Therefore, if these lines are not required, ensure that they are configured with the **no password** and **login** command combination, as shown in Example 4-7.

Example 4-7   Securing the Unused AUX Port

```
R1(config)# line aux 0
R1(config-line)# no password
R1(config-line)# login

% Login disabled on line 1, until 'password' is set
R1(config-line)# exit
R1(config)#
```

Controlling VTYs

By default, all VTY lines are configured to accept any type of remote connection. For security reasons, VTY lines should be configured to accept connections with only the protocols actually needed. This is done with the **transport input** command. For example, a VTY that was expected to receive only Telnet sessions would be configured with **transport input telnet**, and a VTY permitting both Telnet and SSH sessions would have **transport input telnet ssh** configured.

For example, refer to Examples 4-8 and 4-9.

In Example 4-8, the VTY is specifically configured to accept only Telnet and SSH connections.

Example 4-8   Permitting Required Protocols

```
R1(config)# line vty 0 4
R1(config-line)# no transport input
R1(config-line)# transport input telnet ssh
R1(config-line)# exit
```

SSH access is strongly recommended instead of Telnet access. If the Cisco IOS image on the device supports SSH, it is advisable to disable all incoming remote-access protocols and enable only SSH. Example 4-9 configures the VTY to accept only SSH connections.

Example 4-9   Permitting Only SSH

```
R1(config)# line vty 0 4
R1(config-line)# no transport input
R1(config-line)# transport input ssh
R1(config-line)# exit
```

A Cisco IOS device has a limited number of VTY lines, usually five. When all the VTYs are in use, no more additional remote connections can be established. This creates an opportunity for a DoS attack. If an attacker can open remote sessions to all the VTYs on the system, the legitimate administrator may not be able to log in. The attacker does not have to log in to do this. The sessions can simply be left at the login prompt.

One way of reducing this exposure is to configure the last VTY line to accept connections from only a single, specific administrative workstation, whereas the other VTYs can accept connections from any address in a corporate network. This ensures that at least one VTY line is available to the administrator. To implement this, ACLs, along with the **ip access-class** command on the last VTY line, must be configured. This implementation is discussed in Chapter 5.

Another useful tactic is to configure VTY timeouts using the **exec-timeout** command. This prevents an idle session from consuming the VTY indefinitely. Although its effectiveness against deliberate attacks is relatively limited, it provides some protection against sessions accidentally left idle. Similarly, enabling TCP keepalives on incoming connections by using the **service tcp-keepalives-in** global configuration command can help guard against both malicious attacks and orphaned sessions caused by remote system crashes.

Example 4-10 configures the executive timeout to three minutes and enables TCP keepalives.

Example 4-10   Securely Configuring a VTY Connection

```
R1(config)# line vty 0 4
R1(config-line)# exec-timeout 3
R1(config-line)# exit
R1(config)# service tcp-keepalives-in
```

Implementing SSH to Secure Remote Administrative Access

Traditionally, remote administrative access on routers was configured using Telnet on TCP port 23; however, Telnet was developed when security was not the issue that it is today. For this reason, all Telnet traffic is still forwarded in plain text.

SSH has replaced Telnet as the best practice for providing remote router administration with connections that support strong privacy and session integrity. SSH uses port TCP 22 and provides functionality that is similar to that of an outbound Telnet connection, except that the connection is encrypted. With authentication and encryption, SSH allows for secure communications over an insecure network, as shown in Figure 4-35.

Figure 4-35   Secure VTY Lines Using SSH

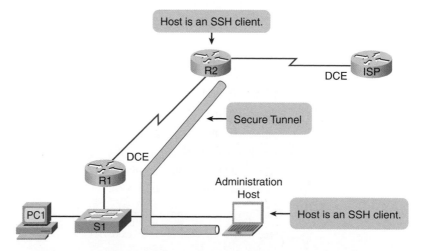

Not all Cisco IOS images support SSH. Only cryptographic images do. Typically, these images have k8 or k9 in their image names. Image names are discussed in the "Secure Router Management" section of Chapter 4.

The SSH terminal-line access feature enables administrators to configure routers with secure access and perform the following tasks:

- Connect to a router that has multiple terminal lines connected to consoles or serial ports of other routers, switches, and devices.

- Simplify connectivity to a router from anywhere by securely connecting to the terminal server on a specific line.

- Allow modems attached to routers to be used for dial-out securely.

- Require authentication to each of the lines through a locally defined username and password, or a security server such as a TACACS+ or RADIUS server.

Cisco routers typically are configured to provide SSH server access to remote SSH clients. However, a router could also be an SSH client and establish a secure connection to another SSH server. By default, both of these functions are enabled on the router when SSH is enabled.

Configuring SSH Security

To enable SSH on a router, the following parameters must be configured:

- Hostname
- Domain name
- Asymmetric keys
- Local authentication

Optional configuration parameters include

- Timeouts
- Retries

To configure SSH on a router, follow these steps:

Step 1.   **Configure the router hostname.** The SSH feature requires a valid router using something other than the default hostname, "Router." A router name is likely already configured. If not, configure it using the **hostname** *hostname* global configuration command:

```
R1(config)# hostname R1
```

Step 2.   **Configure the domain name.** A domain name must exist to enable SSH:

```
R1(config)# ip domain-name cisco.com
```

Step 3. **Generate the RSA asymmetric key.** You need to create a key that the router uses to encrypt its SSH management traffic. Use the **crypto key generate rsa** command from global configuration mode:

```
R1(config)# crypto key generate rsa

The name for the keys will be: R1.cisco.com
Choose the size of the key modulus in the range of 360 to 2048 for your
  General Purpose Keys. Choosing a key modulus greater than 512 may take
  a few minutes.

How many bits in the modulus [512]: 1024
% Generating 1024 bit RSA keys, keys will be non-exportable...[OK]

R1(config)#
*Dec 12 10:13:26.311: %SSH-5-ENABLED: SSH 1.99 has been enabled
```

The router responds with a message showing the naming convention for the keys. It also enables you to specify the key size. The key modulus can be configured in the range of 360 to 2048 for your general-purpose keys. As a best practice, Cisco recommends using a minimum modulus length of 1024, as highlighted in the example.

You should be aware that if you choose a longer modulus, it takes slightly longer to generate the key. It also adds some latency when it is used, but it offers stronger security.

You can learn more about the **crypto key** command in the *Network Security* courses.

Step 4. **Configure local authentication and vty.** You must define a local user, change the login to search the local database using the **login local** command, and assign SSH communication to the VTY lines:

```
R1(config)# username Student secret cisco12345
R1(config)# line vty 0 4
R1(config-line)# no transport input
R1(config-line)# transport input ssh
R1(config-line)# login local
R1(config-line)# exit
```

Step 5. **Configure SSH timeouts (optional).** Timeouts provide additional security for the connection by terminating lingering, inactive connections. Use the **ip ssh time-out** *seconds* **authentication-retries** *integer* command to enable timeouts and authentication retries. The command can also be used to configure the two parameters separately. The following example sets the SSH timeout to 15 seconds and the second command limits the number of retries to 2:

```
R1(config)# ip ssh time-out 15
R1(config)# ip ssh authentication-retries 2
R1(config)#
```

Step 6.   **Establish an SSH client connection.** To connect to a router configured with SSH, you have to use an SSH client application such as PuTTY or Tera Term. You must be sure to choose the SSH option and be sure that it uses TCP port 22.

Figure 4-36 shows the opening Tera Term screen with the settings configured to establish an SSH connection to router R2.

Figure 4-36   Create a New Connection

After the connection is initiated, the R2 router displays a username prompt, as shown in Figure 4-37.

Figure 4-37   Tera Term Username Prompt

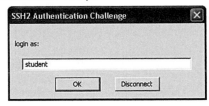

The username is not case-sensitive. This is followed by a password prompt, as shown in Figure 4-38.

Figure 4-38   Tera Term Password Prompt

The password is case-sensitive. Assuming that the correct credentials are provided, Tera Term displays the router R2 user EXEC prompt, as shown in Figure 4-39.

Figure 4-39   Successful Connection

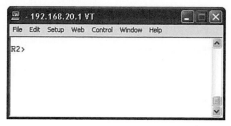

Step 3 of Safeguarding a Router: Log Router Activity

Logs allow you to verify that a router is working properly or to determine whether the router has been compromised. In some cases, a log can show what types of probes or attacks are being attempted against the router or the protected network.

You should carefully configure logging (syslog) on the router. Send the router logs to a designated syslog server that is running syslog software such as KiwiSyslog. The syslog server should be connected to a trusted or protected network or an isolated and dedicated router interface. Harden the server by removing all unnecessary services and accounts.

Routers support different levels of logging. The eight levels range from 0, for emergencies (indicating that the system is unstable), to 7, for debugging messages that include all router information.

Logs can be forwarded to a variety of locations, including router memory or a dedicated syslog server. A syslog server provides a better solution because all network devices can forward their logs to one central station where an administrator can review them. An example of a syslog server application is Kiwi Syslog Daemon.

Also consider sending the logs to a second storage device, such as write-once media or a dedicated printer, to deal with worst-case scenarios (for example, a compromise of the syslog server).

The most important thing to remember about logging is that logs must be reviewed regularly. By doing so, you can gain a feel for your network's normal behavior. A sound understanding of normal operation and its reflection in the logs helps you identify abnormal or attack conditions.

Accurate time stamps are important to logging. Time stamps allow you to trace network attacks more credibly. Example 4-11 enables debug and log messages to be time-stamped on router R2.

Example 4-11   Time-Stamping Log Messages

```
R2(config)# service timestamps ?

debug Timestamp debug messages
log   Timestamp log messages
<cr>
R2(config)# service timestamps
```

All routers can maintain their own time of day, but this usually is insufficient. Instead, direct the router to synchronize with at least two different reliable time servers to ensure the accuracy and availability of time information. A Network Time Protocol (NTP) server could be configured to provide a synchronized time source for all devices. Configuring this option is beyond the scope of this course.

Securing Router Network Services

Cisco routers support a large number of network services at Layers 2, 3, 4, and 7. Some of these services are application layer protocols that allow users and host processes to connect to the router. Others are automatic processes and settings intended to support legacy or specialized configurations that pose security risks. Some of these services can be restricted or disabled to improve security without degrading the operational use of the router. General security practice for routers should be used to support only the traffic and protocols a network needs.

Vulnerable Router Services and Interfaces

Table 4-4 describes general vulnerable router services and their default settings. It also lists best practices associated with those services.

Table 4-4   Vulnerable Router Services

Feature	Description	Default	Recommendation
Cisco Discovery Protocol (CDP)	Proprietary Layer 2 protocol between Cisco devices.	Enabled	CDP is almost never needed. Disable it.
TCP small servers	Standard TCP network services, such as echo and chargen.	Enabled on IOS version 11.2 Disabled on IOS version 11.3 and higher	This is a legacy feature. Disable it explicitly.

Table 4-4   Vulnerable Router Services

Feature	Description	Default	Recommendation
UDP small servers	Standard UDP network services, such as echo and discard.	Enabled on IOS version 11.2 Disabled on IOS version 11.3 and higher	This is a legacy feature. Disable it explicitly.
Finger	UNIX user lookup service. Allows remote listing of users.	Enabled	Unauthorized persons do not need to know this. Disable it.
HTTP server	Some Cisco IOS devices offer web-based configuration.	Varies by device	If not in use, explicitly disable it. Otherwise, restrict access.
BOOTP server	Service to allow other routers to boot from this one.	Enabled	This is rarely needed and may open a security hole. Disable it.
Configuration auto-loading	The router attempts to load its configuration via TFTP.	Disabled	This is rarely used. Disable it if it is not in use.
IP source routing	IP feature that allows packets to specify their own routes.	Enabled	This rarely used feature can be helpful in attacks. Disable it.
Proxy ARP	The router acts as a proxy for Layer 2 address resolution.	Enabled	Disable this service unless the router is serving as a LAN bridge.
IP directed broadcast	Packets can identify a target LAN for broadcasts.	Enabled on IOS version 11.3 and higher	Directed broadcast can be used for attacks. Disable it.
Classless routing behavior	The router forwards packets with no concrete route.	Enabled	Certain attacks can benefit from this. Disable it unless your network requires it.
IP unreachable notifications	The router explicitly notifies senders of incorrect IP addresses.	Enabled	Can aid network mapping. Disabled on interfaces to untrusted networks.

continues

Table 4-4   Vulnerable Router Services

Feature	Description	Default	Recommendation
IP mask reply	The router sends an IP address mask of the interface in response to an ICMP mask request.	Disabled	Can aid IP address mapping. Explicitly disable it on interfaces to untrusted networks.
IP redirects	The router sends an ICMP redirect message in response to certain routed IP packets.	Enabled	Can aid network mapping. Disable it on interfaces to untrusted networks.
NTP service	The router can act as a time server for other devices and hosts.	Enabled (if NTP is configured)	If not in use, explicitly disable it. Otherwise, restrict access.
Simple Network Management Protocol	Routers can support SNMP remote query and configuration.	Enabled	If not in use, explicitly disable it. Otherwise, restrict access.
Domain Name Service	Routers can perform DNS name resolution.	Enabled (broadcast)	Set the DNS server address explicitly, or disable DNS.

Turning off a network service on the router itself does not prevent it from supporting a network where that protocol is employed. For example, a network may require TFTP services to back up configuration files and IOS images. This service typically is provided by a dedicated TFTP server. Although it's unusual, a router could also be configured as a TFTP server. However, in most cases the TFTP service on the router should be disabled.

In many cases, Cisco IOS software supports turning off a service or restricting access to particular network segments or sets of hosts. If a particular portion of a network needs a service but the rest does not, the restriction features should be employed to limit the scope of the service.

Turning off an automatic network feature usually prevents a certain kind of network traffic from being processed by the router or prevents it from traversing the router. For example, IP source routing is a little-used feature of IP that can be used in network attacks. Unless it is required for the network to operate, IP source routing should be disabled.

Note

CDP is used in some IP Phone implementations. Consider this fact before broadly disabling the service.

Disabling Vulnerable Router Services and Interfaces

A variety of commands are required to disable services. The **show running-config** output in Example 4-12 provides a sample configuration of various services that have been disabled.

Example 4-12   *Displaying Disabled Services*

```
!-----IP and network services Section
no cdp run
no ip source-route
no ip classless
no service tcp-small-servers
no service udp-small-servers
no ip finger
no service finger
no ip bootp server
no ip http server
no ip name-server
!-----Boot control section
no boot network
no service config
!-----SNMP Section (for totally disabling SNMP)
!set up totally restrictive access list
no access-list 70
access-list 70 deny any
!make SNMP read-only and subject to access list
snmp-server community aqiytj1726540942 ro 11
!disable SNMP trap and system-shutdown features
no snmp-server enable traps
no snmp-server system-shutdown
no snmp-server trap-auth
!turn off SNMP altogether
```

The following list includes examples of commands that disable the associated service:

- **Small services such as echo, discard, and chargen**: Use the **no service tcp-small-servers** and **no service udp-small-servers** commands.

- **BOOTP**: Use the **no ip bootp server** command.

- **Finger**: Use the **no service finger** and **no ip finger** commands.

- **HTTP**: Use the **no ip http server** command.

- **SNMP**: Use the **no snmp-server** command.

Example 4-13 shows a sample configuration.

Example 4-13   Disabling IP and Network Services

```
R2(config)# no service udp-small-servers
R2(config)# no service tcp-small-servers
R2(config)# no ip bootp server
R2(config)# no service finger
R2(config)# no ip finger
R2(config)# no ip http server
R2(config)# no snmp-server
R2(config)#
```

It is also important to disable services that allow certain packets to pass through the router, that send special packets, or that are used for remote router configuration. The corresponding commands to disable these services are as follows:

- **Cisco Discovery Protocol (CDP)**: Use the **no cdp run** command.

- **Remote configuration**: Use the **no service config** command.

- **Source routing**: Use the **no ip source-route** command.

- **Classless routing**: Use the **no ip classless** command.

Example 4-14 shows a sample configuration to disable these services.

Example 4-14   Disabling CDP, Remote Configuration, Source Routing, and Classless

```
Routing
R2(config)# no cdp run
R2(config)# no service config
R2(config)# no ip source-route
R2(config)# no ip classless
R2(config)#
```

You can make the interfaces on the router more secure by using certain commands in interface configuration mode:

- **Unused interfaces**: Use the **shutdown** command.

- **No Smurf attacks**: Use the **no ip directed-broadcast** command.

- **Ad hoc routing**: Use the **no ip proxy-arp** command.

Example 4-15 shows a sample configuration.

Example 4-15   Securing Interfaces

```
R2(config)# interface FastEthernet0/0
R2(config-if)# no ip directed-broadcast
R2(config-if)# no ip proxy-arp
R2(config-if)# shutdown
R2(config-if)#
```

SNMP, NTP, and DNS Vulnerabilities

SNMP, NTP, and DNS are three management services that should also be secured. The methods for disabling or tuning the configurations for these services are beyond the scope of this course. These services are covered in the *CCNP: Implementing Secure Converged Wide-Area Networks* course.

The following are descriptions and simple guidelines to secure these services:

- **SNMP**: SNMP is the standard TCP/IP protocol for automated remote monitoring and administration. Several different versions of SNMP have different security properties. Versions of SNMP before version 3 shuttle information in clear text. Normally, SNMP version 3 should be used.

- **NTP**: Cisco routers and other hosts use NTP to keep their time-of-day clocks accurate. If possible, network administrators should configure all routers as part of an NTP hierarchy, which makes one router the master timer and provides its time to other routers on the network. However, NTP leaves listening ports open and vulnerable. If an NTP hierarchy is not available on the network, you should disable NTP.

  Disabling NTP on an interface does not prevent NTP messages from traversing the router. To reject all NTP messages at a particular interface, use an access list.

- **DNS**: Cisco IOS software supports looking up hostnames with the Domain Name System (DNS). DNS provides the mapping between names, such as central.mydomain.com, and IP addresses, such as 14.2.9.250—information that an attacker can exploit.

  Unfortunately, the basic DNS protocol offers no authentication or integrity assurance. By default, name queries are sent to the broadcast address 255.255.255.255.

  If one or more name servers are available on the network, and it is desirable to use names in Cisco IOS commands, explicitly set the name server addresses using the global configuration command **ip name-server** *addresses*. Otherwise, turn off DNS name resolution with the command **no ip domain-lookup**. It is also a good idea to give the router a name using the command **hostname**. The name given to the router appears in the prompt.

Securing Routing Protocols

As a network administrator, you have to be aware that your routers are at risk of being attacked just as much as your end-user systems. Anyone with a packet sniffer such as Wireshark can read information propagating between routers. In general, routing systems can be attacked in two ways:

- By disrupting peers
- By falsifying routing information

Disruption of peers is the less critical of the two attacks because routing protocols heal themselves, making the disruption last only slightly longer than the attack itself.

A more subtle class of attack targets the information carried within the routing protocol. Falsified routing information generally may be used to cause systems to misinform (lie to) each other, to cause DoS, or to cause traffic to follow a path it would not normally follow. The effects of falsifying routing information are as follows:

1. It redirects traffic to create routing loops, as shown in Figure 4-40.

2. It redirects traffic so that it can be monitored on an insecure link that would potentially allow a hacker to gain access to confidential information.

3. It redirects traffic to discard it.

Figure 4-40   Attacker Creating a Routing Loop

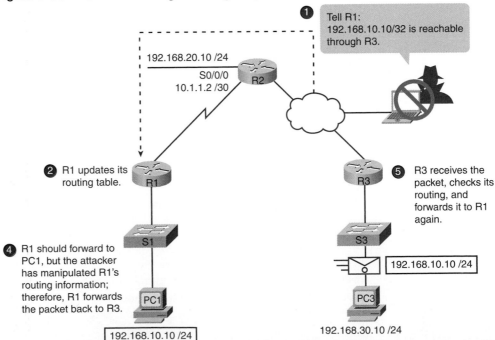

A straightforward way to attack the routing system is to attack the routers running the routing protocols, gain access to the routers, and inject false information. Be aware that anyone "listening" can capture routing updates.

Refer to Figure 4-40 and the following list to see how an attacker can manipulate a router's routing table by creating a routing loop:

1. An attacker connects directly to the link between routers R2 and R3. The attacker injects false routing information destined for router R1 only, indicating that R3 is the preferred destination for the 192.168.10.10/32 host route.

2. Although R1 has a routing table entry to the directly connected 192.168.10.0/24 network, it adds the injected route to its routing table because of the longer subnet mask. A route with a longer matching subnet mask is considered superior to a route with a shorter subnet mask. Consequently, when a router receives a packet, it selects the longer subnet mask because it is a more precise route to the destination.

3. PC3 sends a packet to PC1, located at 192.168.10.10/24.

4. When router R1 receives the packet, it refers to its routing table and does not forward the packet to the PC1 host. Instead, it routes the packet to router R3, because, as far as it is concerned, the best path to 192.168.10.10/32 is through R3.

5. When R3 gets the packet, it looks in its routing table and forwards the packet back to R1, which creates the loop.

Routing Protocol Authentication Overview

The best way to protect routing information on the network is to authenticate routing protocol packets using message digest algorithm 5 (MD5). An algorithm like MD5 allows the routers to compare signatures that should all be the same.

Figure 4-41 shows how each router in the update chain creates a signature.

The three components of a system like the one shown in Figure 4-41 are

- Encryption algorithm

- Key used in the encryption algorithm, which is a secret shared by the routers authenticating their packets

- Contents of the packet itself

The following list describes the steps shown in Figure 4-41. This list shows how routing information is propagated within a network that has been configured to support MD5 routing protocol authentication:

1. Router R3 wants to send an update to routers R1 and R2.

2. R3 produces a signature using the key and routing data it is about to send as inputs into the encryption algorithm.

3. Router R2 receives this routing data and repeats the process using the same key, the data it has received, and the same routing data. If the signature that R2 computes is the same as R3's computed signature, the update is authenticated.

4. Router R2 then repeats the process and forwards the routing update to router R1.

Most of the major routing protocols, such as RIPv2, EIGRP, OSPF, IS-IS, and BGP, all support various forms of MD5 authentication. RIPv1 does not support authentication.

Figure 4-41   Routers Configured with MD5 Routing Authentication

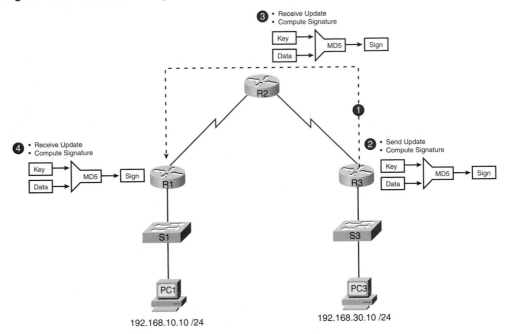

Configuring RIPv2 with Routing Protocol Authentication

Figure 4-42 shows a network configured with the RIPv2 routing protocol.

RIPv2 supports routing protocol authentication. To secure routing updates, each router must be configured to support authentication. The steps to secure RIPv2 updates are as follows:

Step 1.   Prevent RIP routing update propagation.

Step 2.   Prevent unauthorized reception of RIP updates.

Step 3.   Verify the operation of RIP routing.

Figure 4-42 Configuring RIPv2 with Routing Authentication

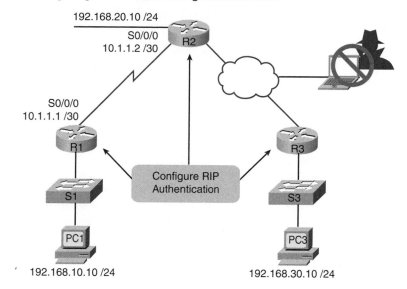

Step 1: Prevent RIP Routing Update Propagation

You need to keep an intruder listening on the network from receiving updates to which he is not entitled. You do this by forcing all interfaces on the router into passive mode and then enabling only those interfaces that are required for sending and receiving RIP updates. An interface in passive mode receives updates but does not send updates. You must configure passive mode interfaces on all the routers in the network.

Routing updates should never be advertised on interfaces that are not connected to other routers. For example, the LAN interfaces on router R1 do not connect to other routers and therefore should not advertise routing updates. Only the S0/0/0 interface on router R1 should advertise routing updates.

In Example 4-16, the **passive-interface default** command disables the forwarding of routing advertisements on all interfaces. This also includes the S0/0/0 interface. The **no passive-interface s0/0/0** command enables the S0/0/0 interface to send and receive RIP updates.

Example 4-16 Configuring Passive Interfaces

```
R1(config)# router rip
R1(config-router)# version 2
R1(config-router)# network 192.168.10.0
R1(config-router)# network 10.0.0.0
R1(config-router)# passive-interface default
R1(config-router)# no passive-interface s0/0/0
```

Step 2: Prevent Unauthorized Reception of RIP Updates

In Example 4-17, RIP MD5 authentication has been enabled on router R1 to ensure that an attacker cannot manipulate the routing tables.

Example 4-17   Configuring RIP Key Chains

```
R1(config)# key chain RIP-KEY
R1(config-keychain)# key 1
R1(config-keychain-key)# key-string cisco
R1(config-keychain-key)# exit
R1(config-keychain)# exit
R1(config)# interface s0/0/0
R1(config-if)# ip rip authentication mode md5
R1(config-if)# ip rip authentication key-chain RIP-KEY
```

Routers R2 and R3 also need to be configured with these commands on the appropriate interfaces. In the example, a key chain named RIP-KEY is created.

Although a key chain can contain multiple keys, our example shows only one key, called key 1. Key 1 is configured to contain a key string called cisco. The key string is similar to a password, and routers exchanging authentication keys must be configured with the same key string.

Interface S0/0/0 is configured to support MD5 authentication. The RIP-KEY chain and the routing update are processed using the MD5 algorithm to produce a unique signature.

After R1 is configured, the other routers receive encrypted routing updates and consequently no longer can decipher the updates from R1. This condition remains until each router in the network is configured with routing protocol authentication.

Step 3: Verify the Operation of RIP Routing

After you have configured all the routers in the network, you need to verify the operation of RIP routing in the network. The **show ip route** command can confirm that router R1 has authenticated and acquired the routes from routers R2 and R3.

Example 4-18 displays output from the **debug ip rip** command.

Example 4-18   debug ip rip Command

```
R1# debug ip rip

RIP protocol debugging is on
R1#
*Dec 12 14:04:24.627: RIP: received packet with MD5 authentication
*Dec 12 14:04:24.627: RIP: received v2 update from 10.1.1.2 on Serial0/0/0
*Dec 12 14:04:24.627:      192.168.20.0/24 via 0.0.0.0 in 1 hops
R1#
```

Notice that the highlighted area confirms that MD5 authentication updates are being received from Router R2.

Overview of Routing Protocol Authentication for EIGRP and OSPF

Routing protocol authentication can also be configured for other routing protocols, such as EIGRP and OSPF. Their implementation is very similar to configuring authentication with RIP. Refer to the topology shown in Figure 4-43 when reviewing EIGRP and OSPF authentication.

Figure 4-43   EIGRP/OSPF Sample Topology

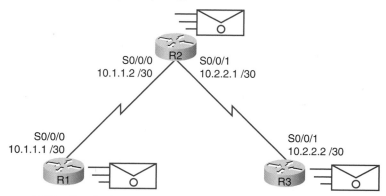

MD5 authentication can be configured for EIGRP and OSPF.

EIGRP

Example 4-19 shows the commands used to configure routing protocol authentication for EIGRP on router R1.

Example 4-19   Configuring EIGRP Authentication

```
R1(config)# router eigrp 1
R1(config-router)# network 192.168.10.0 255.255.255.0
R1(config-router)# network 10.1.1.0 255.255.255.0
R1(config-router)# exit
R1(config)# key chain EIGRP-KEY
R1(config-keychain)# key 1
R1(config-keychain-key)# key-string cisco
R1(config-keychain-key)# exit
R1(config-keychain)# exit
R1(config)# interface s0/0/0
R1(config-if)# ip authentication mode eigrp 1 md5
R1(config-if)# ip authentication key-chain eigrp 1 EIGRP-KEY
```

These commands are very similar to the ones you used for RIPv2 MD5 authentication. The steps to configure EIGRP routing protocol authentication on router R1 are as follows:

Step 1. The first group of highlighted lines shows how to create a key chain to be used by all routers in your network. These commands create a key chain named EIGRP-KEY and place your terminal in keychain configuration mode, with a key number of 1 and a key string value of cisco.

Step 2. The second group of highlighted lines shows how to enable MD5 authentication in EIGRP packets traversing an interface. In the commands, the number 1 after the keyword **eigrp** refers to the autonomous system number.

OSPF

Example 4-20 shows the commands used to configure routing protocol authentication for OSPF on router R1 on interface S0/0/0.

Example 4-20 Configuring OSPF Authentication

```
R1(config)# router ospf 10
R1(config-router)# network 192.168.10.0 0.0.0.255 area 0
R1(config-router)# network 10.1.1.0 0.0.0.255 area 0
R1(config-router)# exit
R1(config)# interface s0/0/0
R1(config-if)# ip ospf message-digest-key 1 md5 cisco
R1(config-if)# ip ospf authentication message-digest
R1(config-if)# exit
R1(config)# router ospf 10
R1(config-router)# area 0 authentication message-digest
R1(config-router)# exit
R1(config)#
```

The steps of configuring OSPF routing protocol authentication on router R1 are as follows:

Step 1. The first two highlighted commands specify the key that will be used for MD5 authentication and enable MD5 authentication.

Step 2. The third highlighted command enables MD5 authentication for area 0.

For more details on routing protocol authentication for EIGRP and OSPF, refer to *CCNP: Building Scalable Internetworks*.

Packet Tracer
☐ Activity

Configuring OSPF Authentication (4.3.2)

This activity covers both OSPF simple authentication and OSPF MD5 authentication. You can enable authentication in OSPF to exchange routing update information in a secure manner. With simple authentication, the password is sent in clear text over the network. Simple authentication is used when devices within an area cannot support the more secure MD5 authentication. MD5 is considered the most secure OSPF authentication mode. When you configure authentication, you must configure an entire area with the same type of authentication. In this activity, you configure simple authentication between R1 and R2, and MD5 authentication between R2 and R3.

Detailed instructions are provided within the activity. Use File e4-432.pka on the CD-ROM that accompanies this book to perform this activity using Packet Tracer.

Locking Down Your Router with Cisco AutoSecure

Cisco *AutoSecure* uses a single command to disable nonessential system processes and services, eliminating potential security threats. You can configure AutoSecure in privileged EXEC mode using the **auto secure** command in one of two modes:

- **Interactive mode** prompts you with options to enable and disable services and other security features. This is the default mode.

- **Noninteractive mode** automatically executes the **auto secure** command with the recommended Cisco default settings. This mode is enabled with the **no-interact** command option.

Perform AutoSecure on a Cisco Router

To start the automated process of securing a router, issue the privilege EXEC **auto secure** command. Example 4-21 displays partial output from a Cisco AutoSecure configuration.

Example 4-21   Implementing Auto Secure

```
R1# auto secure

Is this router connected to internet? [no]:y
Enter the number of interfaces facing internet [1]:1
Enter the interface name that is facing internet:Serial0/1/0
Securing Management plane services

Disabling service finger
Disabling service pad
Disabling udp & tcp small servers
Enabling service password encryption
Enabling service tcp-keepalives-in
Enabling service tcp-keepalives-out
Disabling the cdp protocol
<Output omitted>
```

Cisco AutoSecure asks you for a number of items:

- Interface specifics

- Banners

- Passwords

- SSH

- IOS firewall features

Note

The Cisco Router and Security Device Manager (SDM) provides a similar feature as Cisco AutoSecure, as described in the next section.

Using Cisco SDM

The *Cisco Router and Security Device Manager (SDM)* is an easy-to-use, web-based device-management tool designed for configuring LAN, WAN, and security features on Cisco IOS software-based routers.

SDM helps network administrators of small- to medium-sized businesses perform day-to-day operations. It provides easy-to-use smart wizards, automates router security management, and offers help through comprehensive online help and tutorials.

Cisco SDM Overview

Cisco SDM, shown in Figure 4-44, supports a wide range of Cisco IOS software releases. It is preinstalled by default on all new Cisco Integrated Services Routers (ISR). If it is not preinstalled, you must install it. The SDM files can be installed on the router, a PC, or both. An advantage of installing SDM on the PC is that it saves router memory and allows you to use SDM to manage other routers on the network. If Cisco SDM is preinstalled on the router, Cisco recommends using Cisco SDM to perform the initial configuration.

Cisco SDM simplifies router and security configuration through the use of several intelligent wizards to enable efficient configuration of key router VPN and Cisco IOS firewall parameters. This capability permits administrators to quickly and easily deploy, configure, and monitor Cisco routers.

Cisco SDM smart wizards guide users step-by-step through the router and security configuration workflow by systematically configuring LAN and WAN interfaces, the firewall, IPS, and VPNs.

Figure 4-44   SDM Main Screen

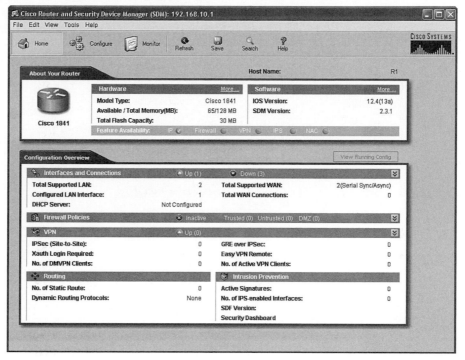

Cisco SDM smart wizards can intelligently detect incorrect configurations and propose fixes, such as allowing DHCP traffic through a firewall if the WAN interface is DHCP-addressed. Online help embedded within Cisco SDM contains appropriate background information, in addition to step-by-step procedures, to help users enter correct data in the Cisco SDM.

Configuring Your Router to Support SDM

Cisco SDM is installed on all new Cisco routers. If you have a router that is already in use but that does not have Cisco SDM, you may be able to download and install SDM without disrupting network traffic, as shown in Figure 4-45.

Figure 4-45   Sample SDM Topology

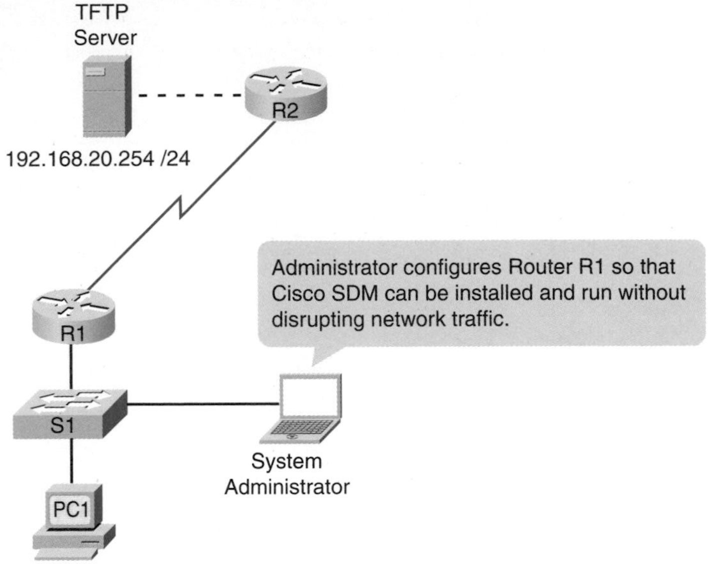

The figure shows a topology in which the system administrator installs Cisco SDM on router R1.

Before you can install SDM on an operational router, you must ensure that a few configuration settings are present in the router configuration file. To configure Cisco SDM on a router that is already in use, without disrupting network traffic, follow these steps:

Step 1.   Access the router's Cisco command-line interface (CLI) using Telnet or the console connection.

Step 2.   Enable the HTTP and HTTPS servers on the router.

Step 3.   Create a user account defined with privilege level 15 (enable privileges).

Step 4.   Configure SSH and Telnet for local login and privilege level 15.

Example 4-22 shows the configuration commands needed to ensure that you can install and run Cisco SDM on a production router without disrupting network traffic.

Example 4-22   Supporting Auto Secure

```
R1(config)# ip http server
R1(config)# ip http secure-server

% Generating 1024 bit RSA keys, keys will be non-exportable...[OK]
R1(config)#
*Dec 12 17:44:10.863: %SSH-5-ENABLED: SSH 1.99 has been enabled
*Dec 12 17:44:11.935: %PKI-4-NOAUTOSAVE: Configuration was modified.  Issue "write
  memory" to save new certificate
R1(config)# ip http authentication local
R1(config)# username Student privilege 15 secret cisco123
R1(config)# line vty 0 4
R1(config-line)# privilege level 15
R1(config-line)# login local
R1(config-line)# transport input telnet ssh
R1(config-line)# exit
R1(config)#
```

If the router has never been configured, it may also require that the FastEthernet interface be configured with an IP address.

Starting SDM

Cisco SDM usually is stored in the router flash memory. However, it can also be stored on a local PC. To launch Cisco SDM, use the HTTPS protocol, and enter the router's IP address into a web browser window. For instance, to access router R1, enter the IP address https://198.162.10.1 and the launch page for Cisco SDM appears.

Figure 4-46 shows the initial launch web page for SDM. This web page can be closed.

Shortly thereafter, the web page shown in Figure 4-47 opens. This web page must remain open while you use SDM.

Figure 4-46   Initial SDM Web Page

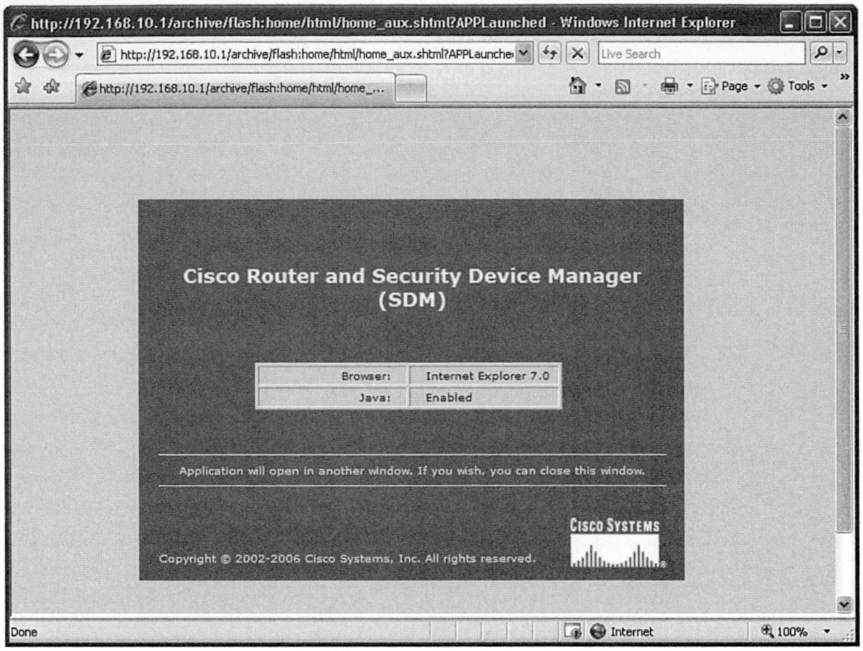

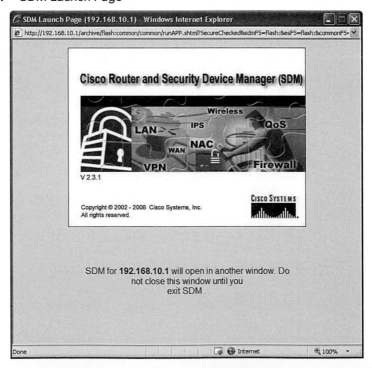

Figure 4-47   SDM Launch Page

The http:// prefix can be used if SSL is unavailable. When the username and password dialog box appears (not shown), enter a username and password for the privileged (privilege level 15) account on the router. After the launch page appears, a signed Cisco SDM Java applet appears; it must remain open while Cisco SDM is running. Because it is a signed Cisco SDM Java applet, you may be prompted to accept a certificate.

Note

The sequence of login steps may vary, depending on whether you run Cisco SDM from a PC or directly from a Cisco ISR.

The SDM Interface

After Cisco SDM has started and you have logged in, the first page displayed is the SDM Home Page, as shown in Figure 4-48.

Figure 4-48   SDM Home Page

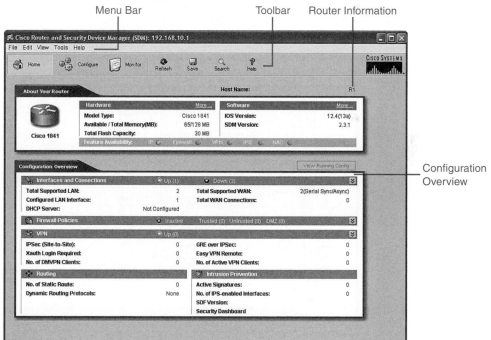

Cisco SDM Home Page Overview

The SDM Home Page displays the router model; the total amount of memory; the versions of flash, IOS, and SDM; the hardware installed; and a summary of some security features, such as firewall status and the number of active VPN connections.

Specifically, it provides basic information about the router hardware, software, and configuration:

- **Menu bar**: The top of the screen has a typical menu bar with File, Edit, View, Tools, and Help menus.

- **Tool bar**: Below the menu bar are the SDM wizards and modes you can select.

- **Router information**: The current mode is displayed on the left side, under the tool bar.

- **Configuration overview**: Summarizes the configuration settings. To view the running configuration, click the **View Running Config** button, located at the top right of this section.

Note

The menu bar, tool bar, and current mode are always displayed at the top of each screen. The other areas of the screen change based on the mode and function you are performing.

About Your Router Area

Figure 4-49 outlines the various parts of the About Your Router section of the SDM Home page.

Figure 4-49   About Your Router Section of the SDM Home Page

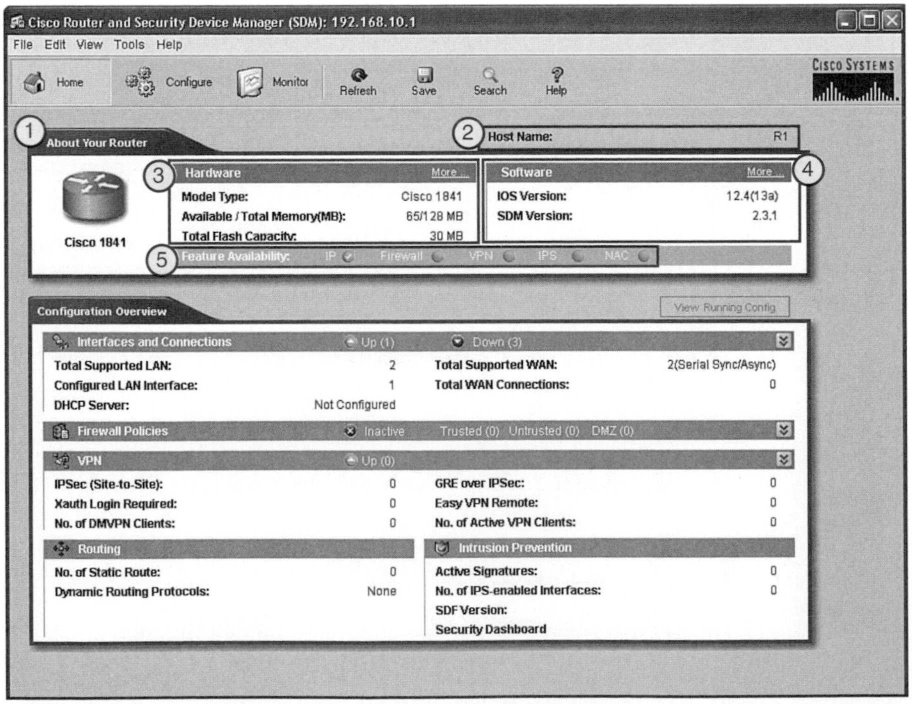

The **About Your Router** section (1) is the area of the Cisco SDM home page that shows basic information about the router hardware and software. It includes the following elements:

- The **Host Name** section (2) displays the router's configured hostname, which in this example is R1.

- The **Hardware** section (3) displays the router model number, the available and total amounts of RAM, and the amount of flash memory available.

- The **Software** section (4) describes the Cisco IOS software and Cisco SDM versions running on the router.

- The **Feature Availability** bar (5) is located across the bottom of the About Your Router tab. It displays the features available in the Cisco IOS image that the router is using. If the indicator beside each feature is green, the feature is available. If the indicator is red, the feature is unavailable. Check marks show that the feature is configured on the router. In the figure, Cisco SDM shows that IP, firewall, VPN, IPS, and NAC are available, but only IP is configured.

Configuration Overview Area

Figure 4-50 outlines the Configuration Overview area (1) of SDM.

Figure 4-50   Configuration Overview Section of the SDM Home Page

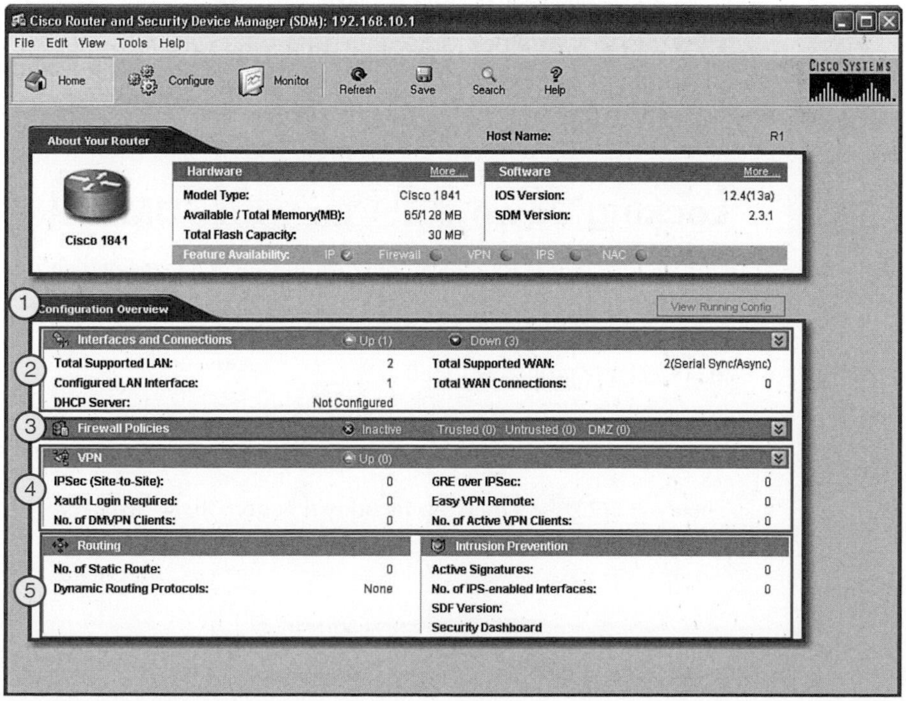

This section contains the following GUI elements:

- The **Interfaces and Connections** section (2) displays interface- and connection-related information, including the number of connections that are up and down, the total number of LAN and WAN interfaces that are present in the router, and the number of LAN and WAN interfaces currently configured on the router. It also shows whether DHCP is configured.

- The **Firewall Policies** section (3) displays firewall-related information, including whether a firewall is in place, and the number of trusted (inside) interfaces, untrusted (outside) interfaces, and DMZ interfaces. It also displays the name of the interface to which a firewall has been applied, whether the interface is designated as an inside or outside interface, and whether the NAT rule has been applied to this interface.

- The **VPN** area (4) displays VPN-related information, including the number of active VPN connections, the number of configured site-to-site VPN connections, and the number of active VPN clients.

- The **Routing** area (5) displays the number of static routes and which routing protocols are configured.

Cisco SDM Wizards

Cisco SDM provides a number of wizards to help you configure a Cisco ISR router. After you have selected a task from the task area in the Cisco SDM GUI, the task pane allows you to select a wizard.

Check *http://www.cisco.com/go/sdm* for the latest information about the Cisco SDM wizards and the interfaces they support.

Locking Down a Router with SDM

One such wizard is the SDM *one-step lockdown wizard*, which implements almost all the security configurations that Cisco AutoSecure offers. It tests your router configuration for potential security problems and automatically makes any necessary configuration changes to correct any problems found.

You access the one-step lockdown wizard from the Configure GUI interface by clicking the **Security Audit** task, as shown in Figure 4-51.

Then you click the **One-step lockdown** button. SDM displays a warning related to the wizard, as shown in Figure 4-52.

Figure 4-51 Security Audit Wizard

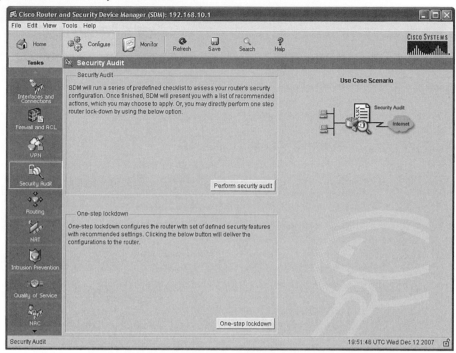

Figure 4-52 SDM Warning Dialog Box

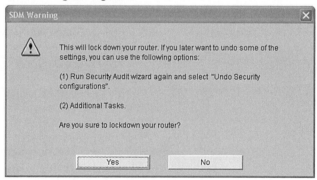

SDM then analyzes the current router configurations and implements best-practice security suggestions, as shown in Figure 4-53.

Figure 4-53   One-Step Lockdown in Operation

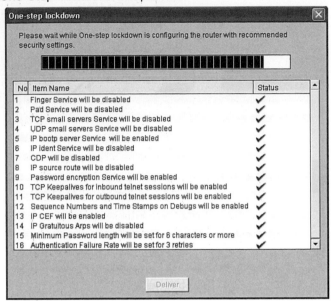

The final step in the process is to deliver the suggested configuration to the actual device, as shown in Figure 4-54.

Figure 4-54   Deliver Commands

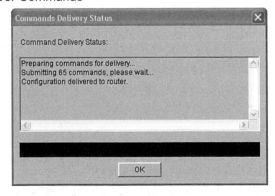

Do not assume that the network is secure simply because you executed a one-step lock-down. In addition, not all the features of Cisco AutoSecure are implemented in Cisco SDM. AutoSecure features that are implemented differently in Cisco SDM include the following:

- Disables SNMP and does not configure SNMP version 3.

- Enables and configures SSH on crypto Cisco IOS images.

- Does not enable Service Control Point or disable other access and file transfer services, such as FTP.

Secure Router Management

Periodically, the router requires updates to be loaded to either the operating system or the configuration file. These updates are necessary to fix known security vulnerabilities, support new features that allow more advanced security policies, or improve performance.

Note

It is not always a good idea to upgrade to the very latest version of Cisco IOS software. Many times that release is not stable.

Maintaining Cisco IOS Software Images

You must follow certain guidelines when changing the Cisco IOS software on a router. Changes are classified as either updates or upgrades. An update replaces one release with another without upgrading the feature set. The software might be updated to fix a bug or to replace a release that is no longer supported. Updates are free.

An upgrade replaces a release with one that has an upgraded feature set. The software might be upgraded to add new features or technologies or replace a release that is no longer supported. Upgrades are not free. Cisco.com offers guidelines to help you determine which method applies.

Cisco recommends that you follow a four-phase migration process to simplify network operations and management. When you follow a repeatable process, you can also benefit from reduced costs in operations, management, and training. The four phases are as follows:

- **Plan**: Set goals, identify resources, profile network hardware and software, and create a preliminary schedule for migrating to new releases.

- **Design**: Choose new Cisco IOS releases and create a strategy for migrating to the releases.

- **Implement**: Schedule and execute the migration.

- **Operate**: Monitor the migration progress and make backup copies of images that are running on your network.

A number of tools available on Cisco.com help you migrate Cisco IOS software. You can use the tools to get information about releases, feature sets, platforms, and images. The following tools do not require a Cisco.com login:

- **Cisco IOS Reference Guide**: Covers the basics of the Cisco IOS software family.

- **Cisco IOS software technical documents**: Documentation for each release of Cisco IOS software.

- **Cisco Feature Navigator**: Finds releases that support a set of software features and hardware, and compares releases.

The following tools require valid Cisco.com login accounts:

- **Download Software**: Cisco IOS software downloads.

- **Bug Toolkit**: Searches for known software fixes based on software version, feature set, and keywords.

- **Software Advisor**: Compares releases, matches Cisco IOS software and Cisco Catalyst OS features to releases, and finds out which software release supports a given hardware device.

- **Cisco IOS Upgrade Planner**: Finds releases by hardware, release, and feature set, and downloads images of Cisco IOS software.

To see a complete list of tools available on Cisco.com, go to *http://www.cisco.com/en/US/support/tsd_most_requested_tools.html*.

Managing Cisco IOS Images

The availability of the network can be at risk if a router configuration or operating system is compromised. Attackers who gain access to infrastructure devices can alter or delete configuration files. They can also upload incompatible IOS images or delete the IOS image. The changes are invoked automatically or when the device is rebooted.

To prevent these problems, you have to be able to save, back up, and restore configuration and IOS images. To do so, you'll learn how to carry out a few file management operations in Cisco IOS software.

Cisco IOS File Systems and Devices

Cisco IOS devices provide a feature called the Cisco IOS Integrated File System (IFS). This system allows you to create, navigate, and manipulate directories on a Cisco device. The directories available depend on the platform.

For instance, Example 4-23 displays the output of the **show file systems** command, which lists all the available file systems on a Cisco 1841 router.

Example 4-23   show file system Command Output

```
R1# show file system

File Systems:

     Size(b)      Free(b)       Type   Flags   Prefixes
           -            -      opaque      rw   archive:
           -            -      opaque      rw   system:
           -            -      opaque      rw   null:
           -            -     network      rw   tftp:
      196600       194247       nvram      rw   nvram:
*   31932416       462848        disk      rw   flash:#
           -            -      opaque      wo   syslog:
           -            -      opaque      rw   xmodem:
           -            -      opaque      rw   ymodem:
           -            -     network      rw   rcp:
           -            -     network      rw   pram:
           -            -     network      rw   ftp:
           -            -     network      rw   http:
           -            -     network      rw   scp:
           -            -     network      rw   https:
           -            -      opaque      ro   cns:
```

This command provides insightful information such as the amount of available and free memory, and the type of file system and its permissions. Permissions include read-only (ro), write-only (wo), and read and write (rw).

Although several file systems are listed, of interest to us are the TFTP, flash, and NVRAM file systems. The other file systems listed are beyond the scope of this course.

Network file systems include using FTP, trivial FTP (TFTP), or Remote Copy Protocol (RCP). This course focuses on TFTP.

Notice that the flash file system has an asterisk (*) preceding it, which indicates that this is the current default file system. Recall that the bootable IOS is located in flash. Therefore, the pound symbol (#) appended to the flash listing indicates that this is a bootable disk.

Example 4-24 lists the contents of the current default file system, which in this case is flash, as indicated by the asterisk preceding the listing in Example 4-23.

Example 4-24   Default File System

```
R1# dir

Directory of flash:/

    1  -rw-         720  Sep 11 2007 15:59:54 +00:00  pre_autosec.cfg
    2  -rw-        1821  Jul 11 2006 10:30:42 +00:00  sdmconfig-18xx.cfg
    3  -rw-     4734464  Jul 11 2006 10:31:20 +00:00  sdm.tar
    4  -rw-      833024  Jul 11 2006 10:31:44 +00:00  es.tar
    5  -rw-     1052160  Jul 11 2006 10:32:14 +00:00  common.tar
    6  -rw-        1038  Jul 11 2006 10:32:36 +00:00  home.shtml
    7  -rw-      102400  Jul 11 2006 10:32:58 +00:00  home.tar
    8  -rw-      491213  Jul 11 2006 10:33:20 +00:00  128MB.sdf
    9  -rw-     1684577  Jul 11 2006 10:34:00 +00:00
  securedesktop-ios-3.1.1.27-k9.pkg
   10  -rw-      398305  Jul 11 2006 10:34:34 +00:00  sslclient-win-1.1.0.154.pkg
   11  -rw-    22149320  Mar 28 2007 16:02:28 +00:00
  c1841-advipservicesk9-mz.124-13a.bin

31932416 bytes total (462848 bytes free)
R1#:
```

The number of files in flash varies based on the feature set and version of IOS. This IOS image also stores the required SDM files and the 128MB.sdf IPS signature file. Of specific interest is the last listing, which is the file image name of the current IOS running in RAM.

Example 4-25 lists the commands to change the directory and view the contents of NVRAM.

Example 4-25   Contents of NVRAM

```
R1# cd nvram:
R1# pwd

nvram:/
R1# dir

Directory of nvram:/

  190  -rw-        1253                 <no date>  startup-config
  191  -- --          24                 <no date>  private-config
  192  -rw-        1253                 <no date>  underlying-config
    1  -rw-           0                 <no date>  ifIndex-table

196600 bytes total (194247 bytes free)
R1#
```

To view the contents of NVRAM, you must change the current default file system using the **cd** (change directory) command. The **pwd** (present working directory) command verifies that we are in the NVRAM directory. Finally, the **dir** command lists the contents of NVRAM. Although a few configuration files are listed, of specific interest to us is the startup-config configuration file.

URL Prefixes for Cisco Devices

When a network administrator wants to move files around on a computer, the operating system offers a visible file structure to specify sources and destinations. Administrators do not have visual cues when working at a router CLI. The **show file systems** command in the preceding section displayed the various file systems available on the Cisco 1841 platform.

File locations are specified in Cisco IFS using the URL convention. The URLs used by Cisco IOS platforms look similar to the format you know from the web.

For instance, Figure 4-55 shows a TFTP example.

Figure 4-55   TFTP File URL

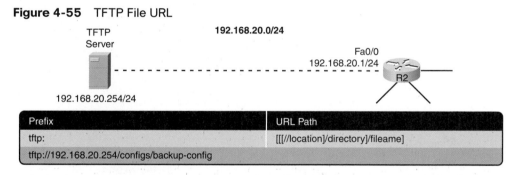

In Figure 4-55, tftp://192.168.20.254/configs/backup-config can be dissected as follows:

- tftp: is the prefix.

- Everything after the double slash (//) defines the location.

- 192.168.20.254 is the location of the TFTP server.

- configs is the master directory on the TFTP server.

- backup-config is a sample filename.

The URL prefix specifies the file system.

Figure 4-56 shows an example for flash memory.

Figure 4-56   Flash File URL

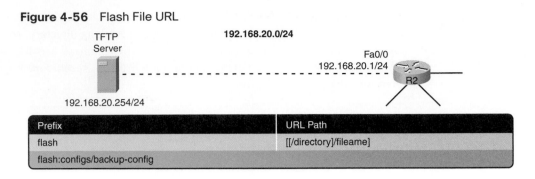

Prefix	URL Path
flash	[[/directory]/fileame]
flash:configs/backup-config	

Figure 4-57 shows an example for RAM memory.

Figure 4-57   RAM File URL

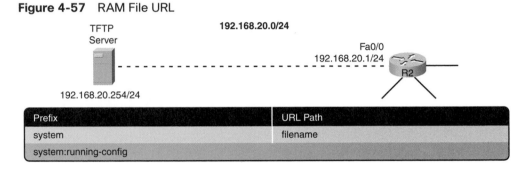

Prefix	URL Path
system	filename
system:running-config	

Figure 4-58 shows an NVRAM example.

Figure 4-58   NVRAM File URL

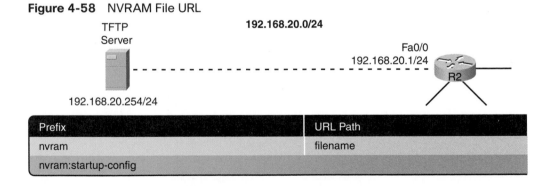

Prefix	URL Path
nvram	filename
nvram:startup-config	

Commands for Managing Configuration Files

Good practice for maintaining system availability is to ensure that you always have backup copies of the startup configuration files and IOS image files. The Cisco IOS software **copy** command is used to move configuration files from one component or device to another, such as RAM, NVRAM, or a TFTP server. Figure 4-59 shows the command syntax.

Figure 4-59   copy Command Syntax

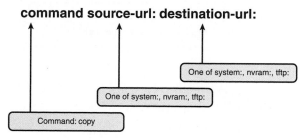

command source-url: destination-url:

Examples 4-26 and 4-27 demonstrate common **copy** command use. The examples list two methods to accomplish the same tasks. The first example is a simple syntax, and the second example is more explicit.

Example 4-26 shows how to copy the running configuration from RAM to the startup configuration in NVRAM.

Example 4-26   Copying the Running Configuration to the Startup Configuration

```
R2# copy running-config startup-config
R2# copy system:running-config nvram:startup-config
```

Example 4-27 shows how to copy the running configuration from RAM to a remote location.

Example 4-27   Copying the Running Configuration to a TFTP Server

```
R2# copy running-config tftp:
R2# copy system:running-config tftp:
```

Example 4-28 shows how to copy a configuration from a remote source to the running configuration.

Example 4-28   Copying from a TFTP Server to RAM

```
R2# copy tftp: running-config
R2# copy tftp: system:running-config
```

Example 4-29 shows how to copy a configuration from a remote source to the startup configuration.

Example 4-29   Copying from TFTP to the Startup Configuration

```
R2# copy tftp: startup-config
R2# copy tftp: nvram:startup-config
```

Cisco IOS File Naming Conventions

The Cisco IOS image file is based on a special naming convention. The name for the Cisco IOS image file contains multiple parts, each with a specific meaning. It is important that you understand this naming convention when upgrading and selecting an IOS.

Figure 4-60 shows a sample IOS image filename.

Figure 4-60   Sample IOS Image Filename

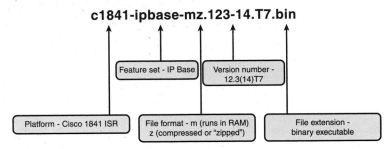

It can be dissected as follows:

- The first part, **c1841**, identifies the platform on which the image runs. In this example, the platform is a Cisco 1841.

- The second part, **ipbase**, specifies the feature set. In this case, ipbase refers to the basic IP internetworking image. Many different feature sets are available:

  - **i** designates the IP feature set.

  - **j** designates the enterprise feature set (all protocols).

  - **s** designates a PLUS feature set (extra queuing, manipulation, or translations).

  - **56i** designates 56-bit IPsec DES encryption.

  - **3** designates the firewall/IDS.

  - **k2** designates 3DES IPsec encryption (168 bit).

- The third part, **mz**, indicates where the image runs and if the file is compressed. In this example, mz indicates that the file runs from RAM and is compressed.

- The fourth part, **123-14.T7**, is the version number.

- The final part, **bin**, is the file extension. The .bin extension indicates that this is a binary executable file.

Managing Cisco IOS Images

Production internetworks usually span wide areas and contain multiple routers. It is important for an administrator to update Cisco IOS images whenever exploits and vulnerabilities are discovered. It is also a sound practice to ensure that all your platforms are running the same version of Cisco IOS software whenever possible. Finally, for any network, it is always prudent to retain a backup copy of the Cisco IOS software image in case the system image in the router becomes corrupted or accidentally erased.

Widely distributed routers need a source or backup location for Cisco IOS software images. Using a network TFTP server allows image and configuration uploads and downloads over the network. The network TFTP server can be another router, a workstation, or a file server.

As any network grows, storing Cisco IOS software images and configuration files on the central TFTP server gives you control over the number and revision level of Cisco IOS images and configuration files that must be maintained. Figure 4-61 shows a sample topology with a TFTP server.

Figure 4-61   Topology with a TFTP Server

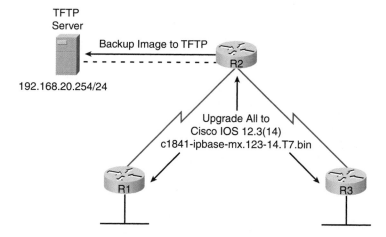

Before changing a Cisco IOS image on the router, you need to complete these tasks:

Step 1.   Determine the memory required for the update, compare it to the amount of existing memory on the router, and install additional memory if necessary.

Step 2.   Set up and test the file transfer capability between the TFTP server and the router.

Step 3.   Schedule the required downtime, normally outside of business hours, for the router to perform the update.

When you are ready to do the update, carry out these steps:

Step 1.   Shut down all interfaces on the router that are not needed to perform the update.

Step 2.   Back up the current operating system and the current configuration file to a TFTP server.

Step 3.   Load the update for either the operating system or the configuration file.

Step 4.   Test to confirm that the update works properly. If the tests are successful, you can reenable the interfaces you disabled. If the tests are not successful, back out of the update, determine what went wrong, and start again.

A great challenge for network operators is to minimize the downtime after a router has been compromised and the operating software and configuration data have been erased. The operator must retrieve an archived copy of the configuration (if one exists) and restore a working image to the router. Recovery must then be performed for each affected router, which adds to the total network downtime.

Bear in mind that the Cisco IOS software resilient configuration feature enables a router to secure and maintain a working copy of the running operating system image and configuration so that those files can withstand malicious attempts to erase the contents of NVRAM and flash.

Backing Up and Upgrading a Software Image

Basic management tasks include saving backups of your configuration files as well as downloading and installing upgraded configuration files when directed to. You create a software backup image file by copying the image file from a router to a network TFTP server.

Backing Up the IOS Software Image

Refer to Figure 4-62. Assume that you want to back up the Cisco IOS of router R1 to the TFTP server located at 192.168.20.254.

To copy a Cisco IOS software image from flash memory to the network TFTP server, you should follow these suggested steps:

Step 1.   Ping the TFTP server to make sure you have access to it:

```
R1# ping 192.168.20.254

!!!!!
```

Step 2. Copy the current system image file from the router to the network TFTP server, using the **copy flash: tftp:** command in privileged EXEC mode. You then are prompted. The command requires that you enter the IP address of the remote host and the name of the source and destination system image files:

```
R1# copy flash: tftp:

Source filename []? c1841-ipbase-mz.123-14.T7.bin
Address or name of remote host []? 192.168.20.254
Destination filename [c1841-ipbase-mz.123-14.T7.bin]? <CR>
!!!!!!!!!!!!!!!!!! !!!!!!!!!!!!! !!!!!!!!!!!!! !!!!!!!
<Output omitted>
13832032 bytes copied in 113.061 secs (122341 bytes/sec)
R1#
```

During the copy process, exclamation points (!) indicate the progress. Each exclamation point signifies that one UDP segment has successfully transferred.

Figure 4-62   Copying an Image to a TFTP Server

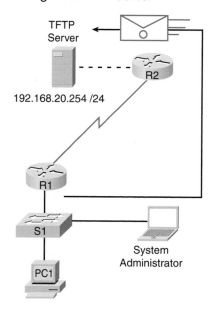

Upgrading IOS Software Images

Upgrading a system to a newer software version requires a different system image file to be loaded on the router. Use the **copy tftp: flash:** command to download the new image from the network TFTP server.

Refer to Figure 4-63. Assume that you will download the Cisco IOS software to router R1 from the TFTP server located at 192.168.20.254.

Figure 4-63   Copying an IOS Image from a TFTP Server

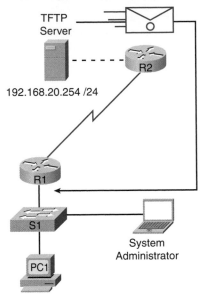

You should verify that the router has sufficient disk space to accommodate the new Cisco IOS software image. Use the **show flash:** command on the router to determine the size of the Cisco IOS image file, as shown in Example 4-30.

Example 4-30   Determining Cisco IOS Image File Size

```
R1# show flash:


System flash directory:
File  Length    Name/status
  1    13832032  c1841-ipbase-mz.123-14.T7.bin
[13832032 bytes used, 18682016 available, 32514048 total]
32768K bytes of processor board System flash (Read/Write)
```

The **show flash:** command is an important tool for gathering information about the router memory and image file. It can determine the following:

- The total amount of flash memory on the router

- The amount of flash memory available

- The names of all the files stored in the flash memory and the amount of flash occupied, as highlighted in Example 4-30

Example 4-31 provides the commands to download the IOS image from a TFTP server.

Example 4-31   Copying from the TFTP Server

```
R1#copy tftp: flash: <CR>

Address or name of remote host []?192.168.20.254
Source filename []? c1841-ipbase-mz.123-14.T7.bin
Destination filename [c1841-ipbase-mz.123-14.T7.bin]?<CR>
Accessing tftp://192.168.20.254/c1841-ipbase-mz.123-14.T7.bin
Erase flash: before copying? [confirm] <CR>
Erasing the flash filesystem will remove all files! Continue? [confirm] <CR>
Erasing device... eeeeeeeeeeeeeeeeeeeeeeeeeeeeeeeeeeeeeeeeeeeeeeeeeeeeeeeeeeeeeeeee
<Output omitted> erased
Erase of flash: complete
Loading c1841-ipbase-mz.123-14.T7.bin from 192.168.20.254 (via Serial 0/0/0): !!!!!
!!!!!!!!!!!!!!!!!!!!!!!!!!!!!!!!!
<Output omitted>
```

The command prompts you for the IP address of the remote host and the name of the source and destination system image file. Enter the appropriate filename of the update image just as it appears on the server.

After these entries are confirmed, the **Erase flash:** prompt appears. Erasing flash memory makes room for the new image. Erase flash memory if there is insufficient flash memory for more than one Cisco IOS image. If no free flash memory is available, the erase routine is required before new files can be copied. The system informs you of these conditions and prompts you for a response.

Note

For fallback purposes, ensure that you have a backup copy of the existing IOS before you erase it. This ensures a backup plan should there be issues with the new IOS image.

Each exclamation point means that one UDP segment has successfully transferred.

Note

Make sure that the Cisco IOS image loaded is appropriate for the router platform. If the wrong Cisco IOS image is loaded, the router could be made unbootable, requiring ROM monitor (ROMmon) intervention.

Using a TFTP Server to Upgrade a Cisco IOS Image (4.5.4)

In this activity, you configure access to a TFTP server and upload a newer, more advanced Cisco IOS image. Although Packet Tracer simulates upgrading the Cisco IOS image on a router, it does not simulate backing up a Cisco IOS image to the TFTP server. In addition, although the image you are upgrading to is more advanced, this Packet Tracer simulation does not reflect the upgrade by enabling more advanced commands. The same Packet Tracer command set is still in effect. Use File e4-454.pka on the CD-ROM that accompanies this book to perform this activity using Packet Tracer.

Recovering Software Images

A router cannot function without its Cisco IOS software. Should IOS be deleted or become corrupt, an administrator must then copy an image to the router for it to become operational again.

One method to accomplish this would be to use the Cisco IOS image that was previously saved to the TFTP server.

Restoring IOS Software Images

When an IOS on a router is accidentally deleted from flash, the router is still operational because the IOS is running in RAM. However, it is crucial that the router is not rebooted at this time, because it would not be able to find a valid IOS in flash.

If the router is rebooted with a missing, invalid, or corrupt IOS image, it enters ROM monitor mode (ROMmon). For example, in Figure 4-64, the IOS on router R1 has accidentally been deleted from flash.

Figure 4-64 Topology with a TFTP Server

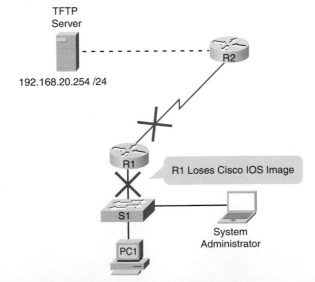

Unfortunately, the router has been rebooted and can no longer load an IOS. Because the router does not have a valid Cisco IOS image, it automatically boots into ROMmon mode. Very few commands are available in ROMmon mode. You can view these commands by entering **?** at the **rommon>** command prompt.

While in this state, router R1 needs to retrieve the IOS image that was previously copied to the TFTP server connected to R2. Because it is in ROMmon mode, **tftpdnld** is a special ROMmon command that must be used to load an IOS from a TFTP server.

To enable the router to use the **tftpdnld** command, first you must set specific ROMmon variables. These variables are syntax- and case-sensitive. When you enter the ROMmon variables, be aware of the following:

- Variable names are case-sensitive.

- Do not include any spaces immediately before or after the = symbol.

- Where possible, use a text editor to cut and paste the variables into the terminal window. The full line must be entered accurately.

- Navigational keys are not operational.

In this scenario, the TFTP server is directly connected to router R1. Having made preparations with the TFTP server, carry out the following procedure:

Step 1.   Connect the devices. Connect the PC of the system administrator to the console port on the affected router, as shown in Figure 4-65.

Figure 4-65   Console to the TFTP Server

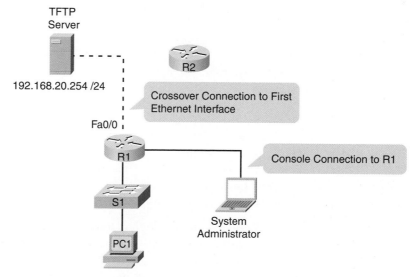

Connect the TFTP server to the first Ethernet port on the router using a crossover cable. In the figure, R1 is a Cisco 1841, so the port is Fa0/0. Assume that the TFTP server is operational and configured with IP address 192.168.20.254/24.

Router R1 must now be configured with the appropriate values to connect to the TFTP server. Remember that the syntax of the ROMmon commands is crucial. The IP address must be on the same subnet as the TFTP server. In this example, we will temporarily assign the Fa0/0 interface of router R1 the IP address 192.168.20.1.

Step 2.   Boot the router and set the ROMmon variables:

```
rommon1> IP_ADDRESS=192.168.20.1
rommon2> IP_SUBNET_MASK=255.255.255.0
rommon3> DEFAULT_GATEWAY=192.168.20.254
rommon4> TFTP_SERVER=192.168.20.254
rommon5> TFTP_FILE=c1841-ipbase-mz.123-14.T7.bin
```

Although the IP addresses, subnet mask, and image name shown here are only examples, it is vital that you use this syntax when configuring the router. Keep in mind that the actual variables vary depending on your configuration.

When you have entered the variables, proceed to the next step.

Step 3.   Enter the tftpdnld command at the ROMmon prompt:

```
rommon7> tftpdnld

           IP_ADDRESS: 192.168.20.1
       IP_SUBNET_MASK: 255.255.255.0
      DEFAULT_GATEWAY: 192.168.20.254
          TFTP_SERVER: 192.168.20.254
            TFTP_FILE: c1841-ipbase-mz.123-14.T7.bin
Invoke this command for disaster recovery only.
WARNING: all existing data in all partitions on flash will be lost!
Do you wish to continue? y/n:  [n]: y
Receiving c1841-ipbase-mz.123-14.T7.bin from 192.168.20.254 !!!!!!!!!!!!!!!!
<Output omitted>!!!!!!!
File reception completed.
Copying file c1841-ipbase-mz.123-14.T7.bin to flash.
Erasing flash at 0x607c0000
program flash location 0x605a0000
```

The **tftpdnld** command displays the required environment variables and warns that all existing data in flash will be erased. Enter **y** to proceed, and press Enter. The router attempts to connect to the TFTP server to initiate the download. When it is connected, the download begins, as indicated by the exclamation points. Each ! indicates that the router has received one UDP segment.

You can use the **reset** command to reload the router with the new Cisco IOS image.

Using Xmodem to Restore an IOS Image

Using the **tftpdnld** command is a quick way to copy the image file. If for some reason you are unable to use the router's Ethernet port, another method for restoring a Cisco IOS image to a router is by using Xmodem. However, the file transfer is accomplished using the console cable; therefore, this is very slow compared to the **tftpdnld** command. The reason is that the default console connection usually is set to 9600 bps instead of the very fast 100-Mbps FastEthernet interface.

Assume that the router R1 host has lost its IOS image, as shown in Figure 4-66.

Figure 4-66   R1 Loses Its Cisco IOS Image

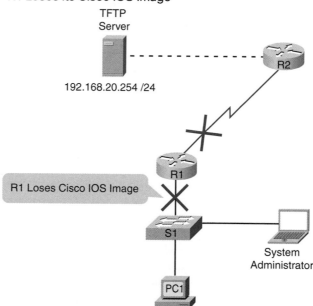

Recall that if the Cisco IOS image is lost, the router goes into ROMmon mode when it boots up. As mentioned, another method to download the IOS using ROMmon is to use the ROMmon **xmodem** command. With that command, the router can communicate with a terminal emulation application, such as HyperTerminal, on the PC of a system administrator. A system administrator who has a copy of the Cisco IOS image on a PC can restore it to the router by establishing a console connection between the router and a PC running terminal emulation software, as shown in Figure 4-67.

Figure 4-67   Establish a Console with R1

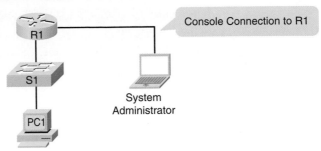

Follow these steps:

Step 1.   Connect the PC of the system administrator to the console port on the affected router. Open a terminal emulation session between the router R1 and the PC of the system administrator.

Step 2.   Boot the router and issue the **xmodem** command at the ROMmon command prompt:

```
rommon1> xmodem -c c1841-ipbase-mz.123-14.T7.bin

Do not start the sending program yet...
device does not contain a valid magic number
dir: cannot open device "flash:"

WARNING: All existing data in bootflash will be lost!
Invoke this application only for disaster recovery.
Do you wish to continue? y/n  [n]:y

Ready to receive file c1841-ipbase-mz.123-14.T7.bin
```

The command syntax is **xmodem** [**-cyr**] [*filename*]. The **cyr** option varies depending on the configuration. For instance, **-c** specifies CRC-16, **y** specifies the Ymodem protocol, and **r** copies the image to RAM. The filename is the name of the file to be transferred.

Accept all prompts when asked, as shown in the preceding configuration.

Step 3.   Figure 4-68 shows the process of sending a file using HyperTerminal. In this case, choose **Transfer > Send File**.

Step 4.   Browse to the location of the Cisco IOS image you want to transfer, and choose the Xmodem protocol, as shown in Figure 4-69.

Figure 4-68 HyperTerminal Transfer Menu

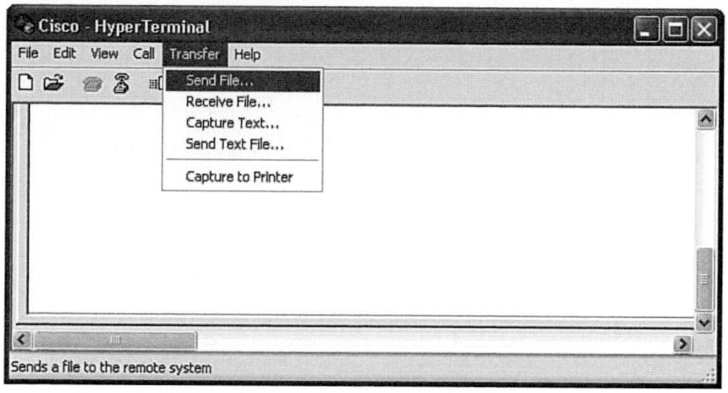

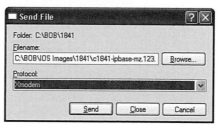

Figure 4-69 HyperTerminal Send File Window

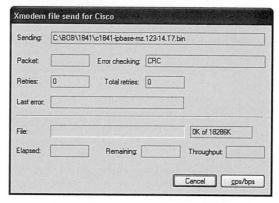

Click **Send**. A dialog box appears, displaying the status of the download, as shown in Figure 4-70. It takes several seconds before the host and router begin transferring the information.

Figure 4-70 Send File Status Window

As the upload begins, the Packet and Elapsed fields increment. Take note of the estimated time remaining indicator.

> **Note**
>
> The download time can be dramatically improved if you change the connection speed of HyperTerminal and the router from 9600 bps to 115000 bps.

When the transfer is complete, the router automatically reloads with the new Cisco IOS.

Troubleshooting Cisco IOS Configurations

When you have a valid Cisco IOS image running on all the routers in the network, and all the configurations are backed up, you can manually tune configurations for individual devices to improve their performance in the network.

Cisco IOS Troubleshooting Commands

Two commands that are extensively used in day-to-day network administration are **show** and **debug**. The difference between the two is significant. A **show** command lists the configured parameters and their values. The **debug** command allows you to trace the execution of a process. Use the **show** command to verify configurations. Use the **debug** command to identify traffic flows through interfaces and router processes.

Table 4-5 summarizes the characteristics of the **show** and **debug** commands.

Table 4-5   Cisco IOS Troubleshooting Commands

	show	debug
Processing Characteristic	Static	Dynamic
Processing Load	Low overhead	High overhead
Primary Use	To gather facts	To observe processes

The best time to learn about the output generated by these commands is when a network is fully operational. This way, you can recognize what is missing or incorrect when using the commands to troubleshoot a problem network.

Using the **show** Command

The **show** command displays static information. Use **show** commands when gathering facts for isolating problems in an internetwork, including problems with interfaces, nodes, media, servers, clients, or applications. Use of the **show** commands can confirm that configuration changes have been implemented.

The Cisco IOS command guide for IOS 12.3 lists 1463 **show** commands. When you are at the command prompt, enter **show ?** for a list of available **show** commands for the level and mode at which you are operating. Example 4-32 shows sample output for the **show protocols** command.

Example 4-32   show protocols Command Output

```
R1# show protocols

Global values:
  Internet Protocol routing is enabled
FastEthernet0/0 is up, line protocol is up
  Internet address is 192.168.10.1/24
FastEthernet0/1 is administratively down, line protocol is down
Serial0/0/0 is up, line protocol is up
  Internet address is 10.1.1.1/30
Vlan1 is administratively down, line protocol is down
```

Using the **debug** Command

When you configure a router, the commands you enter initiate many more processes than you see in the simple line of code. Therefore, tracing your written configurations line by line with a **show** command does not reveal all the possibilities for error. Instead, you need some way of capturing data from the device as each step in a running process is initiated.

By default, the network server sends the output from **debug** commands and system error messages to the console. Remember that you can redirect debug output to a syslog server.

Caution

Debugging output is assigned high priority in the CPU process queue and therefore can interfere with normal production processes on a network. For this reason, use **debug** commands during quiet hours and only to troubleshoot specific problems.

The **debug** command displays dynamic data and events. Use **debug** to check the flow of protocol traffic for problems, protocol bugs, or misconfigurations. The **debug** command provides a flow of information about the traffic being seen (or not seen) on an interface, error messages generated by nodes on the network, protocol-specific diagnostic packets, and other useful troubleshooting data. Use **debug** commands when operations on the router or network must be viewed to determine if events or packets are working properly.

All **debug** commands are entered in privileged EXEC mode, and most **debug** commands take no arguments. To list and see a brief description of all the debugging command options, enter the **debug ?** command in privileged EXEC mode.

Caution

It is important to turn off debugging when you have finished your troubleshooting. The best way to ensure that no lingering debugging operations are running is to use the **no debug all** command.

Example 4-33 shows the sample output of the **debug ip rip** command.

Example 4-33   debug ip rip Command Output

```
R1# debug ip rip

RIP protocol debugging is on
RIP: sending  v1 update to 255.255.255.255 via FastEthernet0/0 (192.168.10.1)
RIP: build update entries
     network 10.0.0.0 metric 1
     network 192.168.20.0 metric 2
     network 192.168.30.0 metric 3
     network 209.165.200.0 metric 2
RIP: sending  v1 update to 255.255.255.255 via Serial0/0/0 (10.1.1.1)
RIP: build update entries
     network 192.168.10.0 metric 1
RIP: received v1 update from 10.1.1.2 on Serial0/0/0
     10.2.2.0 in 1 hops
     192.168.20.0 in 1 hops (output omitted)
R1# no debug all


All possible debugging has been turned off
```

Considerations When Using the **debug** Command

It's one thing to use **debug** commands to troubleshoot a lab network that lacks end-user application traffic. It's another thing to use **debug** commands on a production network that users depend on for data flow. Without proper precautions, the impact of a broadly focused **debug** command could make matters worse.

With proper, selective, and temporary use of **debug** commands, you can obtain potentially useful information without needing a protocol analyzer or other third-party tool.

Keep the following points in mind when using **debug** commands:

- **debug** gets CPU priority. Plan **debug** use carefully. When the information you need from the **debug** command is interpreted and the debug (and any other related configuration setting, if any) is finished, the router can resume its faster switching. Problem-solving can be resumed, a better-targeted action plan can be created, and the network problem can be resolved.

- **debug** can help resolve persistent issues, outweighing its effect on network performance.

- **debug** can generate too much output that is of little use for a specific problem. Know what you are looking for before you start. Normally, knowledge of the protocol or protocols being debugged is required to properly interpret the **debug** outputs.

- Different debugs generate different output formats. Do not be caught by surprise. Some generate a single line of output per packet, and others generate multiple lines of output per packet. Some **debug** commands generate large amounts of output; others generate only occasional output. Some generate lines of text, and others generate information in field format.

Commands Related to the **debug** Command

To effectively use debugging tools, you must consider the following:

- The impact that a troubleshooting tool has on router performance

- The most selective and focused use of the diagnostic tool

- How to minimize the impact of troubleshooting on other processes that compete for resources on the network device

- How to stop the troubleshooting tool when diagnosing is complete so that the router can resume its most efficient switching

To optimize your efficient use of the **debug** command, these commands can help you:

- The **service timestamps** command is used to add a time stamp to a debug or log message. This feature can provide valuable information about when debug elements occurred and the duration of time between events.

- The **show processes** command displays the CPU usage for each process. This data can influence decisions about using a **debug** command if it indicates that the production system is already too heavily used for adding a **debug** command.

- The **no debug all** command disables all **debug** commands. This command frees up system resources after you finish debugging. As an alternative, you could also use the **undebug all** command.

- The **terminal monitor** command displays debug output and system error messages for the current terminal and session. When you telnet to a device and issue a **debug** command, you do not see output unless this command is entered.

Recovering a Lost Password

Passwords can be forgotten, or perhaps an administrator is replaced and the current passwords are unknown. Whatever the reason, passwords can be lost. For this reason, Cisco provides a password recovery process to enable us to recover from lost passwords.

About Password Recovery

The first thing you need to know about password recovery is that for security reasons, you need physical access to the router. You connect your PC to the router through a console cable.

The enable password and enable secret password protect access to privileged EXEC and configuration modes. The enable password can be recovered, but the enable secret password is encrypted and must be replaced with a new password.

In a router, a *configuration register*, represented by a single hexadecimal value, tells the router what specific steps to take when powered on. The configuration register is similar to your PC BIOS settings, which control the bootup process. Among other things, the BIOS tells the PC from which hard disk to boot. Configuration registers have many uses, and password recovery is probably the most popular.

Router Password Recovery Procedure

In Figure 4-71, an administrator can no longer access the privileged EXEC mode of router R1.

Figure 4-71   Recovering the Enable Password of Router R1

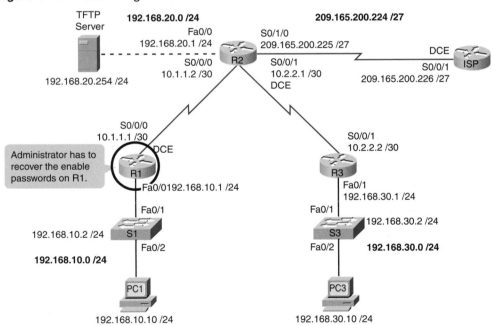

Recovering a lost password involves four steps:

1. Prepare the device.

2. Bypass startup.

3. Access NVRAM.

4. Reset the password(s).

Prepare the Device

To recover a router password, do the following:

Step 1.   Connect to the console port, and open a terminal session.

Step 2.   Even if you have lost the enable password, you still have access to user EXEC mode. Enter **show version** at the prompt, and record the configuration register setting:

```
R1> show version

<Output omitted>
Configuration register is 0x2102
R1>
```

The configuration register usually is set to 0x2102 or 0x102. If you can no longer access the router (because of a lost login or TACACS password), you can safely assume that your configuration register is set to 0x2102.

Step 3.   Use the power switch to turn off the router, and then turn the router back on.

Step 4.   Press **Break** on the terminal keyboard within 60 seconds of power-up to access the ROMmon prompt.

Bypass Startup

It is important to understand that the startup config file still exists. It simply is bypassed when rebooting the router to ignore the unknown passwords.

Step 5.   Enter **confreg 0x2142** at the ROMmon prompt. This causes the router to bypass the startup configuration where the forgotten enable password is stored.

Step 6.   Enter **reset** at the prompt. The router reboots, but it ignores the saved configuration. However, the file still exists in NVRAM.

Step 7.   Enter **no** after each setup question or, better yet, press **Ctrl-C** to skip the initial setup procedure.

Step 8.   Enter **enable** at the **Router>** prompt. This puts you into enable mode, where you should be able to see the **Router#** prompt.

Access NVRAM

Step 9.   Enter **copy startup-config running-config** to copy the backup NVRAM config file into memory.

Caution

Be careful! Do not enter **copy running-config startup-config**, or you will erase your startup configuration.

Step 10. Enter **show running-config**. You can now see the passwords (enable password, enable secret, vty, and console passwords) in either encrypted or unencrypted format. You can reuse unencrypted passwords. If the password is encrypted, you should enter a new one.

> **Note**
>
> A byproduct of using this method is that all interfaces are also shut down. Therefore, you have to manually reenable the required interfaces.

Reset the Password(s)

Step 11. Enter **configure terminal**. The **R1(config)#** prompt appears.

Step 12. Enter **enable secret** *password* to change the enable secret password.

Step 13. Issue the **no shutdown** command on every interface that you want to use.

Step 14. From global configuration mode, enter **config-register** *configuration_register_setting*. The *configuration_register_setting* is either the value you recorded in Step 2 or 0x2102. For example:

```
R1(config)# config-register 0x2102
```

The config register setting is reset to 0x2102.

Step 15. Press **Ctrl-Z** or enter **end** to leave configuration mode. The **R1#** prompt appears.

Step 16. Enter **copy running-config startup-config** to commit the changes.

You can issue the **show ip interface brief** command to confirm that your interface configuration is correct. Every interface that you want to use should display **up up**.

You have now completed password recovery. Entering the **show version** command confirms that the router will use the configured config register setting on the next reboot.

Summary

The importance of network security cannot be underestimated. This chapter stressed the importance of developing an effective security policy and then adhering to what it requires you to do. You now know common threats to your network and the basic steps you need to take to protect yourself from these threats. Moreover, you now understand the requirements to balance security against access.

Network attacks come from all directions and in many forms. Password attacks are easy to launch but also are easily defended against. The tactics of social engineering require users to develop a degree of suspicion and care. When an attacker gains network access, he or she can literally open all the locks. But attackers need not always gain access to wreak havoc. Denial-of-service attacks can overload network resources to the point that they can no longer function. Worms, viruses, and Trojan horses can penetrate networks and continue spreading and infecting devices.

A key task in securing a network is to secure the routers. Routers are the gateway into the network and are obvious targets. Basic administrative tasks, including good physical security, maintaining an updated IOS, and backing up configuration files, are a start. Cisco IOS software provides a wealth of security features to harden routers and close doors opened by used ports and services, most of which can be completed using the one-step lockdown feature of Cisco SDM. Finally, you learned how to perform password recovery.

Labs

The activities and labs available in the companion *Accessing the WAN, CCNA Exploration Labs and Study Guide* (ISBN 1-58713-201-X) provide hands-on practice with the following topics introduced in this chapter:

Lab 4-1: Basic Security Configuration (4.6.1)

In this lab, you learn how to configure basic network security using the network shown in the topology diagram. You learn how to configure router security three different ways: using the CLI, using the AutoSecure feature, and using Cisco SDM. You also learn how to manage Cisco IOS software.

Lab 4-2: Challenge Security Configuration (4.6.2)

In this lab, you configure security using the network shown in the topology diagram. If you need assistance, refer to the Basic Security Configuration lab. However, try to do as much on your own as possible. For this lab, do not use password protection or log in on any console lines, because they might cause accidental logout. However, you should still secure the console line using other means. Use **ciscoccna** for all passwords in this lab.

Lab 4-3: Troubleshooting Security Configuration (4.6.3)

Your company just hired a new network engineer who has created some security issues in the network with misconfigurations and oversights. Your boss has asked you to correct these errors. While correcting the problems, make sure that all the devices are secure but are still accessible by administrators, and that all networks are reachable. All routers must be accessible with SDM from PC1. Verify that a device is secure by using tools such as Telnet and ping. Unauthorized use of these tools should be blocked, but also ensure that authorized use is permitted. For this lab, do not use login or password protection on any console lines to prevent accidental lockout. Use **ciscoccna** for all passwords in this scenario.

Many of the Hands-on Labs include Packet Tracer Companion Activities where you can use Packet Tracer to complete a simulation of the lab. Look for this icon in the *Accessing the WAN, CCNA Exploration Labs and Study Guide* for Hands-on Labs that have a Packet Tracer Companion.

Check Your Understanding

Complete all the review questions listed here to test your understanding of the topics and concepts in this chapter. Answers are listed in the Appendix, "Check Your Understanding and Challenge Questions Answer Key."

1. Match a security category to each security weakness (answers may be used more than once):

   Operating system weaknesses

   Unsecured user accounts

   Network equipment weaknesses

   Unsecured default settings

   Lack of consistency and continuity

   TCP/IP and ICMP weaknesses

   Lack of a disaster recovery plan

   A. Technological weakness

   B. Configuration weakness

   C. Security policy weakness

2. Which pieces of information can you determine from opening a router's Cisco SDM home page? (Choose two.)

A. Routing table

B. CDP neighbors

C. Snapshot of the router configuration

D. A listing of available configuration wizards

E. Features supported by the Cisco IOS software

3. A technician has been asked to perform a Cisco SDM one-step lockdown test. Which mode and SDM page should be used to initiate the test?

A. The Firewall page in Diagnostic mode

B. The Security Audit page in Configure mode

C. The Security Audit page in Test mode

D. The Firewall page in Test mode

4. Match each attack type with its description:

Reconnaissance attack

Password attack

Port redirection

Worm, virus, Trojan horse

DoS attack

A. Dictionary-cracking and brute-force attack

B. Uses a compromised host to pass traffic through a firewall that would otherwise be dropped

C. Uses ping sweeps, port scans, and packet sniffers to gain information about a network

D. Floods a network device with traffic in an attempt to render it unusable for legitimate traffic

E. Malicious software designed to damage a system, replicate itself, or deny services or access to networks, systems, or services

5. What is a major advantage of HIPS over HIDS?

A. HIPS does not require host-based client software.

B. HIPS consumes fewer system resources.

C. HIPS can prevent intrusions.

D. With HIPS, you don't need to update signature files as often.

6. What is the core or "hub" component of the Security Wheel?

   A. Secure

   B. Monitor

   C. Improve

   D. Test

   E. Security policy

7. As part of a network security plan, where does Cisco recommend that administrators send events captured by syslog?

   A. Flash

   B. NVRAM

   C. Designated log hosts

   D. Designated TFTP clients

   E. Designated SNMP clients

8. Which protocol should be used when strong privacy and session integrity are needed for remote administration?

   A. HTTP

   B. SNMP

   C. SSH

   D. Telnet

   E. TFTP

9. Match each network policy with its description:

   Account access request policy

   Remote-access policy

   Risk assessment policy

   Audit policy

   Acceptable user policy

   A. Defines the standards for connecting to the internal network from outside the organization.

   B. Specifies procedures to investigate incidents, ensure conformance to security policies, and monitor user and system activity.

   C. Defines how network resources may and may not be employed.

   D. Formalizes the process of how users request access to systems.

   E. Defines the requirements and provides the authority for the information security team to identify, assess, and remediate risks to the information infrastructure associated with conducting business.

10. What are the three required steps to configure SDM?

    A. Use the **auto secure** command to configure router security.

    B. Enable the HTTP and HTTPS servers on the router.

    C. Create a user account defined with privilege level 15.

    D. Create a user account defined with privilege level 0.

    E. Create an ACL to allow HTTP traffic into the router, and apply it to the VTYs.

    F. Configure SSH and Telnet for local login and privilege level 15.

    G. Configure SSH and Telnet for local login and privilege level 0.

11. Which services should be disabled if they aren't required on a router to prevent security vulnerabilities? (Choose three.)

    A. Network Time Protocol (NTP)

    B. Domain Name System (DNS)

    C. Secure Socket Layer (SSL)

    D. Cisco Express Forwarding (CEF)

    E. Simple Network Management Protocol (SNMP)

    F. Secure Shell (SSH)

12. Which feature provides a straightforward "one-touch" device lockdown for configuring the security posture of routers?

    A. SSH

    B. SDM

    C. AutoSecure

    D. SNMP

13. Match the network management service with its description:

Network Time Protocol (NTP)

Domain Name System (DNS)

Simple Network Management Protocol (SNMP)

    A. An application layer protocol that provides a facility for retrieving and posting data for monitoring and managing devices in a network using TCP port 161

    B. A protocol designed to synchronize the time on a network of machines and that runs over UDP using port 123

    C. A distributed database that maps hostnames to IP addresses using services on a designated server

14. Which feature is a web-based device-management tool for Cisco IOS software-based routers?

    A. SSH

    B. SDM

    C. AutoSecure

    D. SNMP

15. Which SDM wizards are available to configure a router? (Choose three.)

    A. Security audit

    B. Firewall and ACL

    C. DHCP

    D. QoS

    E. Routing

    F. Access list

16. List the four types of reconnaissance attacks, and provide an example of a tool that can be used to carry out each type of attack.

17. List four types of access attacks.

18. List three types of DoS attacks and three types of DDoS attacks.

19. List and explain the anatomy of a worm attack and the four steps to mitigate it.

20. Refer to Figure 4-72.

Figure 4-72   Tera Term Output for Question 20

The following has been configured on router R1:

```
hostname R1

username Student secret cisco123

line vty 0 4

no transport input

transport input telnet
```

To increase administrative access security, you have applied the following configuration. However, you are unable to establish an SSH connection to router R1. Assume that you could telnet to the router before, and that the hostname, IP domain name, and crypto key have been correctly configured. Which changes would correct this problem?

21. List five vulnerable Cisco IOS network services, and provide the best practices associated with them. For example, unused interfaces should be disabled.

22. List the steps to enable the lockdown feature of SDM.

23. List the three steps required to update a router with a new Cisco IOS image file located on a TFTP server.

Challenge Questions and Activities

1. The administrator needs to apply Cisco IOS password security features and secure remote administrative management on router R1. The following is partial output from the **show running-config** command on R1:

```
R1# show running-config

*Dec 14 14:06:19.663: %SYS-5-CONFIG_I: Configured from console by console
Building configuration...

Current configuration : 836 bytes
!
version 12.4
service timestamps debug datetime msec
service timestamps log datetime msec
no service password-encryption
!
hostname R1
ip domain name cisco.com
enable password cisco
!
username Student password 0 cisco
!
!
line con 0
line aux 0
line vty 0 4
 login
!
scheduler allocate 20000 1000
!
end

R1#
```

Assume that the RSA asymmetric key has already been generated. What configurations should be configured on router R1 to address the security requirements?

CHAPTER 5

ACLs

Objectives

After completing this chapter, you should be able to answer the following questions:

- How are ACLs used to secure a medium-size enterprise branch office network? This includes the concept of packet filtering, the purpose of ACLs, how ACLs are used to control access, and the types of Cisco ACLs.

- How do you configure standard ACLs in a medium-size enterprise branch office network? This includes defining filtering criteria, configuring standard ACLs to filter traffic, and applying standard ACLs to router interfaces.

- How do you configure extended ACLs in a medium-size enterprise branch office network? This includes configuring extended ACLs and named ACLs, configuring filters, verifying and monitoring ACLs, and troubleshooting extended ACL issues.

- What are the complex ACLs in a medium-size enterprise branch office network? This includes configuring dynamic, reflexive, and timed ACLs, verifying and troubleshooting complex ACLs, and explaining relevant caveats.

Key Terms

This chapter uses the following key terms. You can find the definitions in the glossary at the end of the book.

Network security is a huge subject, and much of it is far beyond the scope of this book. However, one of the most important skills a network administrator needs is mastery of access control lists (ACL). Administrators use ACLs to stop traffic or permit only specified traffic while stopping all other traffic on their networks. This chapter gives you an opportunity to develop your mastery of ACLs with a series of lessons, activities, and lab exercises.

Network designers use firewalls to protect networks from unauthorized use. Firewalls are hardware or software solutions that enforce network security policies. Consider a lock on a door to a room inside a building. The lock allows only authorized users with a key or access card to pass through the door. Similarly, a firewall keeps unauthorized or potentially dangerous packets from entering the network. On a Cisco router, you can configure a simple firewall that provides basic traffic-filtering capabilities using ACLs.

An *access control list (ACL)* is a sequential list of permit or deny statements that apply to addresses or upper-layer protocols. ACLs provide a powerful way to control traffic into and out of your network. You can configure ACLs for all routed network protocols.

The most important reason to configure ACLs is to provide security for your network. This chapter explains how to use standard and extended ACLs as part of a security solution and teaches you how to configure them on a Cisco router. Included are tips, considerations, recommendations, and general guidelines on how to use ACLs.

Using ACLs to Secure Networks

ACLs enable you to control traffic into and out of your network. This control can be as simple as permitting or denying network hosts or addresses. However, ACLs can also be configured to control network traffic based on the TCP port being used. To understand how an ACL works with TCP, let's look at the dialogue that occurs during a TCP conversation when you download a web page to your computer.

A TCP Conversation

When you request data from a web server, IP takes care of the communication between the PC and the server. TCP takes care of the communication between your web browser (application) and the network server software. When you send an e-mail, look at a web page, or download a file, TCP is responsible for breaking data into packets for IP before they are sent and for assembling the data from the packets when they arrive. The TCP process is very much like a conversation in which two nodes on a network agree to pass data between one another.

Recall that TCP provides a connection-oriented, reliable, byte-stream service. The term connection-oriented means that the two applications using TCP must establish a TCP connection with each other before they can exchange data. TCP is a full-duplex protocol, meaning that each TCP connection supports a pair of byte streams, each stream flowing in one direction. TCP includes a flow-control mechanism for each byte stream that allows the receiver to limit how much data the sender can transmit. TCP also implements a congestion-control mechanism.

Figure 5-1 shows how a TCP/IP conversation takes place. TCP packets are marked with flags that denote their purpose. A SYN starts (synchronizes) the session, an ACK is an acknowledgment that an expected packet was received, and a FIN finishes the session. A SYN/ACK acknowledges that the transfer is synchronized and requires its own ACK. TCP data segments include the higher-level protocol needed to direct the application data to the correct application.

Figure 5-1   TCP Conversation

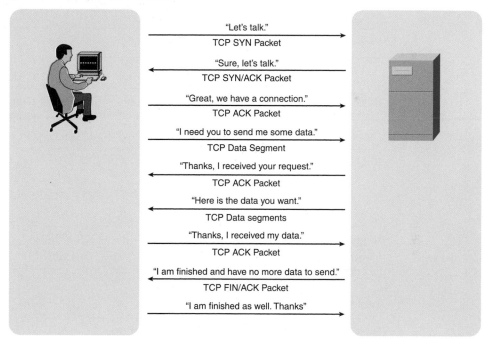

The TCP data segment also identifies the port matching the requested service, as shown in Table 5-1. For example, HTTP is port 80, SMTP is port 25, and FTP is ports 20 and 21. Table 5-1 lists examples of UDP and TCP ports. Table 5-2 lists the different port ranges, which are explained later in this book.

Table 5-1   Examples of TCP/UDP Port Numbers

Type of Port	Port Number	Description
Well-Known TCP Ports	21	FTP
	23	Telnet
	25	SMTP
	80	HTTP
	110	POP3
	194	Internet Relay Chat (IRC)
	443	Secure HTTP (HTTPS)
Well-Known UDP Ports	69	TFTP
	520	RIP
Well-Known TCP/UDP Ports	53	DNS
	161	SNMP
	531	AOL Instant Messenger, IRC
Registered TCP Ports	1863	MSN Messenger
	8008	Alternate HTTP
	8080	Alternate HTTP
Registered UDP Ports	1812	RADIUS Authentication Protocol
	2000	Cisco SCCP (VoIP)
	5004	RTP (Real-time Transport Protocol)
	5060	SIP (VoIP)
Registered TCP/UDP Common Ports	1433	MS SQL
	2948	WAP (MMS)

Table 5-2   Port Numbers

Port Number Range	Port Group
0 to 1023	Well-known (common) ports
1024 to 49151	Registered ports
49152 to 65535	Private and/or dynamic ports

Packet Filtering

Packet filtering, sometimes called static packet filtering, controls access to a network by analyzing the incoming and outgoing packets and passing or halting them based on stated criteria.

A router acts as a packet filter when it forwards or denies packets according to filtering rules. When a packet arrives at the packet-filtering router, the router extracts certain information from the packet header and makes decisions according to the filter rules about whether the packet can pass through or be discarded. Packet filtering works at the network layer of the Open Systems Interconnection (OSI) model or at the Internet layer of the TCP/IP model.

As a Layer 3 device, a packet-filtering router uses rules to determine whether to permit or deny traffic based on source and destination IP addresses, source port and destination port, and the packet's protocol. These rules are defined using ACLs.

Recall that an ACL is a sequential list of permit or deny statements that apply to IP addresses or upper-layer protocols. The ACL can extract the following information from the packet header, test it against its rules, and make "permit" or "deny" decisions based on

- Source IP address
- Destination IP address
- ICMP message type

The ACL can also extract upper-layer information and test it against its rules. Upper-layer information includes

- TCP/UDP source port
- TCP/UDP destination port

Figures 5-2 and 5-3 show an overview of how an ACL allows or denies a packet. Although the figures show packet filtering occurring at Layer 3, it should be noted that filtering can also occur at Layer 4.

Figure 5-2   Packet Filtering: Allowed

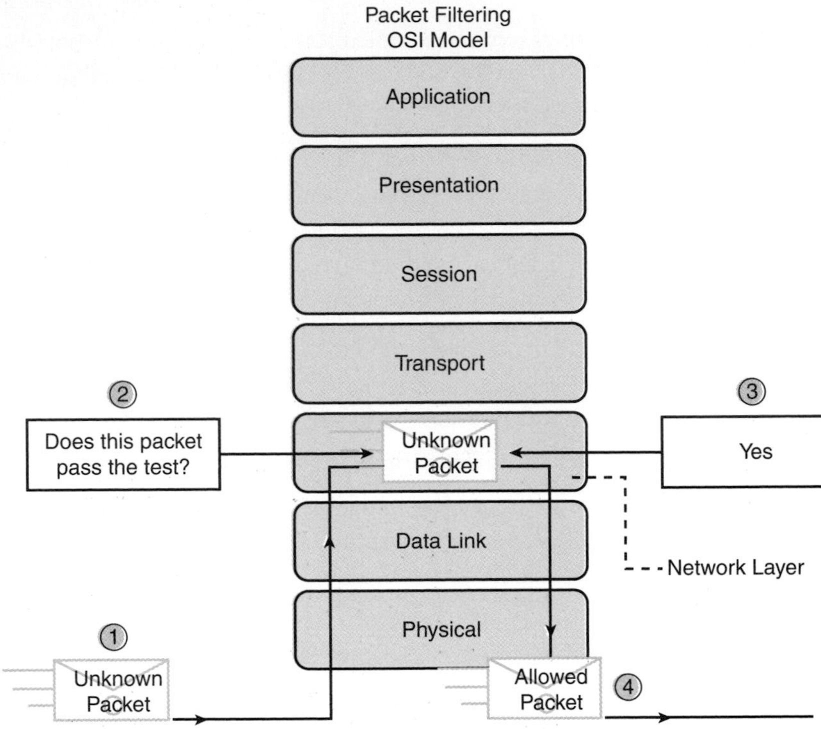

Packet Filtering
OSI Model

Application

Presentation

Session

Transport

② Does this packet pass the test?

Unknown Packet

③ Yes

Data Link

Network Layer

Physical

① Unknown Packet

Allowed Packet ④

To understand how a router uses packet filtering, imagine that a guard has been posted at a locked door. The guard's instructions are to allow only people whose names appear on a list to pass through the door. The guard is filtering people based on the criterion of having their names on the authorized list.

For example, you could say, "Permit only web access to users from network A. Deny web access to users from network B, but permit them to have all other access." Figure 5-4 shows the decision path the packet filter uses to accomplish this task.

Figure 5-3   Packet Filtering: Denied

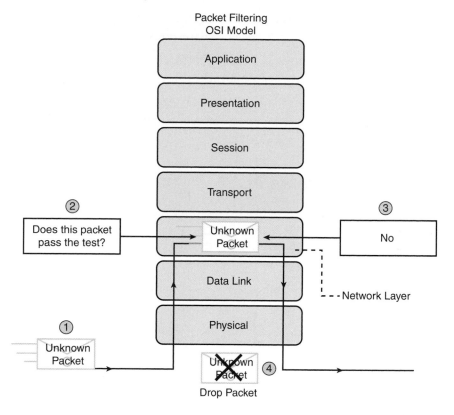

Figure 5-4   Packet Filtering Decision Path

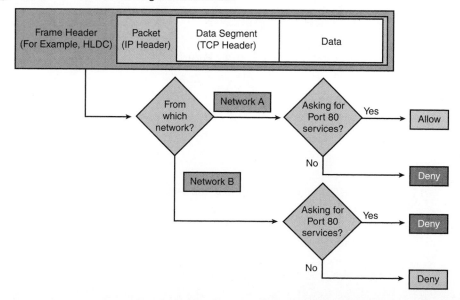

For this scenario, the packet filter looks at each packet as follows:

- If the packet is a TCP SYN from network A using port 80, it is allowed to pass. All other access is denied to those users.

- If the packet is a TCP SYN from network B using port 80, it is blocked. However, all other access is permitted.

This is just a simple example. You can configure multiple rules to further permit or deny services to specific users. You can also filter packets at the port level using an extended ACL, which is covered in the section "Configuring an Extended ACL."

What Is an ACL?

An ACL is a router configuration script that controls whether a router permits or denies packets to pass based on criteria found in the packet header, as shown in Figure 5-5. ACLs are among the most commonly used objects in Cisco IOS software. ACLs are also used to select types of traffic to be analyzed, forwarded, or processed in other ways.

Figure 5-5   What Is an ACL?

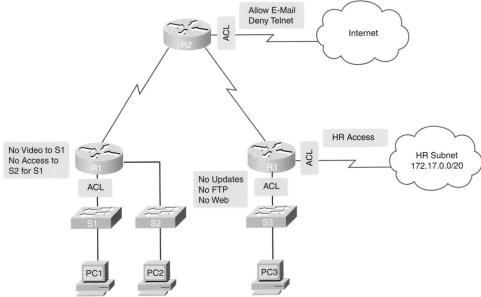

As each packet comes through an interface with an associated ACL, the ACL is checked from top to bottom, one line at a time, looking for a pattern matching the incoming packet. The ACL enforces one or more corporate security policies by applying a permit or deny rule to determine the packet's fate. ACLs can be configured to control access to a network or subnet.

By default, a router does not have any ACLs configured and, therefore, does not filter traffic. Traffic that enters the router is routed according to the routing table. If you do not use ACLs on the router, all packets that can be routed through the router pass through the router to the next network segment.

Here are some guidelines for using ACLs:

- Use ACLs in firewall routers positioned between your internal network and an external network such as the Internet.

- Use ACLs on a router positioned between two parts of your network to control traffic entering or exiting a specific part of your internal network.

- Configure ACLs on border routers—routers situated at the edges of your networks. This provides a basic buffer from the outside network, or between a less controlled area of your own network and a more sensitive area of your network.

- Configure ACLs for each network protocol configured on the border router interfaces. You can configure ACLs on an interface to filter inbound traffic, outbound traffic, or both.

The Three Ps

You can recall a general rule for applying ACLs on a router by remembering the three Ps. You can configure one ACL **p**er protocol, **p**er direction, **p**er interface:

- **One ACL per protocol**: To control traffic flow on an interface, an ACL must be defined for each protocol enabled on the interface (for example, IP or IPX).

- **One ACL per direction**: ACLs control traffic in one direction at a time on an interface. Two separate ACLs must be created to control inbound and outbound traffic.

- **One ACL per interface**: ACLs control traffic for an interface, such as Fast Ethernet 0/0.

Figure 5-6 shows a router with two interfaces and three protocols running, which means that this router could have a total of 12 separate ACLs applied.

Writing ACLs can be a challenging and complex task. Every interface can have multiple protocols and directions defined. The router shown in Figure 5-6 has two interfaces configured for IP—AppleTalk and IPX. This router could possibly require 12 separate ACLs—one ACL for each protocol, times 2 for each direction, times 2 for the number of ports.

Figure 5-6   ACL Traffic Filtering on a Router

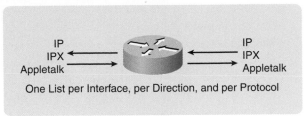

ACL Functions

ACLs perform the following tasks:

- Limit network traffic to increase network performance. For example, if corporate policy does not allow video traffic on the network, ACLs that block video traffic could be configured and applied. This would greatly reduce the network load and increase network performance.

- Provide traffic flow control. ACLs can restrict the delivery of routing updates. If updates are not required because of network conditions, bandwidth is preserved.

- Provide a basic level of security for network access. ACLs can allow one host to access part of the network and prevent another host from accessing the same area. For example, access to the Human Resources network can be restricted to select users.

- Decide which types of traffic to forward or block at the router interfaces. For example, an ACL can permit e-mail traffic but block all Telnet traffic.

- Control which areas a client can access on a network.

- Screen hosts to permit or deny access to network services. ACLs can permit or deny a user access to file types, such as FTP or HTTP.

ACLs inspect network packets based on criteria such as source address, destination address, protocols, and port numbers. In addition to either permitting or denying traffic, an ACL can classify traffic to enable priority processing down the line. This capability is similar to having a VIP pass at a concert or sporting event. The VIP pass gives selected guests privileges not offered to general-admission ticket holders, such as being able to enter a restricted area and being escorted to box seats.

ACL Operation

ACLs define the set of rules that give added control for packets that enter inbound interfaces, packets that relay through the router, and packets that exit outbound interfaces of the router. ACLs do not act on packets that originate from the router itself.

How ACLs Work

ACLs are configured either to apply to inbound traffic or to apply to outbound traffic:

- **Inbound ACLs**: Incoming packets are processed before they are routed to the outbound interface. An inbound ACL is efficient because it saves the overhead of routing lookups if the packet is discarded. If the packet is permitted by the tests, it is then processed for routing.

- **Outbound ACLs**: Incoming packets are routed to the outbound interface, and then they are processed through the outbound ACL.

ACL statements operate in sequential order. They evaluate packets against the ACL, from the top down, one statement at a time.

Figure 5-7 shows the logic for an inbound ACL. If a packet header and an ACL statement match, the rest of the statements in the list are skipped, and the packet is permitted or denied as determined by the matched statement. If a packet header does not match an ACL statement, the packet header is tested against the next statement in the list. This matching process continues until the end of the list is reached.

Figure 5-7   ACL Logic for an Inbound ACL

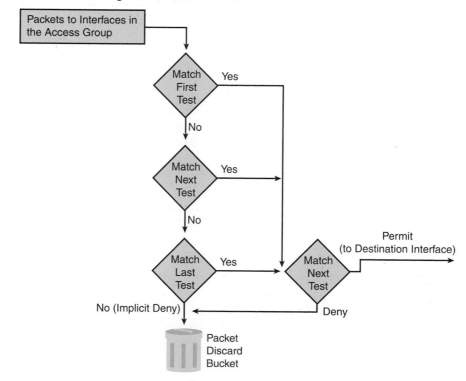

A final implied statement covers all packets for which conditions did not test true. This final test condition matches all other packets and results in a "deny" instruction. Instead of proceeding into or out of an interface, the router drops all these remaining packets. This final statement is often called the "implicit deny any" statement or the "deny all traffic" statement. Because of this statement, an ACL should have at least one permit statement; otherwise, the ACL blocks all traffic.

You can apply an ACL to multiple interfaces. However, there can be only one ACL per protocol, per direction, and per interface.

Figure 5-8 shows the logic for an outbound ACL.

Figure 5-8   ACL Logic for an Outbound ACL

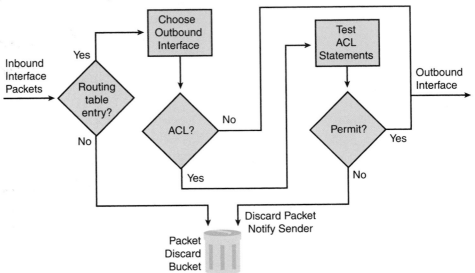

Before a packet is forwarded to an outbound interface, the router checks the routing table to see if the packet is routable. If the packet is not routable, it is dropped. Next, the router checks to see whether the outbound interface is grouped to an ACL. If the outbound interface is not grouped to an ACL, the packet can be sent to the output buffer. Examples of outbound ACL operation are as follows:

- If the outbound interface is not grouped to an outbound ACL, the packet is sent directly to the outbound interface.

- If the outbound interface is grouped to an outbound ACL, the packet is not sent out on the outbound interface until it is tested by the combination of ACL statements that are associated with that interface. Based on the ACL tests, the packet is permitted or denied.

For outbound lists, "to permit" means to send the packet to the output buffer, and "to deny" means to discard the packet.

Routing and ACL Processes on a Router

Figure 5-9 shows the logic of routing and ACL processes on a router.

Figure 5-9   Routing and ACL Processes on a Router

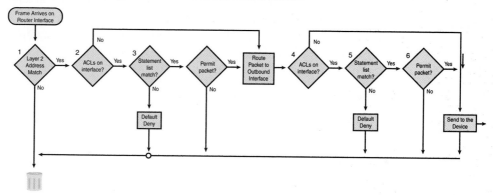

When a packet arrives at a router interface, the router process is the same, whether ACLs are used or not.

1. As a frame enters an interface, the router checks to see if the destination Layer 2 address matches its own or if the frame is a broadcast frame.

2. If the frame address is accepted, the frame information is stripped off, and the router checks for an ACL on the inbound interface. If an ACL exists, the packet is now tested against the statements in the list.

3. If the packet matches a statement, the packet is either accepted or rejected. If the packet is accepted in the interface, it is then checked against routing table entries to determine the destination interface and is switched to that interface. If the packet is rejected, the packet is dropped.

4. The router checks to see whether the destination interface has an ACL. If an ACL exists, the packet is tested against the statements in the list.

5. If the packet matches a statement, it is either accepted or rejected.

6. If there is no ACL or the packet is accepted, the packet is encapsulated in the new Layer 2 protocol and is forwarded out the interface to the next device.

The Implied "Deny All Traffic" Criteria Statement

At the end of every access list is an implied "deny all traffic" criteria statement. It is also sometimes called the "implicit deny any" statement. Therefore, if a packet does not match any of the ACL entries, it is automatically blocked. The implied "deny all traffic" is the default behavior of ACLs and cannot be changed.

A key caveat is associated with this "deny all" behavior. For most protocols, if you define an inbound access list for traffic filtering, you should include explicit access list criteria statements to permit routing updates. If you do not, you might effectively lose communication from the interface when routing updates are blocked by the implicit "deny all traffic" statement at the end of the access list.

Types of Cisco ACLs

The two types of Cisco ACLs are standard and extended:

- Standard ACLs filter packets based on source IP address only.

- Extended ACLs filter packets based on several attributes:

    - Source and destination IP addresses

    - Source and destination TCP and UDP ports

    - Protocol type (IP, ICMP, UDP, TCP, or protocol number)

The following sections describe these two types in greater detail.

Standard ACLs

Standard ACLs allow you to permit or deny traffic from source IP addresses. The packet's destination and the ports involved do not matter. For example, the following ACL statement allows all traffic from the network 192.168.30.0/24:

```
Router(config)# access-list 10 permit 192.168.30.0 0.0.0.255
```

Because of the implied "deny any" at the end, all other traffic is blocked with this ACL. Standard ACLs are created in global configuration mode.

Extended ACLs

Extended ACLs filter IP packets based on several attributes, such as protocol type, source and IP address, destination IP address, source TCP or UDP ports, destination TCP or UDP ports, and optional protocol type information for finer granularity of control. For example, in the following ACL statement, ACL 103 permits traffic originating from any address on the 192.168.30.0/24 network to any destination host port 80 (HTTP):

```
Router(config)# access-list 103 permit tcp 192.168.30.0 0.0.0.255 any eq 80
```

Extended ACLs are created in global configuration mode.

The commands for ACLs are explained in the next few sections.

How a Standard ACL Works

A standard ACL is a sequential collection of permit and deny conditions that apply to source IP addresses. The packet's destination and the ports involved are not examined.

Figure 5-10 maps out the decision process for a standard ACL. Cisco IOS software tests addresses against the conditions one by one. The first match determines whether the software accepts or rejects the address. Because the software stops testing conditions after the first match, the order of the conditions is critical. If no conditions match, the address is rejected.

Figure 5-10   Decision Process for a Standard ACL

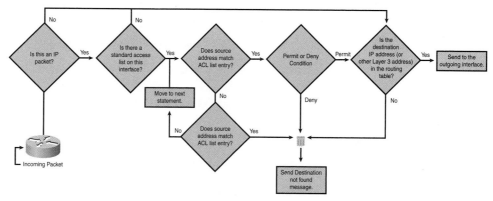

Two main tasks are involved in using ACLs:

Step 1.   Create an access list by specifying an access list number or name and access conditions.

Step 2.   Apply the ACL to interfaces or terminal lines.

Numbering and Naming ACLs

Using numbered ACLs is an effective method for determining the ACL type on smaller networks with more homogeneously defined traffic. However, a number does not tell you the purpose of the ACL. For this reason, starting with Cisco IOS Release 11.2, you can use a name to identify a Cisco ACL.

The rules for numbered ACLs and named ACLs can be summarized as follows:

- **Numbered ACL**: You assign a number based on whether your ACL is standard or extended:
    - 1 to 99 and 1300 to 1999: Standard IP ACL
    - 100 to 199 and 2000 to 2699: Extended IP ACL
    - You cannot add or delete entries within the ACL.

- **Named ACL**: You assign a name by providing the name of the ACL:
    - Names can contain alphanumeric characters.
    - It is suggested that the name be written in CAPITAL LETTERS.
    - Names cannot contain spaces or punctuation and must begin with an alphabetic character.
    - You can add or delete entries within the ACL.
    - You can specify whether the ACL is standard or extended.

Regarding numbered ACLs, in case you are wondering why numbers 200 to 1299 are skipped, it is because those numbers are used by other protocols. This book focuses only on IP ACLs. For example, numbers 600 to 699 are used by AppleTalk, and numbers 800 to 899 are used by IPX.

Where to Place ACLs

The proper placement of an ACL to filter undesirable traffic makes the network operate more efficiently. ACLs can act as firewalls to filter packets and eliminate unwanted traffic. Where you place ACLs can reduce unnecessary traffic. For example, traffic that will be denied at a remote destination should not use network resources along the route to that destination.

Every ACL should be placed where it has the greatest impact on efficiency. The basic rules are as follows:

- Like standard ACLs, extended ACLs can examine the source IP addresses, but they also examine the destination IP address, protocols, and port numbers (or services). Because extended ACLs can filter based on the destination IP address, you can locate extended ACLs as close as possible to the source of the traffic denied. This way, undesirable traffic is filtered without crossing the network infrastructure.

- Because standard ACLs do not specify destination addresses, place them as close to the destination as possible. This way, the ACL does not inadvertently block traffic to more destinations than intended.

Consider the following examples of where to place standard and extended ACLs in the network. The interface and network location are based on what you want the ACL to do.

Placing Standard ACLs

In Figure 5-11, the administrator wants to prevent traffic originating in the 192.168.10.0/24 network from getting to the 192.168.30.0/24 network. An ACL on the outbound interface of R1 keeps R1 from sending traffic to other places as well. The solution is to place a standard ACL on the outbound interface of R3 to stop all traffic from the source address— 192.168.10.0/24. A standard ACL meets these needs because it is concerned with only source IP addresses.

Figure 5-11   Placements of Standard ACLs

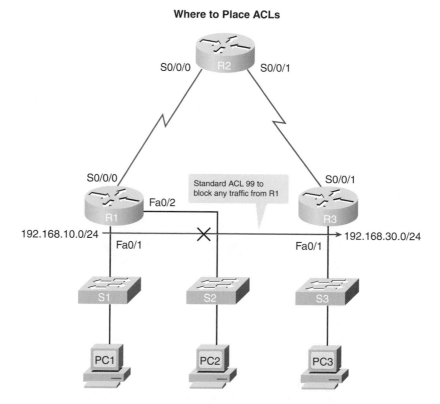

Placing Extended ACLs

Consider that administrators can place ACLs only on devices that they control. Therefore, placement must be determined in the context of where the control of the network administrator extends.

In Figure 5-12, the administrator of the 192.168.10.0/24 and 192.168.11.0/24 networks (referred to in this example as Ten and Eleven, respectively) wants to deny Telnet and FTP traffic from Eleven to the 192.168.30.0/24 network (Thirty, in this example). At the same time, other traffic must be permitted to leave the Eleven network. All traffic from the Ten network is to be permitted.

Figure 5-12 Placements of Extended ACLs

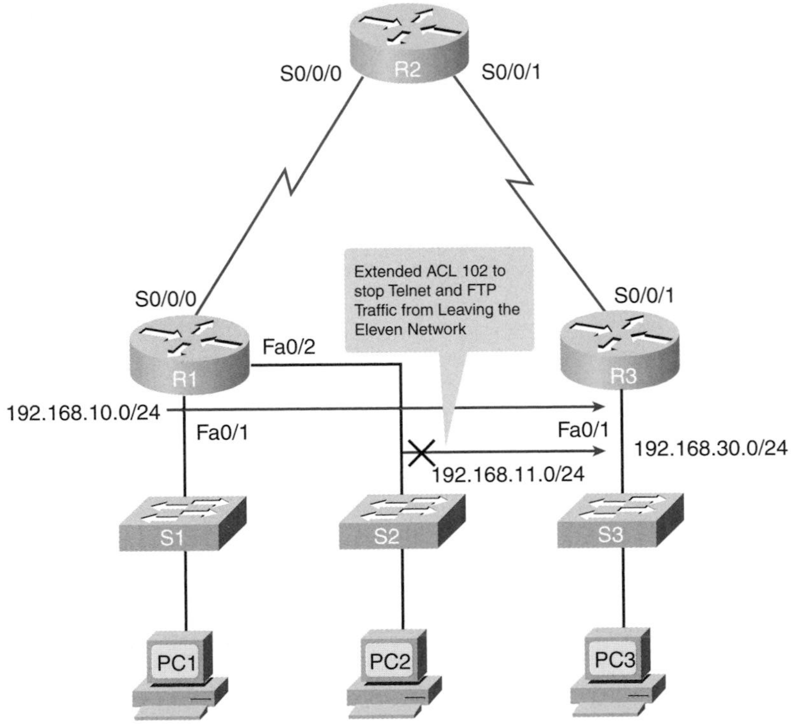

There are several ways to do this. An extended ACL on R3 blocking Telnet and FTP from Eleven would accomplish the task, but the administrator does not control R3. That solution also still allows unwanted traffic to cross the entire network, only to be blocked at the destination. This affects overall network efficiency.

One solution is to use an outbound extended ACL that specifies both source and destination addresses (Ten and Thirty, respectively), and that says, "Telnet and FTP traffic from Eleven is not allowed to go to Thirty." Place this extended ACL on the outbound S0/0/0 port of R1.

A disadvantage of this solution is that traffic from Eleven would also be subject to some processing by the ACL, even though Telnet and FTP traffic is allowed.

The better solution is to move closer to the source and place an extended ACL on the inbound Fa0/2 interface of R1. This ensures that Telnet and FTP packets from Eleven and bound for Thirty do not enter R1 and therefore never need to be processed by R2 or R3. Traffic from Eleven with other destination addresses and ports is still permitted through R1.

General Guidelines for Creating ACLs

Using ACLs requires attention to detail and great care. Mistakes can be costly in terms of downtime, troubleshooting efforts, and poor network service. Before starting to configure an ACL, basic planning is required. Table 5-3 presents guidelines that form the basis of an ACL best-practices list.

Table 5-3   ACL Best Practices

Guideline	Benefit
Base your ACLs on the organization's security policy.	This ensures that you implement organizational security guidelines.
Prepare a description of what you want your ACLs to do.	This helps you avoid inadvertently creating potential access problems.
Use a text editor to create, edit, and save ACLs.	This helps you create a library of reusable ACLs.
Test your ACLs on a development network before implementing them on a production network.	This helps you avoid costly errors.

Configuring Standard ACLs

This section examines how to configure standard ACLs.

Entering Criteria Statements

Before you configure a standard ACL, we will review important ACL concepts covered up to this point in the chapter.

Recall that when traffic comes into the router, it is compared to ACL statements based on the order in which the entries occur in the ACL. The router continues to process the ACL statements until it has a match. For this reason, you should have the more specific entries precede the more general entries. If no matches are found when the router reaches the end of the list, the traffic is denied, because traffic has an implied deny. A single-entry ACL with only one deny entry has the effect of denying all traffic. You must have at least one permit statement in an ACL, or all traffic is blocked.

At the end of every ACL is an implicit "deny any." Although it isn't required, some network administrators like to include this statement for clarity. For example, using the topology shown in Figure 5-13, the two ACLs (101 and 102) shown in Examples 5-1 and 5-2 have the same effect. Network 192.168.10.0 would be permitted to access network 192.168.30, but 192.168.11.0 would not be allowed.

Figure 5-13 Topology for ACLs 101 and 102

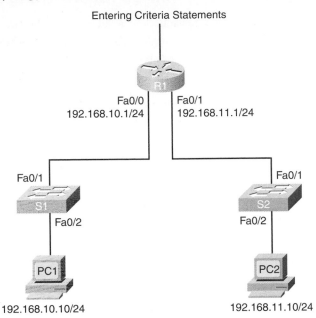

Example 5-1 ACL 101

```
R1(config)# access-list 101 permit ip 192.168.10.0 0.0.0.255 192.168.30.0 0.0.0.255
```

Example 5-2 ACL 102

```
R1(config)# access-list 102 permit ip 192.168.10.0 0.0.0.255 192.168.30.0 0.0.0.255
R1(config)# access-list 102 deny ip any any
```

Configuring a Standard ACL

This section examines the logic used in a standard ACL and shows a sample configuration.

Standard ACL Logic

Using the **access-list 2** statements shown in Example 5-3, Figure 5-14 shows that packets that come into Fa0/0 are checked for their source addresses.

Example 5-3 ACL 2

```
access-list 2 deny 192.168.10.1
access-list 2 permit 192.168.10.0 0.0.0.255
access-list 2 deny 192.168.0.0 0.0.255.255
access-list 2 permit 192.0.0.0 0.255.255.255
```

Figure 5-14   Standard ACL Logic

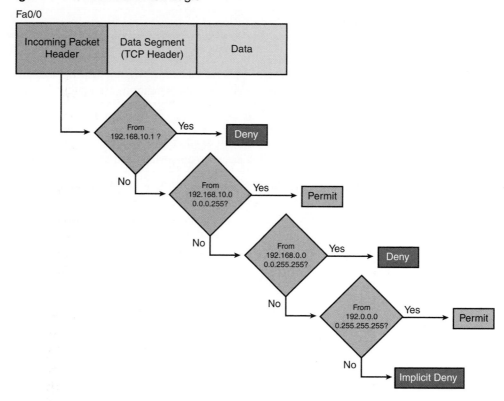

If packets are permitted, they are routed through the router to an output interface. If packets are not permitted, they are dropped at the incoming interface.

Configuring Standard ACLs

To configure numbered standard ACLs on a Cisco router, you must first create the standard ACL and then activate the ACL on an interface.

The **access-list** global configuration command defines a standard ACL with a number in the range of 1 to 99. Cisco IOS Software Release 12.0.1 extended these numbers by allowing 1300 to 1999 to provide a maximum of 798 possible standard ACLs. These additional numbers are called expanded IP ACLs.

The full syntax of the standard ACL command is as follows:

```
Router(config)# access-list access-list-number deny permit remark source
   [source-wildcard] [log]
```

Table 5-4 provides a detailed explanation of the syntax for a standard ACL.

Table 5-4   Standard ACL **access-list** Command Parameters

Parameter	Description
access-list number	Number of an ACL. This is a decimal number from 1 to 99, or 1300 to 1999 (for standard ACL).
deny	Denies access if the conditions are matched.
permit	Permits access if the conditions are matched.
remark	Enables you to add a remark about entries in an IP access list to make the list easier to understand and scan.
source	Number of the network or host from which the packet is being sent. There are two ways to specify the source: Use a 32-bit quantity in four-part dotted-decimal format. Use the keyword **any** as an abbreviation for a source and use a *source-wildcard* of 0.0.0.0 255.255.255.55.
source-wildcard	(Optional) Wildcard bits to be applied to the source. There are two ways to specify the *source-wildcard*: Use a 32-bit quantity in four-part dotted-decimal format. Place 1s in the bit positions you want to ignore. Use the keyword **any** as an abbreviation for a source and use a *source-wildcard* of 0.0.0.0 255.255.255.55.
log	(Optional) Causes an informational logging message about the packet that matches the entry to be sent to the console. (The level of messages logged to the console is controlled by the logging console command.) The message includes the ACL number, whether the packet was permitted or denied, the source address, and the number of packets. The message is generated for the first packet that matches, and then at 5-minute intervals, including the number of packets permitted or denied in the prior 5-minute interval.

For example, to create a numbered ACL designated 10 that would permit network 192.168.10.0/24, you would enter

```
R1(config)# access-list 10 permit 192.168.10.0
```

Removing ACLs

The **no** form of the **access-list** command removes a standard ACL. Example 5-4 provides two outputs of the **show access-list** command. The first part of the output shows that access list 10 has been configured on the router. The second part of the output shows that access list 10 has been removed.

Example 5-4 Removing an ACL

```
R1# show access-list

Standard IP access list 10
    10 permit 192.168.10.0
R1#
R1# conf t

Enter configuration commands, one per line. End with CNTL/Z.
R1(config)# no access-list 10
R1(config)# exit

R1#
*Oct 25 19:59:41.142: %SYS-5-CONFIG_I: configured from console by console
R1# show access-list

R1#
```

To remove the ACL, the global configuration command **no access-list** is used, as shown in Example 5-4. Issuing the **show access-list** command confirms that access list 10 has been removed.

Remarks Within ACLs

Typically, administrators create ACLs and fully understand the purpose of each statement within the ACL. However, when an ACL is revisited later, its purpose may no longer be as obvious as it once was.

The **remark** keyword is used for documentation and makes access lists a great deal easier to understand. Each remark is limited to 100 characters. The fairly simple ACL shown in Example 5-5 provides an example. When you review the ACL in the configuration, the remark is also displayed.

Example 5-5 Remarks Within an ACL

```
R1# conf t

Enter configuration commands, one per line. End with CNTL/Z.
R1(config)# access-list 10 remark Permit hosts from the 192.168.10.0 LAN
R1(config)# access-list 10 permit 192.168.10.0
R1(config)# exit

R1#
*Oct 25 20:12:13.781: %SYS-5-CONFIG_I: configured from console by console
R1# show run

Building configuration...
!
<output omitted>
!
access-list 10 remark Permit hosts from the 192.168.10.0 LAN
access-list 10 permit 192.168.10.0
!
<output omitted>
```

The next section explains how to use wildcard masking to identify specific networks and hosts.

ACL Wildcard Masking

ACLs statements include masks, also called wildcard masks. A *wildcard mask* is a string of binary digits telling the router which parts of the subnet number to look at. Although wildcard masks have no functional relationship to subnet masks, they do provide a similar function. The mask determines how much of an IP source or destination address to apply to the address match. The numbers 1 and 0 in the mask identify how to treat the corresponding IP address bits. However, they are used for different purposes and follow different rules.

Wildcard Masking

Wildcard masks and subnet masks are both 32 bits long and use binary 1s and 0s. Subnet masks use binary 1s and 0s to identify the network, subnet, and host portion of an IP address. Wildcard masks use binary 1s and 0s to filter an individual IP address or groups of IP addresses to permit or deny access to resources based on an IP address. By carefully setting wildcard masks, you can permit or deny a single IP address or several of them.

Wildcard masks and subnet masks differ in how they match binary 1s and 0s. Wildcard masks use the following rules to match binary 1s and 0s:

- **Wildcard mask bit 0**: Match the corresponding bit value in the address.

- **Wildcard mask bit 1**: Ignore the corresponding bit value in the address.

Figure 5-15 shows how different wildcard masks filter IP addresses. As you look at the example, remember that binary 0 signifies a match and that binary 1 signifies ignore.

Figure 5-15   Wildcard Masking

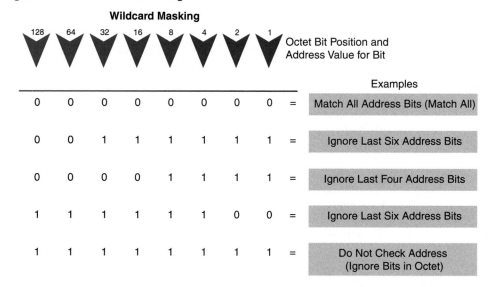

0 means to match the value of the corresponding address bit.
1 means to ignore the value of the corresponding address bit.

> **Note**
>
> Wildcard masks are often called *inverse masks*. The reason is that, unlike a subnet mask, in which binary 1 is equal to a match and binary 0 is not a match, the reverse is true.

Using a Wildcard Mask

Table 5-5 shows the results of applying a 0.0.255.255 wildcard mask to a 32-bit IP address. Remember that a binary 0 indicates a value that is matched.

Table 5-5   Wildcard Mask Example

	Decimal Address	Binary Address
IP Address to Be Processed	192.168.10.0	11000000.10101000.00001010.00000000
Wildcard Mask	0.0.255.255	00000000.00000000.11111111.11111111
Resulting IP Address	192.168.0.0	11000000.10101000.00000000.00000000

Wildcard Masks to Match IP Subnets

Calculating the wildcard mask can be a little confusing at first. This section provides five examples of wildcard masks.

The wildcard mask example shown in Table 5-6 stipulates that every bit in the IP address 192.168.1.1 must match exactly. The wildcard mask 0.0.0.0 functionally corresponds to the subnet mask 255.255.255.255.

Table 5-6   Wildcard Mask: First Example

	Decimal Address	Binary Address
IP Address	192.168.1.1	11000000.10101000.00000001.00000001
Wildcard Mask	0.0.0.0	00000000.00000000.00000000.00000000
Result	192.168.1.1	11000000.10101000.00000001.00000001

The wildcard mask example shown in Table 5-7 stipulates that anything will match. This is similar in function to using a subnet mask of 0.0.0.0.

Table 5-7   Wildcard Mask: Second Example

	Decimal Address	Binary Address
IP Address	192.168.1.1	11000000.10101000.00000001.00000001
Wildcard Mask	255.255.255.255	11111111.11111111.11111111.11111111
Result	0.0.0.0	00000000.00000000.00000000.00000000

The wildcard mask example shown in Table 5-8 stipulates that it will match any host within the 192.168.1.0/24 network. This wildcard mask is similar in function to the subnet mask 255.255.255.0.

Table 5-8   Wildcard Mask: Third Example

	Decimal Address	Binary Address
IP Address	192.168.1.1	11000000.10101000.00000001.00000001
Wildcard Mask	0.0.0.255	00000000.00000000.00000000.11111111
Result	192.168.1.0	11000000.10101000.00000001.00000000

These examples are fairly simple and straightforward. However, calculating wildcard masks can get a little trickier.

The next two examples are more complicated than the last three. In the fourth example, shown in Table 5-9, the first two octets and the first 4 bits of the third octet must match exactly. The last 4 bits in the third octet and the last octet can be any valid number. This results in a mask that checks for 192.168.16.0 to 192.168.31.0

Table 5-9   Wildcard Mask: Fourth Example

	Decimal Address	Binary Address
IP Address	192.168.16.0	11000000.10101000.00010000.00000000
Wildcard Mask	0.0.15.255	00000000.00000000.00001111.11111111
Result Range	192.168.16.0 to 192.168.31.0	11000000.10101000.00010000.00000000 to 11000000.10101000.00011111.00000000

The fifth example, shown in Table 5-10, shows a wildcard mask that matches the first two octets and the least-significant bit in the third octet. The last octet and the first 7 bits in the third octet can be any valid number. Because the last bit in the third octet must be a 1 bit, the result is a mask that will permit or deny all hosts from odd subnets from the 192.168.0.0 major network.

Table 5-10   Wildcard Mask: Fifth Example

	Decimal Address	Binary Address
IP Address	192.168.1.0	11000000.10101000.00000001.00000000
Wildcard Mask	0.0.254.255	00000000.00000000.11111110.11111111
Result Range	192.168.1.0	11000000.10101000.00000001.00000000
	All odd-numbered subnets in the 192.168.0.0 major network	

Calculating wildcard masks can be difficult. When calculating the wildcard mask for a subnet, you can easily calculate the wildcard mask by subtracting the subnet mask from 255.255.255.255.

For example, assume that you want to permit access to all users in the 192.168.3.0/24 network. Because the subnet mask is 255.255.255.0, you could take 255.255.255.255 and subtract the subnet mask 255.255.255.0, as shown in Table 5-11. This solution produces the wildcard mask 0.0.0.255.

Table 5-11   Wildcard Mask Calculation: First Example

	255.255.255.255
Subnet mask	−255.255.255.000
Wildcard mask	000.000.000.255

Now assume that you want to permit network access for the 14 users in subnet 192.168.3.32/28. The subnet mask for the IP subnet is 255.255.255.240. Therefore, take the 255.255.255.255 and subtract the subnet mask 255.255.255.240. The solution this time produces the wildcard mask 0.0.0.15, as shown in Table 5-12.

Table 5-12   Wildcard Mask Calculation: Second Example

	255.255.255.255
Subnet mask	−255.255.255.240
Wildcard mask	000.000.000.015

In the third example, shown in Table 5-13, assume that you want to match only networks 192.168.10.0 and 192.168.11.0. Again, you take the 255.255.255.255 and subtract the regular subnet mask, which in this case is 255.255.252.0. The result is 0.0.3.255.

Table 5-13   Wildcard Mask Calculation: Third Example

	255.255.255.255
Subnet mask	−255.255.252.000
Wildcard mask	000.000.003.255

Although you could accomplish the same result with two statements such as these:

```
R1(config)# access-list 10 permit 192.168.10.0
R1(config)# access-list 10 permit 192.168.11.0
```

it is far more efficient to configure the wildcard mask like this:

```
R1(config)# access-list 10 permit 192.168.10.0 0.0.3.255
```

This may not seem more efficient, but consider if you wanted to match network 192.168.16.0 to 192.168.31.0, as shown in Example 5-6.

Example 5-6 Matching Several Networks

```
R1(config)# access-list 10 permit 192.168.16.0
R1(config)# access-list 10 permit 192.168.17.0
R1(config)# access-list 10 permit 192.168.18.0
R1(config)# access-list 10 permit 192.168.19.0
R1(config)# access-list 10 permit 192.168.20.0
R1(config)# access-list 10 permit 192.168.21.0
R1(config)# access-list 10 permit 192.168.22.0
R1(config)# access-list 10 permit 192.168.23.0
R1(config)# access-list 10 permit 192.168.24.0
R1(config)# access-list 10 permit 192.168.25.0
R1(config)# access-list 10 permit 192.168.26.0
R1(config)# access-list 10 permit 192.168.27.0
R1(config)# access-list 10 permit 192.168.28.0
R1(config)# access-list 10 permit 192.168.29.0
R1(config)# access-list 10 permit 192.168.30.0
R1(config)# access-list 10 permit 192.168.31.0
```

You can see that configuring the following wildcard mask makes it far more efficient:

```
R1(config)# access-list 10 permit 192.168.16.0 0.0.15.255
```

Wildcard Bit Mask Keywords

Working with decimal representations of binary wildcard mask bits can be tedious. To simplify this task, the keywords **host** and **any** help identify the most common uses of wildcard masking:

- The **host** option substitutes for the 0.0.0.0 wildcard mask. This mask states that all IP address bits must match or only one host is matched.

- The **any** option substitutes for the IP address and 255.255.255.255 wildcard mask. This wildcard mask says to ignore the entire IP address or to accept any addresses.

These keywords eliminate the need to enter wildcard masks when identifying a specific host or network. They also make it easier to read an ACL by providing visual clues about the source or destination of the criteria.

Example 1: Wildcard Masking Process with a Single IP Address

As shown in Figure 5-16, instead of entering 192.168.10.10 0.0.0.0, you can use **host** 192.168.10.10:

- 192.168.10.10 0.0.0.0 matches all the address bits.

- Abbreviate the wildcard mask using the IP address preceded by the keyword **host** (**host 192.168.10.10**).

Figure 5-16   Example 1: Wildcard Masking Using **host**

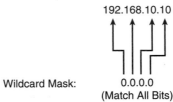

Example 1

192.168.10.10

Wildcard Mask: 0.0.0.0
(Match All Bits)

Example 2: Wildcard Masking Process with a Match Any IP Address

As shown in Figure 5-17, instead of entering 0.0.0.0 255.255.255.255, you can use the keyword **any** by itself:

- 0.0.0.0 255.255.255.255 ignores all address bits.

- Abbreviate the expression with the keyword **any**.

Figure 5-17   Example 2: Wildcard Masking Using **any**

Example 2

0.0.0.0

Wildcard Mask: 255.255.255.255
(Ignores All Bits)

The **host** and **any** Keywords

To use the **host** option to substitute the wildcard mask, you would enter the following:

```
R1(config)# access-list 1 permit 192.168.10.10 0.0.0.0
```

This configuration can be replaced with an alternative statement:

```
R1(config)# access-list 1 permit host 192.168.10.10
```

To use the **any** option to substitute 0.0.0.0 for the IP address with a wildcard mask of 255.255.255.255, you would enter the following:

```
R1(config)# access-list 1 permit 0.0.0.0 255.255.255.255
```

This configuration can be replaced with an alternative statement:

```
R1(config)# access-list 1 permit any
```

Applying Standard ACLs to Interfaces

Before an access list can take effect, it must first be applied to an interface.

Standard ACL Configuration Procedures

After a standard ACL is configured, it is linked to an interface using the following command:

```
Router(config-if)# ip access-group {access-list-number | access-list-name} {in | out}
```

To remove an ACL from an interface, first enter the **no ip access-group** command on the interface, and then enter the global **no access-list** command to remove the entire ACL.

The following steps and syntax show you how to configure and apply a numbered standard ACL on a router:

Step 1. Use the **access-list** global configuration command to create an entry in a standard IP ACL:

```
R1(config)# access-list 1 permit 192.168.10.0 0.0.0.255
R1(config)# access-list 1 remark Permit hosts from the Engineering Building
```

This matches any address that starts with 192.168.10.x. Use the **remark** option to add a description to your ACL.

Step 2. Use the **interface** configuration command to select an interface to apply the ACL to:

```
R1(config)# interface FastEthernet 0/0
```

Step 3. Use the **ip access-group** interface configuration command to activate the existing ACL on an interface:

```
R1(config-if)# ip access-group 1 out
```

To remove an IP ACL from an interface, enter the **no ip access-group** *access-list-number* command on the interface.

Examples 5-7 through 5-9 use the topology shown in Figure 5-18.

Figure 5-18   Topology for a Standard ACL

Example 5-7 shows an ACL that permits a single network. This ACL allows only traffic

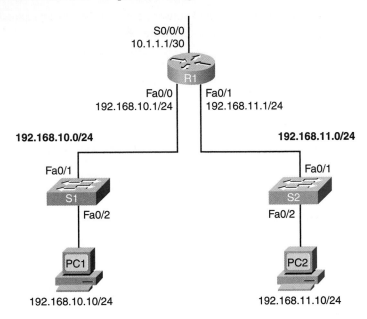

from source network 192.168.10.0 to be forwarded out the serial S0/0/0 interface on router
R1. Traffic from networks other than 192.168.10.0 is blocked.

Example 5-7   ACL to Permit a Single Network

```
R1(config)# access-list 1 permit 192.168.10.0 0.0.0.255
```

```
R1(config)# interface serial 0/0/0
R1(config-if)# ip access-group 1 out
```

The first line identifies the ACL as access list 1. It permits traffic that matches the selected
parameters. In this case, the IP address and wildcard mask identifying the source network is
192.168.10.0 0.0.0.255. Recall that there is an unseen implicit deny all statement that is
equivalent to adding the line **access-list 1 deny 0.0.0.0 255.255.255.255**.

The **ip access-group 1 out** interface configuration command ties ACL 1 to the Serial 0/0/0
interface as an outbound filter.

Therefore, ACL 1 permits only hosts from the 192.168.10.0/24 network to exit R1's serial
S0/0/0 interface. It denies any other network traffic, including 192.168.11.0/24, from being
forwarded out R1's serial S0/0/0 interface.

Example 5-8 shows an ACL that denies a specific host. This ACL replaces the previous example and also blocks traffic from a specific address. The first command deletes the previous version of ACL 1. This is necessary because any new **access-list 1** statements would automatically be appended to the existing list. Because we want to insert a new statement at the beginning of **access-list 1**, we need to delete the entire access list and then enter all the **access-list** statements. The next two statements remove the access list from the interface. This keeps any new **access-list 1** statements from taking effect until the list is completed and added again to the interface. This topic is discussed in more detail later in this chapter.

The next ACL statement denies the PC1 host located at 192.168.10.10. Every other host on the 192.168.10.0/24 network is permitted. Again the implicit deny statement matches every other network. It denies any other network, which in this case is the 192.168.11.0 network.

Example 5-8 ACL to Deny a Specific Host and Permit a Specific Subnet

```
R1(config)# no access-list 1
R1(config)# interface serial 0/0/0
R1(config-if)# no ip access-group 1 out

R1(config-if)# exit

R1(config)# access-list 1 deny 192.168.10.10 0.0.0.0
R1(config)# access-list 1 permit 192.168.10.0 0.0.0.255
R1(config)# interface serial 0/0/0
R1(config-if)# ip access-group 1 out
```

The ACL is again reapplied to interface 2erial 0/0/0 in an outbound direction.

Example 5-9 shows an ACL that denies a specific subnet. This ACL replaces the previous example but still blocks traffic from the host PC1. It also permits all other LAN traffic to exit from router R1.

Example 5-9 ACL to Deny a Specific Subnet and Permit Specific Subnets

```
R1(config)# no access-list 1
R1(config)# interface serial 0/0/0
R1(config-if)# no ip access-group 1 out

R1(config-if)# exit

R1(config)# access-list 1 deny 192.168.10.10 0.0.0.0
R1(config)# access-list 1 permit 192.168.0.0 0.0.255.255
R1(config)# interface serial 0/0/0
R1(config-if)# ip access-group 1 out
```

The first five commands are the same as in Example 5-8. These commands delete the previous version of ACL 1 and **access-group 1** on the interface, along with an ACL statement that denies the PC1 host located at 192.168.10.10.

The next line is new; it permits all hosts from the 192.168.x.x/16 networks. This means that all hosts from the 192.168.10.0/24 network still match, but now the hosts from the 192.168.11.0 network also match.

The ACL is again reapplied to interface Serial 0/0/0 in an outbound direction. Therefore, both LANs attached to router R1 may exit the Serial 0/0/0 interface, with the exception of the PC1 host.

> **Note**
>
> Standard and extended ACLs do not block packets that originate within the router configured with the access list. For example, a router that has an access list that denies Telnet sessions does not block Telnet traffic that originated from that router's own command-line interface.

Using an ACL to Control VTY Access

Cisco recommends using SSH for administrative connections to routers and switches. If the Cisco IOS software image on your router does not support SSH, you can partially improve the security of administrative lines by restricting VTY access. Restricting VTY access is a technique that allows you to define which IP addresses are allowed Telnet access to the router EXEC process. You can control which administrative workstation or network manages your router with an ACL and an **access-class** statement to your VTY lines. You can also use this technique with SSH to further improve administrative access security.

The **access-class** command is used to regulate Telnet sessions to and from the router's virtual terminal lines (vty).

Standard and extended access lists apply to packets that travel through a router. They are not designed to block packets that originate within the router. An outbound Telnet extended ACL does not prevent router-initiated Telnet sessions by default.

Filtering Telnet traffic typically is considered an extended IP ACL function because it filters a higher-level protocol. However, because you are using the **access-class** command to filter incoming or outgoing Telnet sessions by source address and apply filtering to VTY lines, you can use standard ACL statements to control VTY access.

The command syntax of the **access-class** command is as follows:

```
access-class access-list-number {in [vrf-also] | out}
```

The parameter **in** restricts incoming connections between a particular Cisco device and the addresses in the access list. The parameter **out** restricts outgoing connections between a particular Cisco device and the addresses in the access list.

Figure 5-19 shows a topology for the configuration shown in Example 5-10, which allows VTYs 0 and 4. The ACL in Example 5-10 is configured to give networks 192.168.10.0 and 192.168.11.0 access to VTYs 0 to 4. All other networks are denied access to the VTYs.

Figure 5-19   Topology for VTY Access

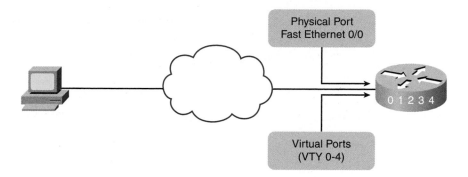

Standard ACLs to Control Virtual Terminal Access

Example 5-10   Standard ACLs to Control VTY Access

```
R1(config)# access-list 21 permit 192.168.10.0 0.0.0.255
R1(config)# access-list 21 permit 192.168.11.0 0.0.0.255
R1(config)# access-list 21 deny any

R1(config)# line vty 0 4
R1(config-line)# login
R1(config-line)# password secret
R1(config-line)# access-class 21 in
```

Consider the following when configuring access lists on VTYs:

- Only numbered access lists can be applied to VTYs.

- Identical restrictions should be set on all the VTYs, because a user can attempt to connect to any of them.

Editing Numbered ACLs

When you configure an ACL, the statements are added in the order in which they are entered at the end of the ACL. However, there is no built-in editing feature that allows you to edit a change in an ACL. You cannot selectively insert or delete lines.

It is strongly recommended that you construct any ACL in a text editor such as Microsoft Notepad. This allows you to create or edit the ACL and then paste it into the router. For an existing ACL, you could use the **show running-config** command to display the ACL, copy and paste it into the text editor, make the necessary changes, and reload it.

For example, assume that the host IP address in an access list was entered incorrectly. Instead of the 192.168.10.100 host, it should have been the 192.168.10.11 host. Here are the steps to edit and correct ACL 20:

Step 1. Display the ACL using the **show running-config** command. This command uses the **include** keyword to display only the ACL statements:

```
R1# show running-config | include access-list
access-list 20 permit 192.168.10.100
access-list 20 deny 192.168.10.0 0.0.0.255
```

Step 2. Highlight the ACL, copy it, and then paste it into Microsoft Notepad. Edit the list as required. As soon as the ACL is correctly displayed in Microsoft Notepad, highlight it and copy it:

```
access-list 20 permit 192.168.10.11
access-list 20 deny 192.168.10.0 0.0.0.255
```

Step 3. In global configuration mode, disable the access list using the **no access-list 20** command. Otherwise, the new statements would be appended to the existing ACL. Then paste the new ACL into the configuration of the router:

```
R1(config)# no access-list 20
R1(config)# access-list 20 permit 192.168.10.11
R1(config)# access-list 20 deny 192.168.10.0 0.0.0.255
```

Caution

When you use the **no access-list** command, no ACL is protecting your network. Also, be aware that if you make an error in the new list, you have to disable it and troubleshoot the problem. In that case, again, your network has no ACL during the correction process.

Commenting Numbered ACLs

You can use the **remark** keyword to include comments (remarks) about entries in any IP standard or extended ACL. The remarks make the ACL easier for you to understand and scan. Each remark line is limited to 100 characters.

The remark can go before or after a **permit** or **deny** statement. You should be consistent about where you put the remark so that it is clear which remark describes which **permit** or **deny** statement. For example, it would be confusing to have some remarks before the associated **permit** or **deny** statements and some remarks after.

To include a comment for IP numbered standard or extended ACLs, use the **access-list** *access-list-number* **remark** *remark* global configuration command. To remove the remark, use the **no** form of this command.

In Example 5-11, the standard ACL allows access to the workstation that belongs to Jones and denies access to the workstation that belongs to Smith.

Example 5-11   Commenting ACLs: Example 1

```
Router(config)# access-list 1 remark Permit only Jones workstation through
Router(config)# access-list 1 permit 192.168.10.13
Router(config)# access-list 1 remark Do not allow Smith through
Router(config)# access-list 1 deny 1 192.168.10.14
```

For an entry in a named ACL, use the **remark** access list configuration command. To remove the remark, use the **no** form of this command. Example 5-12 shows an extended named ACL. Recall from the earlier definition of extended ACLs that they are used to control specific port numbers or services. In Example 5-12, the remark says that the host for Jones is not allowed to use outbound Telnet.

Example 5-12   Commenting ACLs: Example 2

```
Router(config)# ip access-list extended TELNETTING
Router(config-ext-nacl)# remark Do not allow Jones host to Telnet outbound
Router(config-ext-nacl)# deny tcp host 192.168.10.13 any eq telnet
```

Creating Standard Named ACLs

Naming an ACL makes it easier to understand its function. For example, an ACL to deny FTP could be called NO_FTP. When you identify your ACL with a name instead of a number, the configuration mode and command syntax are slightly different.

The following are the steps used to create a standard named ACL:

How To

Step 1.   Starting from global configuration mode, use the **ip access-list standard** *name* command to create a named ACL. ACL names are alphanumeric and must be unique:

```
Router(config) ip access-list [standard | extended] name
```

Step 2.   From named ACL configuration mode, use the **permit** or **deny** statements to specify one or more conditions for determining if a packet is forwarded or dropped:

```
Router(config-std-nacl)# sequence-number [permit | deny | remark] {source
[source-wildcard]} [log]
```

Step 3.   Activate the name IP ACL on an interface with the **ip access-group** command:

```
Router(config-if)# ip access-group name [in | out]
```

In the topology shown in Figure 5-20, Example 5-13 shows the commands used to configure a standard named ACL on router R1, interface Fa0/0, that denies host 192.168.11.10 access to the 192.168.10.0 network.

Figure 5-20 Topology for a Named ACL

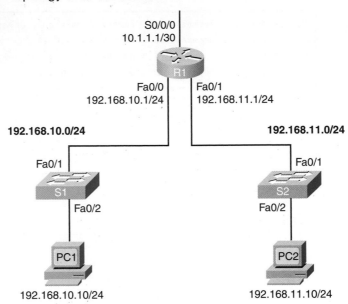

Example 5-13 Named ACL Example

```
R1(config)# ip access-list standard NO_ACCESS
R1(config-std-nacl)# deny host 192.168.11.10
R1(config-std-nacl)# permit 192.168.11.0 0.0.0.255
R1(config-std-nacl)# interface Fa0/0
R1(config-if)# ip access-group NO_ACCESS out
```

Capitalizing ACL names is not required, but it makes them stand out when you view the running-config output.

Monitoring and Verifying ACLs

When you finish an ACL configuration, use Cisco IOS **show** commands to verify the configuration. The following command displays the contents of all ACLs:

```
R1# show access-lists {access-list number | name}
```

Example 5-14 shows the result of issuing the **show access-lists** command on router R1. The capitalized ACL names, SALES and ENG, stand out in the screen output.

Example 5-14   Sample **show access-lists** Output

```
R1# show access-lists

Standard IP access list SALES
    10 deny    10.1.1.0 0.0.0.255
    20 permit 10.3.3.1
    30 permit 10.4.4.1
    40 permit 10.5.5.1
Extended IP access list ENG
    10 permit tcp host 192.168.10.10 any eq telnet (25 matches)
    20 permit tcp host 192.168.10.10 any eq ftp
    30 permit tcp host 192.168.10.10 any eq ftp-data
```

Recall why you started configuring ACLs in the first place: you wanted to implement your organization's security policies. Now that you have verified that the ACLs are configured as you intended, the next step is to confirm that the ACLs work as planned.

The guidelines discussed earlier in this section suggest that you configure ACLs on a test network and then implement the tested ACLs on the production network. Though a discussion of how to prepare an ACL test scenario is beyond the scope of this book, you need to know that confirming that your ACLs work as planned can be a complex and time-consuming process.

Editing Named ACLs

Named ACLs have a big advantage over numbered ACLs in that they are easier to edit. Starting with Cisco IOS software Release 12.3, named IP ACLs allow you to delete individual entries in a specific ACL. You can use sequence numbers to insert statements anywhere in the named ACL. If you are using an earlier Cisco IOS software version, you can add statements only at the bottom of the named ACL. Because you can delete individual entries, you can modify your ACL without having to delete and then reconfigure the entire ACL.

Using the topology shown earlier in Figure 5-20, the configuration in Example 5-15 shows an ACL applied to the Serial 0/0/0 interface of R1. It restricts access to the web server. Note that the last two ACL statements are not needed, because the implicit deny at the end of the list is sufficient. Looking at Example 5-15, you can see two things you have not yet seen in this book:

- In the first **show access-lists** command output, you can see that the ACL named WEB-SERVER has three numbered lines indicating access rules for the web server.

- To grant another workstation access in the list, you only have to insert a numbered line. In the example, the workstation with IP address 192.168.11.10 is being added with the sequence number 15.

- The final **show access-lists** command output verifies that the new workstation is now allowed access.

Example 5-15   Adding a Line to a Named ACL

```
R1# show access-lists

Standard IP access list WEBSERVER
    10 permit 192.168.10.11
    20 deny   192.168.10.0, wildcard bits 0.0.0.255
    30 deny   192.168.11.0, wildcard bits 0.0.0.255
R1# conf t

Enter configuration commands, one per line. End with CNTL/Z.
R1(config)# ip access-list standard WEBSERVER
R1(config-std-nacl)# 15 permit 192.168.11.10
R1(config-std-nacl)# end

R1#
*Nov 1 19:20:57.591: %SYS-5-CONFIG_I: Configured from console by console
R1# show access-lists

Standard access list WEBSERVER
    10 permit 192.168.10.11
    15 permit 192.168.11.10
    20 deny   192.168.10.0, wildcard bits 0.0.0.255
    30 deny   192.168.11.0, wildcard bits 0.0.0.255
```

Packet Tracer
☐ Activity

Configuring Standard ACLs (5.2.8)

Standard ACLs are router configuration scripts that control whether a router permits or denies packets based on the source address. This activity focuses on defining filtering criteria, configuring standard ACLs, applying ACLs to router interfaces, and verifying and testing the ACL implementation.

Detailed instructions are provided within the activity. Use File e4-528.pka on the CD-ROM that accompanies this book to perform this activity using Packet Tracer.

Configuring an Extended ACL

For more precise traffic-filtering control, you can use extended ACLs numbered 100 to 199 and 2000 to 2699, providing a total of 799 possible extended ACLs. Extended ACLs can also be named.

Extended ACLs

Extended ACLs are used more often than standard ACLs because they provide a greater range of control and therefore add to your security solution. Like standard ACLs, extended ACLs check the source packet addresses, but they also check the destination address, protocols, and port numbers (or services). This gives a greater range of criteria on which to base the ACL. For example, an extended ACL can simultaneously allow e-mail traffic from a network to a specific destination while denying file transfers and web browsing.

Testing Packets with Extended ACLs

Figure 5-21 shows the logical decision path used by an extended ACL built to filter on source and destination addresses, and protocol and port numbers. In this example, the ACL first filters on the source address, and then on the port and protocol of the source. It then filters on the destination address, and then on the port and protocol of the destination, and then it makes a final permit-deny decision.

Figure 5-21   Decision Path for Extended ACLs

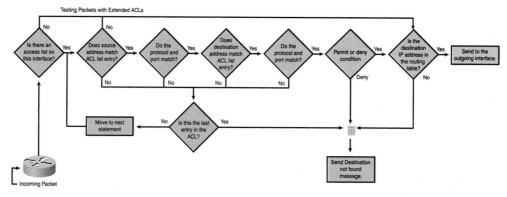

Recall that entries in ACLs are processed one after the other, so a "no" decision does not necessarily equal a "deny." As you go through the logical decision path, note that a "no" means go to the next entry until all the entries have been tested. As soon as there is a match with a permit or deny statement, no further processing of the access list entries occurs. If none of the explicit entries matches, the implicit deny at the end of the list matches, and the traffic is denied.

The next section provides an example of an extended ACL.

Testing for Ports and Services

The ability to filter on protocol and port number allows you to build very specific extended ACLs. Using the appropriate port number, you can specify an application by configuring either the port number or the name of a well-known port.

Example 5-16 shows some examples of how an administrator specifies a TCP or UDP port number or keyword by placing it at the end of the extended ACL statement. Logical operations can be used, such as equal (eq), not equal (neq), greater than (gt), and less than (lt).

Example 5-16   Extended ACL Examples

```
! Using port numbers:
access-list 114 permit tcp 192.168.20.0 0.0.0.255 any eq 23
access-list 114 permit tcp 192.168.20.0 0.0.0.255 any eq 21
! Using keywords:
access-list 114 permit tcp 192.168.20.0 0.0.0.255 any eq telnet
access-list 114 permit tcp 192.168.20.0 0.0.0.255 any eq ftp
```

Example 5-17 shows how to generate a list of port numbers and keywords you can use while building an ACL using the **access-list** command.

Example 5-17   Generating Port Numbers

```
R1(config)# access-list 101 permit tcp any eq ?

  <0-65535>    Port number
  bgp          Border Gateway Protocol (179)
  chargen      Character generator (19)
  cmd          Remote commands (rcmd, 514)
  daytime      Daytime (13)
  discard      Discard (9)
  domain       Domain Name Service (53)
  echo         Echo (7)
  exec         Exec (rsh, 512)
  finger       Finger (79)
  ftp          File Transfer Protocol (21)
  ftp-data     FTP data connections (20)
  gopher       Gopher (70)
  hostname     NIC hostname server (101)
  ident        Ident Protocol (113)
  irc          Internet Relay Chat (194)
  klogin       Kerberos login (543)
  kshell       Kerberos shell (544)
  login        Login (rlogin, 513)
  lpd          Printer service (515)
  nntp         Network News Transport Protocol (119)
  pim-auto-rp  PIM Auto-RP (496)
  pop2         Post Office Protocol v2 (109)
  pop3         Post Office Protocol v3 (110)
  smtp         Simple Mail Transport Protocol (25)
```

```
    sunrpc      Sun Remote Procedure Call (111)
    syslog      Syslog (514)
    tacacs      TAC Access Control System (49)
    talk        Talk (517)
    telnet      Telnet (23)
    time        Time (37)
    uucp        Unix-to-Unix Copy Program (540)
    whois       Nicname (43)
    www         World Wide Web (HTTP, 80)
R1(config)# access-list 101 permit tcp any eq ?
```

Configuring Extended ACLs

The procedural steps for configuring extended ACLs are the same as for standard ACLs. First you create the extended ACL, and then you activate it on an interface. However, the command syntax and parameters are more complex to support the additional features provided by extended ACLs.

The common command syntax for extended ACLs is as follows:

```
access-list access-list-number {deny | permit | remark} protocol source
    source-wildcard [operator operand] [port port-number or name] destination
    destination-wildcard [operator operand] [port port-number or name] [established]
```

Table 5-14 provides details on the keywords and parameters. As you work through this chapter, explanations and examples will further your comprehension.

Table 5-14   Parameters and Descriptions for Extended ACL Command Syntax

Parameter	Description
access-list-number	Identifies the access list using a number in the range 100 to 199 (for an extended IP ACL) or 2000 to 2699 (expanded IP ACLs).
deny	Denies access if the conditions are matched.
permit	Permits access if the conditions are matched.
remark	Used to enter a remark.
protocol	Name or number of an Internet protocol. Common keywords include **icmp**, **ip**, **tcp**, and **udp**. To match any Internet protocol (including ICMP, TCP, and UDP), use the **ip** keyword.

continues

Table 5-14   Parameters and Descriptions for Extended ACL Command Syntax

Parameter	Description
source	Number of the network or host from which the packet is being sent.
source-wildcard	Wildcard bits to be applied to the source.
operand	(Optional) Compares source or destination ports. Possible operands include **lt** (less than), **gt** (greater than), **eq** (equal), **neq** (not equal), and **range** (inclusive range).
port-number or name	(Optional) The decimal number or name of a TCP or UDP port.
destination	Number of the network or host to which the packet is being sent.
destination-wildcard	Wildcard bits to be applied to the destination.
established	(Optional) For the TCP protocol only. Indicates an established connection.

Using the topology shown in Figure 5-22, Example 5-18 shows how you might create an extended ACL specific to your network needs. In Example 5-18, the network administrator needs to restrict Internet access to allow only website browsing. ACL 103 applies to traffic leaving the 192.168.10.0 network, and ACL 104 applies to traffic coming into the network.

Figure 5-22   Topology for Configuring Extended ACLs

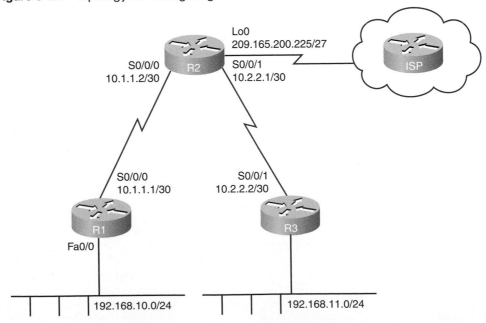

Example 5-18   Configuring Extended ACLs

```
R1(config)# access-list 103 permit tcp 192.168.10.0 0.0.0.255 any eq 80
R1(config)# access-list 103 permit tcp 192.168.10.0 0.0.0.255 any eq 443
R1(config)# access-list 104 permit tcp any 192.168.10.0 0.0.0.255 established
```

These points summarize the **access-list** statements shown in Example 5-18:

- ACL 103 allows requests to ports 80 and 443.

- ACL 104 allows established HTTP and HTTPS replies.

ACL 103 accomplishes the first part of the requirement. It allows traffic coming from any address on the 192.168.10.0 network to go to any destination, subject to the limitation that traffic goes to ports 80 (HTTP) and 443 (HTTPS) only.

The nature of HTTP requires that traffic flow back into the network, but the network administrator wants to restrict that traffic to HTTP exchanges from requested websites. The security solution must deny any other traffic coming into the network. ACL 104 does that by blocking all incoming traffic, except for the established connections. HTTP establishes connections starting with the original request and then through the exchange of ACK, FIN, and SYN messages.

Notice that the example uses the **established** parameter. This parameter allows responses to traffic that originates from the 192.168.10.0/24 network to return inbound on the s0/0/0. A match occurs if the TCP datagram has the ACK or reset (RST) bits set, which indicates that the packet belongs to an existing connection. Without the **established** parameter in the ACL statement, all TCP traffic for the 192.168.10.0/24 network would be permitted.

Applying Extended ACLs to the Interfaces

Now you'll learn how to configure an extended access list by building on the previous example. Recall that you want to allow users to browse both insecure and secure websites. First, consider whether the traffic you want to filter is going in or out. Trying to access websites on the Internet is traffic going out. Receiving e-mails from the Internet is traffic coming into the business. However, when considering how to apply an ACL to an interface, in and out take on different meanings, depending on the point of view.

In Figure 5-23, R1 has two interfaces. It has a serial port, S0/0/0, and a Fast Ethernet port, Fa0/0. The Internet traffic coming in is going in the S0/0/0 interface but is going out the Fa0/0 interface to reach PC1. The configuration shown in Example 5-19 applies the ACL to the serial interface in both directions.

Figure 5-23   Topology for Applying Extended ACLs to Interfaces

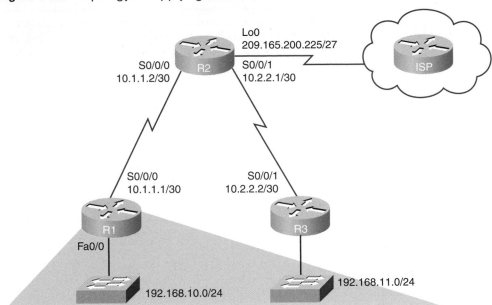

Example 5-19   Applying Extended ACLs to Interfaces

```
R1(config)# interface S0/0/0
R1(config-if)# ip access-group 103 out
R1(config-if)# ip access-group 104 in
```

Using the topology shown in Figure 5-24, Example 5-20 shows the configuration for deny-ing FTP traffic from subnet 192.168.11.0 going to subnet 192.168.10.0 but permitting all other traffic. Note the use of wildcard masks and the explicit deny all. Remember that FTP requires ports 20 and 21, so you need to specify both **eq 20** and **eq 21** to deny FTP.

Example 5-20   Deny FTP

```
R1(config)# access-list 101 deny tcp 192.168.11.0 0.0.0.255 192.168.10.0 0.0.0.255
  eq 21
R1(config)# access-list 101 deny tcp 192.168.11.0 0.0.0.255 192.168.10.0 0.0.0.255
  eq 20
R1(config)# access-list 101 permit ip any any

R1(config)# interface Fa0/1
R1(config-if)# ip access-group 101 in
```

Figure 5-24   Topology for Denying FTP

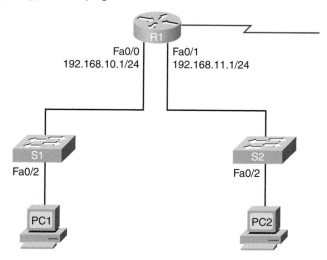

With extended ACLs, you can choose to use port numbers, as in the example, or you can reference a well-known port by name:

```
R1(config)# access-list 101 deny tcp 192.168.11.0 0.0.0.255 192.168.10.0 0.0.0.255 eq
    ftp
R1(config)# access-list 101 deny tcp 192.168.11.0 0.0.0.255 192.168.10.0 0.0.0.255
  eq ftp-data
```

Note that for FTP, both **ftp** and **ftp-data** need to be mentioned.

Again using the topology shown in Figure 5-24, Example 5-21 shows the configuration that denies Telnet traffic from 192.168.11.0 coming into interface Fa0/1 but that allows all other IP traffic from any other source to any destination into Fa0/1. Note the use of the **any** keyword, meaning from anywhere going to anywhere.

Example 5-21   Deny Telnet

```
R1(config)# access-list 101 deny tcp 192.168.11.0 0.0.0.255 any eq 23
R1(config)# access-list 101 permit ip any any

R1(config)# interface Fa0/1
R1(config-if)# ip access-group 101 in
```

Creating Named Extended ACLs

You can create named extended ACLs in essentially the same way you create named standard ACLs. The commands to create a named ACL are similar for standard and extended ACLs, but you have additional options when using extended ACLs.

Follow these steps to create an extended ACL using names:

How To 🔍

Step 1.   Starting in global configuration mode, use the **ip access-list extended** *name* command to define a named extended ACL.

Step 2.   In named ACL configuration mode, specify the conditions you want to allow or deny.

Step 3.   Return to privileged EXEC mode, and verify your ACL with the **show access-lists** [*number* | *name*] command.

Step 4.   Activate the name IP ACL on an interface with the **ip access-group** *name* [**in** | **out**] command.

Step 5.   As an option and a recommended step, save your entries in the configuration file with the **copy running-config startup-config** command.

To remove a named extended ACL, use the **no ip access-list extended** *name* global configuration command.

Using the topology shown in Figure 5-25, the commands in Example 5-22 show the named version of the ACL you created earlier, in Example 5-18.

Figure 5-25   Topology for Named Extended ACLs

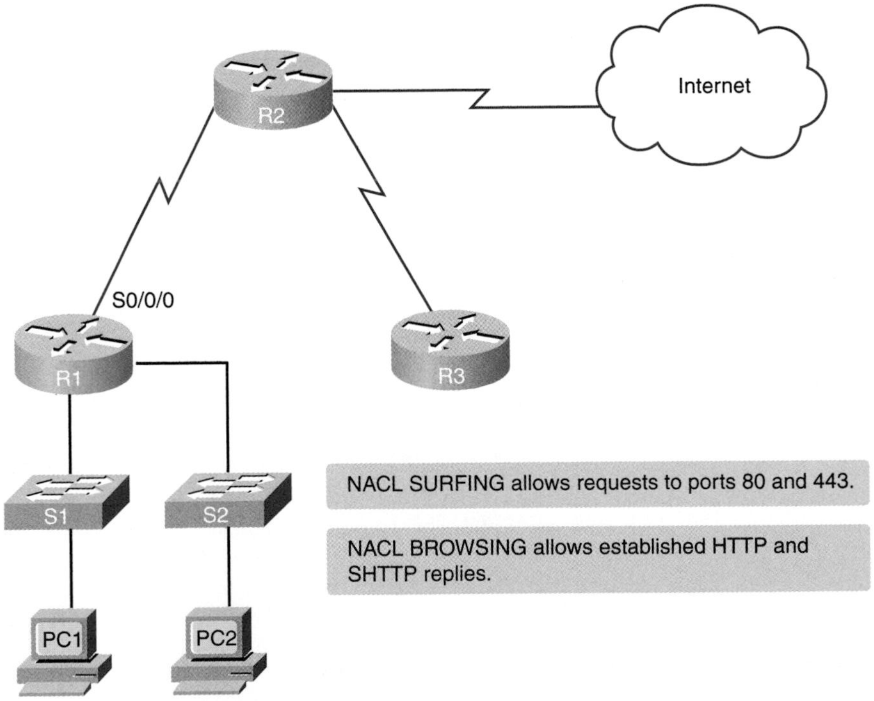

NACL SURFING allows requests to ports 80 and 443.

NACL BROWSING allows established HTTP and SHTTP replies.

Example 5-22   Configuring Named Extended ACLs

```
R1(config)# ip access-list extended SURFING
R1(config-ext-nacl)# permit tcp 192.168.10.0 0.0.0.255 any eq 80
R1(config-ext-nacl)# permit tcp 192.168.10.0 0.0.0.255 any eq 443
R1(config)# access-list extended BROWSING
R1(config-ext-nacl)# permit tcp any 192.168.10.0 0.0.0.255 established
```

Configuring Extended ACLs (5.3.4)

Extended ACLs are router configuration scripts that control whether a router permits or denies packets based on their source or destination address as well as protocols or ports. Extended ACLs provide more flexibility and granularity than standard ACLs. This activity focuses on defining filtering criteria, configuring extended ACLs, applying ACLs to router interfaces, and verifying and testing the ACL implementation.

Detailed instructions are provided within the activity. Use File e4-534.pka on the CD-ROM that accompanies this book to perform this activity using Packet Tracer.

Configure Complex ACLs

We have examined standard, extended, and named ACLs. This section discusses another type of ACL—complex ACLs.

What Are Complex ACLs?

Standard and extended ACLs can become the basis for complex ACLs that provide additional functionality. Table 5-15 summarizes the three categories of complex ACLs.

Table 5-15   Complex ACL Categories

Complex ACL	Description
Dynamic ACLs (lock-and-key)	Users who want to traverse the router are blocked until they use Telnet to connect to the router and are authenticated.
Reflexive ACLs	Allows outbound traffic and limits inbound traffic in response to sessions that originate inside the router.
Time-based ACLs	Allows for access control based on the time of day and the day of the week.

Dynamic ACLs

Lock-and-key is a traffic-filtering security feature that uses dynamic ACLs, which are sometimes called lock-and-key ACLs.

What Are Dynamic ACLs?

Dynamic or lock-and-key ACLs are available for IP traffic only. Dynamic ACLs are dependent on Telnet connectivity, authentication (local or remote), and extended ACLs.

Dynamic ACL configuration starts with the application of an extended ACL to block traffic through the router. Users who want to traverse the router are blocked by the extended ACL until they use Telnet to connect to the router and are authenticated. The Telnet connection is then dropped, and a single-entry dynamic ACL is added to the existing extended ACL. This permits traffic for a particular period; idle and absolute timeouts are possible.

When to Use Dynamic ACLs

Here are some common reasons to use dynamic ACLs:

- When you want a specific remote user or group of remote users to access a host within your network, connecting from their remote hosts via the Internet. Lock-and-key authenticates the user and then permits limited access through your firewall router for a host or subnet for a finite period.

- When you want a subset of hosts on a local network to access a host on a remote network that is protected by a firewall. With lock-and-key, you can enable access to the remote host only for the desired set of local hosts. Lock-and-key requires the users to authenticate through a AAA, TACACS+ server, or other security server before it allows their hosts to access the remote hosts.

Benefits of Dynamic ACLs

Dynamic ACLs have the following security benefits over standard and static extended ACLs:

- Use of a challenge mechanism to authenticate individual users

- Simplified management in large internetworks

- In many cases, a reduction in the amount of router processing that is required for ACLs

- Less opportunity for hackers to break into the network

- Creation of dynamic user access through a firewall, without compromising other configured security restrictions

In Figure 5-26, the user at PC1 is an administrator who requires back-door access to the 192.168.30.0/24 network, located on router R3. A dynamic ACL has been configured to allow FTP and HTTP access through router R3, but only for a limited time.

Figure 5-26   Topology for a Dynamic ACL

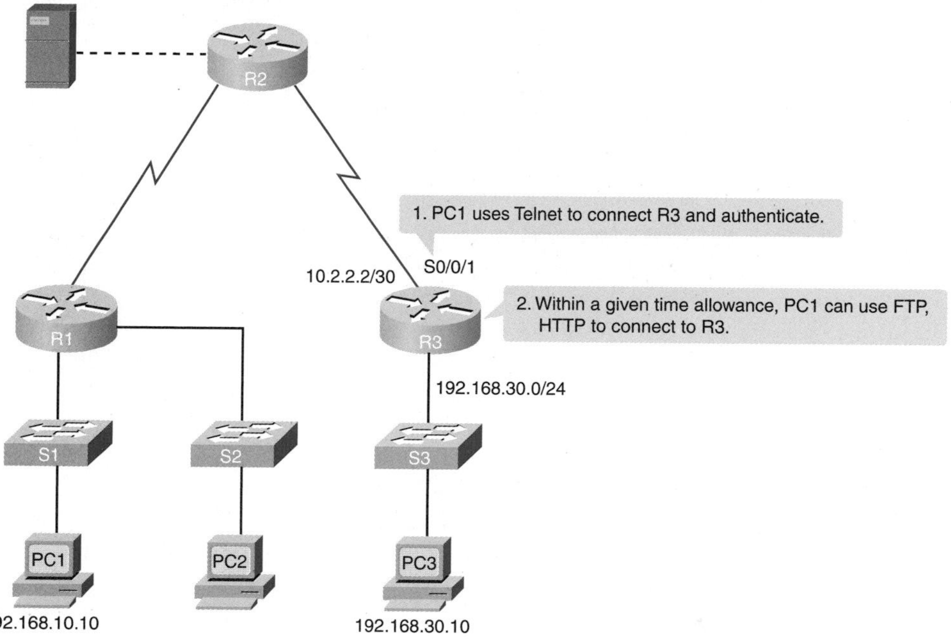

1. PC1 uses Telnet to connect R3 and authenticate.

10.2.2.2/30   S0/0/1

2. Within a given time allowance, PC1 can use FTP, HTTP to connect to R3.

192.168.30.0/24

192.168.10.10

192.168.30.10

Dynamic ACL Examples

Consider a requirement for a network administrator on PC1 to gain periodic access to the network (192.168.30.0/24) through router R3. To facilitate this requirement, a dynamic ACL is configured on the serial interface S0/0/1 on router R3.

Although a detailed description of the configuration for a dynamic ACL is outside the scope of this book, it is useful to review the configuration steps. Again, use the topology shown in Figure 5-26:

Step 1.   Create a login name and password for authentication:

```
R3(config)# username Student password 0 cisco
```

Step 2.   Allow the user to open a Telnet connection to the router. The dynamic ACL entry is ignored until lock-and-key is triggered. The window stays open for 15 minutes and then automatically closes whether it is being used or not.

```
R3(config)# access-list 101 permit any host 10.2.2.2 eq telnet
R3(config)# access-list 101 dynamic router-telnet timeout 15 permit ip
    192.168.10.0
    0.0.0.255 192.168.30.0 0.0.0.255
```

Step 3.   Apply ACL 101 to interface S0/0/1:

```
R3(config)# interface S 0/0/1
R3(config-if)# ip access-group 101 in
```

Step 4.   After the user is authenticated using Telnet, the autocommand executes, and the Telnet session terminates. The user can now access network 192.168.30.0. If up to 5 minutes of inactivity occurs, the window closes:

```
R3(config)# line vty 0 4
R3(config-line)# login local
R3(config-line)# autocommand access-enable host timeout 5
```

Reflexive ACLs

Reflexive ACLs allow IP packets to be filtered based on upper-layer session information. They generally are used to allow outbound traffic and to limit inbound traffic in response to sessions that originate inside the router. This gives you greater control over what traffic you allow into your network and increases the capabilities of extended access lists.

What Are Reflexive ACLs?

Network administrators use reflexive ACLs to allow IP traffic for sessions originating from their network while denying IP traffic for sessions originating outside the network, as shown in Figure 5-27. These ACLs allow the router to manage session traffic dynamically. The router examines the outbound traffic. When it sees a new connection, the router adds an entry to a temporary ACL to allow replies back in. Reflexive ACLs contain only temporary entries. These entries are automatically created when a new IP session begins, for example, with an outbound packet, and the entries are automatically removed when the session ends.

Reflexive ACLs provide a truer form of session filtering than an extended ACL that uses the **established** parameter, introduced earlier. Although similar in concept to the **established** parameter, reflexive ACLs also work for UDP and ICMP, which have no ACK or RST bits. The **established** option also does not work with applications that dynamically alter the source port for the session traffic. The **permit established** statement checks only ACK and RST bits, not source and destination address.

Reflexive ACLs are not applied directly to an interface; they are "nested" within an extended named IP ACL that is applied to the interface.

Reflexive ACLs can be defined only with extended named IP ACLs. They cannot be defined with numbered or standard named ACLs or with other protocol ACLs. Reflexive ACLs can be used with other standard and static extended ACLs.

Figure 5-27   Topology for a Reflexive ACL

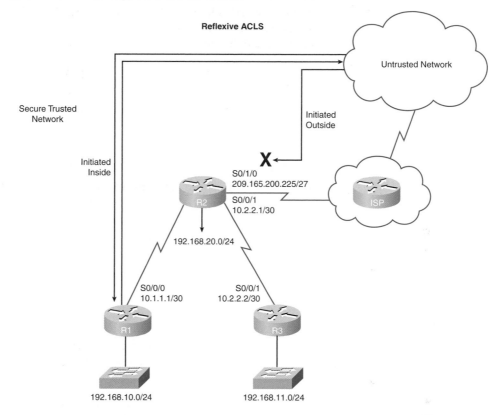

Benefits of Reflexive ACLs

Reflexive ACLs have the following benefits:

- They help secure your network against network hackers and can be included in a fire-wall defense.

- They provide a level of security against spoofing and certain DoS attacks. Reflexive ACLs are much harder to spoof because more filter criteria must match before a packet is permitted through. For example, source and destination addresses and port numbers, not just ACK and RST bits, are checked.

- They are simple to use and, compared to basic ACLs, provide greater control over which packets enter your network.

Reflexive ACL Example

In Figure 5-28, the administrator needs a reflexive ACL that permits ICMP outbound and inbound traffic while permitting only TCP traffic that has been initiated from inside the network. Assume that all other traffic will be denied. The reflexive ACL is applied to the outbound Serial 0/1/0 interface of R2.

Figure 5-28   Reflexive ACL Example

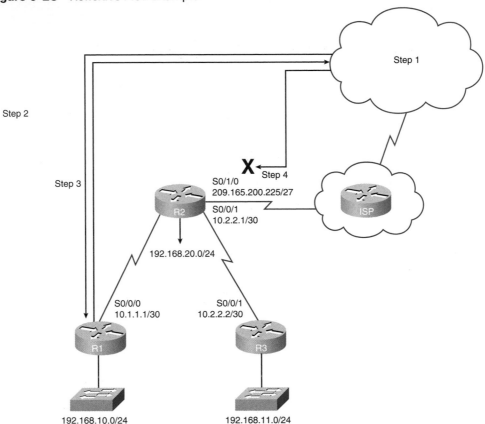

Although the complete configuration for reflexive ACLs is outside the scope of this book, the following steps are required to configure a reflexive ACL:

Step 1.   Configure the router to keep track of traffic that was initiated from inside:

```
R2(config)# ip access-list extended OUTBOUNDFILTERS
R2(config-ext-nacl)# permit tcp 192.168.0.0 0.0.255.255 any reflect
  TCPTRAFFIC
```

Step 2.   Create an inbound policy that requires the route to check incoming traffic to see if it was initiated from inside. It also ties the reflexive ACL part of the OUT-BOUNDFILTERS ACL, called TCPTRAFFIC, to the INBOUNDFILTERS ACL:

```
R2(config)# ip access-list extended INBOUNDFILTERS
R2(config-ext-nacl)# evaluate TCPTRAFFIC
```

Step 3.   Apply both an inbound and an outbound ACL to the interface:

```
R2(config)# interface S0/1/0
R2(config-if)# ip access-group INBOUNDFILTERS in
R2(config-if)# ip access-group OUTBOUNDFILTERS out
```

Time-Based ACLs

Time-based ACLs are similar to extended ACLs in function, but they allow access control based on time, as shown in Figure 5-29. To implement time-based ACLs, you create a time range that defines specific times of the day and days of the week. You identify the time range with a name and then refer to it by a function. The time restrictions are imposed on the function itself.

Figure 5-29   Topology for a Time-Based ACL

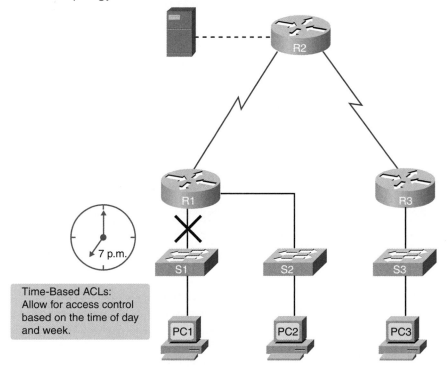

Benefits of Time-Based ACLs

Time-based ACLs have many benefits:

- They give the network administrator more control over permitting or denying access to resources.

■ They allow network administrators to control logging messages. ACL entries can log traffic at certain times of the day, but not constantly.

Time-Based ACL Example

Although the complete configuration details of time-based ACLs are outside the scope of this book, the following example shows the steps that are required. In the example, a Telnet connection is permitted from the inside network to the outside network on Monday, Wednesday, and Friday during business hours:

Step 1.   Define the time range during which to implement the ACL, and give it a name—EVERYOTHERDAY, in this case.

```
R1(config)# time-range EVERYOTHERDAY
R1(config-time-range)# periodic Monday Wednesday Friday 8:00 to 17:00
```

Step 2.   Apply the time range to the ACL:

```
R1(config)# access-list 101 permit tcp 192.168.10.0 0.0.0.255 any eq telnet
    time-range EVERYOTHERDAY
```

Step 3.   Apply the ACL to the interface:

```
R1(config)# interface S0/0/0
R1(config-if)# ip access-group 101 out
```

The time range relies on the router system clock. This feature works best with Network Time Protocol (NTP) synchronization, but the router clock can be used.

Troubleshooting Common ACL Errors

Using the **show** commands described earlier reveals most of the more common ACL errors before they cause problems in your network. Hopefully, you are using a good test procedure to protect your network from errors during the development stage of your ACL implementation.

When you look at an ACL, check it against the rules you learned about how to build ACLs correctly. Most errors occur because these basic rules are ignored. In fact, the most common errors are entering ACL statements in the wrong order and not applying adequate criteria to your rules.

Let's look at a series of common problems and their solutions using the topology shown in Figure 5-30.

Figure 5-30   Topology for Troubleshooting ACLs

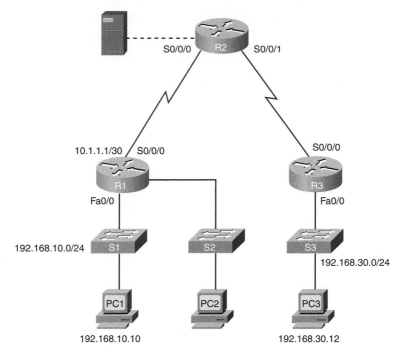

Error #1

Host 192.168.10.10 has no connectivity with 192.168.30.12. Can you see the error in the output of the **show access-lists** command on R3 in Example 5-23? (This access list is applied inbound to R3's s0/0/0 interface.)

Example 5-23   Error #1

```
R3# show access-lists 10

    10 deny tcp 192.168.10.0 0.0.0.255 any
    20 permit tcp host 192.168.10.10 any
    30 permit ip any any
```

The solution to this error reveals itself if you look at the order of the ACL statements on R3. Host 192.168.10.10 has no connectivity with 192.168.30.12 because of the order of rule 10 in the access list. Because the router processes ACLs from the top down, statement 10 denies the entire 192.168.10.0 network, including host 192.168.10.10, so statement 20 does not get processed. Statements 10 and 20 should be reversed. The last line allows all other non-TCP traffic that falls under IP (ICMP, UDP, and so on).

Error #2

The 192.168.10.0/24 network cannot use TFTP to connect to the 192.168.30.0/24 network. Can you see the error in the output of the **show access-lists** command on R1 in Example 5-24? (This access list is applied inbound to R1's Fa0/0 interface.)

Example 5-24   Error #2

```
R1# show access-lists 120

Extended IP access list 120
    10 deny tcp 192.168.10.0 0.0.255.255 any eq telnet
    20 deny tcp 192.168.10.0 0.0.0.255 host 10.100.100.1 eq smtp
    30 permit tcp any any
```

The 192.168.10.0/24 network cannot use TFTP to connect to the 192.168.30.0/24 network because TFTP uses the transport protocol UDP. Statement 30 in access list 120 allows all other TCP traffic. Because TFTP uses UDP, it is implicitly denied. Statement 30 should be **ip any any**.

This ACL works whether it is applied to Fa0/0 of R1 or S0/0/1 of R3, or S0/0/0 or R2 in the incoming direction. However, based on the rule about placing extended ACLs closest to the source, the best option is on Fa0/0 of R1, because it allows undesirable traffic to be filtered without crossing the network infrastructure.

Error #3

The 192.168.10.0/24 network can use Telnet to connect to 192.168.30.0/24, but this connection should not be allowed. Analyze the output from the **show access-lists** command on R1 in Example 5-25, and see whether you can find a solution. Where would you apply this ACL?

Example 5-25   Error #3

```
R1# show access-lists 130

Extended IP access list 130
    10 deny tcp any eq telnet any
    20 deny tcp 192.168.10.0 0.0.0.255 host 192.168.30.0 eq smtp
    30 permit ip any any
```

The 192.168.10.0/24 network can use Telnet to connect to the 192.168.30.0/24 network, because the Telnet port number in statement 10 of access list 130 is listed in the wrong position. Statement 10 currently denies any source with a port number that is equal to Telnet trying to establish a connection to any IP address. If you want to deny Telnet traffic inbound on S0/0/0, you should deny the destination port number that is equal to Telnet—for example, **deny tcp any any eq telnet**.

Error #4

Host 192.168.10.10 can use Telnet to connect to 192.168.30.12, but this connection should not be allowed. Analyze the output from the **show access-lists** command on R1 in Example 5-26.

Example 5-26   Error #4

```
R1# show access-lists 140

Extended IP access list 140
    10 deny tcp host 192.168.10.1 0.0.0.255 any eq telnet
    20 deny tcp 192.168.10.0 0.0.0.255 host 10.100.100.1 eq smtp
    30 permit ip any any
```

Host 192.168.10.10 can use Telnet to connect to 192.168.30.12 because no rules deny host 192.168.10.10 or its network as the source. Statement 10 of access list 140 denies the router interface from which traffic would be departing. However, as these packets depart the router, they have a source address of 192.168.10.10, not the address of the router interface.

As in the solution for Error 2, this ACL should be applied to Fa0/0 of R1 in the incoming direction.

Error #5

Host 192.168.30.12 can use Telnet to connect to 192.168.10.10, but this connection should not be allowed. Look at the output from the **show access-lists** command on R2 in Example 5-27, and find the error. (This access list is applied inbound to R3's S0/0/0 interface.)

Example 5-27   Error #5

```
R3# show access-lists 150

Extended IP access list 150
    10 deny tcp host 192.168.30.12 any eq telnet
    20 permit ip any any
```

Host 192.168.30.12 can use Telnet to connect to 192.168.10.10 because of the direction in which access list 150 is applied to the S0/0/0 interface. Statement 10 denies the source address of 192.168.30.12, but that address would be the source only if the traffic were outbound on S0/0/0, not inbound.

Summary

An ACL is a router configuration script that uses packet filtering to control whether a router permits or denies packets to pass based on criteria found in the packet header. ACLs are also used to select types of traffic to be analyzed, forwarded, or processed in other ways. ACLs are among the most commonly used objects in Cisco IOS software.

There are different types of ACLs—standard, extended, named, and numbered. In this chapter you learned the purpose of each of these ACL types and where they need to be placed in your network. You learned to configure ACLs on inbound and outbound interfaces. Special ACL types—dynamic, reflexive, and timed—were described. Guidelines and best practices for developing functional and effective ACLs were highlighted.

With the knowledge and skills you learned in this chapter, you can now confidently, but with care, configure standard, extended, and complex ACLs, and verify and troubleshoot those configurations.

Labs

The activities and labs available in the companion *Accessing the WAN, CCNA Exploration Labs and Study Guide* (ISBN 1-58713-201-x) provide hands-on practice with the following topics introduced in this chapter:

Lab 5-1: Basic Access Control Lists (5.5.1)

An essential part of network security is being able to control what kind of traffic is being permitted to reach your network, and where that traffic is coming from. This lab teaches you how to configure basic and extended access control lists to accomplish this goal.

Lab 5-2: Access Control Lists Challenge (5.5.2)

In the Basic Access Control Lists lab, you configured for the first time basic and extended access control lists as a network security measure. In this lab, you try to set up as much network security as possible without referring to the Basic Access Control Lists lab. This will allow you to gauge how much you learned in the preceding lab. Where necessary, check your work using either the Basic Access Control Lists lab or the answer key provided by your instructor.

Lab 5-3: Troubleshooting Access Control Lists (5.5.3)

You work for a regional service provider that has recently experienced several security breaches. Your department has been asked to secure customer edge routers so that only the local management PCs can access VTY lines. To address this issue, you will configure ACLs on R2 so that networks directly connected to R3 cannot communicate with networks directly connected to R1, but still allow all other traffic.

Many of the Hands-on Labs include Packet Tracer Companion Activities where you can use Packet Tracer to complete a simulation of the lab. Look for this icon in the *Accessing the WAN, CCNA Exploration Labs and Study Guide* for Hands-on Labs that have a Packet Tracer Companion.

Check Your Understanding

Complete all the review questions listed here to test your understanding of the topics and concepts in this chapter. Answers are listed in Appendix, "Check Your Understanding and Challenge Questions Answer Key."

1. Which statements correctly describe Cisco access control lists? (Choose two.)

   A. Extended ACLs are created in interface configuration mode.

   B. Extended ACLs filter traffic based on source and destination IP, port number, and protocol.

   C. Standard IP ACLs are numbered 1 to 99, and extended ACLs are numbered 100 to 199.

   D. Standard ACLs permit or deny traffic to specific IP addresses.

   E. Standard ACLs do not permit the use of wildcard masks.

2. Which statement is true about applying an access list to an interface?

   A. Access lists are applied in global configuration mode.

   B. Named access lists are applied using the **ip access-name** command.

   C. Standard access lists should be applied to an interface as close as possible to the destination.

   D. The command for applying access list 101 inbound is **ip access-list 101**.

3. Which statement is a guideline to be followed when designing access control lists?

   A. Because ACL tests are executed in order, they should be organized from the most general condition to the most specific.

   B. Because ACL tests are executed in order, they should be organized from the most specific condition to the most general.

   C. Because all statements in an ACL are evaluated before they are executed, an explicit **deny any** statement must be written for an ACL to function properly.

   D. Because all statements in an ACL are evaluated before they are executed, an explicit **permit any** statement must be written for an ACL to function properly.

4. What occurs if the network administrator applies an IP access control list that has no permit statement outbound on an interface? (Choose two.)

A. All traffic outbound is denied.

B. All traffic outbound is allowed.

C. Only traffic originating from the router is allowed outbound.

D. The ACL restricts all incoming traffic and filters outgoing traffic.

5. Which solutions can be implemented with ACLs? (Choose two.)

A. Segment the network to increase available bandwidth.

B. Create a firewall on a router to filter inbound traffic from an external network.

C. Control traffic entering or exiting different areas of a local network.

D. Distribute DHCP traffic to allow easier network availability.

E. Allow or deny traffic into the network based on the MAC address.

6. Match each command with its description:

any

show running-config

show access-list

host

show ip interface

A. Substitutes for the 0.0.0.0 mask.

B. Indicates whether any ACLs are set on an interface.

C. Displays the contents of all ACLs on the router.

D. Represents an IP address and mask pair of 0.0.0.0 255.255.255.255.

E. Reveals the ACLs and interface assignments on a router.

7. Which IP address and wildcard mask test for hosts from an entire subnet of network 192.168.12.0 using a 29-bit mask?

A. 192.168.12.56 0.0.0.15

B. 192.168.12.56 0.0.0.8

C. 192.168.12.56 0.0.0.31

D. 192.168.12.84 0.0.0.7

E. 192.168.12.84 0.0.0.3

F. 192.168.12.84 0.0.0.255

8. What kind of access list is created with the command **ip access-list standard fastaccess**?

   A. Turbo ACL

   B. Reflexive ACL

   C. Named ACL

   D. Dynamic ACL

9. Refer to the following configuration, which shows an ACL that already exists on the router. The network administrator wants to insert the command **access-list 101 deny ip any 192.168.1.0 0.0.0.255 eq ftp** as the third line in the ACL shown. The network administrator enters the command in global configuration mode on the router. What effect does this have?

   ```
   access-list 101 deny ip any 192.168.1.0 0.0.0.255 eq 8080
   access-list 101 deny ip any 192.168.1.0 0.0.0.255 eq 80
   access-list 101 deny icmp any 192.168.1.0 0.0.0.255
   access-list 101 deny icmp any 192.168.2.0 0.0.0.255
   access-list 101 permit ip any 192.168.1.0 0.0.0.255
   access-list 101 permit ip any 192.168.2.0 0.0.0.255
   ```

   A. It inserts the line in the desired position in the ACL.

   B. It inserts the line as the first statement in the ACL.

   C. It inserts the line as the last statement in the ACL.

   D. It deletes the entire list and replaces it with the new line only.

10. Refer to Figure 5-31 and the following configuration. Which statement correctly describes how Router1 processes packets with this configuration?

Figure 5-31 Topology for Question 10

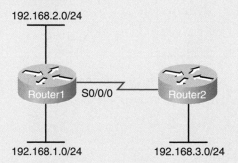

192.168.2.0/24

Router1 S0/0/0 Router2

192.168.1.0/24   192.168.3.0/24

```
Router1(config)# access-list 201 deny icmp 192.168.1.0 0.0.0.255 any
Router1(config)# access-list 201 deny icmp 192.168.2.0 0.0.0.255 any
Router1(config)# access-list 201 permit any any
Router1(config)# access-list 101 deny tcp any 192.168.1.0 0.0.0.255 eq 8080
Router1(config)# access-list 101 deny tcp any 192.168.1.0 0.0.0.255 eq 80
Router1(config)# access-list 101 deny icmp any 192.168.1.0 0.0.0.255
Router1(config)# access-list 101 deny icmp any 192.168.2.0 0.0.0.255
Router1(config)# access-list 101 permit ip any 192.168.1.0 0.0.0.255
Router1(config)# access-list 101 permit ip any 192.168.2.0 0.0.0.255
Router1(config)# interface serial 0/0/0
Router1(config-if)# ip access-group 101 in
Router1(config-if)# ip access-group 201 out
```

A. Traffic exiting interface serial 0/0/0 is filtered by both ACL 101 and ACL 201.

B. If a packet entering interface serial 0/0/0 matches a condition in ACL 101, the router continues comparing the packet to the rest of the statements in ACL 101 to make sure that no other statements might apply.

C. Router1 compares packets entering interface serial 0/0/0 first to all the ACL 101 statements for the IP protocol and then to all the ACL 101 statements for the ICMP protocol.

D. A packet entering interface serial 0/0/0 is compared to each statement in ACL 101 until one statement matches the packet. Then the router drops or forwards the packet without considering the remaining statements in ACL 101.

11. An administrator wants to implement lock-and-key access to a host within the company network for specific users who are connecting from outside the company network. What type of ACL would best suit the situation?

A. Dynamic

B. Reflexive

C. Extended

D. Time-based

12. What type of ACL should the network administrator implement to limit Internet traffic during peak hours of the day?

A. Dynamic

B. Policy-based

C. Reflexive

D. Time-based

13. Which statement correctly describes a reflexive access list?

   A. An ACL that allows IP traffic for sessions originating from inside the network while denying traffic for sessions originating from the outside

   B. An ACL that controls traffic based on the time

   C. An ACL that uses an extended list to block users from traversing a router until they are authenticated

   D. An ACL that identifies only the source of traffic

14. Categorize the following descriptions as belonging to either a standard IP ACL or an extended IP ACL:

   A. Checks only the source address

   B. Access list numbers 100 to 199

   C. Checks protocol and port numbers

   D. Permits/denies only entire protocols based on network address

   E. Access list numbers 1 to 99

   F. Checks source and destination address

15. Refer to the following configuration. Assuming that this ACL is correctly applied to a router interface, which statements describe traffic on the network? (Choose two.)

```
access-list 199 deny tcp 178.15.0.0 0.0.255.255 any eq 23
access-list 199 permit ip any any
```

   A. All FTP traffic from network 178.15.0.0 will be permitted.

   B. All Telnet traffic destined for network 178.15.0.0 will be denied.

   C. Telnet and FTP will be permitted from all hosts on network 178.15.0.0 to any destination.

   D. Telnet will not be permitted from any hosts on network 178.15.0.0 to any destination.

   E. Telnet will not be permitted to any host on network 178.15.0.0 from any destination.

16. Describe the "three Ps" rule associated with access control lists.

17. Describe the two basic rules associated with the placement of standard and extended ACLs.

18. Refer to Figure 5-32 and the following configuration. ACL 10, configured on R1, is designed to deny the host at 192.168.10.10 access to the 192.168.11.0 network, but all other hosts on the 192.168.10.0 network should be permitted access. However, the ACL does not accomplish this. Which changes would correct this problem?

Figure 5-32   Topology for Questions 18 and 19

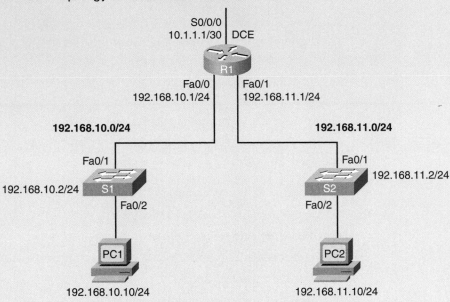

```
R1(config)# access-list 10 deny host 192.168.10.10
R1(config)# interface Fa0/1
R1(config-if)# ip access-group 10 in
```

19. Refer to Figure 5-32 and the following configuration. The named ACL SURFING should enable only the hosts on the 192.168.10.0 network web and secure web access. The hosts on 192.168.11.0 should not be permitted any access. The BROWSING ACL should permit return access only to traffic that originated from the 192.168.10.0 network. However, the ACLs do not accomplish this. Which changes would correct this problem?

```
R1(config)# access-list extended SURFING
R1(config-ext-nacl)# permit tcp 192.168.10.0 0.0.0.255 any eq 23
R1(config-ext-nacl)# permit tcp 192.168.10.0 0.0.0.255 any eq 443
R1(config)# access-list extended BROWSING
R1(config-ext-nacl)# permit tcp any 192.168.10.0 0.0.0.255
R1(config-ext-nacl)# exit
R1(config)# interface S0/0/0
R1(config-if)# ip access-group SURFING out
R1(config-if)# ip access-group BROWSING in
```

20. Describe the three types of complex ACLs and their functions.

Challenge Questions and Activities

1. Configure a time-based ACL that only permits traffic to the server 192.168.1.17, Monday through Friday, from 9:00 a.m. to 5:00 p.m.

2. Configure an **access-list** statement that permits hosts from the 172.30.16.0/20 to 172.30.31.0/20 subnets.

3. RouterA is configured with the following access list that denies ICMP echo requests and echo replies while permitting all other IP traffic. The access list is applied outbound on its single serial interface, serial 0/0/0. None of the devices attached to the LAN on RouterA can ping devices beyond RouterA's serial 0/0/0 interface. However, the network administrator can ping devices outbound on the serial interface when using RouterA's command-line interface (CLI). Why can the router ping devices successfully over the serial link, while devices on the LAN cannot?

```
access-list 101 deny icmp any any echo
access-list 101 deny icmp any any echo-reply
access-list 101 permit ip any any
interface Serial 0/0/0
  ip access-group 101 out
```

CHAPTER 6

Teleworker Services

Objectives

After completing this chapter, you should be able to answer the following questions:

- What are the enterprise requirements for providing teleworker services, and what are the differences between private and public network infrastructure?

- What are the teleworker requirements and recommended architecture for providing teleworker services?

- How do broadband services extend enterprise networks using DSL, cable, and wireless technologies?

- What is the importance of VPN technology, including its role and benefits for enterprises and teleworkers?

- How can VPN technology be used to provide secure teleworker services to an enterprise network?

Key Terms

This chapter uses the following key terms. You can find the definitions in the glossary at the end of the book.

broadband   *page 382*

tunneling   *page 383*

radio frequency (RF)   *page 385*

community antenna television (CATV)   *page 386*

drop cables   *page 386*

frequency   *page 388*

cycles per second   *page 388*

Data-over-Cable Service Interface Specification (DOCSIS)   *page 388*

cable modem termination system (CMTS)   *page 390*

cable modem (CM)   *page 390*

digital subscriber line (DSL)   *page 391*

DSL access multiplexer (DSLAM)   *page 392*

microfilter   *page 393*

splitters   *page 393*

network interface device (NID)   *page 393*

WiMAX (Worldwide Interoperability for Microwave Access)   *page 398*

IEEE 802.11   *page 400*

Wi-Fi Alliance   *page 400*

IEEE 802.11b   *page 400*

IEEE 802.11g   *page 400*

Teleworking (or telecommuting) is when an employee performs his or her job away from a traditional workplace, usually from a home office. The reasons for choosing teleworking vary. They include everything from personal convenience to allowing injured or shut-in employees to continue working during periods of convalescence.

Teleworking is a broad term that refers to conducting work by connecting to a workplace from a remote location with the assistance of telecommunications. Efficient teleworking is possible because of broadband Internet connections, virtual private networks (VPN), and more advanced technologies, including voice over IP (VoIP) and videoconferencing. Teleworking can save money that otherwise would be spent on travel, infrastructure, and facilities support.

Modern enterprises employ people who cannot commute to work every day or for whom working from a home office is more practical. These people, called teleworkers, must connect to the company network so that they can work from their home offices.

This chapter explains how organizations can provide secure, fast, and reliable remote network connections for teleworkers.

Business Requirements for Teleworker Services

More and more companies are finding it beneficial to have teleworkers. With advances in broadband and wireless technologies, working away from the office no longer presents the challenges it did in the past. Workers can work remotely almost as if they were in the next cubicle or office. Organizations can cost-effectively distribute data, voice, video, and real-time applications extended over one common network connection, across their entire workforce, no matter how remote and scattered they might be.

The Business Requirements for Teleworker Services

The benefits of telecommuting extend well beyond the ability for businesses to make profits. Telecommuting affects the social structure of societies and can have positive effects on the environment.

For day-to-day business operations, it is beneficial to be able to maintain continuity in case weather, traffic congestion, natural disasters, or other unpredictable events keep workers from getting to the workplace. On a broader scale, the ability of businesses to provide increased service across time zones and international boundaries is greatly enhanced using teleworkers. Contracting and outsourcing solutions are easier to implement and manage.

From a social perspective, teleworking options increase employment opportunities for various groups, including parents with small children, the handicapped, and people living in remote areas. Teleworkers enjoy more quality family time and less travel-related stress and in general provide their employers with increased productivity, satisfaction, and retention. In the age of climate change, teleworking is another way people can reduce their carbon footprint.

When designing network architectures that support a teleworking solution, designers must balance organizational requirements for security, infrastructure management, scalability, and affordability against the practical needs of teleworkers for ease of use, connection speeds, and reliability of service.

To allow businesses and teleworkers to function effectively, we must balance the selection of technologies and carefully design for telecommuting services.

Table 6-1 summarizes the benefits of teleworking.

Table 6-1   Teleworking Benefits

Organizational Benefits	Social Benefits	Environmental Benefits
Continuity of operations	Increased employment opportunities for marginalized groups	Reduced carbon footprints, for both individual workers and organizations
Increased responsiveness	Less travel- and commuter-related stress	
Secure, reliable, and man ageable access to information		
Cost-effective integration of data, voice, video, and applications		
Increased employee productivity		

The Teleworker Solution

Organizations need secure, reliable, cost-effective networks to connect corporate headquarters, branch offices, and suppliers. With the growing number of teleworkers, enterprises have an increasing need for secure, reliable, and cost-effective ways to connect people working in small offices/home offices (SOHO), and other remote locations, to resources on corporate sites.

Figure 6-1 illustrates the remote connection topologies that modern networks use to connect remote locations. In some cases, the remote locations connect to only the headquarters location, and in other cases, remote locations connect to multiple sites. The branch office in the figure connects to the headquarters and partner sites, whereas the teleworker has a single connection to the headquarters.

Figure 6-1   Remote Connection Options

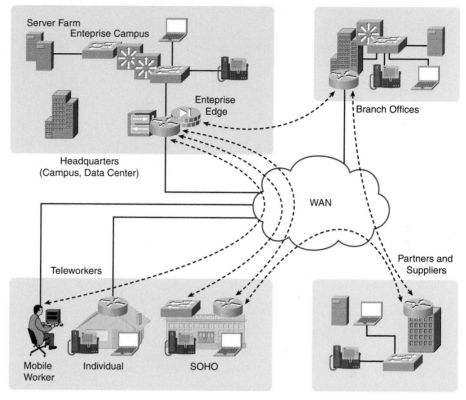

Figure 6-2 shows three remote-connection technologies available to organizations to support teleworker services:

- Traditional private WAN Layer 2 technologies, including Frame Relay, ATM, and leased lines, provide many remote-connection solutions. The security of these connections depends on the service provider.

- IPsec Virtual Private Networks (VPN) offer flexible and scalable connectivity.

- Site-to-site connections can provide a secure, fast, and reliable remote connection to teleworkers. This is the most common option for teleworkers, combined with remote access over broadband, to establish a secure VPN over the public Internet. (A less reliable means of connectivity using the Internet is a dialup connection.)

Figure 6-2 Remote Connection Technologies

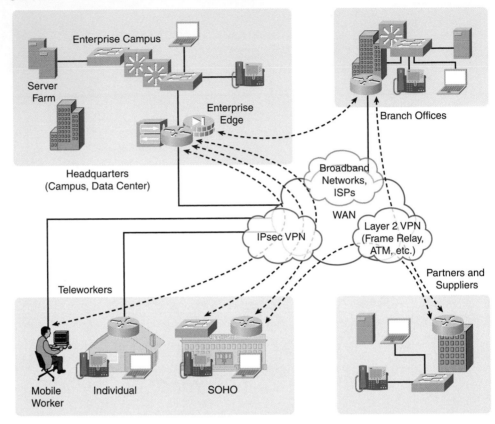

The term *broadband* refers to advanced communications systems that can provide high-speed transmission of services, such as data, voice, and video, over the Internet and other networks. Transmission is provided by a wide range of technologies, including digital subscriber line (DSL), fiber-optic cable, coaxial cable, wireless technology, and satellite. Broadband service data transmission speeds typically exceed 128 kilobits per second (kbps), or 128,000 bits per second, in at least one direction: downstream (from the Internet to the user's computer) or upstream (from the user's computer to the Internet).

This chapter describes how each of these technologies operates and introduces some of the steps needed to ensure that teleworker connections are secure.

To connect effectively to their organization's networks, teleworkers need two key sets of components: home office components and corporate components. The option of adding IP telephony components is becoming more common as providers extend broadband service to more areas. Soon, VoIP and videoconferencing components will become expected parts of the teleworker toolkit.

As shown in Figure 6-3, telecommuting requires the following components:

- **Teleworker and home office components**: The required home office components are a laptop or desktop computer, broadband access (cable or DSL), and a VPN router or VPN client software installed on the computer. Additional components might include a wireless access point. When traveling, teleworkers need an Internet connection and a VPN client to connect to the corporate network over any available dialup, network, or broadband connection. This is represented by the Teleworker section in Figure 6-3.

- **Headquarters and corporate components**: Corporate components are VPN-capable routers, VPN concentrators, multifunction security appliances, authentication, and central management devices for resilient aggregation and termination of the VPN connections. This is represented by the Headquarters section in Figure 6-3.

Figure 6-3   Teleworker Connectivity Requirements

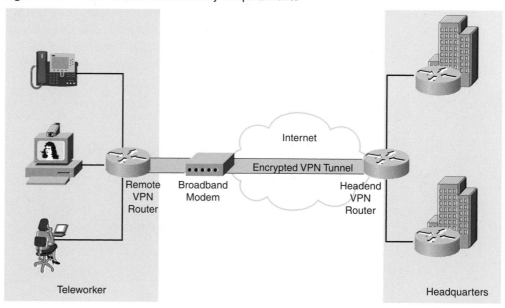

Typically, providing support for VoIP and videoconferencing requires upgrading these components. Routers need quality of service (QoS) functionality to best support VoIP and videoconferencing. QoS refers to a network's capability to provide better service to selected network traffic, as required by voice and video applications. An in-depth discussion of QoS is beyond the scope of this book.

Figure 6-3 shows an encrypted VPN tunnel connecting the teleworker to the corporate network. This is the heart of secure and reliable teleworker connections. A VPN is a private data network that uses the public telecommunication infrastructure. VPN security maintains privacy using a *tunneling* protocol and security procedures.

This chapter presents the IPsec (IP Security) protocol as the favored approach to building secure VPN tunnels. Unlike earlier security approaches that applied security at the application layer of the Open Systems Interconnection (OSI) model, IPsec works at the network or packet processing layer.

Broadband Services

Teleworkers typically use diverse applications (for example, e-mail, web-based applications, mission-critical applications, real-time collaboration, voice, video, and videoconferencing) that require a high-bandwidth connection. The choice of access network technology and the need to ensure suitable bandwidth are the first considerations to address when connecting teleworkers.

Residential cable, DSL, and broadband wireless are three options that provide high bandwidth to teleworkers. The low bandwidth provided by a dialup modem connection usually is insufficient, although it is useful for mobile access while traveling. A modem dialup connection should be considered only when other options are unavailable.

In this section, you will learn how these broadband services extend enterprise networks to enable teleworker access.

Connecting Teleworkers to the WAN

Teleworkers require a connection to an ISP to access the Internet. ISPs offer various connection options, as shown in Figure 6-4.

Figure 6-4   Connecting Teleworkers to the WAN

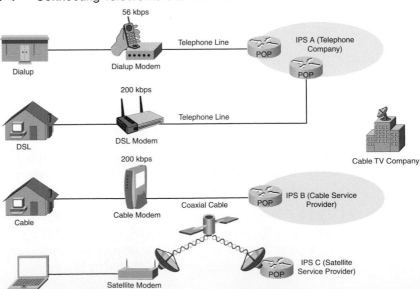

The main connection methods used by home and small business users are as follows:

- **Dialup access** is an inexpensive option that uses any phone line and a modem. To connect to the ISP, a user calls the ISP access phone number. Dialup is the slowest connection option and typically is used by mobile workers in areas where higher-speed connection options are unavailable.

  With speeds up to 56 kbps (the actual physical maximum speed is 53 kbps), dialup access is the slowest connection option. For example, downloading a 5-MB file using a 56-kbps dialup connection takes approximately 12 minutes.

- **DSL** typically is more expensive than dialup but provides a faster connection. DSL also uses telephone lines, but unlike dialup access, DSL provides a continuous connection to the Internet. DSL uses a special high-speed modem that separates the DSL signal from the telephone signal and provides an Ethernet connection to a host computer or LAN.

  DSL provides high-speed broadband access at speeds of 200 kbps and higher. Upload and download speeds vary according to the user's distance from the central office.

  There are many types of DSL. Home users usually use asymmetric DSL (ADSL), in which download speeds are higher than upload speeds. Symmetric DSL has the same speeds for upload and download. SDSL often is more suitable for small-to-medium business applications.

- **Cable modem** service usually is offered by cable television service providers. The Internet signal is carried on the same coaxial cable that delivers cable television. A special cable modem separates the Internet signal from the other signals carried on the cable and provides an Ethernet connection to a host computer or LAN.

  Cable is similar to DSL in that it provides broadband access at speeds of 200 kbps and higher. Unlike DSL, speed is unaffected by the distance to the ISP. However, cable is a shared service, so the bandwidth a customer experiences can be affected to a degree by the number of subscribers sharing a particular section of the distribution network.

- **Satellite** Internet access is offered by satellite service providers. The computer connects through Ethernet to a satellite modem that transmits radio signals to the nearest point of presence (POP) within the satellite network.

  Satellite Internet access speeds range from 128 kbps to 512 kbps, depending on the subscriber plan.

Cable

Accessing the Internet through a cable network is a popular option used by teleworkers to access their enterprise network. The cable system uses a coaxial cable that carries *radio frequency (RF)* signals across the network. Coaxial cable is the primary medium used to build cable TV systems.

What Is Cable?

Cable television began in Pennsylvania in 1948. John Walson, the owner of an appliance store in a small mountain town, needed to solve poor over-the-air TV reception problems experienced by customers trying to receive TV signals from Philadelphia through the mountains. Walson erected an antenna on a utility pole on a local mountaintop. He connected the antenna to his appliance store via a cable and modified signal boosters. This enabled him to demonstrate the televisions in his store with strong broadcasts coming from the three Philadelphia stations. He then connected several of his customers who were located along the cable path. This was the first *community antenna television (CATV)* system in the United States.

Walson's company grew over the years, and he is recognized as the founder of the cable television industry. He also was the first cable operator to use microwave to import distant television stations, the first to use coaxial cable to improve picture quality, and the first to distribute pay television programming.

Most cable operators use satellite dishes to gather TV signals. Early systems were one-way, with cascading amplifiers placed in series along the network to compensate for signal loss. These systems used taps to couple video signals from the main trunks to subscriber homes via *drop cables*. A cable tap is a device that is used to connect into a cable signal and send it to a subscriber.

Modern cable systems provide two-way communication between subscribers and the cable operator. Cable operators now offer customers advanced telecommunications services, including high-speed Internet access, digital cable television, and residential telephone service. Cable operators typically deploy hybrid fiber-coaxial (HFC) networks to enable high-speed transmission of data to cable modems located in a SOHO.

Figure 6-5 illustrates the components of a typical modern cable system, which are summarized in the following list:

- **Antenna site**: The antenna's location is chosen for optimum reception of over-the-air, satellite, and sometimes point-to-point signals. The main receiving antennas and satellite dishes are located at the antenna site.

- **Headend**: This is where signals are first received, processed, formatted, and then distributed downstream to the cable network. The headend facility usually is unmanned and under security fencing. It is similar to a telephone company central office.

- **Distribution network**: In a classic cable system called a tree-and-branch system, the distribution network consists of trunk and feeder cables. The trunk is the backbone that distributes signals throughout the community service area to the feeder. It typically uses 0.750-inch (19-mm) diameter coaxial cable. The feeder branches flow from a trunk and reach all the subscribers in the service area via coaxial cables. The feeder cable usually is a 0.5-inch (13-mm) diameter coaxial cable. (The distribution network is the trunk cable and amplifiers shown in Figure 6-5.)

■ **Subscriber drop**: A subscriber drop connects the subscriber to the cable services. The subscriber drop is a connection between the feeder part of a distribution network and the subscriber terminal device (for example, TV set, videocassette recorder [VCR], high-definition TV set-top box, or cable modem). A subscriber drop consists of radio-grade (RG) coaxial cabling (usually 59-series or 6-series coaxial cable), grounding and attachment hardware, passive devices, and a set-top box.

Figure 6-5   Components of a Cable System

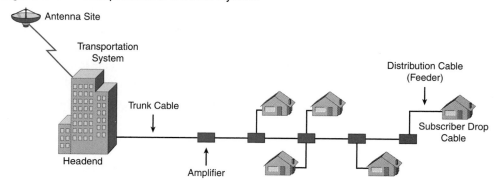

Electromagnetic Spectrum

The electromagnetic spectrum encompasses a broad range of frequencies, as shown in Figure 6-6. Understanding the electromagnetic spectrum is useful not only for cable technology, but also DSL, wireless, and other technologies.

Figure 6-6   Electromagnetic Spectrum

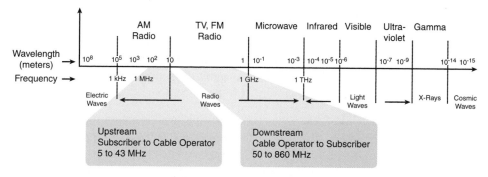

Frequency is the rate at which current (or voltage) cycles occur, computed as the number of "waves" per second. Wavelength is the speed of propagation of the electromagnetic signal divided by its frequency in *cycles per second*.

Radio frequencies or radio waves, generally called RF, constitute a portion of the electromagnetic spectrum between approximately 1 kilohertz (kHz) through 1 terahertz. When users tune a radio or TV set to find different radio stations or TV channels, they are tuning to different electromagnetic frequencies across that RF spectrum. The same principle applies to the cable system.

The cable TV industry uses a portion of the RF electromagnetic spectrum. Within the cable, different frequencies carry TV channels and data. At the subscriber end, equipment such as TVs, VCRs, and high-definition TV set-top boxes tune to certain frequencies that allow the user to view the channel or, using a cable modem, receive high-speed Internet access.

A cable network can transmit signals on the cable in either direction at the same time. The following frequency scope is used:

- **Downstream**: The direction of an RF signal transmission (TV channels and data) from the source (headend) to the destination (subscribers). Transmission from source to destination is called the forward path. Downstream frequencies are in the range of 54 to 860 megahertz (MHz).

- **Upstream**: The direction of the RF signal transmission from subscribers to the headend, or the return or reverse path. Upstream frequencies are in the range of 5 to 42 MHz. Because video needs to be sent in only the downstream direction and only data needs to be sent upstream, the upstream direction can use a lower frequency range.

DOCSIS

The *Data-over-Cable Service Interface Specification (DOCSIS)* is an international standard developed by CableLabs, a nonprofit research and development consortium for cable-related technologies. CableLabs tests and certifies cable equipment vendor devices, such as cable modems and cable modem termination systems, and grants DOCSIS-certified or qualified status.

DOCSIS defines the communications and operation support interface requirements for a data-over-cable system and permits the addition of high-speed data transfer to an existing CATV system. Cable operators employ DOCSIS to provide Internet access over their existing HFC infrastructure.

DOCSIS specifies the OSI Layer 1 and Layer 2 requirements:

- **Physical layer**: For data signals that the cable operator can use, DOCSIS specifies the channel widths (bandwidths of each channel) as 200 kHz, 400 kHz, 800 kHz, 1.6 MHz, 3.2 MHz, and 6.4 MHz. DOCSIS also specifies modulation techniques (the way to use the RF signal to convey digital data).

- **MAC layer**: Defines a deterministic access method—time-division multiple access (TDMA) or synchronous code-division multiple access (S-CDMA). S-CDMA spreads the digital data across a wide frequency band. This allows multiple subscribers to be connected to the network, transmitting and receiving at the same time.

To understand the MAC layer requirements for DOCSIS, an explanation of how various communication technologies divide channel access is helpful. TDMA divides access by time. Frequency-division multiple access (FDMA) divides access by frequency. Code-division multiple access (CDMA) employs spread-spectrum technology and a special coding scheme in which each transmitter is assigned a specific code.

An analogy that illustrates these concepts starts with a room representing a channel. The room is full of people who need to speak to one another. In other words, they need channel access. One solution is for them to take turns speaking (time division). Another is for each person to speak at different pitches (frequency division). In CDMA, they would speak different languages. People speaking the same language can understand each other but not other people. In radio CDMA, used by many North American cell phone networks, each group of users has a shared code. Many codes occupy the same channel, but only users associated with a particular code can understand each other. S-CDMA is a proprietary version of CDMA developed by Terayon Corporation for data transmission across coaxial cable networks.

Plans for frequency allocation bands differ between North American and European cable systems. Euro-DOCSIS is adapted for use in Europe. The main differences between DOCSIS and Euro-DOCSIS relate to channel bandwidths. TV technical standards vary across the world, which affects how DOCSIS variants develop. International TV standards include NTSC (National Television System Committee) in North American and parts of Japan; PAL (Phase Alternating Line) in most of Europe, Asia, Africa, Australia, Brazil, and Argentina; and SECAM (Séquentiel couleurà mémoire, French for "sequential color with memory") in France and some Eastern European countries.

The following list summarizes DOCSIS:

- DOCSIS is a standard for certification of cable equipment vendor devices (cable modem and cable modem termination system).

- DOCSIS specifies the physical and MAC layers.

- DOCSIS defines RF interface requirements for a data-over-cable system.

- Cable equipment vendors must pass certification conducted by CableLabs.

- Euro-DOCSIS is a variation adapted for use in Europe.

You can find more information at the following websites:

- About DOCSIS: *http://www.cablemodem.com/specifications*

- About Euro-DOCSIS: *http://www.euro-docsis.com*

Delivering Services over Cable

Delivering services over a cable network requires different radio frequencies. Downstream frequencies are in the 50- to 860-MHz range, and the upstream frequencies are in the 5- to 42-MHz range.

Figure 6-7 shows the devices involved in sending data over cable. Two types of equipment are required to send digital modem signals upstream and downstream on a cable system:

- *Cable modem termination system (CMTS)* at the headend of the cable operator.

- *Cable modem (CM)* on the subscriber end. The cable modem enables the subscriber to receive data at high speeds. Typically, the cable modem attaches to a standard 10BASE-T Ethernet card in the computer.

Figure 6-7   Sending Data over Cable

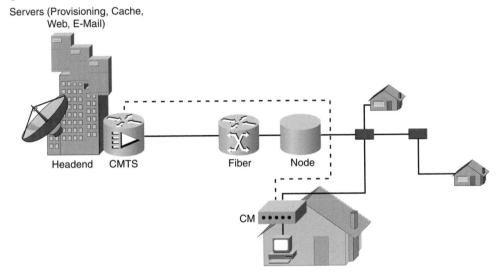

The CMTS is a component that exchanges digital signals with cable modems on a cable network. A headend CMTS communicates with CMs located in subscriber homes. The headend is actually a router with databases for providing Internet services to cable subscribers. The architecture is relatively simple, using a mixed optical-coaxial network in which optical fiber replaces the lower-bandwidth coaxial.

A web of fiber trunk cables connects the headend to the nodes where optical-to-RF signal conversion takes place. The fiber carries the same broadband content for Internet connections, telephone service, and streaming video that the coaxial cable carries. Coaxial feeder cables originate from the node that carries RF signals to the subscribers.

In a modern HFC network, typically 500 to 2000 active data subscribers are connected to a cable network segment, all sharing the upstream and downstream bandwidth. The actual bandwidth for Internet service over a CATV line can be up to 27 Mbps on the download path to the subscriber and about 2.5 Mbps of bandwidth on the upload path. Based on the cable network architecture, cable operator provisioning practices, and traffic load, an individual subscriber typically can get an access speed of between 256 kbps and 6 Mbps.

When high usage causes congestion, the cable operator can add additional bandwidth for data services by allocating an additional TV channel for high-speed data. This addition may effectively double the downstream bandwidth that is available to subscribers. Another option is to reduce the number of subscribers served by each network segment. To reduce the number of subscribers, the cable operator further subdivides the network by laying the fiber-optic connections closer and deeper into the neighborhoods.

DSL

Digital subscriber line (DSL) is a means of providing high-speed connections over installed copper wires. In this section, we look at DSL as one of the key teleworker solutions available.

Several years ago, Bell Labs discovered that a typical voice conversation over a local loop required bandwidth of only 300 Hz to 3 kHz. For many years, the telephone networks did not use the bandwidth above 3 kHz. Advances in technology allowed DSL to use the additional bandwidth from 3 kHz up to 1 MHz to deliver high-speed data services over ordinary copper lines.

For example, asymmetric DSL (ADSL) uses a frequency range from approximately 20 kHz to 1 MHz. Fortunately, only relatively small changes to existing telephone company infrastructure are required to deliver high-bandwidth data rates to subscribers. Figure 6-8 shows a representation of bandwidth space allocation on a copper wire for ADSL. The POTS area identifies the frequency range used by the voice-grade telephone service, which is often called the plain old telephone service (POTS). The ADSL area represents the frequency space used by the upstream and downstream DSL signals.

Figure 6-8   ADSL Bandwidth Allocation

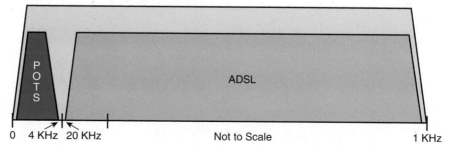

The two basic types of DSL technologies are asymmetric (ADSL) and symmetric (SDSL). All forms of DSL service are categorized as ADSL or SDSL, and there are several varieties of each type. ADSL provides higher downstream bandwidth to the user than upload bandwidth. SDSL provides the same capacity in both directions.

The different varieties of DSL provide different bandwidths, some with capabilities exceeding those of a T1 or E1 leased line. The transfer rates depend on the actual length of the local loop and the type and condition of its cabling. For satisfactory service, the loop must be less than 5.5 kilometers (5460 meters, or 3.5 miles).

DSL Connections

Service providers deploy DSL in the portion of the local telephone network called the local loop or last mile. This is the connection between the service provider's central office and the customer. The connection is set up between a pair of modems on either end of a copper wire that extends between the customer premises equipment (CPE) and the DSL access multiplexer (DSLAM).

Figure 6-9 shows the key equipment needed to provide a DSL connection to a SOHO. The two key components are the DSL transceiver and the DSLAM:

- **Transceiver**: Connects the teleworker's computer to the DSL. Usually the transceiver is a DSL modem connected to the computer using a USB or Ethernet cable. Newer DSL transceivers can be built into small routers with multiple 10/100 switch ports suitable for home office use.

- *DSL access multiplexer (DSLAM)*: Located at the central office (CO) of the carrier, the DSLAM combines individual DSL connections from users into one high-capacity link to an ISP, and thereby to the Internet.

Figure 6-9   DSL Connections

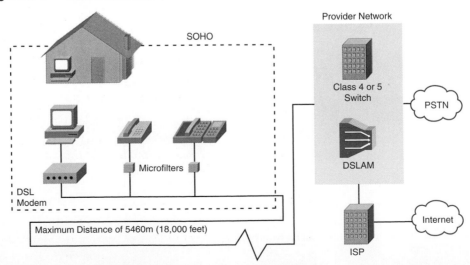

The advantage that DSL has over cable technology is that DSL is not a shared medium. Each user has a separate direct connection to the DSLAM. Adding users does not impede performance, unless the DSLAM Internet connection to the ISP, or the Internet, becomes saturated.

Data and Voice over DSL

The major benefit of ADSL is the ability to provide data services along with POTS voice services using the existing cabling between the central office and the customer.

When the service provider carries analog voice and ADSL on the same wire, the provider splits the POTS channel from the ADSL modem using filters or splitters. This setup guarantees uninterrupted regular phone service even if ADSL fails. When filters or splitters are in place, the user can use the phone line and the ADSL connection simultaneously without adverse effects on either service.

ADSL signals distort voice transmission and are split or filtered at the customer premises. There are two ways to separate ADSL from voice at the customer premises:

- **Using a microfilter**: A *microfilter* is a passive low-pass filter with two ends. One end connects to the telephone, and the other end connects to the telephone wall jack. This solution eliminates the need for a technician to visit the premises and allows the user to use any jack in the house for voice or ADSL service.

- **Using a splitter**: POTS *splitters* separate the DSL traffic from the POTS traffic. The POTS splitter is a passive device. In the event of a power failure, the voice traffic still travels to the voice switch in the carrier's CO. Splitters are located at the CO and, in some deployments, at the customer premises. At the CO, the POTS splitter separates the voice traffic, destined for POTS connections, and the data traffic, destined for the DSLAM.

Figure 6-10 shows the local loop terminating on the customer premises at the demarcation point. The actual device is the *network interface device (NID)*. This point usually is where the phone line enters the customer premises. At this point, a splitter can be attached to the phone line. The splitter forks the phone line: one branch provides the original house telephone wiring for telephones, and the other branch connects to the ADSL modem. The splitter acts as a low-pass filter, allowing only the 0- to 4-kHz frequencies to pass to or from the telephone.

Figure 6-10 Separating Data from Voice in ADSL Connections

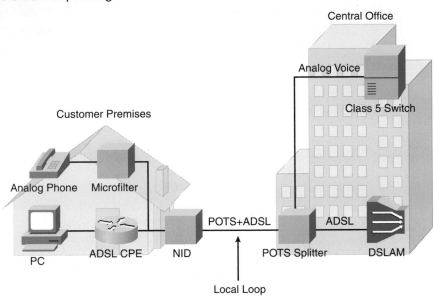

Installing the POTS splitter at the NID usually means that a technician must go to the customer site. Because of this additional labor and technical support, most home installations today use microfilters, as shown in Figure 6-11. Using microfilters also has the advantage of providing wider connectivity through the residence. Because the POTS splitter separates the ADSL and voice signals at the NID, usually only one ADSL outlet is available in the house.

Figure 6-11 Cisco EZ-DSL Microfilters

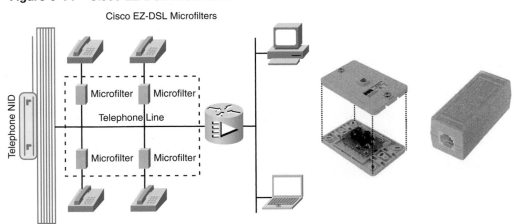

Figure 6-11 shows a typical SOHO DSL layout using microfilters. In this solution, the user can install inline microfilters on each telephone or install wall-mounted microfilters in place of regular telephone jacks.

If the service provider installs a splitter, it is placed between the NID and the inside telephone distribution system, as shown in Figure 6-12. One wire goes directly to the DSL modem, and the other carries the DSL signal to the telephones.

Figure 6-12   DSL Splitter Box

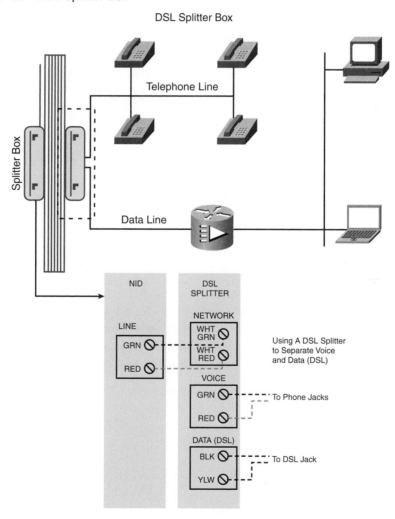

Broadband Wireless

Broadband access by ADSL or cable gives teleworkers faster connections than dialup, but until recently, SOHO PCs had to connect to a modem or router over a Category 5 (Ethernet) cable. Wireless networking, or Wi-Fi (wireless fidelity), has improved that situation, not only in the SOHO, but on enterprise campuses as well.

Using 802.11 networking standards, data travels from place to place on radio waves. What makes 802.11 networking relatively easy to deploy is that it uses the unlicensed radio spectrum to send and receive data. Most radio and TV transmissions are government regulated and require a license to use.

Over the last several years, computer manufacturers have started building wireless network adapters into most laptop computers. As the price of chipsets for Wi-Fi continues to drop, it is becoming a very economical networking option for desktop computers as well.

The benefits of Wi-Fi extend beyond not having to use or install wired network connections. Wireless networking provides mobility. Wireless connections give the teleworker increased flexibility and productivity.

Types of Broadband Wireless

Until recently, a significant limitation of wireless access has been the need to be within the local transmission range (typically less than 100 feet) of a wireless router or wireless access point that has a wired connection to the Internet. As soon as a worker left the office or home, wireless access was not readily available.

However, with advances in technology, the reach of wireless connections has been extended. The concept of hotspots has increased access to wireless connections across the world. A hotspot is the area covered by one or more interconnected access points. Public gathering places, such as coffee shops, parks, and libraries, have created Wi-Fi hotspots, hoping to increase business. By overlapping access points, hotspots can cover many square miles.

New developments in broadband wireless technology are increasing wireless availability. These include

- Municipal Wi-Fi
- WiMAX
- Satellite Internet

Municipal governments have also joined the Wi-Fi revolution. Often working with service providers, cities are deploying municipal wireless networks. Some of these networks provide high-speed Internet access at no cost or for substantially less than the price of other broadband services. Other cities reserve their Wi-Fi networks for official use, providing police, firefighters, and city workers remote access to the Internet and municipal networks.

Single Wireless Router

Figure 6-13 shows a typical home deployment using a single wireless router. This deployment uses the hub-and-spoke model. If the single wireless router fails, all connectivity is lost.

Figure 6-13   Single Wireless Router

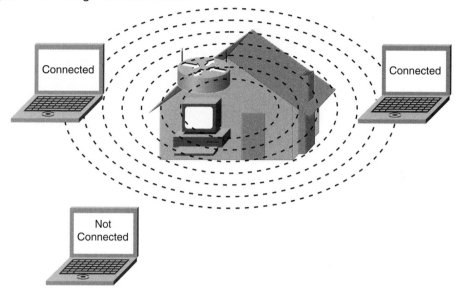

Meshed Municipal Wi-Fi Network

Most municipal wireless networks use a mesh topology rather than a hub-and-spoke model. A mesh is a series of access points (radio transmitters), as shown in Figure 6-14. Each access point is in range and can communicate with at least two other access points. The mesh blankets its area with radio signals. Signals travel from access point to access point through this cloud.

A meshed network has several advantages over single-router hotspots. Installation is easier and can be less expensive because there are fewer wires. Deployment over a large urban area is faster. From an operational point of view, a mesh is more reliable. If a node fails, others in the mesh compensate for it.

Figure 6-14   Meshed Municipal Wi-Fi Network

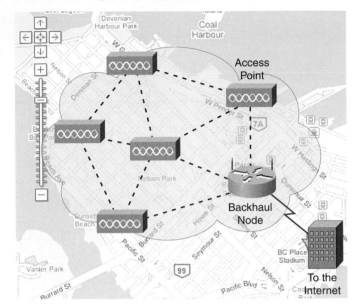

WiMAX

Figure 6-15 shows a WiMAX network. *WiMAX (Worldwide Interoperability for Microwave Access)* is telecommunications technology aimed at providing wireless data over long distances in a variety of ways, from point-to-point links to full mobile cellular-type access. WiMAX operates at higher speeds, over greater distances, and for a greater number of users than Wi-Fi. Because of its higher speed (bandwidth) and falling component prices, it is predicted that WiMAX will soon supplant municipal mesh networks for wireless deployments.

A WiMAX network consists of two main components:

- A tower that is similar in concept to a cellular telephone tower. A single WiMAX tower can provide coverage to an area as large as 3000 square miles, or almost 7500 square kilometers.

- A WiMAX receiver that is similar in size and shape to a PC card (PCMCIA card), or that is built into a laptop or other wireless device.

A WiMAX tower station connects directly to the Internet using a high-bandwidth connection (for example, a T3 line). A tower can also connect to other WiMAX towers using line-of-sight microwave links (backhauling). WiMAX thus can provide coverage to rural areas that are out of reach of "last-mile" cable and DSL technologies.

Figure 6-15   WiMAX

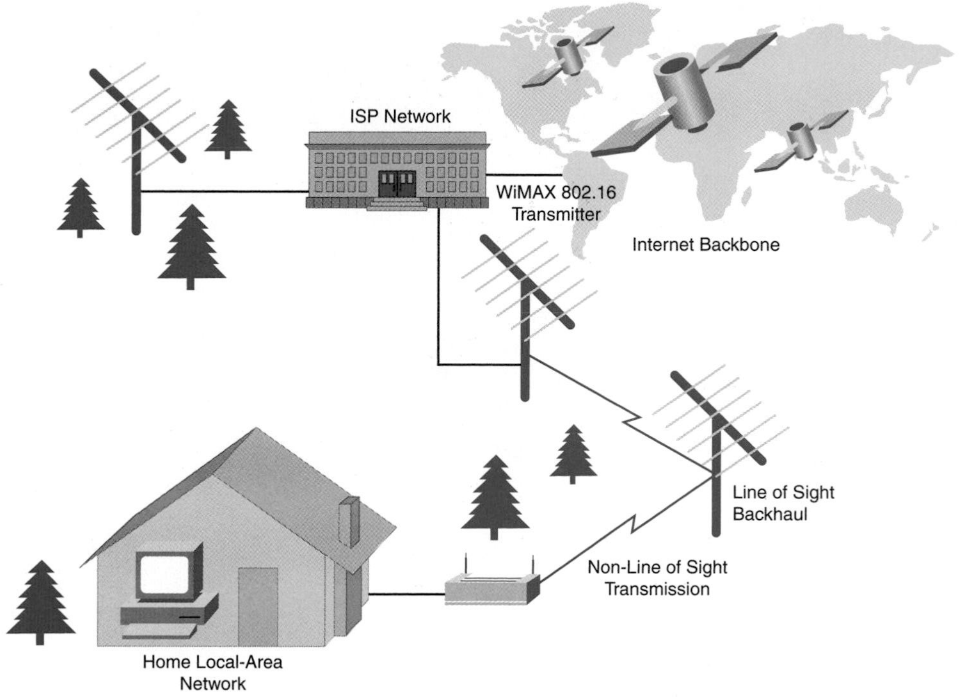

Satellite Internet

Satellite Internet services are used in locations where land-based Internet access is unavailable, or for temporary installations that are continually on the move. Internet access using satellites is available worldwide, including for vessels at sea, airplanes in flight, and vehicles moving on land.

There are three ways to connect to the Internet using satellites:

- **One-way multicast satellite Internet systems** are used for IP multicast-based data, audio, and video distribution. Even though most IP protocols require two-way communication for Internet content, including web pages, one-way satellite-based Internet services can be "pushed" pages to local storage at end-user sites by satellite Internet. Full interactivity is not possible.

- **One-way terrestrial return satellite Internet systems** use traditional dialup access to send outbound (upload) data through a modem and receive downloads from the satellite.

- **Two-way satellite Internet systems** send data from remote sites via satellite to a hub, which then sends the data to the Internet. The satellite dish at each location needs precise positioning to avoid interference with other satellites.

Figure 6-16 illustrates a two-way satellite Internet system. Upload speed is about one-tenth of the download speed, which is in the range of 500 kbps.

Figure 6-16   Satellite Internet Service

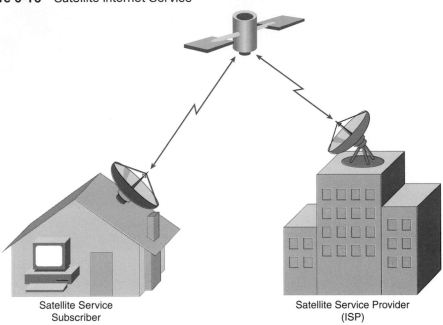

Satellite Service
Subscriber

Satellite Service Provider
(ISP)

The key installation requirement is for the satellite dish to have a clear view of a satellite orbiting the equator, where most orbiting satellites are stationed. Trees and heavy rains can affect signal reception.

Two-way satellite Internet uses IP multicasting technology, which allows one satellite to serve up to 5000 communication channels simultaneously. IP multicast sends data from one point to many points at the same time by sending data in a compressed format. Compression reduces the size of the data and the bandwidth.

Wireless Standards and Security

Wireless networking complies with a range of standards that routers and receivers use to communicate with each other. The most common standards are included in the *IEEE 802.11* wireless local area network (WLAN) standard, which addresses the 5-GHz and 2.4-GHz public (unlicensed) spectrum bands.

The terms 802.11 and Wi-Fi appear to be interchangeable, but this is incorrect. Wi-Fi is an industry-driven interoperability certification based on a subset of 802.11. The Wi-Fi specification came about because market demand led the *Wi-Fi Alliance* to begin certifying products before amendments to the 802.11 standard were complete. The 802.11 standard has since caught up with and passed Wi-Fi.

From the point of view of teleworkers, the most popular access approaches to connectivity are those defined by the *IEEE 802.11b* and *IEEE 802.11g* protocols. Security originally was intentionally weak in these protocols because of the restrictive export requirements of multiple governments. The latest standard, *802.11n*, is a proposed amendment that builds on the previous 802.11 standards by adding multiple-input multiple-output (MIMO).

Figure 6-17 shows a teleworker Linksys wireless router.

Figure 6-17   SOHO Teleworker Router

Teleworker equipment generally uses the 2.4-GHz range, complying with these standards:

■   802.11b: 11 Mbps

■   802.11g: 54 Mbps

■   802.11n: Greater than 54 Mbps (currently up to 300 Mbps), MIMO

The *802.16* (or WiMAX) standard allows transmissions up to 70 Mbps and has a range of up to 30 miles (50 km). It can operate in licensed or unlicensed bands of the spectrum from 2 to 6 GHz.

Packet Tracer
☐ **Activity**

Broadband Services (6.2.4)

In this activity, you demonstrate your ability to add broadband devices and connections to Packet Tracer. Although you cannot configure DSL and cable modems, you can simulate end-to-end connectivity to teleworker devices.

Detailed instructions are provided within the activity. Use File e4-624.pka on the CD-ROM that accompanies this book to perform this activity using Packet Tracer.

VPN Technology

This section examines virtual private network (VPN) technologies, types, components, functional characteristics, and benefits.

VPNs and Their Benefits

The Internet is a worldwide, publicly accessible IP network. Because of its vast global pro-liferation, it has become an attractive way to interconnect remote sites. However, the fact that it is a public infrastructure poses security risks to enterprises and their internal net-works. Fortunately, VPN technology enables organizations to create private networks over the public Internet infrastructure that maintain confidentiality and security.

What Is a VPN?

Organizations use VPNs to provide a virtual WAN infrastructure that connects branch offices, home offices, business partner sites, and remote telecommuters to all or portions of their corporate network. A *VPN* is a means to securely and privately transmit data over an unsecured and shared network infrastructure. Figure 6-18 shows some of the components and technologies used with VPNs, which are explained later in this chapter.

Figure 6-18   VPN Components and Technologies

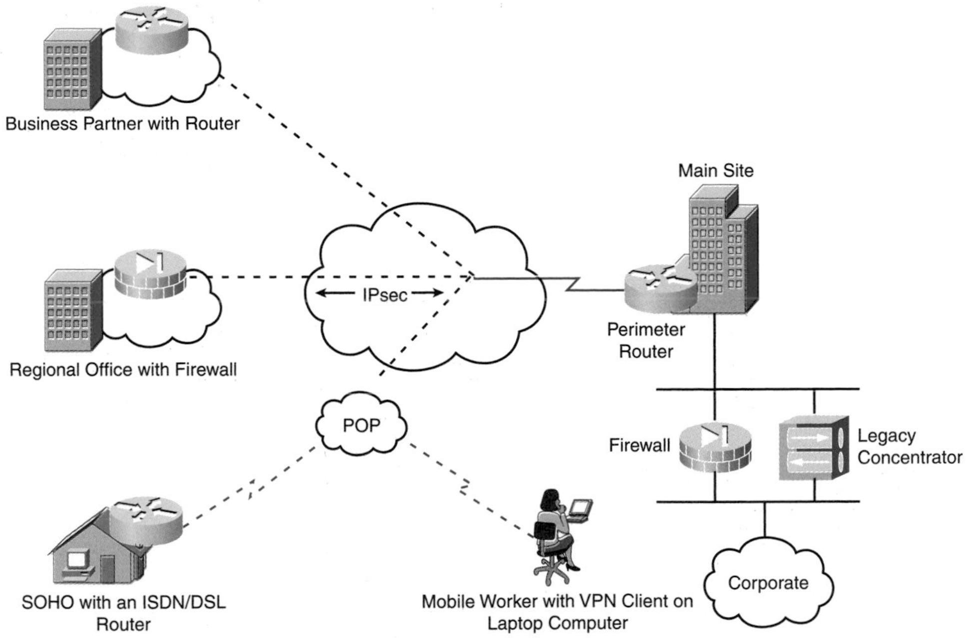

A VPN is

- **Virtual**: Information within a private network is transported over a public network.

- **Private**: The traffic is encrypted to keep the data confidential.

To remain private, the traffic is encrypted. Instead of using a dedicated Layer 2 connection, such as a leased line, a VPN uses virtual connections that are routed through the Internet.

Note

There is no requirement for a VPN to encrypt data, although data encryption typically is part of site-to-site and remote-access VPNs.

An analogy will help explain how a VPN works. Picture a stadium as a public place in the same way the Internet is a public place. When an event at the stadium is over, the public leaves through the public aisles and doorways, jostling and bumping into each other along the way. Pickpockets are threats to be endured.

Consider how the performers leave. The celebrities are whisked through private tunnels into limousines that carry them to their destinations. This section describes how VPNs work in much the same way, bundling data and safely moving it across the Internet through protective tunnels. An understanding of VPN technology is essential to be able to implement secure teleworker services on enterprise networks.

Analogy: Each LAN Is an IsLANd

We will use another analogy to illustrate the VPN concept from a different point of view. Imagine that you live on an island in the ocean. Thousands of other islands are all around you, some very close and others farther away. The normal way to travel is to take a ferry from your island to whichever island you want to visit. Traveling on the ferry means that you have almost no privacy. Other people can see everything you do.

Assume that each island represents a private LAN, and the ocean is the Internet. When you travel by ferry, it is similar to when you connect to a web server or to another device through the Internet. You have no control over the wires and routers that make up the Internet, just as you have no control over the other people on the ferry. This leaves you susceptible to security issues if you try to connect between two private networks using a public resource.

Your island decides to build a bridge to another island to create an easier, more secure, and more direct way to travel between the two. It is expensive to build and maintain the bridge, even though the island you are connecting to is very close. But the need for a reliable, secure path is so great that you do it anyway. Your island would like to connect to a second island that is much farther away, but you decide that this would be too expensive.

This situation is very much like having a leased line. The bridges (leased lines) are separate from the ocean (Internet), yet they can connect the islands (LANs). Many companies have chosen this route because of the need for security and reliability in connecting their remote offices. However, if the offices are very far apart, the cost can be prohibitively high—just like trying to build a bridge that spans a great distance.

So how does VPN fit into this analogy? We could give each inhabitant of the islands his or her own small submarine with these properties:

- Fast

- Easy to take with you wherever you go

- Can hide you completely from any other boats or submarines

- Dependable

Although they are traveling in the ocean along with other traffic, the inhabitants of our two islands could travel back and forth whenever they wanted to with privacy and security. As long as they have access to the ocean, private access exists between any two islands. This is essentially how a VPN works. Each remote member of your network can communicate in a secure and reliable manner using the Internet as the medium to connect to the private LAN. A VPN can grow to accommodate more users and different locations much easier than a leased line. In fact, scalability is a major advantage that VPNs have over typical leased lines. Unlike leased lines, where the cost increases in proportion to the distances involved, the geographic locations of each office matter little in the creation of a VPN.

Benefits of VPNs

Organizations using VPNs benefit from increased flexibility and productivity. Remote sites and teleworkers can connect securely to the corporate network from almost anyplace. Data on a VPN is encrypted and undecipherable to anyone not entitled to have it. VPNs bring remote hosts inside the firewall, giving them close to the same levels of access to network devices as if they were in a corporate office.

Figure 6-19 shows leased lines as solid lines. The dotted lines represent VPN-based connections. Consider these benefits when using VPNs:

- **Cost savings**: Organizations can use cost-effective Internet providers to connect remote offices and users to the main corporate site. This eliminates expensive dedicated WAN links and modem banks. By using broadband, VPNs reduce connectivity costs while increasing remote connection bandwidth.

- **Security**: Advanced encryption and authentication protocols protect data from unauthorized access.

- **Scalability**: VPNs use the Internet infrastructure within ISPs and carriers, making it easy for organizations to add new users. Organizations big and small can add large amounts of capacity without adding significant infrastructure.

Figure 6-19   Benefits of VPNs

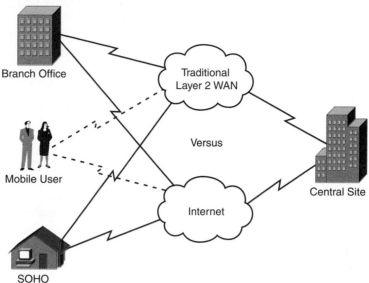

Types of VPNs

This chapter discusses two types of VPNs:

- **Site-to-site VPNs** provide access between two physical sites to an intranet or extranet over a shared infrastructure, such as the Internet. Site-to-site VPNs are used by physical sites such as corporate offices, branch offices, and suppliers.

- **Remote-access VPNs** give remote users access to an intranet or extranet over a shared infrastructure, such as the Internet. Remote-access VPNs typically are used by teleworkers and mobile users.

  VPNs create a private connection or network between two endpoints and typically include authentication and encryption. This topic is discussed in more detail later in this section.

Site-to-Site VPNs

Organizations use site-to-site VPNs to connect distant locations in the same way as a leased line or Frame Relay connection is used. Because most organizations now have Internet access, it makes sense to take advantage of the benefits of site-to-site VPNs. As illustrated in Figure 6-20, site-to-site VPNs also support company intranets and business partner extranets.

Figure 6-20   Site-to-Site VPNs

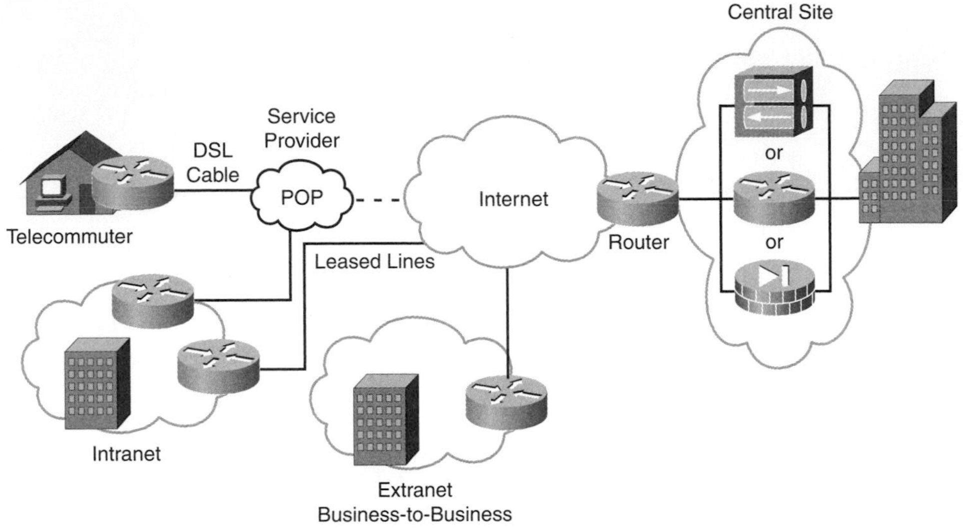

In effect, a site-to-site VPN is an extension of classic WAN networking. Site-to-site VPNs connect entire networks to each other. For example, they can connect a branch office network to a company headquarters network.

In a site-to-site VPN, hosts send and receive TCP/IP traffic through a VPN gateway, which could be a router, PIX firewall appliance, or an Adaptive Security Appliance (ASA). The VPN gateway is responsible for encapsulating and encrypting outbound traffic for all the traffic from a particular site and sending it through a VPN tunnel over the Internet to a peer VPN gateway at the target site. On receipt, the peer VPN gateway strips the headers, decrypts the content, and relays the packet toward the target host inside its private network.

Remote Access VPNs

Mobile users and telecommuters use remote-access VPNs extensively. In the past, organizations (corporations, businesses, and other institutions) supported remote users using dialup networks. This usually involved a toll call and incurring long-distance charges to access the organization.

Most teleworkers now have access to the Internet from their homes and can establish remote VPNs using broadband connections, as shown in Figure 6-21. Similarly, a mobile worker can make a local call to a local ISP to access the organization through the Internet. In effect, this marks an evolutionary advance in dialup networks. Remote-access VPNs can support the needs of telecommuters, mobile users, and extranet consumer-to-business.

Figure 6-21   Remote-Access VPNs

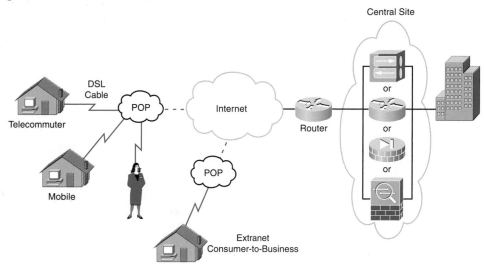

In a remote-access VPN, each host (typically a PC) usually has VPN client software. Whenever the host tries to send any traffic, the VPN client software encapsulates and encrypts that traffic before sending it over the Internet to the VPN gateway at the edge of the target network. On receipt, the VPN gateway handles the data in the same way as it would handle data from a site-to-site VPN. The VPN gateway could be a router, PIX firewall appliance, Adaptive Security Appliance (ASA), or VPN concentrator.

VPN Components

A VPN creates a private network over a public network infrastructure while maintaining confidentiality and security. VPNs use cryptographic tunneling protocols to provide sender authentication, message integrity, and protection from packet sniffing.

Figure 6-22 illustrates a typical VPN topology. Components required to establish this VPN include the following:

- An existing enterprise network with servers and workstations

- A connection to the Internet

- VPN gateways, such as routers, firewalls, VPN concentrators, and ASAs, that act as endpoints to establish, manage, and control VPN connections

- Appropriate software to create and manage VPN tunnels

Figure 6-22   VPN Components

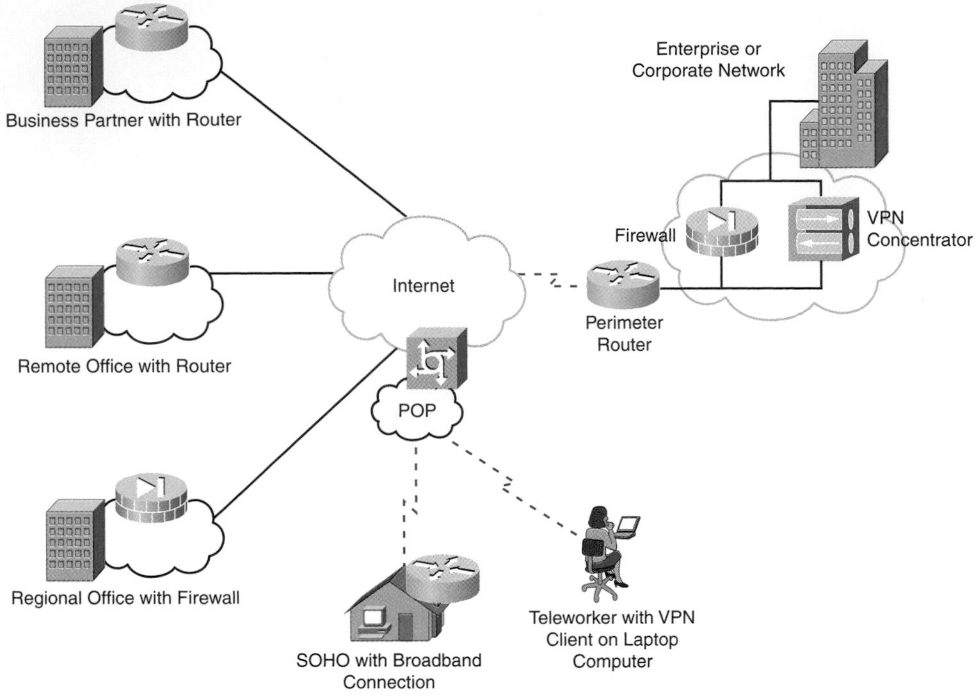

The key to VPN effectiveness is security. VPNs secure data by encapsulating or encrypting it. Most VPNs can do both.

- Encapsulation is also called tunneling, because encapsulation transmits data transparently from source network to destination network through a shared network infrastructure.

- Encryption codes data into a different format using a secret key. Decryption decodes encrypted data into the original unencrypted format.

Encapsulation and encryption are discussed in more detail later in this chapter.

Characteristics of Secure VPNs

VPNs use advanced encryption techniques and tunneling to permit organizations to establish secure, end-to-end, private network connections over the Internet.

The foundation of a secure VPN is data confidentiality, data integrity, and authentication:

- **Data confidentiality**: A common security concern is protecting data from eavesdroppers. As a design feature, data confidentiality aims to protect the contents of messages from interception by unauthenticated or unauthorized sources. VPNs achieve confidentiality using mechanisms of encapsulation and encryption.

- **Data integrity**: Receivers have no control over the path the data traveled and therefore do not know if the data was seen or handled while it journeyed across the Internet. There is always a possibility that the data has been modified. Data integrity guarantees that no tampering or alterations to the data occur while the data travels between the source and destination. VPNs typically use hashes to ensure data integrity. A hash is like a checksum or seal that guarantees that no one has read the content, but it is more robust. Hashes are explained in a later section.

- **Authentication**: Authentication ensures that a message comes from an authentic source and goes to an authentic destination. Authentication gives you confidence that the party with whom you establish communication is who you think it is. VPNs can use passwords, digital certificates, smart cards, and biometrics to establish the identity of parties at the other end of a network.

VPN Tunneling

Incorporating appropriate data confidentiality capabilities into a VPN ensures that only the intended sources and destinations can interpret the original message contents.

Tunneling allows the use of public networks like the Internet to carry data for users as though the users had access to a private network. Tunneling encapsulates an entire packet within another packet and sends the new, composite packet over a network. Tunneling uses three classes of protocols:

- **Carrier protocol**: The protocol over which information travels (Frame Relay, ATM, MPLS).

- **Encapsulating protocol**: The protocol that is wrapped around the original data (GRE, IPsec, L2F, PPTP, L2TP).

- **Passenger protocol**: The protocol over which the original data was carried (IPX, AppleTalk, IPv4, IPv6).

To illustrate the concept of tunneling and the classes of tunneling protocols, consider an example of sending a holiday card through traditional mail. The holiday card has a message inside. The card is the passenger protocol. The sender puts the card in an envelope (encapsulating protocol) with proper addressing applied. The sender then drops the envelope into a mailbox for delivery. The postal system (carrier protocol) picks up and delivers the envelope to the recipient's mailbox. The two endpoints in the carrier system are the "tunnel interfaces." The recipient removes the holiday card from the envelope (extracts the passenger protocol) and reads the message.

Figure 6-23 illustrates an e-mail message traveling through the Internet over a VPN connection. PPP carries the message to the VPN device, where the message is encapsulated within a *Generic Route Encapsulation (GRE)* packet. GRE is a tunneling protocol developed by Cisco Systems that can encapsulate a wide variety of protocol packet types inside IP tunnels, creating a virtual point-to-point link to Cisco routers at remote points over an IP internetwork. In Figure 6-23, the outer packet source and destination addressing are assigned to "tunnel interfaces" and are made routable across the network. As soon as a composite packet reaches the destination tunnel interface, the inside packet is extracted.

Figure 6-23   Packet Encapsulation

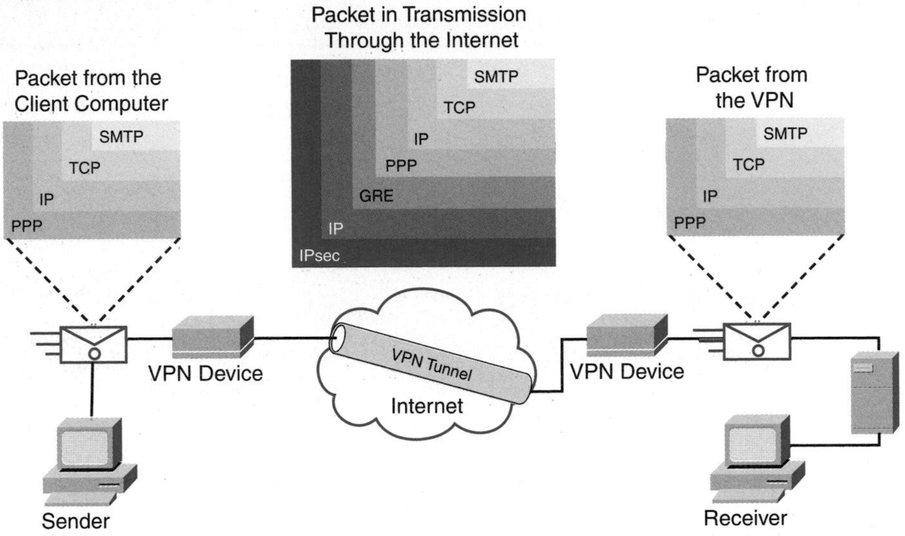

VPN Data Confidentiality and Integrity

If plain-text data is transported over the public Internet, it can be intercepted and read. To keep the data private, it needs to be encrypted. VPN encryption encrypts the data and renders it unreadable to unauthorized receivers.

VPN Encryption

Encryption is the act of coding a given message into a different format to alter the data's appearance, making it incomprehensible to those who are not authorized to view it. For encryption to work, both the sender and the receiver must know the rules used to transform the original message into its coded form. VPN encryption rules include an algorithm and a key. An algorithm is a mathematical function that combines a message, text, digits, or all three with a key. The output is an unreadable cipher string. Decryption is extremely difficult or impossible without the correct key.

There are various ways to encapsulate and encrypt the data while leaving the IP header unencrypted so that the packet can be routed. The IP header may or may not be the original IP header created by the source device. However, this topic is beyond the scope of this book.

In Figure 6-24, Gail wants to send a financial document to Jeremy across the Internet. Gail and Jeremy previously agreed on a secret shared key. At Gail's end, the VPN client software combines the document with the secret shared key and passes it through an encryption algorithm. The output is undecipherable cipher text. The cipher text is then sent through a VPN tunnel over the Internet. At the other end, the message is recombined with the same shared secret key and is processed by the same encryption algorithm. The output is the original financial document, which Jeremy can read.

Figure 6-24   VPN Encryption

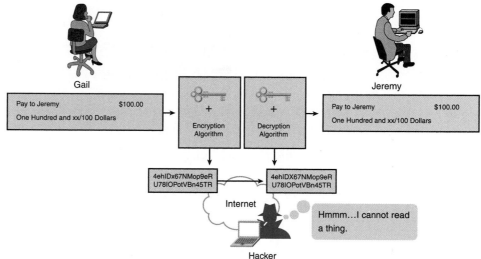

VPN Encryption Algorithms

The degree of security provided by any encryption algorithm depends on the key's length. For any given key length, the time that it takes to process all the possibilities to decrypt cipher text is a function of the computer's computing power. Therefore, the shorter the key, the easier it is to break, but at the same time, the easier it is to pass the message.

Some of the more common encryption algorithms and the length of the keys they use are as follows:

- *Data Encryption Standard (DES)* **algorithm**: Developed by IBM, DES uses a 56-bit key, ensuring high-performance encryption. DES is a symmetric key cryptosystem. Symmetric and asymmetric keys are explained in Table 6-2.

- *Triple DES (3DES)* **algorithm**: A newer variant of DES that encrypts with one key, decrypts with a different key, and then encrypts a final time with another key. 3DES makes the encryption process significantly stronger.

- *Advanced Encryption Standard (AES)*: The National Institute of Standards and Technology (NIST) adopted AES to replace the existing DES encryption in cryptographic devices. AES provides stronger security than DES and is computationally more efficient than 3DES. AES offers three different key lengths: 128-, 192-, and 256-bit keys.

- *Rivest, Shamir, and Adleman (RSA)*: An asymmetric key cryptosystem. The keys use a bit length of 512, 768, 1024, or larger.

Encryption or cryptographic processes use three basic components:

- A key

- A cryptographic mathematical function (also called a cipher)

- A message to be encrypted or decrypted

In some cases, the encryption key and decryption key may be the same. This is called *symmetric encryption*. In other cases, the encryption key and decryption key may be intentionally different. This is called *asymmetric encryption*. Figure 6-25 illustrates the difference between symmetric and asymmetric keys, and Table 6-2 summarizes the differences.

Figure 6-25   VPN Encryption Keys

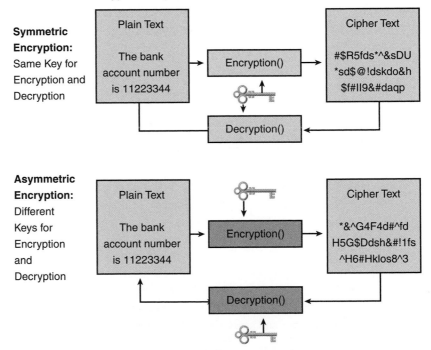

Table 6-2   Symmetric Versus Asymmetric Encryption

Symmetric Encryption	Asymmetric Encryption
Secret key cryptography	Public key cryptography
Encryption and decryption use the same key	Encryption and decryption use different keys
Typically used to encrypt and decrypt a message's content	Typically used in digital certification and key management
Examples: DES, 3DES, AES	Example: RSA

The following sections describe symmetric and asymmetric encryption in greater detail.

Symmetric Encryption

Encryption algorithms such as DES and 3DES require a shared secret key to perform encryption and decryption. Each of the two computers must know the key to decode the information. With symmetric key encryption, also called secret key encryption, each computer encrypts the information before sending it over the network to the other computer. Symmetric key encryption requires knowledge of which computers will be talking to each other so that the same key can be configured on each computer.

For example, suppose a sender creates a coded message in which each letter is substituted with the letter that is two letters down in the alphabet: A becomes C, B becomes D, and so on. In this case, the word SECRET becomes UGETGV. The sender has already told the recipient that the secret key is "shift by 2." When the recipient receives the message UGET-GV, the recipient computer decodes the message by shifting back two letters and calculating SECRET. Anyone else who sees the message sees only the encrypted message, which looks like nonsense unless the person knows the secret key.

The question is, how do the encrypting and decrypting devices both have the shared secret key? You could use e-mail, courier, or overnight express to send the shared secret keys to the administrators of the devices. An easier and more secure method is asymmetric encryption.

Asymmetric Encryption

Asymmetric encryption uses different keys for encryption and decryption. Knowing one of the keys does not allow a hacker to deduce the second key and decode the information. One key encrypts the message, and a second key decrypts it. It is not possible to encrypt and decrypt with the same key.

Public key encryption is a variant of asymmetric encryption that uses a combination of a private key and a public key. The recipient gives a public key to any sender with whom the recipient wants to communicate. The sender uses a private key combined with the recipient's public key to encrypt the message. Also, the sender must share his or her public key with the recipient. To decrypt a message, the recipient uses the sender's public key with his or her own private key.

Hashes

Hashes contribute to data integrity and authentication by ensuring that unauthorized persons do not tamper with transmitted messages. A *hash*, also called a message digest, is a number generated from a string of text. The hash is smaller than the text itself. It is generated using a formula in such a way that it is extremely unlikely that some other text will produce the same hash value.

The original sender generates a hash of the message and sends it with the message itself. The recipient decrypts the message and the hash, produces another hash from the received message, and compares the two hashes. If they are the same, the recipient can be reasonably sure that the message's integrity has not been affected.

In Figure 6-26, Gail is trying to send Jeremy a check for $100. At the remote end, Alex Jones (likely a criminal) is trying to cash the check for $1000. As the check progressed through the Internet, it was altered. Both the recipient and dollar amount were changed. In this case, if a data integrity algorithm was used, the hashes would not match, and the transaction would be invalid.

Figure 6-26   Using Hashes for Data Integrity

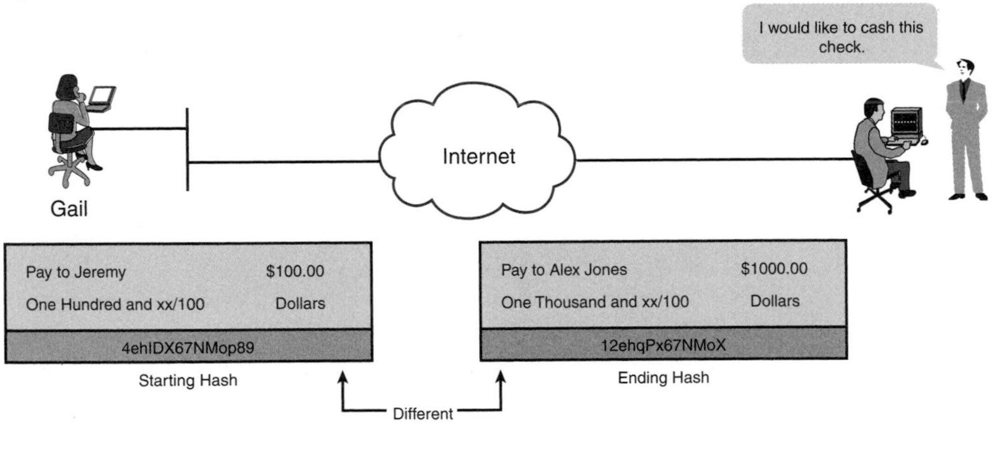

VPN data is transported over the public Internet. As shown, this data could potentially be intercepted and modified. To guard against this threat, hosts can add a hash to the message. If the transmitted hash matches the received hash, the message's integrity has been preserved. However, if there is no match, the message was altered.

VPNs use a keyed *hashed message authentication code (HMAC)* data-integrity algorithm to guarantee a message's integrity and authenticity without using any additional mechanisms.

An HMAC has two parameters: a message input and a secret key known only to the message originator and intended receivers. The message sender uses an HMAC function to produce a value (the message authentication code), formed by condensing the secret key and the message input. The message authentication code is sent along with the message. The receiver computes the message authentication code on the received message using the same key and HMAC function the sender used. Then it compares the result computed with the received message authentication code. If the two values match, the message has been correctly received, and the receiver is assured that the sender is a member of the community of users who share the key. The cryptographic strength of the HMAC depends on the cryptographic strength of the underlying hash function, on the key's size and quality, and the size of the hash output length in bits.

There are two common HMAC algorithms:

- *Message Digest 5 (MD5)* uses a 128-bit shared secret key. The variable-length message and 128-bit shared secret key are combined and run through the MD5 hash algorithm. The output is a 128-bit hash. The hash is appended to the original message and is forwarded to the remote end.

- *Secure Hash Algorithm 1 (SHA-1)* uses a 160-bit secret key. The variable-length message and 160-bit shared secret key are combined and run through the SHA-1 hash algorithm. The output is a 160-bit hash. The hash is appended to the original message and is forwarded to the remote end.

Authentication

When conducting business long distance, it is necessary to know who is at the other end of the phone, e-mail, or fax. The same is true of VPN networks, as shown in Figure 6-27. The device on the other end of the VPN tunnel must be authenticated before the communication path is considered secure. There are two peer authentication methods:

- *Preshared key (PSK)*: A secret key that is shared between the two parties using a secure channel before it needs to be used. PSKs use symmetric key cryptographic algorithms. A PSK is entered into each peer manually and is used to authenticate the peer. At each end, the PSK is combined with other information to form the authentication key.

- *RSA signature*: Uses the exchange of digital certificates to authenticate the peers. The local device derives a hash and encrypts it with its private key. The encrypted hash (digital signature) is attached to the message and is forwarded to the remote end. At the remote end, the encrypted hash is decrypted using the public key of the local end. If the decrypted hash matches the recomputed hash, the signature is genuine.

Figure 6-27   VPN Authentication

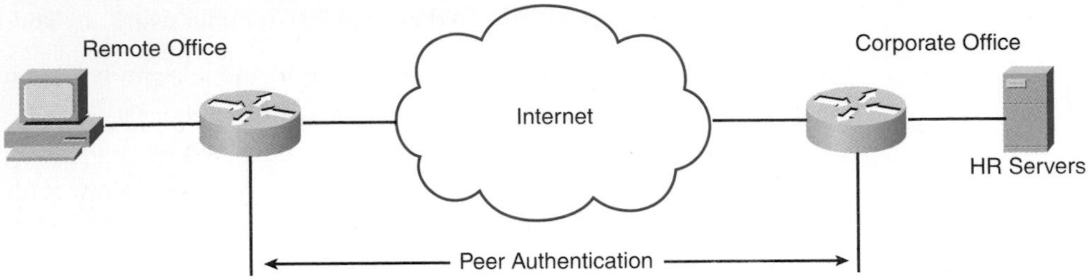

Take a look at an RSA demonstration for an example of RSA encryption at
http://www.securecottage.com/demo/rsa2.html.

IPsec Security Protocols

IPsec is protocol suite for securing IP communications that provides encryption, integrity,
and authentication. IPsec spells out the messaging necessary to secure VPN communications but relies on existing algorithms.

There are two main IPsec framework protocols, as shown in Figure 6-28:

- *Authentication Header (AH)* is used when confidentiality is not required or permitted.
  AH provides data authentication and integrity for IP packets passed between two systems. It verifies that any message passed from R1 to R2 has not been modified during
  transit. It also verifies that the data originated at either R1 or R2. AH does not provide
  data confidentiality (encryption) of packets. Used alone, the AH protocol provides
  weak protection. Consequently, it is used with the ESP protocol to provide data encryption and tamper-aware security features.

- *Encapsulating Security Payload (ESP)* provides confidentiality and authentication by
  encrypting the IP packet. IP packet encryption conceals the data and the identities of
  the source and destination. ESP authenticates the inner IP packet and ESP header.
  Authentication provides data origin authentication and data integrity. Although both
  encryption and authentication are optional in ESP, at a minimum, one of them must be
  selected.

Figure 6-28   IPsec Protocols

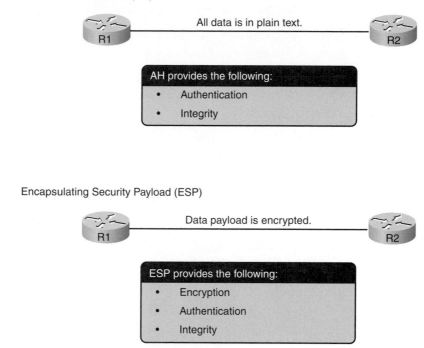

IPsec relies on existing algorithms to implement encryption, authentication, and key exchange. Some of the standard algorithms that IPsec uses are as follows:

- **Data Encryption Standard (DES)** encrypts and decrypts packet data.

- **Triple DES (3DES)** provides significant encryption strength over 56-bit DES.

- **Advanced Encryption Standard (AES)** provides stronger encryption, depending on the key length used, and faster throughput.

- **Message Digest 5 (MD5)** authenticates packet data using a 128-bit shared secret key.

- **Secure Hash Algorithm 1 (SHA-1)** authenticates packet data using a 160-bit shared secret key.

- *Diffie-Hellman (DH)* allows two parties to establish a shared secret key used by encryption and hash algorithms, such as DES and MD5, over an insecure communications channel.

Figure 6-29 shows how IPsec is structured. IPsec provides the framework, and the administrator chooses the algorithms used to implement the security services within that framework. Four IPsec framework squares need to be filled:

■ When configuring an IPsec gateway to provide security services, first choose an IPsec protocol. The choices are ESP, AH, and ESP with AH.

■ The second square is an encryption algorithm if IPsec is implemented with ESP. Choose the encryption algorithm that is appropriate for the desired level of security: DES, 3DES, or AES.

■ The third square is authentication. Choose an authentication algorithm to provide data integrity: MD5 or SHA.

■ The last square is the Diffie-Hellman (DH) algorithm group, which establishes the sharing of key information between peers. Choose which group to use—DH1, DH2, or DH5.

Figure 6-29   IPsec Framework

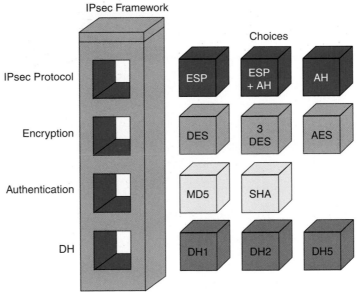

Summary

In this chapter, you learned about the growing importance of teleworkers. You can describe an organization's requirements for providing teleworker services in terms of what the teleworker needs and what the organization must provide: reliable, cost-effective connectivity. Among the favored ways to connect teleworkers, you can describe how to use broadband services including DSL, cable, and wireless. Further, you know how VPN technology can be used to provide secure teleworker services in organizations, including the importance, benefits, role, and impact of VPN technology, and the types of access, components, tunneling, and encryption.

Labs

No labs are affiliated with this chapter of the *Accessing the WAN* online curriculum.

Check Your Understanding

Complete all the review questions listed here to test your understanding of the topics and concepts in this chapter. Answers are listed in Appendix, "Check Your Understanding and Challenge Questions Answer Key."

1. A technician is attempting to explain broadband technology to a customer. Which descriptions should he use to educate the customer? (Choose two.)

   A. It includes dialup connections using POTS.

   B. It is incompatible with multiplexing.

   C. It uses a wide band of frequencies.

   D. It offers sustained speeds of 128 kbps or more.

   E. It requires line-of-sight connection with the service provider.

2. When accommodating a teleworker, which type of connection should be used when mobile access during traveling is required and broadband options are available?

   A. Residential cable

   B. DSL

   C. Dialup

   D. Satellite

3. When comparing DOCSIS and Euro-DOCSIS, what is the primary difference between the two specifications?

   A. Flow-control mechanisms

   B. Maximum data rates

   C. Access methods

   D. Channel bandwidths

4. If asked to describe DSL technology, which statements would help the user develop a better understanding of the technology? (Choose three.)

   A. DSL is available in any location that has a telephone.

   B. ADSL typically has a higher download bandwidth than available upload bandwidth.

   C. In home installations, a splitter separates the ADSL and voice signals at the NID, allowing multiple ADSL outlets in the house.

   D. DSL speed can exceed the speed available with a typical T1 line.

   E. Transfer rates vary according to the length of the local loop.

   F. All varieties of DSL provide the same bandwidth, although they use different technologies to achieve upload and download.

5. In a DSL installation, which devices are installed at the customer site? (Choose two.)

   A. CM

   B. DOCSIS

   C. DSLAM

   D. Microfilter

   E. DSL transceiver

6. Refer to Figure 6-30. On the basis of the network topology shown, which devices or software applications provide encapsulation and encryption for the VPN traffic?

   A. VPN client software installed on the machines of the users at the regional office only

   B. PIX firewall appliance at the corporate network and regional office only

   C. Routers and PIX firewall appliance at the corporate network and the routers and PIX appliance at all remote locations

   D. LAN switches and routers at the remote locations only

   E. Router and PIX firewall appliance at the remote locations only

Figure 6-30   Topology for Question 6

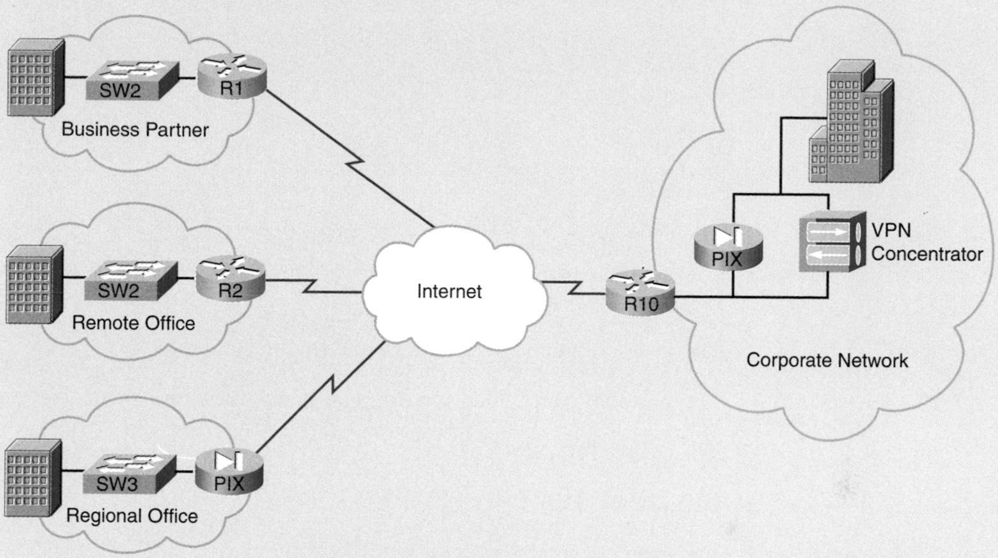

7. Which techniques can be used to secure the traffic sent over a VPN connection? (Choose two.)

   A. Data labeling, used to mark and separate the VPN traffic to different customers

   B. Data encapsulation, used to transmit data transparently from network to network through a shared network infrastructure

   C. Data encryption, used to code data into a different format using a secret key

   D. Use of a second routing protocol to transport the traffic over the VPN tunnel

   E. Use of a dedicated connection over the company private leased line

8. Match each description with its corresponding VPN characteristic:

   Uses passwords, digital certificates, smart cards, and biometrics

   Prevents tampering and alterations to data while data travels between the source and destination

   Protects the contents of messages from interception by unauthenticated or unauthorized sources

   Uses hashes

   Ensures that the communicating peers are who they say they are

   Uses encapsulation and encryption

   A. Data confidentiality

   B. Data integrity

   C. Authentication

9. Which is an example of a tunneling protocol developed by Cisco?

   A. AES

   B. DES

   C. RSA

   D. ESP

   E. GRE

10. Match each description with its corresponding type of tunneling protocol:

    Frame Relay, ATM, MPLS

    The protocol that is wrapped around the original data

    The protocol over which the original data was being carried

    IPX, AppleTalk, IPv4, IPv6

    GRE, IPsec, L2F, PPTP, L2TP

    The protocol over which the information travels

    A. Carrier protocol

    B. Encapsulating protocol

    C. Passenger protocol

11. Match each description with the correct algorithm:

    Encryption and decryption use the same key

    Public key cryptography

    Encryption and decryption use different keys

    DES, 3DES, AES

    RSA

    Shared secret key cryptography

    A. Symmetric algorithm

    B. Asymmetric algorithm

12. What type of connection is the most cost-effective to adequately support SOHO tele-worker access to the Internet?

    A. A direct T1 link to the Internet

    B. 56-kbps dialup

    C. A one-way multicast satellite Internet system

    D. DSL to an ISP

13. Which wireless standard operates in both licensed and unlicensed bands of the spectrum from 2 to 6 GHz and allows for transmission rates of 70 Mbps at a range of up to 50 kilometers?

    A. 802.11g

    B. 802.11n

    C. 802.11b

    D. 802.16

    E. 802.11e

14. What do cable providers typically deploy to support high-speed transmissions of data to SOHO cable modems?

    A. Hybrid fiber-coaxial (HFC)

    B. High-speed dialup cable modems

    C. Broadband copper coaxial

    D. 1000BASE-TX

15. Describe the organizational, social, and environmental benefits of teleworking.

16. Describe the four main connection methods used by homes and SOHO businesses.

17. Describe the two types of VPN networks.

Challenge Questions and Activities

1. In this activity, a small company has set up Internet connectivity using two Linksys WRVS4400N business-class routers. One is located at the central site, and the other is at the branch site. The company wants to access resources between sites but is concerned that Internet traffic will not be secure. To address this concern, it has been suggested that the company implement a site-to-site VPN between the two sites. A VPN would enable the branch site office to connect to the central site office securely by creating a VPN tunnel that would encrypt and decrypt data.

Referring to the topology shown in Figure 6-31, you will use the Linksys router's web configuration utility to configure the settings and enable a VPN called **Site-to-Site** using MD5 authentication, 3DES encryption, and a preshared key of **cisco123**.

Figure 6-31   Site-to-Site VPN Topology

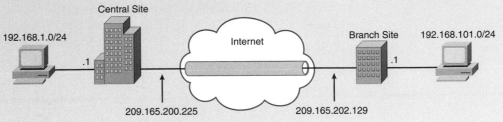

Using the Linksys web configuration utility shown in Figure 6-32, list the correct entries for the central site:

Tunnel Name:

Local Security Group

IP Address:

Remote Security Group

IP Address:

Remote Security Gateway

IP Address:

Key Exchange Method

Encryption:

Authentication:

Pre-Shared Key:

Figure 6-32   Central Site VPN Configuration

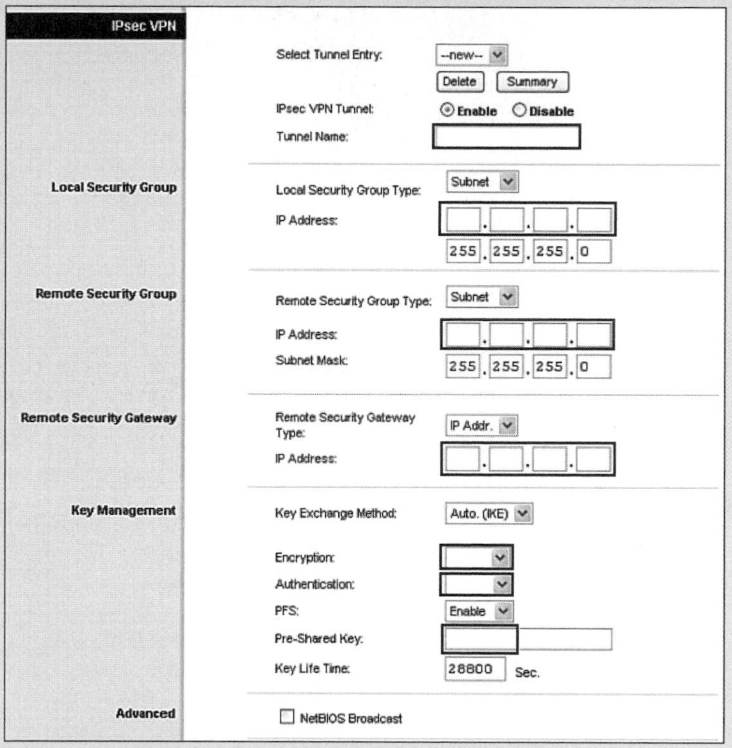

Using the Linksys web configuration utility shown in Figure 6-33, list the correct entries for the branch site:

Tunnel Name:

Local Security Group

IP Address:

Remote Security Group

IP Address:

Remote Security Gateway

IP Address:

Key Exchange Method

Encryption:

Authentication:

Pre-Shared Key:

Figure 6-33   Branch Site VPN Configuration

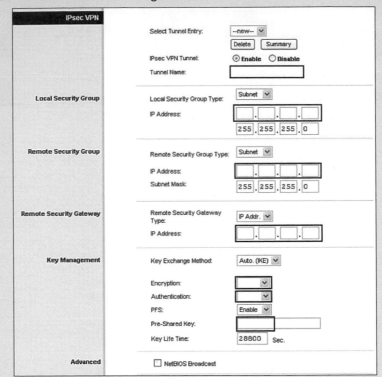

2. A small company has set up Internet connectivity using a Linksys WRVS4400N business-class router at its central site. The company wants to provide remote access to select users from remote locations but is concerned that Internet traffic will not be secure. To address this concern, it has been suggested that the company implement a remote-access VPN, which would allow telecommuters to securely access the central site network. Using the Linksys QuickVPN client software, remote users would be able to connect and establish a remote-access VPN connection, which would encrypt and decrypt data.

   Referencing the topology shown in Figure 6-34, you will use the Linksys router's web configuration utility to configure the remote VPN settings and configure a user account. The user's name is **BobV**, and his password is **cisco123**.

Figure 6-34   Remote-Access VPN Topology

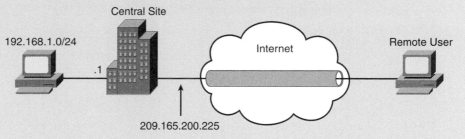

Next, Bob initiates a remote VPN connection to the central site router using the Linksys QuickVPN client software. The profile name should be **Central Site**, and the correct username, password, and IP address should be referenced.

Using the Linksys web configuration utility shown in Figure 6-35, list the remote VPN settings for Central Site:

Username:

Password:

Re-enter to Confirm:

Figure 6-35   Central Site VPN Configuration

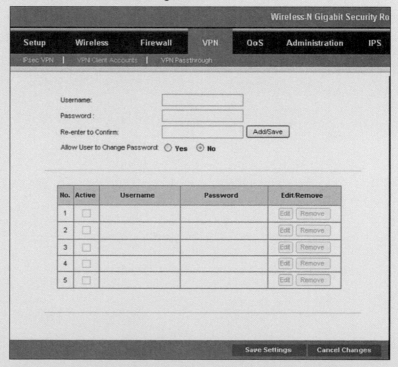

Using the Linksys QuickVPN client software shown in Figure 6-36, list the correct settings for the remote user's PC:

Profile Name:

User Name:

Password:

Server Address:

Figure 6-36   Remote User VPN Configuration

CHAPTER 7

IP Addressing Services

Objectives

After completing this chapter, you should be able to answer the following questions:

- How do I configure DHCP in an enterprise branch network? This includes being able to explain DHCP features and benefits, the differences between BOOTP and DHCP, DHCP operation, and configuring, verifying, and troubleshooting DHCP.

- How do I configure NAT on a Cisco router? This includes explaining key features and operation of NAT and NAT overload, explaining advantages and disadvantages of NAT, configuring NAT and NAT overload to conserve IP address space in a network, configuring port forwarding, and verifying and troubleshooting NAT configurations.

- How do I configure next-generation RIP (RIPng) to use IPv6? This includes explaining how IPv6 solves the problem of IP address depletion, explaining how to assign IPv6 addresses, describing transition strategies for implementing IPv6, and configuring, verifying, and troubleshooting RIPng for IPv6.

Key Terms

This chapter uses the following key terms. You can find the definitions in the glossary at the end of the book.

Introduction

The Internet and IP-related technologies have experienced rapid growth. One reason for the growth has been in part the flexibility of the original design. However, that design did not anticipate the Internet's popularity and the resulting demand for IP addresses. For example, every host and device on the Internet requires a unique IP version 4 (IPv4) address. Because of the dramatic growth, the number of available IP addresses is quickly running out.

To cope with the depletion of IP addresses, several short-term solutions were developed. One short-term solution is to use private addresses and *Network Address Translation (NAT)*.

An inside host typically receives its IP address, subnet mask, default gateway IP address, DNS server IP address, and other information from a *Dynamic Host Configuration Protocol (DHCP)* server. Instead of providing inside hosts with valid Internet IP addresses, the DHCP server usually provides IP addresses from a private pool of addresses. The problem is that these hosts may still require valid IP addresses to access Internet resources. This is where NAT comes in.

NAT enables inside network hosts to borrow a legitimate Internet IP address while accessing Internet resources. When the requested traffic returns, the legitimate IP address is repurposed and available for the next Internet request by an inside host. Using NAT, network administrators need only one or a few IP addresses for the router to provide to the hosts, instead of one unique IP address for every client joining the network. Although it sounds inefficient, this process is actually very efficient, because host traffic occurs very quickly.

Although private addresses with DHCP and NAT have helped reduce the need for IP addresses, it is estimated that we will run out of unique IPv4 addresses by 2010. For this reason, in the mid-1990s, the IETF requested proposals for a new IP addressing scheme. The *IP Next Generation (IPng)* working group responded. By 1996, the IETF started releasing a number of RFCs defining IPv6.

The main feature of IPv6 that is driving adoption today is the larger address space: addresses in IPv6 are 128 bits long versus 32 bits in IPv4.

This chapter describes how to implement DHCP, NAT, and IPv6 on enterprise networks.

DHCP

Every device that connects to a network needs an IP address. Network administrators manually assign static IP addresses to routers, servers, and other network devices whose locations (physical and logical) are not likely to change. These static addresses also enable administrators to manage those devices remotely.

However, desktop and laptop computers often change physical locations within an organization. Administrators attempting to provide manual IP address assignment for these hosts would be faced with the monumental task of readdressing the host every time an employee moves to a different office or cubicle.

Unlike servers and printers, client computers do not require a static address. Instead, administrators can identify a pool of addresses which clients can borrow IP addresses from. A workstation can use any address within the pool of addresses. Because this range typically is within an IP subnet, a workstation can be assigned any address in the range associated with its subnet.

Other items, such as the subnet mask, default gateway, and Domain Name System (DNS) server, are assigned a value that is common to either that subnet or the entire administered network. For example, all hosts within the same subnet receive different host IP addresses but receive the same subnet mask and default gateway IP address.

Introduction to DHCP

Recall from *CCNA Exploration: Network Fundamentals* that DHCP makes the process of assigning new IP addresses almost transparent. DHCP assigns IP addresses and other important network configuration information dynamically. Because desktop clients typically make up the bulk of network nodes, DHCP is an extremely useful and time-saving tool for network administrators. RFC 2131 describes DHCP.

Administrators typically prefer that a network server offer DHCP services, because these solutions are scalable and relatively easy to manage. However, in a small branch or SOHO location, a Cisco router can be configured to provide DHCP services without the need for an expensive dedicated server. A Cisco IOS feature set called Easy IP offers an optional, full-featured DHCP server.

DHCP Operation

Providing IP addresses to clients is the most fundamental task performed by a DHCP server. DHCP includes three different address allocation mechanisms to provide flexibility when assigning IP addresses:

- **Manual allocation**: The administrator assigns a preallocated IP address to the client, and DHCP only communicates the IP address to the device.

- **Automatic allocation**: DHCP automatically assigns a static IP address permanently to a device, selecting it from a pool of available addresses. There is no lease, and the address is permanently assigned to a device.

- **Dynamic allocation**: DHCP automatically dynamically assigns, or leases, an IP address from a pool of addresses for a limited period of time chosen by the server, or until the client tells the DHCP server that it no longer needs the address.

Figure 7-1 highlights devices that require manual IP address assignment and those that require dynamic IP address assignment.

Figure 7-1   Manual Versus Dynamic IP Address Assignment

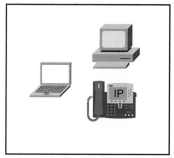

Manual Configuration

Dynamic Configuration

Network devices in the same place (logically and physically) are assigned static IP addresses.

Network devices that are added, moved, or changed (physical and logical) need new addresses. Manual configuration is unwieldy.

This section focuses on dynamic allocation.

DHCP works in a client/server mode and operates like any other client/server relationship. When a PC connects to a DHCP server, the server assigns or leases an IP address to that PC. The PC connects to the network with that leased IP address until the lease expires. The host must contact the DHCP server periodically to extend the lease. This lease mechanism ensures that hosts that move or power off do not hold onto addresses that they do not need. The DHCP server returns these addresses to the address pool and reallocates them as necessary.

Refer to Figure 7-2 and the following list to see how a DHCP server allocates an IP address configuration to a DHCP client.

Figure 7-2   DHCP Server Allocation

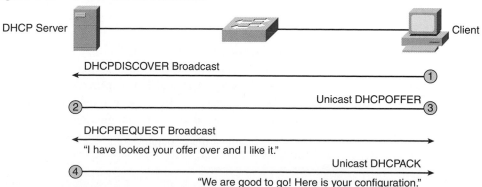

Step 1.   DHCP discover

When the client boots or otherwise wants to join a network, it follows four steps in obtaining a lease. In the first step, the client broadcasts a DHCPDISCOVER message. The DHCPDISCOVER message finds DHCP servers on the network. Because the host has no valid IP information at bootup, it uses Layer 2 and Layer 3 broadcast addresses to communicate with the server.

Step 2.   DHCP offer

When the DHCP server receives a DHCPDISCOVER message, it finds an available IP address to lease. Then it creates an ARP entry consisting of the MAC address of the requesting host and the leased IP address. Finally, it transmits a binding offer with a DHCPOFFER message. The DHCPOFFER message is sent as a unicast, using the server's Layer 2 MAC address as the source address and the client's Layer 2 address as the destination.

Note

Under certain circumstances, the DHCP message exchange from the server may be broadcast and not unicast.

Step 3.   DHCP request

When the client receives the DHCPOFFER from the server, it sends back a DHCPREQUEST message. This message has two purposes: lease origination and lease renewal and verification. When used for lease origination, the client's DHCPREQUEST requests that the IP information be verified just after it has been assigned. The message provides error checking to ensure that the assignment is still valid. The DHCPREQUEST also serves as a binding acceptance notice to the selected server and an implicit decline to any other servers that may have given the host a binding offer.

Many enterprise networks use multiple DHCP servers. The DHCPREQUEST message is sent in the form of a broadcast to inform this DHCP server and any other DHCP servers about the accepted offer.

Step 4.   DHCP acknowledge

On receiving the DHCPREQUEST message, the server verifies the lease information, creates a new ARP entry for the client lease, and replies with a unicast DHCPACK message. The DHCPACK message is a duplicate of the DHCPOFFER, except for a change in the Message Type field. When the client receives the DHCPACK message, it logs the configuration information and performs an ARP lookup for the assigned address. If it does not receive a reply, it knows that the IP address is valid and starts using it as its own.

Clients lease the information from the server for an administratively defined period. Administrators configure DHCP servers to set the leases to time out at different intervals. Most ISPs and large networks use default lease durations of up to three days. When the lease expires, the client must ask for another address, although the client typically is reassigned the same address.

The DHCPREQUEST message also addresses the dynamic DHCP process. The IP information sent in the DHCPOFFER might have been offered to another client during the dynamic allocation. Each DHCP server creates pools of IP addresses and associated parameters. Pools are dedicated to individual, logical IP subnets. The pools allow multiple DHCP servers to respond and IP clients to be mobile. If multiple servers respond, a client can choose only one of the offers.

BOOTP and DHCP

The *Bootstrap Protocol (BOOTP)*, defined in RFC 951, is the predecessor of DHCP and shares some of its operational characteristics. BOOTP gives a diskless workstation a way to acquire an IP address and boot configurations. A diskless workstation does not have a hard drive or operating system. The automated cash register systems at your local supermarket are examples of diskless workstations.

Both DHCP and BOOTP are client/server-based and use UDP ports 67 and 68. Those ports are still known as BOOTP ports. Figure 7-3 shows the client/server relationship of DHCP and BOOTP.

Figure 7-3   DHCP and BOOTP Components

BOOTP/DHCP Server   Client

The server is a host with a static IP address that allocates, distributes, and manages IP and configuration data assignments. Each allocation (IP and configuration data) is stored on the server in a data set called a binding. The client is any device using either BOOTP or DHCP as a method for obtaining IP addressing or supporting configuration information.

To understand the functional differences between BOOTP and DHCP, consider the four basic IP parameters needed to join a network:

- IP address
- Gateway address
- Subnet mask
- DNS server address

There are three primary differences between DHCP and BOOTP:

- The main difference is that BOOTP was designed for manual preconfiguration of the host information in a server database, whereas DHCP allows for dynamic allocation of network addresses and configurations to newly attached hosts. When a BOOTP client requests an IP address, the BOOTP server searches a predefined table for an entry that matches the MAC address for the client. If an entry exists, the corresponding IP address for that entry is returned to the client. This means that the binding between the MAC address and the IP address must have already been configured in the BOOTP server.

- DHCP allows for recovery and reallocation of network addresses through a leasing mechanism. Specifically, DHCP defines mechanisms through which clients can be assigned an IP address for a finite lease period. This lease period allows for reassignment of the IP address to another client later, or for the client to get another assignment if the client moves to another subnet. Clients may also renew leases and keep the same IP address. BOOTP does not use leases. Its clients have reserved IP addresses that cannot be assigned to any other host.

- BOOTP provides a limited amount of information to a host. DHCP provides additional IP configuration parameters, such as WINS and domain name.

Table 7-1 summarizes the differences between BOOTP and DHCP.

Table 7-1   BOOTP and DHCP Differences

BOOTP	DHCP
Static mappings	Dynamic mappings
Permanent assignment	Lease
Supports only four configuration parameters	Supports more than 20 configuration parameters

DHCP Message Format

The developers of DHCP needed to maintain compatibility with BOOTP and consequently used the same BOOTP message format. However, because DHCP has more functionality than BOOTP, the DHCP Options field was added. When communicating with older BOOTP clients, the DHCP Options field is ignored.

Figure 7-4 displays the format of a DHCP message.

Figure 7-4   DHCP Message Format

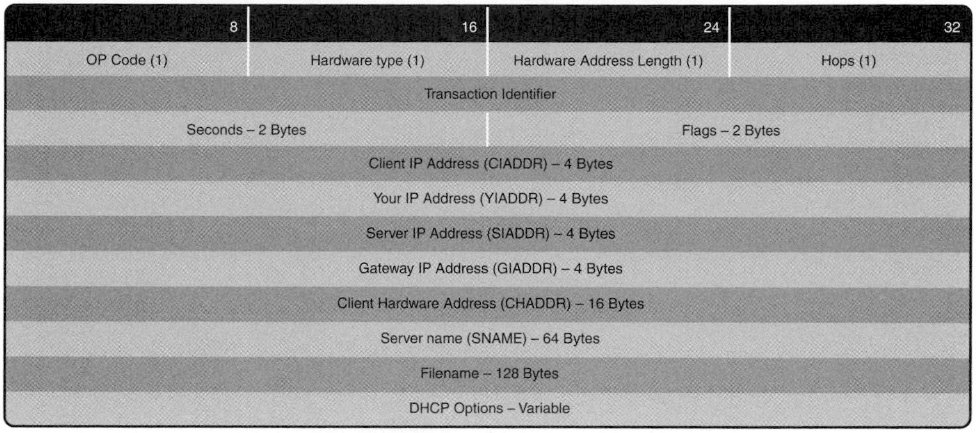

	8	16	24	32
OP Code (1)	Hardware type (1)	Hardware Address Length (1)		Hops (1)
Transaction Identifier				
Seconds – 2 Bytes		Flags – 2 Bytes		
Client IP Address (CIADDR) – 4 Bytes				
Your IP Address (YIADDR) – 4 Bytes				
Server IP Address (SIADDR) – 4 Bytes				
Gateway IP Address (GIADDR) – 4 Bytes				
Client Hardware Address (CHADDR) – 16 Bytes				
Server name (SNAME) – 64 Bytes				
Filename – 128 Bytes				
DHCP Options – Variable				

The fields are as follows:

- **Operation (OP) Code**: Specifies the general type of message. A value of 1 indicates a request message; a value of 2 is a reply message.

- **Hardware Type**: Identifies the type of hardware used in the network. For example, 1 is Ethernet, 15 is Frame Relay, and 20 is a serial line. These are the same codes used in ARP messages.

- **Hardware Address Length**: 8 bits to specify the length of the address.

- **Hops**: Set to 0 by a client before transmitting a request. Used by relay agents to control the forwarding of DHCP messages.

- **Transaction Identifier**: 32-bit identification generated by the client to allow it to match the request with replies received from DHCP servers.

- **Seconds**: The number of seconds elapsed since a client began attempting to acquire or renew a lease. Busy DHCP servers use this number to prioritize replies when multiple client requests are outstanding.

- **Flags**: Only one of the 16 bits is used, which is the broadcast flag. A client that does not know its IP address when it sends a request sets the flag to 1. This value tells the DHCP server or relay agent receiving the request that it should send back the reply as a broadcast.

- **Client IP Address**: The client puts its own IP address in this field if and only if it has a valid IP address while in the bound state; otherwise, it sets the field to 0. The client can use this field only when its address is actually valid and usable, not during the process of acquiring an address.

- **Your IP Address**: The IP address that the server assigns to the client.

- **Server IP Address**: The address of the server the client should use for the next step in the bootstrap process, which may or may not be the server sending this reply. The sending server always includes its own IP address in a special field called the Server Identifier DHCP option.

- **Gateway IP Address**: Routes DHCP messages when DHCP relay agents are involved. The gateway address facilitates communications of DHCP requests and replies between the client and a server that are on different subnets or networks.

- **Client Hardware Address**: Specifies the client's physical layer.

- **Server Name**: The server sending a DHCPOFFER or DHCPACK message may optionally put its name in this field. This can be a simple text nickname or a DNS domain name, such as dhcpserver.netacad.net.

- **Boot Filename**: Optionally used by a client to request a particular type of boot file in a DHCPDISCOVER message. Used by a server in a DHCPOFFER to fully specify a boot file directory and filename.

- **Options**: Holds DHCP options, including several parameters required for basic DHCP operation. This field is variable in length. Both client and server may use this field.

DHCP Discovery and Offer Methods

When a client wants to join the network, it requests addressing values from the network DHCP server. If a client is configured to receive its IP settings dynamically, it transmits a DHCPDISCOVER message on its local physical subnet when it boots or senses an active network connection. Because the client has no way of knowing to which subnet it belongs, the DHCPDISCOVER is an IP directed broadcast (a destination IP address of 255.255.255.255). The client does not have a configured IP address, so the source IP address of 0.0.0.0 is used. In Figure 7-5, the question marks in the fields for the client IP address (CIADDR), default gateway address (GIADDR), and subnetwork mask actually contain 0.0.0.0.

The DHCP server manages the allocation of the IP addresses and answers configuration requests from clients. In the simplest case, a DHCP server on the same subnet picks up the client's request. The server notes that the GIADDR field is blank, so the client is on the same subnet. The server also notes the client's hardware address in the request packet.

When the DHCP server receives the DHCPDISCOVER message, it responds with a DHCPOFFER message. The server selects an IP address from the available pool for that segment, as well as the other segment and global parameters. It adds them to the appropriate fields in the DHCPOFFER packet. This message contains initial configuration information for the client, including its MAC address, followed by the IP address that the server is offering, the subnet mask, the lease duration, and the IP address of the DHCP server making the offer. The subnet mask and default gateway are specified in the Options field parameters subnet mask and router options, respectively. The DHCPOFFER message can be configured to include other information, such as the lease renewal time, domain name server, and NetBIOS Name Service (Microsoft Windows Internet Name Service [Microsoft WINS]).

Figure 7-5   DHCP Discovery

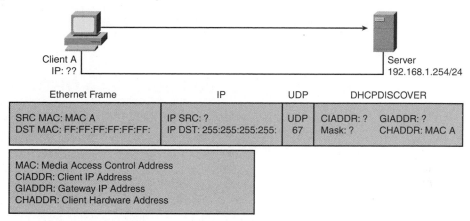

As shown in Figure 7-6, the DHCP server has responded to the DHCPDISCOVER by assigning values to the CIADDR and subnetwork mask.

Figure 7-6   DHCP Offer

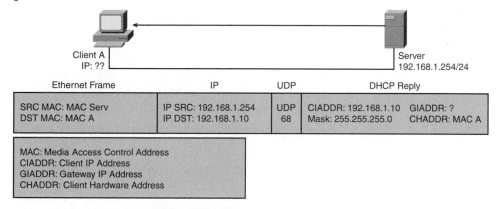

Administrators set up DHCP servers to assign addresses from predefined pools. Most DHCP servers also allow the administrator to define specifically which client MAC addresses can be serviced and automatically assign them the same IP address each time.

DHCP uses User Datagram Protocol (UDP) as its transport protocol. The client sends messages to the server on port 67. The server sends messages to the client on port 68.

The client and server use a DHCPREQUEST and DHCPACK messages to acknowledge and complete the proposed DHCP offer. Finally, the client does a gratuitous ARP using the new IP address. If no other clients on the subnet reply with the proposed IP address, it starts using the new IP address.

> **Note**
>
> For more information on DHCP, see "Cisco IOS DHCP Server" at ***http://www.cisco.com/univercd/cc/td/doc/product/software/ios120/120newft/120t/120t1/easyip2.htm#wp4363***.

Configuring a Cisco Router as a DHCP Server

Cisco routers running Cisco IOS software provide full support for a router to act as a DHCP server. The Cisco IOS DHCP server assigns and manages IP addresses from specified address pools within the router to DHCP clients.

The steps to configure a router as a DHCP server are as follows:

Step 1.   A best practice is to identify addresses to exclude before creating the DHCP pool. This ensures that DHCP does not assign reserved addresses accidentally. These addresses usually are static addresses reserved for the router interface, switch management IP addresses, servers, and local network printers.

The **ip dhcp excluded-address** *low-address* [*high-address*] global configuration command is used to define addresses to exclude, as shown in the following two examples:

```
R1(config)# ip dhcp excluded-address 192.168.10.1 192.168.10.9
R1(config)# ip dhcp excluded-address 192.168.10.254
```

The first line defines a range from 192.168.10.1 to 192.168.10.9. The second line specifically excludes IP address 192.168.10.254. Multiple lines can be used to define ranges to exclude.

Step 2.   Configuring a DHCP server involves defining a pool of addresses to assign. Create the DHCP pool using the **ip dhcp pool** *pool-name* command. The *pool-name* argument is the alphanumeric "name" of the DHCP pool to be configured. The following example defines a pool called LAN-POOL-1:

```
R1(config)# ip dhcp pool LAN-POOL-1
R1(dhcp-config)#
```

Step 3.   Notice that you are now in DHCP config mode. Next you need to configure the specifics of the pool. You must configure the available addresses and specify the subnet network number and mask of the DHCP address pool. Use the **network** statement to define the range of available addresses.

You should also define the default gateway or router for the clients to use with the **default-router** command. Typically, the gateway is the router's LAN interface. One address is required, but you can list up to eight addresses. Table 7-2 lists the required DHCP configuration tasks and commands.

Table 7-2   Required DHCP Tasks

Required Task	Command
Define the address pool	**network** *network-number* [*mask* | */prefix-length*]
Define the default router or gateway	**default-router** *address* [*address2...address8*]

Other DHCP tasks are optional. For example, you can configure the IP address of the DNS server that is available to a DHCP client using the **dns-server** command. When it is configured, one address is required, but up to eight addresses can be listed.

Other parameters include configuring the duration of the DHCP lease. The default setting is one day, but you can change this using the **lease** command. You can also configure a NetBIOS WINS server that is available to a Microsoft DHCP client. Usually, this would be configured in an environment that supports pre-Windows 2000 clients. Because most installations now have clients with a newer Windows operating system, this parameter usually is not required. Table 7-3 lists optional DHCP configuration tasks and commands.

Table 7-3   Optional DHCP Tasks

Optional Task	Command
Define a DNS server	**dns-server** *address* [*address2...address8*]
Define the domain name	**domain-name** *domain*
Define the duration of the DHCP lease	**lease** {*days* [*hours*] [*minutes*] | **infinite**}
Define the NetBIOS WINS server	**netbios-name-server** *address* [*address2...address8*]

Example 7-1 provides a sample DHCP configuration for router R1.

Example 7-1   DHCP Configuration Example

```
R1(config)# ip dhcp excluded-address 192.168.10.1 192.168.10.9
R1(config)# ip dhcp excluded-address 192.168.10.254
R1(config)# ip dhcp pool LAN-POOL-1
R1(dhcp-config)# network 192.168.10.0 255.255.255.0
R1(dhcp-config)# default-router 192.168.10.1
R1(dhcp-config)# domain-name span.com
R1(dhcp-config)# end
```

Disabling DHCP

The DHCP service is enabled by default on versions of Cisco IOS software that support it. To disable the service, use the **no service dhcp** command. Use the **service dhcp** global configuration command to reenable the DHCP server process. Enabling the service has no effect if the parameters are not configured.

Verifying DHCP

To see how a Cisco router can be configured to provide DHCP services, refer to the sample topology shown in Figure 7-7. Router R1 has been configured as specified in Example 7-1. PC1 has not been powered up and therefore does not have an IP address.

Figure 7-7   DHCP Sample Topology

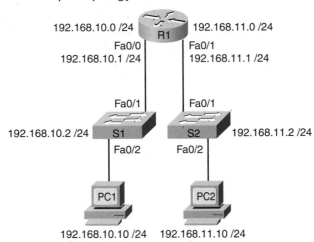

To verify the operation of DHCP, use the **show ip dhcp binding** command. This command displays a list of all IP-address-to-MAC-address bindings that have been provided by the DHCP service. Example 7-2 shows the output of the command with no clients listed.

Example 7-2   **show ip dhcp binding** Command

```
R1# show ip dhcp binding

Bindings from all pools not associated with VRF:
IP address              Client-ID/              Lease expiration        Type
                        Hardware address/
                        User name


R1#
```

To verify that messages are being received or sent by the router, use the **show ip dhcp server statistics** command. This command displays count information about the number of DHCP messages that have been sent and received. Example 7-3 shows the command's output.

Example 7-3   **show ip dhcp server statistics** Command

```
R1# show ip dhcp server statistics

Memory usage          23543
Address pools         1
Database agents       0
Automatic bindings    0
Manual bindings       0
Expired bindings      0
Malformed messages    0
Secure arp entries    0


Message               Received
BOOTREQUEST           0
DHCPDISCOVER          0
DHCPREQUEST           0
DHCPDECLINE           0
DHCPRELEASE           0
DHCPINFORM            0


Message               Sent
BOOTREPLY             0
DHCPOFFER             0
DHCPACK               0
DHCPNAK               0
R1#
```

Notice that a pool is configured. However, no DHCP messages have been exchanged with clients.

Now, assume that PC1 has been powered up and has completed its booting process. Example 7-4 provides the DHCP verification output.

Example 7-4   Verifying DHCP

```
R1# show ip dhcp binding

Bindings from all pools not associated with VRF:
IP address              Client-ID/              Lease expiration        Type
                        Hardware address/
                        User name
192.168.10.10           0100.e018.5bdd.35       Oct 03 2007 05:05 PM    Automatic


R1# show ip dhcp server statistics

Memory usage            23786
Address pools           1
Database agents         0
Automatic bindings      1
Manual bindings         0
Expired bindings        0
Malformed messages      0
Secure arp entries      0

Message                 Received
BOOTREQUEST             0
DHCPDISCOVER            6
DHCPREQUEST             1
DHCPDECLINE             0
DHCPRELEASE             0
DHCPINFORM              0

Message                 Sent
BOOTREPLY               0
DHCPOFFER               1
DHCPACK                 1
DHCPNAK                 0
R1#
```

Notice that the binding information now shows that the IP address of 192.168.10.10 has been bound to a MAC address. The statistics are also displaying DHCPDISCOVER, DHCPREQUEST, DHCPOFFER, and DHCPACK activity.

Example 7-5 shows the output of the **ipconfig /all** command on PC1 and confirms the TCP/IP configured parameters.

Example 7-5   DHCP Client Configuration

```
C:\Documents and Settings\SpanPC> ipconfig /all

Windows IP Configuration

        Host Name . . . . . . . . . . . . : ciscolab
        Primary Dns Suffix  . . . . . . . :
        Node Type . . . . . . . . . . . . : Unknown
        IP Routing Enabled. . . . . . . . : No
        WINS Proxy Enabled. . . . . . . . : No

Ethernet adapter Local Area Connection:

        Connection-specific DNS Suffix  . : span.com
        Description . . . . . . . . . . . : SiS 900 PCI Fast Ethernet Adapter
        Physical Address. . . . . . . . . : 00-E0-18-5B-DD-35
        Dhcp Enabled. . . . . . . . . . . : Yes
        Autoconfiguration Enabled . . . . : Yes
        IP Address. . . . . . . . . . . . : 192.168.10.10
        Subnet Mask . . . . . . . . . . . : 255.255.255.0
        Default Gateway . . . . . . . . . : 192.168.10.1
        DHCP Server . . . . . . . . . . . : 192.168.10.1
        Lease Obtained. . . . . . . . . . : Tuesday, October 02, 2007 1:06:22 PM

        Lease Expires . . . . . . . . . . : Wednesday, October 03, 2007 1:06:22 PM

C:\Documents and Settings\SpanPC>
```

Because PC1 is connected to the network segment 192.168.10.0 /24, it automatically receives an IP address, DNS suffix, and default gateway from that pool. No IP interface configuration is required. If a PC is connected to a network segment that has a DHCP pool available, it can obtain an IP address automatically.

So how does PC2 receive an IP address? Router R1 would have to be configured to provide a 192.168.11.0 /24 DHCP pool, as shown in Example 7-6.

Example 7-6   Configuring LAN-POOL-2

```
R1(config)# ip dhcp excluded-address 192.168.11.1 192.168.11.9
R1(config)# ip dhcp excluded-address 192.168.11.254
R1(config)# ip dhcp pool LAN-POOL-2
R1(dhcp-config)# network 192.168.11.0 255.255.255.0
R1(dhcp-config)# default-router 192.168.11.1
R1(dhcp-config)# domain-name span.com
R1(dhcp-config)# end
```

When PC2 has completed its booting process, it is provided with an IP address for the network segment to which it is connected. Example 7-7 shows the DHCP verification output.

Example 7-7   Verifying DHCP

```
R1# show ip dhcp binding

Bindings from all pools not associated with VRF:
IP address              Client-ID/              Lease expiration        Type
                        Hardware address/
                        User name
192.168.10.10           0100.e018.5bdd.35       Oct 03 2007 06:14 PM    Automatic
192.168.11.10           0100.b0d0.d817.e6       Oct 03 2007 06:18 PM    Automatic


R1# show ip dhcp server statistics

Memory usage            25307
Address pools           2
Database agents         0
Automatic bindings      2
Manual bindings         0
Expired bindings        0
Malformed messages      0
Secure arp entries      0

Message                 Received
BOOTREQUEST             0
DHCPDISCOVER            8
DHCPREQUEST             3
DHCPDECLINE             0
DHCPRELEASE             0
DHCPINFORM              0

Message                 Sent
BOOTREPLY               0
DHCPOFFER               3
DHCPACK                 3
DHCPNAK                 0
R1#
```

Notice that the DHCP bindings now indicate that two hosts have been provided with IP addresses. The DHCP statistics also reflect the exchange of DHCP messages.

Another useful command to view multiple pools is **show ip dhcp pool**, as shown in Example 7-8.

Example 7-8   show ip dhcp pool Command

```
R1# show ip dhcp pool

Pool LAN-POOL-1 :
 Utilization mark (high/low)     : 100 / 0
 Subnet size (first/next)        : 0 / 0
 Total addresses                 : 254
 Leased addresses                : 1
 Pending event                   : none
 1 subnet is currently in the pool :
 Current index        IP address range                Leased addresses
 192.168.10.11        192.168.10.1    - 192.168.10.254    1

Pool LAN-POOL-2 :
 Utilization mark (high/low)     : 100 / 0
 Subnet size (first/next)        : 0 / 0
 Total addresses                 : 254
 Leased addresses                : 1
 Pending event                   : none
 1 subnet is currently in the pool :
 Current index        IP address range                Leased addresses
 192.168.11.11        192.168.11.1    - 192.168.11.254    1
R1#
```

This command summarizes the DHCP pool information and confirms that one address has been allocated from each pool.

Configuring a DHCP Client

Typically, small broadband routers for home use, such as Linksys routers, can be configured to connect to an ISP using a DSL or cable modem. In most cases, small home routers are set to acquire an IP address automatically from their ISPs.

For example, Figure 7-8 shows the default WAN setup page for a Linksys WRVS4400N router.

Figure 7-8   Linksys WRVS4400N WAN Setup Page

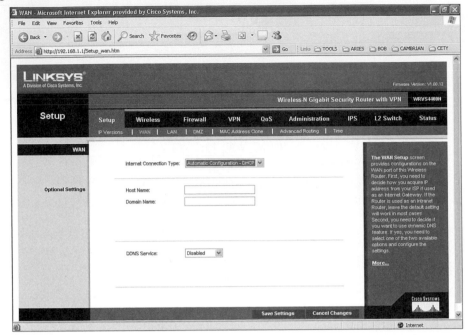

Notice that the Internet connection type is set to **Automatic Configuration - DHCP**. This means that when the router is connected to a cable modem, for example, it is a DHCP client and requests an IP address from the ISP.

Sometimes, Cisco routers in SOHO and branch sites have to be configured in a similar manner. The method used depends on the ISP. However, in its simplest configuration, the Ethernet interface is used to connect to a cable modem. To configure an Ethernet interface as a DHCP client, the **ip address dhcp** command must be configured. For example, consider the topology shown in Figure 7-9.

Assume that an ISP has been configured to provide select customers with IP addresses from the 209.165.201.0 / 27 range. The SOHO is to be configured as a DHCP client. Example 7-9 provides a sample DHCP client configuration and verification of the SOHO router.

Figure 7-9   Sample DHCP Client Topology

Example 7-9   Configuring a DHCP Client

```
SOHO(config)# interface fa0/0
SOHO(config-if)# ip address dhcp
SOHO(config-if)# no shut

SOHO(config-if)#
*Oct  2 17:57:36.027: %DHCP-6-ADDRESS_ASSIGN: Interface FastEthernet0/0 assigned
 DHCP address 209.165.201.12, mask 255.255.255.224, hostname SOHO
SOHO(config-if)# end
SOHO# show ip int fa0/0

FastEthernet0/0 is up, line protocol is up
  Internet address is 209.165.201.12/27
  Broadcast address is 255.255.255.255
  Address determined by DHCP from host 209.165.201.1
  MTU is 1500 bytes
  Helper address is not set
  Directed broadcast forwarding is disabled
  Outgoing access list is not set
  Inbound  access list is not set
  Proxy ARP is enabled

<Output omitted>
```

Notice that after the interface is enabled, it automatically receives an IP address from the ISP. The **show ip interface** output confirms that the FastEthernet 0/0 interface has been assigned a DHCP address from the ISP router located at 209.165.201.1.

DHCP Relay

In a complex hierarchical network, enterprise servers usually are contained in a server farm. These servers may provide DHCP, DNS, TFTP, and FTP services for the clients. The problem is that the network clients typically are not on the same subnet as those servers. Therefore, the clients must locate the servers to receive services, and often these services are located using broadcast messages.

For example, in Figure 7-10, router R1 is not configured as a DHCP server. However, a dedicated DHCP server is located at 192.168.11.5.

Figure 7-10   Sample Topology

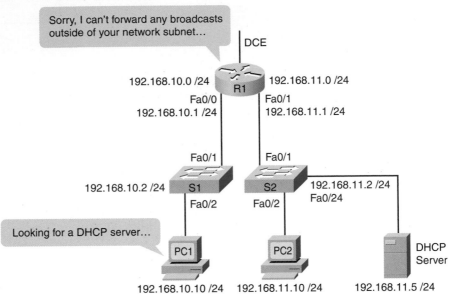

The problem is that PC1 is not located on the same subnet as the DHCP server.

To illustrate this problem, refer to Example 7-10.

Example 7-10   PC1 Releases Its Current IP Address

```
C:\Documents and Settings\Administrator> ipconfig /release

Windows IP Configuration

Ethernet adapter Local Area Connection:

        Connection-specific DNS Suffix  . :
        IP Address. . . . . . . . . . . : 0.0.0.0
        Subnet Mask . . . . . . . . . . : 0.0.0.0
        Default Gateway . . . . . . . . :

C:\Documents and Settings\Administrator>
```

PC1 attempts to renew its IP address. To do so, it must first release its current IP address using the MS-DOS command-line **ipconfig /release** command. Notice that the IP address is released and the current address is now 0.0.0.0.

Next, the **ipconfig /renew** command is issued, as shown in Example 7-11.

Example 7-11   PC1 Renews Its IP Address

```
C:\Documents and Settings\Administrator> ipconfig /renew

Windows IP Configuration

An error occurred while renewing interface Local Area Connection : unable to
  contact your DHCP server. Request has timed out.

C:\Documents and Settings\Administrator>
```

This initiates the host to broadcast a DHCPDISCOVER message. However, PC1 is unable to locate the DHCP server, as highlighted in the example. The reason is that PC1 and the DHCP server are not on the same subnet.

What happens when the server and the client are separated by a router and therefore are not on the same network segment? Remember, routers do not forward broadcasts.

Note

Certain Windows clients have a feature called *Automatic Private IP Addressing (APIPA)*. With this feature, a Windows computer can automatically assign itself an IP address in the 169.254.*x.x* range in the event that a DHCP server is unavailable or does not exist on the network.

To make matters worse, DHCP is not the only critical service that uses broadcasts. For example, Cisco routers and other devices may use broadcasts to locate TFTP servers or to locate an authentication server such as a TACACS server.

As a solution to this problem, an administrator could add DHCP servers on all the subnets. However, running these services on several computers creates both cost and administrative overhead.

A simpler solution is to configure the *Cisco IOS helper address* feature on intervening routers and switches. This solution enables routers to forward broadcasts for specific protocols to corresponding servers. When a router forwards address assignment/parameter requests, it is acting as a *DHCP relay agent*.

For example, PC1 would broadcast a request to locate a DHCP server. If router R1 were configured as a DHCP relay agent, it would intercept this request and forward it to the DHCP server located on subnet 192.168.11.0.

To configure router R1 as a DHCP relay agent, you need to configure the nearest interface to the client with the **ip helper-address** interface configuration command. This command relays broadcast requests for key services to a configured address. Configure the IP helper address on the interface receiving the broadcast. Example 7-12 provides a sample configuration for router R1 to forward DHCP broadcast traffic to the DHCP server.

Example 7-12   DHCP Relay Agent

```
R1# config t
R1(config)# interface Fa0/0
R1(config-if)# ip helper-address 192.168.11.5
R1(config-if)# end
```

Router R1 is now configured as a DHCP relay agent. It accepts broadcast requests for the DHCP service and then forwards them as a unicast to the IP address 192.168.11.5.

Example 7-13 shows PC1 releasing and renewing its IP address.

Example 7-13   PC1 Renews Its IP Address

```
C:\Documents and Settings\Administrator> ipconfig /release

Windows IP Configuration

Ethernet adapter Local Area Connection:

        Connection-specific DNS Suffix  . :
        IP Address. . . . . . . . . . . : 0.0.0.0
        Subnet Mask . . . . . . . . . . : 0.0.0.0
        Default Gateway . . . . . . . . :

C:\Documents and Settings\Administrator> ipconfig /renew

Windows IP Configuration

Ethernet adapter Local Area Connection:

        Connection-specific DNS Suffix  . :
        IP Address. . . . . . . . . . . : 192.168.10.11
        Subnet Mask . . . . . . . . . . : 255.255.255.0
        Default Gateway . . . . . . . . : 192.168.10.1

C:\Documents and Settings\Administrator>
```

As you can see, PC1 now can acquire an IP address from the DHCP server.

DHCP is not the only service that the router can be configured to relay. By default, the **ip helper-address** command forwards the following eight UDP services:

- Port 37: Time

- Port 49: TACACS

- Port 53: DNS

- Port 67: DHCP/BOOTP client

- Port 68: DHCP/BOOTP server

- Port 69: TFTP

- Port 137: NetBIOS name service

- Port 138: NetBIOS datagram service

To specify additional ports, use the **ip forward-protocol** command to specify exactly which types of broadcast packets to forward.

Configuring a DHCP Server Using SDM

Cisco routers also can be configured as a DHCP server using the *Cisco Router and Security Device Manager (SDM)*. Refer to the sample topology shown in Figure 7-11.

Figure 7-11   SDM Sample Topology

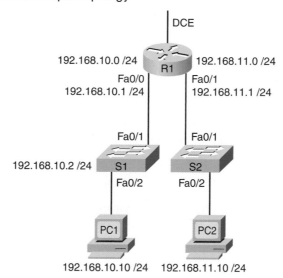

In this example, router R1 is configured as the DHCP server on the Fa0/0 and Fa0/1 interfaces.

The DHCP server function is enabled under Additional Tasks on the Configure tab, as shown in Figure 7-12.

Figure 7-12   SDM DHCP Pools Window

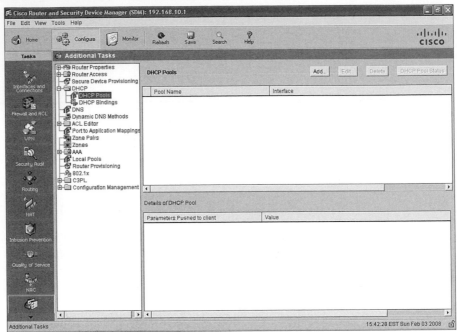

In the list of tasks, click the **DHCP** folder icon. This expands to display the DHCP Pools and DHCP Bindings options. Select the **DHCP Pools** option to add a new pool.

The DHCP Pools window usually displays a summary of configured pools with their specific settings. However, no pools are currently configured.

In the DHCP Pools window, click the **Add** button to create the new DHCP pool. This opens the Add DHCP Pool window, as shown in Figure 7-13.

The Add DHCP Pool window contains the options you need to configure the DHCP IP address pool. The IP addresses that the DHCP server assigns are drawn from a common pool. To configure the pool, specify the starting and ending IP addresses of the range.

Cisco SDM configures the router to automatically exclude the LAN interface IP address in the pool. You must not use the network or subnetwork IP address or broadcast address on the network in the range of addresses that you specify.

If you need to exclude other IP addresses in the range, you can do so by adjusting the starting and ending IP addresses. For instance, if you needed to exclude IP addresses 192.168.10.1 through 192.168.10.9, you would set the starting IP address to 192.168.10.10. This allows the router to begin address assignment with 192.168.10.10.

Figure 7-13   SDM Add DHCP Pool Window

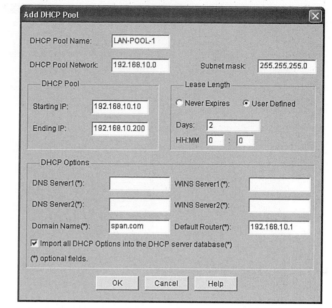

The other available options are as follows:

- **DNS Server1 and DNS Server2**: The DNS server typically is a server that maps a known device name with its IP address. If you have a DNS server configured for your network, enter its IP address here. If the network has an additional DNS server, you can enter the IP address for that server in this field.

- **WINS Server1 and WINS Server2**: Recall that WINS configuration typically is in environments that support pre-Windows 2000 clients.

- **Import all DHCP Options into the DHCP server database**: Allows the DHCP options to be imported from a higher-level server. This option typically is used in conjunction with an Internet DHCP server. This option allows you to pull higher-level information without having to configure it for this pool.

Figure 7-14 shows the DHCP Pools window. Two pools are configured—one for each of the Fast Ethernet interfaces on the R1 router.

Figure 7-14   Configured DHCP Pools Window

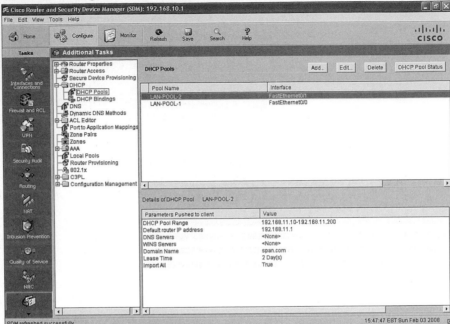

Troubleshooting DHCP Configuration

DHCP problems can arise for a multitude of reasons, such as software defects in operating systems, corrupt NIC drivers, or misconfigured DHCP/BOOTP relay agents. However, the most common problems are configuration issues. Because of the number of potentially problematic areas, a systematic approach to troubleshooting is required. The following sections address some problems you might encounter when configuring DHCP. The list is not exhaustive, but it will help you understand how to troubleshoot DHCP.

Troubleshooting Task 1: Resolve IP Address Conflicts

An IP address lease can expire on a client that is still connected to a network. If the client does not renew the lease, the DHCP server can reassign that IP address to another client. When the client reboots, it requests an IP address. If the DHCP server does not respond quickly, the client uses the last IP address. Then two clients are using the same IP address, which creates a conflict.

The **show ip dhcp conflict** command displays all address conflicts recorded by the DHCP server. The server uses the **ping** command to detect conflicts. The client uses Address Resolution Protocol (ARP) to detect clients. If an address conflict is detected, the address is removed from the pool and is not assigned until an administrator resolves the conflict.

Example 7-14 shows the detection method and detection time for all IP addresses that the DHCP server has offered that have conflicts with other devices.

Example 7-14   Verify IP Address Conflicts

```
R1# show ip dhcp conflict

IP address Detection Method Detection time

192.168.1.32 Ping Dec 16 2007 12:28 PM

192.168.1.64 Gratuitous ARP Dec 23 2007 08:12 AM
```

Troubleshooting Task 2: Verify Physical Connectivity

First, use the **show interface** *interface* command to confirm that the router interface acting as the default gateway for the client is operational. If the state of the interface is anything other than up, the port does not pass traffic, including DHCP client requests. If the interface is down, be sure to enable it by using the **no shutdown** command on the interface.

Troubleshooting Task 3: Test Network Connectivity by Configuring a Client Workstation with a Static IP Address

When troubleshooting any DHCP issue, verify network connectivity by configuring a static IP address on a client workstation. If the workstation is unable to reach network resources with a statically configured IP address, the root cause of the problem is not DHCP. At this point, network connectivity troubleshooting is required.

Troubleshooting Task 4: Verify Switch Port Configuration (STP PortFast and Other Commands)

If the DHCP client is unable to obtain an IP address from the DHCP server on startup, attempt to obtain an IP address from the DHCP server by manually forcing the client to send a DHCP request.

If there is a switch between the client and the DHCP server, verify that the port has STP PortFast enabled and trunking/channeling disabled. The default configuration is PortFast disabled and trunking/channeling auto, if applicable. These configuration changes resolve the most common DHCP client issues that occur with an initial installation of a Catalyst switch. A review of the *CCNA Exploration: LAN Switching and Wireless* course will help you solve this issue.

Troubleshooting Task 5: Distinguishing Whether DHCP Clients Obtain an IP Address on the Same Subnet or VLAN as the DHCP Server

It is important to distinguish whether DHCP is functioning correctly when the client is on the same subnet or VLAN as the DHCP server. If DHCP is working correctly, the problem may be the DHCP/BOOTP relay agent. If the problem persists even with testing DHCP on the same subnet or VLAN as the DHCP server, the problem may actually be with the DHCP server. Verify the DHCP server configuration. If the router is providing DHCP services, verify the DHCP configuration on the router.

Verify Router DHCP/BOOTP Relay Configuration

When the DHCP server is located on a LAN separate from the client, the router interface facing the client must be configured to relay DHCP requests. This is accomplished by configuring the IP helper address. If the IP helper address is not configured properly, client DHCP requests are not forwarded to the DHCP server.

Follow these steps to verify the router configuration:

Step 1. Verify that the **ip helper-address** command is configured on the correct interface. It must be present on the inbound interface of the LAN containing the DHCP client workstations and must be directed to the correct DHCP server. The following output from the **show running-config** command verifies that the DHCP relay IP address is referencing the DHCP server address at 192.168.11.5:

```
R1# show running-config

<Output omitted>
!
interface FastEthernet0/0
 ip address 192.168.10.1 255.255.255.0
 ip helper-address 192.168.11.5
 duplex auto
 speed auto
!
<Output omitted>
```

Step 2. Verify that the global configuration command **no service dhcp** has not been configured. This command disables all DHCP server and relay functionality on the router. The command **service dhcp** does not appear in the configuration, because it is the default configuration.

Verify That the Router Is Receiving DHCP Requests Using debug Commands

The DHCP process fails if the router does not receive DHCP requests from the client. As a troubleshooting task, verify that the router is receiving the DHCP request from the client using the **debug ip packet detail** command.

The **debug** command displays all types of IP traffic. To help narrow the scope of the generated output, the **debug** command can be used with an access control list (ACL). The **debug** access control list is not as intrusive to the router.

Example 7-15 shows the commands to verify that the DHCP server is receiving messages from the DHCP client.

Example 7-15   Debugging DHCP

```
R1# access-list 100 permit ip host 0.0.0.0 host 255.255.255.255
R1# debug ip packet detail 100

IP packet debugging is on (detailed) for access list 100
R1#
00:16:46: IP: s=0.0.0.0 (Ethernet0/0), d=255.255.255.255, len 604, rcvd 2
00:16:46: UDP src=68, dst=67
00:16:46: IP: s=0.0.0.0 (Ethernet0/0), d=255.255.255.255, len 604, rcvd 2
00:16:46: UDP src=68, dst=67
```

The output shows that the router is receiving the DHCP requests from the client.

The source IP address is 0.0.0.0 because the client does not yet have an IP address.

The destination is 255.255.255.255 because the DHCP discovery message from the client is a broadcast. DHCP uses the UDP source, and destination ports are port 68 (BOOTP client) and port 67 (BOOTP server).

This output shows only a summary of the packet, not the packet itself. Therefore, it is not possible to determine if the packet is correct. Nevertheless, the router did receive a broadcast packet with the source and destination IP and UDP ports that are correct for DHCP.

Verify That the Router Is Receiving and Forwarding DHCP Request Using **debug ip dhcp server** Command

Another useful command for troubleshooting DHCP operation is the **debug ip dhcp server** command. This command reports server events, such as address assignments and database updates. It is also used to decode DHCP receptions and transmissions.

Packet Tracer
☐ **Activity**

Configuring DHCP Using Easy IP

DHCP assigns IP addresses and other important network configuration information dynami-cally. Cisco routers can use the Cisco IOS feature set, Easy IP, as an optional, full-featured DHCP server. Easy IP leases configurations for 24 hours by default. In this activity, you configure DHCP services on two routers and test your configuration. Use File e4-718.pka on the CD-ROM that accompanies this book to perform this activity using Packet Tracer.

Scaling Networks with NAT

All public Internet addresses must be registered with a *Regional Internet Registry (RIR)*. Organizations can lease public addresses from an ISP. Only the registered holder of a public Internet address can assign that address to a network device.

There are currently five RIRs in the world:

- *American Registry for Internet Numbers (ARIN)*
- *Réseaux IP Européens Network Coordination Centre (RIPE NCC)*
- *Asia Pacific Network Information Centre (APNIC)*
- *Latin America and Caribbean Internet Addresses Registry (LACNIC)*
- *AfriNIC*

Figure 7-15 shows the RIRs' areas of responsibility.

Figure 7-15   Regional Internet Registries

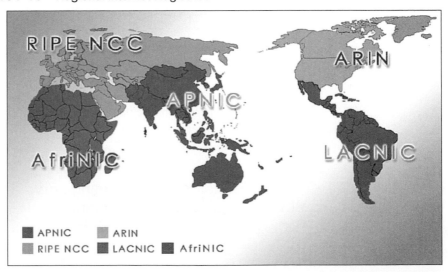

You may have noticed that most examples in this course use private IP addresses. Recall that these are reserved private Internet addresses, as specified in *RFC 1918, Address Allocation for Private Internets*, and are drawn from the three blocks shown in Table 7-4.

Table 7-4   Private Internet Addresses (RFC 1918)

Class	RFC 1918 Private IP Address Range	CIDR Prefix
A	10.0.0.0 to 10.255.255.255	10.0.0.0/8
B	172.16.0.0 to 172.31.255.255	172.16.0.0/12
C	192.168.0.0 to 192.168.255.255	192.168.0.0/16

These addresses are for private, internal network use only. Packets containing these addresses are not routed over the Internet and are called nonroutable addresses.

Unlike public IP addresses, private IP addresses are a reserved block of numbers that anyone can use. This means that two networks, or two million networks, can each use the same private addresses. To protect the public Internet address structure, ISPs configure the border routers to prevent privately addressed traffic from being forwarded over the Internet.

By providing more address space than most organizations could obtain through a RIR, private addressing gives enterprises considerable flexibility in network design. This enables operationally and administratively convenient addressing schemes as well as easier growth.

However, you cannot route private addresses over the Internet, and there are not enough public addresses to allow organizations to provide one to every one of their hosts. Therefore, networks need a mechanism to translate private addresses into public addresses at the edge of their network that works in both directions. Without a translation system, private hosts behind a router in the network of one organization cannot connect with private hosts behind a router in other organizations over the Internet.

Network Address Translation (NAT) provides this mechanism. Before NAT, a host with a private address could not access the Internet. Using NAT, individual companies can address some or all of their hosts with private addresses and can use NAT to provide access to the Internet.

Note

For a more in-depth look at the development of the RIR system, see the Cisco Internet Protocol Journal article at *http://www.cisco.com/web/about/ac123/ac147/archived_issues/ipj_4-4/regional_internet_registries.html*.

What Is NAT?

NAT is like the receptionist in a large office. Assume that you ask the receptionist not to forward any calls to you unless you request it. Later, you call a potential client and leave a message for him to call you back. You tell the receptionist that you are expecting a call from this client, and you ask her to put him through to your telephone.

The client calls the main number for the entire office, which is the only number he knows. When he tells the receptionist who he wants to speak to, she checks a lookup table that matches your name to your extension. The receptionist knows that you are expecting this call, so she forwards the call to your extension.

So although private addresses are assigned to devices inside the network, NAT-enabled routers retain one or many valid Internet IP addresses outside the network. When the client sends packets out of the network, NAT translates the client's internal IP address into an external address. To outside users, all traffic coming to and going from the network has the same IP address or is from the same pool of addresses.

NAT has many uses, but its key use is to save IP addresses by allowing networks to use private IP addresses. NAT translates nonroutable, private, internal addresses into routable, public addresses. NAT has the added benefit of adding a degree of privacy and security to a network, because it hides internal IP addresses from outside networks.

A NAT-enabled device typically operates at the border of a stub network. In Figure 7-16, R2 is the border router.

Figure 7-16   Sample NAT Topology

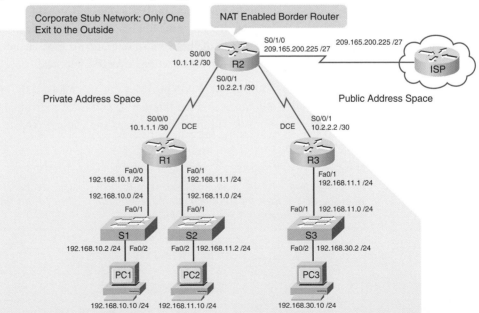

From the perspective of router ISP, R2 is a stub network. A stub network has a single connection to its neighbor network.

When a host inside the stub network—such as PC1, PC2, or PC3—wants to transmit to a host on the outside, the packet is forwarded to R2, the border gateway router. R2 performs the NAT process, translating the host's internal private address to a public, outside, routable address.

In NAT terminology, the inside network is the set of networks that are subject to translation. The outside network refers to all other addresses. IP addresses have different designations based on whether they are on the private network or the public network (Internet) and whether the traffic is incoming or outgoing.

Figure 7-17 shows how to refer to the interfaces when configuring NAT.

Figure 7-17   NAT Terminology

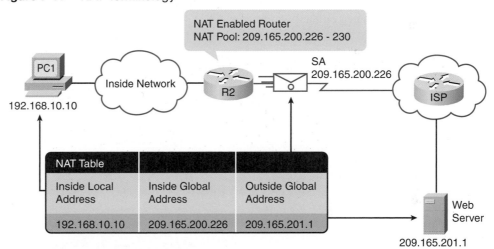

Assume that router R2 has been configured to provide NAT features. It has a pool of publicly available addresses to lend to inside hosts. This section uses the following terms when discussing NAT:

■ *Inside local address*: Usually not an IP address assigned by a RIR or service provider; is most likely an RFC 1918 private address. In the figure, the IP address 192.168.10.10 is assigned to the host PC1 on the inside network.

■ *Inside global address*: A valid public address that the inside host is given when it exits the NAT router. When traffic from PC1 is destined for the web server at 209.165.201.1, router R2 must translate the address. In this case, IP address 209.165.200.226 is used as the inside global address for PC1.

- *Outside global address*: A reachable IP address assigned to a host on the Internet. For example, the web server can be reached at IP address 209.165.201.1.

- **Outside local address**: The local IP address assigned to a host on the outside network. In most situations, this address is identical to the outside global address of that outside device.

Note

We will discuss the inside local address, inside global address, and outside global address. The use of the outside local address is outside the scope of this course.

The "inside" of a NAT configuration is not synonymous with private addresses as defined by RFC 1918. What we call "nonroutable" addresses are not always unroutable. An administrator can configure any router to pass traffic over private subnets. However, if they try to pass a packet to the ISP for any private address, the ISP drops it. Nonroutable means not routable on the Internet.

How Does NAT Work?

In Figure 7-18, the user on PC1 wants to download a web page from a web server. PC1 is an inside host with the IP address 192.168.10.10, and the outside web server is located at 209.165.200.1.

Figure 7-18   NAT Topology

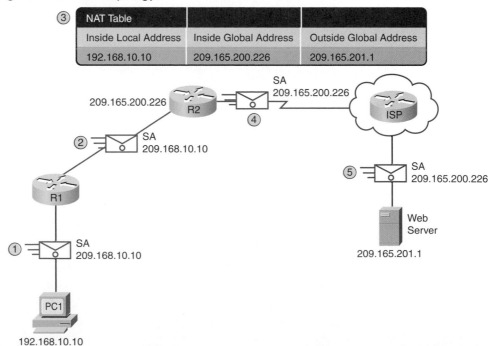

The following steps illustrate the NAT process:

1. PC1 sends a packet destined for the Internet to R1, the default gateway.

2. The R1 router forwards the packet to R2, as directed by its routing table.

3. Router R2 refers to its routing table and identifies the next hop as the ISP router. It then checks to see if the packet matches the criteria specified for translation. R2 has an ACL that identifies the inside network as a valid host for translation. Therefore, it translates an inside local IP address to an inside global IP address, which in this case is 209.165.200.226. It stores this mapping of the local to global address in the NAT table.

4. R2 sends the packet to the ISP router.

5. The packet eventually reaches its destination.

When the web server responds to the NAT-assigned IP address 209.165.200.226, the packet eventually arrives at router R2.

R2 refers to its NAT table and sees that this was a previously translated IP address. It then translates the inside global address (209.165.200.226) to the inside local address (192.168.10.10), and the packet is forwarded to PC1. If it does not find a mapping, the packet is dropped.

Dynamic Mapping and Static Mapping

The two types of NAT translation are as follows:

- *Dynamic NAT* uses a pool of public addresses and assigns them on a first-come, first-served basis. When a host with a private IP address requests access to the Internet, dynamic NAT chooses an IP address from the pool that is not already in use by another host. This is the mapping described so far.

- *Static NAT* uses a one-to-one mapping of local and global addresses, and these mappings remain constant. Static NAT is particularly useful for web servers or hosts that must have a consistent address that is accessible from the Internet. These internal hosts may be enterprise servers or networking devices.

Both static and dynamic NAT require that enough public addresses are available to satisfy the total number of simultaneous user sessions.

Note

For another look at how dynamic NAT works, go to
http://www.cisco.com/warp/public/556/nat.swf.

NAT Overload

NAT overloading (sometimes called *Port Address Translation [PAT]*) maps multiple private IP addresses to a single public IP address or a few addresses. This is what most home routers do. Your ISP assigns one address to your router, yet several members of your family can simultaneously surf the Internet.

With NAT overloading, multiple addresses can be mapped to one or a few addresses because each private address is also tracked by a port number. When a client opens a TCP/IP session, the NAT router assigns a port number to its source address. NAT overload ensures that clients use a different TCP port number for each client session with a server on the Internet. When a response comes back from the server, the source port number, which becomes the destination port number on the return trip, determines to which client the router routes the packets. It also verifies that the incoming packets were requested, thus adding a degree of security to the session.

Figure 7-19 and the following steps illustrate the NAT overload process:

1. PC1 and PC2 send packets destined for the Internet.

2. The packets sent to the NAT overload router, R2, contain the source addresses and their dynamic source port number. NAT overload uses unique source port numbers on the inside global IP address to distinguish between translations.

3. When the packets arrive at R2, NAT overload changes the source address to the inside global IP address and keeps the assigned port numbers (1555 and 1331 in this example) to identify the client from which the packet originated. R2 adds this information to its NAT table. Notice the assigned ports.

4. The packets continue the journey to their destinations.

Figure 7-19 NAT Overload Process

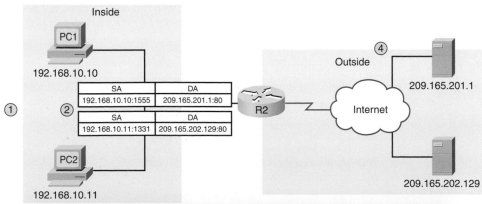

When the web server replies, the same path is followed, but in reverse.

Port numbers are encoded in 16 bits. The total number of internal addresses that can be translated into one external address could theoretically be as high as 65,536 per IP address. However, realistically, about 4000 internal addresses can be assigned a single IP address.

In Figure 7-19, the client source port numbers in the two SAs, 1331 and 1555, do not change at the border gateway. This is not a very likely scenario, because there is a good chance that these numbers may have already been attached to other ongoing sessions.

It should be clarified that NAT overload attempts to preserve the original source port. However, if this source port is already used, NAT overload assigns the first available port number starting from the beginning of the appropriate port group 0 to 511, 512 to 1023, or 1024 to 65535. When no more ports are available and more than one external IP address is configured, NAT overload moves to the next IP address to try to allocate the original source port again. This process continues until NAT overload runs out of available ports and external IP addresses.

Figure 7-20 and the following steps illustrate the NAT overload process when the same source port is used:

1. PC1 sends a packet destined for the Internet with a source port number of 1444.

2. The NAT Overload router, R2, translates the address and assigns it the source port number 1444, as shown in the NAT table.

3. PC2 sends a packet destined for the Internet as well. Coincidently, it also uses the source port number 1444.

4. PC1 and PC2 have somehow chosen the same source port number, 1444. This is acceptable for the inside address, because they both have unique private IP addresses. However, R2 needs to change the port number. Otherwise, two packets from two hosts would leave R2 with the same source address and port number combination. To solve this problem, NAT overload gives the second address the first available port number, which in this case is 1445.

Figure 7-20   NAT Overload Process: Same Source Ports

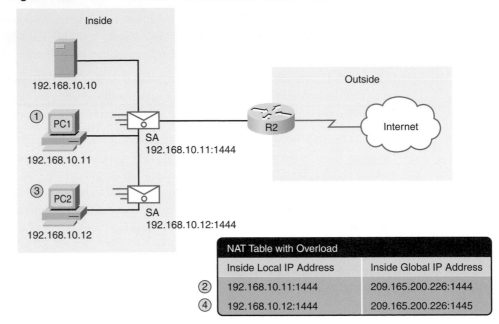

Differences Between NAT and NAT Overload

Summarizing the differences between NAT and NAT overload will help your understanding. NAT generally translates IP addresses only on a 1:1 correspondence between publicly exposed IP addresses and privately held IP addresses. NAT overload modifies both the private IP address and port number of the sender. NAT overload chooses the port numbers seen by hosts on the public network.

NAT routes incoming packets to their inside destination by referring to the incoming source IP address given by the host on the public network. NAT overload generally has only one or very few publicly exposed IP addresses. Incoming packets from the public network are routed to their destinations on the private network by referring to a table in the NAT overload device that tracks public and private port pairs. This is called connection tracking.

Benefits and Drawbacks of Using NAT

NAT provides many benefits and advantages. However, NAT has some drawbacks, including the lack of support for some types of traffic.

The benefits of using NAT include the following:

- **NAT conserves the legally registered addressing scheme by allowing the privatization of intranets.** NAT conserves addresses by applying port-level multiplexing. With NAT overload, internal hosts can share a single public IP address for all external communications. In this type of configuration, very few external addresses are required to support many internal hosts.

- **NAT increases the flexibility of connections to the public network.** Multiple pools, backup pools, and load-balancing pools can be implemented to ensure reliable public network connections.

- **NAT provides consistency for internal network addressing schemes.** On a network without private IP addresses and NAT, changing public IP addresses requires renumbering all hosts on the existing network. The costs of renumbering hosts can be significant. NAT allows the existing scheme to remain while supporting a new public addressing scheme. This means an organization could change ISPs and not need to change any of its inside clients.

- **NAT provides network security.** Because private networks do not advertise their addresses or internal topology, they remain reasonably secure when used in conjunction with NAT to gain controlled external access. However, NAT does not replace firewalls.

NAT has some drawbacks as well. The fact that hosts on the Internet appear to communicate directly with the NAT device, rather than with the actual host inside the private network, creates a number of issues. In theory, a single globally unique IP address can represent many privately addressed hosts. This has advantages from a privacy and security point of view, but in practice, drawbacks exist.

The disadvantages of using NAT include the following:

- **Performance is degraded.** NAT increases switching delays because translating each IP address within the packet headers takes time. The first packet is process-switched, meaning that it always goes through the slower path. The router must look at every packet to decide whether it needs to be translated. The router needs to alter the IP header, and possibly alter the TCP or UDP header. Remaining packets go through the fast-switched path if a cache entry exists; otherwise, they too are delayed.

- **End-to-end functionality is degraded.** Many Internet protocols and applications depend on end-to-end functionality, with unmodified packets forwarded from the source to the destination. By changing end-to-end addresses, NAT prevents some applications that use IP addressing. For example, some security applications, such as digital signatures, fail because the source IP address changes. Applications that use physical addresses instead of a qualified domain name do not reach destinations that are translated across the NAT router. Sometimes, this problem can be avoided by implementing static NAT mappings.

- **End-to-end IP traceability is lost.** It becomes much more difficult to trace packets that undergo numerous packet address changes over multiple NAT hops, making troubleshooting challenging. On the other hand, hackers who want to determine the source of a packet find it difficult to trace or obtain the original source or destination address.

- **Tunneling is more complicated.** Using NAT also complicates tunneling protocols, such as IPsec, because NAT modifies values in the headers that interfere with the integrity checks done by IPsec and other tunneling protocols.

- **Services that require the initiation of TCP connections from the outside network, or stateless protocols such as those using UDP, can be disrupted.** Unless the NAT router makes a specific effort to support such protocols, incoming packets cannot reach their destination. Some protocols can accommodate one instance of NAT between participating hosts (passive mode FTP, for example) but fail when both systems are separated from the Internet by NAT.

Note

Most of the disadvantages of NAT are addressed in IPv6.

Configuring Static NAT

Remember that static NAT is a one-to-one mapping between an inside address and an outside address. Static NAT allows connections initiated by external devices to inside devices. For instance, you may want to map an inside global address to a specific inside local address that is assigned to your web server.

Configuring static NAT translations is a simple task. You need to define the addresses to translate and then configure NAT on the appropriate interfaces.

Table 7-5 explains the steps and commands required to configure static NAT.

Table 7-5   Configuring Static NAT

Step	Action	Command
1	Establish static translation between an inside local address and an inside global address.[*]	Router(config)# **ip nat inside source static** *local-ip global-ip*
2	Specify the inside interface.	Router(config)# **interface** *type number*
3	Exit interface configuration mode.	Router(config-if)# **exit**
4	Specify the inside interface.	Router(config)# **interface** *type number*
5	Mark the interface as connected to the inside.	Router(config-if)# **ip nat inside**
6	Specify the outside interface.	Router(config-if)# **interface** *type number*
7	Mark the interface as connected to the outside.	Router(config-if)# **ip nat outside**

[*]Enter the global command **no ip nat inside source static** to remove the static source translation.

You enter static translations directly into the configuration. Unlike dynamic translations, these translations are always in the NAT table.

Figure 7-21 shows a sample static NAT topology.

Figure 7-21   Static NAT Topology

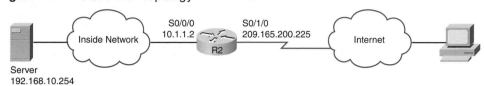

Example 7-16 shows the static NAT configuration.

Example 7-16   Static NAT Configuration

```
R2(config)# ip nat inside source static 192.168.10.254 209.165.200.254
!--Establishes static translation between an inside local address and an inside
!--global address.
R2(config)# interface serial0/0/0
R2(config-if)# ip nat inside
!--Identifies Serial 0/0/0 as an inside NAT interface.
R2(config-if)# interface serial 0/1/0
R2(config-if)# ip nat outside
!--Identifies Serial 0/1/0 as an outside NAT interface.
```

Assume that the server on the inside network with IP address 192.168.10.254 provides web services to outside users. Line 1 of the configuration statically maps the inside IP address of 192.168.10.254 to the outside address of 209.165.10.254. This allows outside hosts to access the internal web server using the public IP address 209.165.10.254.

Configuring Dynamic NAT

Whereas static NAT provides a permanent mapping between an internal address and a specific public address, dynamic NAT maps private IP addresses to public addresses drawn from a *NAT pool*.

Dynamic NAT configuration differs from static NAT, but it also has some similarities. Like static NAT, it requires the configuration to identify each interface as an inside or outside interface. However, rather than creating a static map to a single IP address, a pool of inside global addresses is used.

Table 7-6 explains the steps and commands required to configure dynamic NAT.

Table 7-6 Configuring Dynamic NAT

Step	Action	Command	Notes
1	Define a pool of global addresses to be allocated as needed.	Router(config)# **ip nat pool** *name start-ip end-ip* {**netmask** *netmask* | **prefix-length** *prefix-length*}	Enter the global command **no ip nat pool** *name* to remove the pool of global addresses.
2	Define a standard access list permitting those addresses that are to be translated.	Router(config)# **access-list** *access-list-number* **permit** *source* [*source-wildcard*]	Enter the global command **no access-list** *access-list-number* to remove the access list.
3	Establish dynamic source translation, specifying the access list defined in the preceding step.	Router(config)# **ip nat inside source list** *access-list-number* **pool** *name*	Enter the global command **no ip nat inside source list** *access-list-number* **pool** *name* to remove the dynamic source translation.
4	Specify the inside interface.	Router(config)# **interface** *type number*	
5	Mark the interface as connected to the inside.	Router(config-if)# **ip nat inside**	
6	Specify the outside interface.	Router(config-if)# **interface** *type number*	
7	Mark the interface as connected to the outside.	Router(config-if)# **ip nat outside**	

To configure dynamic NAT, you need an ACL to permit only those addresses that are to be translated. When developing your ACL, remember that each ACL has an implicit "deny all" at the end. An ACL that is too permissive can lead to unpredictable results. Cisco advises against configuring access control lists referenced by NAT commands with the **permit any** command. Using **permit any** can cause NAT to consume too many router resources, which can cause network problems.

Figure 7-22 shows a sample dynamic NAT topology.

Figure 7-22   Dynamic NAT Topology

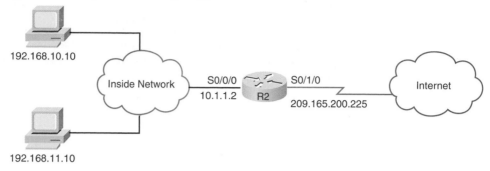

192.168.10.10

192.168.11.10

Example 7-17 shows the dynamic NAT configuration.

Example 7-17   Dynamic NAT Configuration

```
R2(config)# ip nat pool NAT-POOL1 209.165.200.226 209.165.200.240 netmask
  255.255.255.224
!--Defines a pool of public IP addresses under the pool name NAT-POOL1
R2(config)# access-list 1 permit 192.168.0.0 0.0.255.255
!--Defines which addresses are eligible to be translated
R2(config)# ip nat inside source list 1 pool NAT-POOL1
!--Binds the NAT pool with ACL 1
R2(config)# interface serial 0/0/0
R2(config-if)# ip nat inside
!--Identifies interface Serial 0/0/0 as an inside NAT interface
R2(config-if)# interface serial s0/1/0
R2(config-if)# ip nat outside
!--Identifies interface Serial 0/1/0 as the outside NAT interface.
```

This configuration allows translation for all hosts on the 192.168.10.0 and 192.168.11.0 networks when they generate traffic that enters S0/0/0 and exits S0/1/0. These hosts are translated into an available address in the 209.165.200.226 to 209.165.200.240 range.

Configuring NAT Overload for a Single Public IP Address

There are two possible ways to configure overloading, depending on how the ISP allocates public IP addresses. In the first instance, the ISP allocates one public IP address to the organization, and in the other, it allocates more than one public IP address.

Table 7-7 explains the steps and commands required to configure NAT overload with a single IP address.

Table 7-7   Configuring NAT Overload Using a Single IP Address

Step	Action	Command	Notes
1	Define a standard access list permitting those addresses that are to be translated.	Router(config)# **access-list** *access-list-number* **permit** *source* [*source-wildcard*]	Enter the global command **no access-list** *access-list-number* to remove the access list.
2	Establish dynamic source translation, specifying the access list defined in the preceding step.	Router(config)# **ip nat inside source list** *access-list-number* **interface** *interface* **overload**	Enter the global command **no ip nat inside source list** *access-list-number* **interface** *interface* **overload** to remove the dynamic source translation.
3	Specify the inside interface.	Router(config)# **interface** *type number*	
4	Mark the interface as connected to the inside.	Router(config-if)# **ip nat inside**	
5	Specify the outside interface.	Router(config-if)# **interface** *type number*	
6	Mark the interface as connected to the outside.	Router(config-if)# **ip nat outside**	

With only one public IP address, the overload configuration typically assigns that public address to the outside interface that connects to the ISP. All inside addresses are translated into the single IP address when leaving the outside interface.

The configuration is similar to dynamic NAT, except that instead of a pool of addresses, the **interface** keyword is used to identify the outside IP address. Therefore, no NAT pool is defined. The **overload** keyword enables the addition of the port number to the translation.

Refer to the topology shown in Figure 7-22. Example 7-18 shows a NAT overload configuration.

Example 7-18   NAT Overload Configuration for a Single IP Address

```
R2(config)# access-list 1 permit 192.168.0.0 0.0.255.255
!--Defines which addresses are eligible to be translated
R2(config)# ip nat inside source list 1 interface serial 0/1/0 overload
!--Identifies the outside interface Serial 0/1/0 as the inside global address to
!--be overloaded
R2(config)# interface serial 0/0/0
R2(config-if)# ip nat inside
!--Identifies interface Serial 0/0/0 as an inside NAT interface
R2(config-if)# interface serial s0/1/0
R2(config-if)# ip nat outside
```

All hosts from network 192.168.0.0 /16 (matching ACL 1) sending traffic through router R2 to the Internet are translated into IP address 209.165.200.225 (the interface S0/1/0 IP address). The traffic flows are identified by port numbers, because the **overload** keyword is used.

Configuring NAT Overload for a Pool of Public IP Addresses

In the scenario where the ISP has provided more than one public IP address, NAT overload is configured to use a pool. The primary difference between this configuration and the configuration for dynamic, one-to-one NAT is that the **overload** keyword is used. Remember that the **overload** keyword enables port address translation.

Table 7-8 explains the steps and commands required to configure NAT overload using a pool of addresses.

Table 7-8   Configuring NAT Overload Using a Pool of Addresses

Step	Action	Command	Notes
1	Specify the global address, as a pool, to be used for overloading.	Router(config)# **ip nat pool** *name start-ip end-ip* {**netmask** *netmask* | **prefix-length** *prefix-length*}	
2	Define a standard access list permitting those addresses that are to be translated.	Router(config)# **access-list** *access-list-number* **permit** *source* [*source-wildcard*]	Enter the global command **no access-list** *access-list-number* to remove the access list.
3	Establish overload translation.	Router(config)# **ip nat inside source list** *access-list-number* **pool** *name* **overload**	Enter the global command **no ip nat inside source list** *access-list-number* **pool** *name* **overload** to remove the dynamic source translation.
4	Specify the inside interface.	Router(config)# **interface** *type number*	
5	Mark the interface as connected to the inside.	Router(config-if)# **ip nat inside**	
6	Specify the outside interface.	Router(config-if)# **interface** *type number*	
7	Mark the interface as connected to the outside.	Router(config-if)# **ip nat outside**	

Refer to the topology shown in Figure 7-22. Example 7-19 shows a NAT overload configuration.

Example 7-19   NAT Overload Configuration for a Pool of IP Addresses

```
R2(config)# ip nat pool NAT-POOL2 209.165.200.226 209.165.200.240 netmask
  255.255.255.224
!--Defines a pool of addresses named NAT-POOL2 to be used in NAT translation
R2(config)# access-list 1 permit 192.168.0.0 0.0.255.255
!--Defines which addresses are eligible to be translated
R2(config)# ip nat inside source list 1 pool NAT-POOL2 overload
!--Bonds the NAT pool with ACL 1 address to be overloaded
R2(config)# interface serial 0/0/0
R2(config-if)# ip nat inside
!--Identifies interface Serial 0/0/0 as an inside NAT interface
R2(config-if)# interface serial s0/1/0
R2(config-if)# ip nat outside
```

The configuration establishes overload translation for NAT pool NAT-POOL2. The NAT pool contains addresses 209.165.200.226 to 209.165.200.240 and is translated using PAT. Hosts in the 192.168.0.0 /16 network are subject to translation. Finally, the inside and outside interfaces are identified.

Configuring Port Forwarding

Port forwarding (sometimes called tunneling) is the act of forwarding a network port from one network node to another. This technique can allow an external user to reach a port on a private IP address (inside a LAN) from the outside through a NAT-enabled router.

Typically, peer-to-peer file-sharing programs and key operations, such as web serving and outgoing FTP, require that router ports be forwarded or opened to allow these applications to work. Because NAT hides internal addresses, peer-to-peer works only from the inside out, where NAT can map outgoing requests against incoming replies.

The problem is that NAT does not allow requests initiated from the outside. This situation can be resolved with manual intervention. Port forwarding allows you to identify specific ports that can be forwarded to inside hosts.

Recall that Internet software applications interact with user ports that need to be open or available to those applications. Different applications use different ports. For example, Telnet uses port 23, FTP uses ports 20 and 21, HTTP uses port 80, and SMTP uses port 25. This makes it predictable for applications and routers to identify network services. For example, HTTP operates through the well-known port 80. When you enter the address *http://cisco.com*, the browser displays the Cisco Systems, Inc. website. Notice that you do not have to specify the HTTP port number for the page requests, because the application assumes port 80.

Port forwarding allows users on the Internet to access internal servers by using the WAN port address and the matched external port number. When users send these types of requests to your WAN port IP address via the Internet, the router forwards those requests to the appropriate servers on your LAN. For security reasons, broadband routers do not by default permit any external network request to be forwarded to an inside host.

For instance, Figure 7-23 shows the Single Port Forwarding window of a Linksys WVRS4400N business-class SOHO router. Currently, port forwarding is not configured.

Figure 7-23   Single Port Forwarding Window

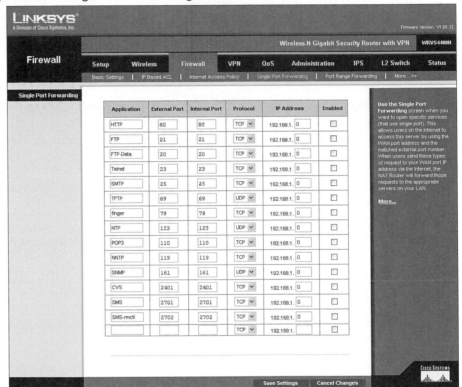

You can enable port forwarding for applications and specify the inside local address to forward the request to. For example, in Figure 7-24, HTTP service requests coming into this Linksys are now forwarded to the web server with the inside local address of 192.168.1.254. If the external WAN IP address of the SOHO router is 209.165.200.158, the external user could enter http://209.165.202.158 and the Linksys router would redirect the HTTP request to the internal web server at IP address 192.168.1.254, using the default port number 80.

Figure 7-24   Single Port Forwarding Window: Inside Local Address Specified

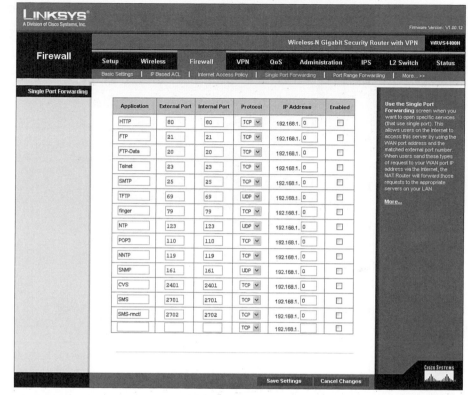

You could specify a port different from the default port 80. However, the external user would have to know the specific port number to use.

The approach you take to configure port forwarding depends on the brand and model of the broadband router in the network. However, there are some generic steps to follow. If the instructions supplied by your ISP or that came with the router do not provide adequate guidance, the website *http://www.portforward.com* provides guides for several broadband routers. You can follow the instructions to add or delete ports as required to meet the needs of any applications you want to allow or deny.

Verifying NAT and NAT Overload

It is important to verify NAT operation. Several useful router commands let you view and clear NAT translations. This section explains how to verify NAT operation using tools available on Cisco routers.

One of the most useful commands when verifying NAT operation is **show ip nat translations**. Before using the **show** command to verify NAT, you must clear any dynamic translation entries that might still be present, because, by default, dynamic address translations remain in the NAT translation table until they time out after a period of nonuse.

Figure 7-25 shows the sample topology used in the next example.

Figure 7-25   Sample Topology

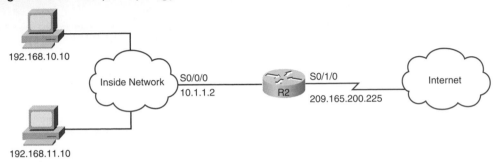

In Example 7-20, router R2 has been configured to provide NAT overload to the 192.168.0.0 /16 clients.

Example 7-20   NAT Overload Configuration

```
R2(config)# access-list 1 permit 192.168.0.0 0.0.255.255
R2(config)# ip nat inside source list 1 interface serial 0/1/0 overload
R2(config)# interface serial 0/0/0
R2(config-if)# ip nat inside
R2(config-if)# interface serial s0/1/0
R2(config-if)# ip nat outside
```

When the internal hosts exit router R2 to the Internet, they are translated into the IP address of the serial interface with a unique source port number.

Assume that the two hosts in the internal network have been accessing web services from the Internet. Notice that the output of the **show ip nat translations** command in Example 7-21 shows the details of the two NAT assignments.

Example 7-21   show ip nat translations Command

```
R2# show ip nat translations

Pro Inside global          Inside local          Outside local
tcp 209.165.200.225:16642  192.168.10.10:16642   209.165.200.254:80
tcp 209.165.200.225:62452  192.168.11.10:62452   209.165.200.254:80
 Outside global
 209.165.200.254:80
 209.165.200.254:80


R2# show ip nat translations verbose

Pro Inside global          Inside local          Outside local
tcp 209.165.200.225:16642  192.168.10.10:16642   209.165.200.254:80
Outside global
 209.165.200.254:80
    create 00:01:45, use 00:01:43 timeout:86400000, left 23:58:16, Map-Id(In): 1,
    flags:
extended, use_count: 0, entry-id: 4, lc_entries: 0
tcp 209.165.200.225:62452  192.168.11.10:62452   209.165.200.254:80
 209.165.200.254:80
    create 00:00:37, use 00:00:35 timeout:86400000, left 23:59:24, Map-Id(In): 1,
    flags:
extended, use_count: 0, entry-id: 5, lc_entries: 0
R2#
```

Adding **verbose** to the command displays additional information about each translation, including how long ago the entry was created and used. The command displays all static translations that have been configured, as well as any dynamic translations that have been created by traffic. Each translation is identified by protocol as well as inside and outside local and global addresses.

The **show ip nat statistics** command displays information about the total number of active translations, NAT configuration parameters, how many addresses are in the pool, and how many have been allocated. In Example 7-22, the hosts have initiated web traffic as well as ICMP traffic.

Example 7-22   show ip nat statistics Command

```
R2# show ip nat translations

Pro Inside global        Inside local         Outside local
icmp 209.165.200.225:3     192.168.10.10:3      209.165.200.254:3
tcp  209.165.200.225:11679 192.168.10.10:11679  209.165.200.254:80
icmp 209.165.200.225:0     192.168.11.10:0      209.165.200.254:0
tcp  209.165.200.225:14462 192.168.11.10:14462  209.165.200.254:80
 Outside global
 209.165.200.254:3
 209.165.200.254:80
 209.165.200.254:0
 209.165.200.254:80

R2# show ip nat statistics

Total active translations: 3 (0 static, 3 dynamic; 3 extended)
Outside interfaces:
  Serial0/1/0
Inside interfaces:
  Serial0/0/0, Serial0/0/1
Hits: 173  Misses: 9
CEF Translated packets: 182, CEF Punted packets: 0
Expired translations: 6
Dynamic mappings:
-- Inside Source
[Id: 1] access-list 1 interface Serial0/1/0 refcount 3
Queued Packets: 0
R2#
```

Alternatively, use the **show run** command and look for NAT, access command list, interface, or pool commands with the required values. Examine these carefully, and correct any errors you discover.

By default, translation entries time out after 24 hours, unless the timers have been reconfigured with the **ip nat translation timeout** *timeout_seconds* command in global configuration mode.

It is sometimes useful to clear the dynamic entries sooner than the default. This is especially true when testing the NAT configuration. To clear dynamic entries before the timeout has expired, use the **clear ip nat translation** global command, as shown in Example 7-23.

Example 7-23   clear ip nat translation Command

```
R2# clear ip nat translation *
R2# show ip nat translations

R2#
```

Table 7-9 shows the various ways to clear the NAT translations.

Table 7-9   Clearing NAT Translations

Command	Description
clear ip nat translation *	Clears all dynamic address translation entries from the NAT translation table.
clear ip nat translation inside *global-ip local-ip* [**outside** *local-ip global-ip*]	Clears a simple dynamic translation entry containing an inside translation or both inside and outside translation.
clear ip nat translation *protocol* **inside** *global-ip global-port local-ip local-port* [**outside** *local-ip local-port global-ip global-port*]	Clears an extended dynamic translation entry.

You can be very specific about which translation to clear, or you can clear all translations from the table using the **clear ip nat translation *** global command.

Only the dynamic translations are cleared from the table. Static translations cannot be cleared from the translation table.

Troubleshooting NAT and NAT Overload Configuration

When you have IP connectivity problems in a NAT environment, it is often difficult to determine the cause of the problem. The first step in solving your problem is to rule out NAT as the cause.

How To

Follow these steps to verify that NAT is operating as expected:

Step 1.   Based on the configuration, clearly define what NAT is supposed to achieve. This may reveal a problem with the configuration.

Step 2.   Verify that correct translations exist in the translation table using the **show ip nat translations** command.

Step 3. Use the **clear** and **debug** commands to verify that NAT is operating as expected. Check to see if dynamic entries are re-created after they are cleared.

Step 4. Review in detail what is happening to the packet, and verify that routers have the correct routing information to move the packet.

Use the **debug ip nat** command to verify the operation of the NAT feature by displaying information about every packet that the router translates. The **debug ip nat detailed** command generates a description of each packet considered for translation. This command also outputs information about certain errors or exception conditions, such as the failure to allocate a global address.

Example 7-24 demonstrates some sample **debug ip nat** output.

Example 7-24   debug ip nat Command Output

```
R2# debug ip nat

IP NAT debugging is on
R2#
*Oct  6 19:55:31.579: NAT*: s=192.168.10.10->209.165.200.225, d=209.165.200.254
  [14434]
*Oct  6 19:55:31.595: NAT*: s=209.165.200.254, d=209.165.200.225->192.168.10.10
  [6334]
*Oct  6 19:55:31.611: NAT*: s=192.168.10.10->209.165.200.225, d=209.165.200.254
  [14435]
*Oct  6 19:55:31.619: NAT*: s=192.168.10.10->209.165.200.225, d=209.165.200.254
  [14436]
*Oct  6 19:55:31.627: NAT*: s=192.168.10.10->209.165.200.225, d=209.165.200.254
  [14437]
*Oct  6 19:55:31.631: NAT*: s=209.165.200.254, d=209.165.200.225->192.168.10.10
  [6335]
*Oct  6 19:55:31.643: NAT*: s=209.165.200.254, d=209.165.200.225->192.168.10.10
  [6336]
*Oct  6 19:55:31.647: NAT*: s=192.168.10.10->209.165.200.225, d=209.165.200.254
  [14438]
*Oct  6 19:55:31.651: NAT*: s=209.165.200.254, d=209.165.200.225->192.168.10.10
  [6337]
*Oct  6 19:55:31.655: NAT*: s=192.168.10.10->209.165.200.225, d=209.165.200.254
  [14439]
*Oct  6 19:55:31.659: NAT*: s=209.165.200.254, d=209.165.200.225->192.168.10.10
  [6338]

<Output omitted>
```

You can see that inside host 192.168.10.10 initiated traffic to outside host 209.165.200.254 and has been translated into address 209.165.200.225.

When decoding the debug output, note what the following symbols and values indicate:

- ***:** The asterisk next to NAT indicates that the translation is occurring in the fast-switched path. The first packet in a conversation is always process-switched, which is slower. The remaining packets go through the fast-switched path if a cache entry exists.

- **s=:** Refers to the source IP address.

- ***a.b.c.d->w.x.y.z*:** Indicates that source address a.b.c.d is translated into w.x.y.z.

- **d=:** Refers to the destination IP address.

- ***[xxxx]*:** The value in brackets is the IP identification number. This information may be useful for debugging because it enables correlation with other packet traces from protocol analyzers.

> **Note**
>
> You can view demonstrations of verifying and troubleshooting NAT.
>
> Flash Animation Case Study: Can Ping Host, But Cannot Telnet: This is a seven-minute flash animation on why a device can ping the host but cannot telnet: ***http://www.cisco.com/warp/public/556/index.swf***.
>
> Flash Animation Case Study: Cannot Ping Beyond NAT: This is a ten-minute flash animation on why a device cannot ping beyond NAT: ***http://www.cisco.com/warp/public/556/TS_NATcase2/index.swf***.

Scaling Networks with NAT

NAT translates nonroutable private, internal addresses into routable, public addresses. NAT has the added benefit of providing a degree of privacy and security to a network because it hides internal IP addresses from outside networks. In this activity, you configure dynamic and static NAT. Use File e4-728.pka on the CD-ROM that accompanies this book to perform this activity using Packet Tracer.

IPv6

To comprehend the IP addressing issues facing network administrators today, consider that the IPv4 address space provides approximately 4,294,967,296 unique addresses. Of these, only 3.7 billion addresses can be assigned, because the IPv4 addressing system separates the addresses into classes and reserves addresses for multicasting, testing, and other specific uses.

Based on figures as recent as January 2007, about 2.4 billion of the available IPv4 addresses are already assigned to end users or ISPs. That leaves roughly 1.3 billion addresses still available from the IPv4 address space. Despite this seemingly large number, the IPv4 address space is running out.

The next three figures highlight the rapid rate of IP address depletion. Figure 7-26 shows the blocks of allocated IP addresses in 1993.

Figure 7-26   Blocks Assigned 1993

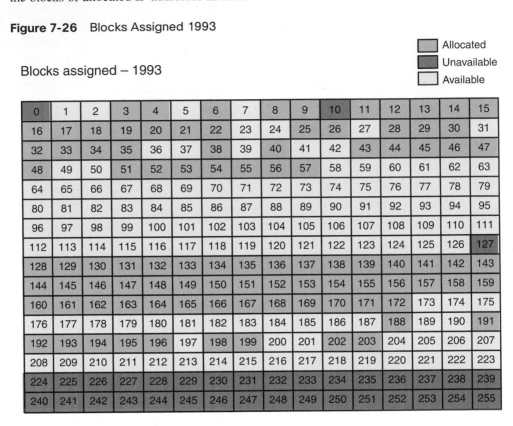

Figure 7-27 shows the blocks of allocated IP addresses in 2000.

Figure 7-27   Blocks Assigned 2000

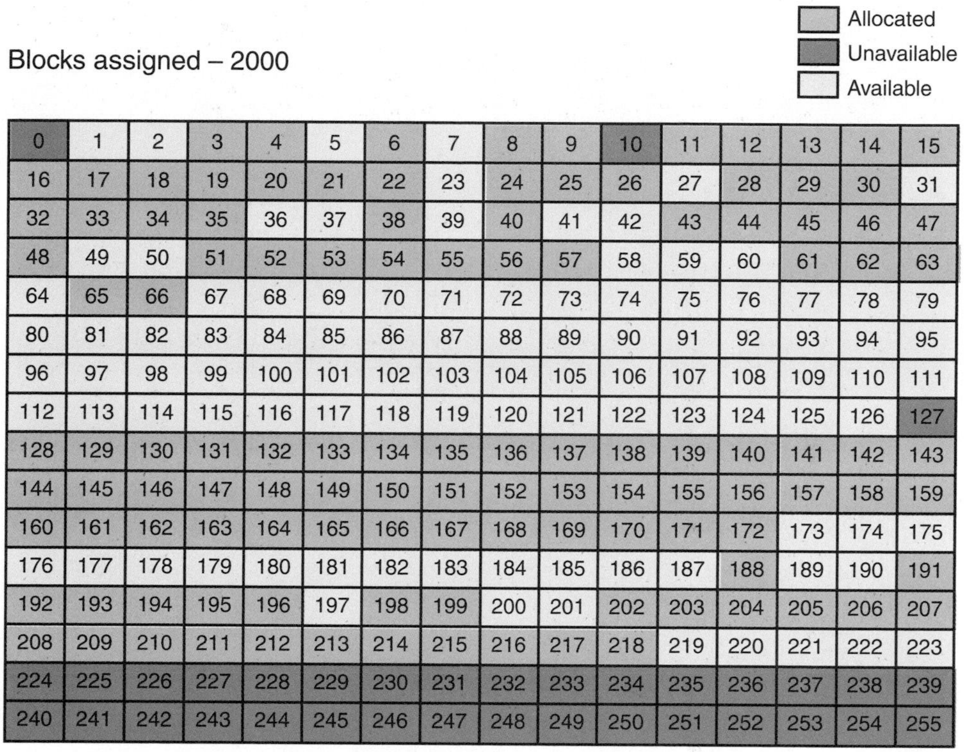

Blocks assigned – 2000

Allocated
Unavailable
Available

0	1	2	3	4	5	6	7	8	9	10	11	12	13	14	15
16	17	18	19	20	21	22	23	24	25	26	27	28	29	30	31
32	33	34	35	36	37	38	39	40	41	42	43	44	45	46	47
48	49	50	51	52	53	54	55	56	57	58	59	60	61	62	63
64	65	66	67	68	69	70	71	72	73	74	75	76	77	78	79
80	81	82	83	84	85	86	87	88	89	90	91	92	93	94	95
96	97	98	99	100	101	102	103	104	105	106	107	108	109	110	111
112	113	114	115	116	117	118	119	120	121	122	123	124	125	126	127
128	129	130	131	132	133	134	135	136	137	138	139	140	141	142	143
144	145	146	147	148	149	150	151	152	153	154	155	156	157	158	159
160	161	162	163	164	165	166	167	168	169	170	171	172	173	174	175
176	177	178	179	180	181	182	183	184	185	186	187	188	189	190	191
192	193	194	195	196	197	198	199	200	201	202	203	204	205	206	207
208	209	210	211	212	213	214	215	216	217	218	219	220	221	222	223
224	225	226	227	228	229	230	231	232	233	234	235	236	237	238	239
240	241	242	243	244	245	246	247	248	249	250	251	252	253	254	255

Figure 7-28 shows the blocks of allocated IP addresses in 2007.

Figure 7-28   Blocks Assigned 2007

Blocks assigned – 2007

| Allocated |
| Unavailable |
| Available |

0	1	2	3	4	5	6	7	8	9	10	11	12	13	14	15
16	17	18	19	20	21	22	23	24	25	26	27	28	29	30	31
32	33	34	35	36	37	38	39	40	41	42	43	44	45	46	47
48	49	50	51	52	53	54	55	56	57	58	59	60	61	62	63
64	65	66	67	68	69	70	71	72	73	74	75	76	77	78	79
80	81	82	83	84	85	86	87	88	89	90	91	92	93	94	95
96	97	98	99	100	101	102	103	104	105	106	107	108	109	110	111
112	113	114	115	116	117	118	119	120	121	122	123	124	125	126	127
128	129	130	131	132	133	134	135	136	137	138	139	140	141	142	143
144	145	146	147	148	149	150	151	152	153	154	155	156	157	158	159
160	161	162	163	164	165	166	167	168	169	170	171	172	173	174	175
176	177	178	179	180	181	182	183	184	185	186	187	188	189	190	191
192	193	194	195	196	197	198	199	200	201	202	203	204	205	206	207
208	209	210	211	212	213	214	215	216	217	218	219	220	221	222	223
224	225	226	227	228	229	230	231	232	233	234	235	236	237	238	239
240	241	242	243	244	245	246	247	248	249	250	251	252	253	254	255

Figure 7-29 provides an alternative view of IP address depletion.

Figure 7-29   Shrinking IP Address Space

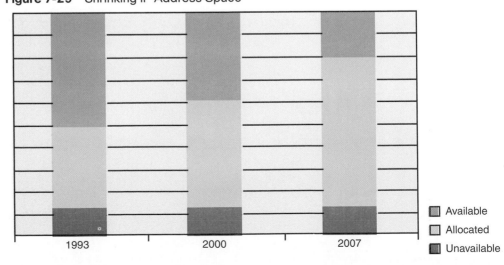

1993   2000   2007

| Available |
| Allocated |
| Unavailable |

Over the past decade, the Internet community has analyzed IPv4 address exhaustion and published mountains of reports. Some reports predict IPv4 address exhaustion by 2010, and others say it will not happen until 2013.

The growth of the Internet, matched by increasing computing power, has extended the reach of IP-based applications.

The pool of numbers is shrinking for the following reasons:

- **Population growth**: The Internet population is growing. In November 2005, Cisco estimated that there were approximately 973 million users. This number has doubled since then. In addition, users stay on longer, reserving IP addresses for longer periods, and are contacting more and more peers daily.

- **Mobile users**: Industry has delivered more than one billion mobile phones. More than 20 million IP-enabled mobile devices, including personal digital assistants (PDA), pen tablets, notepads, and barcode readers, have been delivered. More and more IP-enabled mobile devices are coming online every day. Old mobile phones did not need IP addresses, but new ones do.

- **Transportation**: There will be more than one billion automobiles by 2008. Newer models are IP-enabled to allow remote monitoring to provide timely maintenance and support. Lufthansa already provides Internet connectivity on its flights. More carriers, including ships at sea, will provide similar services.

- **Consumer electronics**: The newest home appliances allow remote monitoring using IP technology. Digital video recorders (DVR) that download and update program guides from the Internet are an example. Home networking can connect these appliances.

Reasons for Using IPv6

Movement to change from IPv4 to IPv6 has already begun, particularly in Europe, Japan, and the Asia-Pacific region. These areas are exhausting their allotted IPv4 addresses, which makes IPv6 all the more attractive and necessary. Japan officially started the move in 2000 when the Japanese government mandated the incorporation of IPv6 and set a deadline of 2005 to upgrade existing systems in every business and public sector. Korea, China, and Malaysia have launched similar initiatives.

In 2002, the European Community IPv6 Task Force forged a strategic alliance to foster IPv6 adoption worldwide. The North American IPv6 Task Force has set out to engage the North American markets to adopt IPv6. The first significant North American advances are coming from the U.S. Department of Defense (DoD). Looking into the future and knowing the advantages of IP-enabled devices, the DoD mandated, as early as 2003, that all new equipment purchased must not only be IP-enabled, but also must be IPv6-capable. In fact, all U.S. government agencies must start using IPv6 across their core networks by 2008, and the agencies are working to meet that deadline.

The ability to scale networks for future demands requires a limitless supply of IP addresses and improved mobility that DHCP and NAT alone cannot meet. IPv6 satisfies the increasingly complex requirements of hierarchical addressing that IPv4 does not provide.

Given the huge installed base of IPv4 in the world, it is not difficult to appreciate that transitioning to IPv6 from IPv4 deployments is a challenge. However, a variety of techniques, including an autoconfiguration option, make the transition easier. Which transition mechanism you use depends on your network's needs.

Table 7-10 compares the binary and alphanumeric representations of IPv4 and IPv6 addresses.

Table 7-10   IPv4/IPv6 Address Comparison

	IPv4 (4 octets)	IPv6 (16 octets)
Binary Representation	11000000.10101000. 00001010.01100101	10100101.00100100. 01110010.11010011. 00101100.10000000 11011101.00000010 00000000.00101001 11101100.01111010 \00000000.00101011 11101010.01110011
Alphanumeric Representation	192.168.10.101	A524:72D3:2C80:DD02: 0029:EC7A:002B:EA73
Total IP Addresses	4,294,467,295 or 2^{32}	$3.4 * 10^{38}$

An IPv6 address is a 128-bit binary value, which can be displayed as 32 hexadecimal digits. IPv6 should provide sufficient addresses for future Internet growth needs for many years to come.

To put the IPv6 address space into perspective, consider the following:

- There are enough IPv6 addresses to allocate more than the entire IPv4 Internet address space to everyone on the planet.

- There are so many IPv6 addresses available that many trillions of addresses could be assigned to every human being on the planet.

- There are approximately 665,570,793,348,866,943,898,599 addresses per square meter of the surface of the Earth!

So what happened to IPv5? IPv5 was used to define an experimental real-time streaming protocol. To avoid confusion, it was decided not to use IPv5 and to name the new IP protocol IPv6.

IPv6 would not exist were it not for the recognized depletion of available IPv4 addresses. However, beyond the increased IP address space, the development of IPv6 has presented opportunities to apply lessons learned from the limitations of IPv4 to create a protocol with new and improved features.

A simplified header architecture and protocol operation translates into reduced operational expenses. Built-in security features mean easier security practices that are sorely lacking in many current networks. However, perhaps the most significant improvement offered by IPv6 is its address autoconfiguration features.

The Internet is rapidly evolving from a collection of stationary devices to a fluid network of mobile devices. IPv6 allows mobile devices to quickly acquire and transition between addresses as they move among foreign networks, with no need for a foreign agent. (A foreign agent is a router that can function as the point of attachment for a mobile device when it roams from its home network to a foreign network.)

Address autoconfiguration also means more robust plug-and-play network connectivity. Autoconfiguration supports consumers who can have any combination of computers, printers, digital cameras, digital radios, IP phones, Internet-enabled household appliances, and robotic toys connected to their home networks. Many manufacturers already integrate IPv6 into their products.

Many of the enhancements that IPv6 offers are explained in this section:

- Enhanced IP addressing

- Simplified header

- Enhanced mobility and security

- Transition richness

Enhanced IP Addressing

A larger address space offers several enhancements:

- Improved global reachability and flexibility.

- Better aggregation of IP prefixes announced in routing tables.

- No broadcasts and thus no potential threat of broadcast storms.

- Multihomed hosts. Multihoming is a technique to increase the reliability of the Internet connection of an IP network. With IPv6, a host can have multiple IP addresses over one physical upstream link. For example, a host can connect to several ISPs.

- Autoconfiguration that can include data link layer addresses in the address space.

- More plug-and-play options for more devices.

- Public-to-private, end-to-end readdressing without address translation. This makes peer-to-peer (P2P) networking more functional and easier to deploy.

- Simplified mechanisms for address renumbering and modification.

Simplified Header

Figure 7-30 compares the simplified IPv6 header structure to the IPv4 header. The IPv4 header has 20 octets and 12 basic header fields, followed by an Options field and a data portion (usually the transport layer segment). The IPv6 header has 40 octets, three IPv4 basic header fields, and five additional header fields.

Figure 7-30   IPv4 Versus IPv6 Header Structure

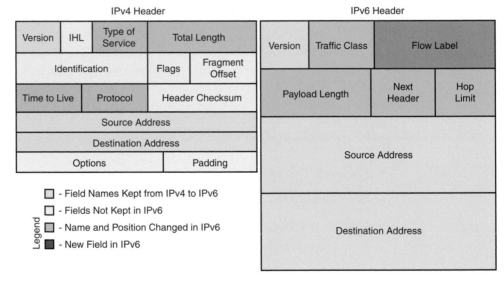

The IPv6 simplified header offers several advantages over IPv4:

- Better routing efficiency for performance and forwarding-rate scalability

- No requirement for processing checksums

- Simplified and more efficient extension header mechanisms

- Flow labels for per-flow processing, with no need to open the transport inner packet to identify the various traffic flows

Enhanced Mobility and Security

Mobility and security help ensure compliance with mobile IP and *IP Security (IPsec)* standards functionality. Mobility enables people with mobile network devices—many with wireless connectivity—to move around in networks.

The IETF Mobile IP standard is available for both IPv4 and IPv6. The standard enables mobile devices to move without breaks in established network connections. Mobile devices use a home address and a care-of address to achieve this mobility. With IPv4, these addresses are manually configured. With IPv6, the configurations are dynamic, giving IPv6-enabled devices built-in mobility.

IPsec is available for IPv4 and is automatically implemented in IPv6. The fact that IPsec is mandatory makes IPv6 more secure.

Transition Richness

IPv4 will not disappear overnight. Rather, it will coexist with and then gradually be replaced by IPv6. For this reason, IPv6 was delivered with migration techniques to cover every conceivable IPv4 upgrade case. However, many were ultimately rejected by the technology community.

Currently, there are three main approaches:

- Dual stack

- 6to4 tunneling

- NAT-PT, ISATAP tunneling, and Teredo tunneling (last-resort methods)

Some of these approaches are discussed in more detail later in this chapter.

The current advice for transitioning to IPv6 is "Dual stack where you can; tunnel where you must!"

IPv6 Addressing

You know the 32-bit IPv4 address as a series of four 8-bit fields, separated by dots. However, larger 128-bit IPv6 addresses need a different representation because of their size.

IPv6 addresses use entries of 16-bit hexadecimal values separated by colons—for example, *x:x:x:x:x:x:x:x*, where *x* is a 16-bit hexadecimal field. IPv6 addresses are not case-sensitive for the hexadecimal A, B, C, D, E, and F values.

IPv4 addresses have a fixed address notation. For example, an IPv4 address cannot be abbreviated. However, an IPv6 address does not require explicit address string notation. It can be abbreviated, but there are rules.

To help explain these IPv6 representation rules, consider the IPv6 address 2031:0000:130F:0000:0000:09C0:876A:130B, shown in Figure 7-31:

- Leading 0s in a field are optional. For example, the 0000 fields equal 0, and the 09C0 field equals 9C0.

- Successive fields of 0s can be represented as two colons (::). However, this shorthand method can be used only once in an address.

Figure 7-31   IPv6 Address Representation

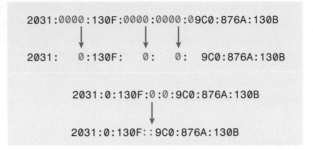

Using the :: notation greatly reduces the size of most addresses.

When an address is read or manipulated, an address parser is responsible for identifying the missing 0s and adding them in until the 128 bits are complete.

Here are some additional examples:

- FF01:0:0:0:0:0:0:1 becomes FF01::1.

- 0:0:0:0:0:0:0:1 becomes ::1.

- 0:0:0:0:0:0:0:0 becomes ::.

- FF01:0000: 0000: 0000: 0000: 0000: 0000:1 becomes FF01:0:0:0:0:0:0:1 becomes FF01::1.

- E3D7:0000:0000:0000:51F4:00C8:C0A8:6420 becomes E3D7::51F4:C8:C0A8:6420.

- 3FFE:0501:0008:0000:0260:97FF:FE40:EFAB becomes 3FFE:0501:8:0:260:97FF:FE40:EFAB becomes 3FFE:501:8::260:97FF:FE40:EFAB.

Note

An unspecified address is written as :: because it contains only 0s.

IPv6 Global Unicast Address

IPv6 has an address format that enables aggregation upward eventually to the ISP. An *IPv6 global unicast address* consists of a 48-bit *global routing prefix* and a 16-bit *subnet ID*, as shown in Figure 7-32.

Figure 7-32   Global Unicast Address

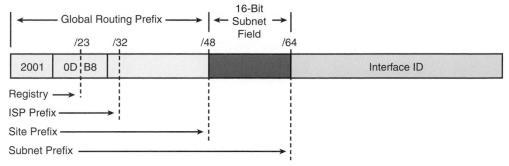

Individual organizations can use a 16-bit subnet field to create their own local addressing hierarchy. This field allows an organization to use up to 65,535 individual subnets.

Notice in Figure 7-32 that the 48-bit global routing prefix can also be used to provide additional hierarchy with the registry prefix, ISP prefix, and site prefix.

> **Note**
>
> When reading about IPv6, you may encounter terms such as top-level aggregator (TLA), next-level aggregator (NLA), and subnet local aggregator (SLA). These terms are historical and have been replaced by the IPv6 Global Unicast Address 48-bit global routing prefix and a 16-bit subnet ID. The new structure is documented in RFC 3587.

The current global unicast address that is assigned by the *IANA* uses the range of addresses that start with binary value 001 (2000::/3), which is one-eighth of the total IPv6 address space and is the largest block of assigned addresses. The IANA is allocating the IPv6 address space in the ranges of 2001::/16 to the five RIR registries (ARIN, RIPE, APNIC, LACNIC, and AfriNIC). Bars A, B, and C in Figure 7-33 reflect this address allocation.

Figure 7-33   IPv6 Address Allocation

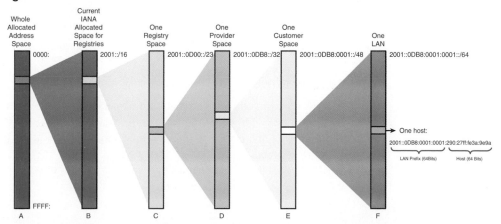

Bars D, E, and F provide a sample hierarchy from a customer's perspective.

For more information, refer to RFC 3587, *IPv6 Global Unicast Address Format*, which replaces RFC 2374.

Reserved Addresses

The IETF reserves a portion of the IPv6 address space for various uses, both present and future. Reserved addresses represent 1/256th of the total IPv6 address space. Some of the other types of IPv6 addresses come from this block.

Private Addresses

A block of IPv6 addresses is set aside for private addresses, just as is done in IPv4. These private addresses are local only to a particular link or site and therefore are never routed outside a particular company network. Private addresses have a first-octet value of FE in hexadecimal notation, with the next hexadecimal digit being a value from 8 to F.

These addresses are further divided into two types, based on their scope:

- **Site-local addresses** are similar to RFC 1918, *Address Allocation for Private Internets*, in IPv4 today. The scope of these addresses is an entire site or organization. However, the use of site-local addresses is problematic and is being deprecated as of 2003 by RFC 3879. In hexadecimal, site-local addresses begin with FE and then C to F for the third hexadecimal digit. So, these addresses begin with FEC, FED, FEE, or FEF.

- **Link-local addresses** are new to the concept of addressing with IP in the network layer. These addresses have a smaller scope than site-local addresses; they refer to only a particular physical link (physical network). Routers do not forward datagrams using link-local addresses, not even within the organization; they are only for local communication on a particular physical network segment. They are used for link communications such as automatic address configuration, neighbor discovery, and router discovery. Many IPv6 routing protocols also use link-local addresses. Link-local addresses begin with FE and then have a value from 8 to B for the third hexadecimal digit. So, these addresses start with FE8, FE9, FEA, or FEB.

Loopback Address

Just as in IPv4, a provision has been made for a special loopback IPv6 address for testing; datagrams sent to this address "loop back" to the sending device. However, IPv6 has just one address, not a whole block, for this function. The loopback address is 0:0:0:0:0:0:0:1, which normally is expressed using zero compression as ::1.

Unspecified Address

In IPv4, an IP address of all 0s has a special meaning: it refers to the host itself, and it is used when a device does not know its own address. In IPv6, this concept has been formalized, and the all-0s address (0:0:0:0:0:0:0:0) is called the "unspecified" address. It typically is used in the source field of a datagram that is sent by a device that seeks to have its IP address configured. You can apply address compression to this address; because the address is all 0s, it becomes just ::.

IPv6 Address Management

IPv6 addresses use interface identifiers to identify interfaces on a link. Think of them as the host portion of an IPv6 address. Interface identifiers are required to be unique on a specific link. Interface identifiers are always 64 bits and can be dynamically derived from a Layer 2 address (MAC).

You can assign an IPv6 address ID statically or dynamically. Static assignment can be accomplished by using

- Manual interface ID
- An *EUI-64* interface ID

Dynamic assignment can be accomplished by using

- *Stateless autoconfiguration*
- *DHCP for IPv6 (DHCPv6)*

Manual Interface ID Assignment

One way to statically assign an IPv6 address to a device is to manually assign both the prefix (network) and interface ID (host) portion of the IPv6 address.

To configure an IPv6 address on a Cisco router interface, use the **ipv6 address** *ipv6-address/prefix-length* command in interface configuration mode, as demonstrated in Example 7-25.

Example 7-25   ipv6 address Command

```
R2(config)# interface FastEthernet 0/0
R2(config-if)# ipv6 address 2001:DB8:2222:7272::72/64
R2(config-if)#
```

EUI-64 Interface ID Assignment

Another way to assign an IPv6 address is to configure the prefix (network) portion of the IPv6 address and interface ID. To derive the interface ID (host) portion, the Layer 2 MAC address of the device is used to create an EUI-64 interface ID.

The EUI-64 standard explains how to stretch IEEE 802 MAC addresses from 48 to 64 bits by separating the 48-bit MAC address into two 24-bit sections, as shown in Figure 7-34.

Figure 7-34 EUI-64 Interface ID

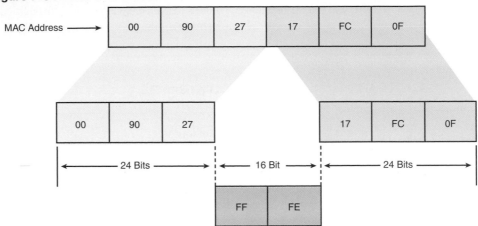

The 16-bit 0xFFFE value is inserted in the middle of the MAC address to create a 64-bit unique interface identifier.

To configure an IPv6 address on a Cisco router interface and enable IPv6 processing using EUI-64 on that interface, use the **ipv6 address** *ipv6-prefix/prefix-length* **eui-64** command in interface configuration mode.

Example 7-26 shows the assignment of an EUI-64 address to the interface of a Cisco router.

Example 7-26 Assigning an EUI-64 Address to a Router Interface

```
R2(config)# interface FastEthernet 0/0
R2(config-if)# ipv6 address 2001:DB8:2222:7272::72/64 eui-64
R2(config-if)#
```

Stateless Autoconfiguration

Stateless autoconfiguration automatically configures the IPv6 address. In IPv6, it is assumed that non-PC devices, as well as computer terminals, will be connected to the network. The autoconfiguration mechanism was introduced to enable plug-and-play networking of these devices to help reduce administrative overhead.

DHCPv6 (Stateful)

DHCPv6 enables DHCP servers to pass configuration parameters, such as IPv6 network addresses, to IPv6 nodes. It offers the capability of automatic allocation of reusable network addresses and additional configuration flexibility. This protocol is a stateful counterpart to

IPv6 stateless address autoconfiguration (RFC 2462). It can be used separately or concurrently with IPv6 stateless address autoconfiguration to obtain configuration parameters.

Note

For more information on IPv6 address assignment, visit
http://www.netbsd.org/docs/network/ipv6/.

IPv6 Transition Strategies

The transition from IPv4 does not require upgrades on all nodes at the same time. Many transition mechanisms enable smooth integration of IPv4 and IPv6. Other mechanisms that allow IPv4 nodes to communicate with IPv6 nodes are available. Different situations demand different strategies.

Different transition mechanisms include

- Dual stack

- Manual tunnel

- 6to4 tunnel

- ISATAP tunnel

- Teredo tunnel

- Proxying and translation (NAT-PT)

Recall the advice "Dual stack where you can; tunnel where you must." These two methods are the most common techniques to transition from IPv4 to IPv6.

Dual Stacking

Dual stacking is an integration method in which a node has implementation and connectivity to both an IPv4 and IPv6 network. This is the recommended option and involves running IPv4 and IPv6 at the same time. Routers and switches are configured to support both protocols, with IPv6 being the preferred protocol.

Tunneling

The second major transition technique is tunneling. Several tunneling techniques are available:

- Manual IPv6-over-IPv4 tunneling: An IPv6 packet is encapsulated within the IPv4 protocol. This method requires dual-stack routers.

- *Dynamic 6to4 tunneling*: Automatically establishes the connection of IPv6 islands through an IPv4 network, typically the Internet. It dynamically applies a valid, unique IPv6 prefix to each IPv6 island, which enables the fast deployment of IPv6 in a corporate network without address retrieval from the ISPs or registries.

Other, less popular tunneling techniques that are beyond the scope of this course include the following:

- **Intrasite Automatic Tunnel Addressing Protocol (ISATAP) tunneling**: An automatic overlay tunneling mechanism that uses the underlying IPv4 network as a link layer for IPv6. ISATAP tunnels allow individual IPv4 or IPv6 dual-stack hosts within a site to communicate with other such hosts on a virtual link, creating an IPv6 network using the IPv4 infrastructure.

- **Teredo tunneling**: An IPv6 transition technology that provides host-to-host automatic tunneling instead of gateway tunneling. This approach passes unicast IPv6 traffic when dual-stacked hosts (hosts that are running both IPv6 and IPv4) are located behind one or multiple IPv4 NATs.

NAT-Protocol Translation (NAT-PT)

Cisco IOS Software Release 12.3(2)T and later (with the appropriate feature set) also include NAT-PT between IPv6 and IPv4. This translation allows direct communication between hosts that use different versions of the IP protocol. These translations are more complex than IPv4 NAT. At this time, this translation technique is the least favorable option and should be used as a last resort.

Cisco IOS Dual Stack

Dual stacking is an integration method that allows a node to have connectivity to an IPv4 and IPv6 network simultaneously. Each node has two protocol stacks with the configuration on the same interface or on multiple interfaces, as shown in Figure 7-35.

Figure 7-35   Cisco IOS Dual Stack

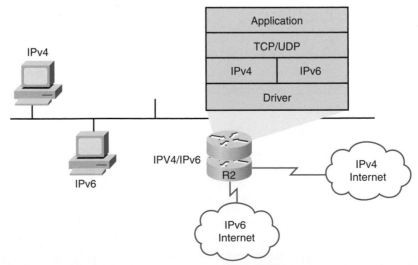

The dual-stack approach to IPv6 integration, in which nodes have both IPv4 and IPv6 stacks, will be one of the most commonly used integration methods. A dual-stack node chooses which stack to use based on the packet's destination address. A dual-stack node should prefer IPv6 when it is available. Old IPv4-only applications continue to work as before. New and modified applications take advantage of both IP layers.

A new application programming interface (API) has been defined to support IPv4 and IPv6 addresses and DNS requests. An API facilitates the exchange of messages or data between two or more different software applications. An example of an API is the virtual interface between two software functions, such as a word processor and a spreadsheet. The API is built into software applications to translate IPv4 into IPv6, and vice versa, using the IP conversion mechanism. New applications can use both IPv4 and IPv6.

Experience in porting IPv4 applications to IPv6 suggests that most applications will see a minimal change in some localized places in the source code. This technique is well known and has been applied in the past for other protocol transitions. It enables gradual application upgrades, one by one, to IPv6.

Figure 7-36 shows a dual-stacked router.

Figure 7-36   Dual-Stacked Router

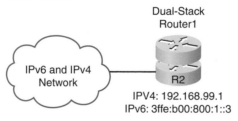

When both IPv4 and IPv6 are configured on an interface, the interface is considered dual-stacked.

Cisco IOS Software Release 12.2(2)T and later (with the appropriate feature set) are IPv6-ready. As soon as you configure basic IPv4 and IPv6 on the interface, the interface is dual-stacked and forwards IPv4 and IPv6 traffic.

Using IPv6 on a Cisco IOS router requires that you use the **ipv6 unicast-routing** global configuration command. This command enables the forwarding of IPv6 datagrams.

All interfaces that forward IPv6 traffic must be configured with an IPv6 address using the **ipv6 address** *IPv6-address* [*/prefix length*] interface command.

Example 7-27 configures an IPv4 and IPv4 address on the router shown in Figure 7-36.

Example 7-27   Dual-Stack Configuration

```
R2(config)# ipv6 unicast-routing
R2(config)# interface FastEthernet 0/0
R2(config-if)# ip address 192.168.99.1 255.255.255.0
R2(config-if)# ipv6 address 3ffe:b00:800:1::3
R2(config-if)#
```

IPv6 Tunneling

Tunneling, as illustrated in Figure 7-37, is an integration method in which an IPv6 packet is encapsulated within another protocol, such as IPv4. This method enables the connection of IPv6 islands without needing to convert the intermediary networks to IPv6. When IPv4 is used to encapsulate the IPv6 packet, a protocol type of 41 is specified in the IPv4 header, and the packet includes a 20-byte IPv4 header with no options and an IPv6 header and payload.

Figure 7-37   IPv6 Tunneling

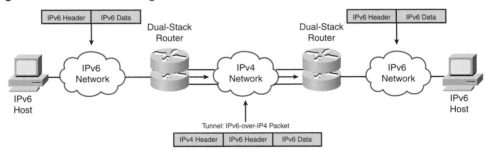

Note

Tunneling also requires dual-stack routers.

Tunneling introduces two issues. The maximum transmission unit (MTU) is effectively decreased by 20 octets if the IPv4 header does not contain any optional fields. In addition, a tunneled network is often difficult to troubleshoot.

Note

Tunneling is an intermediate integration and transition technique and should not be considered a final solution. A native IPv6 architecture should be the ultimate goal.

Manually Configured IPv6 Tunnel

A manually configured tunnel is equivalent to a permanent link between two IPv6 domains over an IPv4 backbone. The primary use is for stable connections that require regular secure communication between two edge routers or between an end system and an edge router, or for connections to remote IPv6 networks. The end routers must be dual-stacked, and the configuration cannot change dynamically as network and routing needs change.

Administrators manually configure a static IPv6 address on a tunnel interface and assign manually configured static IPv4 addresses to the tunnel source and destination. The host or router at each end of a configured tunnel must support both the IPv4 and IPv6 protocol stacks. Manually configured tunnels can be configured between border routers or between a border router and a host. Configured tunnels require dual-stack endpoints and IPv4 and IPv6 addresses configured at each end, as illustrated in Figure 7-38.

Figure 7-38   Manually Configured IPv6 Tunnel

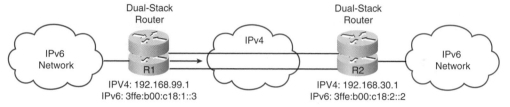

Routing Configurations with IPv6

Like IPv4 *classless interdomain routing (CIDR)*, IPv6 uses longest prefix match routing. IPv6 uses modified versions of most of the common routing protocols to handle longer IPv6 addresses and different header structures.

Larger address spaces make room for large address allocations to ISPs and organizations. An ISP aggregates all the prefixes of its customers into a single prefix and announces the single prefix to the IPv6 Internet. The increased address space is sufficient to allow organizations to define a single prefix for their entire network.

But how does this affect router performance? A brief review of how a router functions in a network helps illustrate how IPv6 affects routing. Conceptually, a router has three functional areas:

- The *control plane* handles the interaction of the router with the other network elements, providing the information needed to make decisions and control the overall router operation. This plane runs processes such as routing protocols and network management. These functions generally are complex.

- The *data plane* handles packet forwarding from one physical or logical interface to another. It involves different switching mechanisms, such as process switching and Cisco Express Forwarding (CEF) on Cisco IOS software routers.

- Enhanced services include advanced features applied when forwarding data, such as packet filtering, quality of service (QoS), encryption, translation, and accounting.

IPv6 presents each of these functions with specific new challenges, as illustrated in Figure 7-39.

Figure 7-39   IPv6 Routing Considerations

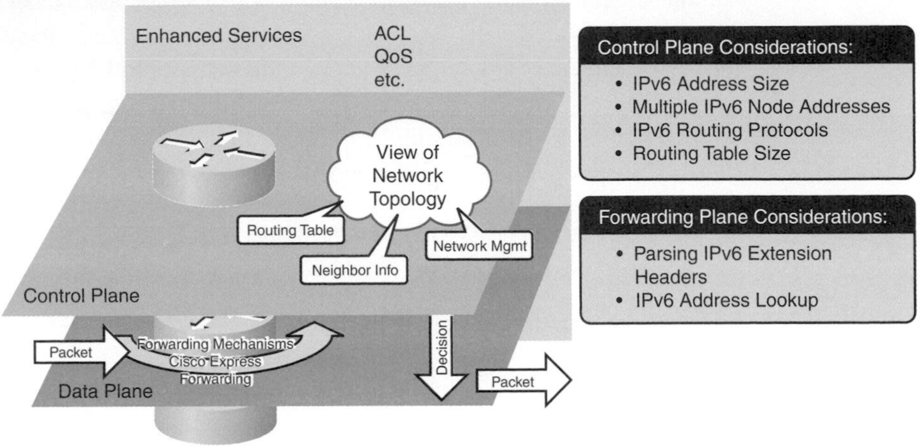

IPv6 Control Plane

Enabling IPv6 on a router starts its control plane operating processes specifically for IPv6. Protocol characteristics shape the performance of these processes and the number of resources necessary to operate them:

- **IPv6 address size**: Address size affects a router's information-processing functions. Systems using a 64-bit CPU, bus, or memory structure can pass both the IPv4 source and destination address in a single processing cycle. For IPv6, the source and destination addresses require two cycles each—four cycles to process source and destination address information. As a result, routers relying exclusively on software processing are likely to perform slower than when in an IPv4 environment.

- **Multiple IPv6 node addresses**: Because IPv6 nodes can use several IPv6 unicast addresses, memory consumption of the Neighbor Discovery cache may be affected.

- **IPv6 routing protocols**: IPv6 routing protocols are similar to their IPv4 counterparts, but because an IPv6 prefix is four times larger than an IPv4 prefix, routing updates have to carry more information.

- **Routing table size**: Increased IPv6 address space leads to larger networks and a much larger Internet. This implies larger routing tables and greater memory requirements to support them.

IPv6 Data Plane

The data plane forwards IP packets based on the decisions made by the control plane. The forwarding engine parses the relevant IP packet information and does a lookup to match the parsed information against the forwarding policies defined by the control plane. IPv6 affects the performance of parsing and lookup functions:

- **Parsing IPv6 extension headers**: Applications, including mobile IPv6, often use IPv6 address information in extension headers, thus increasing their size. These additional fields require additional processing. For example, a router using ACLs to filter Layer 4 information needs to apply the ACLs to packets with extension headers as well as those without. If the length of the extension header exceeds the fixed length of the router's hardware register, hardware switching fails, and packets may be punted to software switching or dropped. This severely affects the router's forwarding performance.

- **IPv6 address lookup**: IPv6 performs a lookup on packets entering the router to find the correct output interface. In IPv4, the forwarding decision process parses a 32-bit destination address. In IPv6, the forwarding decision could conceivably require parsing a 128-bit address. Most routers today perform lookups using an *application-specific integrated circuit (ASIC)* with a fixed configuration that performs the functions for which it was originally designed—IPv4. Again, this could result in punting packets into slower software processing or dropping them altogether.

RIPng Routing Protocol

IPv6 routes use the same protocols and techniques as IPv4. Although the addresses are longer, the protocols used in routing IPv6 are simply logical extensions of the protocols used in IPv4.

RFC 2080 defines *Routing Information Protocol next-generation (RIPng)* as a simple routing protocol based on RIP. RIPng is no more or less powerful than RIP. However, it provides a simple way to configure an IPv6 network without having to build a new routing protocol.

RIPng is a distance vector routing protocol with a limit of 15 hops that uses split horizon and poison reverse updates to prevent routing loops. Its simplicity comes from the fact that it does not require any global knowledge of the network. Only neighboring routers exchange local messages.

RIPng incorporates the following features:

- It's based on IPv4 RIP version 2 (RIPv2) and is similar to RIPv2.

- It uses IPv6 for transport.

- It includes the IPv6 prefix and next-hop IPv6 address.

- It uses the multicast group FF02::9 as the destination address for RIP updates. (This is similar to the multicast function performed by RIPv2 in IPv4.)

- It sends updates on UDP port 521.

- It's supported by Cisco IOS Software Release 12.2(2)T and later.

In dual-stacked deployments, both RIP and RIPng are required.

Configuring IPv6 Addresses

Two basic steps activate IPv6 on a router. First, you must activate IPv6 traffic forwarding on the router, and then you must configure each interface that requires IPv6.

Enabling IPv6 on Cisco Routers

By default, IPv6 traffic forwarding is disabled on a Cisco router. To activate it between interfaces, you must configure the **ipv6 unicast-routing** global configuration command.

The **ipv6 address** command can configure a global IPv6 address. The link-local address is automatically configured when an address is assigned to the interface. You must specify the entire 128-bit IPv6 address or specify the use of the 64-bit prefix by using the **eui-64** option.

Table 7-11 summarizes these two commands.

Table 7-11   Enabling IPv6 on Cisco Routers

Command	Description
RouterX(config)# **ipv6 unicast-routing**	Enables IPv6 traffic forwarding.
RouterX(config-if)# **ipv6 address** *ipv6prefix/prefix-length* **eui-64**	Configures the interface IPv6 addresses.

IPv6 Address Configuration Example

You can completely specify the IPv6 address or compute the host identifier (the rightmost 64 bits) from the interface's EUI-64 identifier.

In Example 7-28, router R2 is configured to provide IPv6 services on interface FastEthernet 0/0 using the IPv6 address EUI-64 format.

Example 7-28   IPv6 Address Configuration Example

```
R2(config)# ipv6 unicast-routing
R2(config)# interface FastEthernet 0/0
R2(config-if)# ipv6 add 2001:db8:c18:1::/64 eui-64
R2(config-if)# no shut
R2(config-if)#
*Dec 18 11:34:30.519: %LINK-3-UPDOWN: Interface FastEthernet0/0, changed state to
  up
*Dec 18 11:34:31.519: %LINEPROTO-5-UPDOWN: Line protocol on Interface FastEthernet0/0,
  changed state to up
R2(config-if)# end
R2#
```

To verify the configuration, refer to Example 7-29.

Example 7-29   Verifying the IPv6 Address Configuration

```
R2# show interface fastethernet 0/0

FastEthernet0/0 is up, line protocol is up
  Hardware is MV96340 Ethernet, address is 000a.b802.d000 (bia 000a.b802.d000)
  MTU 1500 bytes, BW 100000 Kbit, DLY 100 usec,
     reliability 255/255, txload 1/255, rxload 1/255
  Encapsulation ARPA, loopback not set
  Keepalive set (10 sec)
<Output omitted>


R2# show ipv6 interface fastEthernet 0/0

FastEthernet0/0 is up, line protocol is up
  IPv6 is enabled, link-local address is FE80::20A:B8FF:FE02:D000
  No Virtual link-local address(es):
  Global unicast address(es):
    2001:DB8:C18:1:20A:B8FF:FE02:D000, subnet is 2001:DB8:C18:1::/64 [EUI]
  Joined group address(es):
    FF02::1
    FF02::2
    FF02::1:FF02:D000
  MTU is 1500 bytes
<Output omitted>
```

The **show interface** command displays the MAC address of the Fast Ethernet 0/0 interface. The **show ipv6 interface** command verifies that the EUI-64 format has been applied. Configuring an IPv6 address on an interface automatically configures its link-local address.

Notice that the 16-bit FFFE value has been inserted into the MAC address. Although the MAC address begins with hexadecimal **000a.b8**, the new IPv6 address EUI-64 portion begins with **20A:B8**. This is because of a special bit in the IPv6 address called the universal/local (U/L) bit. The change is required to indicate that this IPv6 address has been created by the EUI-64 method and is not manually configured.

Note

The universal/local bit is beyond the scope of this course but is covered in the *CCNP Building Scalable Internetworks* course.

Alternatively, you can specify the entire IPv6 address manually when applying it to a router interface using the **ipv6 address** *ipv6-address*/*prefix-length* command in interface configuration mode.

Cisco IOS IPv6 Name Resolution

As with IPv4, there are two ways to perform name resolution from the Cisco IOS software process, as described in Table 7-12.

Table 7-12   Cisco IOS IPv6 Name Resolution

Command	Example	Description
RouterX(config)# **ipv6 host** *name* [*port*] *ipv6-address1* [*ipv6-address2...ipv6-address4*]	R2(config)# **ipv6 host R1 3ffe:b00:ffff:b::1**	Defines a static name for IPv6 addresses. You can define up to four IPv6 addresses for one hostname. The *port* option refers to the Telnet port to be used for the associated host.
RouterX(config)# **ip name-server address**	R2(config)# **ip name-server 3ffe:b00:ffff: 1::10**	Specifies the DNS server(s) used by the router. The address can be an IPv4 or IPv6 address. You can specify up to six DNS servers with this command.

Configuring RIPng with IPv6

When configuring supported routing protocols in IPv6, you must create the routing process, enable the routing process on interfaces, and customize the routing protocol for your particular network.

Before configuring the router to run IPv6 RIP, globally enable IPv6 using the **ipv6 unicast-routing** global configuration command, and enable IPv6 on any interfaces on which IPv6 RIP is to be enabled.

To enable RIPng routing on the router, use the **ipv6 router rip** *name* global configuration command. The *name* parameter identifies the RIP process. This process name is used later when configuring RIPng on participating interfaces.

For RIPng, instead of using the **network** command to identify which interfaces should run RIPng, you use the command **ipv6 rip** *name* **enable** in interface configuration mode to enable RIPng on an interface. The *name* parameter must match the *name* parameter in the **ipv6 router rip** command.

Enabling RIP on an interface dynamically creates a "router RIP" process if necessary.

Table 7-13 summarizes these two commands.

Table 7-13   Cisco RIPng for IPv6

Command	Description
RouterX(config)# **ipv6 router rip** *name*	Creates and enters RIP router configuration mode.
RouterX(config-if)# **ipv6 rip** *name* **enable**	Configures RIP on an interface.

Example: RIPng for IPv6 Configuration

Refer to the sample topology shown in Figure 7-40.

Figure 7-40   Sample IPv6 Topology

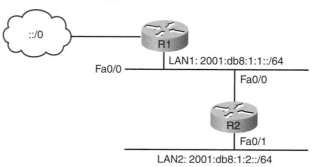

Figure 7-40 shows a network of two routers. Router R1 is connected to the ISP network. Example 7-30 shows the configurations for routers R1 and R2.

Example 7-30   Routers R1 and R2 IPv6 Configuration

```
R1(config)# ipv6 unicast-routing
R1(config)# ipv6 router rip RT0
R1(config)# interface FastEthernet 0/0
R1(config-if)# ipv6 address 2001:db8:1:1:;/64 eui-64
R1(config-if)# ipv6 rip RT0 enable
R1(config-if)#

R2(config)# ipv6 unicast-routing
R2(config)# ipv6 router rip RT0
R2(config)# interface FastEthernet 0/0
R2(config-if)# ipv6 address 2001:db8:1:1::/64 eui-64
R2(config-if)# ipv6 rip RT0 enable
R2(config-if)# interface FastEthernet 0/1
R2(config-if)# ipv6 address 2001:db8:1:2::/64 eui-64
R2(config-if)# ipv6 rip RT0 enable
R2(config-if)#
```

On both routers R1 and R2, the name RT0 identifies the RIPng process. RIPng is enabled on the first Fast Ethernet interface of router R1 and on both Fast Ethernet interfaces of R2.

This configuration allows Fast Ethernet 0/1 on router R2 and the Ethernet 0 interfaces of both routers to exchange RIPng routing information.

Verifying Troubleshooting RIPng for IPv6

After you configure RIPng, verification is required. Table 7-14 lists the various **show** commands you can use for verification.

Table 7-14   Verifying RIPng

Command	Description
show ipv6 interface	Displays the status of interfaces configured for IPv6.
show ipv6 interface brief	Displays a summarized status of interfaces configured for IPv6.
show ipv6 neighbors	Displays IPv6 neighbor discovery cache information.
show ipv6 protocols	Displays the parameters and current state of the active IPv6 routing protocol processes.
show ipv6 rip	Displays information about the current IPv6 RIP processes.
show ipv6 route	Displays the current IPv6 routing table.
show ipv6 route summary	Displays a summarized form of the current IPv6 routing table.
show ipv6 routers	Displays IPv6 router advertisement information received from other routers.
show ipv6 static	Displays only static IPv6 routes installed in the routing table.
show ipv6 static 2001:db8:5555:0/16	Displays only static route information about the specific address given.
show ipv6 static interface serial 0/0	Displays only static route information with the specified interface as the outgoing interface.
show ipv6 static detail	Displays a more detailed entry for IPv6 static routes.
show ipv6 traffic	Displays statistics about IPv6 traffic.

If you discover during verification that RIPng is not working properly, you need to troubleshoot. Table 7-15 lists the various commands you can use for troubleshooting.

Table 7-15   Troubleshooting RIPng

Command	Description
clear ipv6 rip	Deletes routes from the IPv6 RIP routing table and, if installed, routes in the IPv6 routing table.
clear ipv6 route *	Deletes all routes from the IPv6 routing table.
Note: Clearing all routes from the routing table may cause high CPU usage rates as the routing table is rebuilt.	
clear ipv6 route 2001:db8:c18:3::/64	Clears this specific route from the IPv6 routing table.
clear ipv6 traffic	Resets IPv6 traffic counters.
debug ipv6 packet	Displays debug messages for IPv6 packets.
debug ipv6 rip	Displays debug messages for IPv6 RIP routing transactions.
debug ipv6 routing	Displays debug messages for IPv6 routing table updates and route cache updates.

Summary

This chapter has dealt with the key solutions to the problem of diminishing Internet address space. You have learned how to use DHCP to assign private IP addresses inside your network. This conserves public address space and saves considerable administrative overhead in managing additions, moves, and changes. You learned how to implement NAT and NAT overload to conserve public address space and build private secure intranets without affecting your ISP connection. However, NAT has drawbacks in terms of its negative effects on device performance, mobility, and end-to-end connectivity.

Overall, the ability to scale networks for future demands requires a limitless supply of IP addresses and improved mobility that DHCP and NAT alone cannot meet. IPv6 satisfies the increasingly complex requirements of hierarchical addressing that IPv4 does not provide. The emergence of IPv6 not only deals with the depletion of IPv4 addresses and the shortcomings of NAT; it also provides new and improved features. In the brief introduction to IPv6 in this lesson, you learned how IPv6 addresses are structured, how they will enhance network security and mobility, and how the IPv4 world will transition to IPv6.

Labs

The activities and labs available in the companion *Accessing the WAN, CCNA Exploration Labs and Study Guide* (ISBN 1-58713-201-x) provide hands-on practice with the following topics introduced in this chapter:

Lab 7-1: Basic DHCP and NAT Configuration (7.4.1)

In this lab, you configure the DHCP and NAT IP services. One router is the DHCP server. The other router forwards DHCP requests to the server. You also configure both static and dynamic NAT configurations, including NAT overload. When you have completed the configurations, you verify the connectivity between the inside and outside addresses.

Lab 7-2: Challenge DHCP and NAT Configuration (7.4.2)

In this lab, you configure the IP address services using the network shown in the topology diagram. If you need assistance, refer to the Basic DHCP and NAT Configuration lab. However, try to do as much on your own as possible.

Lab 7-3: Troubleshooting DHCP and NAT (7.4.3)

The routers at your company were configured by an inexperienced network engineer. Several errors in the configuration have resulted in connectivity issues. Your boss has asked you to troubleshoot and correct the configuration errors and document your work. Using your knowledge of DHCP, NAT, and standard testing methods, find and correct the errors. Make sure that all clients have full connectivity.

Many of the Hands-on Labs include Packet Tracer Companion Activities where you can use Packet Tracer to complete a simulation of the lab. Look for this icon in the *Accessing the WAN, CCNA Exploration Labs and Study Guide* for Hands-on Labs that have a Packet Tracer Companion.

Check Your Understanding

Complete all the review questions listed here to test your understanding of the topics and concepts in this chapter. Answers are listed in the Appendix, "Check Your Understanding and Challenge Questions Answer Key."

1. Which statements are true about the DHCP server functions? (Choose two.)

   A. When a client requests an IP address, the DHCP server searches the binding table for an entry that matches the client's MAC address. If an entry exists, the corresponding IP address for that entry is returned to the client.

   B. Clients can be assigned an IP address from a predefined DHCP pool for a finite lease period.

   C. DHCP services must be installed on a dedicated network server to define the pool of IP addresses available to the client.

   D. The DHCP server can answer requests and assign IP addresses for a particular subnet only.

   E. Each subnet in the network requires a dedicated DHCP server to assign IP addresses to the host on the subnet.

   F. DHCP provides clients with an IP address, subnet mask, default gateway, and domain name.

2. Refer to the following configuration:

   ```
   R1(config)# ip dhcp pool 10.10.10.0
   ```

   What does the string 10.10.10.0 after the **ip dhcp pool** command specify?

   A. Name of the DHCP pool

   B. Pool of IP addresses available for lease

   C. Range of excluded IP addresses

   D. IP subnet where the DHCP server resides

3. Which statements about DHCP are true? (Choose three.)

   A. DHCP messages use UDP as a transport protocol.

   B. The DHCPOFFER message is sent by the DHCP server after receiving a DHCPDISCOVER message from a client.

   C. DHCP uses ports 67 and 68.

   D. The DHCPREQUEST message is sent by a DHCP client to locate a DHCP server.

   E. The DHCPACK message is sent by the DHCP server to provide the DHCP client with the DHCP server MAC address for further communications.

   F. All DHCP communications are broadcast.

4. Refer to Figure 7-41.

Figure 7-41   DHCP Topology for Question 4

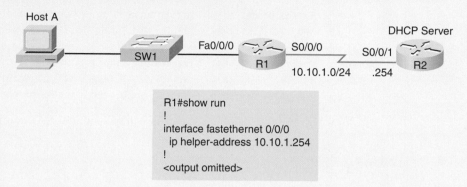

Router R2 is configured as a DHCP server. What happens when Host A sends a DHCP request to the DHCP server?

A. Router R1 drops the request.

B. The request is forwarded to the DHCP server.

C. The request is forwarded to the DHCP server, but the DHCP server does not respond with an IP address.

D. Router R1 responds with an IP address.

5. Refer to the following output:

```
Router# debug ip dhcp server events


DHCPD:DHCPDISCOVER received from client 0b07.1134.a029.
DHCPD:assigned IP address 10.1.0.3 to client 0b07.1134.a029.
DHCPD:Sending DHCPOFFER to client 0b07.1134.a029 (10.1.0.4)
DHCPD:DHCPREQUEST received from client 0b07.1134.a029.
DHCPD:Sending DHCPNACK to client 0b07.1134.a029. (10.1.0.3).
<output omitted>
Router# show ip dhcp conflict


IP address     Detection method      Detection time
10.1.0.3       Ping                  Jan 01 1999 00:00 AM
```

Which statement is true about the DHCP exchange?

A. The client was successfully configured with IP address 10.1.0.3.

B. The DHCP server offered the address 10.1.0.3 to the client.

C. The client requested 10.1.0.3 from the server.

D. The DHCP server could not ping 10.1.0.3.

6. Refer to the following output:

    ```
    NAT1# show ip nat translations

    Pro   Inside global        Inside local          Outside local        Outside global
    udp   198.18.24.211:123    192.168.254.7:123     192.2.182.4:123      192.2.182.4:123
    tcp   198.18.24.211:4509   192.168.254.66:4509   192.0.2.184:80       192.0.2.184:80
    tcp   198.18.24.211:4643   192.168.254.2:4643    192.0.2.71:5190      192.0.2.71:5190
    tcp   198.18.24.211:4630   192.168.254.7:4630    192.0.2.71:5190      192.0.2.71:5190
    tcp   198.18.24.211:1026   192.168.254.9:1026    198.18.24.4:53       198.18.24.4:53
    ```

    Based on the output, which statement is true about the NAT configuration?

    A. Static NAT is configured.

    B. Dynamic NAT is configured.

    C. NAT Overload (PAT) is configured.

    D. NAT is configured incorrectly.

7. If an administrator chooses to avoid using NAT overload, what is the default timeout value for NAT translations?

    A. One hour

    B. One day

    C. One week

    D. Indefinite

8. Match each NAT characteristic with its corresponding NAT technique:

    Provides one-to-one fixed mappings of local and global addresses

    Assigns the translated addresses of IP hosts from a pool of public addresses

    Can map multiple addresses to a single address of the external interface

    Assigns unique source port numbers of an inside global address on a session-by-session basis

    Allows an external host to establish sessions with an internal host

    A. Dynamic NAT

    B. NAT with Overload

    C. Static NAT

9. Refer to the following configuration:

```
R1(config)# ip nat inside source static 192.168.0.100 209.165.200.2
R1(config)# interface serial0/0/0
R1(config-if)# ip nat inside
R1(config-if)# no shut
R1(config-if)# ip address 10.1.1.2 255.255.255.0
R1(config)# interface serial0/0/2
R1(config-if)# ip address 209.165.200.2 255.255.255.0
R1(config-if)# ip nat outside
R1(config-if)# no shut
```

Which host or hosts will have their addresses translated by NAT?

A. 10.1.1.2

B. 192.168.0.100

C. 209.165.200.2

D. All hosts on the 10.1.1.0 network

E. All hosts on the 192.168.0.0 network

10. Based on the following configuration, which addresses will NAT translate?

```
R1(config)# ip nat pool nat-pool1 209.165.200.225 209.165.200.240 netmask
   255.255.255.0
R1(config)# ip nat inside source list 1 pool nat-pool1
R1(config)# interface serial0/0/0
R1(config-if)# ip address 10.1.1.2 255.255.0.0
R1(config-if)# ip nat inside
R1(config)# interface serial s0/0/2
R1(config-if)# ip address 209.165.200.1 255.255.255.0
R1(config-if)# ip nat outside
R1(config)# access-list 1 permit 192.168.0.0 0.0.0.255
```

A. 10.1.1.2 to 10.1.1.255

B. 192.168.0.0 to 192.168.0.255

C. 209.165.200.240 to 209.165.200.255

D. Only host 10.1.1.2

E. Only host 209.165.200.255

11. Refer to Figure 7-42.

Figure 7-42 NAT Topology for Question 11

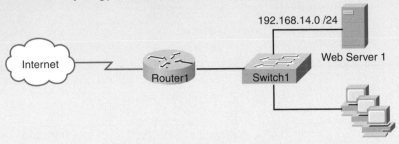

Web server 1 is assigned a single IP address of 192.168.14.5/24. For hosts from the Internet to access web server 1, which type of NAT configuration is required on router R1?

A. Static NAT

B. Dynamic NAT

C. NAT overload

D. Port address translation (PAT)

12. Which NAT solution allows external users to access an internal FTP server on a private network?

A. Dynamic NAT

B. Port address translation (PAT)

C. NAT overload

D. Static NAT

13. Given the following **debug** router output, what kind of address is 24.74.237.203?

```
s=10.10.10.3->24.74.237.203,  d=64.102.252.3 [29854]
s=10.10.10.3->24.74.237.203,  d=64.102.252.3 [29855]
s=10.10.10.3->24.74.237.203,  d=64.102.252.3 [29856]
s=64.102.252.3,  d=24.74.237.203->10.10.10.3 [9935]
s=64.102.252.3,  d=24.74.237.203->10.10.10.3 [9937]
s=10.10.10.3->24.74.237.203,  d=64.102.252.3 [29857]
s=64.102.252.3,  d=24.74.237.203->10.10.10.3 [9969]
s=64.102.252.3,  d=24.74.237.203->10.10.10.3 [9972]
s=10.10.10.3->24.74.237.203,  d=64.102.252.3 [29858]
```

A. Inside local

B. Inside global

C. Outside local

D. Outside global

14. Which statements accurately describe the RIPng routing protocol? (Choose two.)

   A. RIPng has a limit of 15 hops.

   B. RIPng is a link-state routing protocol.

   C. RIPng uses UDP port 238 for updates.

   D. RIPng uses poison reverse.

   E. RIPng forwards IPv6 broadcasts.

15. Which methods of assigning an IPv6 address to an interface are automatic and can be used in conjunction with each other? (Choose two.)

   A. DHCPv6

   B. Stateless autoconfiguration

   C. EUI-64

   D. Static assignment

   E. DNS

16. Match each IPv6 command with its description:

   ipv6 unicast-routing

   ipv6 address

   ip name-server

   ipv6 host name

   ipv6 router rip *name*

   A. Specifies the DNS server used by the router

   B. Defines a static hostname-to-address mapping

   C. Configures a global IPv6 address

   D. Enables IPv6 traffic forwarding between interfaces on the router

   E. Enables RIPng routing on the router and identifies the RIP process

17. Given 2031:0000:0300:0000:0000:00C0:8000:130B, which options are equivalent representations of the full IPv6 address? (Choose three.)

   A. 2031:300::C0:8:130B

   B. 2031:0:300::C0:8000:130B

   C. 2031:0:3::C0:8000:130B

   D. 2031:0:0300:0:0:C0:8000:130B

   E. 2031::300:0:0:0C0:8000:130B

   F. 2031::0300::C0:8:130B

18. Describe the four DHCP discovery and offer messages in sequence of operation and function.

19. Refer to Figure 7-43.

Figure 7-43   Network Topology for Question 19

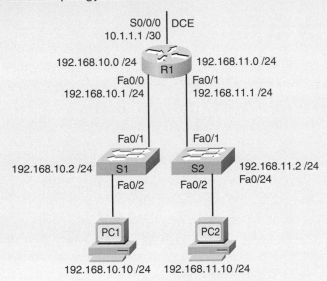

The following has been configured on router R1:

```
hostname R1
ip dhcp excluded-address 192.168.11.1 192.168.11.254
ip dhcp pool LAN-POOL-2
network 192.168.10.0 255.255.255.0
default-router 192.168.2.1
domain-name span.com
```

Router R1 has been configured to provide DHCP services to the hosts on network 192.168.11.0 /24, excluding the first nine IP addresses from the pool. However, after releasing and renewing its IP address, host PC2 still cannot acquire an IP address automatically. Which changes in the configuration would help this problem?

20. Refer to Figure 7-44.

Figure 7-44   Network Topology for Question 20

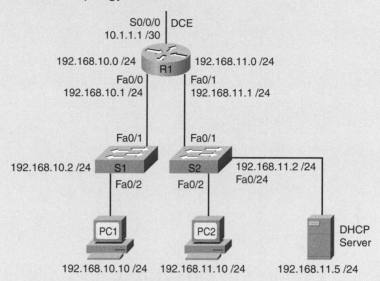

The DHCP server with an IP address of 192.168.11.5 has been configured to provide IP addresses to the hosts on network 192.168.10.0 /24. However, the hosts receive an error stating that their DHCP server request has timed out and that the DHCP server is unreachable. Which configuration commands would correct this problem?

21. Describe the differences between static NAT, dynamic NAT, and NAT overload.

22. Refer to the following output:

```
R2# show ip nat translations

Pro Inside global           Inside local          Outside local
tcp 209.165.200.225:16642   192.168.10.10:16642   209.165.200.254:80
tcp 209.165.200.225:62452   192.168.11.10:62452   209.165.200.254:80
  Outside global
  209.165.200.254:80
  209.165.200.254:80


R2# show ip nat translations verbose

Pro Inside global           Inside local          Outside local
tcp 209.165.200.225:16642   192.168.10.10:16642   209.165.200.254:80
  Outside global
  209.165.200.254:80
    create 00:01:45, use 00:01:43 timeout:86400000, left 23:58:16, Map-Id(In): 1,
    flags:
```

```
      extended, use_count: 0, entry-id: 4, lc_entries: 0
   tcp 209.165.200.225:62452   192.168.11.10:62452    209.165.200.254:80
    209.165.200.254:80
       create 00:00:37, use 00:00:35 timeout:86400000, left 23:59:24, Map-Id(In): 1,
       flags:
   extended, use_count: 0, entry-id: 5, lc_entries: 0
   R2#
```

Router R2 has been configured to provide NAT services. On the basis of the information provided, comment on the NAT translations in the output.

23. Given **2031:0000:130F:0000:0000:09C0:876A:130B**, abbreviate the IPv6 address to its shortest allowable form.

24. Describe the two main IPv4-to-IPv6 transition options, and complete the following IPv6 transition sentence:

"_____ where you can; _____ where you must!"

Challenge Questions and Activities

Refer to Figure 7-45 for the challenge questions.

Figure 7-45   Topology for Challenge Questions

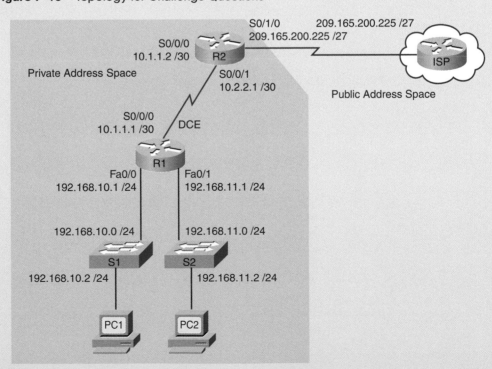

1. The administrator needs to configure DHCP on router R1 for the PC1 and PC2 hosts. Which series of commands would correctly configure router R1 as a DHCP server?

2. The administrator has configured router R2 as a NAT border gateway. Specifically, NAT overload has been configured to translate internal hosts connected to the R1 router to a pool of public addresses in the range of 209.165.200.224/29.

   The following commands were configured on R2:

```
access-list 1 permit 192.168.0.0 0.0.0.255
ip nat pool NAT-POOL 209.165.200.225 209.165.200.239 netmask 255.255.255.240
ip nat inside source list 1 pool NAT-POOL1
interface serial s0/1/0
  ip nat inside
interface serial 0/0/0
  ip nat outside
```

   The PC1 and PC2 hosts can ping router R2 but cannot get Internet access. On the basis of the information presented, which configuration changes would correctly address the current problem?

CHAPTER 8

Network Troubleshooting

Objectives

After completing this chapter, you should be able to answer the following questions:

- How do you establish and document a network baseline?

- What are the various troubleshooting methodologies and troubleshooting tools?

- What are the common issues that occur during WAN implementation?

- How do you identify and troubleshoot common enterprise network implementation issues using a layered model approach?

Key Terms

This chapter uses the following key terms. You can find the definitions in the glossary at the end of the book.

As soon as a network is operational, administrators must monitor its performance for the sake of the organization's productivity. Network outages occasionally will occur. Sometimes they are planned and their impact on the organization easily managed. Other times they are not planned, and their impact on the organization can be severe. A business can suffer lost revenue from its inability to transact business and the cost of unproductive workers; in some cases this can be a substantial dollar amount. Administrators must be able to quickly troubleshoot and correct the problem to restore the network to full production.

This chapter describes a systematic process for troubleshooting network outages.

Establishing the Network Performance Baseline

To efficiently diagnose and correct network problems, a network engineer needs to know how a network has been designed and what the network's expected performance should be under normal operating conditions.

This information is captured and contained in network documentation. *Network documentation* consists of various sources of information that provide a clear picture of the network's design and characteristics.

Documenting Your Network

Network configuration documentation provides a logical diagram of the network and detailed information about each component. Figure 8-1 is a high-level view of these various sources.

Information such as the network's physical and logical topologies, device configuration, end-system configurations, and various network baselines should be included. A hard copy of the documentation should be stored in a central location. The information could also be available on a protected intranet website.

Network documentation should include these components:

- Network topology diagram
- Network configuration table
- End-system configuration table
- Network baseline

The following sections detail the first three components. The network baseline component is covered in the section "Steps for Establishing a Network Baseline."

Figure 8-1   Network Documentation

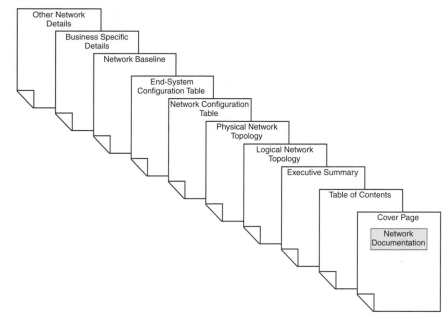

Network Topology Diagram

The ***network topology diagram***, shown in Figure 8-2, is a graphical representation of a network that illustrates how each device in the network is connected and its logical architecture. A topology diagram has many of the same components as the network configuration table. Each network device should be represented on the diagram with consistent notation or a symbol. Also, each logical and physical connection should be represented using a simple line or other appropriate symbol. Routing protocols also can be shown.

At a minimum, the topology diagram should include the following:

- Symbols for all devices and how they are connected

- Interface types, numbers, IP addresses, and subnet masks

- Primary WAN protocols

Note

Various software tools can be used to document the topology. Although many tools are available, Microsoft Visio is considered the de facto standard, so familiarity with it is highly recommended.

Figure 8-2 Sample Network Topology

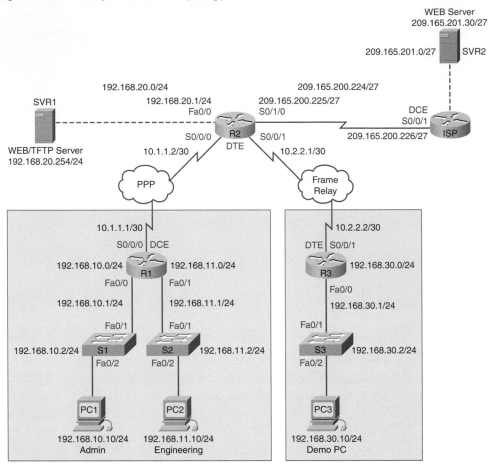

Network Configuration Table

The *network configuration table* contains accurate, up-to-date records of the hardware and software used in a network. It should provide the network engineer with all the documented information necessary to help identify and correct the network fault.

Tables 8-1 and 8-2 show a sample data set that should be included for all components.

Table 8-1   Network Configuration Table: Routers

Device Name, Model	Interface Name	MAC Address	IP Address/ Subnet Mask	IP Routing Protocol(s)
R1, Cisco 1841	fa0/0	000a.b858.a159	192.168.10.1/24	EIGRP 10
	fa0/1	000a.b858.a160	192.168.11.1/24	EIGRP 10
	s0/0/0	—	10.1.1.1/30	EIGRP 10
	s0/0/1	—	Not connected	—
R2, Cisco 1841	fa0/0	000a.b802.d000	192.168.20.1/24	EIGRP 10
	fa0/1	—	Not connected	—
	s0/0/0	—	10.1.1.2/30	EIGRP 10
	s0/0/1	—	10.2.2.1/30	EIGRP 10
	s0/1/0	—	209.165.200.225/27	Default static route
s0/1/1	—	Not connected	—
R3, Cisco 1841	fa0/0	000a.b802.d123	192.168.30.1/24	EIGRP 10
	fa0/1	—	Not connected	—
	s0/0/0	—	Not connected	—
	s0/0/1	—	10.2.2.2/30	EIGRP 10

Note

Table 8-2 reflects the sample topology of Figure 8-2. An actual production network would contain far more information in the table.

Table 8-2   Network Configuration Table: Switches

Switch Name, Model, Management IP Address	Port Name	Speed	Duplex	STP State (Fwd/ Block)	PortFast (Yes/No)	Trunk Status	Ether Channel (Layer 2 or Layer 3)	VLANs	Key
S1, Cisco , WS-C2960-24 192.168.10.2/24	fa0/1	100	Auto	Fwd	No	On	Layer 2	1	Connects to R1
	fa0/2	100	Auto	Fwd	No	On	Layer 2	1	Connects to PC1
	fa0/3 to 0/24	—	—	—	—	—	—	—	Not connected
S2, Cisco WS-C2960-24, 192.168.11.2/24	fa0/1	100	Auto	Fwd	No	On	Layer 2	1	Connects to R1
	fa0/2	100	Auto	Fwd	No	On	Layer 2	1	Connects to PC2
	fa0/3 to 0/24	—	—	—	—	—	—	—	Not connected
S3, Cisco WS-C2960-24, 192.168.30.2/24	fa0/1	100	Auto	Fwd	No	On	Layer 2	1	Connects to R3
	fa0/2	100	Auto	Fwd	No	On	Layer 2	1	Connects to PC3
	fa0/3 to 0/24	—	—	—	—	—	—	—	Not connected

The information in this data set may include but is not limited to the following:

- Type of device, model designation
- IOS image name
- Device network hostname
- Location of the device (building, floor, room, rack, panel)
- If it is a modular device, include all module types and in which module slot they are located
- Data link layer addresses
- Network layer addresses
- Any additional important information about physical aspects of the device

Tables 8-1 and 8-2 display sample forms for capturing router information for routers R1 and R2 and switch information for switch S2. The type of information captured varies depending on the function of the device.

Other types of equipment would require specific information to be captured. For instance, devices such as wireless access points and wireless bridges would require additional unique information, and a custom form would be required.

Note

You can use various software tools to document the device and end-system information. It can be as simple as using a word processor such as Microsoft Word or OpenOffice. However, it is recommended that you use a spreadsheet or database application.

End-System Configuration Table

The *end-system configuration table* contains baseline records of the hardware and software used in end-system devices such as servers, network management consoles, and desktop workstations. An incorrectly configured end system can have a negative impact on the overall performance of a network.

Actual end-system network configuration documentation varies between organizations. However, the documentation should contain the following:

- Device name (purpose)
- Operating system and version
- IP address
- Subnet mask
- Default gateway, DNS server, and WINS server addresses
- Any high-bandwidth network applications that the end system runs

Table 8-3 is a sample end-system configuration table.

Table 8-3 End-System Configuration Table

Device Name (Purpose)	Operating System/ Version	IP Address/ Subnet Mask	Default Gateway Address	DNS Server Address	WINS Server Address	Network Applications	High-Bandwidth Applications
SVR1 (Web/TFTP server)	UNIX	192.168.20.254/24	192.168.20.1/24	192.168.20.1/24	—	HTTP, FTP	—
SVR2 (Web server) colocated at ISP	UNIX	209.165.201.30/27	209.165.201.1/27	209.165.201.1/27	—	HTTP	—
PC1 (Admin terminal)	UNIX	192.168.10.10/24	192.168.10.1/24	192.168.10.1/24	—	FTP, SSH, Telnet	VoIP
PC2 (user PC— Engineering)	Windows XP Pro SP2	192.168.11.10/24	192.168.11.1/24	192.168.11.1/24	—	HTTP, FTP	VoIP
PC3 (demo PC— Marketing)	Windows XP Pro SP2	192.168.30.10/24	192.168.30.1/24	192.168.30.1/24	—	HTTP	Streaming video, VoIP

Note

Network devices including network printers and network VoIP phones also should be documented. No VoIP icon was included in the sample topology because the PCs are configured with the Cisco IP Communicator softphone software-based application that enables the PCs to be used as an IP phone.

Network Documentation Process

Although the documentation process is a very time-consuming task, you'll appreciate its importance whenever you perform network troubleshooting. Having complete and accurate network information at your disposal makes it far easier to pinpoint an anomaly causing a network problem.

The initial documentation could take a substantial amount of time to generate. However, after it is generated, the documentation becomes a maintenance task and is updated on a scheduled basis.

In fact, maintaining up-to-date documentation is very important. Polices and procedures must be in place to ensure accuracy. Any changes in the topology, devices, or end system must be revised and reflected in the documentation.

Figure 8-3 is a flowchart that documents network devices. It is described in the following list:

Step 1.   Log in to an undocumented device.

Step 2.   Discover relevant information about the device.

Step 3.   Record device information in the network configuration table.

Step 4.   Is this device important enough to add to the topology diagram?

Step 5.   Transfer relevant device information from the network configuration table to the topology diagram.

Step 6.   Is there any more information to discover for this device?

Step 7.   What neighboring devices are connected to this device?

Step 8.   Are any other neighbor devices undocumented?

Step 9.   If no undocumented devices exist, documentation is complete.

When you document your network, you have to gather information directly from routers and switches. Here are some commands that are useful to the network documentation process:

- The **ping** command tests connectivity with neighboring devices before logging in to them. Pinging to other PCs in the network also initiates the MAC address autodiscovery process.

- The **telnet** command logs in remotely to a device for accessing configuration information.

- The **show ip interface brief** command displays the up or down status and IP address of all interfaces on a Cisco router or switch.

- The **show ip route** command displays the routing table in a router to discover the directly connected neighbors, more remote devices (through learned routes), and the routing protocols that have been configured.

- The **show cdp neighbor detail** command displays detailed information about directly connected Cisco neighbor devices.

Figure 8-3   Network Documentation Flowchart

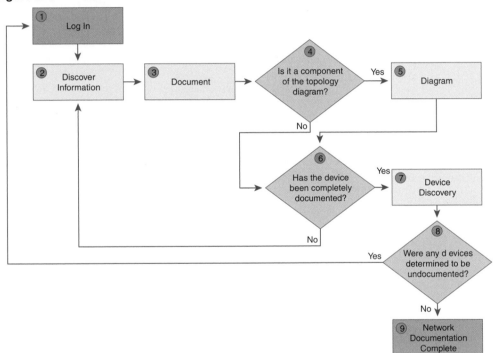

Network Discovery and Documentation (8.1.2)

This activity covers the steps you take to discover a network using primarily the **telnet**, **show cdp neighbors detail**, and **show ip route** commands. This is Part I of a two-part activity.

The topology displayed in the Packet Tracer activity does not reveal all the details of the network. The details have been hidden using the cluster function of Packet Tracer. The network infrastructure has been collapsed, and the topology in the file shows only the end devices. Your task is to use your knowledge of networking and discovery commands to learn about the full network topology and document it.

Detailed instructions are provided within the activity. Use File e4-812.pka on the CD-ROM that accompanies this book to perform this activity using Packet Tracer.

Why Is Establishing a Network Baseline Important?

Many networking problems are easy to identify. For instance, a failure between routers would be very noticeable. However, some network problems are not as easy to identify or notice. Problems such as suboptimal routing, excessive traffic, or excessive errors may not cause a network to fail, but they would definitely be detrimental to its performance.

Users on a subnet may be your first indicator. They may report problems with slower access to services. How do you determine if their concerns are genuine?

You need to compare sample network performance data from the current situation to captured data documenting network performance during normal operations. This captured network performance information is documented in a *network baseline* document.

Establishing a network performance baseline requires collecting key performance data from the ports and devices that are essential to network operation. This information helps determine the network's "personality" and provides answers to the following questions:

- How does the network perform during a normal or average day?

- Where are the underutilized and overutilized areas?

- If errors are discovered, where are the most errors occurring?

- What alert thresholds should be set for the devices that need to be monitored?

- Can the network deliver the service identified in the Network Policy document?

Measuring the initial performance and availability of critical network devices and links allows a network administrator to determine the difference between abnormal behavior and proper network performance as the network grows or traffic patterns change. The baseline also provides insight into whether the current network design can deliver the services identified in the Network Policy document. Without a baseline, no standard exists to measure the optimum nature of network traffic and congestion levels.

In addition, analysis after an initial baseline tends to reveal hidden problems. The collected data reveals the true nature of congestion or potential congestion in a network. It may also reveal areas in the network that are underutilized and that quite often can lead to network redesign efforts based on quality and capacity observations.

Steps for Establishing a Network Baseline

Because the initial network performance baseline sets the stage for measuring the effects of network changes and subsequent troubleshooting efforts, it is important to plan for it carefully.

The recommended steps for planning the first baseline are as follows:

Step 1.   Determine what types of data to collect.

Step 2.   Identify devices and ports of interest.

Step 3.   Determine the baseline duration.

The following sections describe these steps in more detail.

Step 1: Determine What Types of Data to Collect

When conducting the initial baseline, start by selecting a few variables that represent the defined policies. If too many data points are selected, the amount of data can be overwhelming, making analyzing the collected data difficult. Start out simply, and fine-tune along the way. Generally, some good starting measures are interface utilization and CPU utilization.

Figure 8-4 shows the device status of a server named VPC-05. The screen capture is from the WhatsUp Gold network management software from Ipswitch, Inc.

Figure 8-4   WhatsUp Gold

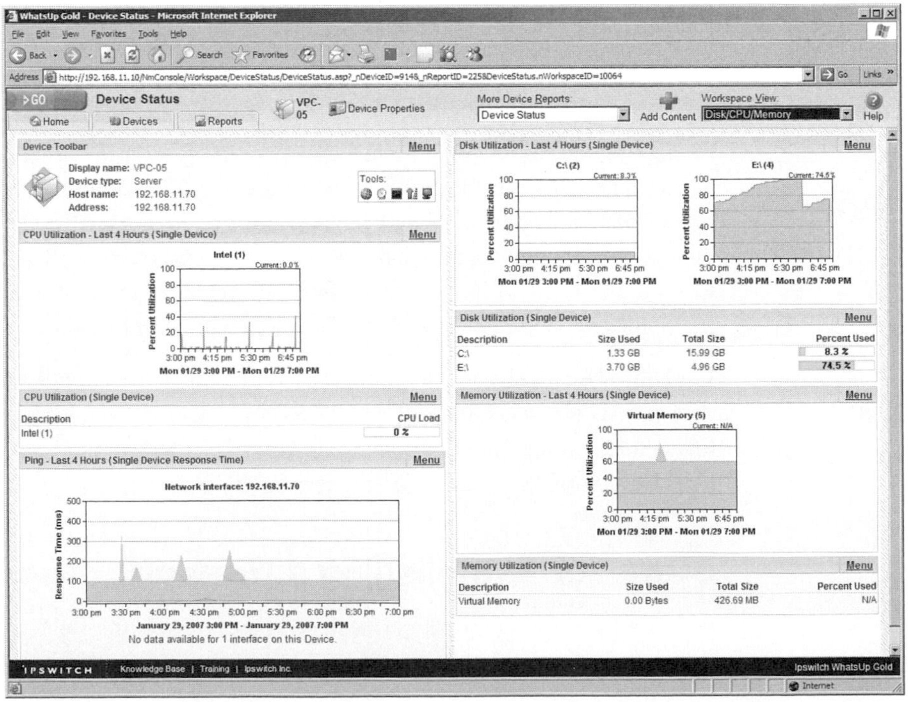

Step 2: Identify Devices and Ports of Interest

The next step is to identify key devices and ports for which performance data should be measured. Devices and ports of interest include

- Network device ports that connect to other network devices

- Servers

- Key users

- Anything else considered critical to operations

In Figure 8-5, the network administrator has highlighted the devices and ports of interest to monitor during the baseline test.

Figure 8-5   Highlighted Ports of Interest

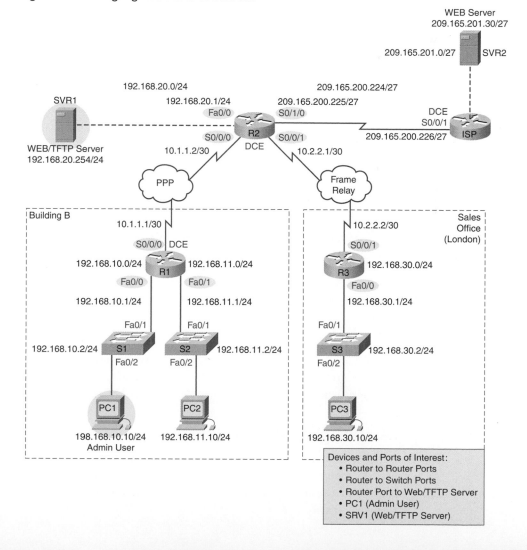

The devices of interest include routers R1, R2, and R3, PC1 (the Admin terminal), and SVR1 (the Web/TFTP server). The ports of interest include those on R1, R2, and R3 that connect to the other routers or to switches, and on router R2, the port that connects to SVR1 (Fa0/0).

When you narrow the ports polled, the results are concise, and the network management load is minimized. Remember that an interface on a router or switch can be a virtual interface, such as a loopback or a switch virtual interface (SVI).

This step is easier if you have configured the device port description fields to indicate what connects to the port. For example, for a router port that connects to the distribution switch in the Engineering workgroup, you might configure the interface description as "Engineering LAN distribution switch."

Step 3: Determine the Baseline Duration

It is important that the length of time and the baseline information being gathered are sufficient to establish a typical picture of the network. This period should include several days to capture any daily or weekly trends. Weekly trends are just as important as daily or hourly trends.

Figure 8-6 shows several screen captures of CPU utilization trends captured over a daily, weekly, monthly, and yearly period.

The workweek trends are too short to accurately reveal the recurring nature of the utilization surge that occurs every weekend on Saturday evening when a major database backup operation consumes network bandwidth. This recurring pattern is revealed in the monthly trend. The yearly trend shown in the example is too long a duration to provide meaningful baseline performance details. A baseline should not extend more than six weeks, unless specific long-term trends need to be measured. Generally, a two-to-four-week baseline is ideal.

You should not perform a baseline measurement during times of unique traffic patterns, because the data would provide an inaccurate picture of normal network operations. You would get an inaccurate measure of network performance if you performed a baseline measurement on a holiday or during a month when most of the company is on vacation.

Baseline analysis of the network should be conducted on a regular basis. At a minimum, perform an annual analysis of the entire network, or baseline different sections of the network on a rotating basis. Analysis must be conducted regularly to understand how the network is affected by growth and other changes.

Measuring Network Performance Data

Sophisticated network management software is often used to baseline large and complex networks. For example, the Fluke Network SuperAgent module, shown in Figure 8-7, enables administrators to automatically create and review reports using its Intelligent Baselines feature.

Figure 8-6   CPU Utilization Trends

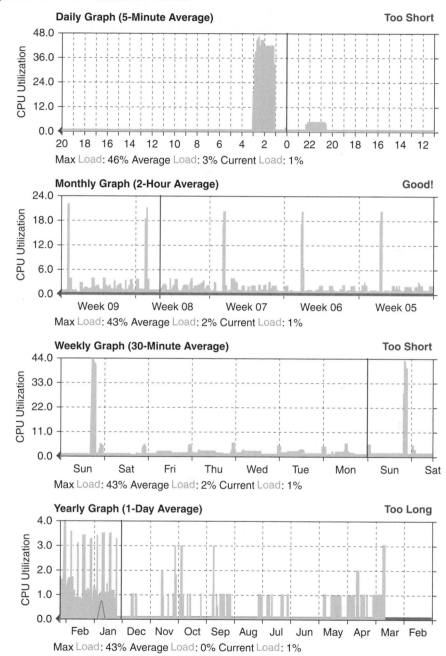

Figure 8-7   Fluke Network SuperAgent

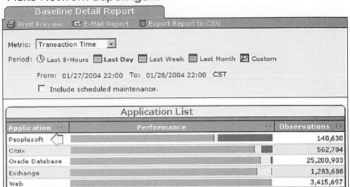

This feature compares current performance levels with historical observations. It can automatically identify performance problems and applications that do not provide expected levels of service.

In simpler networks, the baseline tasks may require a combination of manual data collection and simple network protocol inspectors. Establishing an initial baseline or conducting a performance-monitoring analysis requires several days to accurately reflect network performance. Network management software or protocol inspectors and sniffers may run continuously over the course of the data collection process. Hand collection using **show** commands on individual network devices is extremely time-consuming and should be limited to mission-critical network devices.

Table 8-4 summarizes useful **show** commands.

Table 8-4   Useful **show** Commands

Command	Description
show version	Displays uptime and version information for device software and hardware.
show ip interface [brief]	Displays all the configuration options that are set on an interface. Use the **brief** keyword to show only up/down status of IP interfaces and the IP address of each interface.
show interface [*interface_type interface_num*]	Displays detailed output for each interface. To show detailed output for only a single interface, include the interface type and number in the command (such as **fastethernet 0/0**).
show ip route	Displays the contents of the routing table.
show arp	Displays the contents of the ARP table.
show running-config	Displays the current configuration.

Command	Description
show port	Displays the status of ports on a switch.
show vlan	Displays the status of VLANs on a switch.
show tech-support	Runs other **show** commands and provides many pages of detailed output, designed to be sent to technical support.

Troubleshooting Methodologies and Tools

Network engineers, administrators, and support personnel realize that troubleshooting is a process that takes a significant percentage of their time. Using efficient troubleshooting techniques shortens overall troubleshooting time when you're working in a production environment.

A General Approach to Troubleshooting

Two extreme approaches to troubleshooting almost always result in disappointment, delay, or failure. At one extreme is the theorist, or rocket scientist, approach. At the other extreme is the impractical, or caveman, approach.

The rocket scientist (theorist) analyzes and reanalyzes the situation until the exact cause of the problem has been identified and corrected with surgical precision. Although this process is fairly reliable, few companies can afford to have their networks down for the hours or days that this exhaustive analysis can take.

The caveman's first instinct is to start swapping cards, cables, hardware, and software until miraculously the network begins operating again (the brute-force approach). This does not mean that the network is working properly, just that it is operating. Although this approach may achieve a change in symptoms faster, it is not very reliable, and the root cause of the problem may still be present.

Because both of these approaches are extremes, the better approach is somewhere in the middle, using elements of both. It is important to analyze the network as a whole rather than in a piecemeal fashion. A *systematic approach* minimizes confusion and cuts down on time otherwise wasted with trial and error.

Using Layered Models for Troubleshooting

Logical networking models, such as the OSI and TCP/IP models, separate network functionality into modular layers, as shown in Figure 8-8.

Figure 8-8   OSI and TCP/IP Layered Models

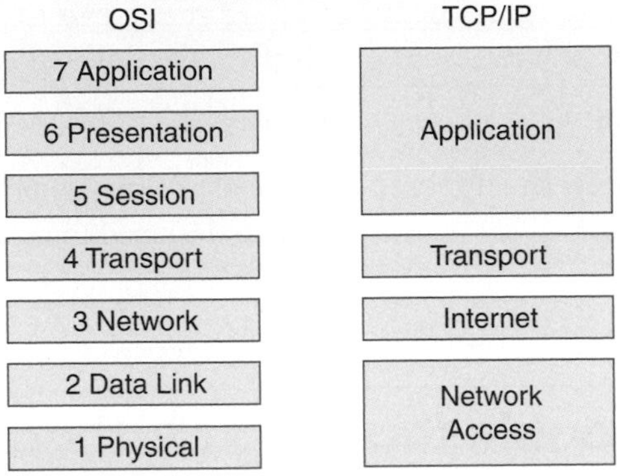

When you're troubleshooting, these layered models can be applied to the physical network to isolate network problems. For example, if the symptoms suggest a physical connection problem, the network technician can focus on troubleshooting the circuit that operates at the physical layer. If that circuit functions properly, the technician looks at areas in another layer that could be causing the problem.

OSI Reference Model

The OSI model provides a common language for network engineers and is commonly used in troubleshooting networks. Problems typically are described in terms of a given OSI model layer.

The OSI reference model describes how information from a software application in one computer moves through a network medium to a software application in another computer.

The upper layers (5 to 7) of the OSI model deal with application issues and generally are implemented only in software. The application layer is closest to the end user. Both users and application layer processes interact with software applications that contain a communications component.

The lower layers (1 to 4) of the OSI model handle data-transport issues. Layers 3 and 4 generally are implemented only in software. The physical layer (Layer 1) and data link layer (Layer 2) are implemented in hardware and software. The physical layer is closest to the physical network medium, such as the network cabling, and is responsible for actually placing information on the medium.

Figure 8-9 shows which OSI layers are commonly used to troubleshoot a particular type of device.

Figure 8-9   Devices Matched to Their OSI Layers

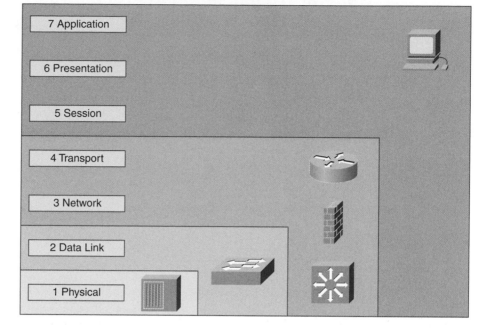

TCP/IP Model

Similar to the OSI networking model, the TCP/IP networking model also divides networking architecture into modular layers. As shown in Figure 8-8, the four layers of the TCP/IP networking model map to the seven layers of the OSI networking model. It is this close mapping that allows the TCP/IP suite of protocols to successfully communicate with so many networking technologies.

The application layer in the TCP/IP suite actually combines the functions of the three OSI model layers: session, presentation, and application. The application layer provides communication between applications such as FTP, HTTP, and SMTP on separate hosts.

The transport layers of TCP/IP and OSI directly correspond in function. The transport layer is responsible for exchanging segments between devices on a TCP/IP network.

The TCP/IP Internet layer relates to the OSI network layer. The Internet layer is responsible for placing messages in a fixed format that allows devices to handle them.

The TCP/IP network access layer corresponds to the OSI physical and data link layers. The network access layer communicates directly with the network media and provides an interface between the architecture of the network and the Internet layer.

General Troubleshooting Procedures

Figure 8-10 shows the stages of the general troubleshooting process.

Figure 8-10   Troubleshooting Stages

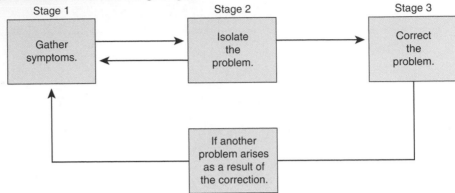

These stages are not mutually exclusive. At any point in the process, it may be necessary to return to previous stages. For instance, you might need to gather more symptoms while isolating a problem.

Also consider that when attempting to correct a problem, you might create another unidentified problem. As a result, it would be necessary to gather the symptoms and isolate and correct the new problem.

A troubleshooting policy should be established for each stage. A policy provides a consistent manner in which to perform each stage. Part of the policy should include documenting every important piece of information.

The following sections describe the three stages of the general troubleshooting process in more detail.

Stage 1: Gather Symptoms

Troubleshooting begins with the process of gathering and documenting symptoms from the network, end systems, and users. In addition, the network administrator determines which network components have been affected and how the network's functionality has changed compared to the baseline. Symptoms may appear in many different forms, including alerts from the network management system, console messages, and user complaints.

While gathering symptoms, use questions as a method of localizing the problem to a smaller range of possibilities.

Stage 2: Isolate the Problem

The problem is not truly isolated until a single problem, or a set of related problems, is identified. To do this, the network administrator examines the characteristics of the problems at the logical layers of the network so that the most likely cause can be selected. At this stage, the network administrator may gather and document more symptoms, depending on the problem characteristics that are identified.

Stage 3: Correct the Problem

Having isolated and identified the cause of the problem, the network administrator works to correct the problem by implementing, testing, and documenting a solution. If the network administrator determines that the corrective action has created another problem, the attempted solution is documented, the changes are removed, and the network administrator returns to gathering symptoms and isolating the problem.

Troubleshooting Methods

The three main methods of troubleshooting networks are

- Bottom-up
- Top-down
- Divide-and-conquer

Each approach has its advantages and disadvantages. The following sections describe the three methods and provide guidelines for choosing the best method for a specific situation.

Bottom-Up Troubleshooting Method

In *bottom-up troubleshooting* you start with the physical components of the network and move up through the layers of the OSI model until the cause of the problem is identified (see Figure 8-11). Bottom-up troubleshooting is a good approach to use when the problem is suspected to be a physical one. Most networking problems reside at the lower levels, so implementing the bottom-up approach often results in effective results.

The disadvantage of bottom-up troubleshooting is that it requires you to check every device and interface on the network until you find the possible cause of the problem. Because each conclusion and possibility must be documented, this approach involves a lot of paperwork. A further challenge is determining which devices to start examining first.

Figure 8-11   Bottom-Up Troubleshooting Approach

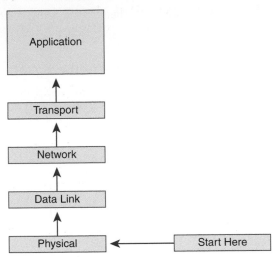

Top-Down Troubleshooting Method

In *top-down troubleshooting* you start with the end-user applications and move down through the layers of the OSI model until the cause of the problem has been identified, as shown in Figure 8-12.

Figure 8-12   Top-Down Troubleshooting Approach

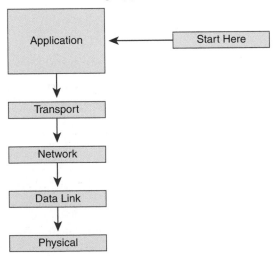

You test end-user applications of an end system before tackling the more specific networking pieces. Use this approach for simpler problems or when you think the problem is with a software application.

The disadvantage of the top-down approach is that it requires you to check every network application until you find the possible cause of the problem. Each conclusion and possibility must be documented. The challenge is to determine which application to examine first.

Divide-and-Conquer Troubleshooting Method

When you apply the *divide-and-conquer troubleshooting* approach toward troubleshooting a networking problem, you select a layer and test in both directions from the starting layer, as shown in Figure 8-13.

Figure 8-13 Divide-and-Conquer Troubleshooting Approach

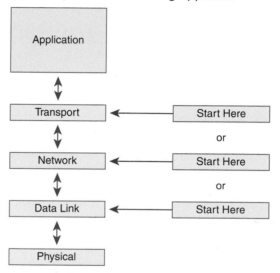

In divide-and-conquer troubleshooting, you start by collecting users' experiences with the problem and document the symptoms. Then, using that information, you decide at which OSI layer to start your investigation. After you verify that a layer is functioning properly, you assume that the layers below it are functioning, and you work up the OSI layers. If an OSI layer is not functioning properly, you work your way down the OSI layer model.

For example, if users can't access the web server and you can ping the server, you know that the problem is above Layer 3. If ICMP error messages are generated and you can't ping the server, you know that the problem is likely at a lower OSI layer.

Guidelines for Selecting a Troubleshooting Method

To quickly resolve network problems, take the time to select the most effective network troubleshooting method. Use the process shown in Figure 8-14 to help select the most efficient troubleshooting method.

Figure 8-14   Guidelines for Selecting a Troubleshooting Method

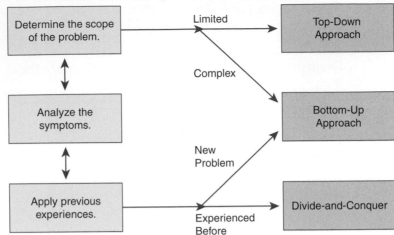

Here is an example of how you would choose a troubleshooting method for a specific problem. Two IP routers are not exchanging routing information. The last time this type of problem occurred, it was a protocol issue. So you choose the divide-and-conquer troubleshooting method. Your analysis reveals that connectivity exists between the routers, so you start your troubleshooting efforts at the physical or data link layer, confirm connectivity, and begin testing the TCP/IP-related functions at the next layer up in the OSI model—the network layer.

Gathering Symptoms

To determine the scope of the problem, gather and document the symptoms, as shown in Figure 8-15.

Figure 8-15   Gathering Symptoms Flowchart

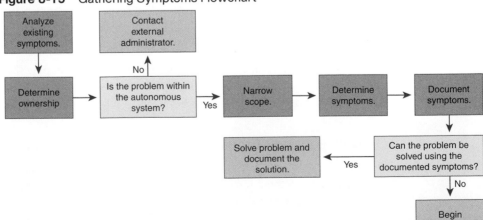

How To Each step in this process is briefly described as follows:

Step 1. **Analyze existing symptoms**: Analyze symptoms gathered from the trouble ticket, users, or end systems affected by the problem to form a definition of the problem.

Step 2. **Determine ownership**: If the problem is within your system, you can move on to the next stage. If the problem is outside the boundary of your control, such as lost Internet connectivity outside the autonomous system, you need to contact an administrator for the external system before gathering additional network symptoms.

Step 3. **Narrow the scope**: Isolate the geographic area involved, and determine if the problem is at the network's core, distribution, or access layer. After you've identified the problem, analyze the existing symptoms, and use your knowledge of the network topology to determine which devices are probably involved.

Step 4. **Gather symptoms from suspect devices**: Using a layered troubleshooting approach, gather hardware and software symptoms from the suspect devices. Start with the most likely possibility, and use knowledge and experience to determine if the problem is more likely a hardware or software configuration problem.

Step 5. **Document symptoms**: Sometimes the problem can be solved using the documented symptoms. If not, begin the isolating phase of the general troubleshooting process.

Table 8-5 describes the common Cisco IOS commands you can use to help gather the symptoms of a network problem.

Table 8-5 Useful Troubleshooting Commands

Command	Description	What Layers It Tests
ping {*host* | *ip-address*}	Sends an echo request packet to an address and then waits for a reply. The *host* | *ip-address* variable is the IP alias or IP address of the target system.	1 to 3
traceroute {*destination*}	Identifies the path a packet takes through the networks. The *destination* variable is the hostname or IP address of the target system.	1 to 3
telnet {*host* | *ip-address*}	Connects to an IP address using the Telnet application.	1 to 7
show ip interface brief	Displays a summary of the status of all interfaces on a device.	1 to 3
show ip route	Displays the current state of the IP routing table.	1 to 3

continues

Table 8-5   Useful Troubleshooting Commands

Command	Description	What Layers It Tests
show running-config interface	Displays the contents of the currently running configuration file for a particular interface.	1 to 4
[no] debug ?	Displays a list of options for enabling or disabling debugging events on a device.	1 to 7
show protocols	Displays the configured protocols and shows the global and interface-specific status of any configured Layer 3 protocol.	1 to 4

Although the **debug** command is an important tool for gathering symptoms, it generates a large amount of console message traffic, and the performance of a network device can be noticeably affected. Make sure that you warn network users that a troubleshooting effort is under way and that network performance may be affected. Remember to disable debugging when you are done.

Use effective questioning techniques when you question end users about a network problem they may be experiencing. This way you get the information you need to effectively document the symptoms of a problem. Table 8-6 provides some guidelines and end-user sample questions.

Table 8-6   Questioning End Users

Guideline	Sample End-User Question
Ask questions that are pertinent to the problem.	What does not work?
Confirm that this is a problem.	What evidence do you have that makes you believe that it is not working properly?
Use each question as a means to either eliminate or discover possible problems.	Are the things that do work and the things that do not work related?
Ask the user when he first noticed the problem.	When did you first notice the problem?
Determine if anything unusual happened since the last time it worked.	What has changed since the last time it worked?
Ask the user to re-create the problem if possible.	Can you reproduce the problem?
Speak at a technical level that the user can understand.	Has the thing that does not work ever worked?

Effectively questioning end users may be one of the most difficult skills to acquire. Remember that when users are experiencing network problems, they probably will be unhappy and maybe even rude.

The following are tips to consider when questioning end users:

- Be patient. Never sigh, take deep breaths, or make derogatory comments.

- Be polite.

- Speak at the user's technical level.

- Always take a moment to collect your thoughts before answering a question.

- Never seem rushed.

- Be compassionate. Let the user know that you are here to help and that together you will identify and rectify the problem.

Troubleshooting Tools

A wide variety of software and hardware tools are available to make troubleshooting easier. These tools may be used to gather and analyze symptoms of network problems. They often provide monitoring and reporting functions that you can use to establish the network baseline.

Software Troubleshooting Tools

Software troubleshooting tools are constantly being produced and are evolving. The following are categories of tools available:

- Network management systems (NMS)

- Knowledge bases

- Baselining tools

- Protocol analyzers

NMS Tools

Network management system (NMS) tools include device-level monitoring, configuration, and fault-management tools. Figure 8-16 shows the WhatsUp Gold NMS software.

Figure 8-16   WhatsUp Gold

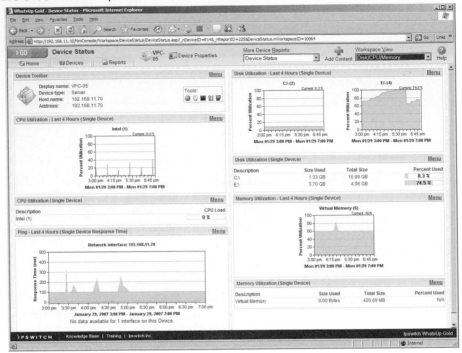

These tools can be used to investigate and correct network problems. Network monitoring software graphically displays a physical view of network devices, allowing network managers to monitor remote devices without actually physically checking them. Device management software provides dynamic status, statistics, and configuration information for switched products. Commonly used network management tools are CiscoView, HP OpenView, SolarWinds, and WhatsUp Gold.

Knowledge Bases

Online network device vendor *knowledge bases* have become indispensable sources of information. When vendor-based knowledge bases are combined with Internet search engines, a network administrator has access to a vast pool of experience-based information.

Figure 8-17 shows the Cisco Support page, which you can access from the Support tab on Cisco.com.

Figure 8-17   Cisco Support Web Page

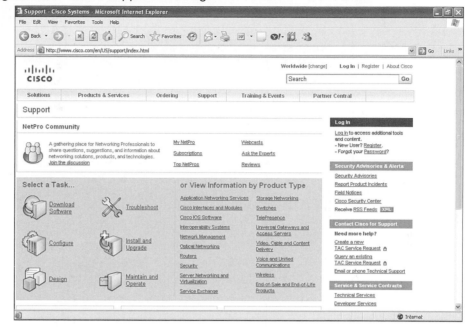

Most vendors provide similar knowledge bases with varying levels of accessibility, usability, and usefulness. The Cisco Support page is comprehensive and useful. However, you must ensure that you are familiar with and accustomed to the resources and tools made available.

Periodically revisit knowledge base sites, because the resources are constantly evolving.

Baselining Tools

There are various approaches to baselining a network, and all of them involve using special software. These software packages have features to automatically draw network diagrams, keep network software and hardware documentation up-to-date, and help measure network bandwidth use.

Figure 8-18 shows the SolarWinds LANsurveyor software, which you can use to help establish a network baseline.

Figure 8-18   LANsurveyor

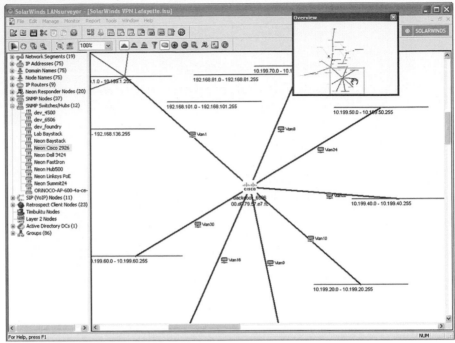

Protocol Analyzers

A *protocol analyzer* captures network traffic as it traverses an identified interface. This captured traffic can then be displayed to reveal the field contents of frames, packets, and segments in a relatively easy-to-understand format. Figure 8-19 shows the Wireshark protocol analyzer.

Figure 8-19   Wireshark

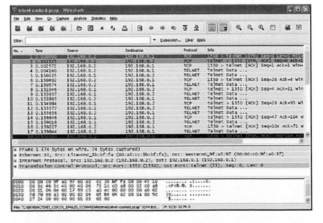

Most protocol analyzers can filter traffic that meets certain criteria so that, for example, all traffic to and from a particular device can be captured. Filtering is also very useful when you want to follow a specific packet stream.

Hardware Troubleshooting Tools

Like software troubleshooting products, hardware troubleshooting products are also constantly being produced and evolving. The following are categories of tools available:

- Network analysis module (NAM)
- Digital multimeters
- Cable testers
- Cable analyzers
- Portable network analyzers

Network Analysis Module

Figure 8-20 shows a *network analysis module (NAM)*.

Figure 8-20   Network Analysis Module (NAM)

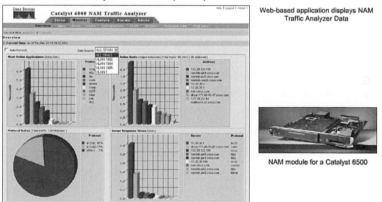

This module can be installed in Cisco Catalyst 6500 series switches and Cisco 7600 series routers to provide a graphical representation of traffic from local and remote switches and routers. The NAM has an embedded browser-based interface that generates reports on the traffic that consumes critical network resources. In addition, the NAM can capture and decode packets and track response times to pinpoint an application problem to the network or server.

Digital Multimeters

Digital multimeters (DMM) are test instruments that are used to directly measure electrical values of voltage, current, and resistance. In network troubleshooting, most of the multimedia tests involve checking power-supply voltage levels and verifying that network devices are receiving power.

Figure 8-21 shows a Fluke digital multimeter.

Figure 8-21   Fluke Digital Multimeter

Cable Testers

Cable testers are specialized handheld devices designed to test the various types of data communication cabling. Cable testers can be used to detect broken wires, crossed-over wiring, shorted connections, and improperly paired connections. These devices can be inexpensive continuity testers, moderately priced data cabling testers, or expensive time-domain reflectometers (TDR).

TDRs are used to pinpoint the distance to a break or short in a cable. These devices send signals along the cable and wait for them to be reflected. The time between sending the signal and receiving it back is converted into a distance measurement. The TDR function normally is packaged with data cabling testers. TDRs used to test fiber-optic cables are known as *optical time-domain reflectometers (OTDR)*.

Figure 8-22 shows a Fluke Networks LinkRunner Pro Tester and a CableIQ Qualification Tester.

Figure 8-22   Cable Testers from Fluke Networks

Fluke Networks LinkRunner Pro Tester   Fluke Networks CableIQ Qualification Tester

Cable Analyzers

Cable analyzers are multifunctional handheld devices that are used to test and certify copper and fiber cables for different services and standards. The more sophisticated tools include advanced troubleshooting diagnostics that measure the distance to the performance defect, identify corrective actions, and graphically display crosstalk and impedance behavior. Cable analyzers also typically include PC-based software. After field data has been collected, the handheld can upload the data to a PC, and up-to-date and accurate reports can be created.

Figure 8-23 shows a Fluke Networks DTX CableAnalyzer.

Figure 8-23   Cable Analyzer from Fluke Networks

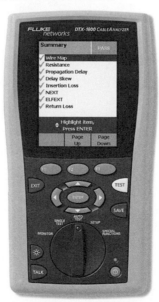

Portable Network Analyzers

Portable network analyzers are custom devices that enable you to troubleshoot switched networks and VLANs in the field. Connecting the network analyzer anywhere on the network enables a network engineer to collect real-time average and peak utilization data for that port. The analyzer can also be used to discover VLAN configuration, identify top network talkers, analyze network traffic, and view interface details. The device typically can output to a PC that has network monitoring software installed for further analysis and troubleshooting.

Figure 8-24 shows a Fluke Networks OptiView Series III network analyzer.

Figure 8-24   Portable Network Analyzer from Fluke Networks

Research Activity

Having the right tool will not help you troubleshoot a network. Having the right tool *and being very familiar with how to use it* will help you troubleshoot a network.

It is very important that you understand how to use a troubleshooting tool and be very familiar with it. Take the time to investigate these tools and become intimately familiar with their features.

Some vendors provide free online training courses, webcasts, podcasts, demos, and learning videos. The software packages also include various learning features. For instance, Figure 8-25 shows the SolarWinds tutorial page.

Figure 8-25   SolarWinds Tutorial

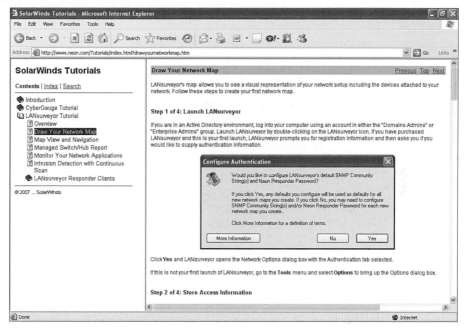

To this end, Table 8-7 documents some links to various troubleshooting tools you should be familiar with.

Table 8-7   Links to Troubleshooting Tools

Software Tools	Network Management Systems	Baselining Tools	Knowledge Bases	Protocol Analyzers
	WhatsUp Gold: *http://tinyurl.com/2glpzy*	Network Uptime: *http://tinyurl.com/2fpjmx*	Cisco: *http://www.cisco.com*	OptiView Protocol Expert: *http://tinyurl.com/268une*
	SolarWinds: *http://tinyurl.com/yuhq9x*	LANsurveyor: *http://tinyurl.com/2ctpa5*		
	OpenView: *http://tinyurl.com/2eb5wj*			
Hardware Tools	Network Analysis Modules (NAM)	Cable Testers	Cable Analyzers	Network Analyzers
	Cisco Network Analysis Module Traffic Analyzer: *http://tinyurl.com/245kso*	CableIQ: *http://tinyurl.com/yt7xvf*	DTX Cable Analyzer: *http://tinyurl.com/2fx24s*	OptiView Series III Integrated Network Analyzer: *http://tinyurl.com/2aj5on*

Review of WAN Communications

A communications provider or a common carrier normally owns the data links that make up a WAN. The links are made available to subscribers for a fee and are used to interconnect LANs or connect to remote networks.

WAN Communications

WAN data transfer speed (bandwidth) is considerably slower than the common LAN bandwidth. The charges for link provision are the major cost element; therefore, the WAN implementation must aim to provide maximum bandwidth at an acceptable cost. With user pressure to provide more service access at higher speeds and with management pressure to contain costs, determining the optimal WAN configuration is not easy.

WANs carry a variety of traffic types, such as data, voice, and video. The design selected must provide adequate bandwidth and transit times to meet the requirements of the enterprise.

Among other specifications, the design must consider the topology of the connections between the various sites, the nature of those connections, and bandwidth capacity.

Older WANs often consisted of data links directly connecting remote mainframe computers. Today's WANs connect geographically separated LANs. WAN technologies function at the lower three layers of the OSI reference model. End-user stations, servers, and routers communicate across LANs, and the WAN data links terminate at local routers.

Routers determine the most appropriate path to the destination for the data from the network layer headers. They also transfer the packets to the appropriate data link connection for delivery on the physical connection. Routers can also provide quality of service (QoS) management, which allots priorities to the different traffic streams.

Steps in WAN Design

Businesses install WAN connectivity to meet the strategic business requirement of moving data between remote branches. Because WAN connectivity is expensive and important to the business, you need to design the WAN in a systematic manner. Figure 8-26 shows the WAN design steps.

Figure 8-26   WAN Design Steps

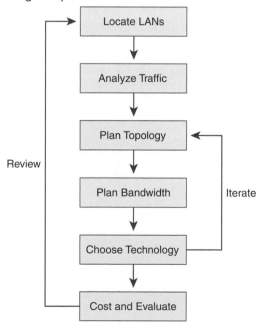

Each time a modification to an existing WAN is considered, these steps should be followed. However, because many WANs have evolved over time, some of the guidelines discussed here may not have been considered. WAN modifications may arise from expanding the enterprise WAN servers or accommodating new work practices and business methods.

As shown in Figure 8-26, the design steps are not a linear process. Several iterations of these steps may be necessary before a design is finalized. To maintain optimal performance of the WAN, continued monitoring and reevaluation are required.

How To

The steps for designing or modifying a WAN are as follows:

Step 1.   **Locate LANs**: Establish the source and destination endpoints that will connect through the WAN.

Step 2.   **Analyze traffic**: Know what data traffic must be carried, its origin, and its destination. WANs carry a variety of traffic types that have varying requirements for bandwidth, latency, and jitter. For each pair of endpoints and for each traffic type, you need information on the various traffic characteristics.

Step 3.   **Plan the topology**: The topology is influenced by geographic considerations but also by requirements such as availability. A high requirement for availability requires extra links that provide alternative data paths for redundancy and load balancing.

Step 4.   **Estimate the required bandwidth:** Traffic on the links may have varying requirements for latency and jitter.

Step 5.   **Choose the WAN technology:** Suitable link technologies must be selected.

Step 6.   **Evaluate costs:** When all the requirements are established, installation and operational costs for the WAN can be determined and compared with the business need driving the WAN implementation.

WAN Traffic Considerations

Table 8-8 shows the wide variety of traffic types and their varying requirements for bandwidth, latency, and jitter that WAN links are required to meet.

Table 8-8   WAN Traffic Considerations

Traffic	Latency Tolerance	Jitter Tolerance	Bandwidth Requirements
Voice	Low	Low	Medium
Transaction data (database)	Medium	Medium	Medium
Messaging (email)	High	High	High
File transfer	High	High	High
Batch data	High	High	High
Network management	High	High	Low
Videoconferencing	Low	Low	High

To determine traffic flow conditions and timing for a WAN link, you need to analyze the traffic characteristics specific to each LAN that is connected to the WAN. Table 8-9 lists various traffic characteristics and provides examples.

Table 8-9   WAN Traffic Characteristics

Characteristic	Example
Connectivity and volume flows	Where does this traffic flow, and how much traffic flows there?
Client/server data	What kind of traffic flows between the client and server?
Latency tolerance, including length and variability	Can the traffic flow tolerate delays? How much and how often?
Network availability tolerance	How critical is user network availability to the enterprise? Can the enterprise tolerate WAN outages, or would production grind to a halt?
Error rate tolerance	Is this noisy traffic?
Priority	Does this traffic have priority over other traffic? For example, network management messages should have higher priority than e-mail.
Protocol type	What types of protocols operate within the network?
Average packet length	What is the average size of packets being transmitted?

Determining traffic characteristics may involve consulting with management and network users to evaluate their needs.

WAN Topology Considerations

After establishing LAN endpoints and traffic characteristics, the next step in implementing a WAN is to design a suitable topology. Doing so essentially consists of the following steps:

■ Selecting an interconnection pattern or layout for the links between the various locations

■ Selecting the technologies for those links to meet the enterprise requirements at an acceptable cost

Many WANs use a star topology, as shown in Figure 8-27.

Figure 8-27   Hub-and-Spoke (Star) Topology

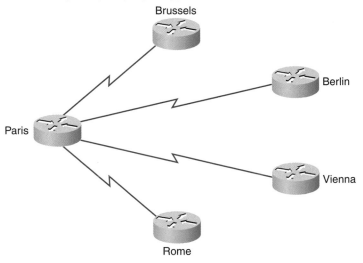

As the enterprise grows and new branches are added, the branches (or spokes) are connected to the head office (or hub), producing a traditional star topology. Star endpoints are sometimes cross-connected, creating a full-mesh or partial-mesh topology, as shown in Figures 8-28 and 8-29.

Figure 8-28   Full-Mesh Topology

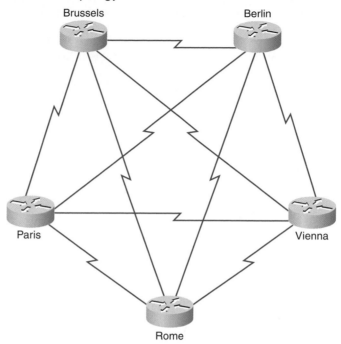

Figure 8-29   Partial-Mesh Topology

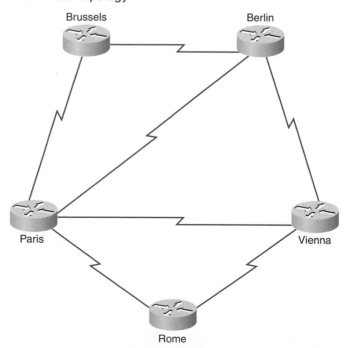

This provides many possible combinations for interconnections. When designing, reevaluating, or modifying a WAN, you must select a topology that meets the design requirements.

When selecting a layout, you must consider several factors. More links increase the cost of the network services, but having multiple paths between destinations increases reliability. Adding more network devices to the data path increases latency and decreases reliability. Generally, each packet must be completely received at one node before it can be passed to the next.

When many locations must be joined, a hierarchical solution is recommended, as shown in Figure 8-30.

Figure 8-30   Hierarchical Topology

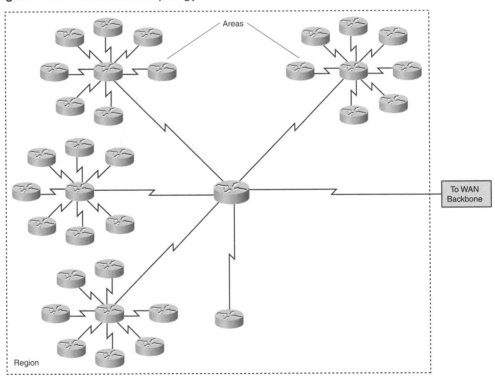

For example, imagine an enterprise that is operational in every country of the European Union. It has a branch in every city with a population of more than 10,000. Each branch has a LAN, and the company has decided to interconnect the branches. A mesh network clearly is not feasible, because there would be hundreds of thousands of links.

The answer is to implement a hierarchical topology. Group the LANs in each area and interconnect them to form a region, and then interconnect the regions to form the core of the WAN. The area could be based on the number of locations to be connected, with an upper limit of between 30 and 50. The area would have a star topology, with the hubs of the stars linked to form the region. Regions could be geographic, connecting between three and ten areas, and the hub of each region could be linked point-to-point.

A three-layer hierarchy is often useful when the network traffic mirrors the enterprise branch structure and is divided into regions, areas, and branches. It is also useful when there is a central service to which all branches must have access but traffic levels are insufficient to justify direct connection of a branch to the service.

The LAN at the center of the area may have servers providing area-based as well as local service. Depending on the traffic volumes and types, the access connections may be dialup, leased, or Frame Relay. Frame Relay facilitates some meshing for redundancy without requiring additional physical connections. Distribution links could be Frame Relay or ATM, and the network core could be ATM or leased line.

When planning simpler networks, you should still consider a hierarchical topology, because it may provide better network scalability. The hub at the center of a two-layer model is also a core, but with no other core routers connected to it. Likewise, in a single-layer solution, the area hub serves as the regional hub and the core hub. This allows easy and rapid future growth, because the basic design can be replicated to add new service areas.

WAN Connection Technologies

A typical WAN uses a combination of technologies that usually are chosen based on traffic type and volume. ISDN, DSL, Frame Relay, or leased lines are used to connect individual branches into an area. Frame Relay, ATM, or leased lines are used to connect external areas back to the backbone. ATM or leased lines form the WAN backbone. Technologies that require the establishment of a connection before data can be transmitted, such as basic telephone, ISDN, or X.25, are not suitable for WANs that require rapid response time or low latency.

Different parts of an enterprise may be directly connected with leased lines, or they may be connected with an access link to a shared network's nearest point of presence (POP). Frame Relay and ATM are examples of shared networks. Leased lines typically are more expensive than access links but are available at virtually any bandwidth and provide very low latency and jitter.

ATM and Frame Relay networks carry traffic from several customers over the same internal links. The enterprise has no control over the number of links or hops that data must traverse in the shared network. It cannot control how long data must wait at each node before moving to the next link. This uncertainty in latency and jitter makes these technologies unsuitable for some types of network traffic. However, the disadvantages of a shared network often may be outweighed by the reduced cost. Because several customers are sharing the link, the cost to each generally is less than the cost of a direct link of the same capacity.

Although ATM is a shared network, it has been designed to produce minimal latency and jitter through high-speed internal links sending easily manageable units of data, called cells. ATM cells have a fixed length of 53 bytes—48 bytes for data and 5 bytes for the header. ATM is widely used to carry delay-sensitive traffic.

Frame Relay may also be used for delay-sensitive traffic, often using QoS mechanisms to give priority to the more sensitive data.

Table 8-10 summarizes these various WAN connection technologies.

Table 8-10   WAN Connection Technologies

Technology	What the Cost Is Based On	Typical Bit Rate	Other
Leased line	Distance, capacity	Up to 45 Mbps (E3/T3)	Permanent fixed capacity
Basic telephone	Distance, time	33 to 56 kbps	Dialed, slow connection
ISDN	Distance, time	64 or 128 kbps up to 2 Mbps, PRI	Dialed, slow connection
X.25	Volume	Up to 48 kbps	Switched fixed capacity
ATM	Capacity	Up to 155 kbps	Permanent variable capacity
Frame Relay	Capacity	Up to 1.5 Mbps	Permanent variable capacity
DSL	Monthly subscription	Up to 3 Mbps	Always-on shared Internet
Metro Ethernet	Monthly subscription	Up to 500 Mbps	Limited geographic scope

Many enterprise WANs have connections to the Internet. Although the Internet may pose a security problem, it provides an alternative for interbranch traffic. Part of the traffic that must be considered during design is going to or coming from the Internet. Common implementations are to have each network in the company connect to a different ISP, or to have all company networks connect to a single ISP from a core layer connection.

WAN Bandwidth Considerations

Recall that a network supports a company's business needs. Many companies rely on the high-speed transfer of data between remote locations. Consequently, higher bandwidth is crucial, because it allows more data to be transmitted in a given time.

When bandwidth is inadequate or inefficiently managed, competition between various types of traffic may cause delay. This could reduce remote employee productivity if the time to access critical business processes between sites is increased.

A solution would be to provision high-bandwidth links to all remote locations. However, this could result in expensive WAN toll costs. Low-bandwidth links may encounter traffic bottlenecks when the outgoing traffic flows become excessive, as shown in Figure 8-31.

Figure 8-31   Low- and High-Bandwidth Link Comparison

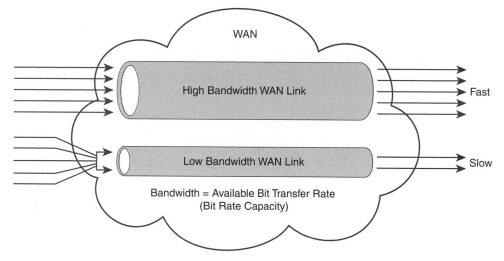

Common WAN Implementations Issues

The following list summarizes common WAN implementation issues and questions you need to answer before you can effectively implement a WAN:

- **Private or public**: Which infrastructure should I use?
- **Latency**: Delays can be a problem for real-time traffic.
- **Confidentiality**: We need to send sensitive company information to our branches across the WAN.
- **Security**: How do we protect ourselves from security threats over the WAN?
- **QoS**: End-to-end quality of service may be hard to obtain across the Internet.
- **Reliability**: Our branch depends on the WAN. Reliability is essential.

WAN Troubleshooting from an ISP's Perspective

Here are typical questions that the technical support desk of an ISP should ask a customer who is calling for support:

- What, if anything, has changed since before you started seeing this problem?

- Have you power-cycled (turned off and back on; rebooted) the router, switch, PC, server? Would you be willing to do it again while I stay on the phone with you?

- Has there been a power outage, lightning strike, or power brownout in your area recently?

- Do you have up-to-date antivirus software on your PCs?

- Ask customers to fax or e-mail you their network diagram.

- Help customers isolate the different parts of the Internet.

A significant proportion of the support calls that an ISP receives relate to the network's slowness. To troubleshoot this problem effectively, you have to isolate the individual components and test each one as follows:

- **Individual PC host**: A large number of user applications open on the PC at the same time may be responsible for the slowness that is being attributed to the network. Tools such as Task Manager on a Windows PC can help determine CPU utilization.

- **LAN**: If the customer has network monitoring software on his or her LAN, the network manager should be able to tell the person whether the bandwidth on the LAN is frequently reaching maximum utilization. The customer company would need to solve this problem internally. This is why a network baseline and ongoing monitoring are so important.

- **Link from the edge of the user network to the edge of the ISP**: To test the link from the customer edge router to the ISP edge router, first ask the customer to log in to his or her router. Then send 100 1500-byte pings (stress pings) to the IP address of the ISP edge router. This problem is not something the customer can fix. Typically it is the ISP's responsibility to engage the link provider to fix this.

- **Backbone of the ISP**: The ISP can run stress pings from the ISP edge router to the customer's edge router. The ISP also can run stress pings across each link that customer traffic traverses. By isolating and testing each link, the ISP can determine which link is causing the problem.

- **Server being accessed**: In some cases the slowness being attributed to the network may be caused by server congestion. This problem is the hardest to diagnose, and it should be the last option you pursue after all other options have been eliminated.

Network Troubleshooting

It is nearly impossible to troubleshoot any type of network connectivity issue without a network diagram that identifies IP addresses, network addresses, routing domains, and infrastructure devices such as routers, firewalls, switches, access points, servers, and so on.

Generally, two types of network maps should be available:

- *Physical topology*

- *Logical topology*

A physical network diagram shows the physical layout of the devices connected to the network. You must know how devices are physically connected to troubleshoot problems at the physical layer, such as cabling or hardware problems. Information recorded on the diagram typically includes

- Device type

- Model and manufacturer

- Operating system version

- Cable type and identifier

- Cable specification

- Connector type

- Cabling endpoints

Figure 8-32 shows a physical network diagram that provides information about the physical location of the network devices, the types of cabling between them, and the cable identification numbers.

This information is used primarily to troubleshoot physical problems with devices or cabling. It is also required when conducting network upgrades and future planning. In addition to the physical network diagram, some administrators also include actual photographs of their wiring closets as part of their network documentation.

A logical network diagram shows how data is transferred on the network. Symbols are used to represent network elements such as routers, servers, hubs, hosts, VPN concentrators, and security devices. Information recorded on a logical network diagram may include

- Device identifiers

- IP address and subnet mask

- Interface identifiers

- Connection type

- DLCI for virtual circuits

- Site-to-site VPNs

- Routing protocols

- Static routes

- Data-link protocols

- WAN technologies used

Figure 8-32   Physical Topology

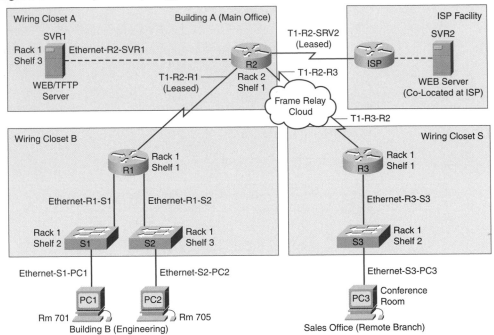

Figure 8-33 shows a logical network diagram. It's the same network as shown in Figure 8-32, but this time it provides logical information such as specific device IP addresses, network numbers, port numbers, signal types, and DCE assignments for serial links. This information could be used to troubleshoot problems at all OSI layers.

Figure 8-33 Logical Topology

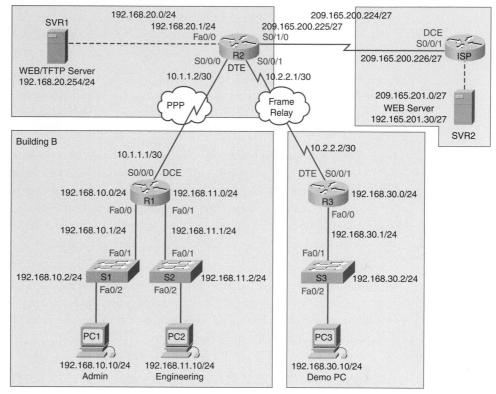

Physical Layer Troubleshooting

The physical layer transmits bits from one computer to another and regulates the transmission of a stream of bits over the physical medium. The physical layer is the only layer with physically tangible properties, such as wires, cards, and antennas.

Symptoms of Physical Layer Problems

Failures and suboptimal conditions at the physical layer not only inconvenience users but also can impact the entire company's productivity. Networks that experience these kinds of conditions usually come to a grinding halt. Because the upper layers of the OSI model depend on the physical layer to function, a network technician must be able to effectively isolate and correct problems at this layer.

A physical layer problem occurs when the physical properties of the connection are substandard, causing data to be transferred at a rate that is consistently less than the rate of data flow established in the baseline. If there is a problem with suboptimal operation at the physical layer, the network may be operational, but performance is consistently or intermittently lower than the level specified in the baseline.

Common symptoms of physical layer problems include the following:

- **Loss of connectivity**: If a cable or device fails, the most obvious symptom is a loss of connectivity between the devices that communicate over that link or with the failed device or interface. This can be discovered through a simple ping test. Intermittent loss of connectivity could indicate a loose or oxidized connection.

- **Error indicators**: Error messages reported on the device console indicate a physical layer problem. Special LEDs on infrastructure equipment can also provide visual clues to physical problems. Either the LED is inactive, or the color indicates a problem.

- **High collision counts**: High collision count usually is not a problem in a modern switched network. However, Ethernet networks using shared media hubs could suffer greatly. Although collisions are expected in a shared media environment, the average collision counts generally should be less than 5 percent. Collision-based problems may often be traced back to a bad cable or interface. As well, if the collision count gets too high and overwhelms the device, the physical layer could fail.

Unlikely symptoms related to the physical layer include network congestion and high CPU utilization. For example, assume that a link has failed because of a physical problem such as a faulty cable, causing traffic to be redirected to a lower-capacity link. This could create a network bottleneck and cause congestion on the router interface. The router would also experience a higher CPU utilization rate.

Causes of Physical Layer Problems

The following list describes the common causes of network problems at the physical layer:

- **Power-related**: Power-related issues are the most fundamental reason for network failure. A power-related problem could be local, such as when a device's power supply fails. It could also be external should electrical power be interrupted. If a power-related issue is suspected, a physical inspection of the power module is often carried out. Check the operation of the fans, and ensure that the chassis intake and exhaust vents are clear. If other nearby units have also powered down, suspect a power failure at the main power supply.

- **Hardware faults**: Faulty network interface cards (NIC) can be the cause of network transmission errors due to late collisions, short frames, and jabber. *Jabber* is often defined as the condition in which a network device continually transmits random, meaningless data onto the network. Likely causes of jabber are faulty or corrupt NIC driver files, bad cabling, or grounding problems.

- **Cabling faults**: Many problems can be corrected by simply reseating cables that have become partially disconnected. When performing a physical inspection, look for damaged cables, improper cable types, and poorly crimped RJ-45s. Suspect cables should be tested or exchanged with a known functioning cable.

Check for incorrectly used crossover cables or hub-and-switch ports that are incorrectly configured as a crossover. Split-pair cables operate either poorly or not at all, depending on the Ethernet speed used, the length of the split segment, and how far it is located from either end.

Problems with fiber-optic cables may be caused by dirty connectors, excessively tight bends, or swapped RX/TX connections when polarized.

Problems with coaxial cable often occur at the connectors. When the center conductor on the coaxial cable end is not straight and of the correct length, a good connection is not achieved.

- **Attenuation**: An attenuated data bitstream is when the bits' amplitude is reduced while they are traveling across a cable. If attenuation is severe, the receiving device cannot always successfully distinguish the component bits of the stream from each other. This ends in a garbled transmission and causes the receiving device to ask the sender to retransmit the missed traffic. Attenuation can be caused if a cable length exceeds the design limit for the medium. (For example, a Category 5 network cable is limited to 100 meters [328 feet] for good performance.) Attenuation also can occur when a poor connection exists, resulting from a loose cable or dirty or oxidized contacts.

- **Noise**: Local electromagnetic interference (EMI) is commonly called noise. Four types of noise are most significant to data networks:

  - Impulse noise is caused by voltage fluctuations or current spikes induced on the cabling.

  - Random (white) noise is generated by many sources, such as FM radio stations, police radios, building security systems, and avionics for automated landing.

  - Alien crosstalk is noise induced by other cables in the same pathway.

  - Near-end crosstalk (NEXT) is noise that originates from crosstalk from adjacent cables. NEXT also can come from nearby electric cables, devices with large electric motors, or anything that includes a transmitter more powerful than a cell phone.

- **Interface configuration errors**: Many things can be misconfigured on an interface and can cause it to go down, causing a loss of connectivity with attached network segments. Examples of configuration errors that affect the physical layer include

  - Serial links were reconfigured as asynchronous instead of synchronous.

  - The interface is not turned on.

- **Exceeding design limits**: A component may be operating suboptimally at the physical layer because it is being used at a higher average rate than the rate at which it is configured to operate. When you troubleshoot this type of problem, it becomes evident that resources for the device are operating at or near the maximum capacity and that the number of interface errors is increasing.

■ **CPU overload**: High traffic can also cause CPU overload in a router. If some interfaces are regularly overloaded with traffic, consider redesigning the traffic flow in the network or upgrading the hardware.

Isolating Problems at the Physical Layer

To isolate problems at the physical layers, do the following:

Step 1.   **Check for bad cables or connections**: Verify that the cable from the source interface is properly connected and is in good condition. Your cable tester (such as Fluke CableIQ tester) might reveal an open wire. If you doubt a cable's integrity, swap the suspect cable with a known working cable. If you think the connection might be bad, remove the cable, physically inspect both the cable and the interface, and then reseat the cable. Use a cable tester with suspect wall jacks to ensure that the jack is properly wired. Devices with modular NICs, WAN interface cards (WIC), network modules, or network blades could also need to be carefully reseated.

Step 2.   **Check that the correct cabling standard is adhered to throughout the network**: Verify that the proper cable is being used. A crossover cable may be required for direct connections between some devices. Ensure that the cable is correctly wired. For example, your Fluke CableIQ meter might detect that although a cable is good for Fast Ethernet, it is not qualified to support 1000BASE-T because wires 7 and 8 are not correctly connected. These wires are not required for Fast Ethernet, but they are required in Gigabit Ethernet and Power over Ethernet (PoE).

Step 3.   **Check that devices are cabled correctly**: Check to make sure that all cables are properly labeled and connected to their correct ports or interfaces. Make sure that any cross-connects are properly patched to the correct location. This is where having a neat and organized wiring closet and good documentation saves you a great deal of time.

Step 4.   **Verify proper interface configurations**: Check that all switch ports are set in the correct VLAN and that spanning-tree, speed, and duplex settings are correctly configured. Confirm that any active ports or interfaces are not shut down.

Step 5.   **Check operational statistics and data error rates**: Use Cisco **show** commands to check for statistics such as collisions and input and output errors. The characteristics of these statistics vary depending on the protocols used on the network.

Data Link Layer Troubleshooting

Troubleshooting Layer 2 problems can be a challenging process. The configuration and operation of these protocols are critical to creating a functional, well-tuned network.

Symptoms of Data Link Layer Problems

Data link layer problems cause common symptoms that help you identify Layer 2 issues. Recognizing these symptoms helps you narrow down the number of possible causes.

Here are some common symptoms of network problems at the data link layer:

- **No functionality or connectivity at the network layer or above**: Some Layer 2 problems can stop the exchange of frames across a link, and others only cause network performance to degrade. Amber LED link lights are useful indicators on switches.

- **The network is operating below baseline performance levels**: Two distinct types of suboptimal Layer 2 operation can occur in a network:

  - Frames take an illogical path to their destination but do arrive. This causes slow performance. An example of a problem that could cause frames to take a suboptimal path is a poorly designed Layer 2 spanning-tree topology. In this case, the network might experience high-bandwidth usage on links that should not have that level of traffic.

  - Some frames are dropped. These problems can be identified through error counter statistics and console error messages that appear on the switch or router. In an Ethernet environment, an extended or continuous ping also reveals if frames are being dropped.

- **Excessive broadcasts**: Modern operating systems use broadcasts extensively to discover network services and other hosts. Where excessive broadcasts are observed, it is important to identify the source of the broadcasts. Generally, excessive broadcasts result from one of the following situations:

  - Poorly programmed or poorly configured applications

  - Large Layer 2 broadcast domains

  - Underlying network problems, such as Spanning Tree Protocol (STP) loops or route flapping

- **Console messages**: In some instances, a router recognizes that a Layer 2 problem has occurred and sends alert messages to the console. Typically, a router does this when it detects a problem with interpreting incoming frames (encapsulation or framing problems) or when keepalives are expected but do not arrive. The most common console message that indicates a Layer 2 problem is a line protocol down message.

Causes of Data Link Layer Problems

Issues at the data link layer that commonly result in network connectivity or performance problems include the following:

- **Encapsulation errors**: An encapsulation error occurs because the bits placed in a particular field by the sender are not what the receiver expects to see. This condition occurs when the encapsulation at one end of a WAN link is configured differently from the encapsulation used at the other end.

- **Address mapping errors**: In topologies such as point-to-multipoint, Frame Relay, or broadcast Ethernet, it is essential that an appropriate Layer 2 destination address be given to the frame. This ensures its arrival at the correct destination. To achieve this, the network device must match a destination Layer 3 address with the correct Layer 2 address using either static or dynamic maps.

  When you use static maps in Frame Relay, an incorrect map is a common mistake. Simple configuration errors can result in a mismatch of Layer 2 and Layer 3 addressing information.

  In a dynamic environment, the mapping of Layer 2 and Layer 3 information can fail for the following reasons:

  - Devices may have been specifically configured not to respond to ARP or Inverse ARP requests.

  - The Layer 2 or Layer 3 information that is cached may have physically changed.

  - Invalid ARP replies are received because of a misconfiguration or a security attack.

- **Framing errors**: Frames usually work in groups of 8 bits (a byte). A framing error occurs when a frame does not end on an 8-bit boundary. When this happens, the receiver may have problems determining where one frame ends and another frame starts. Depending on the severity of the framing problem, the interface may be able to interpret some of the frames. Too many invalid frames may prevent valid keepalives from being exchanged.

  Framing errors can be caused by a noisy serial line, an improperly designed cable (too long or not properly shielded), or an incorrectly configured clock rate.

- **STP failures or loops**: The purpose of STP is to resolve a redundant physical topology into a tree-like topology by blocking redundant ports. Most STP problems revolve around these issues:

  - Forwarding loops that occur when no port in a redundant topology is blocked and traffic is forwarded in circles indefinitely. When the forwarding loop starts, it usually congests the lowest-bandwidth links along its path. If all the links are the same bandwidth, they all are congested. This congestion causes packet loss and leads to a downed network in the affected Layer 2 domain.

- Excessive flooding because of a high rate of STP topology changes. The role of the topology change mechanism is to correct Layer 2 forwarding tables after the forwarding topology has changed. This is necessary to avoid a connectivity outage because, after a topology change, some MAC addresses previously accessible through particular ports might become accessible through different ports. A topology change should be a rare event in a well-configured network. When a link on a switch port goes up or down, eventually a topology change occurs when the port's STP state is changing to or from forwarding. However, when a port is flapping (oscillating between up and down states), this causes repetitive topology changes and flooding.

- Slow STP convergence or reconvergence. This can be caused by a mismatch between the real and documented topology, a configuration error such as an inconsistent configuration of STP timers, an overloaded switch CPU during convergence, or a software defect.

Troubleshooting Layer 2: PPP

The difficulty in troubleshooting Layer 2 technologies, such as Point-to-Point Protocol (PPP) and Frame Relay, is the unavailability of common Layer 3 troubleshooting tools, such as ping, to assist with anything but figuring out that the network is down. Only by thoroughly understanding the protocols and their operation can a network technician choose the appropriate troubleshooting methodology and Cisco IOS commands to solve the problem efficiently.

Most of the problems that occur with PPP involve link negotiation. Refer to Figure 8-34 and Example 8-1.

Figure 8-34   Sample Topology for Troubleshooting PPP

Example 8-1   Verifying the R2 WAN Interface

```
R2# show interfaces serial 0/0/0

Serial0/0/0 is up, line protocol is up
  Hardware is GT96K Serial
  Internet address is 10.1.1.2/30
  MTU 1500 bytes, BW 128 Kbit, DLY 20000 usec,
     reliability 255/255, txload 1/255, rxload 1/255
  Encapsulation HDLC, loopback not set
  . . .
```

The steps for troubleshooting PPP are as follows:

Step 1.   Check that the appropriate encapsulation is in use at both ends, using the **show interfaces serial** command. In Example 8-1, the command output reveals that the encapsulation on R2 has not been configured correctly.

To solve the problem, reconfigure the interface with the **encapsulation ppp** command.

Step 2.   Confirm that the PPP Link Control Protocol (LCP) negotiations have succeeded by checking the output for the LCP Open message. Output from the **show interfaces serial** command reveals that PPP has been configured:

```
R2# show interfaces serial 0/0/0

Serial0/0/0 is up, line protocol is up
   Hardware is GT96K Serial
   Internet address is 10.1.1.2/30
   MTU 1500 bytes, BW 128 Kbit, DLY 20000 usec,
       reliability 255/255, txload 1/255, rxload 1/255
   Encapsulation PPP, LCP Open
     . . .
```

The output also shows the LCP Open message, which indicates that the LCP negotiations have succeeded.

Step 3.   Verify authentication on both sides of the link using the **debug ppp authentication** command, as shown in the following debug output on router R1:

```
R1# debug ppp authentication

Serial0/0/0: Unable to authenticate. No name received from peer
Serial0/0/0: Unable to validate CHAP response. USERNAME R2 not found.
Serial0/0/0: Unable to validate CHAP response. No password defined for
  USERNAME R2
Serial0/0/0: Failed CHAP authentication with remote.
Remote message is Unknown name
   . . .    . . .
```

The output from the **debug ppp authentication** command shows that R1 is unable to authenticate R2 using CHAP, because the username and password for R2 have not been configured on R1.

Refer to Chapter 2, "PPP," for further details on troubleshooting PPP implementations.

How To 🔍

Troubleshooting Layer 2: Frame Relay

Troubleshooting Frame Relay network issues can be broken into four steps:

Step 1.   Verify the physical connection between the channel service unit/data service unit (CSU/DSU) and the router. In Figure 8-35, the physical connections between routers R2 and R3 and their corresponding CSU/DSU can be verified using a cable tester and by verifying that all status LEDs on the CSU/DSU unit are green.

Figure 8-35   Sample Frame Relay Topology

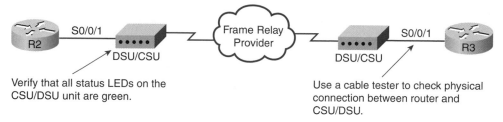

Verify that all status LEDs on the CSU/DSU unit are green.

Use a cable tester to check physical connection between router and CSU/DSU.

In Figure 8-35, some of the status lights for the CSU/DSU at R3 are red, indicating a potential connectivity problem between the CSU/DSU and router R3.

Step 2.   Verify that the router and Frame Relay provider are properly exchanging Local Management Interface (LMI) information by using the **show frame-relay lmi** command:

```
R2# show frame-relay lmi

LMI Statistics for interface Serial0/0/1 (Frame Relay DTE) LMI TYPE = CISCO
    Invalid Unnumbered info 0        Invalid Prot Disc 0
    Invalid dummy Call Ref 0         Invalid Msg Type 0
    Invalid Status Message 0         Invalid Lock Shift 0
    Invalid Information ID 0          Invalid Report IE Len 0
    Invalid Report Request 0         Invalid Keep IE Len 0
    Num Status Enq. Sent 76          Num Status msgs Rcvd 76
    Num Update Status Rcvd 0         Num Status Timeouts 0
Last Full Status Req 00:00:48    Last Full Status Rcvd 00:00:48
```

The output from the **show frame-relay lmi** command shows no errors or lost messages. This indicates that R2 and the Frame Relay provider switch are properly exchanging LMI information.

Step 3.   Verify that the PVC status is active by using the **show frame-relay pvc** command:

```
R2# show frame-relay pvc 201

PVC Statistics for interface Serial0/0/1 (Frame Relay DTE)
DLCI = 201, DLCI USAGE = LOCAL, PVC STATUS = ACTIVE, INTERFACE =
  Serial0/0/1.201
  input pkts 11            output pkts 8            in bytes 3619
  out bytes 2624          dropped pkts 0           in pkts dropped 0
  out pkts dropped 0            out bytes dropped 0
  in FECN pkts 0          in BECN pkts 0           out FECN pkts 0
  out BECN pkts 0         in DE pkts 0             out DE pkts 0
  out bcast pkts 8        out bcast bytes 2624
  5 minute input rate 0 bits/sec, 0 packets/sec
  5 minute output rate 0 bits/sec, 0 packets/sec
pvc create time 00:08:23, last time pvc status changed 00:08:23
```

The output from the **show frame-relay pvc** command verifies that the PVC status is active. Other states include inactive and deleted. The inactive state indicates a successful connection from your router to the local Frame Relay switch but a problem at the remote end of the PVC. The deleted state indicates that the DTE is configured for a DLCI that the local Frame Relay switch does not recognize as valid for that interface.

Step 4.   Verify that the Frame Relay encapsulation matches on both routers with the **show interfaces serial** command, as shown in the following output for interface serial 0/0/1 on both routers R2 and R3:

```
R2# show interfaces serial 0/0/1

Serial0/0/1 is up, line protocol is up
  Hardware is GT96K Serial
  Internet address is 10.2.2.1 /24
  MTU 1500 bytes, BW 1544 Kbit, DLY 20000 usec, reliability 255/255,
  txload 1/255, rxload 1/255
  Encapsulation FRAME-RELAY, loopback not set
  . . .
```

```
R3# show interfaces serial 0/0/1

Serial0/0/1 is up, line protocol is up
  Hardware is GT96K Serial
  Internet address is 10.2.2.2 /24
  MTU 1500 bytes, BW 1544 Kbit, DLY 20000 usec, reliability 255/255,
  txload 1/255, rxload 1/255
  Encapsulation HDLC, loopback not set
  . . .
```

The output of the **show interfaces serial** command at routers R2 and R3 reveals an encapsulation mismatch between them. The encapsulation on R3 has been configured incorrectly.

For further details on troubleshooting Frame Relay implementations, see Chapter 3, "Frame Relay."

Troubleshooting Layer 2: STP Loops

If you suspect that an STP loop is causing a Layer 2 problem, verify that Spanning Tree Protocol is running on each of the switches. A switch should have STP disabled only if it is not part of a physically looped topology. To verify STP operation, use the **show spanning-tree** command on each switch. If you discover that STP is not operating, you can enable it using the **spanning-tree** *vlan-ID* command.

Follow these steps to troubleshoot forwarding loops for the sample topology shown in Figure 8-36:

Step 1. **Identify that an STP loop is occurring**: When a forwarding loop has developed in the network, these are the usual symptoms:

■ Loss of connectivity to, from, and through the affected network regions

■ High CPU utilization on routers connected to affected segments or VLANs

■ High link utilization (often 100 percent)

■ High switch backplane utilization (compared to the baseline utilization)

■ Syslog messages that indicate packet looping in the network (for example, Hot Standby Router Protocol duplicate IP address messages)

■ Syslog messages that indicate constant address relearning or MAC address flapping messages

■ An increasing number of output drops on many interfaces

Figure 8-36   STP Topology

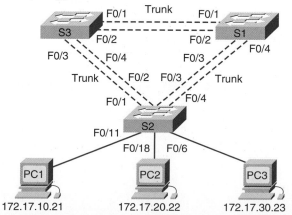

Step 2.   **Discover the loop's topology (scope):** The highest priority is to stop the loop and restore network operation. To stop the loop, you must know which ports are involved. Look at the ports with the highest link utilization (packets per second). The **show interface** command displays the utilization for each interface. Make sure that you record this information before proceeding to the next step. Otherwise, it could be difficult later to determine the cause of the loop.

Step 3.   **Break the loop:** Shut down or disconnect the involved ports one at a time. After you disable or disconnect each port, check whether the switch backplane utilization is back to a normal level. Document your findings. Keep in mind that some ports may not be sustaining the loop but rather are flooding the traffic arriving with the loop. When you shut down such flooding ports, you reduce backplane utilization by only a small amount, but you do not stop the loop.

Step 4.   **Find and fix the cause of the loop:** Determining why the loop began is often the most difficult part of the process, because the reasons can vary. It is also difficult to formulate an exact procedure that works in every case. First, investigate the topology diagram to find a redundant path.

For every switch on the redundant path, check for these issues:

- Does the switch know the correct STP root?
- Is the root port identified correctly?
- Are Bridge Protocol Data Units (BPDU) received regularly on the root port and on ports that are supposed to be blocking?
- Are BPDUs sent regularly on nonroot designated ports?

Step 5.   **Restore the redundancy:** After the device or link that is causing the loop has been found and the problem has been resolved, restore the redundant links that were disconnected.

We have only touched on the subject of troubleshooting STP loops. Troubleshooting loops and other STP problems is complex, and a detailed discussion is beyond the scope of this course. If you want to learn more about troubleshooting STP problems, an excellent technical note is available at *http://cisco.com/en/US/tech/tk389/tk621/technologies_tech_note 09186a0080136673.shtml#troubleshoot*.

Network Layer Troubleshooting

Network layer problems include any problem that involves a Layer 3 protocol, both routed protocols and routing protocols. This section focuses primarily on IP routing protocols.

Symptoms of Network Layer Problems

Common symptoms of network problems at the network layer are

- Network failure

- Network performance below the baseline

Problems at the network layer can cause network failure or suboptimal performance. Network failure is when the network is nearly or completely nonfunctional, affecting all users and applications using the network. Users and network administrators usually notice these failures quickly, so obviously they are critical to a company's productivity. Network optimization problems usually involve a subset of users, applications, destinations, or a particular type of traffic. Optimization issues in general can be more difficult to detect and even harder to isolate and diagnose, because they usually involve multiple layers or even the host computer itself. Determining that the problem is a network layer problem can take time.

Troubleshooting Layer 3 Problems

In most networks, static routes are used in combination with dynamic routing protocols. Improper configuration of static routes can lead to less-than-optimal routing and, in some cases, can create routing loops or cause parts of the network to become unreachable.

Troubleshooting dynamic routing protocols requires a thorough understanding of how the specific routing protocol functions. Some problems are common to all routing protocols, and other problems are particular to the individual routing protocol.

No single template exists for solving Layer 3 problems. Routing problems are solved with a methodical process, using a series of commands to isolate and diagnose the problem.

When you're diagnosing a possible problem involving routing protocols, a good methodology to explore is as follows:

Step 1.   **Check the network topology changes**: Often a change in the topology, such as a down link, may affect other areas of the network in ways that might not be obvious at the time. This may include the installation of new routes, static or dynamic, the removal of other routes, and so on.

Here are a couple of considerations:

- Has anything in the network changed recently?

- Is anyone currently working on the network infrastructure?

Step 2.   **Check for equipment and connectivity problems**: Check for any equipment and connectivity problems, including power problems such as outages and environmental problems such as overheating. Also check for Layer 1 problems, such as cabling problems, bad ports, and ISP problems.

Step 3.   **Check routing neighbor relationships**: If the routing protocol establishes an adjacency with a neighbor, check to see if there are any problems with the routers forming neighbor relationships.

Step 4.   **Check for topology database issues**: If the routing protocol uses a topology table or database, check the table for anything unexpected, such as missing or unexpected entries.

Step 5.   **Check for routing table issues**: Check the routing table for anything unexpected, such as missing or unexpected routes. Use **debug** commands to view routing updates and to perform routing table maintenance.

Transport Layer Troubleshooting

Network problems can arise from transport layer problems on the router, particularly at the edge of the network, where security technologies are examining and modifying the traffic. Some common symptoms of transport layer problems are

- Intermittent network problems

- Security problems

- Address translation problems

- Problems with specific traffic types

This section discusses two of the most commonly implemented transport layer security technologies—access control lists (ACL) and Network Address Translation (NAT).

Common Access List Symptoms and Troubleshooting

The most common issues with ACLs are caused by improper configuration. Misconfigurations commonly occur in eight areas:

- **Incorrect traffic direction**: The most common router misconfiguration is applying the ACL to the correct traffic direction. Traffic is defined by both the router interface through which the traffic is traveling and the direction in which the traffic is traveling. An ACL must be applied to the correct interface, and the correct traffic direction must be selected.

- **Incorrect control element order**: The order of the elements in an ACL should be from specific to general. Although an ACL may have an element to specifically permit a particular traffic flow, packets will never match that element if they are being denied by another element earlier in the list. For example, permit and deny specific hosts first, and then permit or deny general networks.

- **Implicit deny any any**: In a situation in which high security is not required on the ACL, forgetting about this implicit access control element may be the cause of an ACL misconfiguration.

- **Addresses and wildcard masks**: If the router is running both ACLs and NAT, the order in which each of these technologies is applied to a traffic flow is important:

  - Inbound traffic is processed by the inbound ACL before being processed by outside-to-inside NAT.

  - Outbound traffic is processed by the outbound ACL after being processed by inside-to-outside NAT.

  Complex wildcard masks provide significant improvements in efficiency but are more subject to configuration errors. An example of a complex wildcard mask is using the address 10.0.32.0 and wildcard mask 0.0.0.15 to select the first 14 host addresses in the 10.0.32.0 network.

- **TCP/UDP selection**: When configuring ACLs, it is important that you specify only the correct transport layer protocols. Many network engineers, when unsure if a particular traffic flow uses a TCP port or UDP port, configure both or incorrectly configure one. Specifying both opens a hole through the firewall, possibly giving intruders an avenue into the network. It also introduces an extra element into the ACL, so the ACL takes longer to process, introducing more latency into network communications.

- **Source and destination ports**: Properly controlling the traffic between two hosts requires symmetric access control elements for inbound and outbound ACLs. Address and port information for traffic generated by a replying host is the mirror image of address and port information for traffic generated by the initiating host.

- **Use of the established keyword**: The **established** keyword increases the security provided by an ACL. The **established** keyword can be used for only the TCP protocol to indicate an established connection. It ensures that only traffic that originated from the internal network can return. However, if the keyword is applied to an outbound ACL, unexpected results may occur.

- **Uncommon protocols**: Misconfigured ACLs often cause problems for less common protocols than TCP and UDP. Uncommon protocols that are gaining popularity are VPN and encryption protocols.

A useful command for viewing ACL operation is the **log** keyword on ACL entries. This keyword instructs the router to place an entry in the system log whenever that entry condition is matched. The logged event includes details of the packet that matched the ACL element.

The **log** keyword is especially useful for troubleshooting and also provides information on intrusion attempts being blocked by the ACL.

Common NAT Issues

A common problem with NAT technologies is interoperability with other network technologies, especially those that contain or derive information from host network addressing in the packet. Some common NAT issues (at the transport layer—Layer 4) are as follows:

- Interoperability issues

- Incorrect static NAT

- Improperly configured NAT timers

Some of the problematic NAT technologies are as follows:

- **BOOTP and DHCP**: Both protocols manage the automatic assignment of IP addresses to clients, although DHCP has superseded BOOTP. Recall that the first packet that a new client sends is a DHCP-Request broadcast IP packet. The DHCP-Request packet has a source IP address of 0.0.0.0. Because NAT requires both a valid destination and source IP address, BOOTP and DHCP can have difficulty operating over a router running either static or dynamic NAT. Configuring the IP helper feature can help solve this problem.

- **DNS and WINS**: A router running dynamic NAT changes the relationship between inside and outside addresses regularly as table entries expire and are re-created. Therefore, a DNS or WINS server outside the NAT router does not have an accurate representation of the network inside the router. Configuring the IP helper feature can help solve this problem.

- **SNMP**: Similar to DNS packets, NAT cannot alter the addressing information stored in the packet's data payload. Because of this, an SNMP management station on one side of a NAT router may not be able to contact SNMP agents on the other side of the NAT router. Configuring the IP helper feature can help solve this problem.

- **Tunneling and encryption protocols**: Encryption and tunneling protocols often require that traffic be sourced from a specific UDP or TCP port, or use a protocol at the transport layer that NAT cannot process. For example, NAT cannot process IPsec tunneling protocols and generic routing encapsulation protocols used by VPN implementations.

    If encryption or tunneling protocols must be run through a NAT router, the network administrator can create a static NAT entry for the required port for a single IP address on the inside of the NAT router.

One of the more common NAT configuration errors is forgetting that NAT affects both inbound and outbound traffic. An inexperienced network administrator might configure a static NAT entry to redirect inbound traffic to a specific inside backup host. This static NAT statement also changes the source address of traffic from that host, possibly resulting in undesirable and unexpected behaviors or suboptimal operation.

Improperly configured timers can also result in unexpected network behavior and suboptimal operation of dynamic NAT. If NAT timers are too short, entries in the NAT table may expire before replies are received, so packets are discarded. The loss of packets generates retransmissions, consuming more bandwidth. If timers are too long, entries may stay in the NAT table longer than necessary, consuming the available connection pool. In busy networks, this may lead to memory problems on the router, and hosts may be unable to establish connections if the dynamic NAT table is full.

Refer to Chapter 7, "IP Addressing Services," for further details on troubleshooting NAT configuration.

Application Layer Troubleshooting

Recall that two reference models are used in networking. OSI Layers 5 through 7 include the session, presentation, and application layers, and the TCP/IP application layer combines these into one layer. For the purposes of this section, we will refer to the TCP/IP application layer.

Most of the application layer protocols provide user services, as shown in Figure 8-37.

Figure 8-37   Application Layer Overview

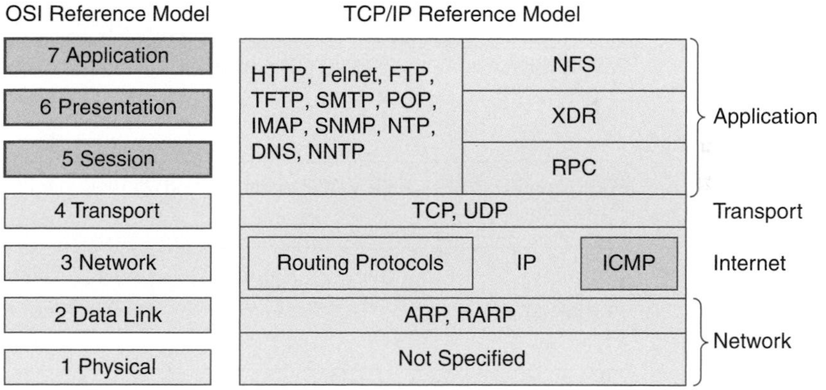

Application layer protocols typically are used for network management, file transfer, distributed file services, terminal emulation, and e-mail. However, new user services are often added, such as VPNs, VoIP, and so on.

The most widely known and implemented TCP/IP application layer protocols include the following:

- **Telnet** enables users to establish terminal session connections with remote hosts.

- **Hypertext Transfer Protocol (HTTP)** supports the exchange of web pages that consist of text, graphic images, sound, video, and other multimedia files on the web.

- **File Transfer Protocol (FTP)** performs interactive file transfers between hosts.

- **Trivial File Transfer Protocol (TFTP)** performs basic interactive file transfers, typically between hosts and networking devices.

- **Simple Mail Transfer Protocol (SMTP)** supports basic message delivery services between mail servers.

- **Post Office Protocol version 3 (POP3)** is used by clients to connect to mail servers and download e-mail.

- **Simple Network Management Protocol (SNMP)** collects management information from network devices.

- **Domain Name Resolution (DNS)** maps IP addresses to the names assigned to network devices.

- **Network File System (NFS)** enables computers to mount drives on remote hosts and operate them as if they were local drives. Originally developed by Sun Microsystems, it combines with two other application layer protocols, external data representation (XDR), and remote-procedure call (RPC), to allow transparent access to remote network resources.

Table 8-11 lists application protocols and their associated ports.

Table 8-11   Application Protocols and Ports

Application	Protocol and Port	Description
WWW browser	HTTP (TCP port 80)	Web browsers and servers use HTTP to transfer the files that make up web pages.
File transfer	FTP (TCP ports 20 and 21)	FTP provides a way to move files between computer systems.
Terminal emulation	Telnet (TCP port 23)	The Telnet protocol provides terminal emulation services over a reliable TCP stream.
E-mail	POP3 (TCP port 110) SMTP (TCP port 25) IMAP4 (TCP port 143)	SMTP is used to transfer e-mail between mail servers. Mail clients use it to send mail. Mail clients use either POP3 or Internet Message Access Protocol (IMAP) to receive mail.
Network management	SNMP (UDP port 161)	SNMP is a network management protocol used to report anomalous network conditions and set network threshold values.

Table 8-11   Application Protocols and Ports

Application	Protocol and Port	Description
Domain name resolution	DNS (TCP/UDP port 53)	Resolves IP addresses to domain names.
Distributed file service	X Window (UDP ports 6000 to 6063) NFS (TCP/UDP port 2049), XDR, RPC (TCP/UDP port 111)	X Window is a popular protocol that permits intelligent terminals to communicate with remote computers as if they were directly attached. NFS, XDR, and RPC combine to allow transparent access to remote network resources.

Symptoms of Application Layer Problems

Application layer problems prevent services from being provided to application programs. A problem at the application layer can result in unreachable or unusable resources when the physical, data link, network, and transport layers are functional. It is possible to have full network connectivity, but the application simply cannot provide data.

Another type of problem at the application layer occurs when the physical, data link, network, and transport layers are functional, but the data transfer and requests for network services from a single network service or application do not meet a user's normal expectations.

A problem at the application layer may cause users to complain that the network or the particular application that they are working with is sluggish or slower than usual when they transfer data or request network services.

Some of the possible symptoms of application layer problems are as follows:

- No network services are available
- User complaints about slow application performance
- Application error messages
- Console error messages
- System log file messages
- Network management system alarms

Troubleshooting Application Layer Problems

The same general troubleshooting process that is used to isolate problems at the lower layers can also be used to isolate problems at the application layer. The concepts are the same, but the technological focus has shifted to involve things such as refused or timed-out connections, access lists, and DNS issues.

How To

The steps for troubleshooting application layer problems are as follows:

Step 1. **Ping the default gateway**: To rule out problems at Layers 1 to 3, use the **ping** command. If it's successful, Layer 1 and Layer 2 services are functioning properly.

Step 2. **Verify end-to-end connectivity**: Use an extended ping if you're attempting the ping from a Cisco router. If it's successful, Layer 3 is operating correctly. If Layers 1 to 3 are functioning properly, the issue must exist at a higher layer.

Step 3. **Verify access list and NAT operation**: Verify Layer 4 ACL and NAT operations. To troubleshoot access control lists, follow these steps:

- Use the **show access-list** command. Could any ACLs be stopping traffic? Notice which access lists have matches.

- Clear the access list counters with the **clear access-list counters** command, and try to reestablish a connection.

- Verify the access list counters. Have any increased? Should they increase?

To troubleshoot NAT, follow these steps:

- Use the **show ip nat translations** command. Are there any translations? Are the translations as expected?

- Clear the NAT translations with the **clear ip nat translation *** command, and try to access the external resource again.

- Use the **debug ip nat** command, and examine the output.

- Look at the running configuration file. Are the **ip nat inside** and **ip nat outside** commands located on the right interfaces? Is the NAT pool correctly configured? Is the ACL correctly identifying the hosts?

If the ACLs and NAT are functioning as expected, the problem must lie in a higher layer.

Step 4. **Troubleshoot upper-layer protocol connectivity**: Even though IP connectivity may exist between a source and a destination, problems may still exist for a specific upper-layer protocol, such as FTP, HTTP, or Telnet. These protocols ride on top of the basic IP transport but are subject to protocol-specific problems related to packet filters and firewalls. It is possible that everything except e-mail works between a given source and destination.

Troubleshooting an upper-layer protocol connectivity problem requires understanding the process of the protocol. This information usually is found in the latest RFC for the protocol or on the application developer web page.

Correcting Application Layer Problems

Figure 8-38 shows a flowchart for correcting application layer problems.

Figure 8-38   Correcting Application Layer Problems

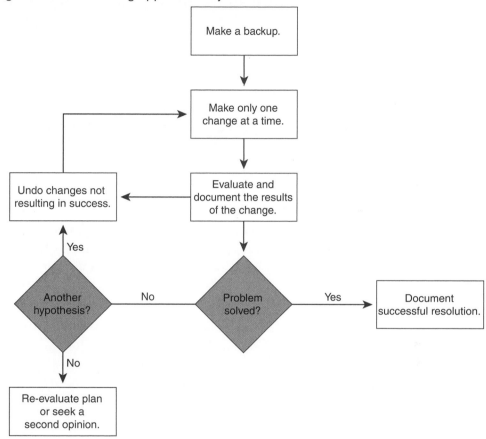

The following list describes these steps in more detail:

Step 1.   **Make a backup**: Before proceeding, ensure that a valid configuration has been saved for any device on which the configuration may be modified. This provides for recovery to a known initial state.

Step 2.   **Test the hypothesis, and make an initial hardware or software configuration change**: From your list of possible causes, test the first hypothesis. If the correction requires more than one change, make only one change at a time.

Step 3.   **Evaluate and document each change and its results**: If the results of any problem-solving steps are unsuccessful, immediately undo the changes. If the problem is intermittent, wait to see if the problem occurs again before evaluating the effect of any change.

Step 4.   **Determine if the change solves the problem**: Verify that the change actually resolves the problem without introducing any new problems. The network should be returned to the baseline operation, and no new or old symptoms should be present. If the problem is not solved, test the next likely hypothesis, and undo all the changes. If new or additional problems are discovered, modify the correction plan.

Step 5.   **Stop when the problem is solved**: Stop making changes when the original problem appears to be solved.

Step 6.   **If necessary, get assistance from outside resources**: This may be a coworker, a consultant, or the Cisco Technical Assistance Center (TAC). On rare occasions, a core dump may be necessary; it creates output that a specialist at Cisco Systems can analyze.

Step 7.   **Document**: After the problem is resolved, document the solution.

Troubleshooting Network Problems (8.4.6)

To successfully complete this activity, you need your final documentation for Packet Tracer Activity 8.2.1: Documenting Your Network, which you completed earlier in this chapter. This documentation should have an accurate topology diagram and addressing table. If you do not have this documentation, ask your instructor for accurate versions.

Detailed instructions are provided within the activity. Use File e4-846.pka on the CD-ROM that accompanies this book to perform this activity using Packet Tracer.

Summary

In this chapter, you learned that a network baseline is required for effective troubleshooting. Creating a baseline begins with ensuring that network documentation is up to date and accurate. Proper network documentation includes a network configuration table for all devices and a topology diagram that reflects the network's current state. When the network has been fully documented, a baseline measurement of network performance should be carried out over a period of several weeks to a month to establish the network's personality. The first baseline is created during a time of stable and normal operation.

The most effective way to troubleshoot is with a systematic approach using a layered model, such as the OSI model or the TCP/IP model. Three methods commonly used to troubleshoot are bottom-up, top-down, and divide-and-conquer. Each method has its advantages and disadvantages, and you learned the guidelines for choosing which method to apply. You also learned about the various software and hardware tools that network professionals use to gather symptoms and troubleshoot network problems.

Although they operate primarily at the first three OSI layers, WANs have implementation issues that can affect the operation of the rest of the network. You learned about some of the considerations for implementing WANs and common problems that WANs introduce into networks, such as security threats, bandwidth problems, latency, and QoS issues.

Finally, you explored the symptoms and causes of common problems at each of the OSI layers and the steps for troubleshooting them.

Labs

The activities and labs available in the companion *Accessing the WAN, CCNA Exploration Labs and Study Guide* (ISBN 1-58713-201-x) provide hands-on practice with the following topics introduced in this chapter:

Note

Because these labs are cumulative, you will use all the knowledge and troubleshooting techniques that you have acquired from the previous material to successfully complete the following lab.

Lab 8-1: Troubleshooting Enterprise Networks 1 (8.5.1)

You have been asked to correct configuration errors in the company network. For this lab, do not use login or password protection on any console lines to prevent accidental lockout. Use **ciscoccna** for all passwords in this lab.

Lab 8-2: Troubleshooting Enterprise Networks 2 (8.5.2)

For this lab, do not use login or password protection on any console lines to prevent accidental lockout. Use **ciscoccna** for all passwords in this lab.

Lab 8-3: Troubleshooting Enterprise Networks 3 (8.5.3)

For this lab do not use login or password protection on any console lines to prevent accidental lockout. Use **ciscoccna** for all passwords in this lab.

Check Your Understanding

Complete all the review questions listed here to test your understanding of the topics and concepts in this chapter. Answers are listed in the Appendix, "Check Your Understanding and Challenge Questions Answer Key."

1. Match each item with its appropriate diagram type:

   Cable type

   IP address and subnet

   Connection type

   Device ID

   Operating system version

   Device type and model

   Routing protocols

   Connector type

   A. Physical diagram

   B. Logical diagram

2. What is one symptom of a physical layer problem?

   A. High CPU utilization

   B. Excessive broadcasts

   C. Slow STP convergence

   D. Routing loops

3. A network administrator receives the output "Serial0 is up, line protocol is down" from the **show interface s0** command. At what layer is this problem most likely being caused?

    A. Physical layer

    B. Data link layer

    C. Network layer

    D. Transport layer

4. Which statement is true about network models?

    A. Although it's similar to the OSI model in construction, the TCP/IP model has more layers.

    B. The network access layer in the OSI model incorporates both physical and data link layers in the TCP/IP model.

    C. Both users and application layer processes interact with software applications that contain a communications component in the OSI model.

    D. TCP/IP communications relate to only the TCP/IP model.

5. Which protocols can be involved in network layer problems? (Choose three.)

    A. DNS

    B. EIGRP

    C. IP

    D. RIP

    E. TCP

    F. UDP

6. Match the application layer protocol with the port number it is commonly associated with:

    FTP

    HTTP

    POP3

    SMTP

    SNMP

    Telnet

    A. 20 and 21

    B. 23

    C. 25

D. 80

E. 110

F. 161

7. A technician has been asked to troubleshoot a simple network problem that seems to be caused by software. Which troubleshooting approach would you suggest?

A. Bottom-up

B. Top-down

C. Divide-and-conquer

D. Middle-out

8. Which questions are appropriate to ask when gathering information from a user? (Choose three.)

A. What does work?

B. Who did you call after the problem appeared?

C. When did you first notice the problem?

D. When does the problem occur?

E. What is your password?

F. What did you do after the problem occurred?

9. Which network troubleshooting tool can you use to test the physical medium for defects, such as near-end crosstalk?

A. Cable analyzer

B. Cable tester

C. Digital multimeter

D. Baselining tool

10. Which documents are needed to efficiently diagnose and correct network problems? (Choose three.)

A. Network management command reference

B. Network configuration tables

C. Network device installation guide

D. Network topology diagrams

E. End-system configuration tables

F. Service provider documentation

11. What are the steps for establishing a network baseline? (Choose three.)

    A. Determine the type of network management traffic to be collected and evaluated.

    B. Determine the types of data to be collected and evaluated.

    C. Identify devices and ports to be monitored.

    D. Identify the virtual interfaces, VLANs, and virtual routing tables to be monitored.

    E. Determine the number of baseline tests to establish a typical picture of the network.

    F. Determine the duration for baseline testing to establish a typical picture of the network.

12. What is associated with the first step of correcting application layer problems?

    A. Analyzing existing symptoms

    B. Making a backup of configurations

    C. Making the initial hardware or software changes

    D. Pinging the default gateway to verify Layer 1 to Layer 3 functionality

13. Explain the function and contents of network documentation, including router, switch, and end-user documentation, as well as network topology diagrams.

14. Explain the recommended steps for planning the first network baseline.

15. Explain the three stages of the general troubleshooting process.

16. Explain the three main troubleshooting methods.

17. Explain the six steps of designing or modifying a WAN.

18. List at least three things to check when troubleshooting Layer 1 problems.

Challenge Questions and Activities

1. A user reports problems with accessing the network. Which questions should you ask to help diagnose the problem?

2. Refer to Figure 8-39.

Figure 8-39 Topology for Challenge Question 2

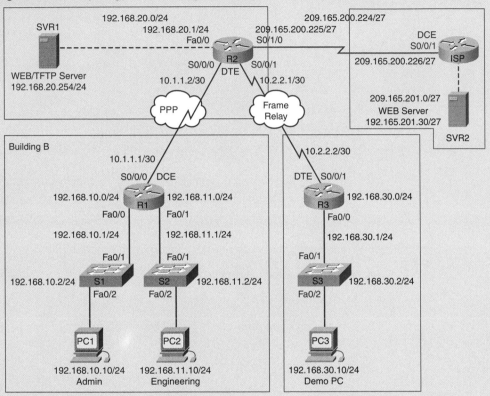

The user on PC3 reports that she no longer can access the SVR2 server on the Internet using its web URL. After questioning her, you decide to use the divide-and-conquer method to troubleshoot the problem using the **ping** command.

The user can successfully **ping** the following locations:

- Her default gateway, which in this case is 192.168.30.1

- The IP address of router R2, which in this case is 10.2.2.1

- The address of the ISP, which in this case is 209.165.200.226

- The IP address of the SVR2 web server, which in this case is 209.165.201.30

Given the preceding information, what is the most likely cause of the problem?

Check Your Understanding and Challenge Questions Answers Key

Chapter 1

Check Your Understanding

1. B, C, and E. Ethernet switches and repeaters typically are found in LANs. Routers can be considered both LAN and WAN devices, used to route packets within a company's network, to an ISP, or between autonomous systems. An access server concentrates dial-in and dial-out user communications. It may have a mixture of analog and digital interfaces supporting hundreds of simultaneous users connecting to the provider's WAN.

2. D. The core layer is also known as the network backbone, designed to switch packets as fast as possible.

3. Circuit switching: D

   Packet switching: C

   Connection-oriented packet switching: B

   Connectionless packet switching: A

4. Metro Ethernet: A

   X.25: D

   ATM: B

   Frame Relay: C

5. C. The DTE transmits the data from a customer network or host computer over the WAN. The DTE connects to the local loop through the DCE. A router is a DTE device and uses a CSU/DSU (DCE device) when connecting to the WAN.

6. E. A leased line is a dedicated point-to-point link usually leased from a carrier.

7. Frame Relay virtual circuits are uniquely identified by a DLCI, which ensures bidirectional communication from one DTE device to another.

8. Asynchronous Transfer Mode (ATM) technology can transfer voice, video, and data through private and public networks. It is built on a cell-based architecture rather than on a frame-based architecture.

9. C. The Cisco Enterprise Branch Architecture allows businesses to extend the applications and services found at the campus network to various remote locations and users independent of size and location.

10. B. The access layer is used to connect users to the network. Layer 2 and Layer 3 switches typically are used at this layer.

11. C. ISDN PRI in North America delivers 23 B channels with 64 kbps and one D channel with 64 kbps in North America, for a total bit rate of up to 1.544 Mbps.

12. E. VPNs are used to tunnel data securely between two private networks over a public network such as the Internet.

13. C. The distribution layer segments workgroups, which isolates any network problems within that subnet or VLAN. Routing between VLANs typically occurs at the distribution layer.

14. C. The local loop cabling that connects the CPE at the subscriber site to the CO of the service provider. The local loop is also sometimes called the "last mile."

15. The Enterprise Teleworker Architecture connects individual employees to network resources remotely, typically from their homes.

16. **Access layer:**

   - Grants user access to network devices.

   - In a network campus, the access layer generally incorporates switched LAN devices with ports that provide connectivity to workstations and servers.

   - In the WAN environment, it may give teleworkers or remote sites access to the corporate network across WAN technology.

   Distribution layer:

   - Aggregates the wiring closets, using switches to segment workgroups and isolate network problems in a campus environment.

   - Similarly, the distribution layer aggregates WAN connections at the edge of the campus and provides policy-based connectivity.

   Core layer (also called the backbone):

   - A high-speed backbone that is designed to switch packets as fast as possible.

   - Because the core is critical for connectivity, it must provide a high level of availability and adapt to changes very quickly. It also provides scalability and fast convergence.

17. Enterprise Campus Architecture:

   - An enterprise campus network is a building or group of buildings connected into one network that consists of many LANs.

   - It is generally limited to a fixed geographic area, but it can span several neighboring buildings.

   - The architecture is modular and scalable and can easily expand to include additional buildings or floors as required.

Enterprise Branch Architecture:

- This module allows businesses to extend the applications and services found at the enterprise campus to thousands of remote locations and users or to a small group of branches.

Enterprise Data Center Architecture:

- Data centers are responsible for managing and maintaining the many data systems that are vital to modern business operations.

- This module centrally houses the data and resources to enable users to effectively create, collaborate, and interact.

Enterprise Teleworker Architecture:

- This module leverages the network resources of the enterprise from home using broadband services such as cable modem or DSL to connect to the corporate network.

- Typically implemented using remote-access VPNs.

Enterprise Edge Architecture:

- This module often functions as a liaison between the campus module and the other modules in the Enterprise Architecture.

18. Customer Premises Equipment (CPE):

- The devices and inside wiring located at the subscriber's premises and connected with a carrier's telecommunication channel.

- The subscriber either owns the CPE or leases it from the service provider.

Central office (CO):

- A local service provider facility or building where local telephone cables link to long-haul, all-digital, fiber-optic communications lines through a system of switches and other equipment.

Local loop:

- Often called the "last mile," it is the copper or fiber telephone cable that connects the CPE at the subscriber site to the CO of the service provider.

Data Communications Equipment (DCE):

- Also called data circuit-terminating equipment, the DCE consists of devices that put data on the local loop.

- The DCE primarily provides an interface to connect subscribers to a communication link in the WAN cloud.

Data Terminal Equipment (DTE):

- The customer devices that pass the data from a customer network or host computer for transmission over the WAN.

- The DTE connects to the local loop through the DCE.

Demarcation point:

- Physically, the demarcation point is the cabling junction box, located on the customer premises, that connects the CPE wiring to the local loop and officially separates the customer equipment from service provider equipment.

- It is the place where the responsibility for the connection changes from the user to the service provider.

19. **Modem:**

- A voiceband modem converts and reconverts the digital signals produced by a computer into voice frequencies that can be transmitted over the analog lines of the public telephone network.

- Faster modems, such as cable modems and DSL modems, transmit using higher broadband frequencies.

CSU/DSU:

- Digital lines, such as T1 or T3 carrier lines, require a channel service unit (CSU) and a data service unit (DSU).

- The two are often combined into a single piece of equipment called the CSU/DSU.

- The CSU provides termination for the digital signal and ensures connection integrity through error correction and line monitoring. The DSU converts the T-carrier line frames into frames that the LAN can interpret.

Access server:

- Concentrates dial-in and dial-out user communications. It may have a mixture of analog and digital interfaces and support hundreds of simultaneous users.

WAN switch:

- A multiport internetworking device used in carrier networks to support Frame Relay, ATM, or X.25.

Router:

- Provides internetworking and WAN access interface ports that are used to connect to the service provider network.

- These interfaces may be serial connections or other WAN interfaces. They may require an external device such as a DSU/CSU or modem (analog, cable, or DSL) to connect to the service provider.

20. X.25:

- An older, low-capacity WAN technology with a maximum speed of 48 kbps. Typically used in dialup mode with point-of-sale card readers to validate transactions on a central computer.

- For these applications, the low bandwidth and high latency are not a concern, and the low cost makes X.25 affordable.

- Frame Relay has replaced X.25 at many service provider locations.

  Frame Relay:

- A Layer 2 WAN protocol that typically offers data rates of 4 Mbps or higher.

- It provides permanent, shared, medium-bandwidth connectivity using virtual circuits that can carry both voice and data traffic.

- VCs are uniquely identified by a DLCI, which ensures bidirectional communication from one DTE device to another.

  ATM:

- Asynchronous Transfer Mode technology is based on a cell-based architecture rather than a frame-based architecture, using fixed-length cells of 53 bytes.

- These small, fixed-length cells are well suited for carrying delay-sensitive voice and video traffic.

Challenge Questions and Activities

1. The advantage of a circuit-switched network is the fixed circuit that provides guaranteed bandwidth between two end devices, such as two telephones or two computers. The disadvantage is that it is an inefficient use of the communications channel. When two devices are communicating over the circuit, no other devices can use that circuit, even during idle periods.

2. Site-to-site VPNs connect users in two remote networks, such as a branch office network with the headquarters network. The VPN is created using a router, firewall, VPN concentrator, or security appliance at each site. Remote-access VPNs are similar to site-to-site VPNs, except that only one end of the VPN tunnel (connection) is a typical company network. The other end of the tunnel is the remote user, such as a teleworker working from home, a hotel room, or a café.

Chapter 2

Check Your Understanding

1. Step 1: C

   Step 2: D

   Step 3: A

   Step 4: B

   Step 5: E

2. B. This is the state of the interface when the local or remote router is misconfigured with a different Layer 2 encapsulation. In our labs, a missing clock rate would also cause this message to appear.

3. A. Cisco HDLC is the default encapsulation method used by Cisco devices on synchronous serial lines.

4. D. The protocol field in a PPP frame indicates the type of Layer 3 information is carried in the frame's Data field.

5. Error control: B

   Authentication protocols: D

   Allows load balancing: C

   Compression protocols: A

6. A, D, E.

7. B. HDLC is a bit-oriented synchronous data link layer protocol developed by the International Organization for Standardization (ISO). HDLC was developed from the Synchronous Data Link Control (SDLC) standard proposed in the 1970s. HDLC provides both connection-oriented and connectionless service.

8. C. Authentication takes place after link establishment and before any network layer protocol configuration.

9. D. PPP uses the Network Control Protocol (NCP) process to negotiate the Layer 3 protocols to operate over the link. IPCP is an example of an NCP for IP.

10. B. PAP uses a two-way handshake, whereas CHAP uses a three-way handshake. The other three possible answers are features of CHAP.

11. B and F. This state can be caused by the router's not sensing a CD signal, which means that the CD is not active. This state can also be caused by faulty or incorrect cabling. Other causes include a WAN carrier service provider problem, which means that the line is down or is not connected to the CSU/DSU, or a hardware failure (CSU/DSU).

12. Configure the username and password: A

Enter interface configuration mode: C

Specify the encapsulation type: D

Configure authentication: G

13. With CHAP authentication, the hostname on one router must match the username the other router has configured. The passwords must also match on both routers.

14. Two-way handshake: PAP

Three-way handshake: CHAP

Open to trial-and-error attacks: PAP

Password sent in clear text: PAP

Periodic verification: CHAP

Uses a one-way hash function: CHAP

15. Negotiates link establishment parameters: LCP

Negotiates Layer 3 protocol parameters: NCP

Maintains/debugs a link: LCP

Can negotiate multiple Layer 3 protocols: NCP

Terminates a link: LCP

16.

- **HDLC**: The default encapsulation type on point-to-point connections, dedicated links, and circuit-switched connections when the link uses two Cisco devices.

- **PPP**: Provides router-to-router and host-to-network connections over synchronous and asynchronous circuits. PPP works with several network layer protocols, such as IP and IPX. PPP also has built-in security mechanisms such as PAP and CHAP.

- **Serial Line Internet Protocol (SLIP)**: A standard protocol for point-to-point serial connections using TCP/IP. SLIP has been largely displaced by PPP.

- **X.25/Link Access Procedure, Balanced (LAPB)**: An ITU-T standard that defines how connections between a DTE and DCE are maintained for remote terminal access and computer communications in public data networks. X.25 specifies LAPB, a data link layer protocol. X.25 is a predecessor to Frame Relay.

- **Frame Relay**: Industry-standard, switched, data link layer protocol that handles multiple virtual circuits. Frame Relay is a next-generation protocol after X.25. Frame Relay eliminates some of the time-consuming processes (such as error correction and flow control) employed in X.25.

- **ATM**: The international standard for cell relay in which devices send multiple service types (such as voice, video, or data) in fixed-length (53-byte) cells. Fixed-length cells allow processing to occur in hardware, thereby reducing transit delays. ATM takes advantage of high-speed transmission media such as E3, SONET, and T3.

17. **Link Control Protocol (LCP) layer**

- Sits on top of the physical layer and has a role in establishing, configuring, and testing the data-link connection.

- Establishes the point-to-point link.

- Provides automatic configuration of the interfaces at each end. This includes handling varying limits on packet size, detecting common misconfiguration errors, terminating the link, and determining when a link is functioning properly or when it is failing.

- Is also used to negotiate authentication, compression, error detection, multilink, and PPP callback after the link is established.

- Negotiates and sets up control options on the WAN data link, which are handled by the NCPs.

Network Control Protocol (NCP) layer

- Includes functional fields containing standardized codes to indicate the network layer protocol that PPP encapsulates.

- Handles the assignment and management of IP addresses in IPCP.

- Encapsulates and negotiates options for multiple network layer protocols.

18. Authentication using PAP or CHAP

- If all you need is password authentication, configure PAP using the **ppp authentication pap** command.

- If you want a challenge handshake, configure CHAP using the **ppp authentication chap** command (it's more secure).

Compression

- Increases the effective throughput by reducing the amount of data in the PPP frame that must travel across the link.

- To configure Stacker, use the **compress stac** command. To configure Predictor, use the **compress predictor** command.

Error detection

- Identifies fault conditions to help ensure a reliable, loop-free data link.

- Configured using the **ppp quality** *percentage* command.

Multilink

- Provides load balancing over the router interfaces that PPP uses using the command **ppp multilink**.

PPP callback

- Enhances security by making a Cisco router a callback client. It makes the initial call, requests that the other Cisco router configured as a server call it back, and terminates its initial call.

- The command is **ppp callback** [**accept** | **request**].

19. On Router R1:

- The **username** command has two errors. The router name should be **R3,** and the password should be **cisco**. Therefore, the correct command is **username R3 password cisco**.

- The third error is in the **ppp authentication** command. It should be **ppp authentication chap**.

Challenge Questions and Activities

1. Serial1 PPP: Phase is AUTHENTICATING, by both indicates that the routers are performing two-way authentication using PAP.

Serial1 PPP: Phase is AUTHENTICATING, by the peer and **Serial1 PPP: Phase is AUTHENTICATING, by this end** indicate that the routers are performing one-way authentication challenge and response messages using CHAP.

Chapter 3

Check Your Understanding

1. B. VCs are identified by DLCIs. DLCI values typically are assigned by the Frame Relay service provider (for example, the telephone company).

2. D. Unlike leased lines, there are no dedicated circuits in the carrier's Frame Relay network for end-to-end customer connectivity. Most providers use PVCs (some use SVCs) to create and discard circuits as customers purchase them without needing to deploy additional cabling.

3. D. Whether using a single physical interface, or an interface configured as a multipoint subinterface, when the remote ends of the virtual circuits are on the same subnet, it is subject to split horizon. If point-to-point subinterfaces are used with each virtual circuit on a separate subnet, split horizon is no longer an issue.

4. B and D. Frame Relay requires a single access line or circuit to the provider's frame network cloud, regardless of the number of remote networks. A router with a single WAN interface and CSU/DSU is needed, along with a single access circuit. Frame Relay allows a provider to efficiently share the bandwidth within its cloud instead of deploying a large number of individual dedicated point-to-point links.

5. Active: C

   Inactive: A

   Deleted: D

6. B. A Frame Relay cloud typically is a meshed network of circuits and Layer 2 switches (usually ATM). This allows for redundancy within the provider's network that does not exist with a dedicated leased line.

7. E. The Layer 2 encapsulation is Frame Relay, with the local DLCI used as the address.

8. A. Point-to-point topologies typically requires a separate subnet for each point-to-point connection. In many networks VLSM is used to subnet one of the subnets as /30 networks. If this is not an option, multipoint topology can be used. Multipoint topology means that all the VCs share the same subnet address. (Note: In today's modern networks, VLSM usually is an option.)

9. C. When point-to-point subinterfaces are used, each VC is on a separate subnet; therefore, split horizon is not an issue. From the perspective of the router, each VC is on a separate (logical) interface. This eliminates split horizon as an issue.

10. D. Frame Relay does not provide any error correction. Only the upper-layer protocol TCP, used by the host, provides any error detection when Frame Relay is used as the Layer 2 transport.

11. **show interface:** C

    show frame-relay lmi: D

    show frame-relay pvc: A

    show frame-relay map: E

    debug frame-relay lmi: B

12. D. The CIR is the amount of data that the network receives from the access circuit. The service provider guarantees that the customer can send data at the CIR. All frames received at or below the CIR are accepted.

13. C. The DLCI numbers are assigned by the service provider. Most providers allow the customer to choose its own DLCI numbers as long as they are valid numbers.

14. A. Frame Relay maps are used to map the remote network address to the local DLCI.

15. CIR: C

DE: A

FECN: B

BECN: D

16. DLCI: Data Link Connection Identifier

- VCs are identified by DLCIs, and the DLCI values are assigned by the Frame Relay service provider.

- Frame Relay DLCIs have local significance and no significance beyond the single link.

- A DLCI identifies a VC to the equipment at an endpoint.

LMI: Local Management Interface

- LMI is a keepalive mechanism that provides status information about Frame Relay connections between the router (DTE) and the Frame Relay switch (DCE).

- Cisco routers support three types of LMIs: Cisco, ANSI, and q933a.

Inverse ARP

- Inverse Address Resolution Protocol (ARP) obtains Layer 3 addresses of other stations from Layer 2 addresses, such as the DLCI in Frame Relay networks (which is the reverse of what ARP does).

- It is primarily used in Frame Relay and ATM networks, where Layer 2 addresses of VCs are sometimes obtained from Layer 2 signaling, and the corresponding Layer 3 addresses must be available before these VCs can be used.

17. frame-relay map ip 10.1.1.2 102 broadcast

18. Access rate (or port speed)

- The capacity of the local loop.

- This line is charged based on the port speed between the DTE and the DCE (customer to service provider).

CIR: Committed Information Rate

- The capacity through the local loop guaranteed by the provider.

- Customers normally choose a CIR lower than the access rate to allow them to take advantage of bursts.

CBIR: Committed Burst Information Rate

- The maximum number of frames allowed in a burst.

- It cannot exceed the CIR for the link.

BE: Excess Burst

- The amount of data above the CBIR that the network tries to deliver, up to the maximum speed of the access link.

- Packets over CIR are marked discard eligible (DE), indicating that they may be dropped if the network does not have capacity.

19. On router R1

- The main serial interface and subinterfaces should be Serial 0/0/0, Serial 0/0/0.102, and Serial 0/0/0.103, respectively.

- The wrong subnet mask is applied to the subinterfaces. The subnet mask should be **255.255.255.252**.

- The DLCIs in the **frame-relay interface-dlci** command should be 102 and 103, respectively.

Challenge Questions and Activities

1. When static mapping is configured on an interface for a protocol and a specific DLCI, the router automatically disables dynamic Inverse ARP for the protocol and the specific DLCI on the interface. After R2 was reloaded, the Inverse ARP never took place for the mapping to R1. There are several solutions. The simplest one is to add another static map on R2 for reachability to R1:

   frame-relay map ip 172.16.1.1 102

Chapter 4

Check Your Understanding

1. Operating system weaknesses: A

   Unsecured user accounts: B

   Network equipment weaknesses: A

   Unsecured default settings: B

   Lack of consistency and continuity: C

   TCP/IP and ICMP weaknesses: A

   Lack of a disaster recovery plan: C

2. C and E

3. B

4. Reconnaissance attack: C

Password attack: A

Port redirection: B

Worm, virus, Trojan horse: E

DoS attack: D

5. C. A host-based intrusion detection system (HIDS) typically is implemented as inline or passive technology and sends logs to a management console only after the attack has occurred and the damage is done. A host-based intrusion prevention system (HIPS) typically is implemented inline and actually stops the attack, prevents damage, and blocks the propagation of worms and viruses. Active detection can be set to shut down the network connection or to stop impacted services automatically. Corrective action can be taken immediately. Cisco provides HIPS using the Cisco Security Agent software.

6. E. The security policy is the hub upon which the four steps of the Security Wheel (secure, monitor, test, and improve) are based. It drives the application of security measures:

- It identifies the organization's security objectives.

- It documents the resources to be protected.

- It identifies the network infrastructure with current maps and inventories.

- It identifies the critical resources that need to be protected, such as research and development, finance, and human resources. This is called a risk analysis.

7. C. A syslog server provides a better solution because all network devices can forward their logs to one central station, where an administrator can review them. Multiple syslog hosts can be configured to provide fault tolerance. An example of a syslog server application is Kiwi Syslog Daemon.

8. C. Secure Shell (SSH) provides the same functionality and authentication as Telnet but establishes an encrypted connection.

9. Account access request policy: D

Remote-access policy: A

Risk assessment policy: E

Audit policy: B

Acceptable user policy: C

10. Step 1: C

Step 2: B

Step 3: F

11. A, B, and E

12. C

13. Network Time Protocol (NTP): B

Domain Name System (DNS): C

Simple Network Management Protocol (SNMP): A

14. B

15. A, B, and D

16. Internet information queries:

- nslookup
- whois

Ping sweeps:

- fping
- gping

Port scans:

- Nmap
- Superscan

Packet sniffers:

- Wireshark

17.

- Password attack
- Trust exploitation attack
- Port redirection attack
- Man-in-the-middle attack

18. DoS attacks:

- Ping of death attack
- SYN flood attack

- Packet fragmentation and reassembly attack

- E-mail bomb attack

- CPU hogging attack

- Malicious applet attack

    DDoS attacks:

- Smurf attack

- Tribe Flood Network (TFN)

- Stacheldraht

- MyDoom

19. The anatomy of a worm attack is as follows:

- **The enabling vulnerability**: A worm installs itself by exploiting known vulnerabilities in systems, such as naive end users who open unverified executable e-mail attachments.

- **Propagation mechanism**: After gaining access to a host, a worm copies itself to that host and then selects new targets.

- **Payload**: After a host is infected with a worm, the attacker has access to the host, often as a privileged user. Attackers can use a local exploit to escalate their privilege level to administrator.

    The following are the recommended steps for worm attack mitigation:

- **Step 1, Containment**: Contain the spread of the worm into your network and within your network. Compartmentalize uninfected parts of your network.

- **Step 2, Inoculation**: Start patching all systems and, if possible, scanning for vulnerable systems.

- **Step 3, Quarantine**: Track down each infected machine in your network. Disconnect, remove, or block infected machines from the network.

- **Step 4, Treatment**: Clean and patch each infected system. Some worms may require complete core system reinstallations to clean the system.

20. On router R1:

- The transport input command should be transport input ssh.

- The login local command is missing from the line vty 0 4 configuration mode.

- The SSH port number in the Tera Term window should reference TCP port 22.

21.

- Small services such as echo, discard, and chargen should be disabled.

- BOOTP should be disabled.

- Finger should be disabled.

- Hypertext Transfer Protocol (HTTP) should be disabled, and secure HTTPS should be configured (if required).

- Simple Network Management Protocol (SNMP) versions 1 and 2 should be disabled, and SNMPv3 should be configured.

- Cisco Discovery Protocol (CDP) should be disabled unless required.

- Remote configuration should be disabled.

- Source routing should be disabled.

- Classless routing should be disabled.

- **no ip directed-broadcast** should be configured to stop Smurf attacks.

- **no ip proxy-arp** should be configured to stop ad hoc routing attacks.

22.

1. Choose Configure.

2. Choose Security Audit.

3. Click the One-step lockdown button.

4. In the Cisco SDM Warning dialog box, click Yes.

5. Deliver commands to the router.

23.

1. Ping the TFTP server to make sure you have access to it.

2. Use the **show flash:** command to verify that the router has enough room in flash to accommodate the size of the Cisco IOS image file.

3. Copy the new Cisco IOS image from the TFTP server using the **copy tftp flash:** command in privileged EXEC mode. Answer the required prompts.

Challenge Questions and Activities

1.

```
R1# show running-config

*Dec 14 14:06:19.663: %SYS-5-CONFIG_I: Configured from console by console
Building configuration...

Current configuration : 836 bytes
!
version 12.4
service timestamps debug datetime msec
service timestamps log datetime msec
no service password-encryption
!
hostname R1
ip domain name cisco.com
enable password cisco
!
username Student password 0 cisco
!
!
line con 0
line aux 0
line vty 0 4
 login
!
scheduler allocate 20000 1000
!
end

R1#
```

A variety of features can be configured. The following are examples:

Router R1 should have all passwords encrypted:

```
R1(config)# service password-encryption
```

Remove the enable password with the **enable secret** command:

```
R1(config)# no enable password
R1(config)# enable secret cisco12345
```

Remove the current username, and re-create it using the **username** *username* **password** command:

```
R1(config)# no username Student password cisco
R1(config)# username Student secret cisco12345
```

To secure administrative access, the console, aux, and vty lines should be secured. Specifically, SSH should be the only remote administrative protocol supported:

```
R1(config)# line console 0
R1(config-line)# login local
R1(config-line)# exec-timeout 3
R1(config-line)# line aux 0
R1(config-line)# no password
R1(config-line)# login
% Login disabled on line 1, until 'password' is set
R1(config-line)# line vty 0 4
R1(config-line)# no transport input
R1(config-line)# transport input ssh
R1(config-line)# login local
R1(config-line)# exit
```

Chapter 5

Check Your Understanding

1. B and C. Standard ACLs filter packets based solely on the source IP addresses and are numbered 1 to 99. Extended ACLs filter IP packets based on several attributes, such as protocol type, source and IP address, destination IP address, source TCP or UDP ports, destination TCP or UDP ports, and optional protocol type information. Extended ACLs are numbered 100 to 199.

2. C. Because standard ACLs do not specify destination addresses, they should be placed as close to the destination as possible so that they filter traffic only to the destination network.

3. B. An ACL is executed in order of the statements. The most specific condition must be examined before the more general conditions. Otherwise, the packet might pass the test condition of the general condition and never be examined by the more specific condition.

4. A, C. At the end of every ACL is an "implicit deny any" statement or the "deny all traffic" statement. Without any permit statements, all traffic would be denied or dropped on the outbound interface. Traffic originating from the route would be permitted, because access lists do not apply to traffic that originates from the router.

5. B, C. ACLs can be used to help create a firewall by filtering inbound and outbound traffic. This includes controlling the traffic entering and exiting LANs. ACLs don't distribute DHCP traffic.

6. **any**: D

    show running-config: E

    show access-list: C

    host: A

    show ip interface: B

7. D. The wildcard mask can be derived by subtracting the 29-bit mask, 255.255.255.248, from 255.255.255.255. This results in the wildcard mask 0.0.0.7. 192.168.12.84 is a subnet of 192.168.12.0/29.

8. C. A standard named access list is created with the global configuration command **ip access-list standard** *name*.

9. C. Additional access list statements are automatically added to the end of the sequence of statements. Named ACLs can use optional sequence numbers to make this modification easier.

10. D. ACL statements are executed in sequential order. The packet is evaluated against each statement in the ACL, from the top down, one statement at a time. After the packet matches a statement, the packet is forwarded or dropped, and the remaining statements are not examined.

11. A. Lock-and-key ACLs are also called dynamic ACLs.

12. D. Time-based ACLs filter packets based on a time range that defines specific times of the day and week.

13. A. Reflexive ACLs are used to allow IP traffic for sessions originating from their network while denying IP traffic for sessions originating outside the network. These ACLs allow the router to manage session traffic dynamically. The router examines the outbound traffic, and when it sees a new connection, it adds an entry to a temporary ACL to allow replies back in.

14.

    A. Standard IP ACL

    B. Extended IP ACL

    C. Extended IP ACL

    D. Standard IP ACL

    E. Standard IP ACL

    F. Extended IP ACL

15. A and D. The first line of the ACL denies Telnet traffic originating from the 178.15.0.0/16 network to any destination network. The second line permits all other IP traffic, including FTP.

16. One ACL per protocol:

- To control traffic flow on an interface, an ACL must be defined for each protocol enabled on the interface.

    One ACL per direction:

- ACLs control traffic in one direction at a time on an interface. Two separate ACLs must be created to control inbound and outbound traffic.

    One ACL per interface:

- ACLs control traffic for an interface, such as Fast Ethernet 0/0.

17. Standard ACLs:

- Because standard ACLs do not specify destination addresses, place them as close to the destination as possible.

    Extended ACLs:

- Locate extended ACLs as close as possible to the source of the traffic denied. This way, undesirable traffic is filtered without crossing the network infrastructure.

18. On router R1:

- The host address is incorrectly specified. It should be 192.168.11.10.

- Because of the implicit deny statement, the remainder of the subnet is not permitted through. The remainder of the subnet should be permitted using the **access-list 10 permit any** command.

- ACL 10 should be applied to be in an outbound direction on interface Fa0/1.

    Correct configuration:

    ```
    R1(config)# access-list 10 deny host 192.168.11.10
    R1(config)# access-list 10 permit any
    R1(config)# interface Fa0/1
    R1(config-if)# ip access-group 10 out
    ```

19. On router R1:

- The first **permit** statement of the SURFING ACL allows Telnet access (23). It should permit web access (80).

- The BROWSING ACL requires the **established** keyword at the end.

Correct configuration:

```
R1(config)# access-list extended SURFING
R1(config-ext-nacl)# permit tcp 192.168.10.0 0.0.0.255 any eq 80
R1(config-ext-nacl)# permit tcp 192.168.10.0 0.0.0.255 any eq 443
R1(config)# access-list extended BROWSING
R1(config-ext-nacl)# permit tcp any 192.168.10.0 0.0.0.255 established
R1(config-ext-nacl)# exit
R1(config)# interface S0/0/0
R1(config-if)# ip access-group SURFING out
R1(config-if)# ip access-group BROWSING in
```

20. **Dynamic (lock-and-key):**

- Dynamic ACLs use an extended ACL to block users from traversing a router until they use Telnet or SSH to connect to the router and are authenticated.

- After being authenticated, specific dynamic ACL entries are activated on the ACL applied to the interface.

- These entries remain active for a specific period and then expire.

- This enables a user to authenticate and access resources that normally would be denied. Dynamic ACLs can be combined with other types of ACLs, such as extended ACLs.

  Reflexive:

- Reflexive ACLs automatically create temporary entries based on upper-layer session information.

- The entries are automatically deleted when the session ends.

  Time-based:

- Time-based ACLs are similar to extended ACLs in function, but they allow access control based on time.

- A time range defines specific times of the day and days of the week at which the ACLs are implemented.

Challenge Questions and Activities

1.

```
Router(config)# time-range BUSINESSHOURS
Router(config-time-range)# periodic Monday 9:00 to Friday 17:00
Router(config)# access-list 101 permit ip any host 192.168.1.17 time-range
    BUSINESSHOURS
```

2.

```
Router(config)# access-list 20 permit 172.30.16.0 0.0.15.255
```

3. ACLs do not block packets that originate on the router where the access list is applied. An ICMP echo request originated from the router is not blocked by the access list. An ICMP echo request that enters the router from its LAN interface is blocked outbound on the serial interface.

Chapter 6

Check Your Understanding

1. C, D. The term broadband has several meanings, depending on the context. In this context, broadband refers to the capability to provide high-speed transmission of services (usually greater than 128 kbps), such as data, voice, and video, over the Internet and other networks using technologies such as DSL, cable, satellite, and broadband wireless. These technologies use a wide range of frequencies and multiplexing techniques.

2. C. With a maximum speed of 56 kbps (actual speed of 53 kbps), dialup connections are not considered a broadband technology like DSL, cable, satellite, and broadband wireless.

3. D. Euro-DOCSIS is adapted for use in Europe. The main differences between DOCSIS and Euro-DOCSIS relate to channel bandwidths.

4. B, D, E. The different varieties of DSL provide different bandwidths, some with capabilities exceeding those of a T1 or E1 leased line. Within the variety of DSL, transfer rates are less as the distance from the central office decreases. ADSL is asymmetric DSL, which provides higher download bandwidth than upload bandwidth.

5. D, E. The customer site may include devices such as a microfilter and a DSL transceiver, which usually is a DSL modem.

6. C. Figure 6-30 shows the regional offices with routers and PIX firewall devices. The corporate office includes a router and a PIX firewall. The PIX firewall could also be replaced by a VPN concentrator.

7. B and C. VPNs secure data by encapsulating, creating a tunnel, or encrypting the data. Most VPNs can do both.

8. Uses passwords, digital certificates, smart cards, and biometrics: C

   Prevents tampering and alterations to data while data travels between the source and destination: B

   Protects the contents of messages from interception by unauthenticated or unauthorized sources: A

Uses hashes: B

Ensures that the communicating peers are who they say they are: C

Uses encapsulation and encryption: A

9. E. GRE is a tunneling protocol developed by Cisco Systems. It can encapsulate a variety of Layer 3 packets inside IP tunnels, creating a virtual point-to-point link to Cisco routers at remote points over an IP internetwork.

10. Frame Relay, ATM, MPLS: A

The protocol that is wrapped around the original data: B

The protocol over which the original data was being carried: C

IPX, AppleTalk, IPv4, IPv6: C

GRE, IPsec, L2F, PPTP, L2TP: B

The protocol over which the information travels: A

11.

Encryption and decryption use the same key: A

Public key cryptography: B

Encryption and decryption use different keys: B

DES, 3DES, AES: A

RSA: B

Shared secret key cryptography: A

12. D. Given these choices, DSL is the most cost-effective method for broadband teleworker access to the Internet. Cable is another cost-effective technology that competes with DSL. Broadband wireless and two-way satellite Internet are becoming more common and more competitive.

13. The 802.16 (or WiMAX) standard allows transmissions up to 70 Mbps. 802.16 has a range of up to 30 miles (50 km). It can operate inlicensed or unlicensed bands of the spectrum from 2 to 6 GHz.

14. A. Cable operators typically deploy HFC networks to enable high-speed transmission of data to cable modems located in a SOHO. The trunks typically are fiber with coaxial distribution cable to the homes (feeders).

15. Organizational benefits:

- Continuity of operations

- Increased responsiveness

- Secure, reliable, and manageable access to information

- Cost-effective integration of data, voice, video, and applications
- Increased employee productivity, satisfaction, and retention

Social benefits:

- Increased employment opportunities for marginalized groups
- Less traveling and commuter-related stress

Environmental benefits:

- Reduced carbon footprints, for both individual workers and organizations

16. **Dialup access:**

- Dialup access is an inexpensive option that uses any phone line and a modem.
- It is the slowest connection option and typically is used in areas where higher-speed connections are unavailable.

DSL:

- DSL is more expensive than dialup but provides a faster connection.
- It also uses telephone lines, but unlike dialup access, DSL provides a continuous connection to the Internet.
- This connection option uses a special high-speed modem that separates the DSL signal from the telephone signal and provides an Ethernet connection to a host computer or LAN.

Cable modem:

- Cable Internet is a connection option offered by cable television service providers.
- The Internet signal is carried on the same coaxial cable that delivers cable television to homes and businesses.
- A special cable modem separates the Internet signal from the other signals carried on the cable and provides an Ethernet connection to a host computer or LAN.

Satellite:

- Satellite connection is an option offered by satellite service providers.
- The user's computer connects through Ethernet to a satellite modem that transmits radio signals to the nearest POP within the satellite network.

17. **Site-to-site VPNs:**

- A site-to-site VPN is an extension of classic WAN networking and can connect a branch office network to a company headquarters network.
- Hosts send and receive TCP/IP traffic through a VPN "gateway," which could be a router, PIX firewall appliance, or Adaptive Security Appliance (ASA).

- The VPN gateway is responsible for encapsulating and encrypting outbound traffic for all the traffic from a particular site and sending it through a VPN tunnel over the Internet to a peer VPN gateway at the target site.

- On receipt, the peer VPN gateway strips the headers, decrypts the content, and relays the packet toward the target host inside its private network.

Remote-access VPNs:

- Mobile users and telecommuters use remote-access VPNs extensively.

- Remote VPN connections typically take advantage of existing broadband connections.

- Each host typically has VPN client software that encapsulates and encrypts that traffic before sending it over the Internet to the VPN gateway at the edge of the target network.

- On receipt, the VPN gateway handles the data in the same way it would handle data from a site-to-site VPN.

Challenge Questions and Activities

1. Tunnel Name: Site-to-Site

   Local Security Group

   IP Address: 192.168.1.0

   Remote Security Group

   IP Address: 192.168.101.0

   Remote Security Gateway

   IP Address: 209.165.202.129

   Key Exchange Method

   Encryption: 3DES

   Authentication: MD5

   Pre-Shared Key: cisco123

   Tunnel Name: Site-to-Site

   Local Security Group

   IP Address: 192.168.101.0

Remote Security Group

IP Address: 192.168.1.0

Remote Security Gateway

IP Address: 209.165.200.225

Key Exchange Method

Encryption: 3DES

Authentication: MD5

Pre-Shared Key: cisco123

2.

Username: BobV

Password: cisco123

Re-enter to Confirm: cisco123

Profile Name: Central Site

User Name: BobV

Password: cisco123

Server Address: 209.165.200.225

Chapter 7

Check Your Understanding

1. B and F. Specifically, DHCP can provide the IP address, subnet mask, default gateway, domain name, DNS server, NetBIOS, and WINS server. The duration of the DHCP lease is by default one day, but you can change it by using the **lease** command.

2. The *pool-name* argument is the alphanumeric "name" of the DHCP pool to be configured.

3. A, B, and C. DHCP uses User Datagram Protocol (UDP) as its transport protocol. The client sends messages to the server on port 67. The server sends messages to the client on port 68. When the DHCP server receives a DHCPDISCOVER message, it finds an available IP address to lease, creates an ARP entry consisting of the MAC address of the requesting host and the leased IP address, and transmits a binding offer with a DHCPOFFER message. The DHCPOFFER message is sent as a unicast, using the server's Layer 2 MAC address as the source address and the client's Layer 2 address as the destination.

4. B. The **ip helper-address** command has been correctly configured on the LAN interface and is pointing to the IP address of the DHCP server.

5. C. At first glance, A might seem like the correct answer. The DHCPNACK message generated by the **debug** command does confirm that the host was provided with IP address 10.1.0.3. However, the **show** command displays a conflict, which means that the host was unsuccessful, so A is incorrect.

6. C. The output lists port numbers. This occurs only when NAT Overload is configured.

7. B. By default, translation entries time out after 24 hours, unless the timers have been reconfigured with the **ip nat translation timeout** *timeout_seconds* command in global configuration mode.

8. Provides one-to-one fixed mappings of local and global addresses: C

   Assigns the translated addresses of IP hosts from a pool of public addresses: A

   Can map multiple addresses to a single address of the external interface: B

   Assigns unique source port numbers of an inside global address on a session-by-session basis: B

   Allows an external host to establish sessions with an internal host: C

9. B. IP address 192.168.0.100 is the inside local address and will be translated into 209.165.200.2.

10. B. NAT will translate the internal addresses 192.168.0.0 to 192.168.0.255 as identified by access list 1.

11. A. IP address 192.168.14.5 is a private address. Therefore, static NAT must be configured, because it would enable an outside host to contact the inside global address of web server 1.

12. D. An FTP server requires a reachable public Internet address to be statically assigned to its internal address.

13. B. The inside local address 10.10.10.3 is being translated into the inside global address 24.74.237.203.

14. A and D. RIPng is a distance vector routing protocol with a limit of 15 hops. It uses split horizon and poison reverse updates to prevent routing loops.

15. A and B. Stateless autoconfiguration automatically configures the IPv6 address for the host, and DHCPv6 enables the automatic allocation of reusable network addresses. DHCPv6 is a stateful counterpart to IPv6 stateless autoconfiguration. It can be used separately or concurrently with IPv6 stateless autoconfiguration to obtain configuration parameters.

16. ipv6 unicast-routing: D

    ipv6 address: C

    ip name-server: A

    ipv6 host name: B

    ipv6 router rip *name*: E

17. Answer: B, D, and E.

18. The four DHCP messages in sequence are as follows:

    DHCPDISCOVER message:

    - A broadcast is forwarded by the host looking for a DHCP server.

    - Messages are forwarded to the DHCP BOOTP server using UDP port 67.

    DHCPOFFER message:

    - When the DHCPDISCOVER message reaches the DHCP server, the server responds with a unicast DHCPOFFER message containing the client's MAC address, offered IP address and mask, default gateway, and the server's IP address.

    - Messages are forwarded to the DHCP BOOTP client using UDP port 68.

    DHCPREQUEST message:

    - Used for two purposes: to initially negotiate an IP address lease, and to renegotiate (or renew) the IP address halfway through its lease time.

    - The client broadcasts the DHCPREQUEST message to the DHCP server using UDP port 67.

    DHCPACK message:

    - Is nearly identical to the original DHCPOFFER but is sent to the client to confirm that it now can use that address using UDP port 68.

19. Correct the following on router R1:

    - The pool is excluding the entire pool. The command should be **ip dhcp excluded-address 192.168.11.1 192.168.11.9**.

    - The network pool is allocating the wrong subnet. The command should be **network 192.168.11.0 255.255.255.0**.

    - The default router IP address is pointing to the switch. The command should be **default-router 192.168.11.1**.

20. On router R1, configure the DHCP relay feature on interface Fast Ethernet 0/0 using the following commands:

    interface FastEthernet 0/0

    ip helper-address 192.168.11.5

21. **Static NAT:**

    ■ Static NAT uses a one-to-one mapping of local and global addresses, and these mappings remain constant.

    ■ Static NAT is particularly useful for web servers or in general hosts that must have a consistent address that is accessible from the Internet.

    Dynamic NAT:

    ■ Dynamic NAT uses a pool of public addresses and assigns them on a first-come, first-served basis.

    ■ When a host requests access to the Internet, dynamic NAT chooses an IP address from the public pool and temporarily binds it with the internal local address.

    NAT Overload:

    ■ NAT overloading (sometimes called Port Address Translation or PAT) maps inside local IP addresses to a combination of a global IP address and a unique port number.

    ■ When a response returns to the NAT router, the router examines the source port number and forwards the packet to the originating inside local address.

    ■ It also validates that the incoming packets were requested, thus adding a degree of security to the session.

22. Router R2 was configured to provide NAT overload translation to hosts on the 192.168.10.0 and 192.168.11.0 networks.

    The host with the inside local IP address **192.168.10.10** was translated into the overloaded inside global IP address **209.165.200.225** using the unique port number **16642** when accessing the **web server** located at **209.165.200.254**.

    The host with the inside local IP address **192.168.11.10** was translated into the overloaded inside global IP address **209.165.200.225** using the unique port number **62452** when accessing the **web server** located at **209.165.200.254**.

23. The shortest form is **2031:0:130F::9C0:876A:130B**.

24. The sentence is "**Dual-stack** where you can; **tunnel** where you must!"

Dual-stack method:

■ Is an integration method in which a node has implementation and connectivity to both an IPv4 and IPv6 network.

■ This is the recommended option and involves running IPv4 and IPv6 at the same time.

■ Routers and switches are configured to support both protocols, with IPv6 being the preferred protocol.

6to4 tunneling method:

■ Is an integration method in which an IPv6 packet is encapsulated within the IPv4 protocol.

■ This method requires dual-stack routers.

■ The dynamic 6to4 tunneling method automatically establishes the connection of IPv6 islands through an IPv4 network.

Other tunneling methods:

■ Other tunneling protocols include NAT-PT, ISATAP tunneling, and Teredo tunneling.

■ These tunneling protocols are complex and should be considered methods of last resort.

Challenge Questions and Activities

1. The following should be configured on Router R1:

```
R1(config)# ip dhcp excluded-address 192.168.10.1 192.168.10.2
R1(config)# ip dhcp pool LAN-POOL-1
R1(dhcp-config)# network 192.168.10.0 255.255.255.0
R1(dhcp-config)# default-router 192.168.10.1
R1(dhcp-config)# exit
R1(config)# ip dhcp excluded-address 192.168.11.1 192.168.11.2
R1(config)# ip dhcp pool LAN-POOL-2
R1(dhcp-config)# network 192.168.11.0 255.255.255.0
R1(dhcp-config)# default-router 192.168.11.1
R1(dhcp-config)# end
```

2. The configurations have several problems:

■ ACL 1 has an incorrect subnet mask and is too restrictive. It permits only hosts on nonexistent subnet 192.168.0.0/24. This excludes hosts on the 192.168.10.0 and 192.168.11.0 networks. ACL 1 should be **access-list 1 permit 192.168.0.0 0.0.255.255**.

- The NAT pool is incorrectly identified. The router interface should not be included in the pool. The pool should be configured to a 255.255.255.248 (/29), not a 255.255.255.224 (/27). The command should be **ip nat pool NAT-POOL 209.165.200.226 209.165.200.230 netmask 255.255.255.248**.

- In the **ip nat inside** command, the pool name should be NAT-POOL, not NAT-POOL1. Also, the **overload** keyword is missing at the end of the command. The command should be **ip nat inside source list 1 pool NAT-POOL overload**.

- The inside and outside NAT interfaces are incorrectly identified. Interface serial s0/1/0 should be configured with the **ip nat outside** interface command, and serial 0/0/0 with the **ip nat inside** interface command.

The correct configuration is as follows:

```
access-list 1 permit 192.168.0.0 0.0.255.255
ip nat pool NAT-POOL 209.165.200.226 209.165.200.230 netmask 255.255.255.248
ip nat inside source list 1 pool NAT-POOL overload
interface serial s0/1/0
  ip nat outside
interface fastethernet 0/0
  ip nat inside
```

Chapter 8

Check Your Understanding

1. Cable type: A

   IP address and subnet: B

   Connection type: B

   Device ID: B

   Operating system version: A

   Device type and model: A

   Routing protocols: B

   Connector type: A

2. A. Common symptoms of physical layer problems include performance less than the baseline; loss of connectivity; high collision counts; network bottlenecks or congestion; high CPU utilization rates on routers, switches, and servers; and console error messages.

3. B. The first part, "Serial0 is up," indicates that the physical layer is operational. The second part, "line protocol is down," indicates a Layer 2 problem.

4. C.

5. B, C, and D. Only EIGRP, IP, and RIP operate at Layer 3. TCP and UDP operate at Layer 4. DNS operates at Layer 7.

6. FTP: A

   HTTP: D

   POP3: E

   SMTP: C

   SNMP: F

   Telnet: B

7. B. Software interacts with Layer 7. Therefore, the top-down approach is the most logical place to start.

8. A, C, D. These are logical questions that will help you narrow down the specific problem. Questions B, E, and F do not add any value and are not pertinent.

9. A. The only tool listed that detects near-end crosstalk is a cable analyzer. Cable testers, digital multimeters, and baselining tools do not detect NEXT.

10. B, D, E. Although the documents listed in answers A, C, and F could be of help, documents B, D, and E are required.

11. B, C, F. Option A would be trivial to collect. Option D does not make sense. Option E is incorrect because you should conduct the baseline over a period of time and not have multiple baseline tests.

12. B. Before proceeding, ensure that a valid configuration has been saved for any device on which the configuration may be modified. This provides for recovery to a known initial state.

13. **Router documentation:**

- The router documentation should include the router names, model designation, location in the enterprise (building, floor, room, rack, panel), configured interfaces, data link layer addresses, network layer addresses, routing protocols configured, and any additional important information about the device.

    Switch documentation:

- The switch documentation should include the switch names, model designation, location in the enterprise (building, floor, room, rack, panel), management IP address, port names and status, speed, duplex, STP state, PortFast setting, trunk status, Layer 2 or Layer 3 EtherChannel, VLAN IDs, and any additional important information about the device.

End-user documentation:

- The end-user documentation should include the server names and functions, operating system version, IP address, gateways, DNS server, network application, and any additional important information about the device.

  Topology diagrams should be available in a physical and logical variation.

Physical network topology diagram:

- A graphical representation that identifies the physical location of the networking device.

- Also details the types of cabling between them and the cable identification numbers.

Logical network topology diagram:

- A graphical representation that uses symbols to identify each network device and how it is interconnected.

- Also details the logical architecture, including interface types and numbers, IP addresses, subnet masks, routing protocols, autonomous system domains, and any additional important information, such as DLCI numbers and Layer 2 protocol.

14.

Step 1: Determine what types of data to collect:

- Start simply, by selecting a few variables that represent the defined policies, and fine-tune along the way.

- Generally, some good starting measures are interface utilization and CPU utilization.

Step 2: Identify devices and ports of interest:

- Devices and ports of interest must be identified, such as network device ports that connect to other network devices, servers, key users, and anything else considered critical to the operation.

Step 3: Determine the baseline duration:

- This period should be at least seven days to capture daily or weekly trends and should last two to four weeks.

- Do not perform a baseline measurement during times of unique traffic patterns.

- Should be conducted on a regular basis, such as an annual analysis of the entire network or a baseline of different sections of the network on a rotating basis.

15.

Stage 1: Gather symptoms:

- Symptoms may appear in many different forms, including alerts from the network management system, console messages, and user complaints.

- Gather and document symptoms from the network, end systems, and users.

- In addition, determine which network components have been affected and how the network's functionality has changed compared to the baseline.

Stage 2: Isolate the problem:

- The problem is not truly isolated until a single problem, or a set of related problems, is identified.

- Examine the characteristics of problems at the logical layers of the network so that the most likely cause can be selected.

- Depending on the problem characteristics identified, gather and document more symptoms.

Stage 3: Correct the problem:

- Work to correct the problem by implementing, testing, and documenting a solution.

16. **Bottom-up troubleshooting method:**

- Start with the network's physical components, and work up through the layers of the OSI model until you identify the cause of the problem.

- This is a good approach to use when you suspect that the problem is physical.

Top-down troubleshooting method:

- Examine the end-user application first.

- The analysis continues downward from the upper layers of the OSI model until the cause of the problem is identified.

Divide-and-conquer troubleshooting method:

- Select a layer, and test in both directions from the starting layer.

- If you can verify that a layer is functioning properly, typically it is safe to assume that the layers below it are functioning.

- If a layer is not functioning properly, gather symptoms of the problem at that layer, and work your way down.

17.

Step 1: Locate LANs:

- Establish the source and destination endpoints that will connect via the WAN.

Step 2: Analyze traffic:

- Find out what data traffic must be carried, its origin, its destination, bandwidth requirements, latency, and jitter tolerance.

Step 3: Plan the topology:

- Identify the various endpoints, geographic considerations, and requirement for availability.

Step 4: Estimate the required bandwidth:

- After considering the endpoints and the links chosen, you can estimate the necessary bandwidth.

Step 5: Choose the WAN technology:

- After you determine the bandwidth availability, you select suitable link technologies.

Step 6: Evaluate costs:

- Determine installation and operational costs for the WAN, and compare them with the business needs driving the WAN implementation.

18. Check for bad cables or connections:

- Use a cable tester to verify that the cable from the source interface is properly connected and is in good condition.

- When you doubt a cable's integrity, swap the suspect cable with a known working cable.

    Make sure that the correct cabling standard is adhered to throughout the network:

- Verify that the proper cable is being used for the connection.

    Check that devices are cabled correctly:

- Verify that all cables are connected to their correct ports or interfaces.

    Verify proper interface configurations:

- Check that all switch ports are set in the correct VLAN and that spanning-tree, speed, and duplex settings are correctly configured.

- Confirm that any active ports or interfaces are not shut down.

Check operations statistics and data error rates:

- Use Cisco **show** commands to check for statistics such as collisions, input, and output errors.

- The characteristics of these statistics vary depending on the protocols used on the network.

19.

- Address mapping errors

- Framing errors

- STP failures or loops

Challenge Questions and Activities

1. Although there is no one perfect method to follow, the following are some sample questions to ask:

- What does not work?

- Has the thing that does not work ever worked?

- When did you first notice the problem?

- What has changed since the last time it did work? For instance, have you installed any new software or hardware?

- Can you reproduce the problem?

- Are the things that do work and the things that do not work related?

2. The user has an incorrect DNS gateway configured. Have her issue the MS-DOS **ipconfig /all** command to verify her settings.

This glossary defines many of the terms and abbreviations related to networking. It includes all the key terms used throughout the book. As with any growing technical field, some terms evolve and take on several meanings. Where necessary, multiple definitions and abbreviation expansions are presented.

A

access control list (ACL)   A list kept by Cisco routers to control access to or from the router for a number of services. For example, ACLs prevent packets with a certain IP address from leaving a particular interface on the router.

access server   A communications processor that connects asynchronous devices to a LAN or WAN through network and terminal emulation software. Performs both synchronous and asynchronous routing of supported protocols. Sometimes called a network access server.

Advanced Encryption Standard (AES)   The National Institute of Standards and Technology (NIST) adopted AES to replace the existing DES encryption in cryptographic devices. AES provides stronger security than DES and is computationally more efficient than 3DES. AES offers three different key lengths: 128-, 192-, and 256-bit keys.

AfriNIC   One of five Regional Internet Registries. AfriNIC is a nongovernment, not-for-profit, membership-based organization based in Mauritius. AfriNIC is responsible for distributing and registering Internet address resources throughout Africa.

APNIC (Asia-Pacific Network Information Centre)   One of five Regional Internet Registries. APNIC is a not-for-profit membership organization that is responsible for distributing and registering Internet address resources throughout the Asia-Pacific region.

application-specific integrated circuit (ASIC)   A development process for implementing integrated circuit designs that are specific to the intended application, as opposed to designs for general-purpose use.

ARIN (American Registry for Internet Numbers)   One of five Regional Internet Registries. ARIN is a not-for-profit membership organization that is responsible for distributing and registering Internet address resources throughout the North America region.

asymmetric encryption   Uses different keys for encryption and decryption. Knowing one of the keys does not allow a hacker to deduce the second key and decode the information. One key encrypts the message, and a second key decrypts it. It is impossible to encrypt and decrypt with the same key.

Asynchronous Transfer Mode (ATM)   An international standard for cell relay in which multiple service types (such as voice, video, or data) are conveyed in fixed-length (53-byte) cells. Fixed-length cells allow cell processing to occur in hardware, thereby reducing transit delays. ATM is designed to take advantage of high-speed transmission media such as E3, T3, and SONET.

Authentication Header (AH)   Provides data authentication and integrity for IP packets passed between two systems. It verifies that any message passed between two systems has not been modified during transit. It also verifies the origin of the data. AH does not provide data confidentiality (encryption) of packets. Used alone, the AH protocol provides weak protection.

Automatic Private IP Addressing (APIPA)
Certain Windows clients have this feature, with which a Windows computer can automatically assign itself an IP address in the 169.254.*x*.*x* range if a DHCP server is unavailable or does not exist on the network.

AutoSecure   Uses a single command to disable nonessential system processes and services, eliminating potential security threats.

B

backbone   The part of a network that acts as the primary path for traffic that is most often sourced from and destined for other networks.

Backward Explicit Congestion Notification (BECN)   A bit set by a Frame Relay network in frames traveling in the opposite direction of frames encountering a congested path. The DTE receiving frames with the BECN bit set can request that higher-level protocols take flow control action as appropriate.

Basic Rate Interface (BRI)   An ISDN interface composed of two B channels and one D channel for circuit-switched communication of voice, video, and data.

bearer (B) channel   In ISDN, a full-duplex 64-kbps channel used to send user data.

bit-oriented   A class of data link layer communication protocols that can transmit frames regardless of frame content. Compared with byte-oriented protocols, bit-oriented protocols provide full-duplex operation and are more efficient and reliable.

black hat   Someone who uses his knowledge of computer systems to break into systems or networks that he is not authorized to use, usually for personal or financial gain. A cracker is an example of a black hat.

Bootstrap Protocol (BOOTP)   A protocol used by a network node to determine the IP address of its Ethernet interfaces to affect network booting.

bot   An application that runs automated tasks.

bottom-up troubleshooting   You start with the physical components of the network and move up through the layers of the OSI model until you find the cause of the problem. Bottom-up troubleshooting is a good approach to use when you suspect a physical problem.

broadband   A transmission system that multiplexes multiple independent signals onto one cable. In telecommunications terminology, any channel having bandwidth greater than a voice-grade channel (4 KHz). In LAN terminology, a coaxial cable on which analog signaling is used. Also called wideband.

buffer   A storage area used to handle data in transit. Buffers are used in internetworking to compensate for differences in process speed between network devices. Bursts of data can be stored in buffers until they can be handled by slower processing devices. Also known as a packet buffer.

C

cable A transmission medium of copper wire or optical fiber wrapped in a protective cover.

cable analyzer A multifunctional handheld device that is used to test and certify copper and fiber cables for different services and standards. The more sophisticated tools include advanced troubleshooting diagnostics that measure distance to performance defect (NEXT, RL), identify corrective actions, and graphically display crosstalk and impedance behavior.

cable modem (CM) Enables you to receive data at high speeds. Typically, the cable modem attaches to a standard 10BASE-T Ethernet card in the computer.

cable modem termination system (CMTS) A component that exchanges digital signals with cable modems on a cable network. A headend CMTS communicates with cable modems that are located in the subscriber homes.

cable television A communication system in which multiple channels of programming are transmitted to homes using broadband coaxial cable. Formerly called community antenna television (CATV).

cable tester A specialized handheld device designed to test the various types of data communication cabling. Cabling testers can be used to detect broken wires, crossed-over wiring, shorted connections, and improperly paired connections.

call setup time The time required to establish a switched call between DTE devices.

cell 1) The basic unit for ATM switching and multiplexing. Cells contain identifiers that specify the data stream to which they belong. Each cell consists of a 5-byte header and 48 bytes of payload. 2) In wireless technology, a cell is the area of radio range or coverage in which the wireless devices can communicate with the base station. The cell's size depends on the speed of the transmission, the type of antenna used, and the physical environment, as well as other factors.

cell relay A network technology based on the use of small, fixed-size packets, or cells. Because cells are fixed length, they can be processed and switched in hardware at high speeds. Cell relay is the basis of many high-speed network protocols, including ATM, IEEE 802.6, and SMDS.

central office (CO) A local telephone company office to which all local loops in a given area connect and in which circuit switching of subscriber lines occurs.

Challenge Handshake Authentication Protocol (CHAP) A security feature supported on lines using PPP encapsulation that prevents unauthorized access. CHAP does not itself prevent unauthorized access; it merely identifies the remote end. The router or access server then determines whether that user is allowed access.

channel 1) A communication path. Multiple channels can be multiplexed over a single cable in certain environments. 2) In IBM, the specific path between large computers (such as mainframes) and attached peripheral devices.

channel service unit (CSU) A digital interface device that connects end-user equipment to the local digital telephone loop. Often mentioned with DSU as CSU/DSU.

circuit A communications path between two or more points.

circuit switching   A switching system in which a dedicated physical circuit path must exist between sender and receiver for the duration of the "call." Used heavily in the telephone company network. Circuit switching can be contrasted with contention and token passing as a channel access method, and with message switching and packet switching as a switching technique.

Cisco 7000   Any of the Cisco 7000 series of routers. A high-end router platform that supports a wide range of network interface and media types and is designed for use in enterprise networks.

Cisco IOS helper address   An address configured on an interface to which broadcasts received on that interface are sent.

Cisco Router and Security Device Manager (SDM)   An easy-to-use web-based device-management tool designed for configuring LAN, WAN, and security features on Cisco IOS software-based routers.

classless interdomain routing (CIDR)   A technique supported by BGP4 and based on route aggregation. CIDR allows routers to group routes to reduce the quantity of routing information carried by the core routers. With CIDR, several IP networks appear to networks outside the group as a single, larger entity. With CIDR, IP addresses and their subnet masks are written as four octets, separated by periods, followed by a slash and a two-digit number that represents the subnet mask.

Clear to Send (CTS)   A circuit in the EIA/TIA-232 specification that is activated when the DCE is ready to accept data from the DTE.

clock skew   A clock's frequency difference, or the first derivative of its offset with respect to time.

coaxial cable   A cable consisting of a hollow cylindrical conductor that surrounds a single inner wire conductor. Two types of coaxial cable are currently used in LANs: 50-ohm cable, which is used for digital signaling, and 75-ohm cable, which is used for analog signal and high-speed digital signaling.

Committed Information Rate (CIR)   The rate at which a Frame Relay network agrees to transfer information under normal conditions, averaged over a minimum increment of time. CIR, measured in bits per second, is one of the key negotiated tariff metrics.

communications line   The physical link (such as a wire or telephone circuit) that connects one or more devices to one or more other devices.

community antenna television (CATV)   A communication system in which multiple channels of programming are transmitted to homes using broadband coaxial cable.

community string   A text string that acts as a password and is used to authenticate messages sent between a management station and a router containing an SNMP agent. The community string is sent in every packet between the manager and the agent.

configuration register   In Cisco routers, a 16-bit user-configurable value that determines how the router functions during initialization. The configuration register can be stored in hardware or software. In hardware, you set the bit position by specifying a hexadecimal value using configuration commands.

congestion   Traffic in excess of network capacity.

connectionless   A term used to describe data transfer without the existence of a virtual circuit.

connection-oriented   A term used to describe data transfer that requires the establishment of a virtual circuit.

control plane   Handles the interaction of the router with the other network elements, providing the information needed to make decisions and control the overall router operation. This plane runs processes such as routing protocols and network management.

core router   In a packet-switched star topology, a router that is part of the backbone and that serves as the single pipe through which all traffic from peripheral networks must pass on its way to other peripheral networks.

cracker   Someone who tries to gain unauthorized access to network resources with malicious intent.

Customer Premises Equipment (CPE) Terminating equipment, such as terminals, telephones, and modems, supplied by the telephone company, installed at customer sites, and connected to the telephone company network.

cycles per second   A measure of frequency.

D

data communications   The sending and receiving of data between two endpoints. Data communications require a combination of hardware (CSU/DSUs, modems, multiplexers, and other hardware) and software.

Data Communications Equipment (DCE)   Data communications equipment is the EIA expansion. Data circuit-terminating equipment is the ITU-T expansion. The devices and connections of a communications network that comprise the network end of the user-to-network interface. The DCE provides a physical connection to the network, forwards traffic, and provides a clocking signal used to synchronize data transmission between DCE and DTE devices. Modems and interface cards are examples of DCE.

Data Encryption Standard (DES)   Developed by IBM, DES uses a 56-bit key, ensuring high-performance encryption. DES is a symmetric key cryptosystem.

Data Link Connection Identifier (DLCI)   A value that specifies a PVC or SVC in a Frame Relay network. In the basic Frame Relay specification, DLCIs are locally significant (connected devices might use different values to specify the same connection). In the LMI extended specification, DLCIs are globally significant (DLCIs specify individual end devices).

Data-Over-Cable Service Interface Specification (DOCSIS)   An international standard developed by CableLabs, a nonprofit research and development consortium for cable-related technologies. CableLabs tests and certifies cable equipment vendor devices, such as cable modems and cable modem termination systems, and grants DOCSIS-certified or qualified status.

data plane   Handles packet forwarding from one physical or logical interface to another. It involves different switching mechanisms such as process switching and Cisco Express Forwarding (CEF) on Cisco IOS software routers.

data service unit (DSU)   A device used in digital transmission that adapts the physical interface on a DTE device to a transmission facility such as T1 or E1. The DSU is also responsible for such functions as signal timing. Often mentioned with CSU as CSU/DSU.

Data Set Ready (DSR)   An EIA/TIA-232 interface circuit that is activated when DCE is powered up and ready for use.

data stream   All data transmitted through a communications line in a single read or write operation.

Data Terminal Equipment (DTE)   A device at the user end of a user-network interface that serves as a data source, destination, or both. DTE connects to a data network through a DCE device (such as a modem) and typically uses clocking signals generated by the DCE. DTE includes such devices as computers, protocol translators, and multiplexers.

Data Terminal Ready (DTR)   An EIA/TIA-232 circuit that is activated to let the DCE know when the DTE is ready to send and receive data.

decryption   The reverse application of an encryption algorithm to encrypted data, thereby restoring that data to its original, unencrypted state.

dedicated line   A communications line that is indefinitely reserved for transmissions, rather than switched as transmission is required.

delta (D) channel   A full-duplex 16-kbps (BRI) or 64-kbps (PRI) ISDN channel.

demarcation point   The point where the service provider or telephone company network ends and connects with the customer's equipment at the customer's site.

demilitarized zone (DMZ)   The interface of a firewall where the publicly accessible segment exists. The host on the outside may be able to reach the host on the public services segment, the DMZ, but not the host on the inside part of the network.

DHCPACK   Unicast message sent by a DHCP server in response to a device sending a DHCPREQUEST. This message is used by the DHCP server to complete the DHCP process.

DHCPDISCOVER   Broadcast messages sent by a client device to discover a DHCP server.

DHCP for IPv6 (DHCPv6)   Dynamic Host Configuration Protocol for IPv6.

DHCPOFFER   Unicast message returned by the DHCP server in response to a client device sending a DHCPDISCOVER broadcast message. This message typically contains an IP address, subnet mask, default gateway address, and other information.

DHCP relay agent   A component that relays DHCP messages between DHCP clients and DHCP servers on different IP networks.

DHCPREQUEST   Broadcast message sent by a client device in response to a DHCP server's DHCPOFFER message. This message is used by the device to accept the DHCP server's offer.

Diffie-Hellman (DH)   An algorithm to securely derive shared keys across an untrusted network infrastructure. Diffie-Hellman is used to generate keys to be used in the ciphers specified in IPsec transforms. IPsec uses these transforms in conjunction with Diffie-Hellman keys to encrypt and decrypt data as it passes through the VPN tunnel.

digital multimeter (DMM)   A test instrument that directly measures electrical values of voltage, current, and resistance. In network troubleshooting, most multimedia tests involve checking power-supply voltage levels and verifying that network devices are receiving power.

digital subscriber line (DSL)   An always-on connection technology that uses existing twisted-pair telephone lines to transport high-bandwidth data and that provides IP services to subscribers. A DSL modem converts an Ethernet signal from the user device into a DSL signal, which is transmitted to the central office.

Discard Eligible (DE)   Also known as tagged traffic. If the network is congested, tagged traffic can be dropped to ensure delivery of higher-priority traffic.

distributed DoS (DDoS) attack   Designed to saturate network links with illegitimate data. This data can overwhelm an Internet link, causing legitimate traffic to be dropped. DDoS uses attack methods similar to standard DoS attacks, but it operates on a much larger scale. Typically, hundreds or thousands of attack points attempt to overwhelm a target.

divide-and-conquer troubleshooting   You start by collecting users' experiences with the problem and document the symptoms. Then, using that information, you make an informed guess about the OSI layer at which to start your investigation. After you verify that a layer is functioning properly, assume that the layers below it are functioning, and work up the OSI layers. If an OSI layer is not functioning properly, work your way down the OSI layer model.

DoS attack   A denial-of-service (DoS) attack is designed to saturate network links with illegitimate data. This data can overwhelm an Internet link, causing legitimate traffic to be dropped.

drop cable   Generally, a cable that connects a network device (such as a computer) to a physical medium. A type of attachment user interface (AUI).

DS0 (digital signal level zero)   A framing specification used to transmit digital signals over a single channel at 64 kbps on a T1 facility.

DSL access multiplexer (DSLAM)   The device located at the provider's central office (CO). Concentrates connections from multiple DSL subscribers.

dual stacking   A common transition mechanism to enable the smooth integration of IPv4 to IPv6.

dynamic 6to4 tunneling   Automatically establishes the connection of IPv6 islands through an IPv4 network, typically the Internet. It dynamically applies a valid, unique IPv6 prefix to each IPv6 island, which enables the fast deployment of IPv6 in a corporate network without address retrieval from the ISPs or registries.

Dynamic Host Configuration Protocol (DHCP)   Makes the process of assigning new IP addresses almost transparent. DHCP assigns IP addresses and other important network configuration information dynamically.

dynamic NAT   Uses a pool of public addresses and assigns them on a first-come, first-served basis. When a host with a private IP address requests access to the Internet, dynamic NAT chooses an IP address from the pool that is not already in use by another host.

E

E1   A wide-area digital transmission scheme used predominantly in Europe that carries data at a rate of 2.048 Mbps. E1 lines can be leased for private use from common carriers.

E3   A wide-area digital transmission scheme used predominantly in Europe that carries data at a rate of 34.368 Mbps. E3 lines can be leased for private use from common carriers.

Encapsulating Security Payload (ESP)   Provides a combination of security services for IPsec-processed IP packets. Examples of the services offered by ESP include data confidentiality, data origin authentication, data integrity, and data confidentiality.

encryption   Applying a specific algorithm to data to alter its appearance, making it incomprehensible to those who are not authorized to see the information.

end-system configuration table   Contains baseline records of the hardware and software used in end-system devices such as servers, network management consoles, and desktop workstations. An incorrectly configured end system can have a negative impact on a network's overall performance.

enterprise network   A large and diverse network connecting most major points in a company or other organization. Differs from a WAN in that it is privately owned and maintained.

EUI-64 (Extended Universal Identifier 64)   An IPv6 address format created by taking an interface's MAC address (which is 48 bits long) and inserting another 16-bit hexadecimal string (FFFE) in the OUI (first 24 bits) of the MAC address. To ensure that the chosen 48-bit address is a unique Ethernet address, the seventh bit in the high-order byte is set to 1 (equivalent to the IEEE U/L, Universal/Local bit).

Excess Burst Size (BE)   A negotiated tariff metric in Frame Relay internetworks. The number of bits that a Frame Relay internetwork attempts to transmit after the committed burst (BC) is accommodated. In general, BE data is delivered with a lower probability than BC data, because BE data can be marked as DE by the network.

exchange identification (XID)   Request and response packets exchanged before a session between a router and a Token Ring host. If the parameters of the serial device contained in the XID packet do not match the host's configuration, the session is dropped.

F

firewall   A router or access server designated as a buffer between any connected public network and a private network. A firewall router uses access lists and other methods to ensure the security of the private network.

Forward Explicit Congestion Notification (FECN)   A bit set by a Frame Relay network to inform the DTE receiving the frame that congestion occurred in the path from source to destination. DTE receiving frames with the FECN bit set can request that higher-level protocols take flow-control action as appropriate.

fragmentation   The process of breaking a packet into smaller units when transmitting over a network medium that cannot support the packet's original size.

Frame Relay   An industry-standard switched data link layer protocol that handles multiple virtual circuits using HDLC encapsulation between connected devices. Frame Relay is more efficient than X.25, the protocol for which it is generally considered a replacement.

Frame Relay access device (FRAD)   Any network device that provides a connection between a LAN and a Frame Relay WAN.

frequency   The number of cycles, measured in hertz, of an alternating current signal per unit of time.

full-mesh topology   A network in which each network node has either a physical circuit or a virtual circuit connecting it to every other network node. A full mesh provides a great deal of redundancy, but because it can be prohibitively expensive to implement, it is usually reserved for network backbones.

G

Generic Route Encapsulation (GRE)   A tunneling protocol developed by Cisco that can encapsulate a wide variety of protocol packet types inside IP tunnels. This creates a virtual point-to-point link to Cisco routers at remote points over an IP internetwork. By connecting multiprotocol subnetworks in a single-protocol backbone environment, IP tunneling using GRE allows network expansion across a single-protocol backbone environment.

global routing prefix   Part of the IPv6 address that is a hierarchically structured value assigned to a site.

H

hacker   A general term that has historically been used to describe a computer programming expert. More recently, this term is often used in a negative way to describe an individual who attempts to gain unauthorized access to network resources with malicious intent.

hash   Contributes to data integrity and authentication by ensuring that unauthorized persons do not tamper with transmitted messages. A hash, also called a message digest, is a number generated from a string of text. The hash is smaller than the text itself. It is generated using a formula in such a way that it is extremely unlikely that some other text will produce the same hash value.

hashed message authentication code (HMAC)   A data integrity algorithm that guarantees the message's integrity.

headend   The endpoint of a broadband network. All stations transmit toward the headend; the headend then transmits toward the destination stations.

High-Level Data Link Control (HDLC)   A bit-oriented synchronous data link layer protocol developed by ISO. Derived from SDLC, HDLC specifies a data encapsulation method on synchronous serial links using frame characters and checksums.

High-Speed Serial Interface (HSSI)   A network standard for high-speed (up to 52 Mbps) serial connections over WAN links.

hub   Generally, a term used to describe a device that serves as the center of a star topology network.

I

IANA (Internet Assigned Numbers Authority)   An organization operated under the auspices of the ISOC as part of the IAB. IANA delegates authority for IP address-space allocation and domain-name assignment to the NIC and other organizations. IANA also maintains a database of assigned protocol identifiers used in the TCP/IP stack, including autonomous system numbers.

IEEE 802.11   An IEEE specification developed to eliminate problems inherent in the proprietary WLAN technologies. It began with a 1-Mbps standard and has evolved into several other standards, including 802.11a, 802.11b, and 802.11g.

IEEE 802.11b   The IEEE WLAN standard for 11 Mbps at 2.4 GHz.

IEEE 802.11g   The IEEE WLAN standard for 54 Mbps at 2.4 GHz.

IEEE 802.11n   The IEEE WLAN standard for 248 Mbps at 2.4 or 5 GHz. As the latest standard, 802.11n is a proposed amendment that builds on the previous 802.11 standards by adding multiple input, multiple output (MIMO).

IEEE 802.16   The WiMAX standard. It allows transmissions of up to 70 Mbps and has a range of up to 30 miles (50 km). It can operate in licensed or unlicensed bands of the spectrum from 2 to 6 GHz.

inside global address   Used with NAT, a valid public address that the inside host is given when it exits the NAT router.

inside local address   Used with NAT, this usually is not an IP address assigned by a RIR or service provider and is most likely an RFC 1918 private address.

Integrated Services Digital Network (ISDN)   A communication protocol, offered by telephone companies, that permits telephone networks to carry data, voice, and other source traffic.

Internetwork Packet Exchange (IPX)   A NetWare network layer (Layer 3) protocol for transferring data from servers to workstations. IPX is similar to IP and XNS.

intrusion detection system (IDS)   Detects attacks against a network and send logs to a management console.

intrusion prevention system (IPS)   Prevents attacks against the network and should provide active defense mechanisms in addition to detection, including prevention and reaction. Prevention stops the detected attack from executing. Reaction immunizes the system from future attacks from a malicious source.

Inverse Address Resolution Protocol (ARP)   A method of building dynamic routes in a network. Allows an access server to discover the network address of a device associated with a virtual circuit.

IP Next Generation (IPng)   Now known as IPv6, a network layer IP standard used by electronic devices to exchange data across a packet-switched internetwork. It follows IPv4 as the second version of the Internet Protocol to be formally adopted for general use. IPv6 includes support for flow ID in the packet header, which can be used to identify flows.

IP Security (IPsec)   A protocol suite for securing IP communications that provides encryption, integrity, and authentication. IPsec spells out the messaging necessary to secure VPN communications, but it relies on existing algorithms.

IPv6 global unicast address   A globally unique address that can be routed globally with no modification. It shares the same address format as an IPv6 anycast address. The IANA assigns global unicast addresses.

J

J1   A wide-area digital transmission scheme used predominantly in Japan that carries data at a rate of 1.544 Mbps. J1 lines can be leased for private use from common carriers.

jabber   The condition in which a network device continually transmits random, meaningless data onto the network.

K

keepalive interval   The amount of time between each keepalive message sent by a network device.

knowledge base   An information database used to assist in the use or troubleshooting of a product. Online network device vendor knowledge bases have become indispensable sources of information. When vendor-based knowledge bases are combined with Internet search engines such as Google, a network administrator has access to a vast pool of experience-based information.

L

LACNIC (Latin America and Caribbean Internet Addresses Registry)   One of five Regional Internet Registries. LACNIC is a not-for-profit membership organization that is responsible for distributing and registering Internet address resources throughout the Latin America and Caribbean region.

leased line   A transmission line reserved by a communications carrier for a customer's private use. A leased line is a type of dedicated line.

Link Access Procedure, Balanced (LAPB)   A data link layer protocol in the X.25 protocol stack. LAPB is a bit-oriented protocol derived from HDLC.

Link Access Procedure for Frame Relay (LAPF) As defined in the ITU Q.922, specifies Frame Mode Services in the Frame Relay network.

Link Control Protocol (LCP)   A protocol that establishes, configures, and tests data-link connections for use by PPP.

local loop   A line from the premises of a telephone subscriber to the telephone company CO.

Local Management Interface (LMI)   A keepalive mechanism that provides status information about Frame Relay connections between the router (DTE) and the Frame Relay switch (DCE).

logical topology   Describes the arrangement of devices on a network and how they communicate with one another.

M

man-in-the-middle (MITM) attack   Carried out by an attacker who positions himself between two legitimate hosts. The attacker may allow the normal transactions between hosts to occur, and only periodically manipulate the conversation between the two.

mesh   A network topology in which devices are organized in a manageable, segmented manner with many, often redundant, interconnections strategically placed between network nodes.

Message Digest 5 (MD5)   An algorithm used for message authentication. MD5 verifies the integrity of the communication, authenticates the origin, and checks for timeliness.

metropolitan-area network (MAN)   A network that spans a metropolitan area. Generally, a MAN spans a larger geographic area than a LAN but a smaller geographic area than a WAN.

microfilter   A device that prevents certain router frequencies from traveling over the telephone line and interfering with telephone calls.

microwave   Electromagnetic waves in the range 1 to 30 GHz. Microwave-based networks are an evolving technology gaining favor due to high bandwidth and relatively low cost.

modem   A device that converts digital and analog signals. At the source, a modem coverts digital signals to a form suitable for transmission over analog communication facilities. At the destination, the analog signals are returned to their digital form. Modems allow data to be transmitted over voice-grade telephone lines.

N

NAT overloading   Sometimes called Port Address Translation (PAT). Maps multiple private IP addresses to a single public IP address or a few addresses.

NAT pool   A list of public IP addresses used in NAT.

Network Address Translation (NAT)   Only globally unique in terms of the public Internet. A mechanism for translating private addresses into publicly usable addresses to be used within the public Internet. An effective means of hiding actual device addressing within a private network.

network analysis module (NAM)   Can be installed in Cisco Catalyst 6500 series switches and Cisco 7600 series routers to provide a graphical representation of traffic from local and remote switches and routers. The NAM is a embedded browser-based interface that generates reports on the traffic that consumes critical network resources. In addition, the NAM can capture and decode packets and track response times to pinpoint an application problem to the network or server.

network baseline   Used to efficiently diagnose and correct network problems. A network baseline documents what the network's expected performance should be under normal operating conditions. This information is captured in documentation such as configuration tables and topology diagrams.

network configuration table   Contains accurate, up-to-date records of the hardware and software used in a network. The network configuration table should provide the network engineer with all the information necessary to identify and correct the network fault.

Network Control Protocol (NCP)   Used to establish and configure different network layer protocols.

network documentation   Provides a logical diagram of the network and detailed information about each component. This information should be kept in a single location, either as hard copy or on the network on a protected website. Network documentation should include a network configuration table, an end-system configuration table, and a network topology diagram.

network interface device (NID)   Connects the customer premises to the local loop at the demarcation point.

network management system (NMS)   Responsible for managing at least part of a network. An NMS is generally a reasonably powerful and well-equipped computer, such as an engineering workstation. NMSs communicate with agents to help keep track of network statistics and resources.

Network Security Wheel   Helps you comply with a security policy. The Security Wheel, a continuous process, promotes retesting and reapplying updated security measures on a continuous basis.

network topology diagram   A graphical representation of a network that illustrates how each device is connected and its logical architecture. A topology diagram has many of the same components as the network configuration table. Each network device should be represented on the diagram with consistent notation or a graphical symbol. Also, each logical and physical connection should be represented using a simple line or other appropriate symbol. Routing protocols also can be shown.

nonbroadcast multiaccess (NBMA)   A term describing a multiaccess network that does not support broadcasting (such as X.25) or in which broadcasting is not feasible (for example, an SMDS broadcast group or an extended Ethernet that is too large).

Novell IPX   See Internetwork Packet Exchange (IPX).

null modem   A small box or cable used to join computing devices directly, rather than over a network.

O

one-step lockdown wizard   Tests your router configuration for potential security problems and automatically makes any necessary configuration changes to correct any problems found.

optical time-domain reflectometer (OTDR) Pinpoints the distance to a break in a fiber-optic cable. This device sends signals along the cable and waits for them to be reflected. The time between sending the signal and getting it back is converted into a distance measurement. The TDR function normally is packaged with data cabling testers.

outside global address   A reachable IP address used in NAT and assigned to hosts on the Internet.

P

packet-switched network   Uses packet-switching technology to transfer data.

packet switching   A networking method in which nodes share bandwidth with each other by sending packets.

partial mesh topology   A network in which some network nodes are organized in a full mesh and others are connected to only one or two other nodes in the network. A partial mesh does not provide the level of redundancy of a full-mesh topology, but it is less expensive to implement. Partial-mesh topologies generally are used in the peripheral networks that connect to a fully meshed backbone.

passphrase   A sentence or phrase that translates into a more secure password. Make sure that the phrase is long enough to be hard to guess but easy to remember and type accurately.

Password Authentication Protocol (PAP)   An authentication protocol that allows PPP peers to authenticate one another. The remote router attempting to connect to the local router is required to send an authentication request. Unlike CHAP, PAP passes the password and username in the clear (unencrypted). PAP does not itself prevent unauthorized access, but merely identifies the remote end. The router or access server then determines if that user is allowed access. PAP is supported only on PPP lines.

password recovery   The process of legitimately accessing a device when the password is unknown.

permanent virtual circuit (PVC)   A virtual circuit that is permanently established. PVCs save bandwidth associated with circuit establishment and are torn down in situations where certain virtual circuits must exist all the time.

phisher   Someone who uses e-mail or other means to trick others into providing sensitive information, such as credit card numbers or passwords. A phisher masquerades as a trusted party that has a legitimate need for the sensitive information.

physical topology   The mapping of a network that shows the physical layout of equipment, cables, and interconnections.

point of presence (POP)   A point of interconnection between the communications facilities provided by the telephone company and the building's main distribution facility.

point-to-point connection   A connection used to connect LANs to service provider WANs and to connect LAN segments within an Enterprise network.

Point-to-Point Protocol (PPP)   A successor to SLIP. Provides router-to-router and host-to-network connections over synchronous and asynchronous circuits.

Port Address Translation (PAT)   Sometimes called NAT overloading. Maps multiple private IP addresses to a single public IP address or a few addresses.

portable network analyzer   A portable device that is used to troubleshoot switched networks and VLANs. By plugging in the network analyzer anywhere on the network, a network engineer can see the switch port to which the device is connected and the average and peak utilization.

port forwarding   Sometimes called tunneling. The act of forwarding a network port from one network node to another. This technique can allow an external user to reach a port on a private IP address (inside a LAN) from the outside through a NAT-enabled router.

preshared key (PSK)   A secret key that is shared between the two parties using a secure channel before it needs to be used. PSKs use symmetric key cryptographic algorithms. A PSK is entered into each peer manually and is used to authenticate the peer. At each end, the PSK is combined with other information to form the authentication key.

Primary Rate Interface (PRI)   An ISDN interface to primary rate access. Primary rate access consists of a single 64-Kbps D channel plus 23 (T1) or 30 (E1) B channels for voice or data.

primary station   In bit-synchronous data link layer protocols such as HDLC and SDLC, a station that controls the transmission activity of secondary stations. Also performs other management functions such as error control through polling or other means. Primary stations send commands to secondary stations and receive responses.

protocol analyzer   Decodes the various protocol layers in a recorded frame and presents this information in a relatively easy-to-use format.

public switched telephone network (PSTN)   A general term referring to the variety of telephone networks and services in place worldwide. Also called the plain old telephone service (POTS).

R

radio frequency (RF)   A generic term referring to frequencies that correspond to radio transmissions. Cable TV and broadband networks use RF technology.

reassembly   The putting back together of an IP datagram at the destination after it has been fragmented at either the source or the intermediate node.

Regional Internet Registry (RIR)   An organization overseeing the allocation and registration of Internet number resources in a particular region of the world. There are currently five RIRs.

RFC 1918, Address Allocation for Private Internets   Private IP addresses that are a reserved block of numbers that can be used by anyone. ISPs typically configure their border routers to prevent privately addressed traffic from being forwarded over the Internet.

RIPE (Réseaux IP Européens) Network Coordination Centre   One of five Regional Internet Registries. RIPE is a not-for-profit membership organization that is responsible for distributing and registering Internet address resources throughout Europe, the Middle East, and parts of Central Asia.

Rivest, Shamir, and Adleman (RSA)   An asymmetric key cryptosystem. The keys use a bit length of 512, 768, 1024, or larger.

Routing Information Protocol next generation (RIPng)   RIP for IPv6.

RSA signature   Uses the exchange of digital certificates to authenticate the peers. The local device derives a hash and encrypts it with its private key. The encrypted hash (digital signature) is attached to the message and is forwarded to the remote end. At the remote end, the encrypted hash is decrypted using the public key of the local end. If the decrypted hash matches the recomputed hash, the signature is genuine.

S

Secure Hash Algorithm 1 (SHA-1)   Uses a 160-bit secret key. The variable-length message and the 160-bit shared secret key are combined and are run through the HMAC-SHA-1 hash algorithm. The output is a 160-bit hash. The hash is appended to the original message and is forwarded to the remote end.

Secure Shell (SSH)   A protocol that allows data to be exchanged over a secure channel between two computers. A secure form of Telnet.

security policy   A policy for an organization that informs users, staff, and managers of their obligations for protecting technology and information assets.

Serial Line Internet Protocol (SLIP)   A standard protocol for point-to-point serial connections using a variation of TCP/IP. A predecessor of PPP.

signaling   The process of sending a transmission signal over a physical medium for purposes of communication.

SNA Control Protocol   Part of the family of Network Control Protocols (NCP), specifically for SNA. Used to establish and configure different network layer protocols.

SONET   A high-speed (up to 2.5 Gbps) synchronous network specification developed by Bellcore and designed to run on optical fiber. STS-1 is the basic building block of SONET. Approved as an international standard in 1988.

spammer   An individual who sends large quantities of unsolicited e-mail messages. Spammers often use viruses to take control of home computers and use them to send bulk messages.

splitter   Separates the DSL traffic from the POTS traffic.

star topology   A LAN topology in which endpoints on a network are connected to a common central switch by point-to-point links.

stateless autoconfiguration   A plug-and-play IPv6 feature that enables devices to connect themselves to the network without any configuration and without any servers (such as DHCP servers). This key feature enables the deployment of new devices on the Internet, such as cell phones, wireless devices, home appliances, and home networks.

Static NAT   Uses a one-to-one mapping of local and global addresses, and these mappings remain constant. Static NAT is particularly useful for web servers or hosts that must have a consistent address that is accessible from the Internet. These internal hosts may be enterprise servers or networking devices.

statistical time-division multiplexing (STDM)   A technique whereby information from multiple logical channels can be transmitted across a single physical channel. Statistical multiplexing dynamically allocates bandwidth only to active input channels, making better use of available bandwidth and allowing more devices to be connected than with other multiplexing techniques.

subnet ID   Individual organizations can use a 16-bit subnet field to create their own local addressing hierarchy. This field allows an organization to use up to 65,535 individual subnets.

switched virtual circuit (SVC)   A virtual circuit that is dynamically established on demand and that is torn down when transmission is complete. SVCs are used in situations where data transmission is sporadic.

symmetric encryption   Encryption algorithms such as DES and 3DES require a shared secret key to perform encryption and decryption. Each of the two computers must know the key to decode the information. With symmetric key encryption, also called secret key encryption, each computer encrypts the information before sending it over the network to the other computer. Symmetric key encryption requires knowledge of which computers will be talking to each other so that the same key can be configured on each computer.

synchronization   The establishment of common timing between sender and receiver.

Synchronous Data Link Control (SDLC)   An SNA data link layer communications protocol. A bit-oriented, full-duplex protocol that has spawned numerous similar protocols, including HDLC and LAPB.

systematic approach   A troubleshooting method that analyzes the network as a whole rather than in a piecemeal fashion. A systematic approach minimizes confusion and cuts down on time that would be wasted with trial and error.

T

T1   A digital WAN carrier facility. T1 transmits DS-1 formatted data at 1.544 Mbps through the telephone switching network, using AMI or B8ZS coding.

T3   A digital WAN carrier facility. T3 transmits DS-3 formatted data at 44.736 Mbps through the telephone switching network.

TACACS/TACACS+   An authentication protocol, developed by the Defense Data Network (DDN) community, that provides remote-access authentication and related services, such as event logging. User passwords are administered in a central database rather than in individual routers, providing an easily scalable network security solution.

T-carrier   A TDM transmission method that usually refers to a line or cable carrying a DS-1 signal.

telephony   The science of converting sound to electrical signals and transmitting it between widely removed points.

teleworker   An employee who enjoys some flexibility in working location and hours. The daily commute to an office is replaced by telecommunication links.

TFTP server   Trivial File Transfer Protocol is a simplified version of FTP that allows files to be transferred from one computer to another over a network. The TFTP server stores and receives the uploaded files for download at the user's request.

time-division multiplexing (TDM)   A technique in which information from multiple channels can be allocated bandwidth on a single wire based on preassigned time slots. Bandwidth is allocated to each channel regardless of whether the station has data to transmit.

top-down troubleshooting   You start with the end-user applications and move down through the layers of the OSI model until you find the cause of the problem. You test end-user applications of an end system before tackling the more specific networking pieces. Use this approach for simpler problems or when you think the problem is with a piece of software.

transaction   A result-oriented unit of communication processing.

transmission link   A network communications channel consisting of a circuit or transmission path and all related equipment between a sender and a receiver. Most often used to refer to a WAN connection.

Triple DES (3DES)   A newer variant of DES that encrypts with one key, decrypts with a different key, and then encrypts a final time with another key. 3DES provides significantly more strength to the encryption process.

Trojan horse   A type of virus in which the application is written to look like something else, when in fact it is an attack tool. An example of a Trojan horse is a software application that runs a simple game on a workstation. While the user is occupied with the game, the Trojan horse mails a copy of itself to every address in the user's address book. The other users receive the game and play it, thereby spreading the Trojan horse to the addresses in each address book.

trunk   Used to create multiple network cables or ports in parallel to increase the link speed beyond the limits of any single cable or port.

tunneling   An architecture that is designed to provide the services necessary to implement any standard point-to-point encapsulation scheme.

U–V

Universal Asynchronous Receiver/Transmitter (UART)   An integrated circuit, attached to a computer's parallel bus, used for serial communications. The UART translates between serial and parallel signals, provides transmission clocking, and buffers data sent to or from the computer.

virtual circuit (VC)   A logical circuit created to ensure reliable communication between two network devices. A virtual circuit is defined by a VPI/VCI pair, and it can be either permanent (PVC) or switched (SVC). Virtual circuits are used in Frame Relay and X.25. In ATM, a virtual circuit is called a virtual channel.

virtual private network (VPN)   A means to securely and privately transmit data over an unsecured and shared network infrastructure.

virus   Malicious software that is attached to another program to execute a particular unwanted function on a workstation.

voice over IP (VoIP)   The capability to carry normal telephony-style voice over an IP-based Internet with POTS-like functionality.

W–X

white hat   Someone who looks for vulnerabilities in systems or networks and then reports them to the system's owners so that they can be fixed. This person is ethically opposed to the abuse of computer systems. A white hat generally focuses on securing IT systems, whereas a black hat (the opposite) wants to break into them.

wide-area network (WAN)   A data communications network that serves users across a broad geographic area and often uses transmission devices provided by common carriers. Frame Relay, SMDS, and X.25 are examples of WANs.

Wi-Fi Alliance   Offers certification for interoperability between vendors of 802.11 products. It helps market a WLAN technology by promoting interoperability between vendors. Certification includes all three 802.11 RF technologies and Wi-Fi Protected Access (WPA).

wildcard mask   A 32-bit quantity used in conjunction with an IP address to determine which bits in an IP address should be ignored when comparing that address to another IP address. A wildcard mask is specified when setting up access lists.

WiMAX (Worldwide Interoperability for Microwave Access)   Described in the IEEE standard 802.16. WiMAX offers high-speed broadband service with wireless access. It provides broad coverage like a cell phone network rather than using small Wi-Fi hotspots.

wiring closet   A specially designed room used to wire a data or voice network. Wiring closets serve as a central junction point for the wiring and wiring equipment that is used to interconnect network devices.

worm   Executes code and installs copies of itself in the memory of the infected computer, which can, in turn, infect other hosts.

X.25   An ITU-T standard that defines how connections between DTE and DCE are maintained for remote terminal access and computer communications in packet data networks (PDN). X.25 specifies LAPB, a data link layer protocol, and PLP, a network layer protocol. Frame Relay has to some degree superseded X.25.

J-K-L